PHILLIPPS' FIELD GUIDE TO THE MAMMALS OF BORNEO

SABAH, SARAWAK, BRUNEI AND KALIMANTAN

SECOND EDITION

QUENTIN PHILLIPPS

ILLUSTRATED BY
KAREN PHILLIPPS

JOHN BEAUFOY PUBLISHING

CONTENTS

MAMMALS

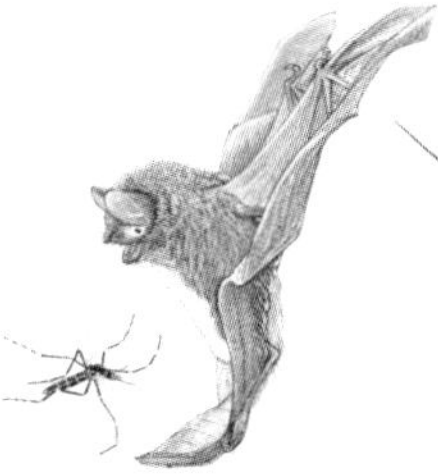

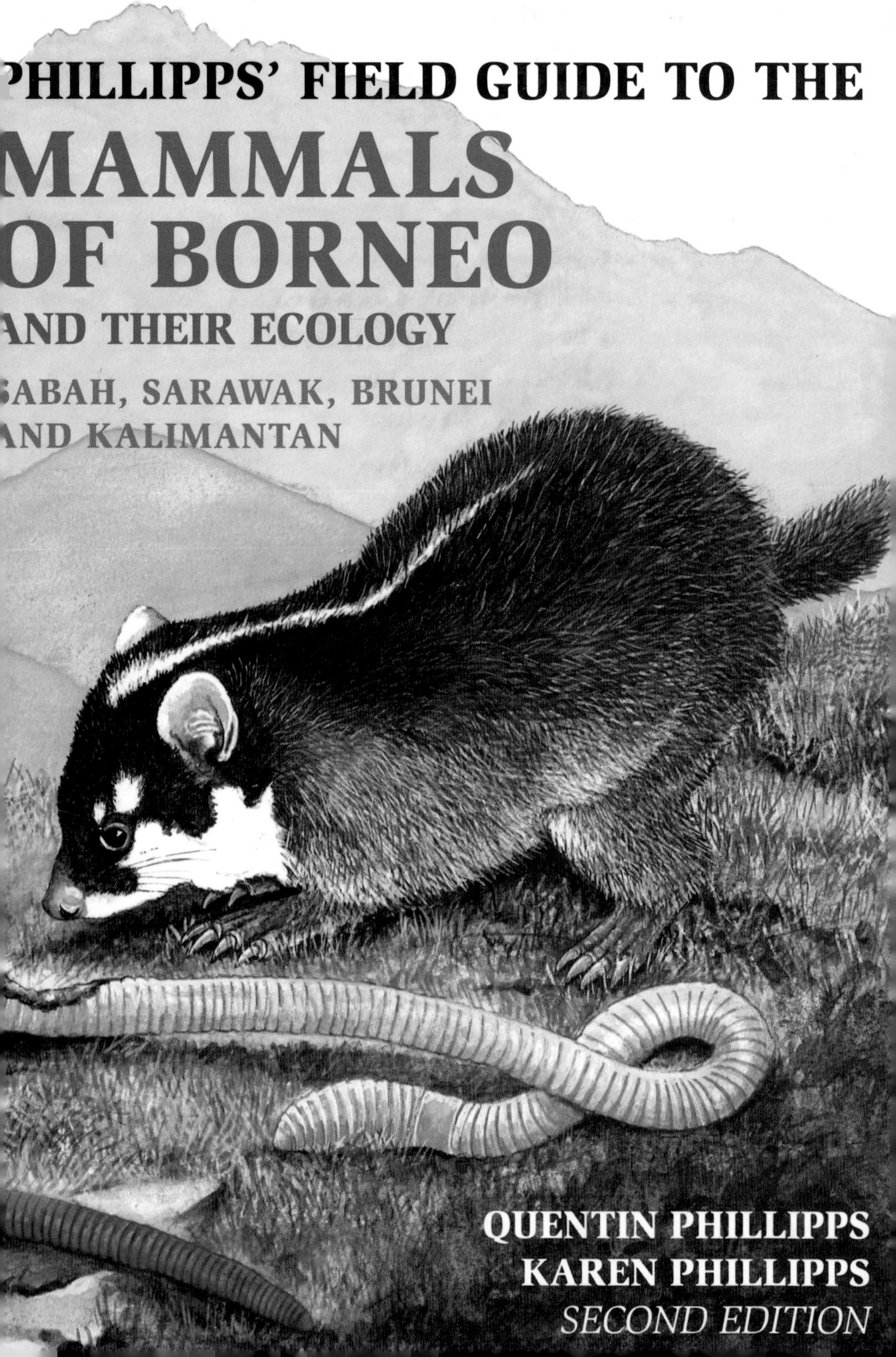

PHILLIPPS' FIELD GUIDE TO THE

MAMMALS OF BORNEO

AND THEIR ECOLOGY

SABAH, SARAWAK, BRUNEI AND KALIMANTAN

QUENTIN PHILLIPPS
KAREN PHILLIPPS

SECOND EDITION

ECOLOGY

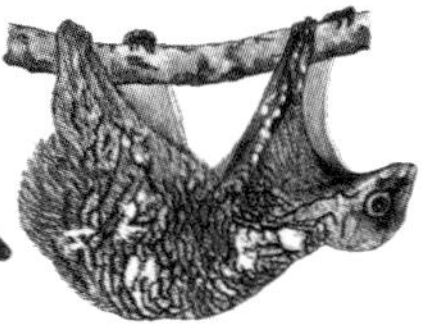

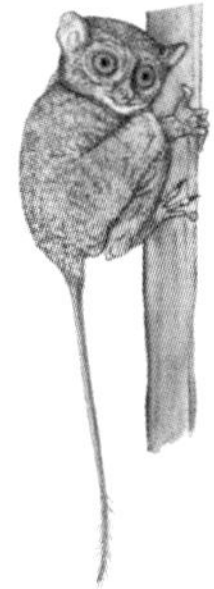

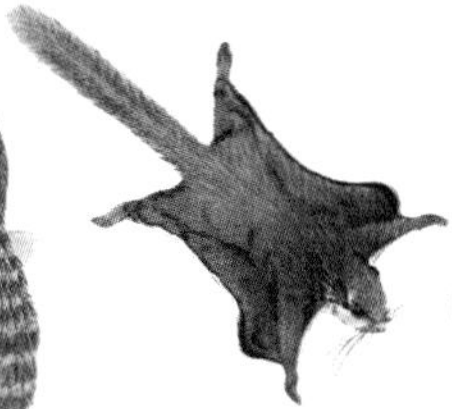

IAPS AND SITES

ACKNOWLEDGEMENTS

The contents of this book are based on the first edition (2016) to which a large number of people contributed, and who are hereby recognized and thanked for their foundation contributions without which this second edition would not have been possible. For additional help with this second edition we would particularly like to thank:

New illustrations: Karen Phillipps.

New photographs: Hans Hazebroek, Zdeněk Mačát, Hanyrol H. Ahmad Sah and Sam Woods.

Help with content and or logistics: Nick Acheson, Liz Bennett, Oriana Bhasin, Chan Chew Lun, Hin Cheung Timothy Chang, Susan Cheyne, Anthony Chieng, Gathorne Cranbook, Jungle Dave, Nick Garbutt, Gabriella Frederiksson, Linus Gokusing, Ulmar Graffe, Benoit Goosens, Tony Lamb, Laslie at the Rasa Ria Resort, C.K Leong, Cynthia Lobato, Martyn at the Ulu Ulu Resort, Miyabi Nakabayashi, Junaidi Payne, Anthea Phillipps, Cosmo Phillipps, Honor Phillipps, Lindsay Porter, Fred Sheldon, Roger Rajah, Albert Teo, Valentine Thiry, Mark Harrison, Elisa Panjang, Rustam (PROFAUNA), Samhan, Danica Stark, Ferry Slik, Ray Tipper, Ken Searle, Salwa, Suhailie (Mincho), Balut and Markiss, Leona Wai, Arlene Walshe, Wong Siew Te and Yeo Siew Teck.

Publishing: John Beaufoy, Rosemary Wilkinson, Chan Chew Lun and John Button.

Front and Back Cover Illustration The Giant Kinabalu Earthworm *Pheretima darnleiensis*, which can grow up to a metre long, provides food for both the Giant Kinabalu Leech *Mimobdella buettikoferi* and the Bornean Ferret Badger *Melogale everetti*. The Giant Leech having no teeth is forced to swallow its favourite prey whole. All three species are endemic to the mountains of Borneo. The Giant Kinabalu Leech is best seen during heavy rain when it chases (very slowly) the Giant Kinabalu Earthworm across the Kinabalu Summit Trail (2,500–3,500m asl.) The Bornean Ferret Badger is best seen raiding the dustbins at night below the Timpohon Gate on Kinabalu (1,850m). See p. 254.

Frontispiece (opposite) A Mountain Treeshrew *Tupaia montana* feeding on the Beccarian food bodies produced by the lid of a giant *Nepenthes raja* pitcher plant. A chemical in the food bodies (possibly sorbitol) stimulates the treeshrew to defecate into the pitcher bowl. Thus the plant feeds the treeshrew and the treeshrew in turn feeds the plant. See pp. 70–71.

Abbott's Gibbon
Hylobates abbotti
p. 185

IN MEMORIAM
Two of the world's rarest primates, Abbott's Gibbon and the black morph of the Sarawak Langur are likely to become extinct when the new Pan-Borneo Highway is pushed through the biodiverse hotspot of Samunsam and Tanjong Datu in south-west Sarawak.

Black *chryosmelas* morph of Sarawak Langur *P. chrysomelas* resident at Samunsam, p. 170

This edition first published in the United Kingdom in 2018
and reprinted in 2024 by John Beaufoy Publishing Ltd,
11 Blenheim Court, 316 Woodstock Road, Oxford OX2 7NS, England
www.johnbeaufoy.com

10 9 8 7 6 5 4

ISBN (Paperback) 978-1-912081-95-0

Designed and typeset by Bookcraft Ltd, Stroud, Gloucestershire, UK
Printed and bound in Malaysia by Times Offset (M) Sdn. Bhd.

Two young Hose's Langurs play in the early morning mist next to the Belalong Canopy Walkway in the Ulu Temburong National Park, Brunei (pp. 167 and 357).
(Photo Hanyrol H. Ahmad Sah, resident researcher at the Ulu Ulu Resort)

INTRODUCTION TO THE SECOND EDITION (2018)

Changes New illustrations: pp. 46–47 Forest Fungi; p. 103 Francis' Bat; p. 160 Sunda Slow Loris; p. 164 Grey Langurs; p. 167 Hose's Langur; p. 197 Prevost's Squirrel; p. 198 Horse-tailed Squirrel; p. 211 Giant Squirrel; p. 266 Giant Millipedes. Major text revisions have been made on pp. 46–47 Forest Fungi; pp. 166–167 Grey Langur Ecology; pp. 278–279 Clouded Leopard Ecology; pp. 280–281 Marbled Cat; pp. 356–357 Temburong, Brunei.

Illegal Poaching and Hunting Since the publication of the first edition of this book (2016) it has become clear that although the major threat to wildlife throughout Borneo remains the conversion of forested areas to oil palm, hunting and poaching are equally important. Logging roads and fragmentation have allowed poachers easy access to areas of previously inaccessible forest. The booming market in wild meat (particularly pigs, pangolins and porcupines), singing birds and Helmeted Hornbill casques means that many locals are now hunting for the market. In Sarawak and Kalimantan, forests are being stripped of their wildlife for sale in markets as far away as Jakarta and Medan.

Wildlife Legislation and the IUCN Red List The Red List designations are not used in this book because taxonomy is moving so fast that the Red List is outdated almost as soon as it is published. Because legally protected animals in Borneo are usually listed based on the Red List this is causing major problems in legal enforcement against poachers.

Mammals of Borneo Total land mammals 247, of which 100 are bats and 63 are endemic to Borneo.

ABBREVIATIONS AND MALAY PLACE NAMES (see also Glossary p. 398)

KYA	Thousands of years ago	**LGM**	Last Glacial Maximum
MYA	Millions of years ago	**YBP**	Years Before Present
Bukit	Hill	**Kg**	Kampong or village
Sg	Sungai or River	**Gng**	Gunung or Mountain

CONVERSION FACTORS

100 mm	**3.93"**
1m	**3.28'**
10 km	**6.2 miles**

1 ha	**10,000 sq m**
100 ha	**1 sq km**
1 ha	**2.47 acres**

2.59 sq km	**1 sq mile**
1 sq km	**247.1 acres**
1 sq mile	**259 ha**

KEY TO DISTRIBUTION MAPS

The distribution maps show the original mammal distributions based on preferred altitude and original habitat, not the fine detail of current fragmented distributions.

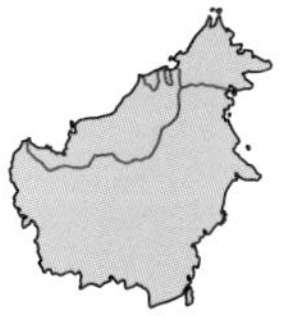

Throughout Borneo

Endemic resident throughout

Coastal

Lowland

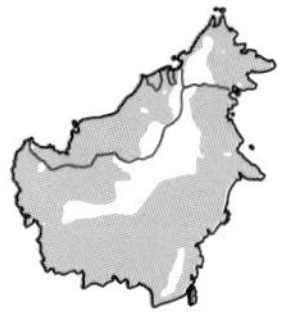

Lowland and hills

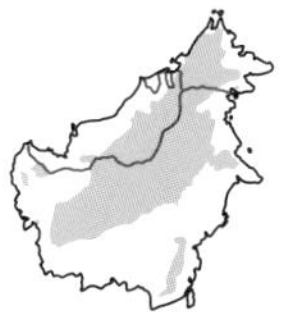

Hills and mountains

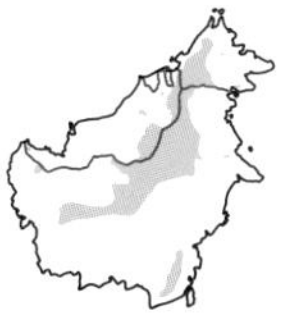

Mountains

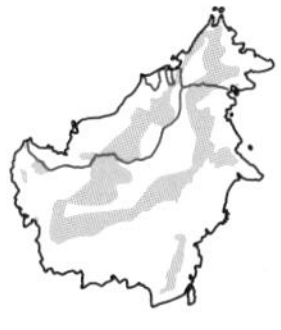

Hills and slopes

Rivers and alluvial habitat

Local distribution

Bay Cat *Felis badia*, the only wild cat endemic to Borneo.
Illustration by Joseph Wolf from
A Monograph of the Felidae (1883) by Daniel Giraud Elliott.

THE TOP TEN BORNEAN MAMMALS AND WHERE TO SEE THEM

(Map inside back cover)

Bornean Orangutan	Sepilok, Kinabatangan, Danum, Tabin, Semengoh, Tg Puting	p. 188
Proboscis Monkey	Bako, Brunei Bay, Labuk Bay, Klias	p. 174
Clouded Leopard	Tabin, Danum, Kinabatangan, Deramakot	p. 276
Sumatran Rhino	Tabin	p. 294
Pygmy Elephant	Kinabatangan River, Tabin, Danum, Deramakot	p. 288
North Borneo Gibbon	Danum, Tabin, Deramakot, Belalong Canopy Walkway	p. 184
Red Langur	Sepilok, Gomantong, Danum, Tawau Hills, Sabangau	p. 162
Hose's Langur	Ulu Temburong, Brunei, Kiudang, Brunei	p. 164
Sun Bear	Danum, Sepilok, Sg Wain, Deramakot	p. 246
Bearded Pig	Bako, Danum, Kinabatangan, Tabin	p. 300

SIXTY-THREE ENDEMIC MAMMALS AND WHERE TO SEE THEM

SUNDA TAILLESS FRUIT BAT	*Megaerops ecaudatus*	Tasek Merimbun, Brunei	p. 94
BORNEAN FRUIT BAT	*Aethalops aequalis*	Kinabalu, Gng Penrissen	p. 92
DAYAK ROUNDLEAF BAT	*Hipposideros dyacorum*	Danum, Mulu, Matang	p. 108
RED-BROWN PIPISTRELLE	*Hypsugo kitcheneri*	Sepilok, Ulu Temburong	p. 118
VORDERMAN'S PIPISTRELLE	*Hypsugo vordermanni*	Samunsam, Tg Puting	p. 118
GOMANTONG MYOTIS	*Myotis gomantongensis*	Gomantong	p. 130
BORNEAN WHISKERED MYOTIS	*Myotis borneoensis*	Sepilok, Lambir	p. 132
BLACK SHREW	*Suncus ater*	Kiau Gap, Kinabalu	p. 138
HOSE'S PIGMY SHREW	*Suncus hosei*	Sepilok, Ulu Ulu	p. 138
BORNEAN SHREW	*Crocidura foetida*	Tabin, Matang	p. 138
KINABALU SHREW	*Crocidura kinabauensis*	Kinabalu Park HQ	p. 138
BORNEAN WATER SHREW	*Chimarrogale phaeura*	Kinabalu streams	p. 138
SMOOTH-TAILED TREESHREW	*Dendrogale melanura*	Crocker Range Park HQ	p. 146
MOUNTAIN TREESHREW	*Tupaia montana*	Summit trail, Kinabalu	p. 146
STRIPED TREESHREW	*Tupaia dorsalis*	Matang, Gng Penrissen	p. 146
SLENDER TREESHREW	*Tupaia gracilis*	Danum, Tabin, Mulu	p. 144
PLAIN TREESHREW	*Tupaia longipes*	Danum, Tabin, Mulu	p. 144
PAINTED TREESHREW	*Tupaia picta*	Lambir, Tasek Merimbun	p. 148
SPLENDID TREESHREW	*Tupaia splendidula*	Tg Puting, Sabangau	p. 148
KAYAN SLOW LORIS	*Nycticebus kayan*	Maliau Basin, Kelabit Hghlds	p. 160
BORNEAN SLOW LORIS	*Nycticebus borneanus*	Sabangau	p. 160
RED LANGUR	*Presbytis rubicunda*	Sepilok, Sabangau	p. 162
HOSE`S LANGUR	*Presbytis hosei*	Ulu Temburong	p. 164
SABAH GREY LANGUR	*Presbytis sabana*	Tabin	p. 164
KUTAI GREY LANGUR	*Presbytis canicrus*	Wehea Community Forest	p. 164
KALIMANTAN GREY LANGUR	*Presbytis frontata*	Lanjak Entimau, Sg Wain	p. 164
SARAWAK LANGUR	*Presbytis chrysomelas*	Samunsam, Maludam	p. 170
NATUNA LANGUR	*Presbytis natunae*	Bunguran Besar, Natunas	p. 168
PROBOSCIS MONKEY	*Nasalis larvatus*	Bako, Kinabatangan	p. 174
ABBOTT'S GIBBON	*Hylobates abbotti*	Samunsam	p. 184
NORTH BORNEO GIBBON	*Hylobates funereus*	Danum, Tabin	p. 184
MÜLLER'S GIBBON	*Hylobates muelleri*	Sg Wain	p. 184
WHITE-BEARDED GIBBON	*Hylobates alibarbis*	Tg Puting, Sabangau	p. 184
BORNEAN ORANGUTAN	*Pongo pygmaeus*	Sepilok, Tg Puting	p. 193
KINABALU SQUIRREL	*Callosciurus baluensis*	Kinabalu Park HQ	p. 195
EAR-SPOT SQUIRREL	*Callosciurus adamsi*	Sepilok	p. 202
BROOKE`S SQUIRREL	*Sundasciurus brookei*	Kinabalu Park HQ	p. 200
JENTINK`S SQUIRREL	*Sundasciurus jentinki*	Kinabalu Summit Trail	p. 200
BORNEAN BLACK-BANDED SQUIRREL	*Callosciurus orestes*	Kinabalu Park HQ	p. 204
BORNEAN MT GROUND SQUIRREL	*Dremomys everetti*	Kinabalu Summit Trail	p. 212
FOUR-STRIPED GROUND SQUIRREL	*Lariscus hosei*	Tawau Hills	p. 212
WHITEHEAD`S PIGMY SQUIRREL	*Exilisciurus whiteheadi*	Kinabalu Park HQ	p. 206
BORNEAN PIGMY SQUIRREL	*Exilisciurus exilis*	Danum, Matang,Tg Puting	p. 206
SCULPTOR SQUIRREL	*Glyphotes simus*	Maliau Basin, KPHQ	p. 208
TUFTED GROUND SQUIRREL	*Rheithrosciurus macrotis*	Malaiu Basin, Tawau Hills	p. 214
HOSE`S PIGMY FLYING SQUIRREL	*Petaurillus hosei*	Sepilok, Tasek Merimbun	p. 216
EMILY'S FLYING SQUIRREL	*Petaurillus emiliae*	Mulu	p. 216
KINABALU RAT	*Rattus baluensis*	Panar Laban, Kinabalu	p. 230
BORNEO GIANT RAT	*Sundamys infraluteus*	Kinabalu Park HQ	p. 230
MOUNTAIN MAXOMYS	*Maxomys alticola*	Kinabalu Park HQ	p. 230
LONG-TAILED MOUNTAIN RAT	*Niviventer rapit*	Kinabalu	p. 232
BAEODON MAXOMYS	*Maxomys baeodon*	Sepilok, Danum, Maliau	p. 236
CHESTNUT-BELLIED MAXOMYS	*Maxomys ochraceiventer*	Maliau, Gng Penrissen	p. 236
LARGE SUNDA TREE-MOUSE	*Chiropodomys major*	Sepilok, Matang	p. 240
GREY-BELLIED SUNDA TREE-MOUSE	*Chiropodomys muroides*	Kinabalu, Poring	p. 240
BORNEAN SUNDA TREE-MOUSE	*Chiropodomys pusillus*	Poring, Mulu	p. 240
EMMON'S TREE-RAT	*Pithecheirops otion*	Danum DVFC	p. 242
RANEE MOUSE	*Haeromys margarettae*	Sepilok, Gng Penrissen	p. 242
BORNEAN PORCUPINE	*Thecurus crassispinis*	Danum. Tabin, Tawau Hills	p. 244
BORNEAN STRIPED PALM CIVET	*Arctogalidia stigmatica*	Poring, Danum, Tabin	p. 264
HOSE`S CIVET	*Hemigalus hosei*	Pulong Tau, Crocker Range	p. 270
BAY CAT	*Felis badia*	Danum. Tabin, Tawau Hills	p. 282
BORNEAN YELLOW MUNTJAC	*Muntiacus atherodes*	Danum. Tabin, Tawau Hills	p. 310

CLIMATE 1: SEASONS

MONSOONS AND ENSO CYCLES Borneo's rainforests, lying across the equator, have the least seasonal climate in the world. Between Pontianak on the equator and Kota Kinabalu at 6° N, day length only varies by 40 minutes between 21 Jun–21 Dec. Daily temperatures hardly vary between 32° C during the day, falling to 22° C at night, and in most of Borneo at least 100mm of rain falls in most months. Constant rainfall enables many Bornean plants, such as bananas and gingers, to flower and fruit continuously. However, it would be a serious mistake to think that the Bornean climate is non-seasonal. Bornean forest ecology is powerfully influenced by variations in rainfall that take two forms.

An annual monsoon cycle with a wettest period at the end of each year caused by the NE monsoon, followed by a 4–8-week period of reduced rainfall – a mini drought. (p. 48, swidden farming.)

An ENSO cycle (average interval 4–5 years) causing a severe drought lasting several months. Droughts are usually most severe in SE Borneo and may result in catastrophic forest fires in logged forest.

Birds breed on an annual cycle based on the NE monsoon In Sabah extra rain results in new leaves in Dec–Jan, followed by flowering in the drier period Mar–May. New leaves and flowers provide extra food for insects, which peak in abundance at the start of each year. Most birds feed their young on insects, so the extra food encourages birds to breed in Feb–May each year. If insects are scarce most birds will not breed. Birds that feed on grain breed continuously (see Phillipps & Phillipps 2014). Note: in SW Sarawak and Kalimantan rainfall and bird breeding peak some 2–3 months later than Sabah.

Mammals breed when food is plentiful The increased flowering in Sabah, Mar–May, results in increased fruiting in Jul–Sep. Wade (1958), reporting on 201 small adult mammals collected in the lowlands of Sabah by Davis (1962) in Apr–Aug, found that the pregnancy rate increased from 0% in Apr to 44% in Aug. Most Bornean small mammals such as treeshrews rely on extra fruit, not insects, to trigger breeding. Treeshrews breed continuously in captivity, but at Danum Emmons found that treeshrew breeding depended on fruit availability. However, fruit availability varies massively due to the interplay of the annual monsoon and irregular ENSO-triggered masting (p. 12). Insectivorous mammals breed at the same time as birds. Large mammals like Sun Bears, Clouded Leopards and Orangutans may need ENSO events to trigger breeding.

Different flowering and fruiting strategies of Bornean plants Over larger areas rainfall varies widely (see maps, opposite), but locally is usually similar. Some plants use water stress (droughts) to coordinate local flowering (and pollination) over small areas, as in a single valley. Other plants flower based on an inbuilt genetic clock or when they have built up sufficient resources. Bornean mammals have co-evolved with plants to exploit the different fruiting strategies described below, cross-referenced to further information in this book.

1 Steady State Fruit continuously, e.g. bananas, some bat figs, providing food for 'trapliners' (pp. 72 and 78).

2 Random Fruit randomly in large crops, providing foods during 'lean periods', e.g. strangling figs (p. 76).

3 Annual Flower annually Mar–May with fruiting Jul–Sep. Most primate fruits (pp. 59, 65 and 74).

4 Masting (Big Bang) Mass flowering at long intervals following a severe drought, a strategy evolved to reduce predation of soft recalcitrant seeds and encourage the hoarding of hard orthodox seeds (pp. 54, 60 and 234).

5 Monocarpic (Big Bang) Plant flowers once, then dies. Strategy evolved to avoid seed predation and encourage dispersal by hoarding rodents, e.g. some palms (pp. 50 and 52), and bamboos (p. 48).

HISTORICAL RECORDS OF EL NIÑO DROUGHTS IN BORNEO

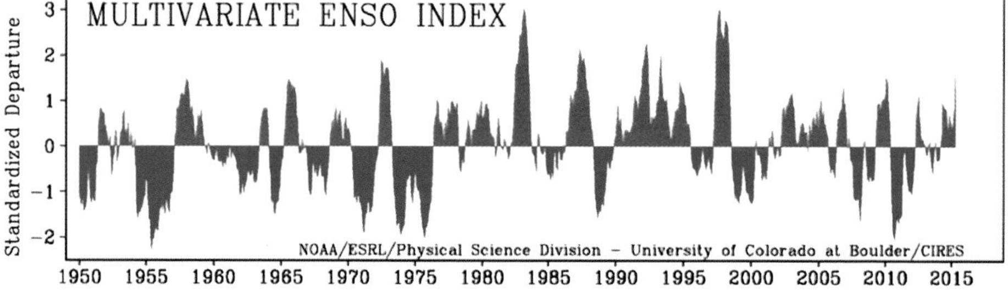

Large positive values show the historical occurrence of El Niño conditions. Comparison with export charts of Illipe nuts (Local: Enkabang or Tenkawang) resulting from the mass flowering of the dipterocarp *Shorea macrophylla* indicate that ENSO events trigger dipterocarp flowering and masting (p. 54).

ENSO El Niño Southern Oscillation, a warming of the E Pacific Ocean every 2–7 years which affects rainfall over the W Pacific.

RAINFALL IN DIFFERENT AREAS OF BORNEO
MONTHLY RAINFALL IN MM, JANUARY TO DECEMBER

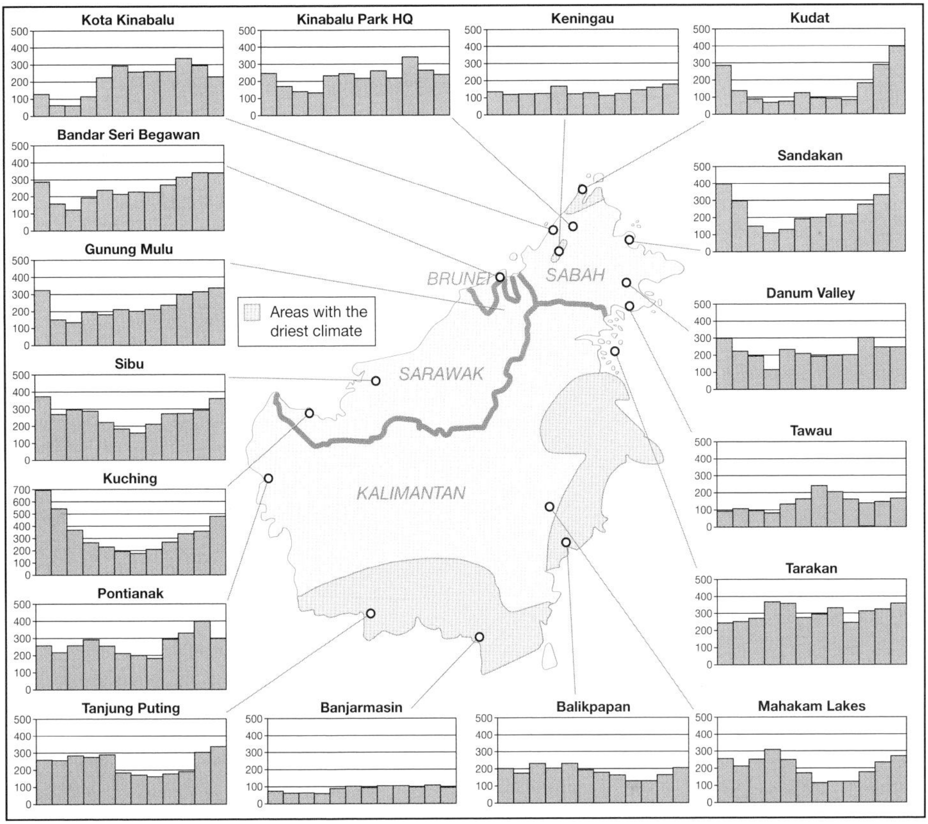

BORNEO'S ANNUAL MONSOONS

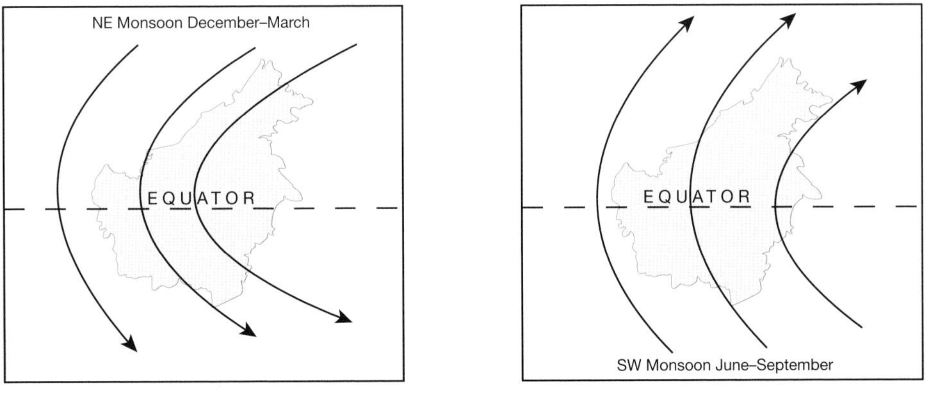

CLIMATE 2: PHENOLOGY

STRONG AND WEAK CLIMATIC TRIGGERS AND RAINFOREST PHENOLOGY Phenology is the study of plant and animal breeding cycles and how these are influenced by variations in temperature, day length and food supply. In the strongly seasonal climates of high latitudes, the phenology of plants and animals is chiefly influenced by day length and to a lesser degree temperature. At London (UK) 52° N, day length varies by 10 hours 50 minutes between mid-summer (21 June) and mid-winter (21 Dec), compared with under an hour anywhere in Borneo (p. 10).

Strong triggers in temperate climates A fixed annual variation in day length at high latitudes acts as a 'strong trigger' to coordinate breeding for each species. Temperature is more variable so it is less important as a trigger. When temperature and day length are out of synchrony, the result (such as late frosts) can be a disaster for both farmers and wildlife. **Important note:** A day-length trigger works because temperate plants and animals have evolved an internal genetic clock with an annual roughly 365-day cycle. Thus temperate rodents hoard food for winter in autumn even though they cannot know that winter (and possible starvation) is coming.

Breeding triggers in Borneo The annual mini-drought that follows the end of the NE monsoon provides a weak annual flowering trigger for many plants, but some, like dipterocarps, are genetically programmed only to react to much stronger triggers. Other plants, such as bananas and gingers, breed continuously.

Cool periods as triggers Pigeon Orchids *Dendrobium crumenatum* flower en masse 9 days after an above-average fall in night temperature. Coffee and a number of other plants in the Rubiaceae family flower on a similar trigger.

Water stress as a trigger Many plants are triggered to flower by water stress, i.e. droughts. The absence of rain affects trees on different soils differently. Thus trees on sandy soils suffer water stress before trees growing on water-retentive clay soils. Trees benefit from coordinating their mass flowering, but just as with 'late frosts' evolution does not always work perfectly. In general the greater the water stress, the stronger the trigger.

The ENSO (El Niño Southern Oscillation) cycle and predator satiation On average, roughly every 4–5 years much of Borneo experiences a severe drought. These droughts have been linked to the ENSO cycle depicted graphically (p. 10). Many Bornean forest trees, especially the dipterocarps, use this strong trigger to coordinate flowering and fruiting at erratic multi-year intervals. This strategy appears to have evolved first to starve dipterocarp seed predators into extinction followed by predator satiation – providing so much seed that seed predators are 'satiated'. Janzen (1974), Walsh & Newberry (1999), Cannon et al. (2007), Roubik et al. (2005).

Internal clocks It is likely that different tree species react differently to water stress, depending on the 'programming' of an internal genetic clock. For example, the clock may be programmed to initiate flowering annually, biannually, every 4 years or every 10 years, and so on.

MASTING BASED ON A 4–5 YEAR CYCLE The SE Asian rainforests, with Borneo at the centre, are the only forests in the world where mass flowering followed by mass fruiting (masting) takes place at long multi-year intervals. Masting events are dominated by the giant dipterocarps, which comprise 60–90% of the forest mass in many lowland areas. Exports of dipterocarp fruits, illipi nuts show that masting events average every 4–5 years but vary unpredictably between 2–10 years (p. 10).

A possible model to explain dipterocarp masting is suggested as follows: Most masting dipterocarp species have evolved a genetic timer to flower/fruit at roughly 4–5 year intervals. This allows individual trees time to build enough resources to power masting. The flowering trigger for dipterocarps is an extended drought. Because most dipterocarps' genetic clock cycle averages 4–5 years (rather than 1 year), a very strong trigger (ENSO drought) is required to initiate masting. The strength of the trigger depends on the time lapse since the last masting. If masting last occurred 2 years ago an ENSO event (strong trigger) may cause masting, but if masting last occurred 6 years ago an annual drought (weak trigger) may cause masting. **The combination of a 4–5-year internal clock combined with varying weak (annual) and strong (irregular ENSO droughts)** may explain the pattern of most dipterocarp masting found in the Bornean forests.

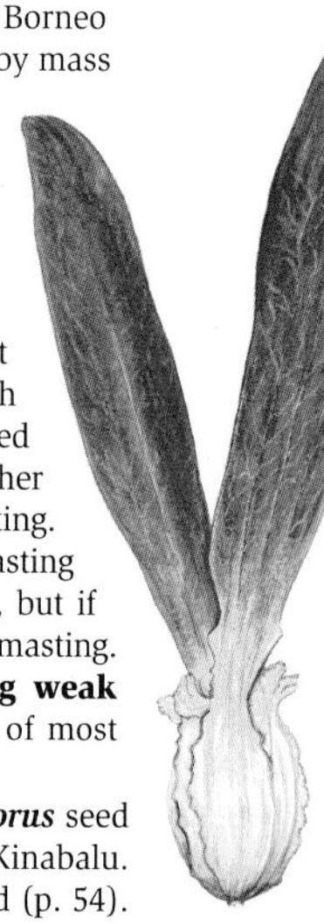

Dipterocarpus grandiflorus seed
The most common dipterocarp on Gaya Island opposite Kota Kinabalu.
Typhoon dispersed (p. 54).

Maxomys rajah feeding on *Dipterocarpus validus* seed (p. 55).

MYTHS ABOUT THE BORNEO CLIMATE Many Western researchers from Wallace onwards have described Borneo as having a perhumid (always wet), aseasonal (non-seasonal) climate, and refer to ENSO events as an unwelcome occasional aberration. Local fishermen, farmers and hunters know better. Their day-to-day activities are governed by annual dry (*musim kemarau*) and wet (*musim landas*) seasons and irregular ENSO droughts. The reality is that cyclical differences in rainfall are of overwhelming importance to plants and animals in Borneo. Differences in rainfall both coordinate plant and mammal breeding, and determine the carrying capacity of the habitat during the long lean season between masts. Emmons at Danum (2000), Cannon et al. at Gng Palung (2007), Sakai et al. (2006) and Roubik et al. at Lambir (2005), Ashton (2014), (p. 10.)

STAGGERED SYNCHRONIZATION OF DIPTEROCARP FLOWERING Most Bornean plants reproduce sexually and need to synchronize flowering so that male pollen is only dispersed when female stigmas are receptive. Dipterocarps are pollinated by tiny insects called thrips. If dipterocarps flower irregularly together at long intervals, how does the thrip population cope with such massive changes in demand for pollination? Research at Lambir found that closely related dipterocarps flower in sequence species by species over a period of up to 4 months, allowing the thrip population to build up, but fruit together in one big bang over a period of just 6 weeks (Ashton 2014). This proves that plants are not slaves to external triggers, but that each species has evolved a sophisticated and precise genetic clock to synchronize pollination and seed dispersal.

The Phenology of 24 Dipterocarp Species at Bukit Soeharto in E Kalimantan was studied by Kiyono et al. (2000). Individual trees flowered for 30–90 days and fruited for 42–200 days. Dry spells triggered flowering in 1993–4, 1994–5 and 1997–8. Different species showed different sensitivities to the drought trigger and differing delays between drought and flowering. For example, *Shorea parvifolia* participated in all episodes, whilst *S. johorensis* only participated in the last two. *S. parvifolia* flowered on average 6 weeks after a drought commenced, whilst *S. johorensis* flowered 16 weeks (average) after a drought began. *Cotylobium lanceolatum*, the most fire- and drought-resistant dipterocarp, flowered on average 34 weeks after the trigger. Staggered flowering benefits pollination, whilst simultaneous fruiting (masting) mimimizes seed predation.

BEARDED PIG MIGRATIONS

When I first visited Pulau Tiga (W Sabah) in 1980, Bearded Pigs were numerous, but 15 years later they were gone. A local fisherman said that all the pigs swam 5km to the mainland during a drought and never returned. Bearded Pigs evolved to deal with a food supply that varies greatly at random times. They cope with this by breeding rapidly when food supplies are abundant and migrating long distances when food is scarce. A population explosion following an increase in food supply is typical of many rats, some of which are then triggered to migrate long distances in search of food (pp. 49 and 278). The curious fact about Pulau Tiga is that all the pigs left simultaneously, even though Pulau Tiga could probably support a small permanent population. See p. 228 (rats); p. 301 (pigs); p. 386 (island extinctions).

Bearded Pig at Bako (p. 300).

ORIGIN AND EVOLUTION OF BORNEO'S MAMMALS

CLIMATE – WARM AND WET OR COLD AND DRY For the last 55 million years Borneo's climate has varied periodically between warm and wet (rainforest) and cold and dry (savannah grassland), each habitat hosting entirely different mammals. Even during long, cold, dry periods, however, pollen studies show that NE Borneo remained a wet rainforest refuge. This explains Borneo's high level of endemism amongst plants and animals, which is highest in NE Borneo and on Kinabalu. During the Pleistocene climate changes speeded up, with long, cold, dry periods alternating with short, warm, wet periods every 100,000 years. The result is the patchy relict mammal distributions we see today. See Sheldon (2015) for an excellent overview and graph (p. 17).

The Pleistocene and Sundaland For the majority of the last 2.6 million years (Pleistocene epoch), Sundaland has been one large area of dry land *c.* 2 million km^2 with vegetation that varied repeatedly at least 30 times from wet rainforest to dry savannah grassland.

Rainforest For around 10% of the Pleistocene (including today) the climate has been warm and wet with rainforest predominating over most of Sundaland. These wet periods resulted from glacial melting, which also caused the sea-level rises that turned Java, Sumatra and Borneo into isolated islands at least 30 times, the last time being around 10,000 years ago (Cannon et al. (2009).

Savannah and rainforest refugia Even during the wettest periods (our current climate), patches of dry savannah grassland continued to exist as in E Java today, and even during the driest periods wet-rainforest refugia continued to exist in NE Borneo and the Kalimantan mountains. During long, cold periods mountain vegetation expanded downhill into the flat lowlands and connected isolated mountains to each other. These changes in vegetation explain the uneven mammal distributions we see today, with examples listed below:

1. Similarity of montane plants and animals on currently isolated mountains, e.g. Borneo Giant Rat, p. 230.
2. Relict populations of montane mammals lingering on in the lowlands, e.g. Bornean Ferret Badger, p. 254.
3. Extinction of savannah-habitat large grazing mammals and their predators, pp. 17 and 19.
4. Montane endemics, e.g. Jentink's Squirrel, p. 200; Black-banded Squirrel, p. 204; Sculptor Squirrel, p. 208.
5. Uneven distribution of big mammals on different Sunda islands, e.g. tiger, Leopard, tapir, pp. 18 and 50.
5. Riau Pocket plants shared between Borneo, Riau Islands and Malaya. See p. 368 re. Lambir.
6. Wallace's Line Absence of Australian mammals in Borneo, e.g. Cuscus, due to deep 2,000m oceanic trench between Sulawesi and Borneo. See map opposite.

Epoch length	Start MYA	End MYA	Climate
Eocene 18 Ma	55	37	Warm and wet
Oligocene 13 Ma	37	24	Cold and dry but N Borneo mountains remained wet
Miocene 17.7 Ma	23	5.3	Warm and wet
Pliocene 2.7 Ma	5.3	2.6	Cold and dry but N Borneo mountains remained wet
Pleistocene 2.6 Ma	2.6	11,700	Alternately cold and dry or warm and wet every 100,000 years
Holocene 11,700	11,700	15.07.1945	Warm and wet. Global warming due to human activities
Anthropocene 80	16.07.1945	?	Global warming accelerates. Sea-level rises inevitable

The future If the Earth follows previous long-term cycles, Borneans are headed for a colder, dryer period with lowered sea levels and land connections re-established between Borneo, Sumatra, Java and Malaya in some 5,000 years time. This natural cycle will probably be interrupted by human-caused global warming, resulting in sea-level rises that will drown large areas of S, C and E Kalimantan under the sea in the next few hundred years.

SARs – Species Area Relationships
Large areas of habitat support both more animals and plants and greater diversity of species (p. 168). The rising seas that turned Borneo into an island *c.* 10,000 years ago also resulted in a large number of mammal extinctions in the Sunda Basin due both to land flooding and the change to rainforest from grassland. Thus the extinction of large megafauna cannot be blamed just on the arrival of human hunter-gatherers from Africa (pp. 16, 18, 21 and 168), but also on the disappearance of suitable habitat.

Stegodon trinocephalus and ***Lepus nigricollis*** Typical residents of savannah grassland during the Pleistocene.

MALESIAN BOTANICAL REGION

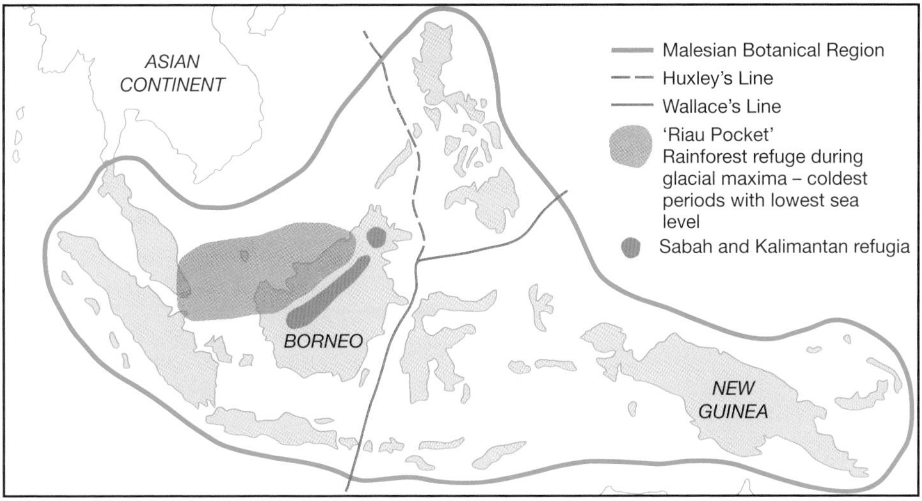

SUNDALAND ZOOLOGICAL REGION TODAY

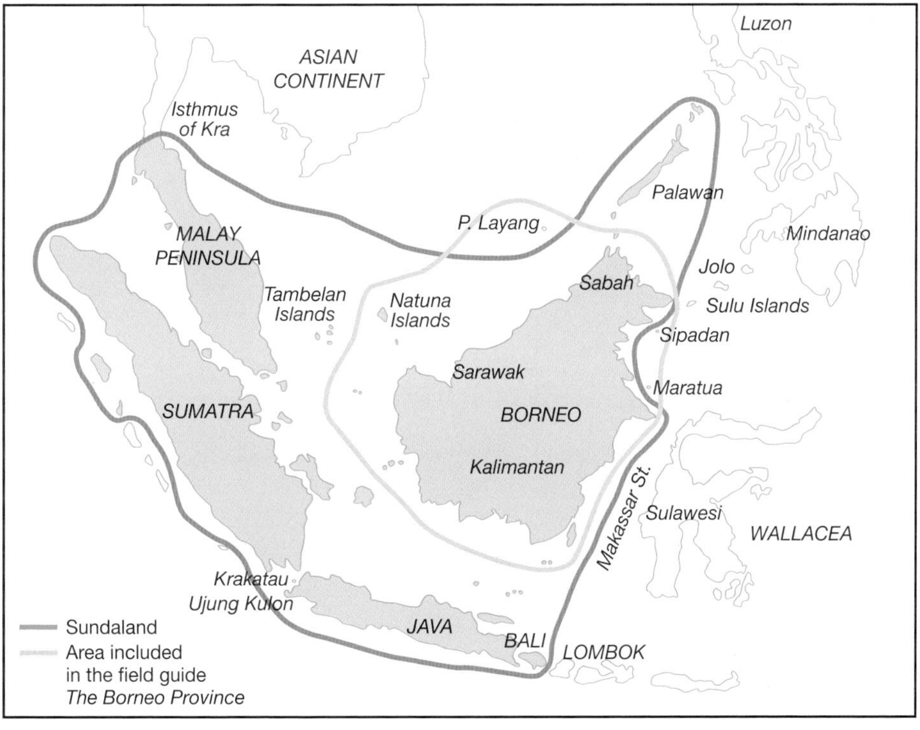

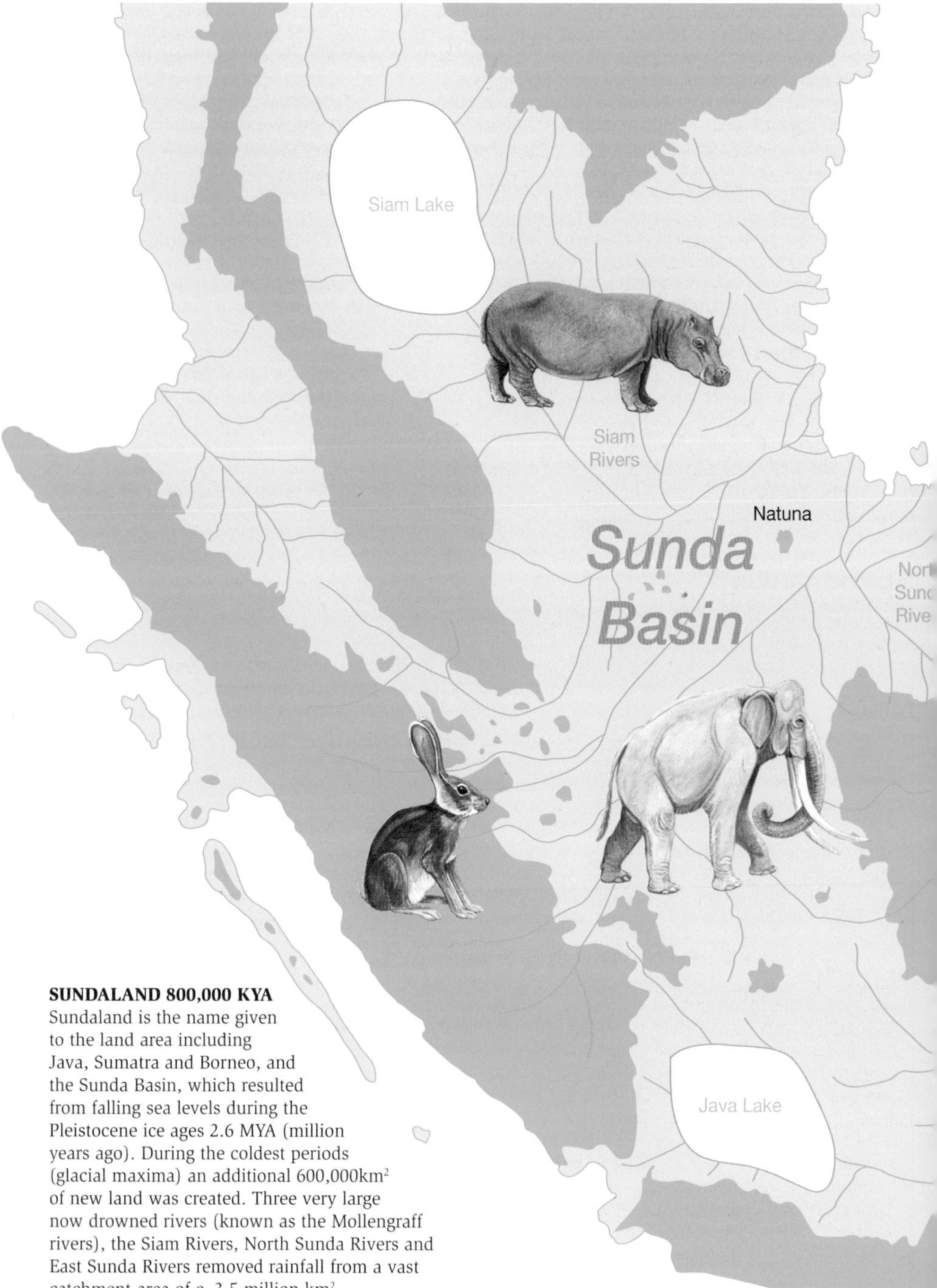

SUNDALAND 800,000 KYA

Sundaland is the name given to the land area including Java, Sumatra and Borneo, and the Sunda Basin, which resulted from falling sea levels during the Pleistocene ice ages 2.6 MYA (million years ago). During the coldest periods (glacial maxima) an additional 600,000km^2 of new land was created. Three very large now drowned rivers (known as the Mollengraff rivers), the Siam Rivers, North Sunda Rivers and East Sunda Rivers removed rainfall from a vast catchment area of c. 3.5 million km^2.

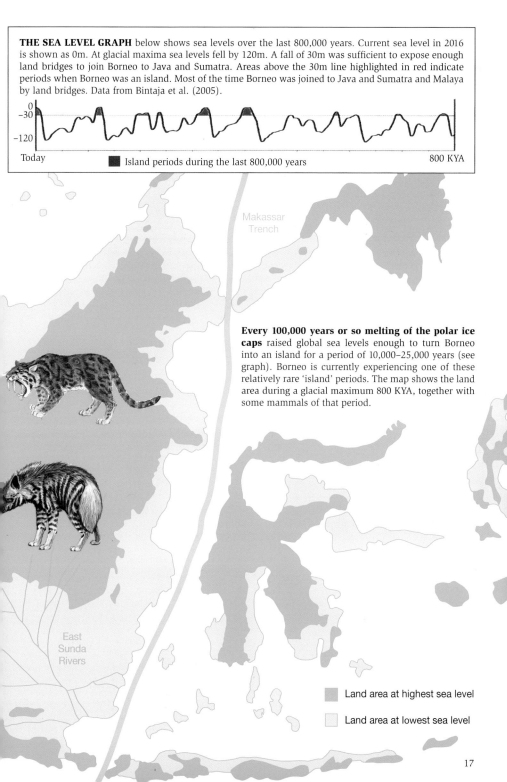

THE SEA LEVEL GRAPH below shows sea levels over the last 800,000 years. Current sea level in 2016 is shown as 0m. At glacial maxima sea levels fell by 120m. A fall of 30m was sufficient to expose enough land bridges to join Borneo to Java and Sumatra. Areas above the 30m line highlighted in red indicate periods when Borneo was an island. Most of the time Borneo was joined to Java and Sumatra and Malaya by land bridges. Data from Bintaja et al. (2005).

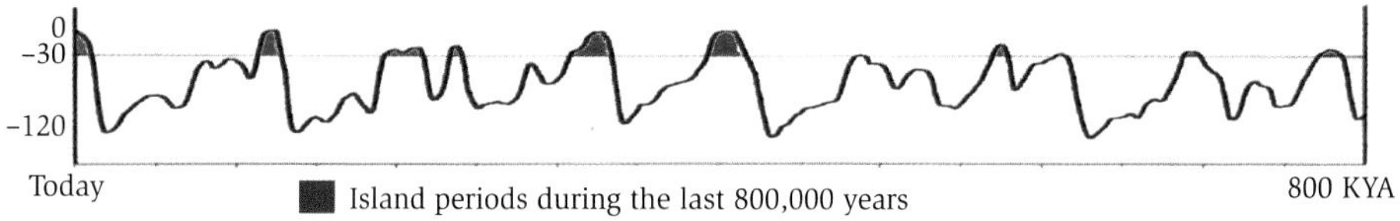

Every 100,000 years or so melting of the polar ice caps raised global sea levels enough to turn Borneo into an island for a period of 10,000–25,000 years (see graph). Borneo is currently experiencing one of these relatively rare 'island' periods. The map shows the land area during a glacial maximum 800 KYA, together with some mammals of that period.

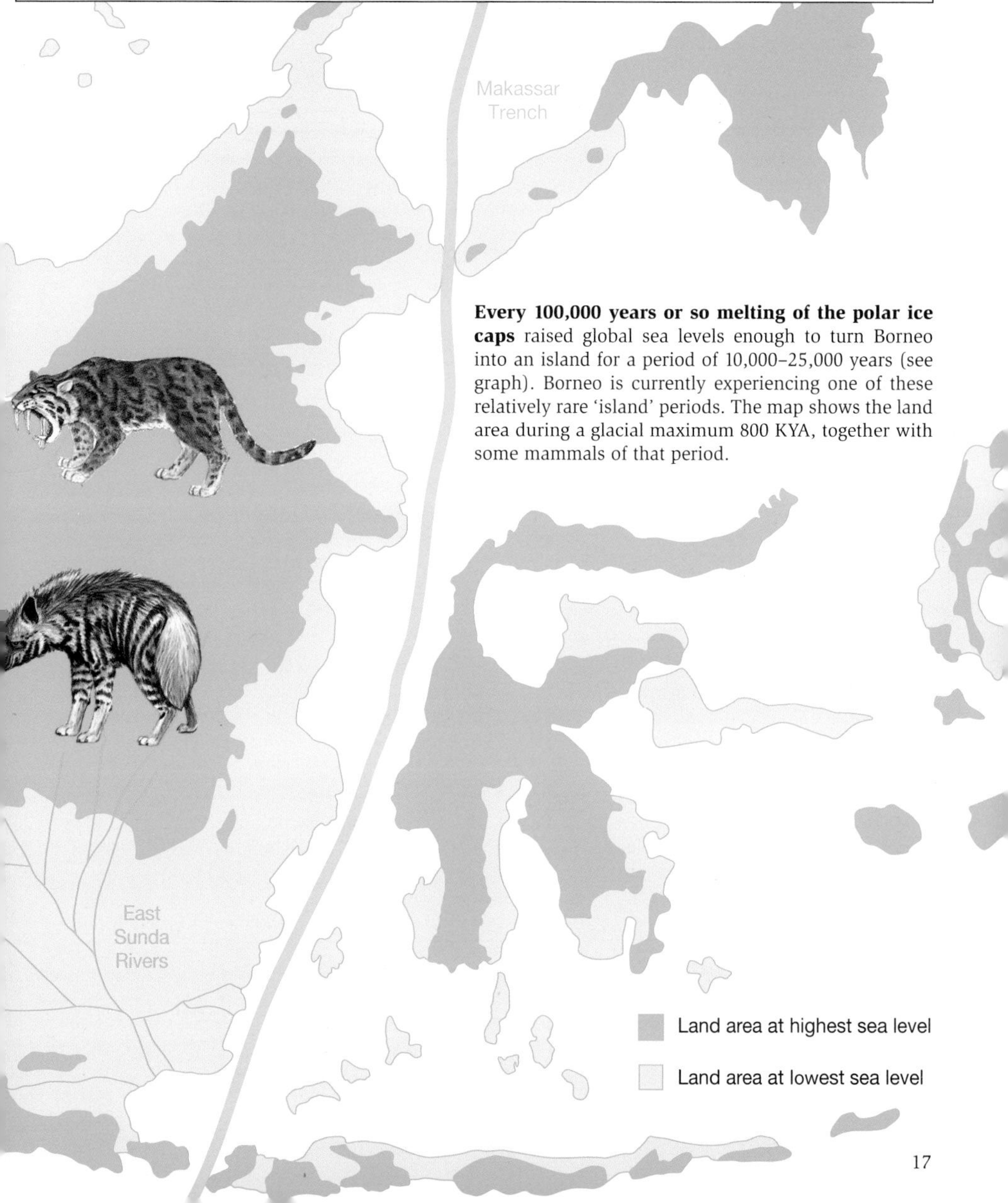

SUNDALAND MAMMALS (40KYA) NOW EXTINCT IN BORNEO

THE MAMMALS OF SUNDALAND 40,000 years ago were the same mammals that are now living in Borneo, Sumatra and Java, except that each island has ended up with a slightly different Sundaland fauna. The explanation for this is not that mammals arrived on different islands by chance on Nipa Palm rafts as many zoologists have claimed (p. 51), but that at least 30 times during the Pleistocene (most of the last 2.6m years), all the large islands probably had a full Sundaland fauna. On each island mammals became extinct when conditions deteriorated and reinvaded from refugia when suitable conditions returned (p. 15). The largest islands (Borneo and Sumatra) retained the most species; only generalist species survived on smaller islands (pp. 14, 168 and 386). Islands with dry seasonal climates such as Java acted as refugia for savannah grazers, whilst the ever-wet Bornean mountains acted as refugia for rainforest mammals and birds (Sheldon 2015).

Savannah corridors Pollen analysis shows that the Sunda forests were a rich mosaic of coastal mangroves, wet rainforest in the north and dry grassland in the south, often described as a savannah corridor, which repeatedly linked Java by land to the Asian continent. The balance between dry savannah and rainforest varied continuously, with forest replacing grassland and vice versa at least 30 times in the Pleistocene. The large Sunda Basin was cut by 3 of the world's largest rivers and the floodplains would have been covered by forests of anachronistic fruit trees as described on p. 38. Dipterocarps would have been scarce during the dryer periods, expanding their range during wetter periods, with *Vatica* spp. probably the most common dipterocarp (p. 54).

JAVAN AND BORNEAN MAMMALS: ABSENCE OF EVIDENCE IS NOT EVIDENCE OF ABSENCE
Some zoologists assume that because there are no Bornean fossils of many Sundaland mammals, it is unlikely that these species ever occurred in Borneo. In this book I take the opposite view and assume that if fossil remains have been found in Java, then at some time that mammal almost certainly occurred on land that is now part of Borneo, which was joined to Java for most of the Pleistocene. These mammals became extinct due to a change in vegetation, a shrinking range and hunting pressure on the reducing populations. Allee Effect (p. 298).

TIGER *Panthera tigris* **HB 1,700–2,300** **Extinct in Borneo**
Tiger bones have been found at the Niah Caves (Sarawak), Madai (Sabah) and Ille Cave (Palawan). Many Bornean folk tales refer to tigers indicating that they became extinct fairly recently. (Piper et al. 2007, 2008, Venz 2013), (p. 370).

LEOPARD *Panthera pardus* **HB 1,050–1,300** **Extinct in Borneo**
Although no Leopard bones have been found, Leopards probably occupied savannah habitat in Kalimantan until some 10,000 years ago. **Orangutans and Leopards**: Nowhere in the world do Leopards and Orangutans co-exist. In Sundaland Orangutans live on Borneo and Sumatra, but are extinct in Java and the Malay Peninsula. Leopards survive on Java and in Malaya, but are extinct in Sumatra and Borneo. A simple explanation is that Leopard prey lives at greater densities in areas of savannah grassland (for example in Java) and Orangutans live only in tall rainforest. In areas reverting to forest from grassland, Leopards are too heavy to climb tall rainforest trees so they would be starved out. Clouded Leopards survive in rainforest because they can feed on canopy primates (p. 279).

JAVAN RHINOCEROS *Rhinoceros sondaicus* **SH 1,600–1,800** **Extinct in Borneo**
The bones of the Javan Rhinoceros have been found both at the Madai Caves in Sabah and the Niah Caves in Sarawak, although the Sumatran Rhino was more common (Cranbrook 1986, Cranbrook & Piper 2007). See p. 294 for a possible reason why the Javan Rhino became extinct in Borneo before the Sumatran Rhino.

TAPIR *Tapirus indicus* **SH 900–1,050** **Extinct in Borneo**
In Malaya tapirs remain widespread, with a known dietary preference for the pioneer shrubs of secondary forest (Medway 1978). Early Bornean zoologists like Low & Everett listed the tapir for Borneo based on local reports, so it is likely that the tapir became extinct in Borneo relatively recently. See opposite.

OPENHEIMER'S EDEN IN THE EAST Openheimer (1998) suggests that the Sunda Basin was a cradle of human civilization until it was swamped by rising sea levels, but the evidence for this is scanty. The Sunda Basin most likely hosted an array of large mammals hunted by Austronesian (negrito) human hunter gatherers at a maximum density of *c.* 1/km², giving the 600,000km² Sunda Basin a maximum human population of *c.* 600,000 at the last glacial maximum, 24 KYA. As rising sea levels drowned the Sunda Basin over the next 14,000 years, these humans would have been squeezed out of flooded land at a rate of *c.* 43 humans per year – hardly a mass migration, but equivalent to a slow pump pushing the human population into the under-populated islands to the east of Java, including New Guinea and Australia.

TIGER Present in Sumatra and Malaya. Extinct in Java, Bali, Borneo and Palawan.

LEOPARD Present in Java, Malaya and Thailand. Extinct in Sumatra and Borneo.

JAVAN RHINO Present in Java. Extinct in Borneo. Recently extinct in Sumatra, Malaya, Thailand and Vietnam.

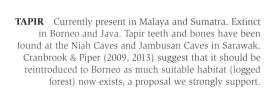

TAPIR Currently present in Malaya and Sumatra. Extinct in Borneo and Java. Tapir teeth and bones have been found at the Niah Caves and Jambusan Caves in Sarawak. Cranbrook & Piper (2009, 2013) suggest that it should be reintroduced to Borneo as much suitable habitat (logged forest) now exists, a proposal we strongly support.

TAPIR ECOLOGY Feeding experiments by Campos-Arceiz et al. (2011) at Singapore Zoo found that tapirs are poor dispersers of large seeds. Like pigs, they are predators of large seeds. Only small seeds such as those of *Dillenia indica* and *Melastoma malabathricum* remain intact in tapir dung.

TAPIR TAXONOMY The tapirs are members of the relict Tapiridae family most closely related to horses and rhinos. Tapiridae were once widespread in N America and Eurasia, but are now restricted to 4 species in tropical America and the Malayan Tapir in SE Asia. At least 2 species of tapir were present in SE Asia for most of the last 1.5 million years. The largest of these is now extinct (Cranbrook & Piper 2013). It would be a terrible loss if the last Asian tapir became extinct as well.

THE ARRIVAL OF HUMANS IN BORNEO

MODERN HUMANS FIRST ARRIVED IN BORNEO AROUND 50 KYA (thousand years ago), but a million years before this a variety of hominids was living in Java, Flores (Indonesia), China, Europe and probably Borneo.

Out of Africa Primates including monkeys, apes and modern humans originally evolved in Africa, later dispersing throughout the world. All humans living today are regarded as 1 species, *Homo sapiens*, but for most of the last 2 million years several species of human (genus *Homo* or 'hominids') co-existed both within and outside Africa. These hominids include *Homo erectus* (Java Man and Peking Man), *H. floresiensis* (the Hobbit from Flores in E Indonesia) and *H. neanderthalensis*, the Neanderthals in Europe.

Modern man Around 200 KYA yet another hominid, *H. sapiens*, evolved in Africa, and some 65 KYA *H. sapiens* began a dispersal out of Africa. *H. sapiens* reached Borneo and Australia at least 50 KYA, and entered the Americas via Siberia and Alaska at least 20 KYA.

Evidence for the first hominids in Borneo has been claimed for Manusili Valley in Ulu Segama, E Sabah, where a stone-tool factory has been found dating back to *c.* 235,000 years (Sabah Museum).

Evidence for the first modern humans in Borneo has been found at the Niah Caves, NW Sarawak (from 50 KYA) and at the Madai Caves, E Sabah (from 21 KYA). There are thousands of caves in Borneo that have yet to be investigated archaeologically (see Barker et al. 2013).

Sundaland The first modern humans reached Borneo *c.* 50 KYA by walking across the dry land of the Sunda Basin now flooded by the S China Sea. These humans (Negritos/Austronesians), looked like curly-haired Australian aboriginals similar to the Orang asli of Malaya. Excavations at Niah show that the Austronesians were hunter gatherers who used fire to clear the surrounding jungle, and hunted pigs, deer, bats, Orangutans and langurs. They also ate tapirs, tigers, and Javan and Sumatran Rhinos, and grew small amounts of yams and wet rice (Barker et al. 2013).

The first farmers and fishermen Around 10 KYA rising sea levels turned Borneo into an island, and *c.* 5 KYA at least 4 groups of mongoloid peoples with straight hair arrived in small boats. The first group established small fishing settlements all around the coast. A second group from the Philippines cleared the jungle for swidden agriculture in the Kudat Peninsula. A third group from Sumatra started swidden farming around Pontiananak (W Borneo) and a fourth group from Java started swidden farming near Bandjarmasin (S Borneo). These areas were the first to suffer local overpopulation, with large areas of primary forest converted to barren lalang grassland (p. 48).

THE ARRIVAL OF IRON AND THE FIRST EXTINCTIONS The first fishermen and farmers built boats and houses and cleared the jungle using only stone tools and fire. Large trees were killed by ring barking. The dead tree was then felled by burning the base. Iron tools and iron-working technology first reached Borneo *c.* 1,300 years ago, enabling rapid expansion in both permanent and swidden agriculture, and the construction of large boats for trading with other islands. Iron-tipped spears and steel-drilled blowpipes made hunting more effective and probably resulted in the first local mammal extinctions.

The first mammal extinctions When James (the white rajah) Brooke arrived in Borneo in 1838, Borneo was still covered in forest, but Orangutans were extinct in W Sabah and Brunei. Tapirs, tigers and Javan Rhinoceroses were already extinct throughout Borneo, and elephants only survived in E Sabah. The majority of Borneo's human population was already settled in small villages or longhouses, and survived by fishing and swidden farming (p. 48). The first wave of curly-haired Austronesian forest dwellers had gone, replaced by straight-haired mongoloid hunter gatherers known as Penans.

Hunter-gatherers, swidden farmers and over-population In 1860, St John estimated the human population as 3 million, yet in ecological terms Borneo was already overpopulated. An explanation for this is that hunter-gathering and swidden farming need very large areas of forest to feed a single family compared with fishing or wet-rice ('sawah') cultivation. Compared with the rich volcanic soils of Java, Sumatra and the Philippines, Bornean soils are poor and land for growing permanent food crops is scarce.

HEADHUNTING IN BORNEO

The Brookes rule in Sarawak from 1841–1946 was generally welcomed by the local tribes as it brought peace, justice and increased trade to W Borneo. Brooke rule was disliked for two reasons (1) A ban on headhunting and (2) A ban on the movement of long houses (villages) to new river valleys. In ecological terms headhunting was a way of expanding or defending tribal territory in an overpopulated habitat. Similarly, moving a longhouse to another river valley when the surrounding land was exhausted was also a response to an expanding population. These two Brooke laws therefore led to an increase in rural malnutrition.

MODERN MAN AT THE NIAH CAVES 40,000 YEARS AGO A curly-haired Austronesian family roasts a tapir's head at the Niah Caves in NW Sarawak *c.* 40,000 years ago, whilst a child plays with a locally common pet Orangutan. Tapirs are now extinct in Borneo and Orangutans have not been recorded around Niah within living history. The earliest humans in Borneo were Austronesians, later driven out, assimilated or killed by straight-haired Mongoloids arriving by sea from the surrounding islands.

HUNTER-GATHERER ECOLOGY

Sometime in the last 5,000 years the early curly-haired Austronesian (negrito) hunter-gatherer population disappeared, replaced by mongoloid straight-haired hunter-gatherers known as Penans. Penans can only survive in forest where there are extensive stands of wild Sago Palm *Eugeissona utilis*. A basic diet of carbohydrate sago is supplemented with hunted meat, mainly wild pig and wild fruit. Wild sago only grows below 1,200m on hill slopes, where it is free from attack by elephants (p. 52). Therefore the Penan population of Borneo was limited to the hilly interior where wild sago groves were abundant. Penan families moved camp frequently to allow sago groves to recover.

By 1838 the hilly forested interior of Borneo was already at 'carrying capacity', fully occupied by hunter-gatherers and swidden farmers with no land to spare, resulting in constant headhunting raids. Apart from the mountains and swamps, the only unpopulated lowland forest was in E Sabah (p. 52).

TRADITIONAL HUNTING TECHNIQUES

Until recently, the large majority of Borneo's coastal dwellers lived on a staple diet of fish and rice or cultivated sago, whilst the inland tribes lived on hill rice, wild sago and hunted meat. In forested areas most meat came from wild pigs. Before shotguns became widely available (in 1945), mammals were hunted in three ways. 1. Hunting Bearded Pigs with trained dogs and spears produced the most meat. 2. When pigs were scarce, blowpipes were used to hunt primates and squirrels in fruiting trees. 3. Before the rice harvest, traps were used to catch crop-raiding deer, pigs, porcupines and macaques. Hunting accidents were common, hence a local tradition that one should never hunt alone. (See Puri 2005.)

HUNTING ACCIDENTS 'The large animals hunted by the Ibans were chiefly bearded pigs, sun bears, clouded leopards and occasionally a rhinoceros or a banteng. Nearly all hunting accidents were due to wild boar or bears. We usually hunted in couples, but this evening one man set off alone. When we returned to camp at nightfall this man was missing and a search failed to find him. In the morning we all continued the search. He was found not far from the camp. He was horribly wounded; his stomach was split open and at least six foot of his intestines were hanging out, grimy with earth and covered with ants. Incredibly he was still alive and conscious. We carried him back to camp but he died soon afterwards. He had surprised a sow with her young, and before he could defend himself with his iron-tipped blow-pipe the mother pig had charged knocking him down. She then turned and charged again, and split open his stomach with a terrible thrust of her snout before running off.' (Adapted from Domalain 1974, Panjamon).

PRESERVING THE RESULTS OF THE HUNT In the past, preservation of surplus game without a freezer was a serious problem. George Jamuh describes how the Tagal Muruts of SW Sabah stored excess meat known as ***jarok*** for up to 6 months. 'The meat was chopped up and placed with salt into a large bamboo section which was then boiled slowly over a fire, sealed air tight with bees wax or resin and buried in the ground. Rats, squirrels and birds can be preserved whole. Jamuh reports that one Tagal used to force feed his dog with pig meat until the dog was over full. The owner would then hit the dog until it vomited up its meal. This tasty pre-digested meat was then stored for future consumption in the manner described above. Note that in most cases the meat is half-chewed by the hunters themselves before being preserved and the use of a dog saved this work! The saliva from dog or man, acts as a tenderizer.' (Condensed from G. Jamuh, *Sarawak Museum Journal*, 1954).

ELEPHANTS AND RHINOS, EAST SABAH – A HAVEN FOR WILDLIFE E Sabah today retains the most wildlife in Borneo because it has been mostly uninhabited until quite recently. A possible explanation for this is that the swampy floodplains of the Sugud, Labuk, Kinabatangan and Segama Rivers hosted abundant mosquitos, whilst the abundant mammals hosted zoonotic diseases such as malaria. The most likely explanation was provided by Banks (1982). He noted that there are no wild sago palms *Eugeissona utilis* in E Sabah, most likely wiped out by elephants. Therefore there was no staple food for Penans and no fallback food for swidden farmers, so E Sabah remained uninhabited. **NOTE:** A common palm used for sago production in E Kalimantan, *Arenga undulatifolia* (Langkap) is less preferred by elephants because all parts contain toxic rhaphides, and the *Arenga* palms in E Sabah are probably too scarce for continual harvesting (pp. 50 and 52).

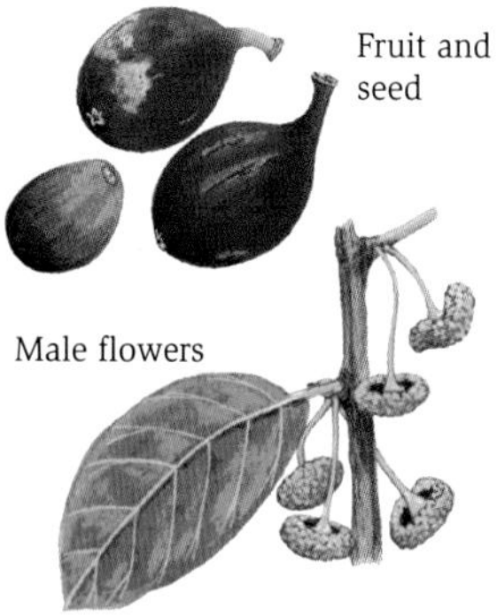

POISONOUS SAP The UPAS or IPOH tree *Antiaris toxicaria* grows sparingly in rainforest from W Africa to Australia and the Pacific. In Borneo, the Upas is a giant forest tree growing to 50m. The oval red fruit with a single seed are dispersed by large pigeons and fruit bats. The Upas is dioecious (separate male and female trees), and is easily recognized by the fallen green male flowers like flattened acorn cups. Sticky white Upas sap is tapped by cutting the bark. The poisonous sap is then dried over a fire and smeared on the tips of blowpipe darts. Upas poison retains toxicity indefinitely (Needham 1988). Some hunters add snake, scorpion or *Strychnos* poison for a more powerful effect when hunting large game. Upas bark was the preferred bark cloth used to make loin cloths (p. 74).

HUNTING WITH BLOWPIPES

SE Asian hunter gatherers originally used bows and arrows for hunting and switched to blowpipes only when Upas poison, the latex of *Antiaris toxicaria*, was discovered (Rambo 1978). Blowpipes were invented independently by hunter gatherers in Borneo and the Amerindians in the Amazon, suggesting that they are the ideal weapon for hunting in tall tropical forests. According to Puri (2005), a skilled blowpipe hunter can pick off a whole troop of Pig-tailed Macaques one by one whilst its unconcerned companions continue feeding. Due to the delayed action and silence of a fired dart a smart hunter can kill as many as a dozen grey langurs at a salt spring in one sitting, whilst the hunter only has one chance when using a shotgun. During the Second World War blowpipes were used to kill straggling enemy soldiers on jungle patrols. Blowpipes were originally constructed from bamboos with long internodes like *Kinabaluchloa nebulosa* (Wong & Dransfield 1996), but are now made from hardwood, hand-drilled with an iron bit.

Upas Tree
Antiaris toxicaria
Note the channels cut in the bark to collect the poisonous latex.

ECOLOGY: FOREST DISEASES AND NATURAL MEDICINES

TROPICAL FORESTS are both a source of many tropical diseases such as malaria, AIDS and Ebola, and a storehouse or natural pharmacy for treating human diseases. Borneo's 15,000 plant species protect their leaves, bark, seeds and roots from being eaten by manufacturing (synthesizing) nasty-tasting, toxic or poisonous chemicals. Plant chemicals range from bitter tannins, as in bark and tea leaves, to powerful oestrogens in yam tubers. The most toxic chemicals are reserved for the seeds.

The dose makes the poison Many plant toxins are used to treat human illnesses but usually only in tiny doses. Human livers can detoxify the small amounts of plant poisons contained in a normal human diet. However, an overload of natural toxins such as asprin can lead to liver failure and death.

The origin of taste Many studies have shown that the tongue can only taste 5 basic substances, sweet, sour, salt, bitter and umami. Thus in humans and most likely all mammals overall taste is decided in the brain. Humans are naturally aware if they have had 'too much of a good thing'. Therefore most mammals are probably self-medicating. If something tastes good to a mammal it most likely will do it good, and vice versa.

How Orangutans self-medicate Orangutans taste dozens of new different plants every day. A hungry 7-year-old Orangutan that has just left its mother cannot possibly know if all the leaves and fruit it encounters are safe to eat. According to researchers, Orangutans have a 6-stage strategy to test new plants for toxicity. 1. The plant is felt with fingers and mouth. 2. It is thoroughly smell tested. 3. It is tasted with lips and tongue. 4. A small piece of the plant is slowly chewed and the results are carefully inspected. 6. If the Orangutan is fully satisfied that there is no danger it will swallow a small taster and wander off. 6. Finally, if there are no negative effects, the Orangutan will return hours later to resume feeding. (See Schuster, Smits & Ulall 2012, *Thinkers of the Jungle.*), (p. 190).

Why are there no drug-addicted wild Orangutans? Psychoactive (brain-stimulant) drugs are abundant in Bornean plants. In Thailand, *Mitragyna speciosa* [kratom] is known as 'poor man's opium' and humans smoke the leaves for their hallucinogenic effects. In Borneo, kratom grows abundantly along the banks of the Kinabatangan River, prime Orangutan habitat, but it is not eaten by Orangutans. A drugged-up Orangutan would soon starve or fall prey to a Clouded Leopard – so undoubtedly kratom must taste very nasty to an Orangutan.

Cryptic medicines The average wild Orangutan diet probably includes numerous cryptic medicines and dietary supplements that most Orangutan researchers will never recognize. Is the Orangutan eating a new leaf because it tastes good or because there is nothing else to eat?

Kutai Grey Langur *Presbytis canicrus* at a mineral spring at Wehea, East Kalimantan
Many Bornean mammals and birds eat soil or visit salt or mineral licks, especially seed predators and leaf eaters. Carnivores and omnivores that gain their salt from the meat in their diet visit less often.
At Deramakot FR, Sabah (p. 338), Matsubayashi et al. (2014) found that 29 different mammals visited 5 salt-water springs. The most frequent were Sambar Deer, Bearded Pig, Lesser Mousedeer, Teledu and Bornean Orangutan. But why do seed-eating langurs and green pigeons visit salt licks so often, whilst fruit-pulp eating gibbons and imperial pigeons never do? The most likely explanation is that fine clay particles bind with and chemically detoxify the plant poisons in seeds and leaves, whilst salt is required by the stomach bacteria to digest cellulose plant fibres.

Slender Squirrel *Sundasciurus tenuis* eating the husk of Pinang Palm fruits *Areca catechu* to prevent intestinal worms as described by Ridley (1930), (p. 200).

Orangutan eating the flowers of *Fordia splendissima*, a common leguminous understorey shrub, as a caffeine stimulant as described by Willie Smits (2012).

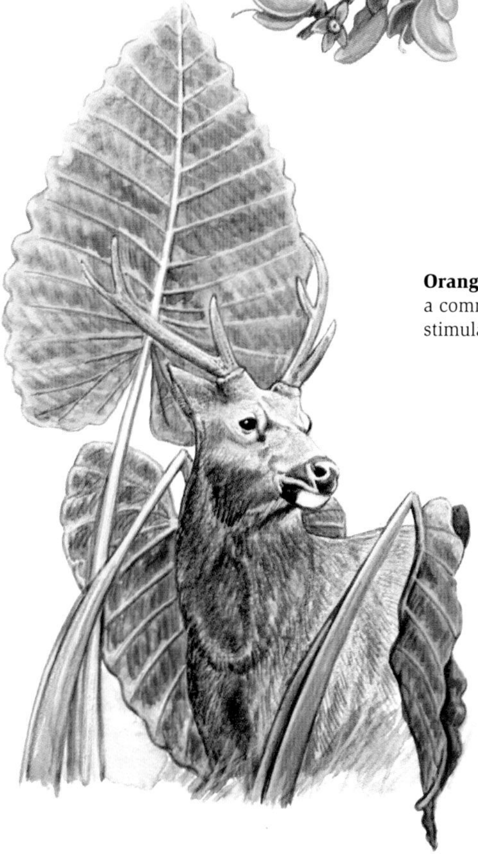

Sambar Deer rubbing its neck on an *Alocasia macrohyzza* leaf that it has damaged so that it can use the poisonous sap to kill ticks on inaccessible parts of its body as described by Palin at Tabin (pp. 308 and 344).

ECOLOGY: DANGER SIGNALS, MIMICRY AND CAMOUFLAGE

Unlike colourful birds that fly off when danger approaches, most mammals (except bats) are less able to escape easily. Mammals use a variety of subtle colours and markings for defence, camouflage and protection. Scent is also very important for sexual signalling and danger warnings when threatened, as in the Moonrat (p. 138) and Teledu (p. 254).

Black and white, black and yellow In all animals the universal signal for extreme danger is a series of black-and-white or black-and-yellow stripes – think of a wasp or a tiger. At long distance these markings may act as camouflage and only appear as a danger signal close up (see slow loris, p. 161 and Clouded Leopard, p. 279).

Mimicry is when harmless animals copy the appearance of poisonous or dangerous animals. A mimicry ring is when both dangerous and harmless animals share the same danger signal, some of which are genuine and some of which are false, as in Large Treeshrew, p. 151; primates, p. 157 and Collared Mongoose, p. 272.

Size matters Relative size is extremely important in judging danger. A predator risks serious injury and death if it attacks an animal much larger than itself. As additional defence some mammals make themselves look as large as possible when frightened, for example porcupines expand their quills, squirrels fluff out their tails and the Sun Bear stands up when threatened.

TARSIER Having ignored the very clear warning colouration, this Tarsier is eating a genuinely dangerous Banded Coral Snake *Maticora intestinalis*, as witnessed by Carsten Niemitz at Semengoh (p. 158).

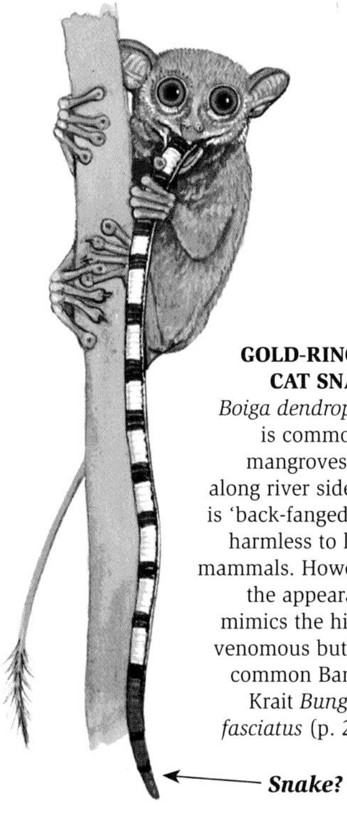

LINSANG The Linsang is a nocturnal carnivore with sharp teeth. The black-and-white danger markings are emphasized by the snake-like appearance of the tail (p. 260).

GOLD-RINGED CAT SNAKE *Boiga dendrophila* is common in mangroves and along river sides. It is 'back-fanged', so harmless to large mammals. However, the appearance mimics the highly venomous but less common Banded Krait *Bungarus fasciatus* (p. 261).

SUN BEAR
When threatened Sun Bears rear upright on their hind legs, exposing pale danger-sign markings on the chest. This young bear has pale soles to its feet, giving the impression of the eyes of a very large, dangerous animal with an open mouth. An adult Sun Bear is the most feared mammal in the Bornean rainforest, so the threat is genuine if the mother is near (p. 246).

PLANTAIN SQUIRREL
Squirrels remain still when threatened and could easily be mistaken for a branch by a gibbon or langur. However, close-up the belly stripes on *Callosciurus* squirrels clearly indicate that the squirrel is not a branch but a rodent with a nasty bite. The eye is also emphasized by a white ring (p. 195).

FLAT-HEADED CAT
hunting for frogs along the Kinabatangan River. Like most fish and otters, the cat is counter-shaded dark above and pale below for camouflage from both above and below. In this incident, witnessed by Baton Bijamin, the cat wisely backed off from the (harmless) snake. Note the black-and-white aposematic danger-warning face markings on the cat, found on most cats, civets and primates in Borneo.

ECOLOGY: LARGE CAVES OF BORNEO

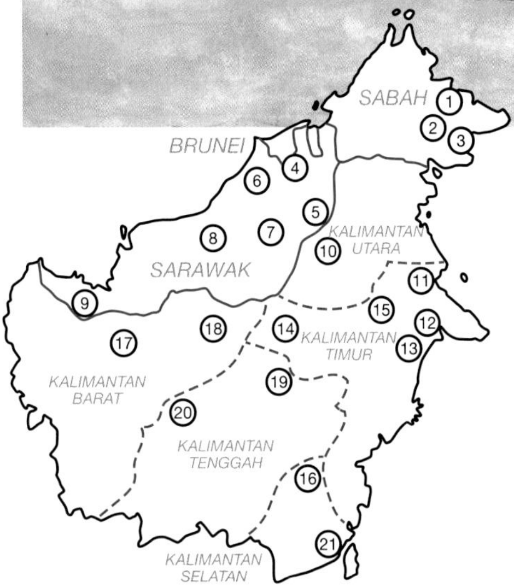

LARGE CAVES OF BORNEO
based on Lim & Cranbrook (2014)

	SABAH		KALIMANTAN
1	Gomantong (42,100*)	10	Talang Bala (166,666*)
2	Kuamut (9,800*)	11	Suaran (58,750*)
3	Madai (80,000*)	12	Sangkulirang
		13	Sengata (164,000*)
	SARAWAK	14	Long Pangahai (178,750*)
4	Mulu (75,000*)	15	Muara Wahau (53,333*)
5	Ulu Baram (22,000*)	16	Tabalong (87,000*)
6	Niah	17	Bukit Kelam (50,000*)
7	Ulu Kakus (125,000*)	18	Putussibau (186,667*)
8	Bkt Sarang (4,500*)	19	Puruk Cahu (833,333*)
9	Bau (37,000*)	20	Menukung (88,000*)
		21	Kota Baru (108,333*)

*Estimated population of Edible-nest Swiftlets in 2000.

LARGE CAVES OF BORNEO Borneo's largest caves are mostly found in scattered limestone hills (karst), the remnants of ancient coral reefs. The large cave list (left) is based on the estimated annual production of Edible-nest Swiftlet nests listed in Lim & Cranbrook (2014), but there are thousands of smaller caves, particularly in large areas of karst, as at Mulu (Melinau formation) and the Sangkulirang (Mangkalihat) Peninsula in E Kalimantan, which support large populations of cave bats and swiftlets.

Niah, Mulu and Gomantong, the largest accessible caves, are popular tourist sites providing a spectacular show as millions of bats and swiftlets swap roosts at dawn and dusk. Predatory hawks, eagles and owls pick off the stragglers. In isolated, undisturbed caves Sambar Deer frequently enter the caves to feed on the mineral-rich guano, whilst porcupines, Malay Civets and Müller's Rats visit nightly to feed on fallen bats and swiftlets. The tons of guano deposited in the caves every 24 hours supports a rich fauna of invertebrates and reptiles, including bat earwigs (pp. 134 and 136).

Foraging distance Bats and swiftlets forage up to 60km from their cave roosts. Conversion of forest to oil palm around the Niah Caves in Sarawak has contributed (along with overharvesting of nests) to a more than 90% collapse in both the bat and swiftlet populations over the last 50 years (pp. 366 and 372).

ECOLOGY: BIODIVERSITY GRADIENTS – FOREST AND OIL PALM

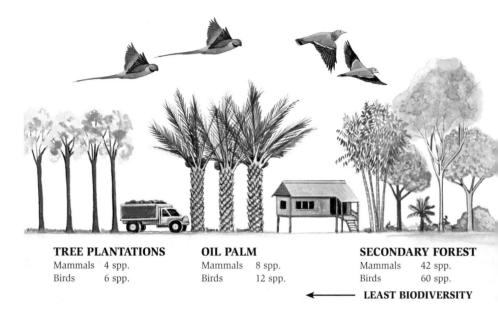

TREE PLANTATIONS		OIL PALM		SECONDARY FOREST	
Mammals	4 spp.	Mammals	8 spp.	Mammals	42 spp.
Birds	6 spp.	Birds	12 spp.	Birds	60 spp.

← **LEAST BIODIVERSITY**

BIODIVERSITY GRADIENTS measure the change in diversity (number of species) across a range of adjacent habitats. For example, on Kinabalu the diversity of both plants and animals falls the higher you climb. Where different habitats overlap (an ecotone), diversity temporarily increases, a phenomenon known as the Hump (pp. 46 and 236). Virgin rainforest in Borneo is some of the most diverse on Earth, so when it is replaced by secondary forest or plantations, the result is a massive loss in biodiversity, as shown in the estimated species figures above.

Invasive rodents benefit from forest destruction When virgin primary forest is degraded into logged forest or monoculture plantations the biodiversity collapses, but the biomass (total weight of mammals) often increases. Virgin lowland forest in Borneo supports 12 species of squirrel at low densities, whilst the abundant Plantain Squirrel is the only squirrel found in oil palm. Lowland forest hosts around 14 rats and mice, often rare species, whilst oil-palm plantations host up to 5 invasive rat species at very high densities of up to several hundred rats per hectare. In oil palm rats are predated by abundant snakes and owls, but rat predators such as civets and wild cats cannot survive in oil-palm plantations because they have nowhere to hide, rest or breed.

NEGATIVE DENSITY DEPENDENCY (NDD) AND THE JANZEN-CONNELL EFFECT In tropical rainforests seeds and saplings have the highest chance of survival the **further** away they grow from the parent tree. The reason for this is that the seed fall of the parent tree attracts species-specific seed predators including fungi, insects and rats. Thus seeds are more likely to grow into trees if they are first dispersed over long distance (p. 34). In the wet rainforests of Borneo pest pressure is continuous, hence the need for masting strategies to reduce seed predation (p. 54). (See also Blundell 1999, 2004, and Webb and Peart (1999, 2006). One result of pest pressure is high species diversity (p. 46). Another is that Bornean trees rarely grow in mono-dominant stands, and different tree species are thinly spread over large areas of forest. (See p. 46, Janzen 1970 and Connell 1970.)

The danger of plantation monocultures is that pests and diseases can spread rapidly from one tree to another. The oil palm is not native to Borneo, so has few natural enemies, but with increasing air travel it is only a matter of time before native oil-palm diseases spread from W Africa and S America to Borneo, devastating millions of hectares of oil-palm plantations. (See Phillipps & Phillipps 2014, p. 340, Jackson (2008), and Grandin (2010).)

LOGGED FOREST
Mammals 119 spp.
Birds 160 spp.

VIRGIN PRIMARY FOREST
Mammals 149 spp.
Birds 220 spp.

MOST BIODIVERSITY ⟶

The oil-palm forest ecotone Oil palm fruits continuously so where oil-palm estates adjoin forest, wildlife is often abundant. Many birds such as hornbills and parrots rely on oil-palm fruit as a fallback food. Owls and eagles feed on the abundant rats. Leopard Cats often hunt for rats along the edge of oil palm next to forest. Common *Cynopterus* fruit bats are often more abundant at the edge of oil palm than in virgin forest (pp. 86 and 96). Macaques, Bearded Pigs, Sun Bears, Porcupines and elephants often enter oil palm to feed both on fruit and palm buds, and these mammals are often hunted or poisoned by estate staff.

OIL PALM
COSTS AND BENEFITS
Oil palm is the world's most profitable plantation crop, 10 times as productive as soybean and 5 times as productive as canola (rape seed) oil. At current (2016) prices a typical 10,000ha (100km^2) plantation with a capital value of *c.* US $100 million will employ 2,500 workers and produce edible oils worth US$20–50 million per annum.

Estimated Mammal Deaths When Converting 100km^2 (10,000ha) of Forest to Oil Palm.

Mammal	Mammals per 100km^2	Est. loss
Large Treeshrew	Emmons (2000)	**4,900**
Colugo	Lim (2007)	**5,000**
Clouded Leopard	(p. 278)	**3**
Malay Civet	Colon (1999)	**100**
Slow Loris	Munds (2013)	**500**
Tarsier	Crompton (1987)	**1,200**
Orangutan	(p. 190)	**200**
Grey Langur	Blough & Gombek (2000)	**700**
Red Langur	Davies (1984)	**1,800**
Gibbon	(p. 186)	**900**
Pig-tailed Macaque	Johns (1982)	**1,580**
Sambar Deer	Kamil et al (2001)	**28**
Mousedeer sp.	Heydon & Bulloh (1997)	**8,400**
Muntjak sp.	Heydon & Bulloh (1997)	**600**
Elephant	Boonratana (1997)	**28**

PANGOLINS AND OIL PALM Mammals that benefit from oil-palm plantations include Plantain Squirrels, rats and surprisingly pangolins. Ants remain abundant in oil palm so there is no shortage of food for pangolins. However, oil palms are harvested every 2 weeks by contract labour paid the minimum wage, and any pangolin encountered is either eaten or sold for traditional Chinese medicine (p. 152). Thus oil-palm estates are death traps for pangolins.

ECOLOGY: SEED DISPERSAL OVERVIEW

FOREST PLANTS use multiple strategies to ensure that their seeds are widely dispersed, including wind and water, but the large majority use food (fruit pulp) as a bait to entice a mammal or bird to swallow the fruit whole, later defecating the seeds far away from the parent tree. With oak acorns and leguminous beans the seed acts as a bait to attract seed-eating, scatter-hoarding rats, porcupines and squirrels.

Dispersal guilds Different plant dispersal strategies are known as *dispersal syndromes* and animal groups that eat similar fruit are known as *dispersal guilds*. Illustrations in the plant section (pp. 48–77) show how some Bornean plant families target specific dispersal guilds with a variety of fruit sizes and colours.

Dispersal syndromes Opposite are given examples of 5 common dispersal syndromes recognizable from key features of the fruit, including 1. fruit size, 2. seed size, 3. fruit signal colour, 4. smell, 5. skin type and 6. pulp content. See also bat dispersal (p. 80) and rodent dispersal (pp. 233, 237 and 245).

Generalists Although we can recognize and categorize dispersal guilds and syndromes, be aware that generalist fruits (which target more than one guild) are common, and also that dispersal guilds are not rigid. For example, primates may eat bulbul fruit or hornbill fruit if primate fruit is scarce. Seed dispersal is extremely important in forest ecology, but because the boundaries between guilds are often fuzzy, not enough attention has been paid to seed dispersal in the past.

DISPERSAL OF A MANGO SEED
Mangifera torquenda Local: Bunitan

Pulp thieves An Orangutan, gibbon or macaque will eat the pulp and dump the seed (too large to swallow) close to the parent tree.

Seed predators A pig or porcupine will eat both the pulp *and* the seed.

Local disperser A Sambar Deer will swallow the fruit and regurgitate the seed locally.

The target Only a Sun Bear, rhino or elephant can swallow the fruit and disperse the seed far from the parent tree in a pile of fertilizer. Small mangoes may be targeted at primates (p. 58).

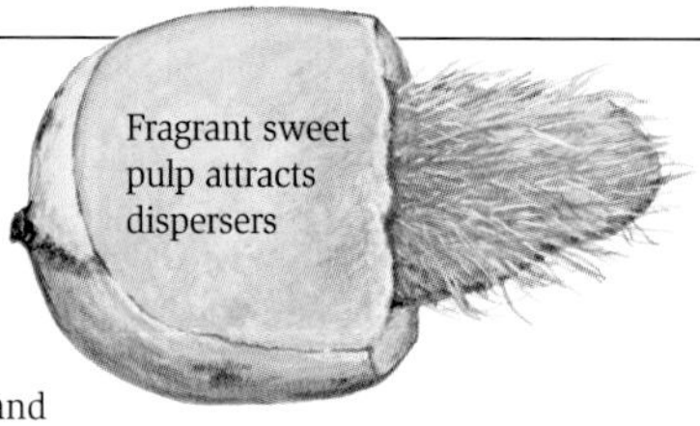
Fragrant sweet pulp attracts dispersers

Pulp is attached by hairs to the toxic seed to ensure that the seed is swallowed whole when the pulp is eaten.

MAMMALS AS SEED DISPERSERS AND SEED PREDATORS IN BORNEO Mammals can be grouped into 5 types in relation to seed dispersal: 1. seed dispersers, 2. seed predators, 3. pulp thieves, 4. all three preceding categories, 5. no relationship, as insectivorous bats. Most mammals are in category 4. They both predate some and disperse other seeds, but in different proportions. See chart below: '%' refers to ripe/unripe fruit/seed consumption only, not other dietary items. **Note:** Even seed predators disperse tiny seeds such as those of figs, wild bananas and gingers, and important seed dispersers like gibbons, elephants and rhinos also predate oaks and dipterocarp seeds during masting periods (p. 44).

MAMMAL	% dispersed	% predated	% pulp thief	Page
Fruit bats	80%	0%	20%	80
Langurs	25%	75%	0%	176
Macaques	25%	5%	70%	182
Gibbon	95%	5%	0%	186
Orangutan	50%	40%	10%	190
Prevost's Squirrel	5%	5%	90%	196
Giant Squirrel	5%	40%	45%	210
Forest rats	20%?	80%?	0%	237
Porcupines	20%?	80%?	0%	244
Sun Bear	95%	5%	0%	248
Palm Civet	95%	5%	0%	264
Elephant	95%	5%	0%	290
Rhinoceros	95%	5%	0%	296
Bearded Pig	20%	80%	0%	302
Mousedeer	95%	5%	0%	306
Sambar	95%	5%	0%	308
Muntjac	95%	5%	0%	310

SOME SEED-DISPERSAL SYNDROMES AND GUILDS

SMALL BIRD-DISPERSED FRUIT

Example: *Antidesma bunius* (Berunai)
Small fruit with no smell.
Ripens to bright red/shiny black.
Sweet pulp, soft skin.
Small, smooth seeds.
Fruit swallowed, seeds defecated.

HORNBILL-DISPERSED FRUIT

Example: *Knema furfuracea*
(Wild nutmeg/Pala hutan)
No smell – birds cannot smell!
Hard shell to deter pulp thieves.
Splits (dehices) when ripe, showing red oily aril and smooth seeds.
Seed and aril swallowed by hornbills, seed later regurgitated.

PRIMATE-DISPERSED FRUIT

Example: *Nepthelium rambutan-ake*
(Wild rambutan, p. 216)
Pleasant smell.
Ripens to dull colours, brown, red.
Thick skin stops pulp-thieving birds.
Sweet pulp sticks to the seed so that pulp and seed are swallowed together – seeds later defecated.
Seed close to maximum width (2.1cm) for primate to swallow whole.

RAT-DISPERSED BEANS (p. 68)

Example: *Mucuna* and *Dioclea* beans
Large, hard, shiny dark beans.
Seeds have long dormancy.
Seeds slightly toxic.
No pulp. The seed is the reward.
Rats scatter-hoard fallen beans, which may later sprout.
Some beans can only grow after being gnawed by rats.

ELEPHANT DISPERSAL (p. 290)

Example: *Citrus grandis* (Wild Pomelo)
Fruit ripens to dull, brown/green/yellow.
Strong, pleasant smell when ripe.
Grows on small trees easily reached by an elephant's trunk.
Thick rind to stop pulp thieves.
Very large fruit. Only elephant is big enough to swallow it whole.
Note all seeds are in centre to deter seed predators.

ECOLOGY: THE SIGNIFICANCE OF SEED SIZE

WHY DO SO MANY TROPICAL TREES HAVE LARGE SEEDS? An estimated 85% of Borneo's tree species are animal dispersed. Large animals prefer to eat large fruit to maximize foraging efficiency. Given a choice an elephant will choose a durian over a fig because it is larger. Thus competition between plants to attract the largest long-distance dispersers results in larger seeds. In addition we can recognize numerous evolutionary strategies and trade-offs that affect the sizes of Bornean fruits and seeds.

Benefits of large seeds include 1. A larger store of food and water, giving the young plant a higher chance of survival. The larger the seedling, the more likely it is to survive and grow when forest gaps open up (Brown & Whitmore 1992). 2. Large fruit are more likely to attract large mammal dispersers like rhinos and elephants.

Disadvantages (costs) of large seeds 1. Bigger stores of food attract more seed predators like rats and porcupines. 2. Large seeds have a lower chance of ending in the right place. A belian seed (p. 39) weighs the same as 50,000 fig seeds, so for the same investment, a fig has 50,000 chances of the seed growing into a tree whilst a belian only has one.

Compound fruit or large fruit with many smaller seeds packed in an edible pocket such as durians, jak fruit and terap (p. 75) are an attempt to attract both large and small dispersers. Even though the fruit may be large the seed packets can be swallowed individually and dispersed by many different smaller mammals.

Targeted dispersal and seed size The benefits of large seeds are such that animal-dispersed plants evolve the largest seed a local disperser can swallow. Thus the majority of primate fruit have seeds close to 2.1cm in width, the maximum size that can be swallowed by gibbons and Orangutans, whilst seeds with oily arils targeted at hornbill dispersal have even larger seeds (2.6cm maximum width), the largest size that can be swallowed (and later regurgitated) by hornbills.

Seeds designed to be swallowed whole Belian seeds are extremely slippery once the pulp has been removed so that the seed will slide easily down the throat of a rhino, whilst the seed itself is toxic to most animals. In many primate fruit the stone is covered in hairs or sticks to the flesh, for example in mangosteen, mango and rambutan, so that the primate is forced to swallow the seed along with the flesh. In contrast, hornbill-dispersed seeds like most durians have smooth seeds, so they can easily be regurgitated (p. 368).

THE LARGER THE SEED, THE GREATER THE INTERVAL BETWEEN FRUITING Trees that produce fruit with very small seeds, like figs, gingers, bananas and laran, tend to flower and fruit almost continuously, whilst trees that produce fruit with large, unprotected (non-toxic) seeds, such as dipterocarps, mangoes and durians, fruit together at long intervals, i.e. trees with large edible seeds are more prone to **masting** than trees with small seeds (pp. 12, 54 and 196).

***Macaranga* seed size and fruiting:** In a study at Lambir that compared the fruiting of 11 sympatric species of *Macaranga*, a common secondary forest tree with large leaves, Davies et al. (1999) found that *Macaranga* with large seeds produced low numbers of seeds at long intervals, whilst *Macaranga* with small seeds produced more seeds more regularly – presumably due to the reduced predation risk from rats and ground doves, which prefer large seeds.

ARGUS PHEASANTS AND TOXIC PRIMATE-DISPERSED SEEDS

Primate-dispersed trees produce seeds just under 2.1cm wide, which are swallowed and defecated by primates. Argus Pheasants also cannot swallow seeds more than 2.1cm wide (Davison 1981). This is unlikely to be a coincidence. Primate-dispersed seeds are very toxic to primates, but obviously not to Argus Pheasants. According to Mjoberg (1930), 'Anyone who chances to eat the flesh of an Argus Pheasant becomes seriously ill with high fever, headache, difficulty in breathing, aching limbs, palpitation of the heart and violent pain in the lymph vessels of the throat. For the flesh is very poisonous owing to the fact that the Argus-pheasant feeds almost entirely on a number of poisonous fruits.'

It is likely that the Argus Pheasant is a specialist predator on toxic primate-dispersed seeds and sequesters the toxins to protect itself, as happens in many butterflies, beetles, bats, slow loris and mongooses. The Argus Pheasant advertises its unpleasant taste with a bright blue head similar to the head of the Bornean Ground-cuckoo, which also has inedible flesh probably tainted by toxins from poisonous beetles and millipedes. This advertising by both birds of their poisonous flesh is an example of Müllerian mimicry (pp. 124 and 156).

The Argus Pheasant is the most common large avian seed predator of the forest floor in Borneo.

1 0.5 cm width

2 1.5 cm width

3 2.1 cm width

4 2.6 cm width

SEVEN SEED DISPERSAL GUILDS ARRANGED BY SIZE
(D) Swallowed and defecated
(R) Swallowed and regurgitated
(P) Seed predated, (S) Seed spit.
Illustrated are the ***seeds*** with the largest width that are ***normally*** swallowed by the animals listed in each guild.
Notes: (A) When swallowed these seeds are covered in pulp which may add 2 + cm to the width shown. (B) Birds and mammals occasionally swallow seeds and fruits of larger sizes. (C) Large seeds often vary in size i.e. they are targeted at more than one seed dispersal guild e.g. belian (p. 39), mezzetia (p. 190) and onion fruit (p. 237). (D) Macaques and mousedeer use cheek pouches to hold large fruit before the seed is spit/regurgitated.

1 Seeds up to 0.5 cm width
Fruit Bat (D), macaque (D), Bearded Pig (D)

2 Seeds up to 1.5 cm width
Fairy Bluebird (R), Bulbul (R), Civet (D)

3 Seeds up to 2.1 cm width
Gibbon (D), Broadbill (R), Sambar Deer (R), Muntjac (R) Argus Pheasant (P) Mousedeer (R)

4 Seeds up to 2.6 cm width
Orangutan (D), Hornbill (R), Barbet (R), Imperial Pigeon (R), Mousedeer (R)

5 Seeds up to 4.0 cm width
Sun Bear (D), Sambar Deer (R)

6 Seeds up to 6.0 cm width
Rhinoceros (D) tapir in Malaya and Sumatra (P)

7 Seeds 6.0 cm–10 cm width
Elephant (D) Cassowary in New Guinea (R)

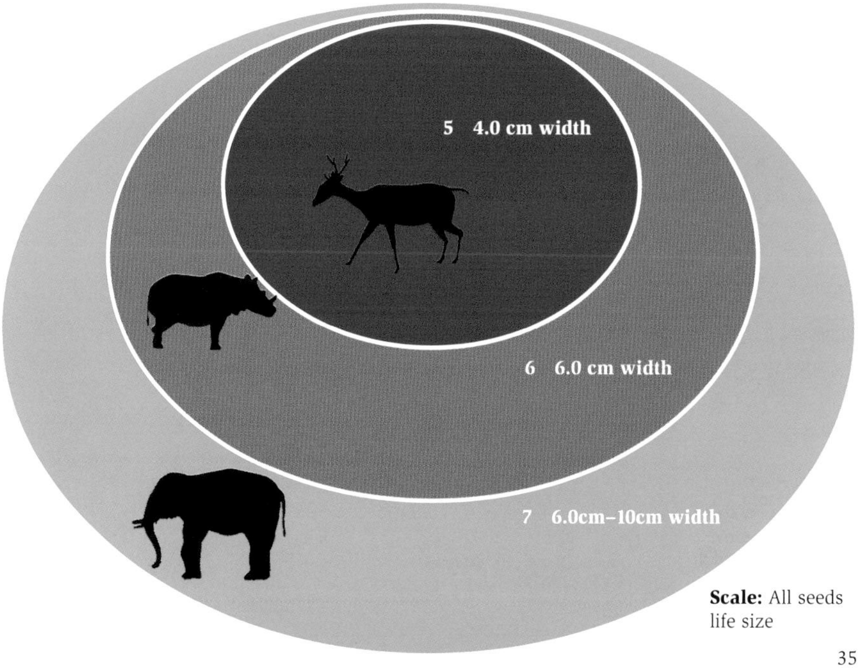

Scale: All seeds life size

ECOLOGY: ANACHRONISTIC FRUITS

DISPERSAL OF SUNDALAND'S FORESTS Anachronistic fruits are fruits that evolved to be dispersed by a vanished megafauna of large mammals. Today we can recognize at least 100 large Bornean fruits targeted at elephant and rhino dispersal growing in localities where megafauna are now extinct (pp. 290 and 296). A subgroup of these fruits produces large, hard seeds that float down rivers from the forested interior of Borneo to appear on coastal beaches as drift seeds. Yet these large seeds cannot survive in sea water or grow in salty sand.

Anachronistic drift seeds The explanation of this anomaly lies in the history of Sundaland (maps, pp. 15–17). For the last 2.6 million years, Sundaland's land area repeatedly expanded and contracted as sea levels rose and fell. At glacial maximums Sundaland was mostly dry land crossed by some of the world's largest and longest rivers and populated by megafauna. Fruits evolved tasty pulp surrounding large, woody seeds. As sea levels fell, the seeds floated down rivers to colonize the new land. When sea levels later rose the megafauna retreated back into the hills, dropping the seeds in their dung. Today these drift seeds grow far into the hills of Borneo. Six of these anachronistic drift seeds are illustrated opposite and elsewhere in this guide, like *Eugeissona* Palms (p. 52), mangoes (p. 58), *Entada* beans (p. 68), *Mezzetia* (p. 190), *Irvingia* (p. 310) and *Lithocarpus* oaks (p. 233). Note that most of these seeds are slow to germinate (orthodox), allowing ample time for dispersal (p. 234).

MEGAFAUNA EXTINCTIONS WORLDWIDE Following the migration of modern humans from Africa to Europe and Asia around 60,000 years ago, many species of large Sundaland mammal became extinct. For much of the last 2.6 million years, Sundaland was populated by at least 3 species of elephant and 3 species of rhino, as well as 2 tapirs and a hippo (pp. 16 and 18). Most of the Pleistocene was dryer and colder than currently. Pollen evidence from oil surveys shows that the vegetation of the Sunda Basin varied from savannah grassland to dipterocarp forest. In the drier southern lowlands a 'savannah corridor' opened up every *c.* 100,000 years, allowing birds from Indochina and large grazers to reach Java from the Asian continent, whilst during wetter periods dipterocarp forest covered the basin from Singapore to Sarawak. The evidence from Javan fossils (p. 14, 16 and 288) is that Sundaland was teeming with megafauna and its predators, including scattered bands of hunter/gatherer hominids. The rapid extinction of megafauna by early humans throughout the world left behind the fruit trees that megafauna had evolved to disperse. The existence of 'anachronistic fruit' was first recognized by Dan Janzen in Costa Rica, e.g. the avocado is an American anachronistic fruit with no known disperser. (See Janzen & Martin 1982, Barlow 2000, Guimaraes et al. 2008, Dinerstein 2013.)

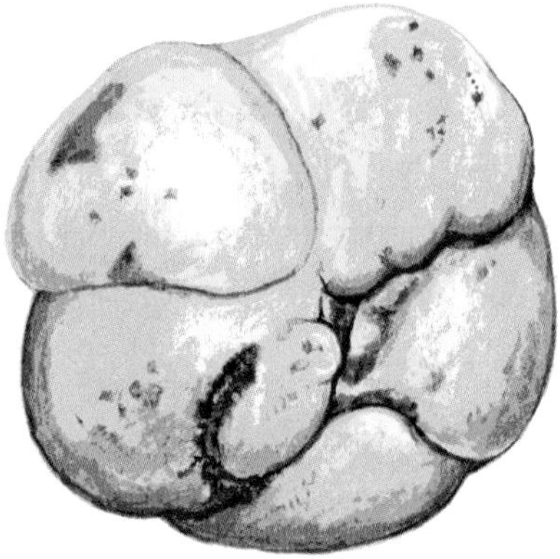

Dillenia indica Simpoh Gajah (Dilleniaceae). Common on river floodplains. John Lim reports that a herd of elephants behaved as if they were drunk after eating the fallen fruit.

Scale: All seeds and fruit are 60% life size apart from the football-sized fruit of *Hodgsonia macrocarpa*. All seeds shown are maximum 6cm width indicating rhino-targeted dispersal.

SOME COMMON DRIFT SEEDS ALSO DISPERSED BY RHINOS AND ELEPHANTS

Hodgsonia macrocarpa Akar Kepayang or Oil Nut (Cucurbitaceae). The football-sized fruit must be targeted at elephant dispersal but rhinos are also likely to disperse the fallen seeds.

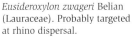

Eusideroxylon zwageri Belian (Lauraceae). Probably targeted at rhino dispersal.

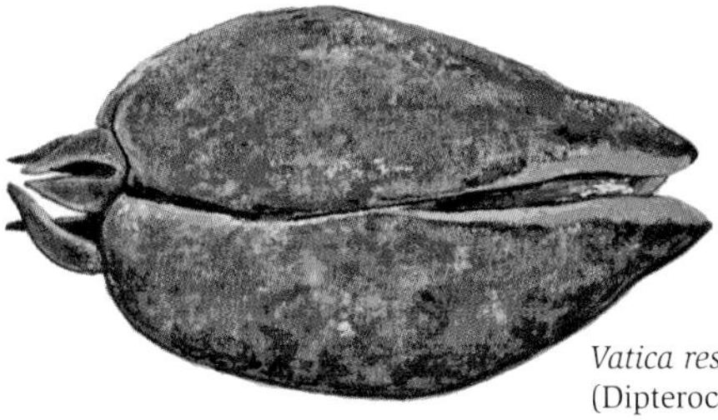

Vatica resak Resak (Dipterocarpaceae). Dispersed by sea from Malaya to N Guinea.

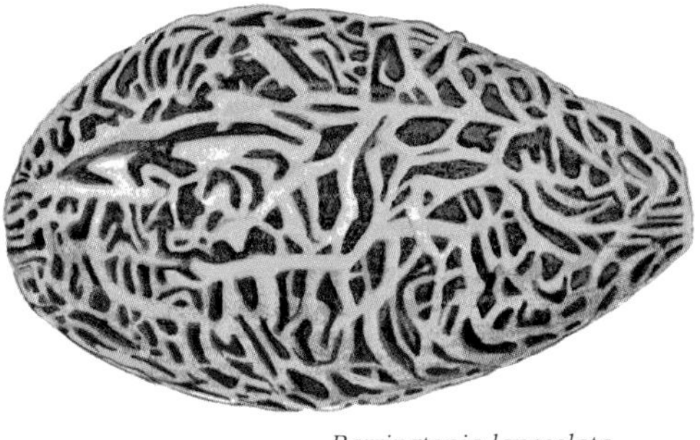

Barringtonia lanceolata Putat hutan seed. Most likely targeted at rhino dispersal.

Barringtonia sarcostachys (Lecythidaceae).
Putat hutan fruit. One of 18 *Barringtonia* found in Bornean forests.

ECOLOGY: HOW PLANTS COLONIZE NEW ISLANDS

BATS, RATS AND HERMIT CRABS Many Bornean coastal trees with sea-dispersed seeds have evolved mutualistic relationships with fruit bats as pollinators or dispersers, or both. Around 30 plants known as the **Barringtonia Association** dominate sandy beaches from E Africa to the Pacific Islands. Their drift seeds are dragged inland by rats and hermit crabs. Bats disperse seeds inland and between islands. Unlike anachronistic fruit (p. 39), the seeds of Barringtonia Association plants survive salt water and thrive in beach sand.

Bats and the Barringtonia Association Many Barringtonia Association plants flower and fruit continuously (Steady State) benefitting 2 guilds of bats. 1. Resident understorey *Cynopterus* and *Macroglossus* bats are ensured a continuous supply of fruit and nectar. 2. Nomadic flying foxes and cave-dwelling *Eonycteris* nectar bats rely on coastal forests as fallback provisions when inland forests are barren. Nomadic bats often roost on islands and in mangrove forests both for safety and for the constant supply of fruit and nectar.

Sundaland and the Barringtonia Association Sundaland's long coastlines host the world's highest diversity of coastal and mangrove plants, a result of forced evolution from continuously changing sea levels during the Pleistocene, and the competition amongst plants to occupy new habitats (p. 39). As pointed out by Whittaker (1994) and Thornton (1996), the rapid colonization of new coastline by mangrove and Barringtonia Association plants has a positive feedback effect, attracting birds and bats that also bring with them seeds of inland forest trees such as figs. Thus the early arrival of Barringtonia Association plants 'kick starts' the return of lowland forest to new land.

KRAKATAU AND PLANT DISPERSAL On 27 August 1883 the volcanic island of Krakatau (300km south-west of Borneo (map, p. 15) exploded, creating a tsunami that killed over 36,000 people on the coasts of Java and Sumatra. Three new sterile islands were rapidly colonized by wind-blown fern spores followed by wind-dispersed plants. Within 3 years drift seeds of the Barringtonia Association were growing along the coast, and within 15 years there were 4 species of bat figs. By 1989 there were 59 sea-dispersed plants, 75 wind-dispersed plants, 81 wind-dispersed ferns and 110 bird- and bat-dispersed plants. According to Thornton (1996) 'animal dispersal has been of overwhelming importance in the development of the Krakatau forests'. Of the 24 species of fig on the Krakatau islands, the first 7 species to arrive were all bat figs. By 1992, 7 species of fruit bat had arrived. Volcanic islands around Borneo include Pulau Tiga, Sipadan, Maratua and the Turtle islands near Sandakan.

A fourth island, **Anak Krakatau**, emerged in 1927. Illustration shows Anak Krakatau in 1989 with Sertung in the background.

HERMIT CRABS Around 15 species of land-based (terrestrial) hermit crab inhabit the small islands around Borneo. Hermit crabs range from 0.5cm across to the giant 40cm Coconut Crab *Birgus latro*. As night falls hermit crabs scavenge along the tide line, dragging drift seeds back to their burrows inland. Hermit crabs are important dispersers of coastal plants. The Coconut Crab is also a seed predator able to open mature coconuts.

Small Hermit Crabs like *Cilibanarius* species burrow in empty seashells to house their soft bodies.

PUTAT LAUT *Barringtonia asiatica*. Sturdy (to 25m) bat-pollinated and sea-dispersed coastal tree. Fine examples can be seen on sandy beaches all round Borneo, e.g. P Mantanani, P Gaya and P Tiga on Sabah's west coast. There are *c*. 18 species of *Barringtonia* tree in Bornean lowland forests. The majority have bat-pollinated flowers and anachronistic fruit most likely targeted at rhinos (p. 39). Sea-dispersed *B. asiatica* is an exception.

Illustration by Susan Phillipps.

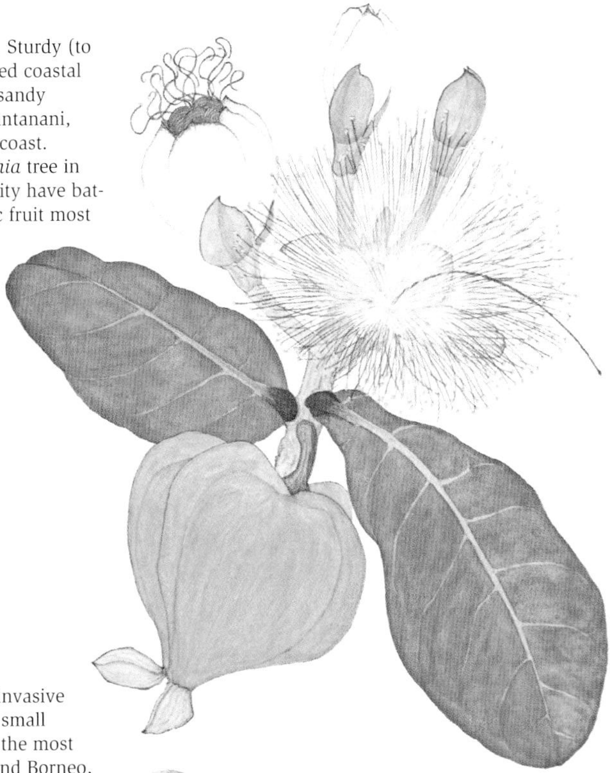

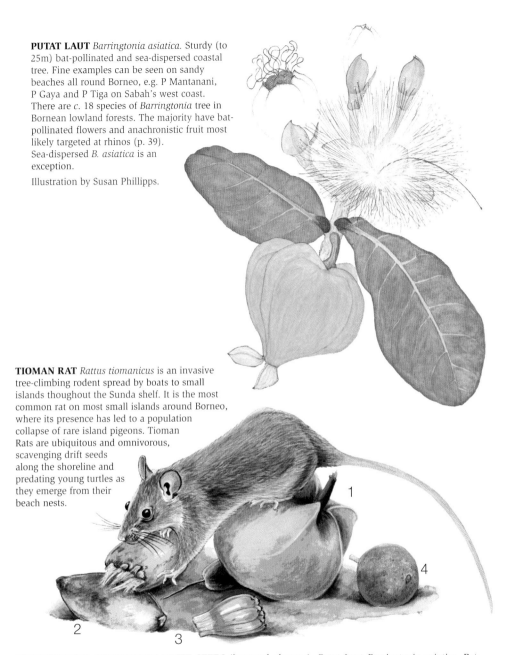

TIOMAN RAT *Rattus tiomanicus* is an invasive tree-climbing rodent spread by boats to small islands thoughout the Sunda shelf. It is the most common rat on most small islands around Borneo, where its presence has led to a population collapse of rare island pigeons. Tioman Rats are ubiquitous and omnivorous, scavenging drift seeds along the shoreline and predating young turtles as they emerge from their beach nests.

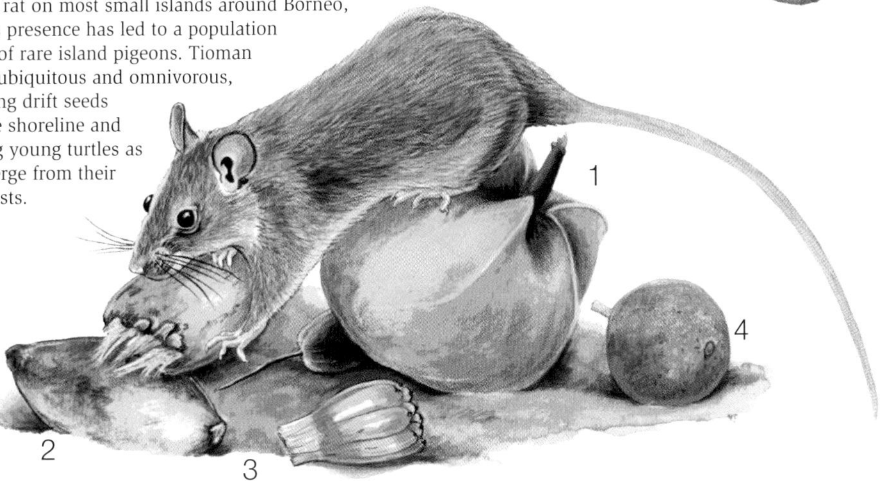

BARRINGTONIA ASSOCIATION DRIFT SEEDS illustrated above: 1. Putat Laut *Barringtonia asiatica*. Bat pollinated and sea dispersed. The toxic seeds are used as a fish poison, but this does not appear to deter rats, which chew holes in the thick, fibrous husk to get at the inner seed. 2. Sea Almond [Ketapang] *Terminalia catappa*. Common coastal tree (p. 81). 3. Pandan *Pandanus tectorius* (p. 83). 4. Bintanggor laut *Calophylum inophyllum*. All members of the Barringtonia Association have sea-dispersed 'drift' seeds. A large number are bat pollinated and a lesser number, 3 of which are illustrated above, are both bat pollinated and bat and sea dispersed.

ECOLOGY: FOREST NOMADS

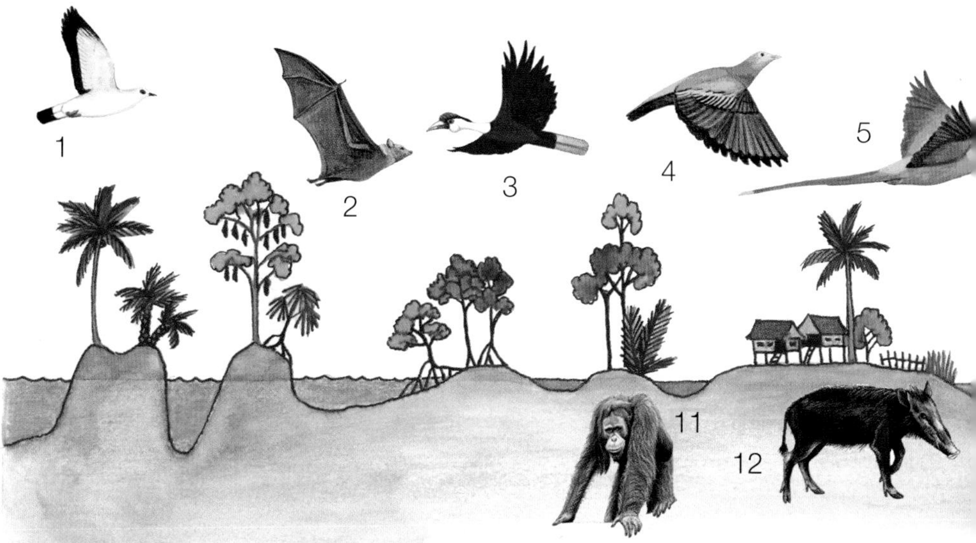

Many fruit trees in Borneo rely on dry periods to trigger simultaneous flowering (masting), on average every 4–5 years (pp. 10 and 12). Borneo's numerous hills and valleys provide multiple differing microclimates so that even annual fruiting varies from valley to valley. More rain falls on the hilly interior than in coastal forest, so that fruiting begins in the lowlands and moves inland up each river valley. The result is a constantly changing mosaic of flowering and fruiting patches in Bornean forests, forcing fruit- and nectar-eating nomads to travel long distances.

NOMADIC BIRDS AND MAMMALS

1 **PIED IMPERIAL PIGEON** Nomadic disperser of large seeds between islands.

2 **FLYING FOX** Roosts in coastal forest. Flies inland to forage for nectar and fruit.

3 **WRINKLED HORNBILL** Important nomadic disperser in peat-swamp forest.

4 **GREEN PIGEONS** Common nomadic seed predators of lowland forests.

5 **PARROTS** of 3 species are common nomadic seed predators in forested areas.

6 **GIANT HONEY BEES** are nomadic pollinators migrating between patches of flowering forest (p. 66).

7 **FIG TREES** fruit year round, providing a steady food supply to resident mammals and birds (p. 76).

8 **LIMESTONE CAVES** provide roost sites for fruit and nectar bats that fly long distances to feed (p. 30).

9 **MOUNTAIN IMPERIAL PIGEON** Breeds in the mountains but often visits coastal mangroves.

10 **WREATHED HORNBILL** Nomadic flocking hornbill that follows fruiting patches in hill forest.

11 **ORANGUTAN** Wanders long distances. Both a seed disperser and seed predator (p. 190).

12 **BEARDED PIGS** do best next to oil palm in cultivated areas (p. 300).

13 **ELEPHANTS** are important dispersers of large fruit with large seeds in lowland forests (p. 290).

14 **BEARDED PIGS** follow fruiting patches over long distances involving mass migrations (p. 302).

15 **RHINOCEROS**, now extinct, was previously a major disperser of anachronistic fruit (p. 296).

16 **PHEASANTS** are major seed predators on fallen fruit and breed only when seeds are abundant.

VERS **LOWLAND FOREST** **LIMESTONE CAVES** **HILLS** **MOUNTAINS** **KINABALU**

MASTING evolved in plants as a strategy to defeat seed predators, but in turn 'guilds' of nomadic seed predators and seed dispersers have also evolved to exploit the erratic supply of nectar and fruit.

Lowland forests are both the most productive and most varied in fruit production. Fruit may be super abundant following ENSO events, to almost absent a few months later – apart from 'fallback' fruits like figs (p. 76).

Peat-swamp forests fruit steadily but in low quantities. **Montane forests** produce fruit erratically and out of synchrony with lowland forests. Thus both peat-swamp and montane forests provide **food refugia** for nomadic frugivores when fruit is scarce in lowland forests. Cultivation that cuts corridors between forests means death by starvation for many ground mammals.

HOW NOMADS FIND FLOWERING AND FRUITING TREES According to local tradition, when the forest starts flowering Giant Honey Bees are the first to arrive, building their huge combs on tall *Koompasia* trees (p. 66). The bees are followed by flying foxes and nectar bats (attracted by scent), which can be seen overhead in large flocks at dusk and at dawn. Bearded Pigs begin mating at this flowering stage. When fruiting begins flocks of screeching parrots, hornbills and pigeons flying overhead signal fruiting trees to nomadic bands of Bearded Pigs below. Pigs also follow the sounds made by feeding gibbons and Pig-tailed Macaques.

Fruiting strangling figs In the 'lean period' between masting episodes, many Bornean mammals are semi-nomadic, relying on large strangling figs that fruit intermittently to provide a 'fallback' diet. Nomadic fig eaters that climb, such as Orangutans, Binturong and Pig-tailed Macaques, can watch the flight paths of bats and hornbills at dawn and dusk from the top of a tall tree to find fruiting figs, but how do terrestrial mammals such as Bearded Pigs and Sun Bears track down these scarce widely separated events? Sun Bear expert Wong Siew Te suggests that both birds and mammals use barbet calls to locate fruiting figs. Normally solitary and territorial, barbets gather to feed in fruiting figs, voicing their distinctive *took took* calls constantly between feeding bouts. Several different barbets all calling from the same location indicates a fruiting strangling fig.

ECOLOGY: SEED PREDATION OVERVIEW

A LARGE STRANGLING FIG like *Ficus caulocarpa* can produce more than 10,000 fruit in each crop. Large figs crop up to 3 times a year. Each fig contains *c.* 300 viable seeds. In a lifetime exceeding 100 years a *F. caulocarpa* produces in excess of 1 billion seeds. Yet only 1 seed is required to perpetuate its genes. What happens to the other 999,999,999? The answer is that they are nearly all predated – by fungi, beetles, ants and birds, and some by mammals. Fig seeds are protected from predation by their tiny size, but large, oil-rich seeds are a major food source for Orangutans, langurs, pigs, squirrels, rats and porcupines. Bornean plants invest heavily in defensive strategies to protect their seeds.

Defensive strategies used against seed predators include 1. Physical protection such as hard seed coats or sharp spines as in Durians (p. 62). 2. Chemical protection like toxic or poisonous seeds (p. 24). 3. Camouflage colours that help seeds blend with the forest floor. 4. Small size – too small for large seed predators. 5. Large size – too heavy for small rats to carry (p. 290). 6. Slippery surfaces so that seeds will rapidly slip through the predators' gut unharmed, as in Belian (p. 38). 7. Predator satiation/starvation via masting (see below) and 8. Recalcitrant seeds (see opposite).

MASTING OR MASS FRUITING is a strategy whereby the majority of forest trees in one locality fruit simultaneously or in rapid sequence in a 3-month masting event. Masting is common in the temperate forests of the northern hemisphere, where most plants flower in the spring and summer but fruit en masse in the autumn. In Borneo masting occurs on an irregular 2–6-year cycle and is believed to be a strategy to provide so much food that seed predators are unable to consume all the seeds (predator satiation), followed by a multi-year lean period causing predator starvation. In turn, many Bornean seed predators have adopted a nomadic lifestyle (pp. 11 and 42). In Borneo masting is dominated by the dipterocarps, the most common large trees throughout the lowland forests of Borneo (p. 54).

SCATTER- AND LARDER-HOARDING – THE PARADOX OF THE SQUIRREL AND THE ACORN Early zoologists assumed that there was an ongoing war between fruiting plants and seed predators. It was Ridley (1930) who first pointed out that although squirrels are significant seed predators of oak-tree acorns, oaks are only common where squirrels are common and vice versa. In northern Europe, America and Asia, oaks mast fruit each autumn, and squirrels typically collect excess acorns and bury them randomly up to 100m from the mother tree – a strategy known as scatter-hoarding. In winter when food is scarce, a squirrel retrieves the acorns. Inevitably, many squirrels die before they collect the acorns, which then sprout the following spring. Thus the relationship between squirrels and oaks is mutualistic rather than predatory, and the oak tree is effectively 'paying' the squirrel community to disperse its acorns.

Borneo is a world centre of diversity of squirrels (34 spp.), oaks (90 spp.) and rats (27 spp.), and scatter-hoarding of hard seeds especially in the mountains is common. Scatter-hoarding squirrels include Low's Squirrel, the Horse-tailed Squirrel, Three-striped Ground Squirrel and Plantain Squirrel. Larder-hoarding, where seeds are taken back to burrows or tree holes for storage, has been recorded for the Sabah Rat, Red Spiny Maxomys and Rajah Maxomys (all at Pasoh), Whitehead's Maxomys and Müller's Rat in peat-swamp forest at Lingga, Sarawak, Long-tailed Porcupine and Bornean Porcupine in Sabah (p. 245) and Rajah Maxomys at Danum. (Miura et al. 1997, Curran & Leighton 2000, Van der Meer et al. 2008, Wells & Bagchi 2005.)

ORTHODOX SEEDS have hard seed coats combined with delayed germination. The Lithocarpus oak acorns being scatter-hoarded by this Three-striped Ground Squirrel (p. 213) germinate after an average of 146 days. Ng (2014), (pp. 232 and 234).

Three-striped Ground Squirrel *Lariscus insignis* (p. 213).

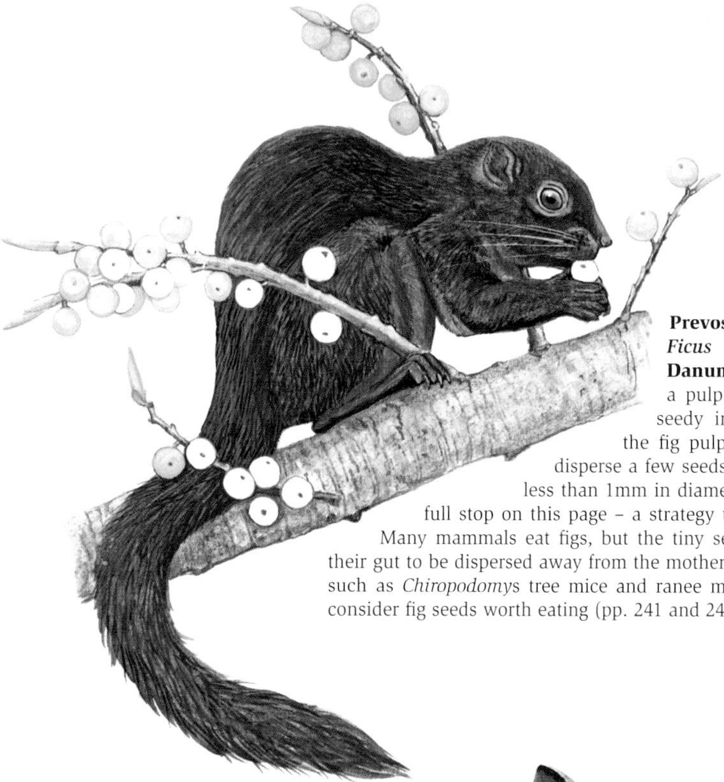

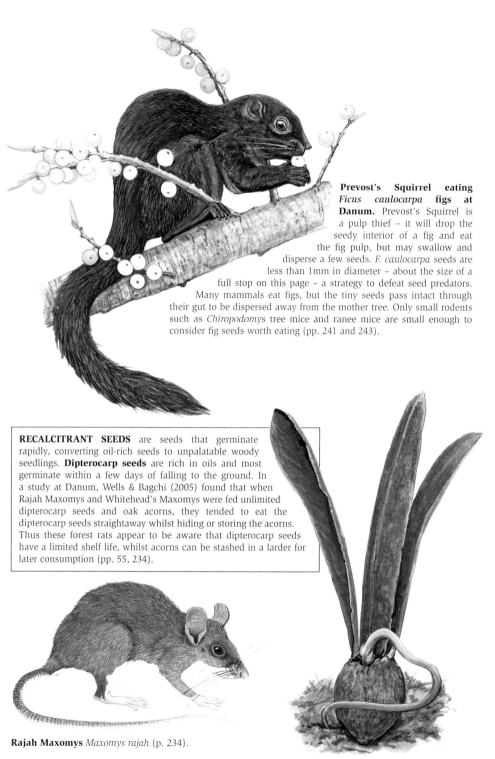

Prevost's Squirrel eating *Ficus caulocarpa* figs at Danum. Prevost's Squirrel is a pulp thief – it will drop the seedy interior of a fig and eat the fig pulp, but may swallow and disperse a few seeds. *F. caulocarpa* seeds are less than 1mm in diameter – about the size of a full stop on this page – a strategy to defeat seed predators. Many mammals eat figs, but the tiny seeds pass intact through their gut to be dispersed away from the mother tree. Only small rodents such as *Chiropodomys* tree mice and ranee mice are small enough to consider fig seeds worth eating (pp. 241 and 243).

RECALCITRANT SEEDS are seeds that germinate rapidly, converting oil-rich seeds to unpalatable woody seedlings. **Dipterocarp seeds** are rich in oils and most germinate within a few days of falling to the ground. In a study at Danum, Wells & Bagchi (2005) found that when Rajah Maxomys and Whitehead's Maxomys were fed unlimited dipterocarp seeds and oak acorns, they tended to eat the dipterocarp seeds straightaway whilst hiding or storing the acorns. Thus these forest rats appear to be aware that dipterocarp seeds have a limited shelf life, whilst acorns can be stashed in a larder for later consumption (pp. 55, 234).

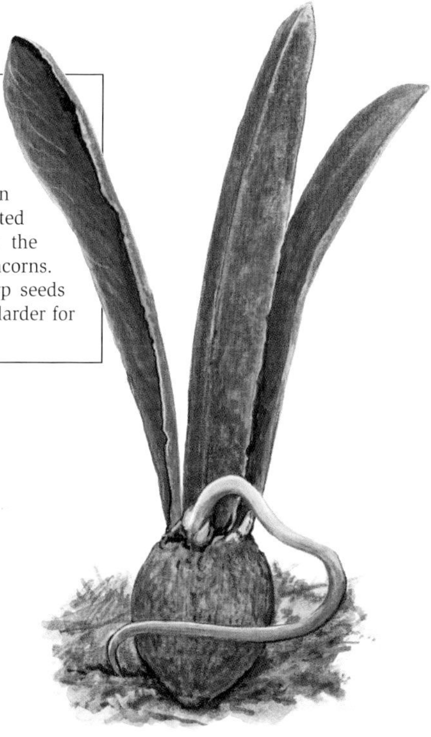

Rajah Maxomys *Maxomys rajah* (p. 234).

ECOLOGY: WHY SO MANY TREES?

WHY DOES BORNEO HAVE SOME OF THE MOST DIVERSE FOREST ON EARTH, by far the richest in Asia, with Lambir's diverse tree list only comparable with Kinabalu and a Peruvian forest (Yasuni) in the headwaters of the Amazon? Each tree species occupies its own special niche, which gives it a competitive advantage within that niche over other species. To understand Lambir's (and Borneo's) tree diversity we need to know 1. Why tree speciation at Lambir has consistently exceeded tree extinction over a very long period, 2. What limits endless speciation, and 3. Are extinction rates likely to exceed speciation in the future?

According to Givnesh's (1999) overview, plant diversity worldwide increases with rainfall, soil fertility, forest height, moderate disturbance, long-term climatic stability and area of habitat. Plant diversity decreases with distance from the equator, seasonality and altitude. In other words, the hottest, wettest, least seasonal, most climatically stable, tall lowland forests with the least catastrophic events produce the greatest species diversity. N Borneo's climate has been relatively stable for at least 23 million years (Ashton 2014), with wet rainforest refugia for 40 million years (Cannon 2003), time for evolution to fill most rainforest niches.

- Borneo's varied soils (edaphic factors) provide microhabitat niches for different species.
- A varied topography of hills, lowlands and mountains (altitudinal gradients) also drives speciation.
- Soils are rich enough for tall forest, providing 3D microhabitats for epiphytes and small animals.
- Birds and mammals coevolved with the plants, providing species-specific pollination and dispersal.
- Lambir's forests were until recently part of the much larger 2 million km^2 Sundaland (p. 168).
- Diversity may arise because plant pests are often species specific and plants speciate to escape attack. See Negative Density Dependency and the Janzen-Connell Effect (p. 32).

The Riau Pocket and Rainforest Refugia When you walk in the forests of Lambir or Matang in Sarawak, you are walking in the same forest with the same tree species that once extended all the way to Singapore. We know this because many of Sarawak's coastal forest trees are shared with Sumatra, the Riau Islands and Johore, first pointed out by Corner (1960). One example is a spiny rattan palm, *Daemonorops scapigera*, first collected by Beccari in Sumatra, but also found at Matang, Singapore and the Natuna Islands. For 90% of the last 2.6 million years, the whole area was covered in forest. At least 25 times rising sea levels drowned the forest, whilst Matang and Lambir remained above sea level, acting as wet-rainforest refugia to Sundaland's plants. These plants then repopulated the Sunda lowlands when sea levels fell (p. 38). The result of 23 million years of relative climatic and habitat stability in NW Borneo is that the tiny remnant patches of Sarawak's lowland forests are living museums, unique relics of Sundaland's now vanished hyper-diverse flora (map, p. 14).

What drives speciation in different plant families? A simplified explanation is that each plant family has its own unique genetic toolkit (phylogenetic history), which gives it a competitive advantage over other plant families. Speciation is the result of local adaption to a particular niche or microhabitat. Dipterocarps dominate the Bornean rainforest in both height (to 80m) and forest mass. Their ability to grow very large, woody trunks in poor soil enables dipterocarps to shade rival trees and win the competition for sunlight. Dipterocarps speciate by specializing in different light environments, or edaphic/soil differences (Ashton 2014). Dipterocarp genera Upuna and Vatica are exceptions (p. 54). Figs, in contrast, have mutualistic relationships with many animals, providing food for birds and mammals throughout the year. Figs speciate by partitioning potential seed dispersers into guilds, providing a targeted food package (the fig) tailored to each group (p. 76).

What limits endless speciation in plants? 1. Coevolution and obligate relationships. Speciation often results from coevolution. Plants gain a competitive advantage by cooperating with animals that provide pollination of flowers, dispersal of seeds and defence against leaf eaters. However, plants and animals that evolve a one-to-one (obligate) relationship, like a banana flower pollinated by a bat, both risk extinction if either plant or animal populations collapse – so most plant/animal relationships are 'generalist' not obligate. The closer the relationship, the higher the risk of extinction – so this limits endless speciation through coevolution.
2. The need for pollination. There are c. 450,000 trees of 1,200 species in the 52ha Lambir plot. The greater the proportion of rare tree species, the greater the problems with pollination and sexual reproduction. Lambir's tree diversity is probably close to a practical pollination limit. See Allee Effect (p. 296).

A species-poor future for Lambir The recent extinction of Lambir's large mammals and birds will inevitably increase tree-extinction rates, leading to a collapse in Lambir's plant list because many plants will no longer be pollinated or their seeds dispersed. Eventually, only generalist species with multiple pollinators and dispersers will survive (p. 368).

Coevolution of Plants and Animals Tall tropical rainforest trees provides three-dimensional (3D) space with structural support for thousands of species of liana and epiphyte, which in turn provide myriad feeding and foraging niches for insects, birds and mammals.
Relationships between plants and animals may be mutualistic (beneficial) to both parties, e.g. flower pollination, seed dispersal, or antagonistic, e.g. wood-eating termites or seed predation. Each relationship may result in the evolution of a new species as animals and plants compete to survive. The higher the diversity of plants, the higher the diversity of mammals, birds and insects.

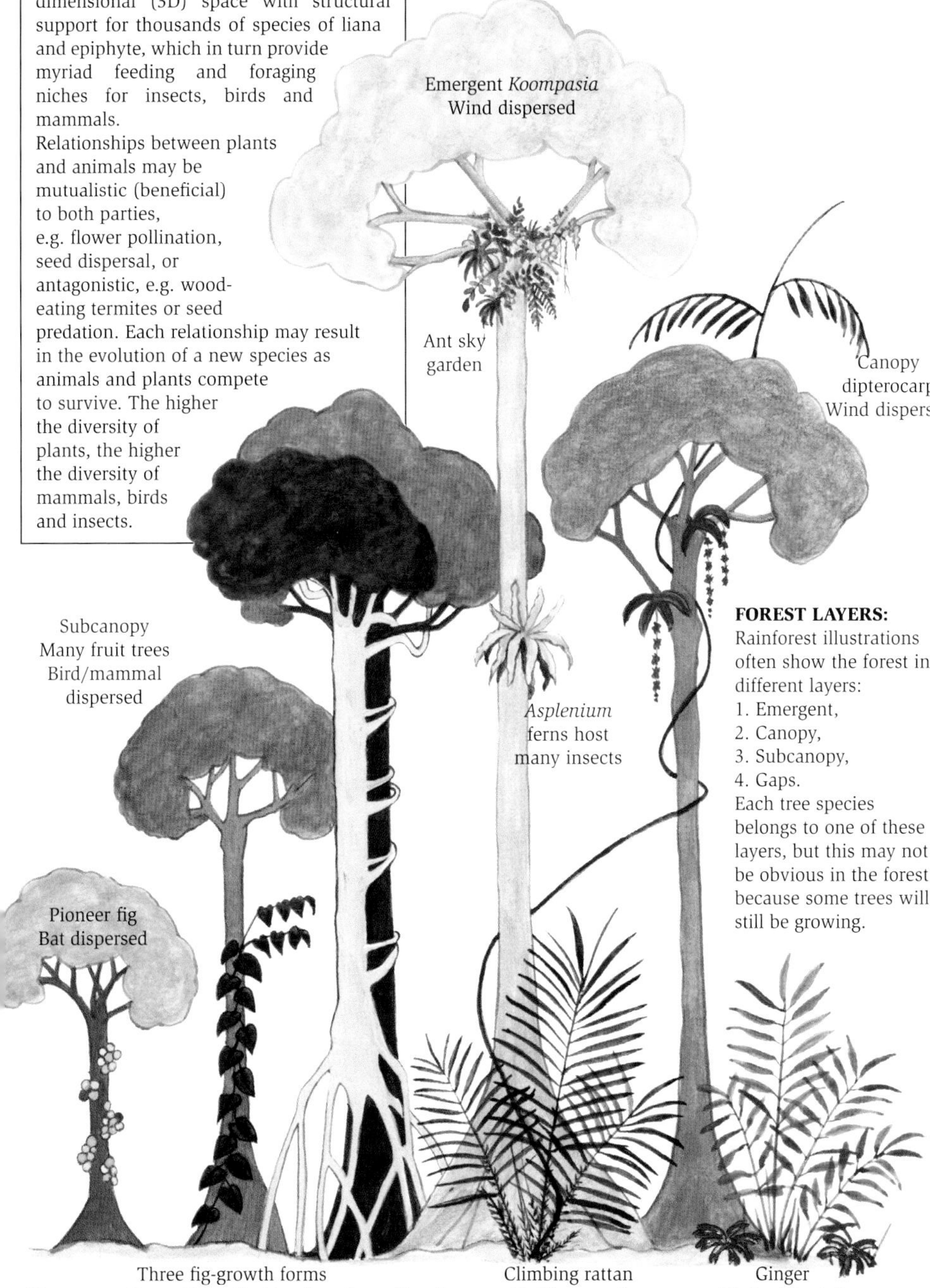

FOREST LAYERS:
Rainforest illustrations often show the forest in different layers:
1. Emergent,
2. Canopy,
3. Subcanopy,
4. Gaps.
Each tree species belongs to one of these layers, but this may not be obvious in the forest because some trees will still be growing.

PLANTS: HOW FOREST FUNGI AFFECT TREE DIVERSITY IN BORNEO

In very simplified terms forest fungi can be split into two main types:

1 **Ectomycorrhizas (ECM)** and **arbuscular mycorrhizas (AM)** have a mutualistic (beneficial) association with their host plant. These fungi feed on sugars provided by the plant and in return supply the plant with minerals. In forests these fungi also provide a "**wood-wide web**" of inter-connected roots through which nearby plants share nutrients and water which may assist sick trees against fungal attack.

2 **Saprotrophic fungi** have an antagonistic relationship with a host tree. They attack the tree with enzymes which break down cellulose, resulting in fungal decay and the eventual death of the tree.

Both types of fungus may be host specific (to one plant species) or generalists (attack many species).

How climate change influences saprotrophic fungal attack Fungi and moulds thrive best in warm wet conditions and struggle to survive in cold, dry, salty or water-logged habitats. Globally both tree diversity and fungal diversity increase with temperature and rainfall. Thus the climatic cycles of the 2.8 million year Pleistocene ice ages caused repeated changes in fungal abundance and related changes in the forest diversity in Borneo. However ECM/AM and saprotrophic fungi react differently to climate change. ECM/AM fungi are fed by their host plants underground and outcompete saprotrophic fungi in cold or dry climates.

Negative density dependence (NDD) and the escape hypothesis Janzen and Connell (1970 & 1971) found that tree species survived longer the further they grew from the parent tree (NDD) and suggested that pest pressure was most intense near the parent tree. Trees "escape" host specific attacks by **speciating** resulting in increasing diversity. Wills et al (2006) found that in all the Smithsonian tropical forest plots tree diversity was increasing even whilst large animal diversity was collapsing. Whilst tree pests include insects and many animals, the most likely explanation is that since the end of the last ice age, saprotrophic fungi have benefited from an increasingly warm and wet climate resulting in increased fungal "pest pressure" on forests worldwide.

Forest diversity and saprotrophic fungi In Borneo, wet lowland rainforest is the most diverse (most species). Tree diversity is reduced in montane, peatswamp and mangrove forests probably because these forests are too wet (no oxygen – fungi "breathe" oxygen) or cold for saprotrophic fungi to thrive. Compared with lowland dipterocarp forest, plants in these other forests have a higher proportion of hard (orthodox) seeds, are less prone to masting and often grow in mono-dominant stands. Thus forest type in Borneo is determined by local weather and edaphic (soil) conditions which determine levels of fungal attack (p. 30).

Mycovores: the agents of fungal attack Many fungi have evolved to be dispersed by wind-blown spores from their fruiting bodies (mushrooms). However the forest understory is almost windless and many mushrooms are edible to encourage mycovores such as pheasants, deer, rats, squirrels and pigs to eat the mushrooms and spread the spores via defecation.

Beneficiaries of fungal attack include woodpeckers that eat insects that feed on dead wood, barbets that nest in holes in dead wood, and many animals that sleep in dead logs and or tree holes e.g. bats. Some trees may even benefit. Bracket fungus e.g. *Ganoderma* spp. attack the heartwood of trees hollowing them out and providing roost sites for bats and birds whose droppings in turn provide nutrients for the host tree (p. 380). For an overview see: LaManna, J.A., Mangan, et al. (2017).

SAPROTROPHIC FUNGI THAT ATTACK DEAD WOOD

1 Yellow Stagshorn *Calocera viscosa*
2 Smooth Tropical Goblet *Cookeina sulcipes*

ECTOMYCORRHIZAL FUNGI (ECM) THAT BENEFIT PLANTS

3 Velvet Brittlegill *Russula violaleipes*
4 Greencracked Brittlegill *Russula virescens*

SAPROTROPHIC BRACKET FUNGI THAT ATTACK HEARTWOOD

5 *Ganoderma* species
6 Blood-red Bracket *Pycnoporus sanguineus*

PLANTS: POACEAE GRASSES AND BAMBOOS

GRASSES **World**: *c.* 10,000 spp. **Borneo**: *c.* 250 spp. including *c.* 150 spp. of bamboos and less than 100 grasses. **Grasses** including native bamboos are the world's most valuable (to man) plant family. Native grasses include the giant *Pennisetum macrostachys* (Elephant grass), *Saccharum robustum* (Wild Sugar Cane), and the Common Reed *Phragmites karka*, which grow on river banks. Common introduced grasses in Borneo include Love Grass *Eragrostis* sp. and Buffalo Grass *Paspalum conjugatum*.

Cultivated Grasses include rice *Oryza sativa* which was first introduced to Borneo from S China via the Philippines *c.* 5, 000 years ago. Other important 'grass' crops include maize, sugar cane, sorghum and Job's tears.

Large Mammals and Grasses Before the arrival of man in Borneo both grasses and grassland were scarce, found only in coastal swamps and along river banks, and this is the most probable explanation for the absence or rarity of large grazing mammals in Borneo in the recent past, including elephants (p. 290), Banteng and wild water buffalo (p. 304). Grasses thrive in dryer, cooler 'fire climax' climates where there is a mutualistic relationship with grazing mammals such as antelopes, deer and wild cattle. Grasses grow from underground corms or roots that enable survival even when above ground shoots are eaten or burnt by fire. Grazing mammals and fire destroy the shoots of invading shrubs and trees and grazers disperse the grass seeds in their dung, effectively creating or farming their ideal habitat by zoochory, pp. 32, 290.

LALANG *Imperata cylindrica* [alang alang] [cogon]

A fire-tolerant sword grass that grows to the height of a man and flourishes in degraded soils subject to regular fires. Until recently large areas of the Kudat Peninsula (Sabah), W. Kalimantan and SE Borneo (Bandjarmasin) were covered by lalang – now mostly replaced with tree plantations. Lalang invades when the swidden cycle is too short (under 7 years), the result of human over-population. These lalang areas were the first parts of Borneo to be settled by swidden farmers arriving thousands of years ago from the Philippines, Sumatra and Java. The razor sharp adult leaf blades of lalang deter ungulate grazers, but after burning, pigs, deer and Banteng are attracted to graze on the new shoots. See also Dove (1985).

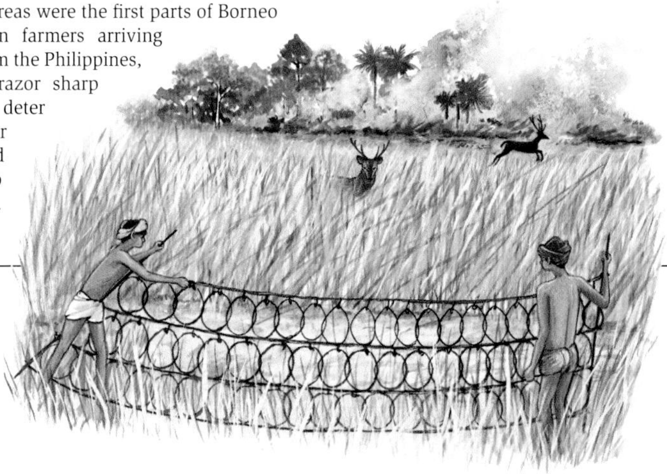

Rungus Dusuns burn mature lalang and use panels of rattan nets to catch Sambar deer fleeing from the flames in the Kudat Peninsula.

SWIDDEN FARMING OF HILL RICE Until recently the majority of rice in Borneo was grown in temporary forest clearings on a 7–10 year cycle known as 'slash and burn' or swidden farming. The first year the forest was felled and burnt in the dry season, May–August. Rice seed was sown at the beginning of the wet season September–November, signalled by the rising of the Pleiades star constellation at dusk in the east. Rice was harvested between March and May. After harvest, secondary crops such as tapioca, maize and vegetables were planted and the land was left to revert to secondary forest. In over-populated areas reducing swidden cycles to less than 7 years led to the invasion of lalang grass. Shortage of land meant that distant swiddens required 'field huts' for overnight stays. Swidden fields needed fencing against macaques, Sambar deer and Bearded Pigs which ate the young rice. Although each family 'owned' their own swidden fields, the village chief was responsible for co-coordinating synchronous planting and subsequent harvesting using reciprocal labour in order to minimise crop predation by mammals and birds, a defensive strategy equivalent to forest masting. See p. 12 for predator satiation. Note: months are based on Sabah. In Sarawak and Kalimantan activities take place *c.* 3 months later.

BAMBOOS World: c. 1,200 spp. **Borneo**: c.150 spp. Bamboos are giant forest grasses that include both the massive bamboo clumps of forest clearings and the thin climbing bamboos that grow in logged forest and at 2,000m in a 'bamboo belt' high up on Kinabalu. Large bamboos are used to construct houses, rafts, traps, tools, mats and baskets and are often planted around villages. A large bamboo clump in a forest setting is usually evidence of previous human settlement. It has been suggested that the only 'tools' required by prehistoric agriculturalists to settle in Borneo were fire and bamboos, but see Bar-Yosef, Eren et al (2011) regarding the relative merits of stone and bamboo tools.

Mammals and Bamboos Orangutans, elephants, rhinoceros and Banteng eat bamboo shoots and leaves, but they are so rich in hard silica crystals and toxic cyanide that they play a minor part in mammalian diets. Porcupines eat both bamboo roots and shoots but only a few Bornean mammals rely on bamboo clumps for survival. The Bamboo Mouse (p. 241) and at least 5 bat species use hollow bamboo nodes for roosting. Two species, *Tylonycteris tomesi* and *T. robustula*, roost only in bamboos, and have evolved flat skulls to squeeze through the narrow entrance slits less than 5mm wide created by beetles (p. 121).

Bamboo clumps flower and fruit at multi-year intervals before the whole clump dies This 'masting' strategy resembles that of many monocarpic palms (p. 50), and is designed to defeat seed predators (p. 42). Masting bamboos produce so much seed that the local rodent population is 'satiated', leaving seeds to grow into new bamboo clumps. Rodents may also scatter-hoard the seed helping to disperse bamboos (pp. 32, 213, 233, 237, 245).

Botanists have discovered that the trigger for masting differs in each of three masting plant groups. **Dipterocarp masting** is triggered by irregular El Niño droughts (p. 10). **Monocarpic palms** flower individually when the store of starch in their stem is adequate to power fruiting (p. 52). **Many bamboos** in contrast possess a genetically programmed timer, so that all closely related bamboos fruit simultaneously wherever they are in the world (Janzen 1976). Different *Racemobambos* bamboo species on Kinabalu flower in patches at 10 to 23 year intervals (Wong & Dransfield 1996), satiating the local rodents but also providing food for flocks of nomadic Pin-tailed Parrot Finches. When the bamboo seed is exhausted, hordes of these finches descend on ripening crops of hill rice – the most feared rice pest of Borneo's swidden farmers (Harrisson in Smythies 1999).

Pin-tailed Parrot Finch *Erythrura prasina*

Swidden Farm
Illustration shows a bamboo clump, bamboo field hut, bamboo fencing and bamboo 'whistling windmill' deer scare which has failed to deter crop raiding Bearded Pigs in a typical hill rice swidden in interior Borneo.

PLANTS: PALMS

Langkap
Arenga undulatifolia
Monocarpic, Big Bang

Rotan
Rattan
Steady State

Pinang Palm
Areca catechu
Cultivated, Steady State

ARECACEAE **World**: 2,300 spp. **Borneo**: 283 spp., making Borneo a world centre of palm diversity. Palms grow upwards from a single bud [palm cabbage, palm heart], [malay-ubud] at the top of the trunk. This bud is eaten by elephants, Sun Bears, Orangutans, macaques and humans. Most native palms are heavily armed with thorns and/or irritant crystals (raphides) to deter leaf and bud predators. Most native palms grow in clumps so that the death of one stem will not kill the whole plant (p. 52).

Introduced palms including the Oil Palm, Betel-nut Palm, Coconut Palm, Sago Palm and Sugar Palm provide Borneo's most important food crops after grasses (rice, maize). As individuals, palms provide abundant fruit and nectar to wildlife, but grown in mono-cultures they are an ecological disaster (p. 30).

Rattans Just under half (138 spp.) of Borneo's palms are rattans, viciously spiked climbing palms common in most forests. Most rattan leaves end in thorny whips used both as defence and to aid their rapid growth. The small scaly brown fruit are dispersed by hornbills, pigeons, primates and bats.

Monocarpic (suicide) 'Sago' palms 13 spp. of Bornean palms in the genera *Eugeissona, Caryota, Corypha, Metroxylon*, and *Arenga* are monocarpic. Mature palms accumulate a massive store of starch, dissipated in one Big Bang of flowering and seeding before dying – a strategy to satiate seed predators. Mature stems may be harvested by humans for sago just prior to flowering (p. 52). However most palms flower and fruit continuously (Steady State).

Palms, Bats and Alcohol Palms produce giant spathes of tiny pale flowers rich in nectar, favoured by nectar bats. The flowers remain open 24 hours and are also pollinated by bees and nectar-loving sunbirds. Locals tap the flower buds for nectar which ferments naturally into palm wine, toddy. Distilled toddy is known as arak, previously a common trade good. Evaporated nectar makes palm sugar, gula Malacca or jaggery. Palm civets or toddy cats (p. 264) and fruit bats (p. 86) raid toddy containers at night. In Malaya, colugos damage coconut flower buds to obtain nectar (Lim 1967), (p. 154). See also p. 52 re. the curious pollination of *Eugeissona* Palms..

Rhinoceros Hornbill feeding on ripe *Caryota* palm fruit

Oil Palm
Elaeis guineensis
Cultivated, Steady State

Talipot Palm in flower
Corypha umbraculifera
Monocarpic, Big Bang

Fish-tail Palm
Caryota no
Big Bang

RAPHIDES are the needle-sharp crystals of calcium oxalate present in many plants. Raphides physically damage the mouth and internal organs of mammals, opening skin to burning oxalic acid. Raphides are present in the leaves, fruit pulp and seeds of many genera of Bornean palms including *Areca, Arenga, Caryota, Cyrtostachys, Iguanura, Livistonia, Oncosperma* and *Pinanga* (Zona 2004). One of Corner's botanical macaques (p. 182) died after eating *Caryota* fruit. However hornbills and palm civets appear to swallow the ripe fruit of these palms with impunity. For humans, just handling the ripe red fruit can cause severe skin irritation.

A NIPA PALM RAFT floats past P. Sangkalaki opposite the Berau River mouth, E. Kalimantan. Nipa Palms *Nypa fructans* dominate muddy river mouths in Borneo. The prostrate trunks float off during floods. After storms, floating Nipa Palm Rafts up to the size of a bungalow may be seen out at sea. The snakes and lizards so common on oceanic islands such as Maratua must have arrived on these Nipa rafts. Some reptiles are parthenocarpic (a single female can reproduce without sex), so a lone female reptile could kick-start an island population. Zoologists such as Wallace (1876), Hickson (1889), Chasen (1940) and D. Brandon-Jones (1998) have used 'Nipa palm rafting' between islands to explain the distribution of Sundaland's mammals on different islands (p. 386).

It is more likely that Sundaland's 'missing mammals' e.g. tiger, Javan Rhino, tapir, arrived when falling sea levels created 'land bridges' and later became extinct due to climate change and a shrinking habitat when sea levels rose again. However, Long-tailed Macaques may have colonised remote islands by Nipa rafts. Abegg & Thierry (2002), Meijaard & Groves (2004), Fooden (1995), (pp. 16, 180).

***EUGEISSONA* PALMS** **World:** 6 spp. **Malaya**: 2 endemics. **Borneo:** 4 endemics, making Borneo the world centre of distribution. *Eugessona minor* is an understorey palm in Borneo with stilt roots known as the Walking Palm, common along ridges at Lambir. *E. ambigua* is very rare. *E. insignis* is a spiny trunkless palm common around Kuching and at Bako. *E. utilis* Wild Sago Palm is found wild throughout the Bornean forests usually on ridges or steep slopes, but now often near areas of human habitation. The unique flower structure common to all *Eugeissonas* indicates that they are pollinated by small mammals rewarded with alcoholic nectar and edible pollen.

POLLINATION OF *EUGEISSONA TRISTIS* IN MALAYA In the Malay Peninsula the endemic *E. tristis* [Local: *Bertam*] is considered a foresters' weed. It flourishes in sunlit gaps after logging and prevents regeneration of the natural dipterocarp forest. *Bertam* grows in large clumps of spiny-leaved rosettes but with no proper trunks. Each rosette produces a giant flower stalk taller than a man and then dies. These flower stalks are covered with numerous small flowers protected by hard spiny petals like long thin finger nails. (See illustration). Pollination studies by Wiens et al (2008) found that the flowers leaked copious amounts of fermented alcoholic nectar for 5 weeks before the protective bracts opened at night for 24 hours to allow access by pollinators to the flowers. A barren period of 6 weeks was then followed by a further 7 weeks of nectar production followed by 48 hours when the bracts opened again at night to allow further pollination.

Alcohol-leaking flower stalks were visited by 5 different mammals at night including Slow Loris (p. 160), Pen-tailed Treeshrew (p. 142), Malayan Field Rat, Grey Tree Rat (p. 232) and Malayan Tree Rat. Two mammals Common Treeshrew and Plantain Squirrel visited during the day or at dusk.

Pollination of the 4 Bornean *Eugeissona* palms has yet to be studied but they are believed to be mammal pollinated. Beccari, the first botanist to describe *E. utilis* (1871) mentions that *E . utilis* produces large amounts of purple pollen. When the palms are harvested for sago this pollen is eaten by Borneans as a snack. It appears therefore that *Eugeissona* palms use edible pollen as an additional reward for pollinators. *E. tristis* (Malaya) and *E. insignis* (Borneo) are very similar – both without a trunk. *E. utilis* (Borneo), (see opposite) is the only *Eugeissona* with a tall trunk (to 15m), and is therefore the only *Eugeissona* palm which can be harvested for sago.

THE WILD SAGO PALM OF BORNEO Sago [Local: *Sagu*] is a carbohydrate rich flour extracted from the trunk of several different palm species. These palms flower just once in their lifetime (monocarpic) and then die (See p. 10 re masting strategies and p. 50 re palms). Just before flowering the palm trunk is felled and split open and the sago flour is washed out of the central pith. The sago is then dried into hard biscuits or small round 'pearls' for later consumption. Although considered inferior to rice as a food, sago is a staple part of the diet for many Borneans. The Sarawak Melanaus and other coastal tribes in W Borneo cultivate the introduced Sago Palm *Metroxylon sagu* in fresh water swamps. Interior hill tribes such as the Muruts, Ibans, Kenyah and Kayans harvest sago from Pantu (*E. utilis*) as a fallback food when their hill rice crops fail, but only the nomadic Penans have traditionally relied on Pantu sago as a staple part of their diet (See p. 21 Penan ecology). It is probable that the Malay/Indonesian name for Borneo [Kalimantan] is derived from the word *lemantah*, the Malay name for raw sago, a popular trade good in the Indonesian archipelago even today (Beccari 1904).

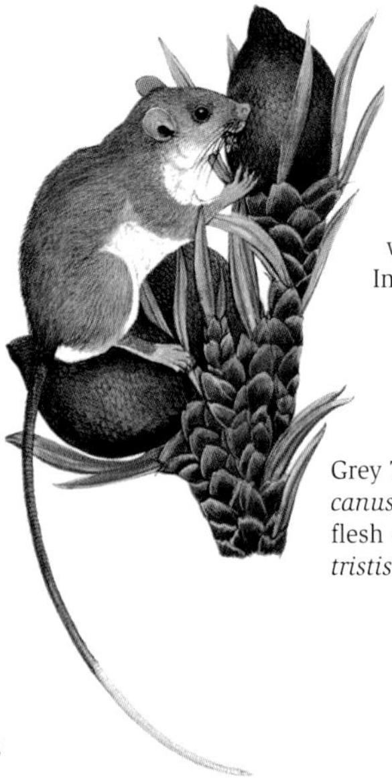

Grey Tree Rat *Lenothrix canus* feeding on the oily flesh of scaly *Eugeissona tristis* fruit in Malaya.

Pantu *Eugeissona utilis* drift seed common along river banks and coastal beaches in Borneo. Scale: 50%

SEED DISPERSAL OF PANTU BY SUMATRAN RHINOCEROS *Eugeissona utilis* occurs naturally throughout the Bornean forests but is found most often along the ridge tops of forested hills. As the large seeds (see opposite) are often found washed up on river banks and coastal beaches, it has been suggested that they are water dispersed. This does not explain why Pantu palms prefer ridge tops to valley bottoms. The fiberous oily flesh of *Eugeissona* palm fruits is eaten by rats, squirrels, pigs and macaques, however the large hard inner seed means that whole fruits can only be swallowed by the largest mammals and the most likely targeted disperser is the Sumatran Rhinoceros which, in the past, was known to establish permanent trails along the tops of ridges in hill country. It is likely therefore that when you recognise the giant flowers of Pantu emerging from a forested ridge you are looking at what was once a Sumatran Rhinoceros trail route for many thousands of years. Pantu palms can be seen throughout the interior hills of Sarawak and Kalimantan, on the hill slopes of Gunung Mulu, along the Temburong River in Brunei and on the lower slopes of the Crocker Range (Sabah). Pantu fruit are an important fallback food for many mammals, especially Bearded Pigs in the Kayan Mentarang N. Park in Kalimantan (Puri 2005). See also p. 36 re Anachronistic fruits.

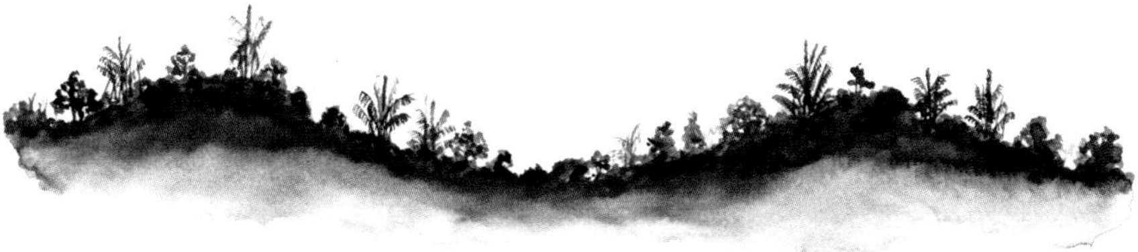

A ridge line of flowering *Eugeissona* Palms at Batang Duri, Brunei, probably indicates an ancient Sumatran Rhino trail.

Pen-tailed Treeshrew *Ptilocercus lowii* sipping nectar from a flowering *Eugeissona tristis* palm in Malaya.

Clump of wild Sago Palm *Eugeissona utilis* [Pantu]. Each trunk flowers and fruits only once before dying. When harvested for sago the trunk is felled just before flowering and the sago starch is washed from the pith in a nearby river. The dried starch can be stored as biscuits for later human consumption.

PLANTS: DIPTEROCARPS — MALAY: MERANTI, SERAYA, KERUING, RESAK

DIPTEROCARPACEAE **World:** *c.* 490 spp**. Africa:** *c.* 10 spp. **S. America** *c.* 10 spp. **Borneo:** 269 spp. with 155 endemics. Dipterocarps originated over 60 million years ago in the southern continent of Gondwana and later spread throughout the wet tropics. Borneo is now the world centre of distribution. In Sundaland's rainforests dipterocarps average 30–50% of forest trees but in some Bornean forests reach 70%. By their overwhelming dominance in the forest dipterocarps exclude other plant families that benefit mammals and birds either by pollination or dispersal. By fruiting simultaneously at irregular intervals (masting) dipterocarps alternately starve their seed predator enemies and then provide them with so much food during a short 3 month period that the predators leave most seeds uneaten, a strategy known as 'predator satiation' (Janzen 1974). For many Bornean mammals surviving in a dipterocarp forest means alternating cycles of feast and famine.

FEAST OR FAMINE Records over the last 100 years show that major masting takes place on average every 4–5 years, with a minor event every 2 years. However masting is irregular and may occur twice in two years or not at all for up to 8 years. The result for Bornean mammals is 3 months of feasting at irregular intervals, followed by a famine that may last 2–8 years. Bornean animals that predate dipterocarp seeds include Bearded Pigs, Orangutans, Sun Bears, langurs, macaques, gibbons, squirrels, fruit bats, porcupines, rats, parrots and pheasants. Nomadic animals in particular rely on masting events to provide the extra food needed for breeding and have adapted to this cycle of feast and famine by breeding during food abundance whilst surviving on a semi-starvation diet in between masting periods (p. 42).

DIPTEROCARP SEED DISPERSAL STRATEGIES Borneo's 269 dipterocarp species are divided into 9 genera *Anisoptera* (5), *Cotyelobium* (3), *Dipterocarpus* (41), *Dryobalanops* (7), *Hopea* (42), *Parashorea* (6), *Shorea* (127), *Upuna* (1) and *Vatica* (35). Most of the genera have fruit with 5 wings with 2 or 3 wings used for wind dispersal, the others remaining vestigial. In some genera there are also species with no wings on the seeds often described as 'water dispersed'. *Vatica* fruits have mostly lost their wings. Unlike the other dipterocarps most *Vaticas* have mutualistic or beneficial relationships with mammalian dispersers as described below, but their fruiting habits are unrecorded.

LOCAL DISPERSAL In Borneo's windless forests winged dipterocarp seeds do not normally travel far. Provided they are not predated, dipterocarp saplings wait close to the parent tree until a nearby tree fall allows them to start a growth spurt that ends in the canopy. Dipterocarps spread by competitive exclusion, growing taller than other forest trees and shading them out. Dipterocarp saplings may also gain a competitive advantage from an exclusive mutualistic fungal network (mycorrhiza) originating from the parent tree that allows scarce nutrients to be shared locally between the roots of related dipterocarps, Smits (1994).

Scale: All seeds 50% life size

RESAK DEGONG *Vatica havilandii* has edible bracts that encircle the hard seed and is probably targeted at bat dispersal

RESAK AYER *Vatica umbonata*. The fruit shape indicates the seed is most likely targeted at scatter-hoarding squirrels for dispersal

KERUING BELIMBING *Dipterocarpus grandiflorus* is an example of several *dipterocarp* seeds with very long wings believed to be typhoon dispersed. They are most common on the islands of the S. Philippines and in coastal N Borneo. During Typhoon Greg (26 Dec 1996) the worst storm in living memory in Sabah most of the *D. grandiflorus* on Gaya Island (opposite Kota Kinabalu) were snapped in half, but soon re-grew.

RAJAH MAXOMYS *Maxomys rajah* feeding on *Dipterocarpus validus* fruit. At Danum during masting in 1985 Emmons (2000) found that the population of treeshrews and 3 common forest rats, *M. surifer*, *L.sabanus* and *N. cremoriventer* remained unchanged whilst the population of *Maxomys rajah* increased by over 6 times. At Lambir trapping by Nakagawa et al (2007) showed that *M. rajah* populations exploded following general masting and collapsed during inter-mast intervals.

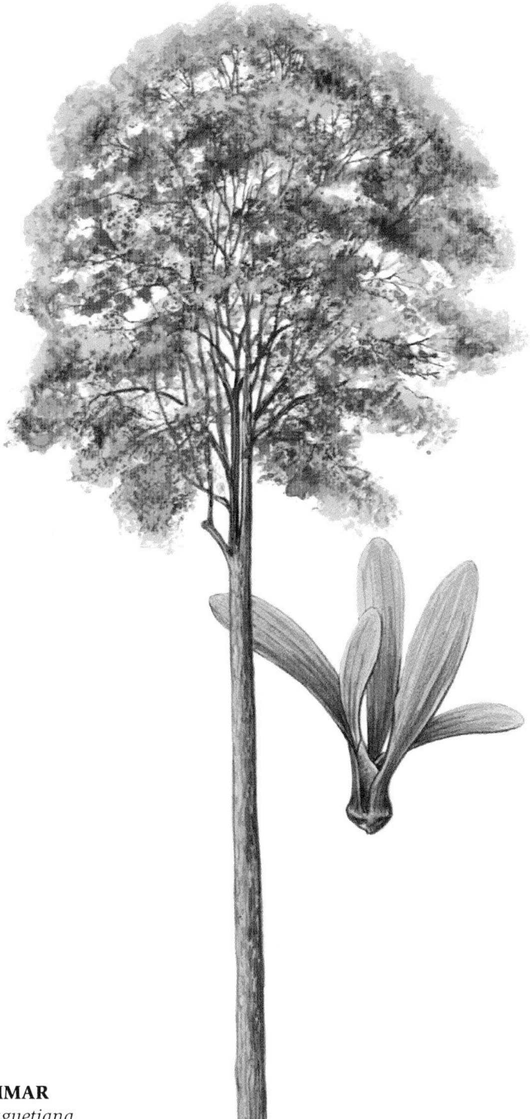

MERANTI DAMMAR SIPUT *Shorea faguetiana* fruit are typical of seeds aimed at local wind dispersal. Common in Sundaland forests this tree growing in Tawau Hills Park has been measured at 88.33m – the tallest rainforest tree in the world.

RAFFLESIACEAE **World**: 18 spp. **Borneo**: 8 spp. with 7 endemics. *Rafflesia* are the some of the world's largest flowers – with gigantic leathery petals but with no leaves or stem. *Rafflesia* grow parasitically on corky barked *Tetrastigma* vines in the understorey of the great tropical forests of SE Asia. *Tetrastigma* vines, which belong to the grape family Vitiaceae, are common in Bornean forests, but *Raffflesia* are exceedingly rare and it has long been a mystery as to how *Rafflesia* manage to propagate.

Rafflesia Propagation *Rafflesia* are dioecious, which means that each plant produces only male or female flowers. For successful propagation 4 stages are needed: 1. Male and female *Rafflesia* must flower simultaneously in the same locality, a rare event. 2. Pollen must be transferred from a male to a female flower 3. The resultant seed (s) must then be dispersed to another host *Tetrastigma* vine and 4. The seed must then be able to establish roots in the exceedingly thick corky bark of the new host *Tetrastigma* vine. Studies by Meijer (1997) show that the strong corpse-like smell of rotting flesh emitted by *Rafflesia* when open attracts carrion flies, which can carry pollen over a kilometer between distant flowers. Studies by Emmons, Nais and Biun (1991) revealed that giant Rafflesia fruit, which are the size of a husked coconut, are full of an oily mush containing thousands of small seeds. The seeds are swallowed by treeshrews and squirrels and are most likely dispersed in their faeces. However, the method by which the seeds establish on a new host vine has been the subject of much debate.

Cultivation of Rafflesia In cultivation Rafflesia has been propagated both by slip grafting tissue from an infected *Tetrastigma* vine into a new host vine and by inoculating Rafflesia seeds into the bark of an uninfected *Tetrastigma* vine. See also Nais (2001) Linton, Lamb & Lim (2005) and Mat Salleh (2007). In Sabah local entrepreneurial Dusun farmers near Ranau are planting cuttings from infected *Tetrastigma* vines to attract fee-paying tourists when the Rafflesias eventually flower.

RAFFLESIA SEED DISPERSAL The relict distribution of Rafflesias and the large anachronistic fruit indicate that the targeted disperser of Rafflesias is now extinct in Sundaland's forests. The most likely candidate is probably the Sumatran Rhino once common on the forested hill sides preferred by parasitic Rafflesia flowers and their host *Tetrastigma* vines.

Rafflesia Seed Establishment It has been hypothesized that the heavy hooves of rhinos or pigs that eat Rafflesia might damage the bark of nearby *Tetrastigma* vines. Faeces full of Rafflesia seeds deposited on damaged vines would allow the seeds to establish. An alternative theory (Anthony Lamb) is that the mammal that swallows Rafflesia seeds also eats ripe *Tetrastigma* fruit at the same time. Their faeces therefore contain seeds of both species and the host-parasite relationship is established at the seedling stage when they are growing together in a pile of dung. The likelihood of this happening would be greatly enhanced if the parasitic Rafflesia timed its fruiting to coincide with that of its host *Tetrastigma* vine. However this has yet to be researched

RAFFLESIA
Illustration shows a fruiting *Tetrastigma* vine growing up a forest tree at Poring in the Kinabalu Park with a Plantain Squirrel on the trunk head down. On the left is a *Rafflesia keithii* flower. In the centre are two Large Treeshrews *Tupaia tana* with a Raffleisia bud at the front and an open *Rafflesia* fruit at the rear.

SIR THOMAS STAMFORD RAFFLES 1781–1826 is best known for the conquest of Java in 1812 and the foundation of Singapore in 1819. Raffles was also a keen naturalist, one of the founders of the Zoological Society of London in 1825. Raffles was the first person to describe the Long-tailed Macaque, the Lesser Mousedeer and Raffles Malkoha. Two Bornean birds are named in honour of Raffles, the rare Olive-backed Woodpecker and the common Red-crowned Barbet. As Raffles was the discoverer of the first Rafflesia flower (*R. arnoldii*) in Sumatra, all Rafflesias now bear Raffles' name.

ANACARDIACEAE **World:** 69 spp. **Borneo:** 28 spp. which vary in size from 1–20cm in width. Borneo is the world centre of mango diversity with both the most species and the largest fruit, the giant endemic Bambangan *(Mangifera pajang)*, which reaches 18cm in length and 20cm diameter. The smooth oval shape of the seed, the numerous threads which attach the sweet flesh to the seed and the strong turpentine smell indicate that Borneo's largest mangoes were designed to be swallowed whole by very large mammals. The only possible candidates in Borneo's recent history are the tapir, the Sumatran and Javan rhinos and the Elephant (megafauna), once abundant in Bornean forests (p. 38).

Wild Mangoes Have Evolved a Variety of Sizes and Colours each designed to target a particular guild of dispersers, including 1. Primates 2. Fruit bats and 3. Megafauna. The cultivated mango is SE Asia's most popular fruit with humans. Orangutans, gibbons and macaques are pulp thieves of most large mangoes. Several small mango exceptions include the Wahab *Mangifera griffithii*, with a seed designed to be swallowed whole by large primates.

Masting and Mangoes Forest mangoes fruit irregularly at intervals of 2–3 or more years (For *Mangifera lagenifera*, Bompard 1988 quotes intervals of 3–8 years). Flowering follows a dry spell and often coincides with dipterocarp masting events triggered by El Niño droughts. The explanation for dipterocarp masting is predator satiation (pp. 12, 54). So why do elephant dispersed mangoes join dipterocarps in masting? The explanation is that mango seeds are dispersed and predated by entirely different mammals. Large mangoes are swallowed whole by large frugivores such as elephants. Elephants digest the mango pulp only, and defecate the seed, which is more likely to survive rodent seed predators when surrounded by fallen dipterocarp seeds. Both dipterocarp and mango seeds are recalcitrant (rapid sprouting, p. 44), but mango seeds are pre-programmed with a dormancy period of around 10 days compared with *c.* 2 days for most dipterocarps. This extra dormant period is to allow time for the mango seed to pass through the elephant's gut before sprouting. Thus both mangoes and dipterocarps benefit by fruiting simultaneously- a joint strategy to defeat seed predators.

BELUNO ***Mangifera caesia***
Dispersed by elephants and rhinos. Ripens green and fragrant. The hard seed case is covered in threads which prevent the flesh separating from the seed. Grows to 54+m.

Scale: All fruits 70% life size.

RAWA or WAHAB ***Mangifera griffithii*** Primate dispersed. A common swamp mango of Sundaland. Fruit ripen red or black but are very variable in size from 2 to 3.5cm. The small stringy seeds are normally swallowed whole by both humans and other primates because the pulp is attached to the stone with numerous fibres.

DODOL ***Mangifera pentandra*** Bat dispersed. Ripens green and fragrant. Most likely bat dispersed. Bats carry large fruit to a feeding roost away from the fruiting tree and the stone is dropped below.

BAMBANGAN ***Mangifera pajang*** Elephant dispersed. Ripens brown and fragrant.

PLANTS: OAKS AND CHESTNUTS — MALAY: MEMPENING

FAGACEAE **World:** *c.* 600 spp. **Borneo**: *c.* 100 spp. (49 endemic). **Kinabalu:** 62 spp. When you follow the forest trails around Kinabalu Park HQ, you are walking in the most diverse oak and chestnut forests on earth. Towards the end of each year you can find up to 20 different species of fallen acorns and chestnuts along the Mempening Trail at Kinabalu Park, including the giant acorn of *Lithocarpus turbinatus* (illustrated opposite). The diversity of oaks and chestnuts on Kinabalu indicates that northern Borneo has provided a climatically stable refuge for this plant family for the last 40 million years (Cannon 2003).

Oaks and chestnuts occur throughout Borneo's lowland forests, however they are most common in the mountains between 1,000–3,000 m. All Fagaceae have relatively hard orthodox seeds, e.g. castanopsis nuts average 308 days to germinate (Ng 2014) (pp. 43, 245). Kinabalu also hosts the highest diversity of squirrels and rats per unit area in the world, which is no coincidence as these rodents both predate and disperse acorns in a strategy known as 'scatter-hoarding' or 'larder-hoarding' (p. 42). Rodents collect and bury acorns in the ground for later recovery or remove them to their nests. Inevitably some of these rodents die before the acorns can be eaten and the acorns sprout into new trees (pp. 212, 232, 234, 245).

THREE DIFFERENT FAGACEAE DISPERSAL STRATEGIES Bornean oaks and chestnuts produce 3 types of seed nuts demonstrating 3 different general strategies to handle seed dispersal and seed predation. Within these general types the 100 differing fruit/acorn shapes in Borneo indicate an even more specialized targeting of specific mammalian dispersers. Three different dispersal techniques are described below.

1 Dispersal of spike covered Chestnuts, e.g. *Castanopsis megacarpa* [Malay: Berangan]**:** 'A squirrel seizes a bundle of chestnuts and breaks it off, and, holding it in its paws, attempts to nibble through the prickly husk to eat the nut. Often, due to the prickles being too sharp for its paws, it drops the whole bundle before it has eaten more than one nut (Ridley).

2 Dispersal of large hard nuts fully covered in a thin edible rind e.g. *Lithocarpus turbinatus*: These massive nuts have a thick woody endocarp (shell) protecting an oil-rich seed. The endocarp is itself covered in an edible green flesh (mesocarp). There are at least two possible explanations for this 'design' and probably both are correct. A squirrel, rat or porcupine will drag the nut away to a 'larder' to nibble on the rind storing the hard nut for later consumption. Another explanation is that this 'design' attracts megafauna such as deer and rhino that swallow the fruit whole and regurgitate or defecate the hard nut intact. Abandoned nuts are then collected for larder-hoarding or scatter-hoarding by rats and squirrels (secondary dispersal), (p. 213).

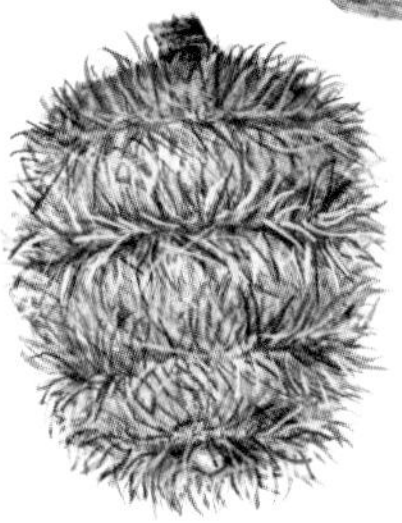

1

Giant Chestnut *Castanopsis megacarpa*

3 Dispersal of smooth shiny acorns in rough cups e.g. *Lithocarpus niewenhuis* Acorns are the commonest type of Fagaceae fruit. A squirrel finds it easy to break a bunch of acorns from the tree, but the smooth surface of the acorn deflects attempts to gnaw the surface with the teeth and the slippery surface makes the acorn easy to drop. As squirrels usually remove the acorn away from the mother tree to feed, the dropped acorn is effectively dispersed, and may also be secondarily dispersed by ground squirrels and rats.

OAK MASTING ATTRACTS SPECIALISED SEED PREDATORS IN THE HILLS OF BORNEO
Unlike the Dipterocarps (p. 50) which fruit en-mass (masting), lowland Fagaceae do not synchronize flowering. **Lowland oaks and chestnuts** flower and fruit in small flushes almost continuously (Kaul 1986). **In the hills and mountains** however, where Fagaceae become dominant, local populations do mast at annual intervals. These masting episodes are triggered by dry periods, but being subject to local topography and weather patterns will vary in time from valley to valley. It is believed that both the Giant Tufted Ground Squirrel and the endemic Bulwer's Pheasant are nomadic seed predators on acorns, following fruiting oaks from valley to valley. In many hilly areas e.g. Danum, Maliau Basin, Pulong Tau and Kayan Mentarang, large herds of Bearded Pigs also arrive from the lowlands when Fagaceae are fruiting, and create large areas of bare, churned-up ground as they search for fallen acorns under the fruiting oaks (pp. 215, 302).

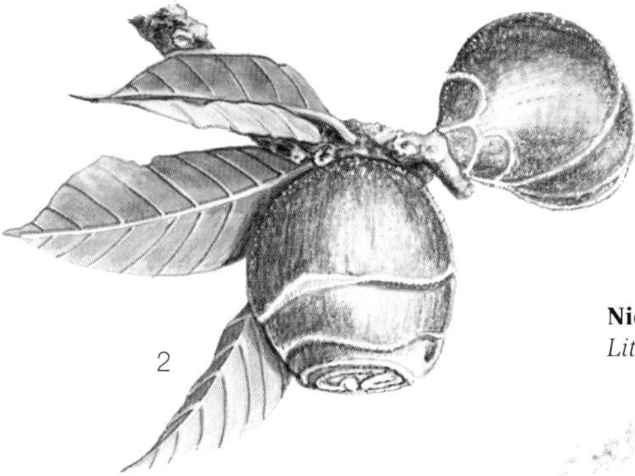

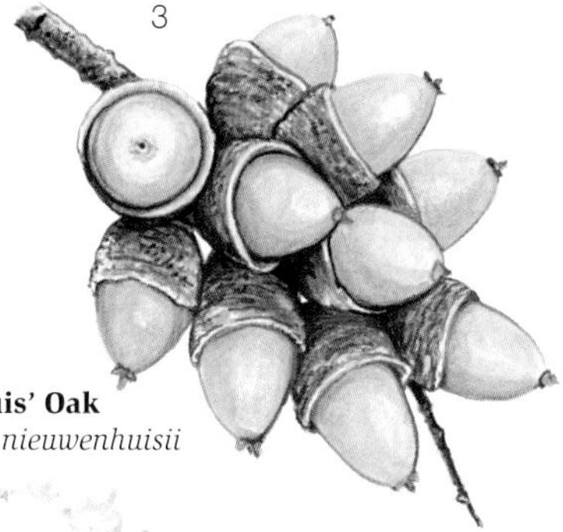

Nieuwenhuis' Oak
Lithocarpus nieuwenhuisii

Scale: All nuts 50% life size.

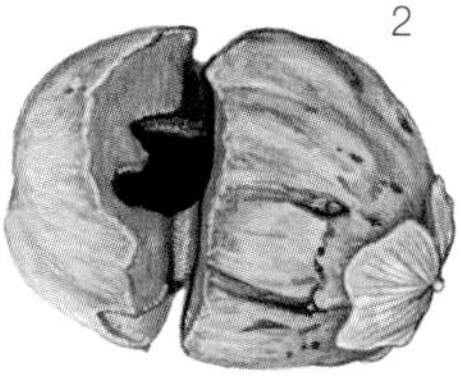

Turban Oak *Lithocarpus turbinatus* (above) with the internal seed predated by Mountain Ground Squirrel (p. 212).

Mountain Ground
Squirrel (p. 212).

MALVACEAE **World:** 30 spp. **Borneo:** 21 spp., of which 16 are endemic, making Borneo the world centre of durian distribution. In Borneo durians are medium to tall (to 50m) forest trees found throughout the lowlands and hills. Smaller trees with larger fruits, *Durio zibethinus,* are cultivated in home orchards. The large smelly thorny durian is considered Borneo's finest fruit by local primates and is equally popular with squirrels, civets, Sun Bears, and Clouded Leopards. Elephants are known to roll durians in leaves and swallow the whole bundle. Most durian seeds are too large for primates to swallow but are swallowed intact by ground mammals, from mousedeer up to sambar deer. Mature durian seeds are toxic (unless first boiled by humans for their own consumption), and are therefore not eaten by most mammals. According to Ridley (1930), 'I gave a tame sun bear a wild durian. It tore the fruit to bits with its powerful claws and ate the aril but would not eat the seed and spat it out. Another bear saw the seed fall and bit it but did not like the taste and would not eat it.' Unripe seeds are not toxic and durians are covered in sharp spines to resist seed predation whilst on the tree. This does not stop Orangutans predating immature durians before they ripen (p. 340).

Scale: All fruit 50% life size.

FALLEN RIPE DURIANS emit a powerful smell to attract terrestrial mammalian dispersers.
Wallace (1865) describes eating durian: 'A rich custard highly flavoured with almonds gives the best general idea of it, but there are occasional wafts of flavour that call to mind cream-cheese, onion-sauce, sherry-wine, and other incongruous dishes. Then there is a rich glutinous smoothness in the pulp which nothing else possesses, but which adds to its delicacy. It is neither acid nor sweet nor juicy; yet it wants neither of these qualities, for it is in itself perfect. It produces no nausea or other bad effect, and the more you eat of it the less you feel inclined to stop. In fact, to eat Durians is a new sensation worth a voyage to the East to experience'.

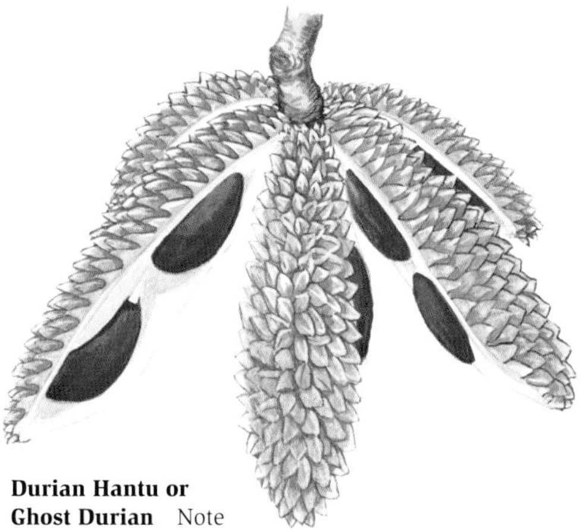

Durian Hantu or Ghost Durian Note oily red aril covering the large durian seed of *Durian Hantu*. Hornbills swallow the whole package and regurgitate the seed, p. 368.

DURIAN HANTU *Durio grandiflorus*. Six species of small wild durians are hornbill dispersed and have no smell. They split into 3 or 5 capsules whilst on the tree exposing seeds covered in bright red arils. Hornbill dispersed durians include *D. graveolens, D. acutifolius, D. griffithii, D. crassipes* and *D. lanceolatus* (p. 368).

DURIAN SUKANG *Durio oxleyanus* (See right): 'This small fruited wild durian is very popular with both humans and Orangutans. Rijksen (1978) reports that Orangutans ate the seeds of *Durio oxleyanus* at Ketambe in Sumatra. He concludes that humans, Sun Bears, and possibly tigers are the main dispersal agents for this wild durian in Sumatra. Observations during 9 years indicate this is generally not the case at Tg Puting in Borneo. While Orangutans may consume the crisp seeds of very unripe fruits, wild Orangutans generally eat only the flesh of ripe fruits, discarding mouthfuls of intact stones. Wild Orangutans function as dispersal agents for this species because they discard stones up to 50m away from a mother tree.' Galdikas (1982). However at Deramakot Nakashima et al (2008) found that Orangutans were usually seed predators of durians, eating the unripe fruit and seeds (p. 338).

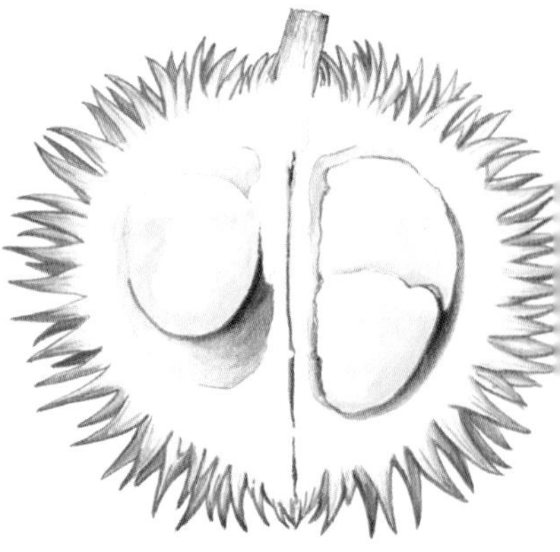

Cave Nectar Bat
Eonycteris spelaea

BATS POLLINATE DURIAN FLOWERS at night whilst spiderhunters pollinate durian flowers by day (Yumoto 2000). Bat-pollinated flowers are white whilst bird-pollinated flowers are pink or red. Durian flowers are ramiflorus (growing on the branches) and the branches themselves tend to spread out flat in a wagon wheel structure (terminalia branching) giving easy access at night to the nocturnal bat pollinator (p. 83).
In the illustration above a Cave Nectar Bat *Eonycteris spelea* is about to sip nectar from an orchard durian *Durio zibethinus*.

DURIAN SUKANG
Durio oxleyanus
Wild tree harvested for fruit. Note the open branching to give access to nocturnal pollinating bats.

DURIAN SUKANG
Durio oxleyanus

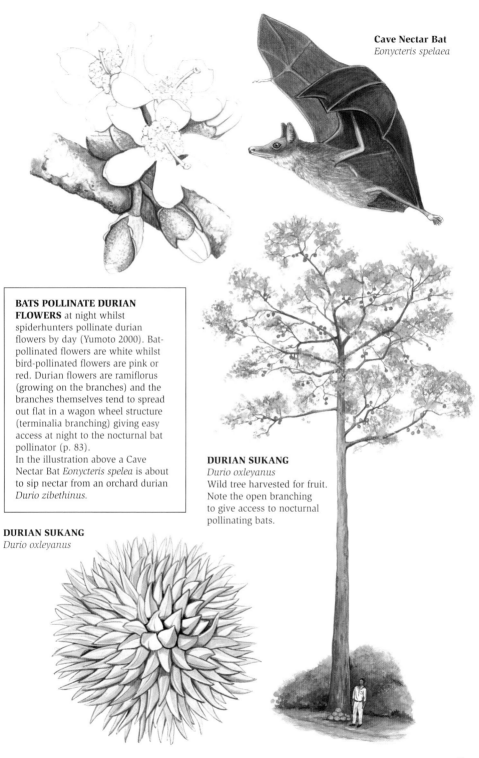

MELIACEAE World: c.565 spp**. Borneo:** 131 spp. in 15 genera of which Aglaia with 60 spp. of small to medium (to 40m) forest trees are the most common e.g. 55 spp. in 52 ha at Lambir (LaFrankie, 2010).

The Pan-Tropical Meliaceae are widely known for the S. American wind-dispersed *Swietenia* mahoganies often grown as street trees in Borneo. In Asia the bat-dispersed *Azadirachta indica* [Neem] is cultivated for traditional medicine and insecticides.

Borneo's Meliaceae have evolved a wide range of dispersal strategies for their seeds, targeting river, sea, wind, fish, bird and mammals for dispersal. Genera such as *Chisocheton* (21 spp.) and *Dysoxylum* (22 spp.) target dispersal by birds such as broadbills, hornbills and imperial pigeons whilst *Sandoricum* (5 spp.), *Walsura* (7 spp.), and *Lansium* (1 sp.) target bat and primate dispersal. The Asian Meliaceae and in particular Aglaia have been extensively researched by Dr Caroline Pannell who found that most Aglaia can be divided into two dispersal syndromes Primates and Birds, distinguished by the shape, size, colour, smell and chemical content of the fruit as illustrated below. Pannell's innovative approach to the recognition of targeted dispersal (functional syndromes) has been adopted throughout this book. See Pannell et al. (1992, 1997a, 1997b), Hopins and Pannell et al. (1998) and pp. 34, 36 and 38.

PRIMATE DISPERSED e.g. ***Aglaia korthalsii***
Seeds swallowed and dispersed by large primates such as gibbons and Orangutans, and later defecated.

* Fruit does not open when ripe (indehiscent).
* Seed covered by thin transparent sweet aril
* Aril sticks to the seed.
* Fruit has pleasant smell.

Range: NE India to Philippines, Borneo, Sumatra, Sulawesi. **Tree** to 26m. **Fruit size**: Up to 4 x 5cm. **Seed size:** Up to 1.5 x 2cm.
Note: At Ketambe in Sumatra Rijksen found that this was the most favoured fruit of Orangutans which swallowed whole seeds.

BIRD DISPERSED e.g. ***Aglaia spectabilis***
Seeds are swallowed whole by imperial pigeons and hornbills and later regurgitated.

* Fruit splits open on tree (dehices) when ripe.
* Seed covered by oily aril.
* Aril is easily removed from the seed
* Red aril contrasts with white fruit interior.
* Fruit has no smell.

Range: NE India to Sumatra, Borneo Sulawesi, Australia. **Tree** to 40m. **Fruit size**: Up to 9 x 9cm. **Seed size:** Up to 2.7 x 5cm.
Note that Imperial Pigeons and hornbills are capable of swallowing much larger seeds than large primates. These seeds are regurgitated not defecated.

Seed is covered in an oily red aril.

Scale: All fruit and seeds 50% life size.

Neem *Azadirachta indica* Commonly cultivated in Borneo for medicinal use. The fibrous fruit are dispersed by fruit bats and primates.

angsat *ansium omesticum* ommon rchard tree.

A family of Pig-tailed Macaques *Macaca nemestrina* raid a fruiting langsat *Lansiun domesticum* in a village orchard whilst the dominant male keeps watch. Langsat grows wild throughout the forests of Malaysia from Thailand to New Guinea. Domesticated varieties known as *duku* or *dokong* produce larger, sweeter fruit. The relatively small cauliferous pale fruit of wild langsats indicate that they may be targeted at bat dispersal. Macaques hold the fruit in their cheek pouches before retiring to a secure place to separate the pulp and spit the seeds. They therefore provide local dispersal for the langsat. However, the seeds are small enough to be swallowed by larger primates such as Orangutans and gibbons and so dispersed long distances (p. 182).

PLANTS: LEGUMES (BEAN TREES)

FABACEAE World: 20,000 spp. **Borneo:** *c.* 300 spp. Despite being the world's third largest plant family (after orchids and daisies), the bean family (Fabaceae) is species poor in Borneo represented by *c.* 250 species of lianas (p. 69) and shrubs and *c.* 50 species of trees, as shown below. Legumes thrive in the dry seasonal forests of Africa, Australia and C America. In the wet forests of Borneo they cannot compete with giant Dipterocarps and abundant fruit trees of the Anarcardiacea, Meliaceae, Myrtaceae, Sapindaceae and Sapotaceae plant families. Even so Bornean legumes are important for mammals in four different ways

1 Pollination. Many legumes are pollinated by bats e.g. Parkia, Entada (p. 69).

2 Protein and calcium-rich leaves and young pods provide food for fruit bats, langurs, and large browsers such as deer and elephants e.g. *Koompasia, Parkia, Cassia.*

3 Mature beans of many genera are surrounded by a tasty pulp or an oily aril that attract mammalian seed disperses including bats, primates and large ground mammals e.g. *Afzelia, Cassia, Copaifera, Cynometra, Dialum, Sindora, Uittienia.*

4 Hard beans are larder-hoarded by rodents (pp. 33, 69).

LEGUME TREE PLANTATIONS Legumes can grow rapidly in nitrogen-deficient soil due to a symbiotic relationship with nitrogen-fixing bacteria in their root nodules and make ideal plantation trees in the poor soils of Borneo. As a result over one million ha of Borneo's forests have been converted to ecologically barren mono-culture plantations of *Albizia lebek* and *Acacia mangium* for wood pulp production, which provide virtually no food to wildlife (p. 30).

KOOMPASIA World: 3 spp. **Borneo:** 2 spp. These giant leguminous trees, which grow to 80m [Local names: mangaris (Sabah) tapang (Sarawak) bangris (Kalimantan)], are common reminders of land that was once forested in many parts of Borneo, e.g. Tabin, Sepilok and Gng Penrissen, saved from destruction for both spiritual and practical reasons. *Koompasia* often host multiple colonies of nomadic giant honey bees, *Apis dorsata.* The honeycombs are harvested at night by recklessly brave locals who climb the trees using bamboo pegs driven into the trunk linked with rattan to create a flimsy ladder. It is believed that the bees prefer these giant trees for nesting because they are too tall and smooth to be climbed by honey-loving Sun Bears. In turn the extremely vicious bees protect the tree from leaf and seed predators, especially langurs, who eat the leaves when bees are absent (p. 249).

CASSIA World: 24 spp. **Borneo:** 1 sp. *Cassia javanica* produces a long, round, hard pod up to 100cm long (illustrated far right). These pods are full of tiny hard seeds enclosed in circular cross-sections filled with a sweet pulp. In India and Africa related *Cassia* species are dispersed by large ground mammals, such as wild cattle and antelopes. *Cassia fistula* is a similar but much smaller ornamental tree with yellow flowers and similar pods often grown in town gardens. *Cassia javanica* grows wild along the forest edge e.g. at Poring (Sabah). Here a group of Tembadau, or Banteng *Bos javanica* are shown feeding on the fallen pods (p. 304).

CASSIA JAVA

Cassia javanica
seed pods are up to 1m long

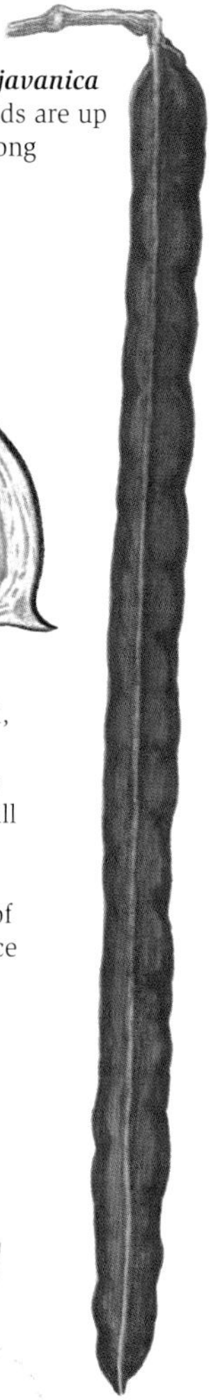

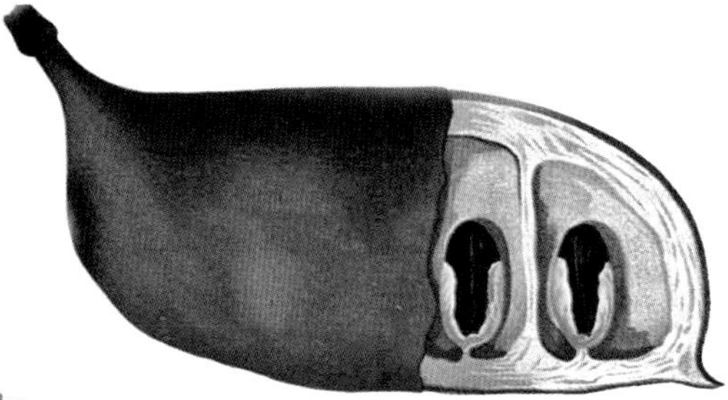

Afzelia rhomboidea Ripe pod split open, advertising the small, smooth, black, toxic seeds surrounded by an edible orange oily aril. This is a typical hornbill fruit which is also dispersed by gibbons and Orangutans. The valuable hard timber, Merbau, of this 40m forest tree is now scarce due to logging (p. 30).

MPASIA ***PARKIA***

PARKIA **World:** 40 spp.
Borneo: 6 spp.
[Local: Petai]
Parkia are important bat-pollinated trees in the wet forests of Asia, Africa and S America. The green pods are eaten by primates and humans. In Borneo *Parkia* are common trees of the forest edge and secondary forest, often found growing near old settlements. Look out for the tall straight white trunks (to 25m), with either pendulous pom-pom flowers or bunches of long green pods.

Cave Nectar Bat
Eonycteris spelaea feeding on *Parkia* flowers (p. 96).

LEGUMINOUS LIANAS of the bean family Fabaceae (See p. 67 for bean trees) are ubiquitous in Borneo's forests, climbing up tall trees in virgin forest and smothering saplings in logged forest. At Sepilok lianas averaged 1,348 stems per ha in alluvial forest. Of these, 26% (300 stems) were legumes of 17 different species dominating the liana community (DeWalt 2006). Leguminous vines provide nectar for bats and bean pods for rhinos but are most important because their young leaves provide a staple food for many mammals. The leaves of the abundant *Spatholobus* (16 spp.) and *Bauhinia* (31 spp.) vines are a favourite food of primates, elephants and rhinoceros. Legume leaves are particularly high in protein compared with fruits, and therefore provide an essential component of primate diets.

How do leguminous lianas benefit from providing a high protein salad to Bornean mammals? There are two competing theories. 1. Lianas gain no benefit from having their leaves eaten, but it is more efficient to allocate scarce resources to rapid growth rather than investing in poisonous leaf toxins and thorns to deter leaf predators. 2. Lianas do benefit but in a currently unknown manner, e.g. primate folivores might destroy leaf-eating caterpillars before they can become a plague. It is also possible that by trampling broken pieces of liana into the muddy ground, elephants and rhinos may help the vines to disperse to new locations. Finally, the edible leaves may act as a 'taster' to attract bean-dispersing mammals (p. 74).

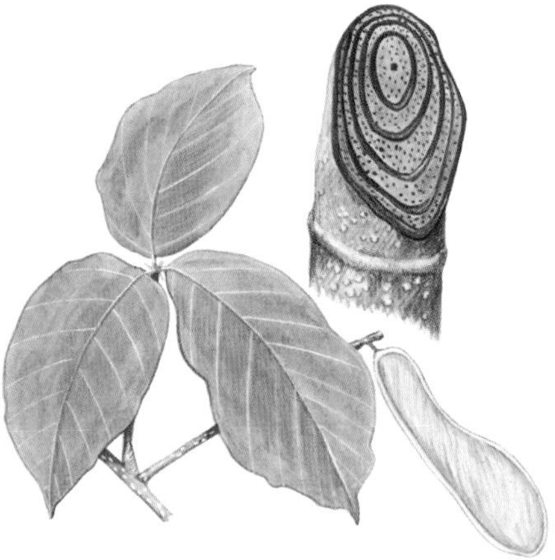

Spatholobus vine. Borneo is the world centre of *Spatholobus* distribution with 16 species. Tea made from the dried stem of various *Spatholobus* species is famed in Chinese herbal medicine as a powerful blood tonic (p. 24).

Bauhinia excelsa Bauhinias are the commonest flowers of the forest canopy and Borneo is a world centre with 31 species. Most bauhinias can be distinguished by their 'goats hoof' leaves, here being eaten by a Long-tailed Macaque.

Illustration by Susan Phillipps.

ENTADA LIANAS **World:** *c.* 30 pan-tropical spp. **Borneo:** 3 spp. *Entadas* produce the largest bean pod in the world containing giant beans, as illustrated below. The lianas are common along roadsides and in forest gaps throughout Borneo. These beans are common drift seeds along the Bornean coast and have been found in the gut of a dead Sumatran rhinoceros indicating that *Entadas* are anachronistic fruits, as described on p. 38. Entada beans have been found larder-hoarded by Long-tailed Porcupines (Linus Gokusing).

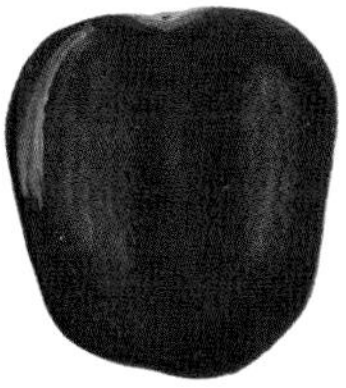

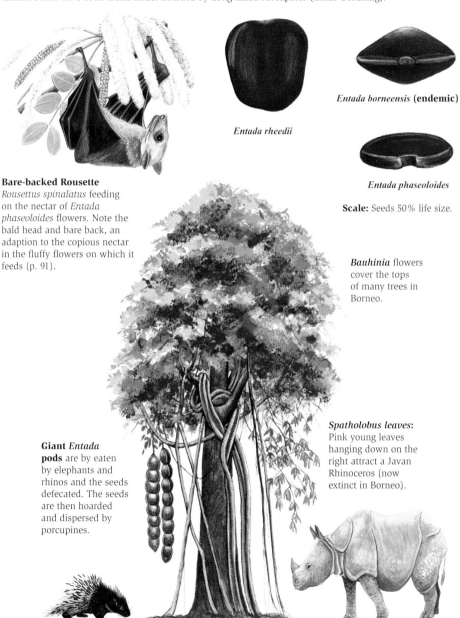

Entada rheedii

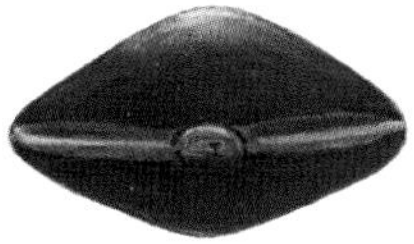

Entada borneensis **(endemic)**

Entada phaseoloides

Scale: Seeds 50% life size.

Bare-backed Rousette *Rousettus spinalatus* feeding on the nectar of *Entada phaseoloides* flowers. Note the bald head and bare back, an adaption to the copious nectar in the fluffy flowers on which it feeds (p. 91).

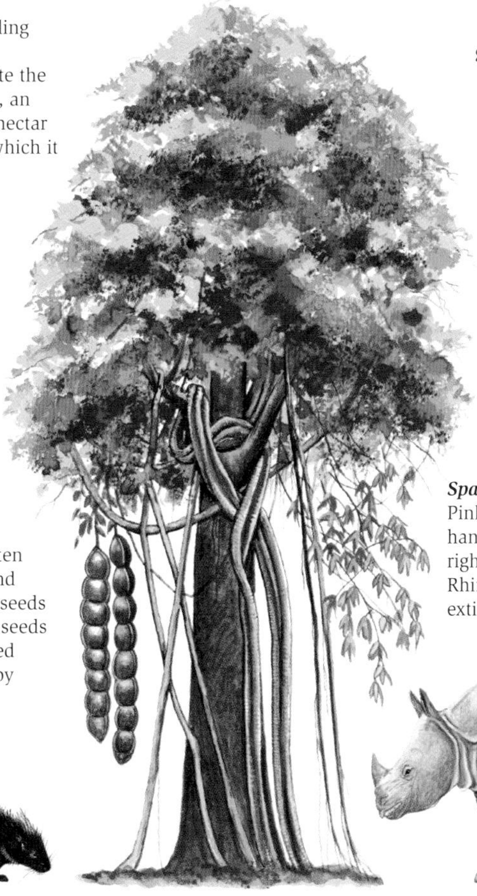

Bauhinia flowers cover the tops of many trees in Borneo.

***Spatholobus leaves*:** Pink young leaves hanging down on the right attract a Javan Rhinoceros (now extinct in Borneo).

Giant *Entada* pods are by eaten by elephants and rhinos and the seeds defecated. The seeds are then hoarded and dispersed by porcupines.

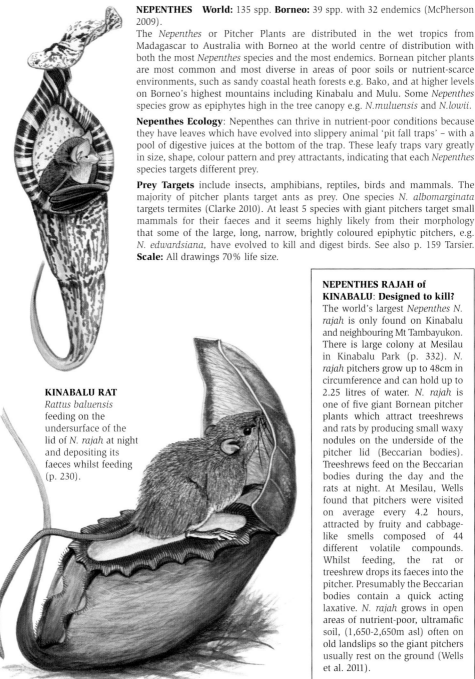

NEPENTHES World: 135 spp. **Borneo:** 39 spp. with 32 endemics (McPherson 2009).

The *Nepenthes* or Pitcher Plants are distributed in the wet tropics from Madagascar to Australia with Borneo at the world centre of distribution with both the most *Nepenthes* species and the most endemics. Bornean pitcher plants are most common and most diverse in areas of poor soils or nutrient-scarce environments, such as sandy coastal heath forests e.g. Bako, and at higher levels on Borneo's highest mountains including Kinabalu and Mulu. Some *Nepenthes* species grow as epiphytes high in the tree canopy e.g. *N.muluensis* and *N.lowii*.

Nepenthes Ecology: Nepenthes can thrive in nutrient-poor conditions because they have leaves which have evolved into slippery animal 'pit fall traps' – with a pool of digestive juices at the bottom of the trap. These leafy traps vary greatly in size, shape, colour pattern and prey attractants, indicating that each *Nepenthes* species targets different prey.

Prey Targets include insects, amphibians, reptiles, birds and mammals. The majority of pitcher plants target ants as prey. One species *N. albomarginata* targets termites (Clarke 2010). At least 5 species with giant pitchers target small mammals for their faeces and it seems highly likely from their morphology that some of the large, long, narrow, brightly coloured epiphytic pitchers, e.g. *N. edwardsiana,* have evolved to kill and digest birds. See also p. 159 Tarsier.
Scale: All drawings 70% life size.

NEPENTHES RAJAH of KINABALU: Designed to kill?
The world's largest *Nepenthes N. rajah* is only found on Kinabalu and neighbouring Mt Tambayukon. There is large colony at Mesilau in Kinabalu Park (p. 332). *N. rajah* pitchers grow up to 48cm in circumference and can hold up to 2.25 litres of water. *N. rajah* is one of five giant Bornean pitcher plants which attract treeshrews and rats by producing small waxy nodules on the underside of the pitcher lid (Beccarian bodies). Treeshrews feed on the Beccarian bodies during the day and the rats at night. At Mesilau, Wells found that pitchers were visited on average every 4.2 hours, attracted by fruity and cabbage-like smells composed of 44 different volatile compounds. Whilst feeding, the rat or treeshrew drops its faeces into the pitcher. Presumably the Beccarian bodies contain a quick acting laxative. *N. rajah* grows in open areas of nutrient-poor, ultramafic soil, (1,650-2,650m asl) often on old landslips so the giant pitchers usually rest on the ground (Wells et al. 2011).

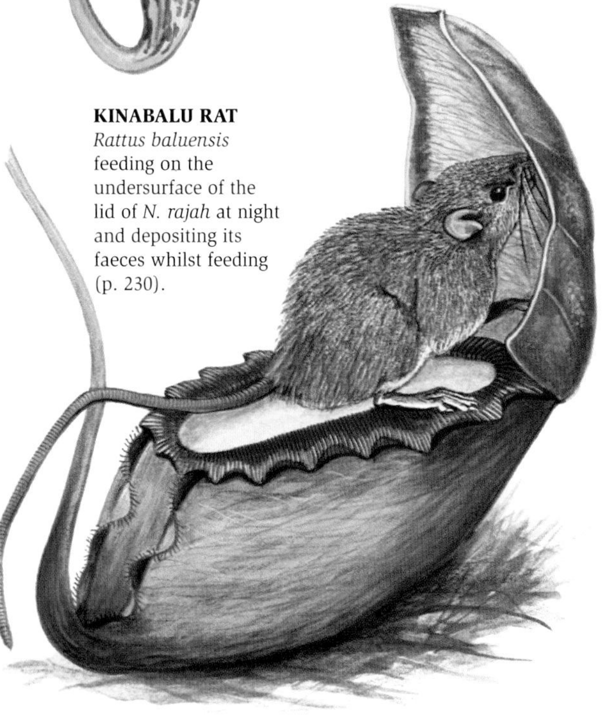

KINABALU RAT
Rattus baluensis
feeding on the undersurface of the lid of *N. rajah* at night and depositing its faeces whilst feeding (p. 230).

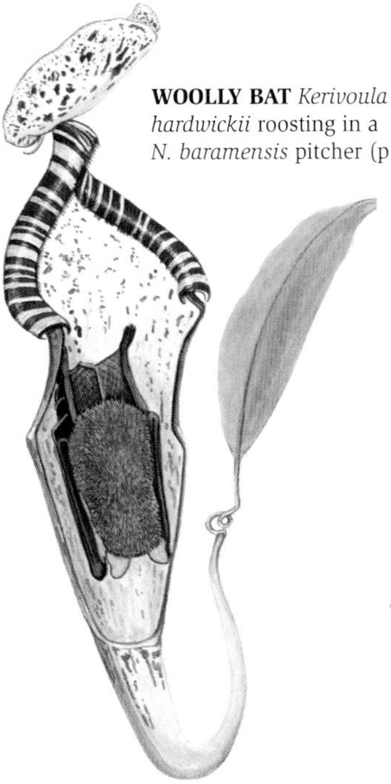

WOOLLY BAT *Kerivoula hardwickii* roosting in a *N. baramensis* pitcher (p. 116).

NEPENTHES AND BATS In 2009 Ulmar Grafe discovered that 29% of the *Nepenthes baramensis* pitchers in his Brunei study area were used as day roosts by Woolly Bats, *Kerivoula hardwickii,* which preferred them over other roosting sites. Spectroscopic analysis revealed that a majority of the nitrogen uptake by *N. baramensis* resulted from bat faeces (Grafe et al., 2010). Schoner at al (2015) found that *K. hardwickii* used an acoustic reflector at the base of the pitcher lid to locate *N. baramensis* pitchers amongst dense forest vegetation. This is the first recorded instance of bats using echo-location to identify specific vegetation in Asia. Bats have also been recorded roosting in 2 other species of *Nepenthes*: *N. bicalcarata* (Clarke 2010), and *N. ampularia* (Metzger).

DROWNED RATS Different *Nepenthes* species produce pitchers in a variety of sizes from small to very large, suitable for different sized prey. However only *N. rajah* has a bowl large enough to drown a rat or a squirrel. On at least eight occasions drowned rats or treeshrews have been found dead in *N. rajah* bowls and it seems too much of a coincidence to be a matter of chance. In contrast, *N. lowii,* which also produces Beccarian bodies to attract treeshrews, has a width restriction at the base of the bowl. The most likely explanation is that *N. lowii* is an epiphyte growing in trees and may have difficulty in supporting the weight of a dead rat during digestion, whilst the ground loving *N. rajah* experiences no such difficulty and the occasional death of one of its many visitors is a welcome bonus to its normal 'diet' of faeces.

MOUNTAIN TREESHREW *Tupaia montana* feeds on Beccarian food bodies under the lid of *Nepenthes lowii* during the day, p. 146.

PLANTS: BANANAS AND GINGERS

BANANAS AND GINGERS are large fleshy herbs, extremely common along roadsides, riverbanks and logged forest throughout Borneo. Banana fruits are produced on hanging stems providing easy access to bats, squirrels and primates, whilst ginger fruit are produced at ground level for dispersal by deer, pigs and rats.

Steady State Fruiting Bananas and gingers are of enormous importance to Borneo's wildlife because both the flowers and fruit are produced continuously, not in seasonal bursts or masts. Both bananas and gingers grow in clumps from underground roots or rhizomes and are therefore tolerant of damage to their above-ground leaves. The fleshy stems of bananas are much loved by elephants and as a result, where elephants are common, such as at Tabin, Danum or along the Kinabatangan River, wild bananas are replaced by gingers, which are less preferred by elephants. Bananas are commonest in the hills e.g. Poring (Sabah) and Ulu Temburong in Brunei, where elephants have long been absent.

BANANAS (MUSACEAE) **World:** *c.* 40 spp. **Borneo:** *c.* 20 spp. The islands stretching from Borneo and the Philippines to New Guinea are the world centre of diversity for bananas. Inevitably Borneo's forests host many banana pests which prevent bananas being grown as a plantation crop in Borneo, although small holders grow over 100 different cultivars, often seen for sale on roadside stalls.

24 Hour Pollination Most bananas have a dual pollination strategy, the flowers providing nectar both day and night. During the day banana flowers are pollinated by at least 5 species of traplining, spiderhunter birds. At night the diurnal pollinators are replaced by numerous nocturnal fruit and nectar feeding bats (p. 94). Like the diurnal spiderhunters during the day the Long Tongued Nectar Bat is a trapliner, flying from clump to clump in a nocturnal circuit (see opposite and p. 97).

Banana Seed Dispersal Wild banana fruits are packed with small, hard, black seeds. The whole fruit is carried away by fruit bats (p. 81) to a feeding roost where the flesh is pulped and swallowed and the seeds dropped. Banana fruit attract most of Borneo's frugivorous mammals, including squirrels, tree rats, treeshrews, primates, civets and elephants. In all banana clumps there is usually one stem fruiting providing a constant supply of fruit and nectar to both resident and nomadic fruit bats.

Small ***Cynopterus*** **fruit bats** construct **harem tents** by biting through the structural veins of banana leaves until they collapse to make a cosy shelter (pp. 87 and 130).

Small bats often roost in rolled-up banana and ginger leaves (pp. 128, 130).

Wild banana clump Elephants destroy the whole clump, not just the fruit.

CULTIVATED BANANA
Male flowers being nectar robbed by a Plantain Squirrel, *Callosciurus notatus*. Both the squirrel and the banana are common in disturbed forest. The cultivated banana is closely related to *M. acuminata*, a Sundaland native (p. 202).

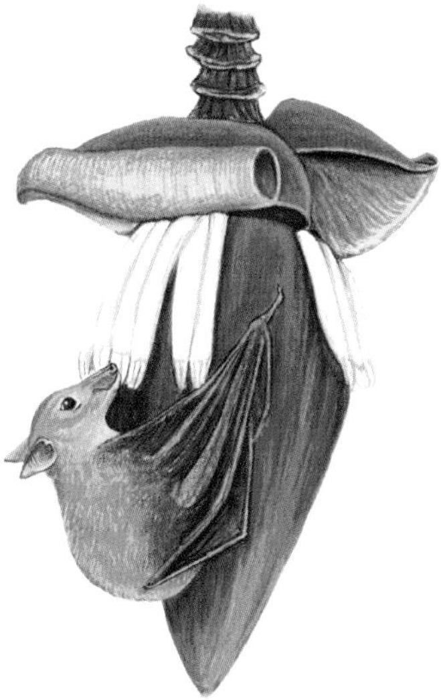

BAU BANANA *Musa bauensis*. Female flowers being pollinated by Long-tongued Nectar Bat *Macroglossus minimus*. A typical banana flower spike opens one bract each night from the top down exposing the female flowers. After pollination, small banana fruit appear. Subsequent opening bracts expose male flowers each night. At this stage the flower bud is often collected for local consumption (p. 96).

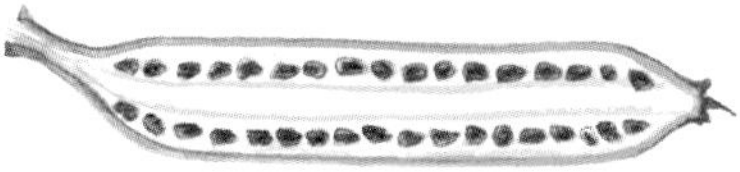

BAU BANANA
Musa bauensis Fruit split to show numerous seeds. Endemic to the limestone area of Bau near Kuching.

GINGERS (ZINGIBERACEAE) World: c.1,300 spp. **Borneo:** c.250+ spp. Gingers protect their leafy stems with strong smelling volatiles (aromas/scents). Whilst rejected by elephants, ginger roots, inner stems and flowers are widely used both as vegetables and herbs in local cooking. Orangutans are known to descend to ground level specifically to feed on the inner stems of gingers. **Ground Level Fruit and Flowers:** Unlike bananas, which flower from a prominent heart-shaped flower bud jantung (heart) hanging from a spike at the top of plant, most gingers produce flowers and their fruit at ground level or on short stalks. The small hard black seeds are encased in a sweet fleshy aril surrounded by a hard shell in heads like a small pineapple.

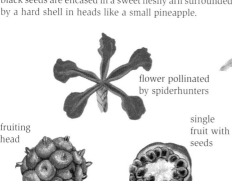

flower pollinated by spiderhunters

fruiting head

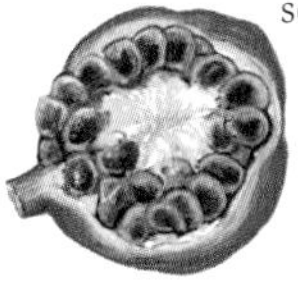

single fruit with seeds

Etlingera megalocheilos. The seeds of this wild ginger, common at Danum, are dispersed by mousedeer (p. 306).

MORACEAE World: 60 spp. **Borneo:** 22 wild spp. making Borneo the world centre of *Artocarpus* diversity. In most forest plots *Artocarpus* are abundant, comprising 4-6% of the trees. *Artocarpus* are one of the most important fruit providers to Bornean mammals. Small smooth fruit (fig mimics) are swallowed by hornbills; medium to large hairy fruit are eaten by primates, including humans. *Artocarpus* nectar is of major importance to nectarivorous bats. The world's largest compound fruit is the domesticated jakfruit. The jakfruit's wild relative the cempedak (*Artocarpus integer*) evolved to be dispersed by rhinos, elephants and tapirs.

BURUNI *Artocarpus lacucha* (*A. dadah*) is an irregularly shaped apple sized fruit that ripens yellow with soft pink flesh. The small seeds are targeted at dispersal by fruit bats and primates especially gibbons.

Buruni are common throughout the forests of Borneo and some people believe that the nation state of Brunei Darussalam derives its name from the Buruni fruit. Etymologists (people who study the origin of words) are confident that the name Borneo is derived from Brunei, and it is therefore most likely that the great island of Borneo is named after this popular primate fruit.

BINTAWAK (TERAP IKAL) *Artocarpus anisophyllus* produces a large fruit with blunt spines and a powerful smell that attracts large primates, such as Orangutans and humans. It is common throughout the Bornean forests, and a fruiting tree will also attract flying squirrels, civets and fruits bats at night as well as primates during the day. Deer and Bearded Pigs gather to eat the fallen fruit. The large seeds are eaten by humans once roasted, but are toxic if uncooked, and Orangutans normally eat the flesh but reject the seeds thus acting as 'pulp thieves'. *Illustration based on a photograph taken by Robert Ong from the canopy walkway at Sepilok.*

THE CEMPADAK AND THE SUMATRAN RHINOCEROS The cempedak *(A. integer)* a wild relative of the jakfruit produces very strong-smelling, large fruits on its lower trunk and branches twice a year targeted at dispersal by large ground mammals such as rhinos, elephants, tapir and deer. The fruit bunches are invariably accompanied by a bunch of leaves known to be a favoured food of the Sumatran Rhinoceros. It is likely that the edible leaves are a 'taster' to encourage the rhinos to include the cempadak trees on their regular forest circuit, so that the seeds will be dispersed by the rhinos before they can be eaten by seed predators, such as Argus Pheasants and porcupines. According to Ridley (1930), 'The Sumatran Rhino often wanders great distances. It has a regular route for very many miles which it constantly travels, a march occupying a month or more. It generally evacuates only at special spots, frequently a long way from where it has been feeding, and consequently may carry and distribute seeds a long distance.'

TAMPANG *Artocarpus nitidus* produces small shiny fruits the size of a large grape (fig mimics), which ripen pink/orange and are designed to be swallowed whole and dispersed by hornbills and large imperial pigeons and carried away by fruit bats at night.

CEMPEDAK
Sumatran Rhinos eat both the leaves and the fruit of cempedak.

MORACEAE **World**: *c.* 800 spp. **Borneo**: *c.* 150 spp., making Borneo the world centre of *Ficus* distribution. Figs originated in the tropical forests of Gondwanaland (previously joined to S. America via Antarctica) over 60 million years ago, but have reached their highest diversity in Borneo with at least 11 recognizable dispersal syndromes (p. 35). Below we describe 5 *Ficus* dispersal syndromes targeted primarily at mammals. For figs dispersed by bats see p. 78.

Plastic Genes and and Genetic Toolkits Over the last 60 million years two Bornean plant families, in particular the beans Fabaceae (pp. 66, 68) and the Moraceae, *Artocarpus* (p. 74), and *Ficus* have developed highly plastic 'genetic tool kits' enabling a rapid morphological adaption to new environments. Thus the 150 *Ficus* species of Borneo may be found growing from coastal beaches to the tree line on Kinabalu. In form they vary from giant forest stranglers, providing food for hornbills to diminutive rheophytes growing in the beds of fast-flowing streams. It can truly be said that where ever you are in Borneo you are rarely more than 100m from a fig, although that fig may be a seedling in the rain gutter of a hotel in Kota Kinabalu. Plastic genes and rapid evolution are the reason figs are overwhelmingly important for the survival of Borneo's animals but have made *Ficus* classification a taxonomic puzzle. See Berg (2005).

FICUS SEED DISPERSAL AND PREDATION Fig seeds are tiny, nearly always less than 2mm diameter. This gives figs both advantages and disadvantages. A single fruiting fig tree may produce hundreds of thousands of fruits and millions of seeds. The small seeds are swallowed and dispersed by many birds and mammals. One advantage is that *Ficus* seeds can establish almost anywhere, from tiny cracks in concrete roofs to gaps in tree bark high in the canopy. One disadvantage is that due to the tiny seeds the young plant has no food reserves and will die soon after germination unless nutrients and water are readily available. Another disadvantage is that guilds of animals have evolved specifically to predate fig seeds. Avian fig seed predators include canopy green pigeons and ground-living pheasants and partridges. Both groups swallow small stones in order to grind up fig seeds in their tough elastic gizzards. Pencil-tailed Tree Mice also predate fig seeds, although the most important fig seed predators are seed-eating Bruchid beetles (p. 44).

Scale: All fruit 70% life size

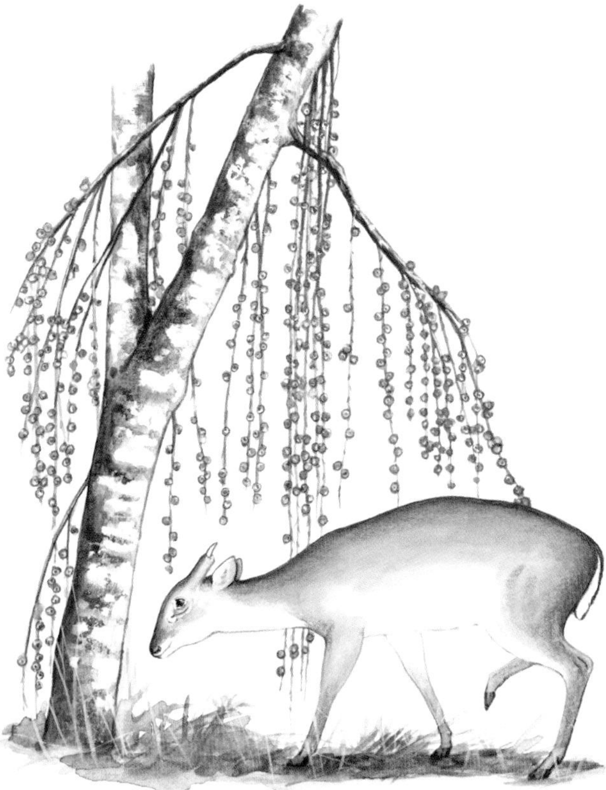

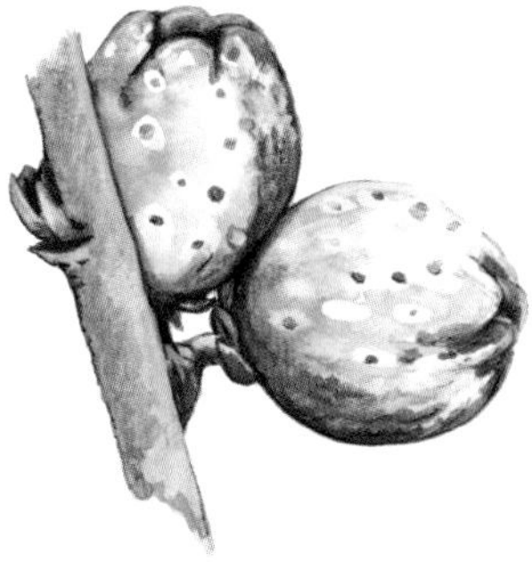

TREUB'S FIG *Ficus treubii*. A small tree of the forest understorey, e.g. at Sepilok. The small figs hang in curtains from aerial roots. They ripen green and are probably eaten by understorey bats and large ground mammals, such as barking deer and mousedeer.

LEPEROUS FIG *Ficus lepicarpa*. A small tree of the forest edge, e.g. at Tabin. The figs are ramiflorus and are eaten by fruit bats and palm civets. The figs ripen green with rough brown patches hence the latin name – leperous skin.

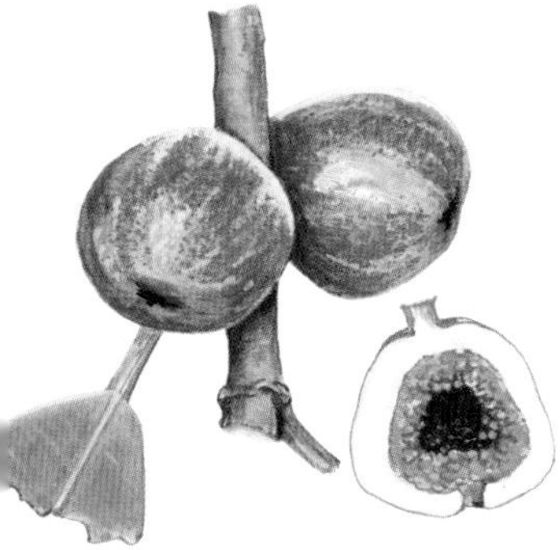

KEYSTONE SPECIES Ficus are a keystone species in the ecology of tropical forests and in Borneo they are by far the most important source of food for animal life. Figs provide the primary food source for gibbons, mousedeer, several species of civets, many species of fruit bats, 3 species of hornbills, green pigeons, and pheasants and partridges. Figs are even more important as a 'fallback food' for frugivorous mammals. Figs fruit asynchronously at odd times on an irregular pattern so Orangutans, macaques, deer, pigs squirrels, rats, treeshrews and Sun Bears rely on figs when no other fruit is available.

DUBIOUS FIG *Ficus dubia* is a large strangling fig of primary forest with one of the largest canopy fig fruits just small enough for a hornbill to swallow whole, but too large for a seed predator green pigeon. The figs are eaten by Orangutans and hornbills.

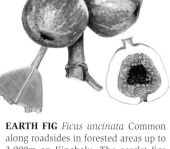

EARTH FIG *Ficus uncinata* Common along roadsides in forested areas up to 2,000m on Kinabalu. The scarlet figs grow on stolons (roots) half buried in the earth. Dispersed by pigs, deer, rats and ground squirrels. The spines (bracts) are to prevent ground-level seed predators e.g. pheasants and partridges swallowing the fig whole.

TANGKOL or RED RIVER FIG *Ficus racemosa* A common generalist fig popular with elephants, primates, bats, hornbills and cat fish. Common along river banks in Sabah, such as the Kinabatangan with trunk (cauliflorus) and branches (ramiflorus) covered in figs that ripen pink to red. Tangkol is important in Kadazan/Dusun (Sabah) culture, celebrated by an annual Nunuk Ragang festival. A fine example of Tangkol grows in the car park of the Shangrila Tg Aru Resort, Kota Kinabalu.

FRUIT BAT ECOLOGY 1: BAT FIGS

1 *Ficus callosa*: Tall tree to 35m with a straight trunk and large buttresses. Common on Signal Hill, KK. Figs ripen yellow green in a **Big Bang.**

2 *Ficus annulata*: Large climber which may later turn into a strangler to 30 m. Figs ripen yellow green in a **Big Bang.**

3 *Ficus variegata*: Tall tree to 30 m. Figs ripen green when they are eaten by bats later turning red when eaten by gibbons and birds. **Steady State.**

BAT FIGS OF BORNEO Illustrated above are five bat fig trees and their figs, along with a common bird fig, *Ficus microcarpa,* sometimes also eaten by bats. At least 15 species of Borneo's figs (10% of a total of *c.* 150 species) are recognisably targeted at bat dispersal. Bat figs occur in all shapes and sizes, from tall stranglers to small shrubs. Bat figs ripen greenish yellow or brown and usually hang from trunks (cauliflorus) or branches (ramiflorus). Bats do eat 'bird' figs but prefer 'bat' figs. Palm civets also prefer bat figs to bird figs. Bats detect ripe figs by their smell. Differences in nutrients, sugars etc. between bat and bird figs are being investigated (Nakabayashi 2015). Birds cannot recognize ripe bat figs because (a) Most birds cannot smell and (b) Bat figs ripen green not red. *Ficus variegata* is an exception.

4 *Ficus microcarpa*: A Borneo native 'banyan' with stilt roots. Common in coastal areas. The small pink figs are bird dispersed. **Big Bang.**

5 *Ficus fistulosa*: Common along forest margins to 20m. Figs ripen yellow green. Abundant on Signal Hill, Kota Kinabalu. **Steady State.**

6 *Ficus septica*: Shrub to 15m. Common cultivated areas. Figs ripen yellow green. Common on Signal Hill, Kota Kinabalu. **Steady State.**

CANOPY BATS AND UNDERSTOREY BATS Amongst the specialist bat figs two sub-guilds can also be recognized 1. Big Bang canopy figs which fruit irregularly providing fruit for nomadic bats e.g. *Cynopterus horsfieldi*, *Pteropus vampyrus*, *Dyacopterus spadiceus*, and *Megaerops* spp. and 2. Steady State understorey and secondary forest figs e.g. *Ficus fistulosa* and *F. septica* which fruit continuously and feed small resident bats such as *Cynopterus brachyotis* and *C. minimus*. *F. variegata* is very widespread, found from S China to Australia and targets multiple dispersers. *F. variegata* has a two-stage ripening process, first attracting bats and civets when green, and later turning red to attract birds and primates (Nakabayashi 2015).

FRUIT BAT ECOLOGY 2: BAT-DISPERSED SEEDS

BAT FRUIT TREES AND SEED DISPERSAL Over 300 Bornean tree species target fruit bats for seed dispersal. Bat-dispersed trees are scarce in the canopy, common in the forest understorey, and abundant along the forest edge and in secondary forest. Illustrated above are 6 bat fruit trees of which the seeds are primarily dispersed by bats.

Bat Fruit 1. Ripen green/yellow/brown rather than the pink/red/black of bird-dispersed fruit. 2. Are usually larger than bird fruit and often covered in sharp hairs to prevent seed predator green pigeons from swallowing them whole but are 3. Smaller than primate fruit such as mangosteens and rambutans (pp. 217, 376).

Bat Fruits may be further divided into two types (a) With large seeds covered in edible flesh e.g. *Elaeocarpus, Prunus, Livistonia* and *Terminalia,* which are carried to local feeding perches and then dropped or (b) With tiny seeds (max 2 mm diameter) evolved to be swallowed whole and defecated e.g. Bananas, Figs, *Muntingia.*

Recognizing Bat Trees Most bat trees have distinctive straight white trunks, open pagoda type branching and leaves with prominent white veins. Fruit and flowers are often caulifórous or ramiflorus or held pendant on long stalks to make access easy for bats (pp. 78, 82).

Steady State and Big Bang Bat Feeding Guilds Resident fruit bats e.g. *Cynopterus, Balionycteris* and *Chironax*, tend to feed on Steady State secondary forest trees which fruit continuously, whereas nomadic bats such as the *Pteropus, Dyacopterus* and *Megaerops* arrive only when canopy trees are fruiting in one Big Bang (p. 94).

1 MEDANG KELEWAR ***Prunus polystacha***: Bat plum. [Local: Akil] Common small Big Bang bat-dispersed tree of the forest edge with a single large seed.

2 MUNTINGIA [Malay cherry: Buah cheri] A small S American tree often planted in kampungs for its Steady State sweet red berries with numerous tiny seeds. *Muntingia* fruit are eaten by Green Pigeons by day and *Cynopterus* bats at night. Green Pigeons are seed predators so the reason you often see *Muntingia* growing in vacant building plots is because the seeds were dispersed by bats as they flew over at night.

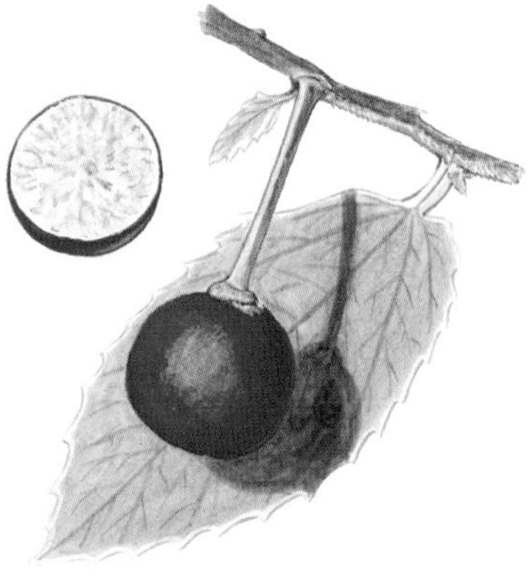

4 KETAPANG
Terminalia catappa.
Sea Almond. A common Steady State sea shore tree which is both pollinated and dispersed by bats (p. 40).

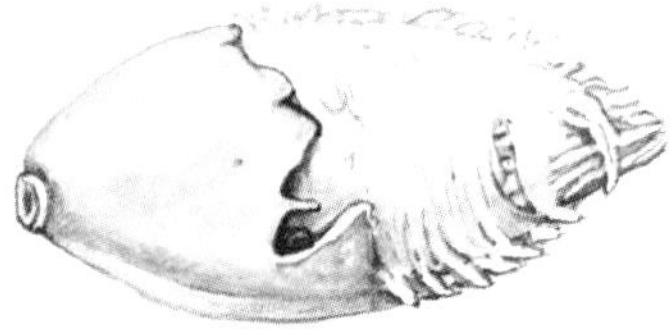

5 MEDANG MUSANG
Elaeocarpus parvifolius Civet Plum. *Elaeocarpus* are common small trees of the forest edge from islands to high on Kinabalu. The Big Bang blue fruit are eaten by hornbills and pigeons. Green fruit preferred by bats. A single hard seed.

6 LIVISTONIA PALMS
Locally common palms of seasonal dry forest, often planted in gardens. Palms produce vast amounts of nectar almost continuously (Steady State) and bats are important pollinators. *Livistonia* fruit are dispersed by bats, civets and hornbills.

3 BANANA (Steady State)
A Short-nosed Fruit Bat *Cynopterus brachyotis* carries a banana back to its feeding perch.

FRUIT BAT ECOLOGY 3: BAT-POLLINATED TREES

1 KAPOK (BB) *Ceiba pentandra*. (Malvaceae). Branches held straight out so that nectar bats have easy access to the ramiflorus white flowers. Seeds wind dispersed.

2 BINUANG (SS) *Octomeles sumatrana* (Tetramelaceae). A common fast growing tree of river banks. Bat pollinated. Seeds wind dispersed.

3 MIDNIGHT HORROR (SS) [Beka]. *Oroxylum indicum* (Bignoniaceae). Seeds wind dispersed. Pods look like parangs (bush knives).

4 PULAI (BB) *Alstonia angustiloba* (Apocynaceae). Seeds wind dispersed from long thin twin seed pods. Large trees common in peat-swamp, secondary forests.

KEY **(BB)** Trees which flower in one big bang. **(SS)** Trees which flower year round or steady state.

BAT-POLLINATED TREES IN BORNEO Bat-pollinated trees are both common and easy to recognise. Illustrated here are 8 of the most common (of several hundred) trees with flowers that are primarily bat pollinated. In his classic book *The Wayside Trees of Malaya* (1952), Corner describes and lists numerous 'pagoda trees with terminalia type branching' (p. 81), without reference to the fact these distinctive features evolved to allow easy access for bat pollinators and/or dispersers. Most bat trees have tall straight pale white trunks to advertise their location at night. Bat pollinated trees may also be pollinated by moths, bees and birds. In addition to trees which 'target' bat pollinators, many tree families e.g. the Mangoes (Anacardiaceae) and Legumes (Mimosoidea) produce 'generalist' flowers pollinated by insects, birds and bats.

1 KAPOK *Ceiba pentandra* (Malvaceae) is a very large tree with giant buttresses common around rural kampungs in Borneo. Kapok was one of the first S American (New World) tropical trees introduced to Asia and Africa (Old World) for the white fluff contained in the large pods, used for stuffing pillows. Kapok is bat pollinated in S America. Despite their divergent evolutionary pathways Kapok flowers are very popular with Old World bats, and to date 4 different bats found in Borneo have been recorded feeding on Kapok nectar including *Cynopterus brachyotis*, *Cynopterus sphinx*, *Eonycteris spelaea* and *Microglossus minimus*.

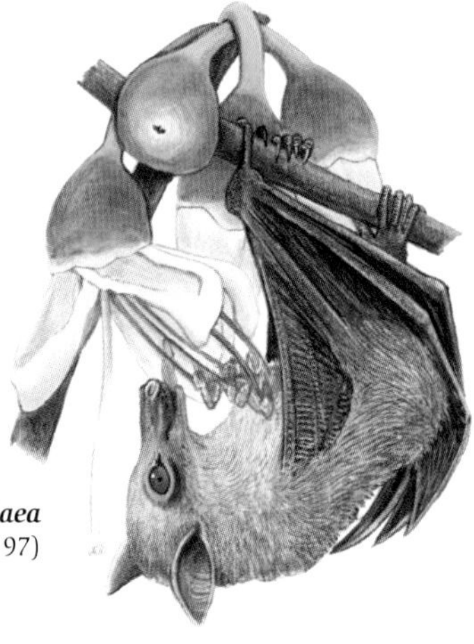

Cave Nectar Bat ***Eonycteris spelaea***
pollinating Kapok flower (pp. 67, 97)

5 NIBONG (SS)
Oncosperma tigillarium
Common in coastal swamps. In the hills replaced by *O. horridum*. Seeds dispersed by large pigeons and bats.

6 PETAI (BB)
Parkia speciosa
(Leguminosae). Common around kampongs. The green beans are cooked and eaten. Large pom pom flowers (illus. p. 66).

7 COCONUT (SS)
[Kelapa] *Cocos nucifera*
Evolved on small Pacific islands, now ubiquitous. Bat, bee, bird pollinated. Dispersed by sea and coconut crabs (p. 84)

8 PANDAN (SS)
Pandanus tectorius
c. 56 species of pandans are common along coasts and in swamp forest. Giant fruit are bat and sea dispersed (p. 92).

2 BINUANG FLOWER Fast-growing pioneer tree of flat river floodplains. Common along the Labuk river, Kinabatangan, and next to the river at Danum and Tabin. Distinguished by large leaves (often heavily attacked by insects) and straight white trunk. The pendant strings of small white flowers attract nocturnal Flying Foxes.

3 MIDNIGHT HORROR FLOWER Named by Corner (1952) after the strong bat-attracting smell of the flowers which open before midnight. A common slender tree of kampungs and secondary forest. Distinguished by very large, sword-shaped bean pods containing papery wind-dispersed seeds. Also known as the Broken Bones tree from the bone-shaped leaf stalks that fall below. Gould (1978) suggests that *Oroxylum indicum* may be an obligate bat-pollinated tree with flowers 'designed' to provide regular small amounts of nectar each night, throughout the year (Steady State) for Cave Nectar Bats *Eonycteris spelaea* (pp. 63, 67, 97).

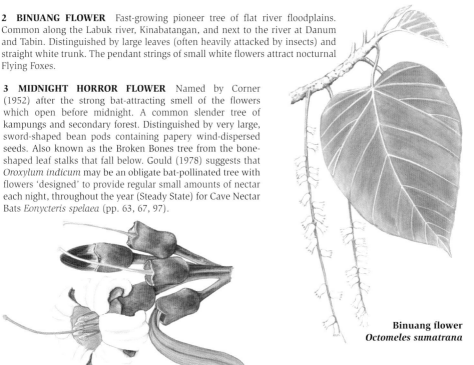

Binuang flower
Octomeles sumatrana

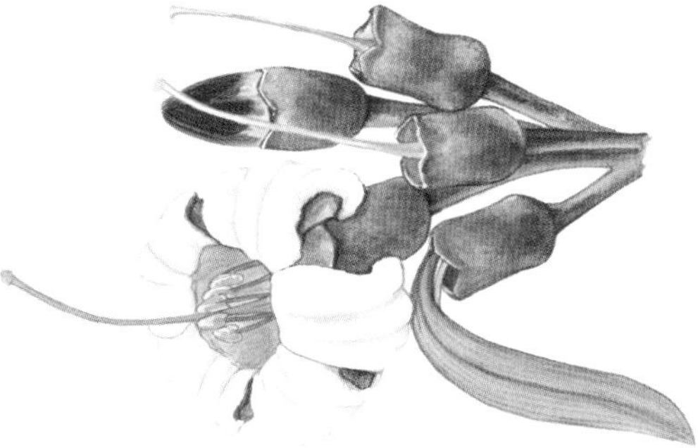

***Oroxylum indicum* flower**

FRUIT BATS AND FLYING FOXES

PTEROPODIDAE: FRUIT BATS World: 186 spp. **Borneo:** 1+ spp. The Pteropodidae fruit bats are confined to the tropics of the Old World i.e. Africa and Asia and are nocturnal fruit, nectar and leaf eaters.
Echolocation: All of the insectivorous bats in Borneo possess sonar (for hunting insects) and for navigating to roosts in dark caves. In Borneo 2 species of *Rousette* fruit bats also use sonar sounds generated by tongue clicking to navigate to their dark cave roosts. Other fruit bats may use the reflected sound of their wing beats to navigate in darkness (p. 90). **Roosting:** Fruit bats usually roost in groups. Flying foxes roost in large colonies in tree tops, whilst small fruit bats may use buildings, tree holes, or caves. Male *Cynopterus* bats construct harem tents to attract females (pp. 86, 128). **Habits:** Some fruit bats are local residents, others are nomadic with no permanent roosts whilst a third group are 'cave roosters' which fly long distances to feed each night. **Breeding** is co-ordinated with fruiting seasons, so colony females usually synchronize breeding. Fruit bats normally park their single young at a maternity roost whilst they forage at night. **ID:** All fruit bats (apart from the 2 *Eonycteris* species) have a small claw on the second finger as well as a large claw on the thumb. None of the insectivorous Bornean bats have a second claw (Diagram p. 99). **Ecology:** Small fruit bats are abundant in all habitats throughout Borneo and are important seed dispersers and flower pollinators having co-evolved with their host plants (pp. 80, 82).
Conservation Larger fruit bats in Borneo are severely threatened by hunting for food and need urgent legal protection. www.batcon.org, www.seabcru.org

FLYING FOXES: (Genus *Pteropus*) **World:** 59 spp. **Borneo:** 2 spp. The world's largest bats confined to the wet tropics, from the Pacific Islands to W Africa. Flying Foxes are commonest on small tropical islands where they play a key ecological role as the primary pollinator and seed disperser of many coastal and forest trees. In Borneo the Large Flying Fox is (was) a key ecological partner of many lowland forest trees, roosting during the day in coastal nipah and mangrove forest where food is limited but continuous and flying long distances each evening to feed on masting patches of forest trees. Feeding bats arrive in flocks soon after dusk, but once feeding are highly territorial defending their feeding patch with high-pitched screeching and wing flapping.

1 LARGE FLYING FOX *Pteropus vampyrus* FA 185–200 **Scarce nomad [Malay: Kalong]**

The world's largest bat with a wingspan reaching 1,700mm. Large flocks of this giant bat, flying high overhead at dusk used to be a common sight in many areas of Borneo. **Habits:** Epstein et al (2009) found that satellite tracked Flying Foxes from roosts in Malaya foraged as far as W Sumatra, a distance of 500 km over several months. Thus these bats have co-evolved to pollinate and disperse masting forest trees that flower and fruit erratically over very large areas (p. 42). **Breeding:** Flying Foxes gather in large roosts for breeding (See opposite). Colonies on Gaya Island and P. Tiga (Sabah) have vanished. A colony on P. Siarau, Brunei Bay is one of the last in coastal W Borneo. **Hunting:** Flying foxes are hunted with guns and nets for food in most areas of Borneo and are on the brink of extinction in many areas (Harrison, Cheyne et al 2011). **Captivity:** Flying foxes rapidly become tame and are easy to feed on local fruits. Flying foxes have lived to 31 years in captivity. **Diet:** Regarded as a pest by fruit farmers. It eats a wide variety of both forest fruits and nectar. Favoured nectar trees include Binuang (p. 82), Petai (p. 66) and palm flowers (p. 50).

2 ISLAND FLYING FOX *Pteropus hypomelanus* FA 121–140 **Locally common**

Can only be told apart from the Large Flying Fox by size (measurements). Normally roosts on islands and feeds locally but flocks may fly long distances to feed on the mainland e.g. at the Mantanani Islands, W Sabah. The Bornean coast and small offshore islands are largely inhabited by Muslim fisherfolk e.g. Bajaus, Suluks, who do not hunt bats and usually leave bat colonies undisturbed, and easy to watch.
Habits: On Maratua a colony of several hundred bats which fed on the nectar of coconut flowers, figs, breadfruit and papayas near the main village of Boheybukut was wiped out in 2013 by Javanese workers constructing the new airport. Tame colonies survive on some Semporna Islands' resorts and Nabucco Island Dive Resort, Maratua Lagoon. **Food**: Seven different species of figs were found growing on the roots of coconut palms below the bat colony on Maratua.
Range: Small islands from Thailand south to Borneo and the Lesser Sundas.

2

1 *Pteropus vampyrus* Large broad wings. Flies slowly long distances. Feeds in canopy.
2 *Pteropus hypomelanus* Shorter broad wings. Forages in dense coastal forest on islands.
3 *Macroglossus minimus* Small with short broad wings. Forages for nectar in understorey.
4 *Rousettus* sp. Roosts in caves. Flies fast long distance to feed on canopy flowers.

LARGE FLYING FOX IN SINGAPORE BOTANIC GARDEN
'When breeding, the Fox-Bats collect in immense numbers in some part of a forest, often in a mangrove swamp, and remain for some months, till the young are able to fly. In the Botanic Gardens in Singapore, on rare occasions – about once in 10 years – they used to come to breed in the Garden jungle, and it was calculated that between 70,000 and 80,000 at a time used to occupy the loftiest trees there. At dusk the greater number used to start in every direction in search of fruit, and could be seen flying for miles. Those with young seldom flew to any distance, but remained in the jungle, and ate the buds and leaves of the trees till they were almost leafless. Every evening, even after the colony had gone, these bats could be seen flying over, usually at great heights. I have often seen them a good long way out at sea, and from the fact that there is an endemic species on Christmas Island (*Pteropus natalis*), 240 miles from the nearest land, and furthermore, that a number of other species occur on remote islets, it may be concluded that they can fly very long distances.' Ridley (1930).

ISLAND FLYING FOX feeding on coconut flower nectar on Pulau Maratua E. Kalimantan.
It is likely that coconut palms, flying foxes (pollinators) and coconut crabs (dispersers) all originated and co-evolved together on isolated Pacific islands (p. 40).

CYNOPTERUS FRUIT BATS — MALAY: CECADU

Cynopterus fruit bats are the most common small fruit bats throughout Borneo in most habitats including oil palm (p. 96). *Cynopterus* bats have distinctive 1. White ear rims (which darken with age). 2. Pale wing bones. 3. Short tails. 4. Breeding males have yellow-orange collars (p. 99). *Cynopterus* bats are easily caught in mist nets set at night and must be untangled rapidly before the net is chewed to shreds. **Diet:** *Cynopterus* are generalist fruit, leaf and nectar eaters with an often noted preference for 'bat figs' (p. 78). **Habits:** Small fruit are snatched in flight and taken to a nearby secluded feeding roost where the flesh is pulped and swallowed along with small seeds. The fibre wad and large seeds are dropped in a pile below. Thus *Cynopterus* bats are local dispersers of large seeds but disperse small seeds by defecation in flight. **Breeding:** *Cynopterous* bats are polygynous. *Cynopterus* males bite through the ribs of large leaves to construct harem tents (p. 128)**.** Harems of a single male and 3–5 females are also found in bell holes near cave entrances and under roofs. The 4 Bornean *Cynopterus* bats are listed below in size order. The 3 smallest *Cynopterus* species can only be distinguished by forearm (**FA**) length. The largest, *C. horsfieldi* has distinctive teeth. See diagrams.

1 FOREST SHORT-NOSED FRUIT BAT *Cynopterus minutus* **FA less than 60, Wt 19–24 Common**

[Dog-faced Fruit Bat] Confined to tall and adjacent disturbed forest throughout Borneo up to 1,800m at Gng Emas (Crocker Range). Overlaps with *C. brachyotis* in forest and at the forest edge. **ID:** Smallest *Cynopterus.* **Habits:** Benda (2010) found that *C. brachyotis* was 20 x more common than *C. minutus* in disturbed forest at Sapulot and 4 x more common in primary forest at Batu Punggul (SW Sabah)**.** In Brunei**,** Kofron (2002) found that *C. minutus* was confined to primary forest and *C. brachyotis* to disturbed forest. **Taxonomy:** Split from *C. brachyotis* by Kitchener & Mahardatunkamsi (1991). See Wilson and Reeder (2005), Benda (2010), Abdullah et al (2003, 2009, 2012). **Range:** Malaya, Sumatra, Java, Sulawesi, Borneo**.**

2 SUNDA SHORT-NOSED FRUIT BAT *Cynopterus brachyotis* **FA 60–62, Wt 25–30 Abundant**

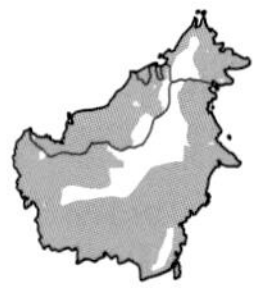

[Dog-faced Fruit Bat] [Lesser Short-nosed Fruit Bat]. Abundant in orchards, oil palm, coastal and secondary forest, mangroves and on small islands throughout and around Borneo. Overlaps with *C. minutus* in tall forest up to 1,800m at Gng Emas (Crocker Range). **ID:** Distinguished by FA length. **Habits:** At Tg Aru, Kota Kinabalu these bats feed on the fruit of Barringtonia Association, sea-dispersed coastal trees and roost under coconut palm leaves (p. 40). **Breeding:** In Brunei females give birth to a single young twice a year coinciding with mango fruiting (Kofron 2009). Females move between groups or may form single sex groups of up to 20. Old males may roost alone. **Range:** Sri Lanka to Malaya, Philippines, Sumatra, Java, **Borneo race**: *C. b. brachyotis* (Type from Dewei River, C Kalimantan).

3 SPHINX FRUIT BAT *Cynopterus sphinx* **FA 65 + , E 19 + , Wt 26–35 Rare**

[Greater Short-nosed Fruit Bat]. An abundant fruit bat in the seasonal forests of India to N. Malaya. In Borneo a mystery fruit bat reported from at least 4 localities possibly in error. See Payne (1985), Paeadiso (1971), Benda (2010), Mohd. Azlan (2003). **ID**: Similar to *C. brachyotis* but larger with FA always 65 +. Lower cheek teeth are rounded without extra cusps. **Habits:** In India up to 10 males and 15 females share the same breeding 'tent'. After mating, individuals split into single sex groups of 8 or 9. *C. sphinx* breeds twice a year. Females breed at 5 months of age, but males do not breed until they are a year old. Females are more common than males, (Balasing et al 1993, Tan et al 2009). **Diet:** Eats larger fruit than *C. brachyotis* Bumrungsri et all (2007). **Range:** India to S China south to Malaya, Sumatra, Java, Timor. **Borneo race**: *C. s. angulatus*. See p. 386 re Serasan Island, Natunas, South China Sea.

4 HORSFIELD'S FRUIT BAT *Cynopterus horsfieldi* **FA 68–76, E 16–18, Wt 30–40 Locally common**

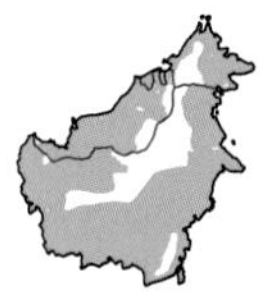

[Peg-toothed Short-nosed Fruit Bat] The largest and heaviest *Cynopterus* bat in Borneo. A locally common nomad throughout Borneo up to 1,400m on Kinabalu. **ID:** The largest *Cynopterus* with distinctive square cheek teeth which have "pegs" in the centre of the largest. See diagram. **Habits:** Similar to *C. brachyotis* and often shares the same roost (Lekagul 1977). At Krau, a nomadic bat which arrived when canopy level Big Bang trees were fruiting. (Hodgkison) (p. 94). In Malaya prefers oil palm to secondary forest (Shafie et al 2011). (p 96). **Range:** S Thailand, Malaya, Sumatra, Java. **Borneo race***:* *C. h. persimilis.*

Cynopterus species. (Photo: Ch'ien C. Lee)

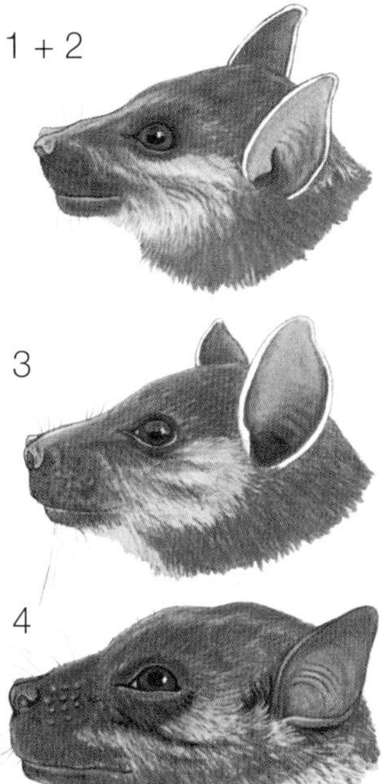

Cynopterus species harem group, Ulu Ulu Resort, Temburong, Brunei

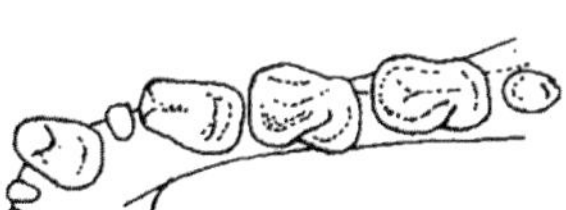

Cynopterus brachyotis teeth

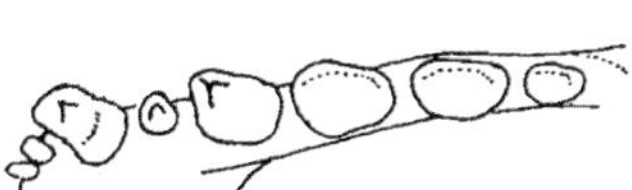

Cynopterus sphinx teeth

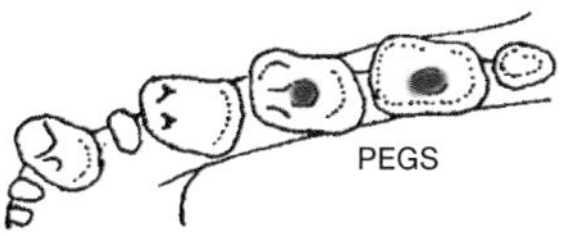

Cynopterus horsfeldi teeth

DYAK AND DUSKY FRUIT BATS

1 DAYAK FRUIT BAT *Dyacopterus spadiceus* FA 77–81, T 19–24, Wt 55–110 Scarce

Generally very scarce but sometimes locally common in the upper canopy most often recorded feeding in fruiting strangling figs. As these fig trees tend to be scattered and fruit erratically, this indicates nomadic habits. Recorded from Bukit Tudal, Brunei, at 1,181m (Bennett). Found at Poring, Sepilok and the Baturong Caves in Sabah, and throughout the Sarawak lowlands. In Kalimantan trapped in peat-swamp forest near Pontianak (feeding on figs), and at Tg Puting feeding in a flowering leguminous *Sindora* tree. **ID:** Similar to *Cynopterus* but with a larger, heavier head, a short muzzle and heavy cheek teeth designed for crushing or grinding. Breeding adults have orange tufts of fur on each side of the neck. **Habits:** Males produce milk, but there are as yet no records of males feeding young (Francis 1994). Roosting includes caves, a hollow tree trunk and tree hollows. Roosting sites are likely to be temporary. **Diet:** Powerful jaw and teeth indicate a specialized diet, possibly including crushed fig seeds. See Nogueira and Peracchi (2003), Bonaccorso (1979), and Wagner et al. A flock at Sepilok was feeding in a fruiting fig tree with Horsfield's Fruit Bat (Payne 1985). At Krau in Malaya, Hodgkison (2004) found that *D. spadiceus* was nomadic with a Big Bang foraging strategy, feeding on canopy-level green bat figs *Ficus depressa* and *F. annulata* (p. 78). Only undamaged fig seeds were defecated despite many damaged seeds being present in the figs. **Taxonomy**: The type was collected by Hose in Sarawak. Two larger montane *Dyacopterus* species are known from SE Asia including *D. brooksi* (Sumatra) and *D. ricarti* (Philippines). Helgen et al. (2007) provisionally classify a bat collected at Lalut Birai WWF Field Station, Kayan Mentarang, as *D. brooksi* indicating that there are 2 species of Dayak Fruit Bat in Borneo, *D. spacideus* in the lowlands and the larger *D. brooksi* in the mountains. **Range:** S Thailand, Malaya, Sumatra, **Borneo race:** *D. s. spadiceus*.

2 DUSKY FRUIT BAT *Penthetor lucasi* FA 57–62, E 14–16.5, Wt 24–45 Locally abundant

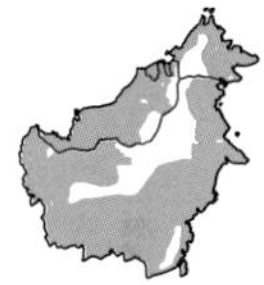

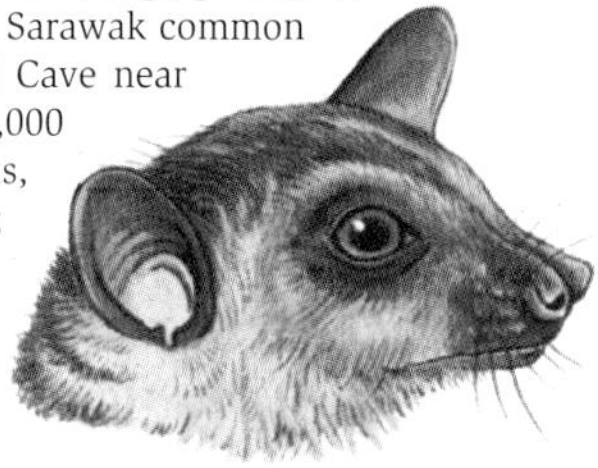

The most common fruit bat in areas of limestone caves (map, p. 30). In Sabah found at Gomantong, Sg Kuamut and Sapulot. In Sarawak common at Mulu, Niah, Bukit Sarang, Matang, Bako and Wind Cave near Kuching, where the population was estimated at 71,000 (Barapoi 2004). **ID:** Distinguished from *Cynopterus* bats, which also have short tails by 1. no white rim to ears; 2. no colourful collar; 3. fur is much duller, dark grey brown above and paler below; 4. one pair of lower incisors compared with two pairs for *Cynopterus*; 5. wing bones not as pale as *Cynopterus*; 6. distinctive smell (Khan 2008). **Diet:** Forages on locally available fruit and nectar from a permanent roost cave. Roosts deep within the cave (unlike *Cynopterus*) indicating some sonar ability (p. 90). The seeds of fruit brought to the roost later sprout indicating a roost above (Payne 1985). In Brunei females produce a single young in Oct out of synchrony with the April–June fruit season (Kofron 2007). **Habits:** Population is increasing at Wind Cave and Niah as secondary forest and orchards replace primary forest. No records from oil palm, unlike *C. brachyotis* (Fukuda 2009) (p. 96). **Taxonomy:** Genetic studies and measurements by Mohd Ridwan (2010) indicate 2 species in Borneo, one of which is genetically closer to *P. lucasi* in Malaya, probably the result of separate immigrations to Borneo during the Pleistocene (p. 14). **Range:** Malaya, Riau Islands, Borneo.

DUSKY FRUIT BAT ON KINABALU

Griswold collected 15 *P. lucasi* on Kinabalu in 1937 and noted 'All 15 bats were caught at Labang Cave (1,460m). This is a huge overhanging rock by a little stream, which is the beginning of the Kadaimaian River, on the western slopes of Kinabalu. The Dusuns made excursions there to secure bats to eat, as could be seen by the branches left at the mouth of the cave which they used to knock the bats down. The native I went with made a sacrifice of rice and called to the spirits of the mountain before he would enter. Most of the bats would leave at the slightest noise' (Allen and Coolidge 1940).

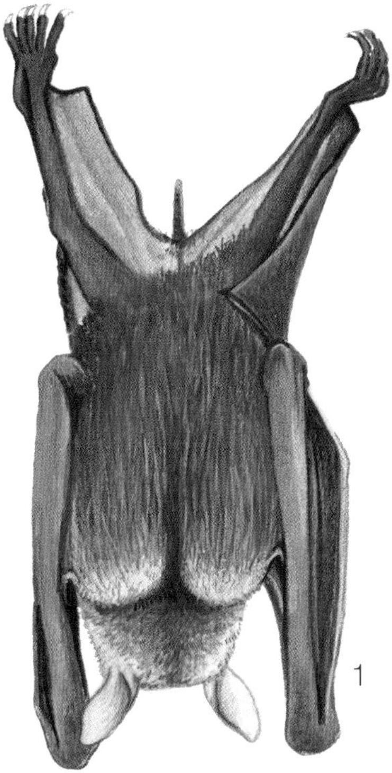

1

Dayak Fruit Bat, Sarawak. (Photo: Ch'ien C. Lee)

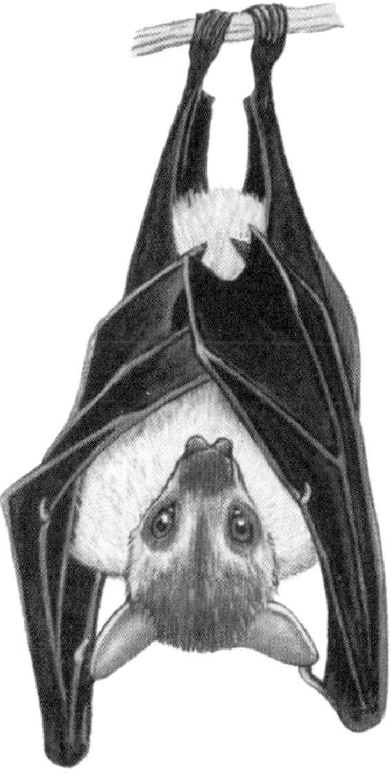

2

Dusky Fruit Bat, Samarakan. (Photo: Ch'ien C. Lee)

ROUSETTE FRUIT BATS

GENUS ROUSETTUS **World:** 10 spp. **Borneo:** 2 spp. Large fruit bats that live in colonies in caves often in association with *Eonycteris* nectar bats. Unlike all other fruit bats, they use low-resolution sonar to navigate in the dark cave interior and roost in complete darkness, giving greater safety against predators. **Rousette diet** includes soft fruit such as figs, together with flower nectar and pollen, unlike *Eonycteris* bats, which eat minimal amounts of fruit. Both *Eonycteris* and Rousette bats have obvious tails. **Distinguish from *Eonycteris* bats:** by the normal fruit bat, 2 claws on each wing. *Eonycteris* bats are missing a claw on their second digit (see diagram, p. 99). **ID:** In both species males are slightly larger and heavier than females. The wings of *R. spinalatus* are joined down middle of back, giving the appearance of a partly furless back. With *R. amplexicaudatus* the wings are separated by a band of fur. Rousette bats have short, thin hair with straggling longer hairs around the neck. In both species adult breeding males have pale yellow tufts of hair on sides of neck. **Sonar**: 'In flight, in darkness, both rousettes utter a high pitched buzzing call, composed of short bursts of rapid clicks, which are caused by movements of the tongue against the palate' (Medway 1978). These buzzing clicks are audible to humans. The resolution may be good enough to assist in finding large distinctive nectar flowers e.g. *Oroxylum indicum* at night (p. 83).

1 GEOFFROY'S ROUSETTE *Rousettus amplexicaudatus* **FA 78–87, T 21, E 16.5–18.5, Wt 60–93**

Locally common in Sabah near roosting caves, e.g. Pulau Balambangan, Pulau Mantanani, Gomantong and Madai Caves. Lakim et al. (1998) recorded a roost of 1,000+ in a cave on Pulau Boheydulang (Semporna). In Brunei both rousette species occur, probably visitors from the Mulu caves in Sarawak (p. 372.). In Sarawak and Kalimantan caves the population has collapsed due to unsustainable hunting (pp. 137, 366). A single record from Sangkulirang (E. Kalimantan). The commonest bat in cave deposits at Niah but absent today (Cranbrook & Piper 2007). **ID:** See above. **Habits:** Important pollinator of coconuts and other palms and orchard fruit trees. Heavily hunted in the Philippines, where the protected Montfort Cave in a Mindanao coconut plantation holds 1.8 million roosting bats. See Carpenter et al. (2014). **Range:** Myanmar south to Malaya, Sumatra, Java, Borneo, Philippines to New Guinea and Solomons.

2 BARE-BACKED ROUSETTE *Rousettus spinalatus* **FA 83–89, T 12–18, E 15.5–18, Wt 88–94**

Scarce. Recorded from caves at Gomantong, and Sg Kuamut (Sabah), Niah, Bintulu and Bukit Sarang in Sarawak; also at Sg Ingei (Brunei) near Mulu, but rare and much less common than *R. amplexicaudatus*. Cave roosts may contain both species. **ID:** See above. **Habits:** A colony of 300 individuals contained both adult males and pregnant females (Payne 1985). Swiftlet nest collectors claim that *R. spinalatus* damages and eats swiftlet nests. Andersen (1912) notes that *R. aegypticus* (Middle East) have been seen feeding on molluscs along the seashore at low tide and it is highly likely that *R. spinalutus* is a predator on young swiftlets and swiftlet eggs. **Taxonomy:** The type from Niah was first described in 1980 by Bergmans & Hill. **Range:** Sumatra, Borneo, with a relict distribution on both islands.

HOW ANIMALS USE SOUND FOR ECHO LOCATION (SONAR) IN BORNEO'S FORESTS

Made by	*Resolution*	*Purpose*	*How made*
Insectivorous Bats	Tiny flying insects	Catching insects, Cave roosting	Throat/Larynx
Edible-nest Swiftlets	Swiftlet nest c 3 x 5cm	Nesting in dark caves	Throat/Larynx
Rousette Fruit Bat	Swiftlet nest c 3 x 5cm	Roosting in dark caves	Tongue movements
Other Fruit Bats	*c.* $0.5m^2$	Navigating caves and tree gaps	Wing movements

Boonman et al (2014) found that some fruit bats could navigate a blacked-out room by using clicking noises generated by their wings. Species included *Cynopterus brachyotis*, *Macroglossus sobrinus* and *Eonycteris spelea*. The resolution was not good enough to find food, but could detect cave passages in dark caves and vegetation gaps. The ability probably varies amongst different species, e.g. *Penthetor lucasi* typically roosts in dark cave interiors, whilst *Cynopterus brachyotis* typically roosts near the cave entrance indicating that *P. lucasi* has superior echolocating ability to *C. brachyotis*.

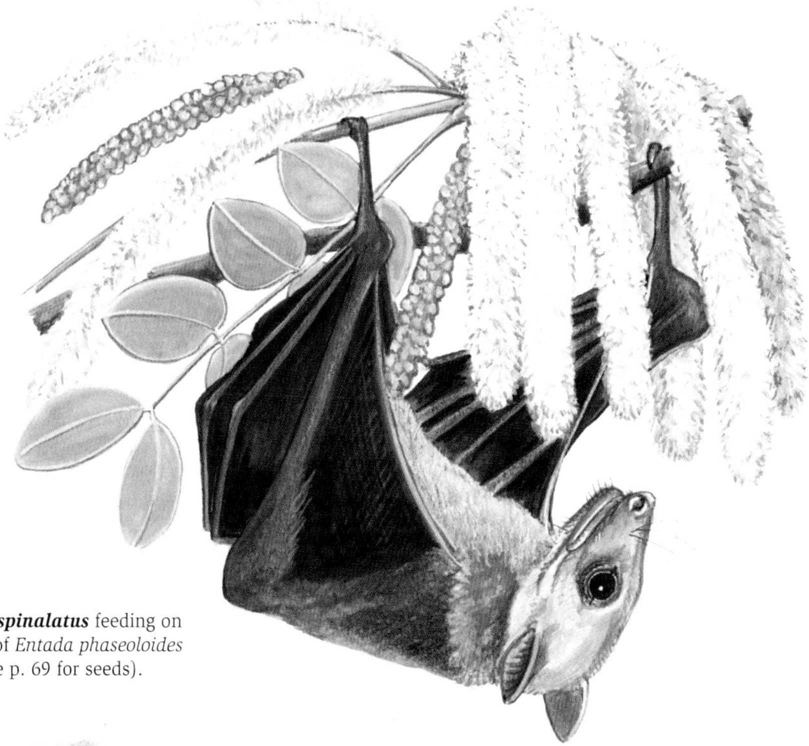

Rousettus spinalatus feeding on the nectar of *Entada phaseoloides* flowers (see p. 69 for seeds).

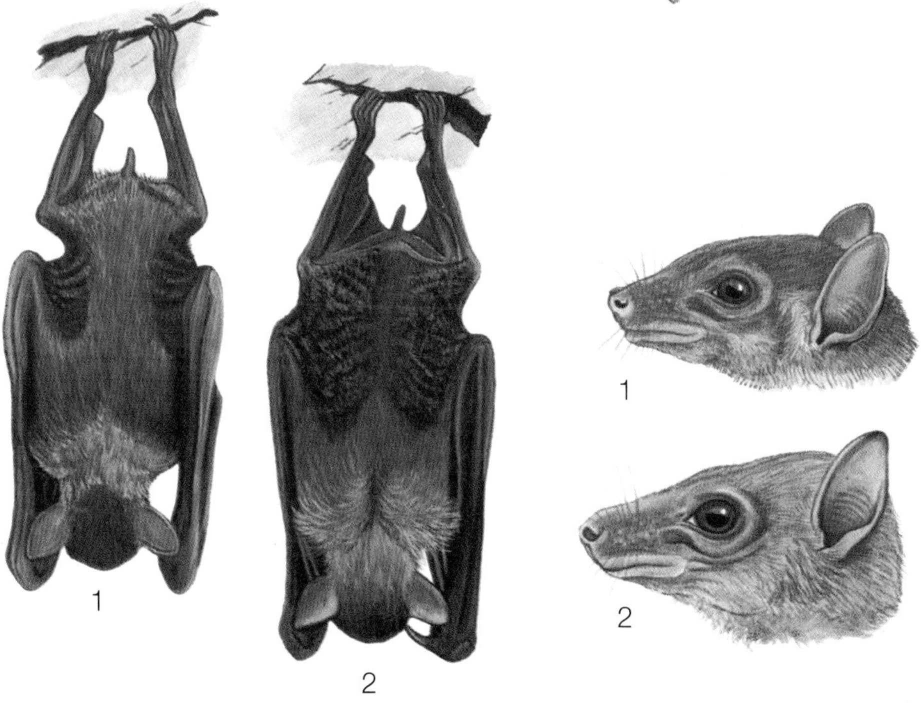

TAIL-LESS FRUIT BATS: AETHALOPS, CHIRONAX AND BALIONYCTERIS

1 BORNEAN FRUIT BAT *Aethalops aequalis* FA 42–46, T none, E 10–13, Wt 14–18

Local montane endemic [Pygmy Fruit Bat] [Grey Fruit Bat] Tiny, locally common, endemic fruit bat confined to the central mountain chain of Borneo above 1,000m from Kinabalu along the Crocker Range south to Ulu Temburong, Brunei throughout the Sarawak mountains south to Bukit Baka on the border of W and C Kalimantan. **ID:** Tiny, delicate fruit bat covered in long fur and with no tail. Narrow, pointed muzzle. **Habits:** On Kinabalu forages in gaps in montane mossy cloud forest 1,000–2,700m. The most common fruit bat at Gng Emas, Crocker Range 1,800m (Benda 2010). At Gng Penrissen (1,000m) near Kuching 2 were caught near flowering bananas along with 36 other fruit bats of 7 species (Kumaran et al. 2005). **Taxonomy:** The type was collected at Lumu Lumu (Kiau Gap) on Kinabalu by Griswold in 1937 and described by Allen (1938). In Payne (1985) listed as *A. alecto* Grey Fruit Bat, also found in Malaya, Sumatra and Java, but split by Kitchener et al. (1993a). Genetic studies by Tingga & Abdullah (2012) found that the populations on 1. Bukit Baka and 2. Sarawak and Sabah can be considered separate races of an endemic Bornean species.

2 BLACK-CAPPED FRUIT BAT *Chironax melanocephalus* FA 43–46, T none, E 13, Wt 16–20

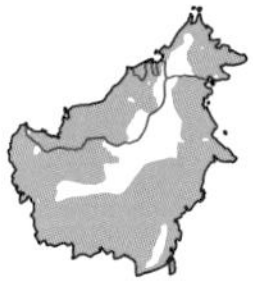

Rare bat with records scattered throughout the lowland and hills of Borneo, including Sepilok in Sabah, Ulu Temburong in Brunei, Kubah, Lambir and Samunsam in Sarawak and W, C and E Kalimantan. **ID:** Similar to *Cynopterus* but no tail. Most adults have yellow-orange tufts on the sides of the neck. Distinguished by two pairs of lower incisors. All other small tail-less fruit bats have only one pair. **Habits:** Most records are from the understorey of dipterocarp forest, but four were caught in the canopy at Lambir and at Samunsam it has been caught in beach forest. In Malaya regarded as common in hill forest. Roosts in groups in caves and rock shelters. At Krau a Steady State resident with similar morphology and foraging habits to *C. brachyotis* only *c.* 20% smaller and around half as common. **Range:** S. Thailand, Malaya, Sumatra, Java, Sulawesi. **Borneo race**: *C. m. dyasae* (See Maharadatunkamsi 2012).

3 SPOTTED-WINGED FRUIT BAT *Balionycteris maculata* FA 40–45, T none, E 10–12, Wt 10–15

Endemic. Borneo's smallest fruit bat is common in the forest understorey. Recorded from mangrove, secondary and primary forest up to *c.* 1,000m at Gng Penrissen. Also found in peat-swamp forest at Tg Puting and Sabangau in Kalimantan. **ID:** Unmistakable. Tiny fruit bat, distinctively spotted white/yellowish on a black background. **Habits:** At Krau in Malaya, Hodgkison and Balding frequently mist-netted this bat at ground level. The wings are short and broad, making this bat highly manouverable in the lowest level of the cluttered understorey. Abdullah (1999) recorded mist-netted bats killed by a tarsier at Semengoh near Kuching (p. 159). **Diet:** Forages at all levels in the forest. The nightly foraging range is *c.* 1 km^2 and this bat is a generalist feeder on a wide variety of both Big Bang and Steady State fruits, including both understorey and canopy figs (Hodgkison). **Breeding:** Kofron (2007) found that females in Brunei produce one young once a year in Oct–Dec in the main wet season, out of synchrony with the flowering and fruiting season Apr.–Jun. Females breed at 6 months old. Hodgkison found that males constructed small, bell-shaped harem tents in the base of epiphytic ferns and gingers, and in ant and termite nests. The tents were occupied by 1–14 individuals including a male and up to 9 adult females and their dependent young. **Range:** S Thailand, Malaya, Riau islands. **Taxonomy**: In Payne (1985) considered conspecific with *B. seimundi* of Malaya. Split by Khan (2008) based on DNA.

Spotted-winged Fruit Bat, Bukit Sarang, Sarawak, (photo: Ch'ien C. Lee)

1

2

3

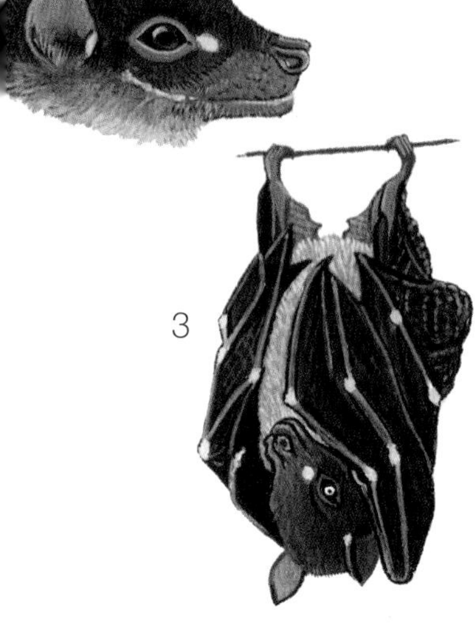

BORNEAN FRUIT BAT
Aethalops aequalis eating the edible bracts of an epiphytic pandan ***Freycinetia javanica*****,** which grows in the Mountain Garden at Kinabalu Park HQ and by doing so helps to pollinate the flower.

Males construct harem roosts under epiphytic ferns to attract females.

TAIL-LESS FRUIT BATS: MEGAEROPS

1 SUNDA TAILLESS FRUIT BAT *Megaerops ecaudatus* FA 50–58, T none, Wt 20–40

Scarce, endemic

Locally common small bat of forest throughout Borneo recorded to 1,800m at Gng Emas (Crocker Range). Most common in areas of poor soils (kerangas) including peat-swamp, mangrove and montane forest. **ID:** No tail. Pale bat, the size of *Cynopterus* but with none of the distinctive markings of a *Cynopterus* (p.86). Distinguish by short muzzle with prominent 'divided' nostrils. Base of thumb is partially enveloped in wing membrane, so that it folds inwards when the wing is folded (Yasuma 2005). Always larger than *M. wetmorei*. **Habits:** At Krau in Malaya, Hodgkison & Balding (2005), and Kingston (2009) report that this bat is a nomadic forager, which feeds on fruit at all levels in the forest. The distinctive nostrils are most likely an aid to locate ripe cauliferous figs in the understorey of dense forest, based on the habits of the similar *Nyctimene* tube-nosed fruit bats of Australia and Wallacea (Richards & Hall, 2012). Wing shape resembles *C. brachyotis* indicating that it is a temporary local resident. *M. ecaudatus* has been found in caves, but the low numbers suggest that caves provide temporary roosts only. **Taxonomy:** Khan (2008) says the high divergence in DNA suggests that Malayan and Bornean forms should be split. **Range:** S Thailand, Malaya, Sumatra, Borneo.

2 WHITE-COLLARED FRUIT BAT *Megaerops wetmorei* FA 45–50, T none, Wt 16–26 Rare

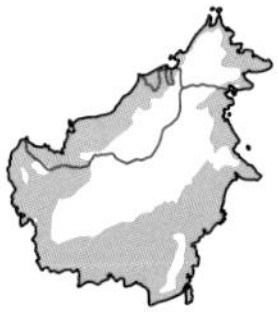

Payne (1985) listed a single Borneo record at Tasek Merimbun in Brunei, but recent records are from forested areas all over Borneo. It appears to be most common in Brunei's peat-swamp forests. Recorded from peat-swamp forest at Tg Puting in C Kalimantan (Struebig 2006). **ID:** No tail. A small bat. Distinguished from *Cynopterus* bats by the short muzzle with prominent 'divided nostrils'. Distinguished from *M. ecaudatus* by the prominent white tufts of fur on necks of some individuals of both sexes (presumably breeding) and the smaller size, which does not overlap in measurements or weight. Note the white wing bones as illustrated. **Habits:** At Krau in Malaya this bat was an irregular visitor in small numbers. Recorded feeding on *Palaquium obovatum* fruit (Sapotaceae), Kingston (2009). The Sapotaceae are a common tree family in lowland forests prone to masting, i.e. flowering and fruiting together in one Big Bang. See p. 196 re *Madhuca* (Sapotaceae). **Taxonomy:** Francis (1989) split *M. wetmorei* in Borneo as a separate race from the Malayan, Sumatran and Philippine forms. As the Philippine *M. wetmorei* is likely to be split off as a separate species it is probable that *M. w. albicolis* will end up as a Bornean endemic. **Range:** S Malay Peninsula, Sumatra, Philippines. **Borneo race**: *M. w. albicolis*.

BIG BANG (BB) FLOWERING AND NOMADIC BATS Hodgkison & Balding (2005) classified the 8 fruit bats at Krau in Malaya into 2 main feeding guilds. We extend this analysis below for all Borneo's fruit bats.

1 **Steady State (SS):** Resident bats that feed **under** the canopy on continuously flowering and fruiting plants.

2 **Big Bang (BB):** Nomadic bats that visit to feed on canopy level trees that flower and fruit in one 'big bang'. See pp. 50 and 78–81 for illustrations.

Steady State Resident Bats	*Preferred food*
Aethalops aequalis	Generalist small fruit
Balionycteris maculata	Generalist small fruit
Cynopterus brachyotis	Generalist medium fruit
Cynopterus minutus	Generalist medium fruit
Cynopterus sphinx	Generalist large fruit
Chironax melanocephalus	Generalist small fruit
Macroglossus minimus	Banana nectar (p. 72)
Penthetor lucasi	Generalist fruit
Petropus hypomelanus	Coconut nectar (p. 85)

Big Bang Nomadic Bats	*Preferred food*
Cynopterus horsfieldi	Canopy bat figs
Dyacopterus spadiceus	Canopy bat figs
Eonycteris major	Canopy tree nectar
Eonycteris spelaea	Canopy tree nectar
Petropus vampyrus	Nectar and soft fruit
Megaerops ecaudatus	Understorey figs
Megaerops wetmorei	Understorey figs
Rousettus amplexicaudatus	Canopy nectar + fruit
Rousettus spinalatus	Canopy nectar + fruit

BANANA FRUIT AND NECTAR AS FRUIT BAT FALLBACK FOOD Kumaran (2004) describes extraordinary success in trapping fruit bats over two nights in Jan. 2004 at Gng Penrissen at a clump of bananas next to the golf course. The catch was 38 fruit bats of 8 different species including 14 *C. brachyotis*, one *C. horsfieldi*, 4 *P. lucasi*, 4 *M. ecaudatus*, 2 *A. aequalis*, one *E. spelaea* and one *E. major*. The list includes both resident and nomadic bats, and the obvious explanation is that there was a shortage of flowering canopy trees at Gng Penrissen at that time, so the nomadic bats used banana nectar and fruit as a fallback food (pp. 80, 72).

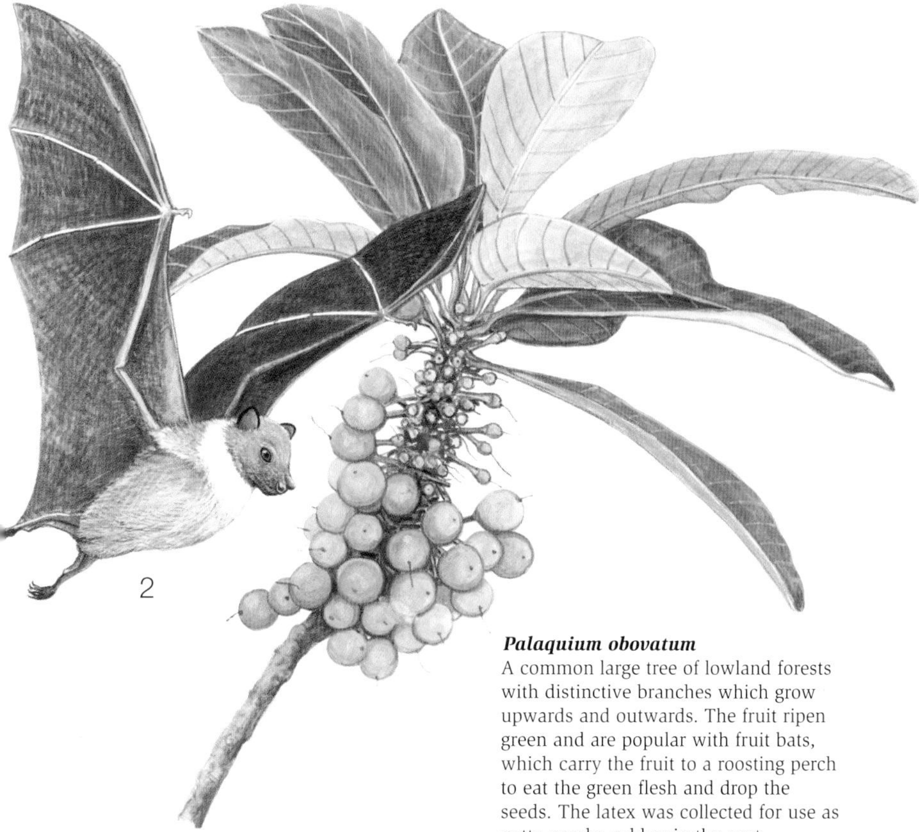

Palaquium obovatum
A common large tree of lowland forests with distinctive branches which grow upwards and outwards. The fruit ripen green and are popular with fruit bats, which carry the fruit to a roosting perch to eat the green flesh and drop the seeds. The latex was collected for use as gutta-percha rubber in the past.

1

2

The tube noses of *Megaerops* bats are similar to those of the *Nyctimene* tube-nosed fruit bats of Sulawesi, which are used for locating ripe fruit in dense vegetation.

MACROGLOSSUS AND EONYCTERIS NECTAR BATS

1 LONG-TONGUED NECTAR BAT *Macroglossus minimus* FA 38–42, T none, E 13–15.5, Wt 11–19

[*Macroglossus lagochilus*] **Common**, tiny bat of the forest understorey and the forest edge, including mangroves throughout Borneo, strongly associated with wild bananas (p. 73). **ID:** By small size and long muzzle. **Habits:** Roosts alone in young rolled-up banana leaves, a habit shared with several *Kerivoula* insect bats (p. 130). **Diet:** Although the preferred diet is banana nectar, also recorded feeding on coconut, *Sonneratia* mangrove, *Syzygium* (jambu) and durian flowers (p. 63). **Breeding**: In Brunei, Kofron (2008) found that females produced single young twice a year coinciding with two wet seasons Oct–Dec and Apr–May. **Range:** Coastal Thailand, Malaya, S Philippines, Java to New Guinea, Solomons and N Australia. **Taxonomy**: Khan (2008) notes that the DNA of a Borneo specimen showed only a 2% difference from *M. sobrinus* in Malaya, indicating a close relationship. **Borneo race:** *M. m. lagochilus*.

2 CAVE NECTAR BAT *Eonycteris spelaea* FA 62–70, T 15–18, E 17–20, Wt 41–72 Locally common

[Dawn Bat] Most common large nectar bat in many caves but the population at Niah has been hunted to extinction (p. 366). **ID:** Both *Eonycteris* nectar bats are missing a claw on the second digit unlike all other fruit bats. *E. major*, is larger, darker and with a longer downturned muzzle. Illustrated pp. 63 & 67. **Habits:** Roosts in caves in large noisy colonies. Males are 20% heavier than females. Krutszch et al. (2005) at the Batu Caves, Kuala Lumpur found that *E. spelaea* breeds year round with a peak coinciding with the wettest months. **Diet:** Tony Start (Ashton 2014) collected pollen weekly from *E. spelaea* bat guano at the Batu Caves. Start found that *E. spelaea* regularly flew over 38km each way to feed on the nectar of *Sonneratia* coastal mangrove flowers. The most regular supplies of nectar came from *Duabanga grandiflora* and *Artocarpus* fruit trees (p. 75). Nectar was also sourced from jambu (syzygium) and durian flowers, both common orchard trees. In Borneo often mist-netted near bananas. **Range:** N India east to S China south to Malaya, Philippines, Sumatra, Java, Borneo.

3 GREATER NECTAR BAT *Eonycteris major* FA 71–80, T 18, E 21 Wt 91 Scarce cave dweller

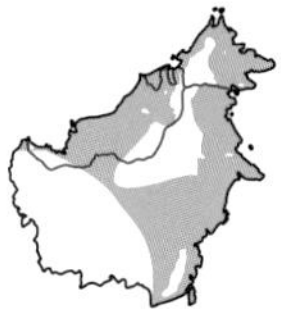

Uncommon but widespread. No records from C and W Kalimantan. Most common in the hills, e.g. Ranau, Sabah, and Gng Dulit and Gng Penrissen but also in the lowlands e.g. Kubah near Kuching. In Kalimantan recorded from Kutai and upper S Tengah in S Kalimantan. Cave roosts have been found in Sarawak along the S Tinjar and in the Bintulu district (Payne 1985). **ID:** See above. *Eonycteris spelaea*, is smaller, paler in colour with a shorter muzzle; *Rousettus* bats have shorter muzzles and a claw on the second digit. **Habits:** Roosts in caves and sometimes hollow trees. **Range:** Philippines, Borneo.

FRUIT BATS AND OIL PALM Fukuda et al (2009) investigated the use of different habitats by fruit bats at Lambir NP (primary forest) and in adjacent secondary forest, orchards and oil palm. They found that 2 species of *Cynopterus* were strongly attracted to oil palm fruit, whilst *Eonycteris spelaea* visited oil palm for nectar and pollen (p. 32). The chart shows the numbers trapped in the different habitats. Shafie et al. (2011) found that in Malaya C. *horsfieldi* was also more common in oil palm than secondary forest (p. 86)

Bat Species	***Primary Forest***	***Secondary Forest***	***Orchards***	***Oil Palm***	***Total***
Balionycteris maculata	16	2	0	0	18
C. brachyotis	4	49	106	201	360
C. minutus	8	11	6	9	34
Eonycteris spelaea	4	1	44	12	61
Macroglossus minimus	5	3	31	0	39
Penthetor lucasii	13	3	0	0	16
Total	**50**	**69**	**187**	**222**	**528**

Duabanga grandiflora

Sonneratia

Syzygium grandis

1

2

3

Long-tongued Nectar Bat *M. minimus* feeding on banana nectar. (Photo: Ch'ien C. Lee)

INTRODUCTION TO INSECTIVOROUS BATS

MALAY: KELAWAR

World: *c.* 1,000 spp. in 18 families. **Borneo:** *c.* 79+ spp. in 8 families. More bat species are likely to be discovered in Borneo in the future either from collecting in previously unexplored habitats or as a result of splitting cryptic species using genetic analysis (p. 108). All bats are nocturnal, but on some remote islands like Maratua bats may be seen hunting in daylight.

Echolocation Insectivorous bats use sophisticated echolocation (SONAR) for both catching insect prey and navigating in caves and dark forests at night. Most Bornean bats generate echolocation sounds in the larynx (voice box) and emit the sounds through the mouth. *Rhinolophus* and *Hipposideros* bats use their ornate noseleaves to focus and modulate the emitted sound. Most bat sonar is too high in frequency to be heard by most humans, although children can often hear faint buzzing and low-frequency clicks (www.seabcru.org).

TWO DIFFERENT TYPES OF SONAR Bat sonar evolved separately twice around 50 million years ago. *Rhinolophus* and *Hipposideros* bats use constant frequency (CF) sounds to detect movement (flutter) of their prey. In contrast, vesper bats use FM (frequency modulation) and vary the intensity in decibels (dB) and duration in milliseconds (ms) of their sonar to build a 'sound picture' of their environment that can even detect beetles sitting on leaves. This means that insect bats can be surveyed at night with a bat detector and compared with an echolocation database. See Arjan Boonman, www.Batecho.EU, Chris Corben, Anabat, www.hoarybat.com, Kingston et al. (2006).
Sonar jamming: Research has shown that some tiger moths and hawk moths 'jam' the sonar of bats if they are targeted. *Tadarida* bats have also been recorded jamming each other (Corcoran & Conner, 2014).

Endemic Bornean Tiger Moth ***Spilosoma groganae*** uses a vibrating membrane on the thorax (tymbals) to jam bat sonar.

Morphological Differences and Feeding Strategies Bird ecology can be guessed from the shape of birds' wings (flight strategies) and beaks (feeding strategies), and the same approach can be used for bats. Bats with long, narrow wings fly faster and for longer distances than bats with short, narrow wings, which have evolved for flying in the cluttered forest understorey. Bats with large interfemoral membranes surrounding the tail, such as *Kerivoula* species, use them to scoop up their prey, whereas bats with small membranes catch insects in flight with their mouths (Emballonuridae), or large, hairy feet (*Myotis*, *Tadarida*).

Feeding Guilds Denzinger & Schnitzler (2013) identified 7 feeding strategies in insectivorous bats, the result of specialized wing shapes and echolocation techniques.

INDEX TO INSECT BATS

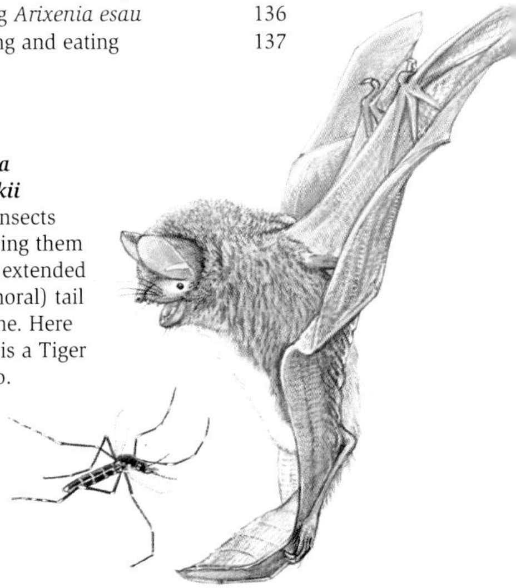

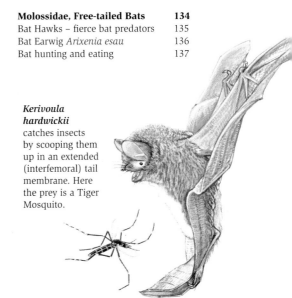

Kerivoula hardwickii catches insects by scooping them up in an extended (interfemoral) tail membrane. Here the prey is a Tiger Mosquito.

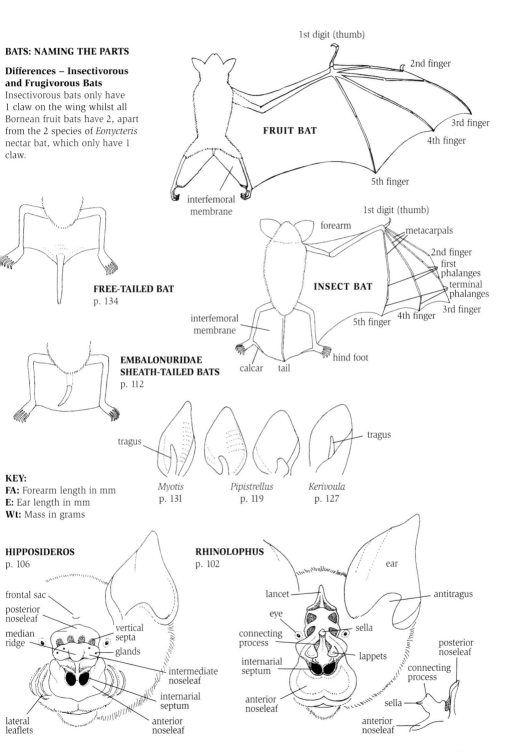

BATS: NAMING THE PARTS

Differences – Insectivorous and Frugivorous Bats
Insectivorous bats only have 1 claw on the wing whilst all Bornean fruit bats have 2, apart from the 2 species of *Eonycteris* nectar bat, which only have 1 claw.

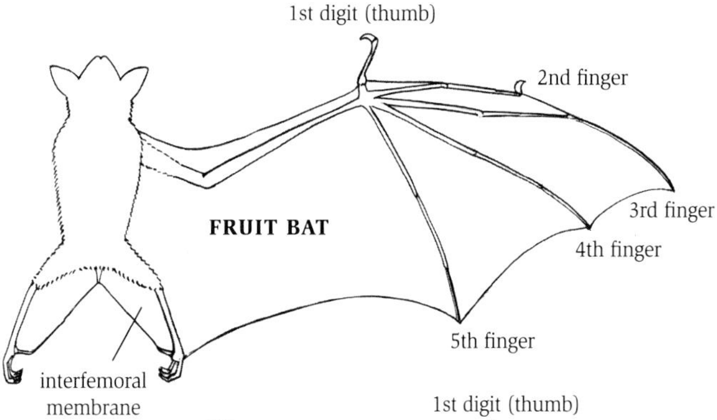

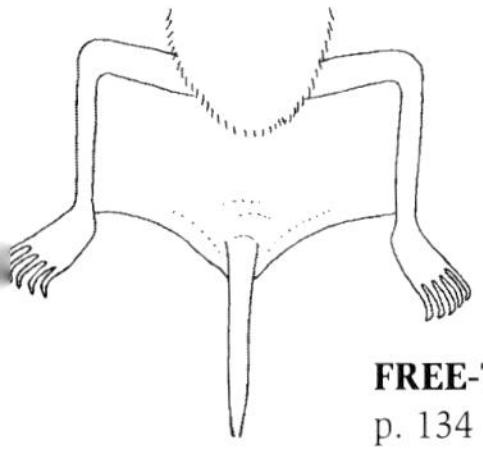

FREE-TAILED BAT
p. 134

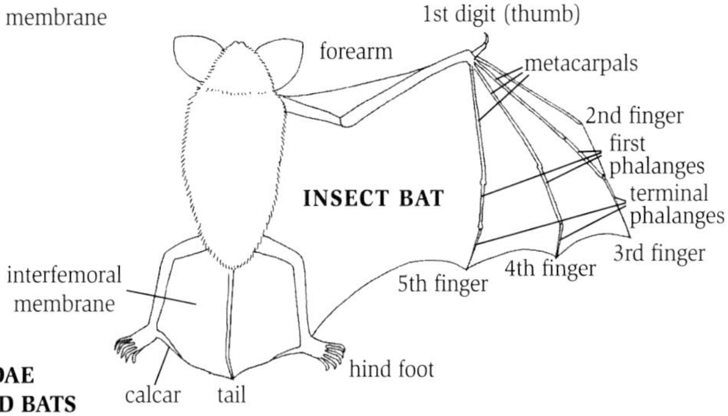

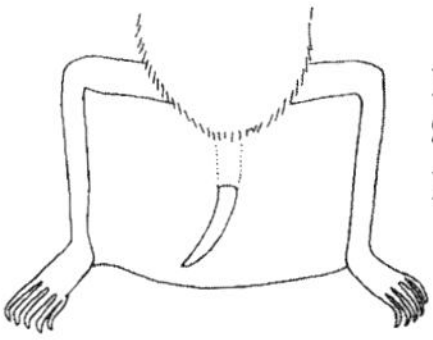

EMBALONURIDAE SHEATH-TAILED BATS
p. 112

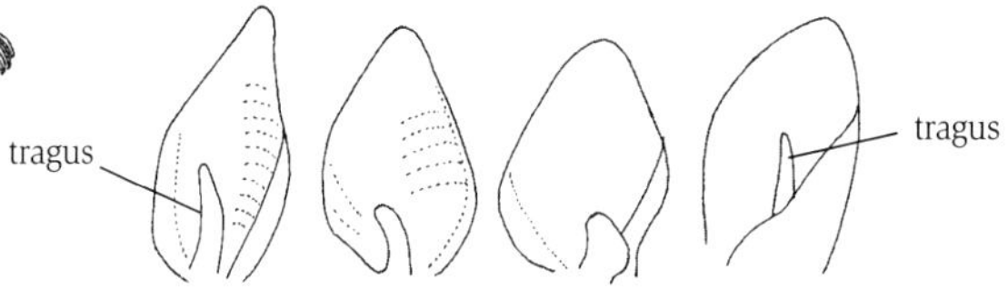

Myotis p. 131 *Pipistrellus* p. 119 *Kerivoula* p. 127

KEY:
FA: Forearm length in mm
E: Ear length in mm
Wt: Mass in grams

HIPPOSIDEROS
p. 106

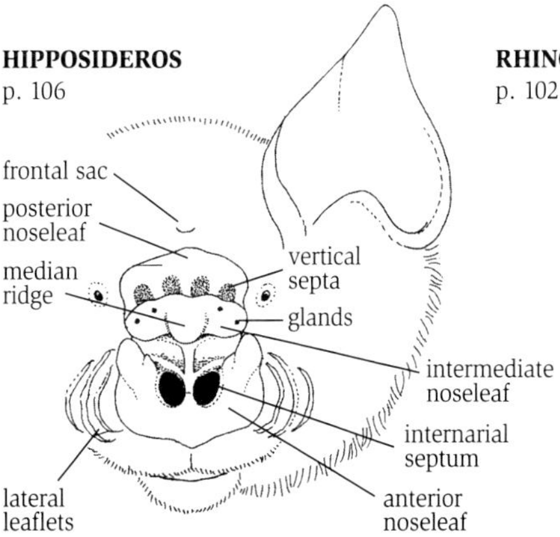

RHINOLOPHUS
p. 102

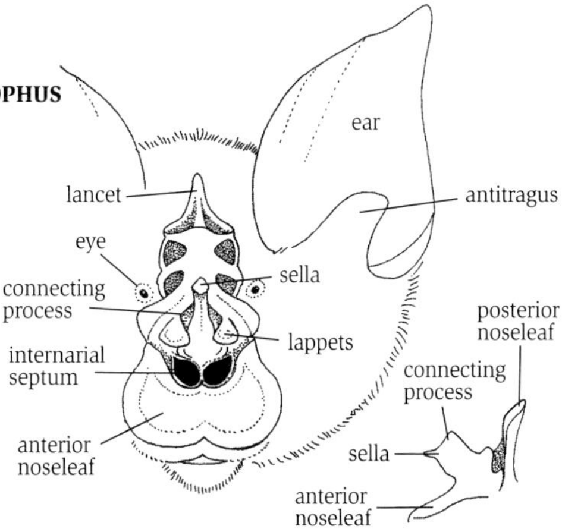

INSECT BAT-FORAGING GUILDS

SEVEN INSECTIVOROUS BAT-FORAGING GUILDS Above and opposite we follow the guild classification used by Denzinger & Schnitzler (2013), which takes into account the use of echolocation in different habitats by insectivorous bats. A foraging guild is a group of species that hunt for food in a similar way. Members of a foraging guild may come from different genera (an example of convergent evolution). According to the definition of a species, each member of the same guild must occupy its own separate feeding niche. In the *Rhinolophus* and *Hipposideros* bats, which occupy guilds 4 and 5, different species use differences in sonar (as exemplified by their nose leaves) to catch different types and sizes of insects in different habitats.

Catching Prey Bats use at least 4 non-exclusive preferred methods. 1. Chase with open mouth, e.g. *Taphozous*, p. 115; *Emballonura*, p. 113. 2. Chase and scoop with an interfemoral membrane, *Pippistrellus, Miniopterus* and *Kerivoula*, p. 126. 3. Trawling, catch with sharp, often hairy claws, e.g. *Myotis*, p. 133. 4. Flycatching by flying out to capture an insect, then returning to perch, some *Rhinolophus*, p. 102; *Hipposideros*, p. 104.

	SEVEN FORAGING GUILDS	EXAMPLES
1	**Open Space Aerial Foragers** Hunt above canopy	*Emballonura*, p. 112; *Tadarida*, p. 134
2	**Edge Space Aerial Foragers** Hunt over edge buildings, trees	*Taphozous*, p. 114; *Miniopterus*, p. 116
3	**Edge Space Trawling Foragers** Hunt over water, mudflats	*Myotis*, p. 132; *Hypsugo vordermanii*, p. 118
4	**Narrow Space Flutter Detecting Foragers** 'Flycatchers'	*R. luctus*, p. 102; *H. diadema*, p. 106
5	**Narrow Space Active Gleaning Foragers** Forest understorey	Most *Rhinolophus, Hipposideros, Kerivoula*
6	**Narrow Space Passive Gleaning Foragers** Listens for prey	*Nycteris tragata*, p. 110
7	**Narrow Space Passive/Active Foragers** Hunts large prey	*Megadema spasma*, p. 110

1 *Tadarida*

4/5 *Hipposideros*

1 *Emballonura taphozous*

7 *Megaderma*

3 *Myotis*

6 *Nycteris*

5 *Kerivoula*

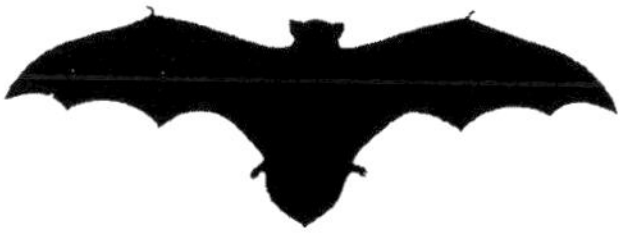

2 *Miniopterus*

4/5 *Rhinolophus*

RHINOLOPHUS: HORSESHOE BATS 1

World: *c.* 50 spp. **Malaya:** 18 spp. **Borneo:** 10 spp. Both *Rhinolophus* and roundleaf (*Hipposideros*) bats use elaborate nose leaves on their face to focus sonar for navigation and catch insect prey. Both groups chase insects in flight or use flycatching, where a bat hanging from a forest perch flies out to catch passing insects. There is no tragus but a prominent antitragus (p. 99). The large interfemoral membrane encloses the tail and is used for scooping up insects in flight. Moths, the major prey of bats, use many techniques to avoid capture, including sonar jamming and distraction tails. See below and opposite.

1 GREAT WOOLLY HORSESHOE BAT *Rhinolophus luctus* **FA 63–67, T 38–50, E 31–35, Wt 29–37**
Generally scarce but found throughout the lowlands of Borneo to 1,600m in the mountains. Usually alone or in small groups and not restricted to areas with caves. **ID:** Largest horseshoe bat with long, dark blackish fur. All 3 *Rhinolophus* species illustrated opposite have similar lateral (side) lappets at base of sella. *R. sedulous* is a much smaller bat. *R. trifoliatus* is also smaller and the noseleaf is yellow not grey. **Habits:** Breeds year round. Roosts alone or in small groups in rock crevices or hollow trees. Recorded flycatching. At Kubah hand netted inside a road-drain culvert (Khan 2008). **Range:** Sri Lanka, India through S China, Taiwan, Southeast Asia, Sumatra, Java, Bali. **Borneo race:** *R. l. foetidus*.

2 LESSER WOOLLY HORSESHOE BAT *Rhinolophus sedulus* **FA 40–44, T 20–25, Wt 8.4–11**
Third most common *Rhinolophus* bat, found in all habitats. At Tg Puting second most common *Rhinolophus* in heath forest. **ID:** See under *R. luctus* above. **Habits:** Roosts in hollow trees or leaf bunches, singly or in pairs not restricted to caves. Forages in the understorey of tall forest to 1,500m. Caught roosting with *R. luctus* in a culvert at Kubah (Khan 2008). **Range:** Malaya. **Borneo race:** *R. s. sedulus*.

3 TREFOIL HORSESHOE BAT *Rhinolophus trifoliatus* **FA 47–52, T 27–37, E 22–26, Wt 10.5–18**
Locally common throughout Borneo including mangroves, mostly in the lowlands but to 1,800m (Gng Trus Madi). Often found far from caves. Locally abundant in heath forest at Tg Puting (Struebig et al. 2006). **ID:** Noseleaf is similar to that of *R. sedulous* and *R. trifoliatus*, but yellow not grey. Has fluffy fur like *R. luctus* and *R. sedulous* but overall fur is paler than that of the other 2 species. **Habits:** Breeds year round but most births at Krau are early in the year (Kingston). Hunts by flycatching. Roosts alone in bunches of leaves or under palm leaves in undisturbed forest and often switches roosts. Rarely found in caves. **Range:** NE India, Myanmar south to Malaya, Sumatra, Java. **Borneo race:** *R. t. trifoliatus*.

4 FRANCIS' BAT *Rhinolophus francisi* **FA 53–55** **Rare**
Soisook et al (2015) used DNA and measurements to describe a new bat species similar to *R. trifoliatus* but darker and larger (FA 53–55) that is found throughout Borneo. *R. francisi* is named after Charles Francis who first collected this bat on Trus Madi in 1983. Currently 5 Borneo records and one Thai record.

DISTRACTION TAILS ON MOTHS
Studies by Barber, Kawahara et al. (2015) compared insectivorous bat attacks on moon moths with long tails and moths in which the tails had been removed, and found that that in 47% of attacks on tailed moths the bat attacked the long tail and the moth escaped unharmed. Thus a long tail distracts the bat and confers a survival advantage on the moth (p. 233).

Moon Moth *Argemna maenas*
Each twisted tail-tip appears in constant-frequency bat sonar as a single fluttering moth, increasing the confusion.

Illustration by Susan Phillipps.

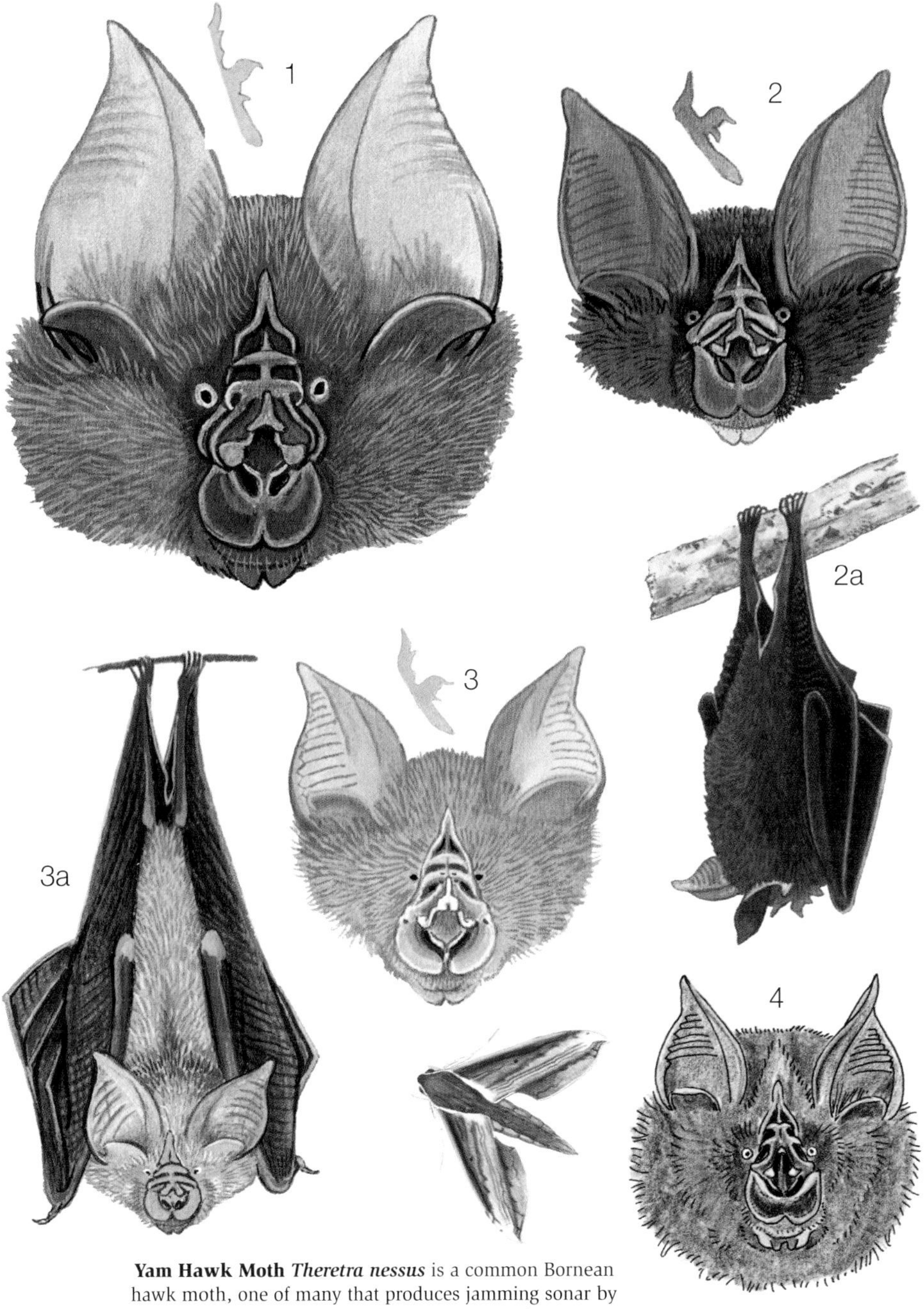

Yam Hawk Moth ***Theretra nessus*** is a common Bornean hawk moth, one of many that produces jamming sonar by scraping scales on the genitalia in response to bat sonar. The ability to jam bat sonar has evolved at least twice in the moths. Barber & Kawahara (2013) (p. 98).

RHINOLOPHUS: HORSESHOE BATS 2

1 PHILIPPINE HORSESHOE BAT *Rhinolophus philippinensis* **FA 48–53, T 25–33, E 27–31, Wt 8.5–11.5**
Locally abundant in some large caves throughout most of Borneo, but scarce or absent away from areas of karst limestone caves (Suyanto et al. 2007). **ID:** Distinctive noseleaf shape and very large ears. **Habits:** Roosts in loose colonies in caves. **Taxonomy:** Sedlock et al. (2008) point out that this bat occurs in 3 size morphs, possibly cryptic species. Kingston & Rossiter (2004) suggest at least 2 cryptic species may be involved. **Range:** Philippines, Sulawesi, Timor, Australia. **Borneo race:** *R. p. sanborni.*

2 CREAGH'S HORSESHOE BAT *Rhinolophus creaghi* **FA 46–51, E 19, Wt 10.5–13.5 Abundant**
Locally abundant in some large caves in Sabah, Sarawak and Sangkulirang, E Kalimantan, but scarce or absent away from caves (Suyanto et al. 2007). At Sg Ingei, Brunei, close to Mulu, the most common bat in the forest understorey. Rare at Niah. **ID:** Distinguished by tuft of stiff hairs on rear of connecting process. **Habits:** Large roosting colonies up to 100,000. **Range:** Madura, Java, Timor. **Borneo race:** *R. c. creaghi.*

3 ACUMINATE HORSESHOE BAT *Rhinolophus acuminatus* **FA 48–50, T 21–31, E 20–21, Wt 11.5–13.5**
Locally common in Sabah in lowland forest to 1,600m on Kinabalu; not normally associated with caves. **ID:** By sharply upwards pointed sella. **Habits:** Found in lowland forest. There is a roost under Danau Girang FC, Kinabatangan (Fletcher & Baylis). At Krau roosts singly or in pairs under palm leaves (Kingston et al. 2009). **Range:** Vietnam, Thailand, Malaya, Balabac, Palawan, Sumatra, Java. **Borneo race:** *R. a. sumatranus.*

4 ARCUATE HORSESHOE BAT *Rhinolophus arcuatus* **FA 46–48 Rare**
Least common *Rhinolophus* bat. No records for Sabah and Brunei. Known from Kubah and Bungoh Cave near Bau near Kuching, and some caves in Kalimantan. **ID:** Note rounded connecting process with tuft of hairs. **Habits:** Cave roosting. **Range:** Philippines, Sumatra, Flores. **Borneo race:** *R. a. proconsulis.*

5 INTERMEDIATE HORSESHOE BAT *Rhinolophus affinis* **FA 49–54, T 22–26, Wt 12.5**
Rare in Sabah. Locally common around Kuching where there are numerous records, including Kubah, Matang, Gng Gading, Gng Pueh, Gng Penrissen and Samunsam. Widespread in W and S Kalimantan. **ID:** Upperparts bright orange to dark brown, underparts paler. Often confused with *R. acuminatus* and can only be distinguished by shape of sella (Sazali 2008). **Habits:** In Malaya roosts in caves and forages in the forest understorey at all elevations (Medway 1983). Has been netted at canopy level (Kingston et al. 2009). **Range:** India through China, south to Malaya, Sumatra, Java. **Borneo race:** *R. a. nesites.*

6 LEAST HORSESHOE BAT *Rhinolophus pusillus* **FA 37–40, T 13, E 12.5 Scarce**
Generally scarce but locally common in Sabah caves. Abundant at Sangkulirang. Karst dependent and patchily distributed (Suyanto 2007). **ID:** Smallest horseshoe bat in Borneo, with relatively large ears. Distinguished by size. **Range:** India to S China, south to Malaya. Java and **Borneo race:** *R. p. pusillus.*

7 BORNEAN HORSESHOE BAT *Rhinolophus borneensis* **FA 40–44, T 21–26, E 17–19, Wt 7–8.5**
Most common and most widespread *Rhinolophus* bat throughout Borneo recorded to 1,000m in the Hose Mountains. **ID:** Fur varies from orange to brown. Smaller and paler than very similar *R. acuminatus*. **Habits:** Roosts in caves, in colonies of up to several hundred. At Kubah found roosting in a culvert and caught in mist nets over a frog pond (Khan 2008). **Range:** Con Son Island (Vietnam), Malaya (rare), Java. **Borneo races:** 1. *R. b. borneensis* (throughout), 2. *R. b. spadix* (P Karimata and P Serutu), W Kalimantan.

Rhinolophus borneensis
Bukit Sarang, Sarawak.
(Photo: Ch'ien C. Lee)

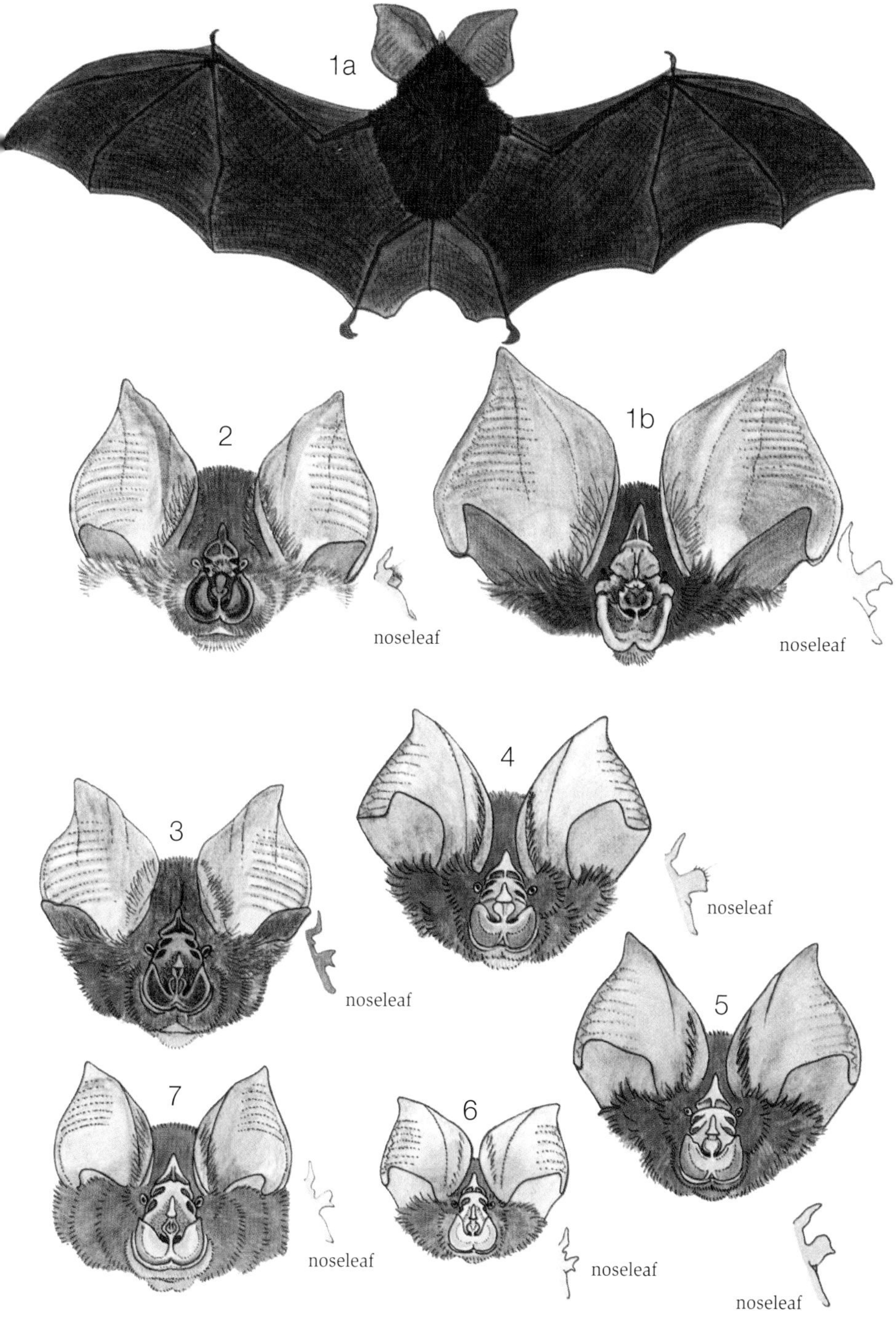
1a
2
1b
noseleaf
noseleaf
4
3
noseleaf
noseleaf
5
7
6
noseleaf
noseleaf
noseleaf

HIPPOSIDEROS: ROUNDLEAF BATS 1

World: *c.* 60 spp. **Malaya:** 21 spp. **Borneo:** 12 spp. in 2 genera. The roundleaf bats are the most common bats of the forest understorey. Outside Borneo they are found in tropical and subtropical forests from Africa to Australia. Distinguished from horseshoe bats by 4 chambered vertical septa (posterior noseleaf) between the eyes and the lack of a sella (p. 99).
Foraging Roundleaf bats forage in the understorey or along the forest edge. The large ears, tiny eyes and varied nose leaves indicate that sonar is more important for them than sight for navigation and hunting. The broad, short wings enable tight manoeuvres in cluttered forest.
Roosting Like the *Rhinolophus* bats, roundleaf bats are of 2 types. 1. Obligate cave dwellers with maternal (breeding) roosts to *c.* 300,000, like *H. cervinus*, restricted to cave areas (map, p. 30). 2. Bats that roost alone or in small groups in tree hollows and drains throughout Borneo, like *H. dyacorum.*

1 DIADEM ROUNDLEAF BAT *Hipposideros diadema* **FA 76–87, T 53, E 27–18.5, Wt 30–47 Abundant**
Abundant bat of large caves, but usually less common than *H. cervinus*. Medway (1958) estimated over 5,000 at Subis (Niah Caves), now reduced to hundreds (Hall et al. 2002), (p. 366). **ID:** Largest *Hipposideros* in the world with the widest range. Distinctive orange to grey fur with white patches on shoulders and sides. Adult females dark brown with orange-buff shoulders and sides. Juveniles dark grey and white. **Habits:** In Borneo roosts in caves; in Malaya roosts in tree hollows. Forms large maternity colonies of females and young. **Diet:** In Australia 'flycatches' in gaps in the forest understorey, often near streams. Eats moths and small birds caught in flight. **Range:** SE Asia to Australia. **Borneo race:** *H. d. niasoni.*

2 CANTOR'S ROUNDLEAF BAT *Hipposideros galeritus* **FA 47–51, T 30–43, Wt 5.7–8.5 Common**
(Formerly included in *H. cervinus*). Less common than *H. cervinus* and *H. diadema*, but widespread. Found throughout Borneo near caves. Most common insect bat trapped at the Bau Caves near Kuching (Mohd Azlan 2005). **ID:** Fur usually dark grey-brown, occasionally with reddish tinge. Noseleaf pinkish-grey. Noseleaf has 2 lateral leaflets. Tail always longer than that of *H. cervinus*. **Habits:** Roosts in caves, often with *H. cervinus*, in groups up to several hundred. Roosts in palms at Sg Liang, Brunei (Wong 1997). **Range:** India to Thailand, Malaya, Java. **Borneo race:** *H. g. insolens.*

3 ASHY ROUNDLEAF BAT *Hipposideros cineraceus* **FA 36–40.5, T 24–30, E 18.5–21, Wt 4–5.5 Scarce**
[Least Roundleaf Horseshoe Bat] Widespread but scarce, recorded throughout Borneo near caves. Locally common around Kuching (Khan 2008). Collected on Mt Murud at 1,335m asl (Sazali et al. 2011). **ID:** Distinguished by simple noseleaf with raised bump on internarial septum and small size. **Habits:** Locally common in cave roosts, often with other *Hipposideros* bats. **Taxonomy:** Khan (2011) suggests records include more than 1 species. **Range:** Pakistan to Vietnam south to Malaya. **Borneo race:** *H. c. cineraceus.*

4 BICOLORED ROUNDLEAF BAT *Hipposideros bicolor* **FA 45–48, T 27–31, E 17.5–20, Wt 7–8.5 Scarce**
Uncommon cave-roosting bat found in caves throughout Borneo, including Kuching and caves of the Sankulirang Peninsula (Suyanto et al. 2007). **ID:** Upperparts grey-brown; underparts paler, usually buffy-white. Noseleaf pale pinkish-brown, simple and small, lacking lateral leaflets. **Taxonomy:** According to Kingston et al. (2009), in Malaya *H. bicolour* comprises a pair of cryptic species that are genetically and acoustically divergent but show morphological overlap, that is the 2 species appear similar but use different echolocation frequencies. Khan (2011) says that DNA indicates the Borneo race is an endemic species. **Range:** India to S China, Taiwan south to Malaya, Philippines, Sumatra, Java, Sulawesi. **Borneo:** *H. b. bicolor.*

5 RIDLEY'S ROUNDLEAF BAT *Hipposideros ridleyi* **FA 47–49, T 25–29, E 25–27, Wt 6.5–9.5 Scarce**
Scarce bat throughout Borneo. Locally common in caves near Kuching. Records include Sg Wain and Tg Puting in Kalimantan. **ID:** Fur uniformly dark brown. Ears, noseleaf and wing membranes dark grey. Ears very large and rounded. Noseleaf large, covering whole muzzle; no lateral leaflets; internarial septum expanded into large disk that nearly obscures nostrils. ***H. coxi*** also has large noseleaf, but with a quite different structure and 2 lateral leaflets. **Habits:** Found in lowland forest including kerangas. At Sg Wain, 12 roosted in a forest hut. Enters lighted houses to feed on insects (Yasuma 2005). **Range:** Malaya, Borneo.

6 DORIA'S ROUNDLEAF BAT *Hipposideros doriae* **FA 34–37, Wt 4.2 Rare**
[Least Roundleaf Bat *H. sabanus*] Type was collected near Kuching. One of the rarest *Hipposideros* but widespread records throughout Borneo, including the Crocker Range, Brunei, Lawas, Gng Penrissen and C and E Kalimantan. **ID:** Smallest *Hipposideros* bat. Similar to *H. cinereous* and *H. bicolor* but smaller. Distinguished by lack of septa (partitions) on posterior noseleaf. **Range:** Sumatra, Malaya, Borneo.

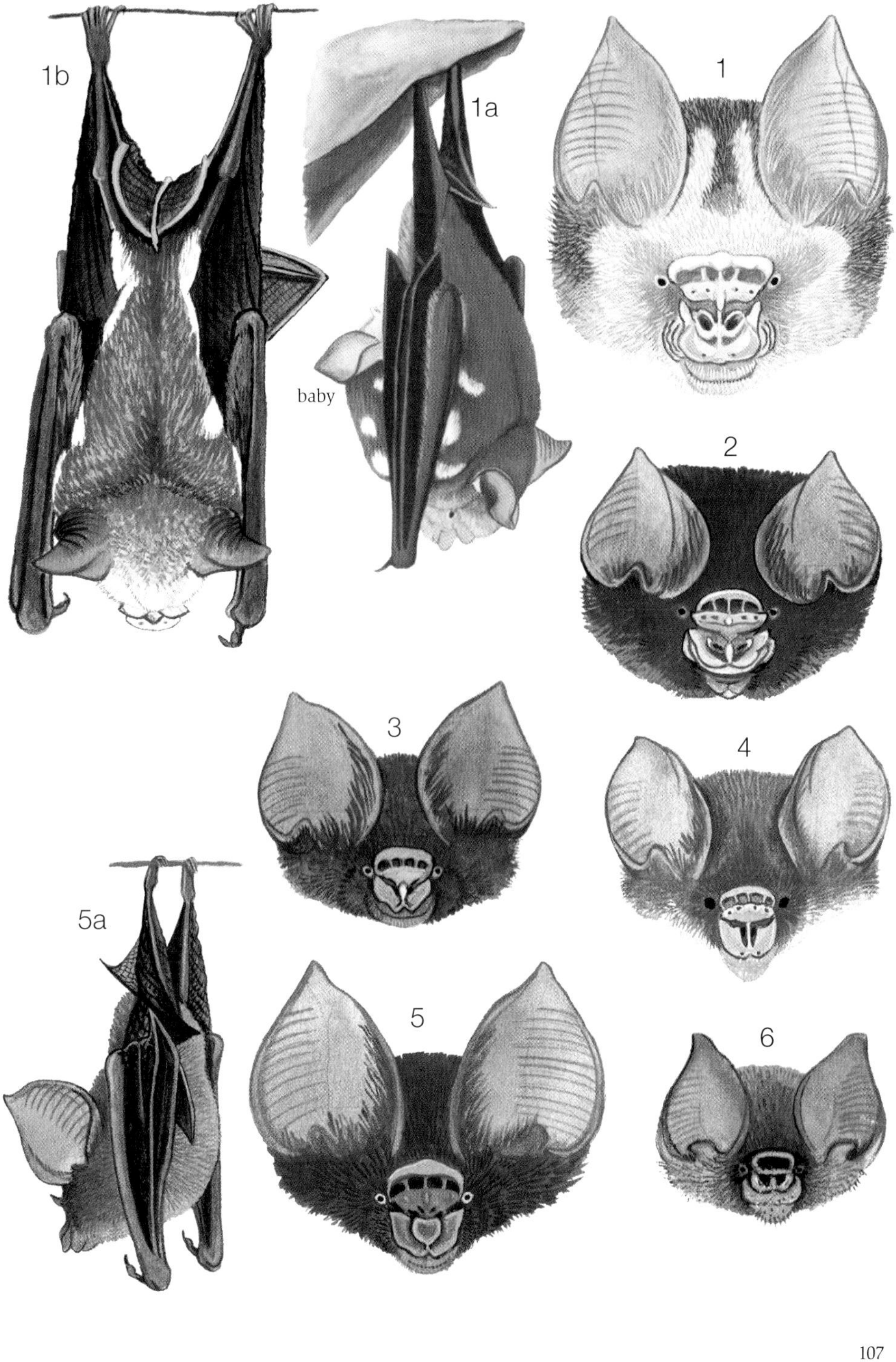

1b
1a
1
baby
2
3
4
5a
5
6

HIPPOSIDEROS: ROUNDLEAF BATS 2

1 COX'S ROUNDLEAF BAT *Hipposideros coxi* **FA 53–55, Wt 10** **Rare Borneo endemic**
No records from Sabah or Brunei. Most records are from SW Sarawak, including Gng Penrissen, Bungoh, the Jambusan Caves and Bako, all near Kuching. Also recorded from C Kalimantan (Struebig et al. 2010). **ID:** Upperparts dark brown; underparts dull brown. Distinguished by large, dark brown noseleaf, completely covering muzzle. **Habits:** Recorded from a hill cave at 1,200m. At Bako netted in mangrove near rock crevices.

2 INTERMEDIATE ROUNDLEAF BAT *Hipposideros larvatus* **FA 56–64, Wt 15–20**
Locally common in S Borneo from Kuching south to Gng Kenepai in W Kalimantan, S Pangkalahan and S Pasir in S Kalimantan. Common in the Sangkulirang Caves, E Kalimantan (Suyanto et al. 2007). **ID:** Noseleaf has 3 lateral leaflets similar to those of *H. diadema*, which is much larger with prominent pale shoulder-marks. Other Bornean *Hipposideros* are smaller with maximum of 2 lateral leaflets. **Habits:** Karst dependent and patchily distributed (Suyanto 2007). Roosts in caves. **Range:** Bangladesh to S China, south to Malaya, Sumatra, Java. **Taxonomy:** Future split likely (Khan 2011). **Borneo race:** *H. l. neglectus.*

3 FAWN ROUNDLEAF BAT *Hipposideros cervinus* **FA 44–50, T 21–28, E 14–17, Wt 5–10** **Abundant**
Most common and widespread insectivorous bat in Borneo's caves. Medway (1958) estimated the Niah population at 250,000. Common in most island caves, including on P Balembangan, P Mantanani and P Labuan. **ID:** Fur colour variable from grey to bright orange. Noseleaf has 2 lateral leaflets. *H. galeritus* also has 2 lateral leaflets, but noseleaf otherwise differs. Tail shorter than that of *H. galeritus.* **Habits:** In caves, roosts with and previously confused with *H. galeritus*, but also roosts outside caves. Feeds in the forest understorey. **Range:** Malaya, the Philippines, Sumatra, Java, Borneo to Australia. **Borneo race:** *H. c. labuanensis.*

4 DAYAK ROUNDLEAF BAT *Hipposideros dyacorum* **FA 38–42, T 19–24, E 15–18, Wt 5–7.5** **Endemic**
Locally common endemic that forages in the forest understorey throughout Borneo at altitudes to 900m. **ID:** Fur plain dark brown. Noseleaf simple, without lateral leaflets, similar to that of *H. ater*, which has a pale pink, not grey/brown, noseleaf and pale fur underneath. Distinctive short tail. **Habits:** Roosts in caves, rock crevices and hollow trees. Yasuma (2005) records feeding by flycatching.

5. DUSKY ROUNDLEAF BAT *Hipposideros ater* **FA 39–43, T 22–26, E 15–17.5, Wt 5–7.5** **Scarce**
Scarce cave dweller throughout Borneo. **ID:** Distinguished by pale pinkish, simple noseleaf lacking lateral leaflets. Roosts in caves in colonies of up to a few hundred individuals. **Taxonomy:** Khan (2011) says that DNA suggests that Borneo has 2 cryptic species. **Range:** Sri Lanka to Australia.

6 LESSER TAILLESS ROUNDLEAF BAT *Coelops robinsoni* **FA 34–37, T none, E 12–14** **Rare**
Very rare bat. In Sarawak known from 1. Deer Cave, Mulu, 2. Bintulu Planted Forest, 3. Lobang Gan Kira Niah (Abdul Rahman et al. 2010). Also C and E Kalimantan (Struebig 2010). **ID:** Small with long, soft grey fur. Large ears rounded without internal ridges. Large lateral leaflets. Interfemoral membrane with no visible tail is distinctive. **Habits:** At Krau recorded roosting with *Hipposideros ridleyi* in tree hollow (Kingston 2009). Enters lighted houses to feed on insects (Yasuma 2005). **Taxonomy:** 1. Greater Tailless Roundleaf Bat *C. frithi*, which ranges from India east to Sumatra, Java and Bali, is not recorded for Borneo, but might occur – it is larger (FA 43–47), with the lower lobes of the noseleaf elongated and narrow (Payne et al. 1985). 2. *C. hirsutus* of Mindoro, the Philippines, may be conspecific (Hill 1972). **Range:** Thailand, Malaya, Borneo.

DNA BARCODING OF BORNEO'S BATS Borneo bat researchers are increasingly using DNA analysis to discover 'cryptic' (concealed) bat species in Borneo. See Khan et al. (2008) and Ridwan (2010) for *Penthetor lucasi*; Csorba et al. (2011) for *Murina*; Francis & Habersetzer (2011) for *Hipposideros larvatus*; Khan et al. (2011) for *Hipposideros bicolor*; Wiantoro (2011) for *Myotis muricola*; Esselstyn et al. (2012) for the Asian *Hipposideros*; Soisook et al. (2013) for *Murina cyclotis*; Gorfol et al. (2013) for *Myotis montivagu.* Comparison of genetic codes can be carried out on many different sections of an animal's DNA, but for the best results it is important that the same standardized section of DNA is used for all animal species (see Valentini 2008). Worldwide DNA barcoding is organized by the Consortium for the Barcode of Life (CBOL, http:// barcoding.si.edu), which aims to both promote global standards and coordinate research. Francis et al. (2010) compared the DNA barcodes from 1,900 SE Asian bats and concluded that regional bat species richness was underestimated by at least 50%. This implies that Borneo hosts not *c.* 100 but closer to 200 bat species! The existence of new species should always be confirmed by measurement, morphology and differences in echolocation and habits. (Ivanova et al. 2012)

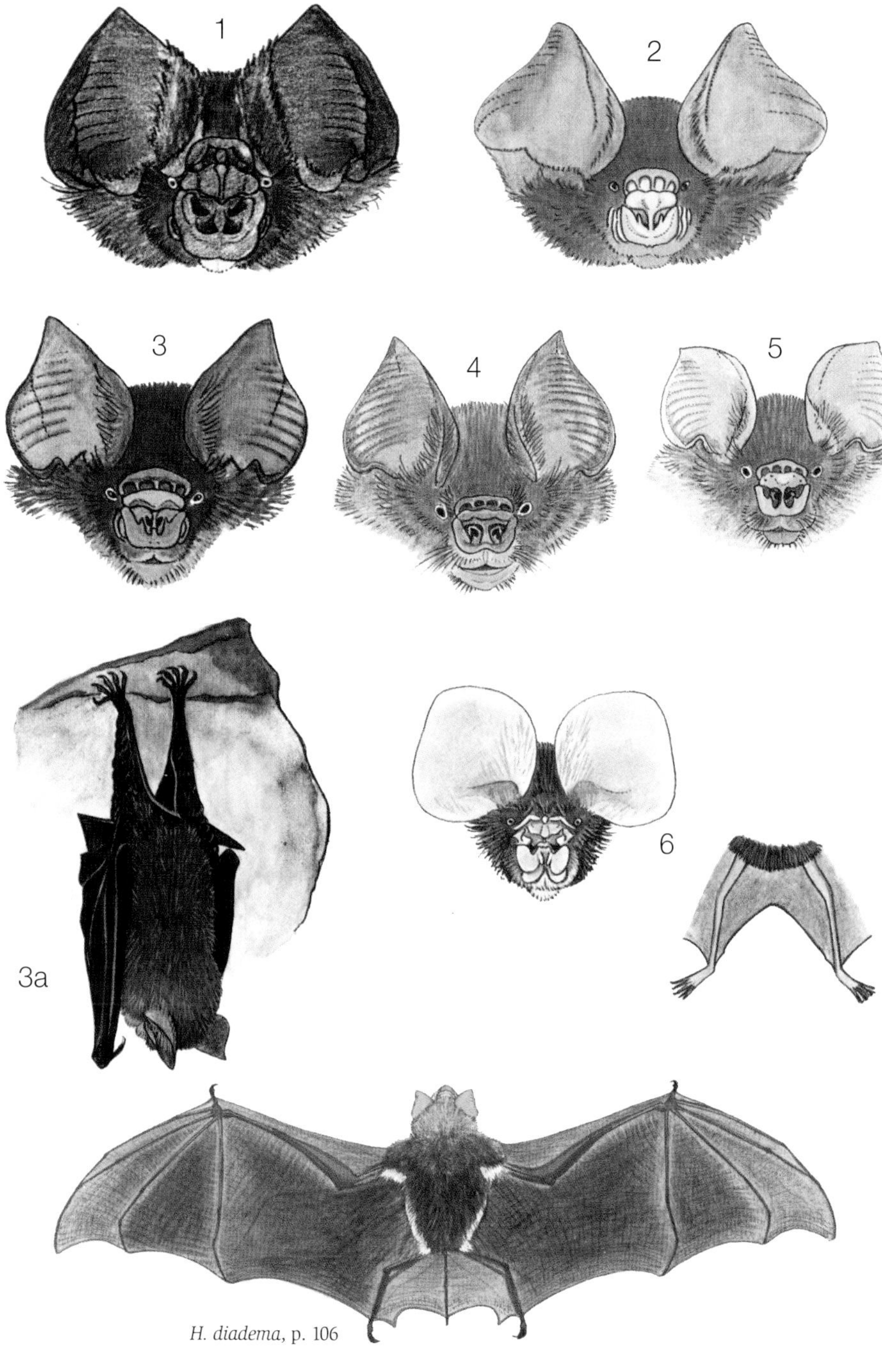

H. diadema, p. 106

FALSE VAMPIRE AND HOLLOW-FACED BATS

1 LESSER FALSE VAMPIRE *Megaderma spasma* **FA 54–61, E 35–40, Wt 23–28 Locally common**
Recorded throughout Borneo from Tg Puting in Kalimantan to 1,000m on Kinabalu. Most common in coastal districts, including mangrove, peat-swamp and islands. Sabah records include Labuk Bay, Sepilok and P Boheydulang (Semporna) in a cave with *Rousettus amplexicaudatus* and *Hipposideros cervinus*. **Brunei:** P Berembang (Kofron). **Sarawak:** Niah and Kuching. **Kalimantan:** Sg Kapuas in W Kalimantan and Sg Tengah in S Kalimantan. **ID:** Distinctive noseleaf and large ears joined at bases. **Habits:** In Malaya roosts in small groups in caves, tunnels or hollow trees. Feeds on large insects, and also small birds and mammals, including other bats (Kingston et al. 2009). In India uses sonar to find and feed on frogs (Brock Fenton 1992), which would classify this bat as a Narrow Space Passive/Active Forager (p. 101). **Range:** Sri Lanka, to Malaya, the Philippines, Sumatra, Java, Sulawesi, Moluccas. **Borneo races:** 1. *M. s. trifolium* (widespread). 2. *M. s. kinabalu* (Kinabalu and the Crocker Range). 3. *M. s. carimatae* (P Karimata).

2 HOLLOW-FACED BAT *Nycteris tragata* **FA 46–51, T 65–72, E 29–31, Wt 12–17 Locally common**
[Slit-faced Bat] Recorded from Sepilok, Sukau and Tawau in Sabah; most parts of Sarawak including Niah and the Kuching area; upper S Tengah in S Kalimantan; Sangkulirang Peninsula and nearby Sg Lesan (Struebig 2007). **ID:** Distinctive split noseleaf and very large ears separated at bases. Tail is T-shaped, fully surrounded by interfemoral membrane. **Habits:** Roosts in small groups in hollow trees or caves in forested areas. Listens passively with large ears for rustling of large insects. Low wing loading enables it to lift off the ground with heavy prey (Kingston et al. 2009), which would classify the bat as a Narrow Space Passive Forager (p. 101). Large tail-membrane pouch holds struggling prey whilst it is carried to a feeding perch. **Taxonomy:** Borneo *Nycteris* were thought to be *N. javanica*, but Simmons (2005) states that they are *N. tragata*. **Range:** Myanmar south to Malaya, Sumatra. **Borneo race:** *N. t. tragata*.

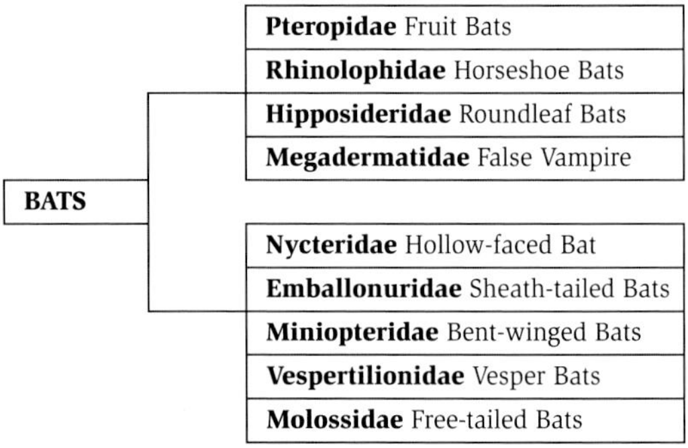

CONVERGENT EVOLUTION IN BATS
Fifty million years ago the world's bats split into 2 groups as illustrated. Both groups separately evolved sonar (p. 98), and later on converged in habits. *Megaderm spasma* and *Nycteris tragata* are common Bornean bats with similar appearance and ecology, yet their last common ancestor was 50 MYA. Taxonomy diagram follows Dietz et al. (2009).

Megaderma spasma, Bau, Sarawak. (Photo: Ch'ien C. Lee)

EMBALLONURIDAE 1: SHEATH-TAILED BATS

EMBALLONURA World: *c.* 50 spp. **Malaya:** 4 spp. **Borneo:** 5 spp. The 5 species of Bornean sheath-tailed bat are some of the most common insectivorous bats in open countryside, around towns and in coastal areas, and are easily distinguished from other bats by 2 key features. 1. Tail emerges from sheath in middle of skin between hind legs known as the interfemoral membrane (p. 99). 2. Roosting posture favoured by *Emballonura* and *Taphozous* bats, in which the bat hangs from its hind claws, but rests its front claws against a wall below, with one wing often placed at an angle. The 2 *Emballonura* species can be distinguished in the field by a loud alarm squeak when the roost is approached. **Ecology:** Long, narrow wings, preferred roosts (often on offshore islands) and observations indicate that these bats hunt high above the canopy or in open spaces, often flying long distances to feed. Insect prey is caught in the wide mouth (gape). **Range:** Worldwide in tropical and subtropical areas.

1 GREATER SHEATH-TAILED BAT *Emballonura alecto* **FA 45–48, T 14–15, E 12–13, Wt 4.5–7.5**

Common throughout the lowland and hill forests of Borneo, including Sungai Wain and caves on the Sangkulirang Peninsula (E Kalimantan). **ID:** Distinguished from *E. monticola* by larger size of FA (see listed measurements); by differences in teeth – a diastema (gap) between the upper anterior and posterior premolars (Corbet & Hill 1992); and by larger skull (Payne et al. 1985). However, Suyanto & Struebig (2007) give various examples of instances where these supposed differences do not coincide and suggest that a full taxonomic and genetic review of both species is required to distinguish them. They often roost together and museum collections are often mislabelled. **Habits:** Often roosts in areas that are relatively well lit, including the roof eaves of forest buildings, earth banks, rocky overhangs and fallen tree trunks, and cave mouths. **Range:** The Philippines, Sulawesi. **Borneo race:** *E. a. rivalis.*

2 LESSER SHEATH-TAILED BAT *Emballonura monticola* **FA 43–45, T 11–14, E 12–13, Wt 4.5–5.5**

Common throughout the lowland forests of Borneo. There is a record for P Karimata (off the coast of SW Kalimantan). Locally common in heath forest at Tg Puting (Struebig et al. 2006). **ID:** Both this bat and *E. alecto* (above) look similar, with reddish-brown fur, and have similar habits; even museum specimens are easily confused (see Suyanto & Struebig 2007). **Habits:** *E. alecto* and *E. monticola* often roost together, when they may be distinguished by the relative differences in size. Unlike most forest-roosting insectivorous bats, which forage below the canopy, *Emballonura* bats forage above the canopy and for this reason are often under-recorded in forest-bat surveys. *Emballonura* bats are often the first bats to start foraging before dusk (Kingston et al. 2009). **Range:** S Thailand, Malaya, Sumatra, Java, Sulawesi, Borneo.

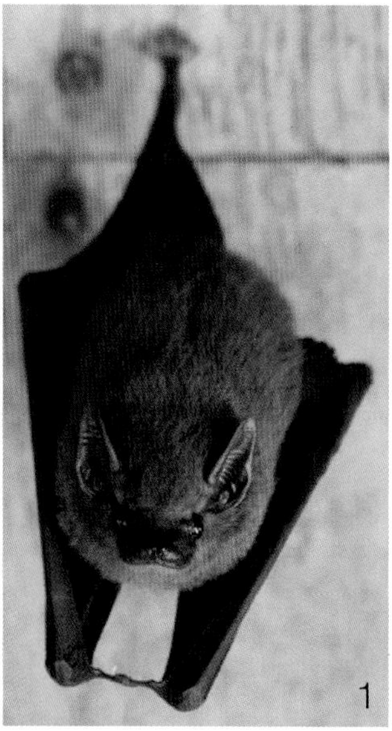

E. alecto

E. monticola

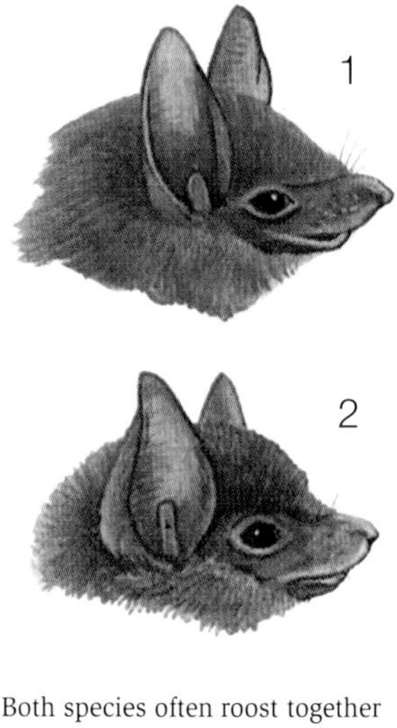

Both species often roost together as photographed here by Wong Tsu Shi at the entrance gate of the orchid garden at Tawau Hills Park.

Black-bearded Tomb Bat *Taphozous melanopogon*, like *Emballonura alecto* and *E. monticola*, often uses a distinctive roosting posture, resting on its elbows with a wing stretched out to one side. The tail, like that of all the emballonurid bats, emerges from a sheath in the interfemoral skin between the hind legs, not from the edge of the membrane, although this may be difficult to see.

Black-bearded Tomb Bat (p. 114), Waikiki apartments, Tg Aru beach Kota Kinabalu.

Lesser Sheath-tailed Bat in a rocky overhang, Johore, West Malaysia. (Photo: Nick Baker)

EMBALLONURIDAE 2: TAPHOZOUS SHEATH-TAILED BATS

These are 3 species of medium-sized insectivorous bats often locally common in coastal towns. They have several distinctive features. 1. The roosting position is similar to the 2 *Emballonura* bats', which hang from flat walls by hooking their front claw over a projection whilst resting the wing claws against the wall. 2. Long, narrow, translucent (white) wings. 3. Loud echolocating clicks in flight as they emerge before dusk. 4. The prominent tail emerges from the skin of the interfemoral wing membrane (not from the edge as in most bats, as illustrated (p. 99). The only other bats with this feature are the 2 *Emballonura* sheath-tailed bats, although in their case the very small tail ends short of the edge.

1 POUCHED TOMB BAT *Saccolaimus saccolaimus* **FA 71–78, T 33–34, E 19–21, Wt 40–50 Common**
[*Taphozous saccolaimus*] Largest tomb bat. Found throughout the lowland forests of Borneo; often locally abundant. **ID:** Bare skin on face normally black or dark grey. Upperparts dark black or brown, sometimes marked with white spots. Underparts usually white, but a brown morph has been recorded. Both sexes have a glandular chin-pouch. Legs and feet hairless. **Habits:** Often roosts in large colonies in roofs of houses. Also roosts in hollow trees and rock crevices. Emerges just before dusk, feeding up to 90m height (Yasuma 2005). **Range:** India to Australia. **Borneo race:** *T. s. saccolaimus*.

2 BLACK-BEARDED TOMB BAT *Taphozous melanopogon* **FA 60–63, T 25–28, E 19–22, Wt 22–30**
Locally common in the lowlands, often in coastal areas and towns, throughout Borneo. Roosts in sea caves at Kudat, Sandakan and Samunsam, and in limestone caves at Baturong, Tepadong and Niah. A colony of hundreds lives in a cave on the tiny tern-breeding islet of Pelong Rocks, *c.* 1km offshore Muara Brunei (Wong & Ibrahim 1996). On Bunguran Besar (Natunas), Everett found it abundant amongst large beach boulders above high tide. **ID:** Bare skin on face is normally pink. Translucent wings. Body fur varies from pale grey-brown to dark brown. Underparts always paler, sometimes almost white. Males have a patch of black hairs covering a gland on throat. Legs and feet hairless. **Habits:** Because this bat emerges before dusk it is targeted by diurnal predators. For many years a migrant Peregrine Falcon that roosted in the casuarinas at Tg Aru beach fed on these bats as they emerged from their tree holes each evening. Often roosts in buildings in exposed positions, for example above the car-park exit at the Merdeka shopping complex in KK. **Range:** India to S China south to Malaya, Sumatra, Java. **Borneo race:** *T. m. fretensis*.

3 LONG-WINGED TOMB BAT *Taphozous longimanus* **FA 54–58, Wt ? Rare**
Smallest tomb bat, with scattered records including Ranau and P Labuan in Sabah; Gng Penrissen in Sarawak; S Kapuas in W Kalimantan. **ID:** Colour varies from dark brown to black, sometimes with white speckles. In Thailand females are grey and males brown. Chin naked; throat-pouch in males only. Unlike in the other 2 tomb bats, legs are covered with short fur. **Habits:** In Malaya roosts in hollow trees, rock crevices and houses. **Range:** Sri Lanka, east to Vietnam, south to Malaya, Sumatra, Java to Flores. **Borneo race:** *T. l. albipinnis*.

4 THEOBALD'S TOMB BAT *Taphozous theobaldi* **FA 70-76 T 25-30 E 22-28 (Not illustrated)**
In Borneo a rare bat recorded only from Kalimantan. **ID:** Very similar to *T. melanopogon*. Distinguished by longer FA and lack of any hairs on the interfemoral membrane. **Range:** Locally common in caves in seasonally dry areas of the Asian continent from India to Java. The distribution is obviously relict with no records from the Malay Peninsula or Sumatra. See Hill, Robinson & Boeadi (1990), Bates & Harrison (1997), and Lekagul (1977).

Purpose of wing-sacs Males of the 51 species of S American sac-winged bats (Emballonuridae) fill small pockets (sacs) on their wings with a mixture of glandular secretions and urine to use in mating displays, in which they hover in front of females fanning their wings. Males also fan their wings to warn off rival males. This suggests that wing sacs (radio-metacarpal pouches) on Borneo's sheath-tailed bats are used by males to signal to females when breeding. Other possible uses of glandular secretions may be to waterproof and condition the fur, and application as an external toxin to deter predators (p. 125).

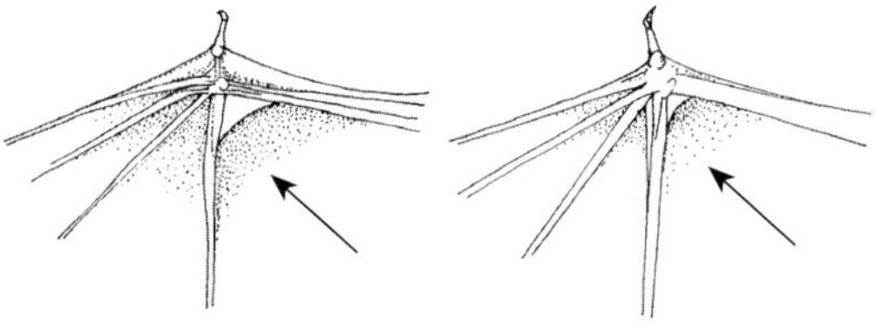

Wing-sacs (radio metacarpal pouches)
(a) *Saccolaimus saccolaimus*
(b) *Taphozous melanopogon*.

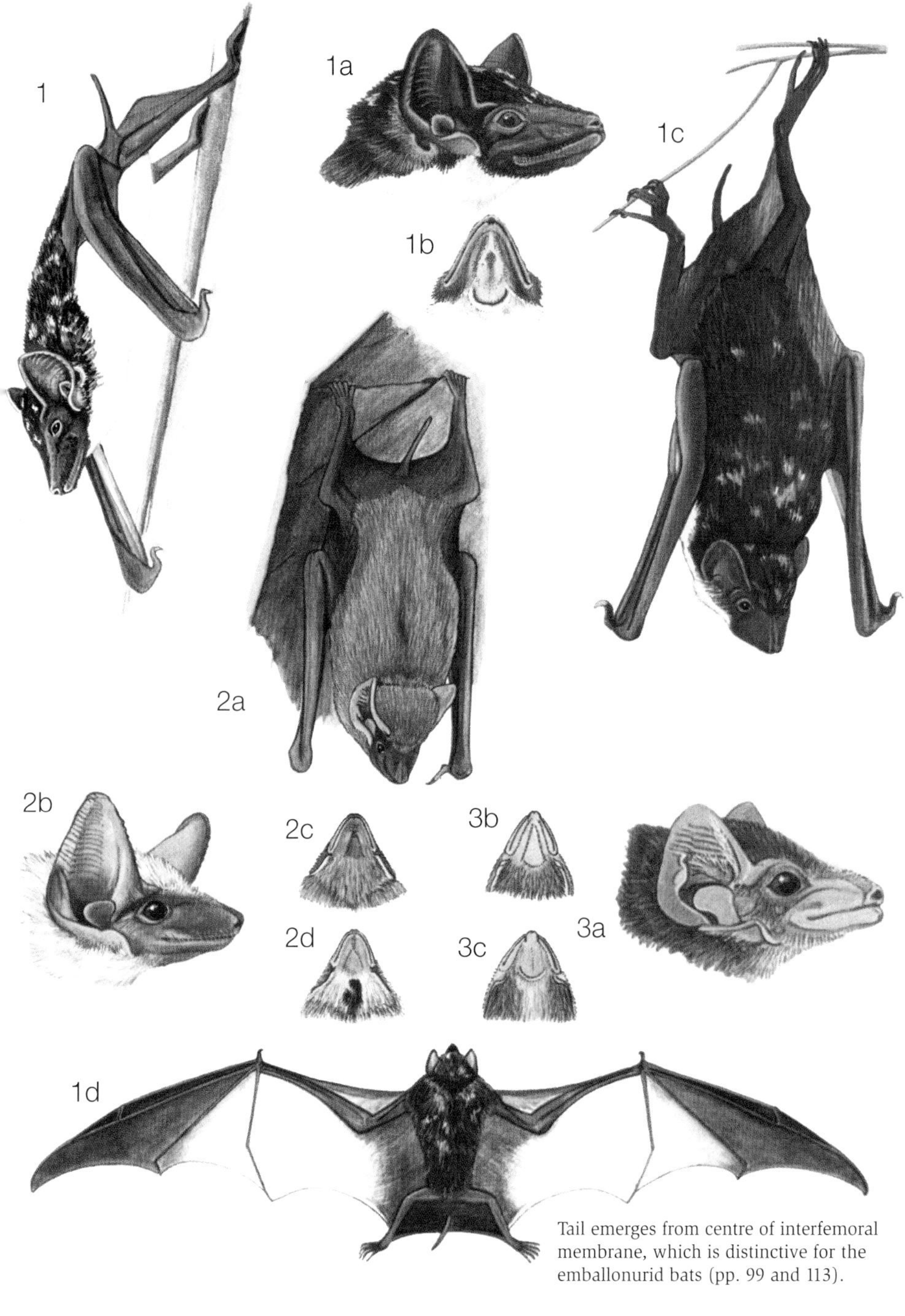

Tail emerges from centre of interfemoral membrane, which is distinctive for the emballonurid bats (pp. 99 and 113).

BENT-WINGED OR LONG-FINGERED BATS

MINIOPTERIDAE **World:** 20 spp. **Borneo:** 6 spp. Bent-winged bats are small bats with long, distinctive wings. The third finger has a short first phalanx (finger bone) and a very long terminal phalanx that is three times the length of the first, causing the wing to bend up at the third finger when the bat is at rest (Kingston et al. 2009). Different species are distinguished by size and sometimes skull measurements (see Kitchener & Suyanto 2002 and Koopman 1989). At Danum Valley DVFC, Chris Corben (Anabat) found that *Miniopterus* were the most commonly recorded bats. 'This bat arrived later than others, but was ubiquitous once it appeared. Seen hunting around the DVFC buildings and hunted well below the canopy, with direct, fast flight.'
Breeding: At the Subis caves (Niah), Medway (1970) found that *M. australis* bred annually, and all births took place in a synchronized peak period of 12 days in late Apr/early May.

1 LARGE BENT-WINGED BAT *Miniopterus magnater* **FA 49.5 avg., Wt 13–16** **Locally common**
[Western Long-fingered Bat]. Common in Sabah. At Kinabalu Park headquarters, Poring and Monggis, often forages around street lamps. **ID:** Largest *Miniopterus*, with a wide mouth (gape). **Habits:** Cave roosts on P Balembangan, Gomantong, Madai and the upper S Kuamut in Sabah. On the Sangkulirang Peninsula at Gua Kelawar, found roosting along with 500 *M. australis* (Suyanto et al. 2007). **Range:** SE Asia to N Guinea and Australia. **Borneo race:** *M. m. macrodens.*

2 SCHREIBERS'S BENT-WINGED BAT *Miniopterus schreibersii* **FA 46.5 avg., Wt 10–12.5** **Common**
The world's most widespread bat, found from Portugal to Japan, south to Australia. In Borneo a locally common inhabitant of many large caves, including Gomantong, Madai, S Kuamut (Sabah). Sarawak records from the First and Fourth Divisions (Long Lama). **ID:** Slightly smaller than *M. magnater*, but with some overlap. **Habits:** In Australia a local migrant travelling to 1,300km between winter and summer roosts. Cave roosts number up to 300,000 and are often shared with *M. magnater* and *M. australis.* **Taxonomy:** Probably more than 1 species (Simmons 2005). **Range:** Africa and Europe to Australia. **Borneo race:** *M. s. blepotis.*

3 SMALL BENT-WINGED BAT *Miniopterus pusillus* **FA 42.6 avg.** **Rare**
One specimen reported from Kalimantan (Payne et al. 1985). Given the wide range of this bat and abundance elsewhere, the rarity in Borneo is puzzling. **ID:** FA is always under 45mm, but always averages larger than that of *M. australis* (Kitchener). **Range:** Nicobar Islands, India, Hong Kong, Sumatra, Java east to New Guinea.

4 MEDIUM BENT-WINGED BAT *Miniopterus medius* **FA 41.5 avg., Wt 7.3–8.3** **Locally common**
Reported from the Tapadong Caves in Sabah and a cave at Kutai in E Kalimantan. **ID:** Intermediate in size between *M. schreibersi* and *M. australis.* Fur generally paler than that of both. **Habits:** Roosts in caves, often with *M. australis.* **Range:** Thailand, Malaya, Java to New Guinea. **Borneo race:** *M. m. medius.*

5 LESSER BENT-WINGED BAT *Miniopterus australis* **FA 39.2 avg., Wt 5–7** **Locally abundant**
Abundant in caves in Sabah, E Kalimantan and at Niah, Sarawak. The most common bat in limestone caves of the Sangkulirang Peninsula, with 10,000 at Gua Sungai and 500 at Gua Kelawar along with other bats. *M. magnater* was present in smaller numbers in the same cave (Suyanto et al. 2007). **ID:** Second smallest bent-winged bat. Fur black, sometimes with large reddish patches. **Habits:** Large maternity cave roosts often comprise mixed *Miniopterus* species. **Range:** The Philippines through Indonesia to Australia.

6 PHILIPPINE BENT-WINGED BAT *Miniopterus paululus* **FA 36.3 avg** **(Not illustrated)**
[Philippine Long-fingered Bat] Common resident of Philippine caves. Recorded from sea caves Balembangan, N Borneo. Also Gomantong and Kutai in E Kalimantan (Kitchener et al. 2002). **ID:** Smallest *Miniopterus.* FA averages 10% shorter than in *M. australis* (Kitchener). **Taxonomy:** In Payne et al. (1985), listed as race of *M. australis.* Split by Kitchener & Suyanto (2002). **Range:** The Philippines. **Borneo race:** *M. a. witkampi.*

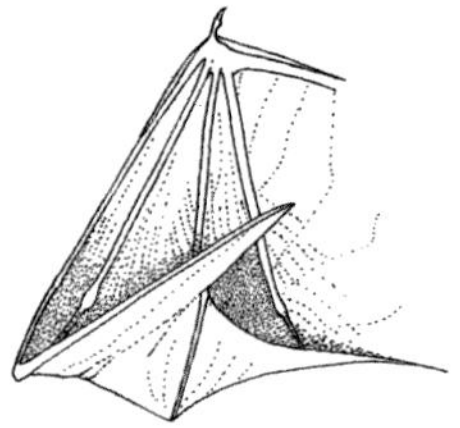

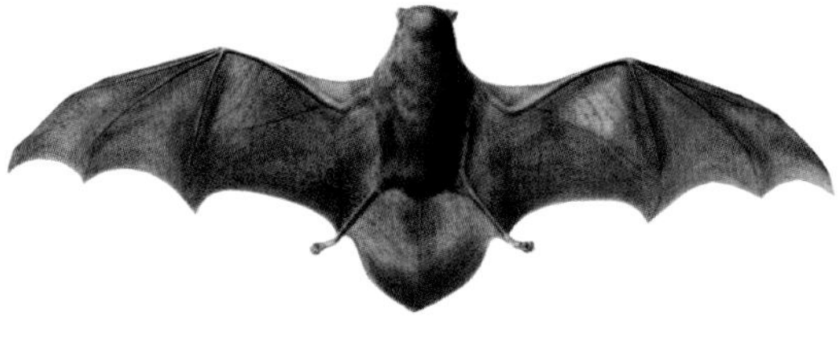

Folded wing-tip at rest, *M. schreibersii.* Silhouette shows long wings and large interfemoral membrane.

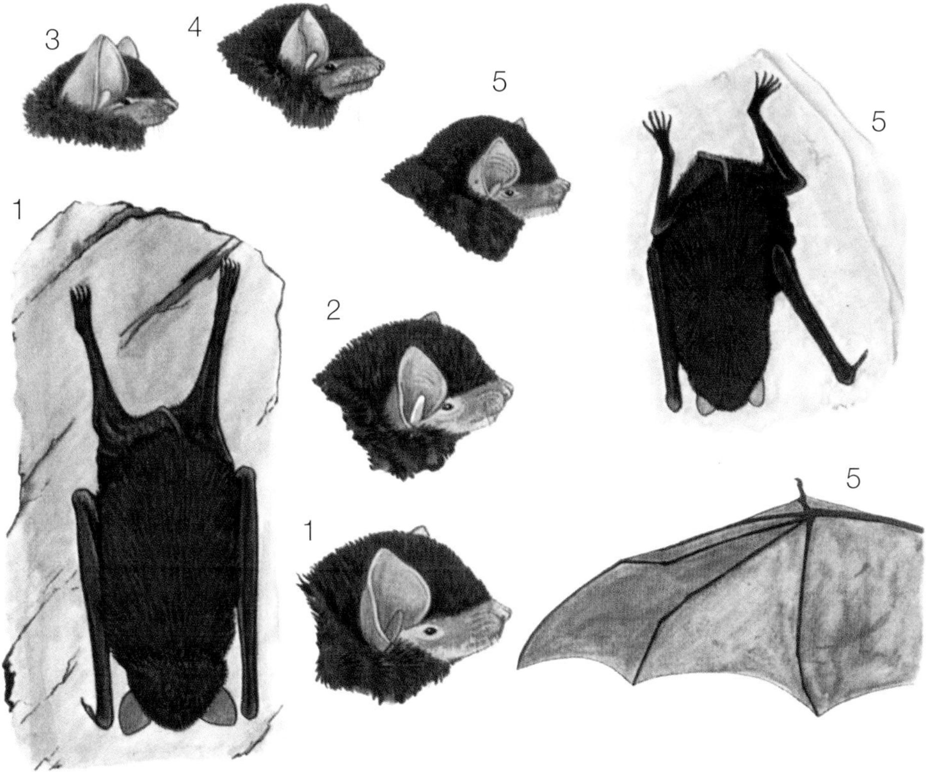

M. australis at Bukit Sarang. (Photo: Ch'ien C. Lee)

VESPER BATS 1: *PIPISTRELLUS, FALSISTRELLUS* AND *HYPSUGO*

VESPERTILIONIDAE World: 300 spp. **Borneo:** 32 spp. in 9 genera, including *Arielulus, Falsistrellus, Hypsugo, Glischropus, Hesperoptenus, Myotis, Philetor, Pipistrellus, Scotophilus* and *Tylonycteris*. Vesper bats, or evening bats, are the world's most widespread bats, found throughout the tropics north to the Arctic Circle. Most *Pipistrellus* and *Hypsugo* use weak, fluttery flight to catch insects close to vegetation, whilst some *Hesperoptenus, Myotis* and *Pipistrellus* 'trawl' over water to catch insects and fish with large claws. The tail is always fully enclosed. Different species are easily confused. Francis (2008) suggests that the baculum (penis bone) may be useful to distinguish species. Habitat descriptions indicate that many listed records are misidentified.

1 JAVAN PIPISTRELLE *Pipistrellus javanicus* **FA 31–35, T 32–351, E 9.0–12.0, Wt 5.6–5.0 Montane**
Locally common in moss forest at 1,200–1,600m on Gng Kinabalu and the Crocker Range in Sabah only. **ID:** Upperpart fur dark brown with dark bases; underparts paler. Ear moderately short and rounded, tragus long but not tapered, with rounded tip (p. 99). **Habits:** In Borneo known only from montane moss forest. Elsewhere in Asia recorded from towns and lowland forest. In Sumatra recorded roosting in thatched roofs of village houses. **Range:** Japan, E China through Southeast Asia, the Philippines, Sumatra, Java. **Borneo race:** *P. j. javanicus*.

2 LEAST PIPISTRELLE *Pipistrellus tenuis* **FA 29–32, T 32, E 8–11, Wt 4.2 Common Sabah**
Locally common in Sabah mangroves. **ID:** Upperpart fur uniformly dark brown; underparts similar or slightly paler. Ear and tragus similar to those of *P. javanicus*. **Taxonomy:** *P. tenuis* is a complex and probably includes several species (Simmons 2005). **Range:** Afghanistan to Moluccas. **Borneo race:** *P.t. nitidus*.

3 WOOLLY PIPISTRELLE *Falsistrellus petersi* **FA 40–42, T 39–41, E 13–15.5, Wt 6–7 Montane Sabah**
[*Pipistrellus petersi*] Known only from the Crocker Range in Sabah at 1,500m. **ID:** Fur very long and shaggy, dark blackish-brown with pale grey-brown tips on upperparts, shorter and browner on head and underparts. Muzzle long and narrow. **Habits:** Colony found roosting under eaves of a house in lower montane forest. **Taxonomy:** May be conspecific with *F. affinis* of the Asian continent (Corbet & Hill 1992). **Range:** The Philippines, Sulawesi, Moluccas, Borneo.

4 NARROW-WINGED PIPISTRELLE *Pipistrellus stenopterus* **FA 38–42 Common**
Widespread in Sabah and Sarawak to 1,200m (Kelabit Highlands). **ID:** Largest *Pipistrellus,* uniformly reddish-brown. Distinguished from all other *Pipistrellus* by length of fifth metacarpal, which is much shorter than fourth metacarpal, creating a narrow wing (Kingston 2009), (p. 99). *Philetor brachypterus* has a similar narrow wing, but is smaller (p. 120). **Habits:** Roosts in buildings. At Krau mist netted over large rivers. Caught hawking insects next to a light (Monggis, Kinabalu). **Range:** Malaya, Mindanao, Sumatra, Borneo.

5 COPPERY SPRITE *Arielulus cuprosus* **FA 34.5–36.5, T 38–39, E 12.5, Wt 5.3–5.6 Rare endemic**
[Coppery Pipistrelle *Pipistrellus cuprosus*] In Sabah recorded from the forest at Sepilok. In Sarawak recorded at Similajau, Kubah, Gng Penrissen (Khan 2008) and Lanjak Entimau (Roberta, Anwarali et al. 2010). **ID:** By distinctive long, thick, reddish-tipped fur on back, yellowish whiskers below ears and pale-tipped fur below.

6 KELLART'S PIPISTRELLE *Pipistrellus ceylonicus* **FA 38, Wt ? Rare**
[Dark-brown Pipistrelle] One specimen from 1,300m on Trus Madi in Sabah. **ID:** Fur dark brown. Ears large, tragus broad (p. 99). **Habits:** Unknown. **Range:** Pakistan to S China, Vietnam. **Borneo race:** *P c. borneanus*.

7 RED-BROWN PIPISTRELLE *Hypsugo kitcheneri* **FA 35–38, Wt ? Rare endemic**
[*Pipistrellus kitcheneri*] Recorded from (Sabah), Buntuk (E Kalimantan), Sg Barito (S Kalimantan). **ID:** Upperparts reddish-brown with black bases to fur, paler below. Ears with short, broad tragus.

8 VORDERMANN'S PIPISTRELLE *Hypsugo vordermanni* **FA 30.5, T 15.1 Rare**
[*Pipistrellus vordermanni*] [White-winged Pipistrelle] Uncommon in mangrove and coastal forest throughout Borneo, including Banggi Island (Nor 1996), Belalong (Brunei), Kuching (Abdullah et al. 2000), Samunsam, Tg Puting (Nash & Nash 1987). **ID:** The only Pipistrelle with translucent white wings. **Habits:** Trawls for insects and fish on rivers and calm seas. **Range:** Borneo and Belitung Island between Sumatra and Borneo.

9 BROWN PIPISTRELLE *Hypsugo imbricatus* **(Not illustrated) Rare**
Recorded from the Kelabit Highlands. **Taxonomy:** Previously considered a race of *H. macrotis*, which forages over coastal mud flats in Malaya. Split by Francis & Hill (1986). See Kingston (2009). **Range:** Java, Bali, Lesser Sundas.

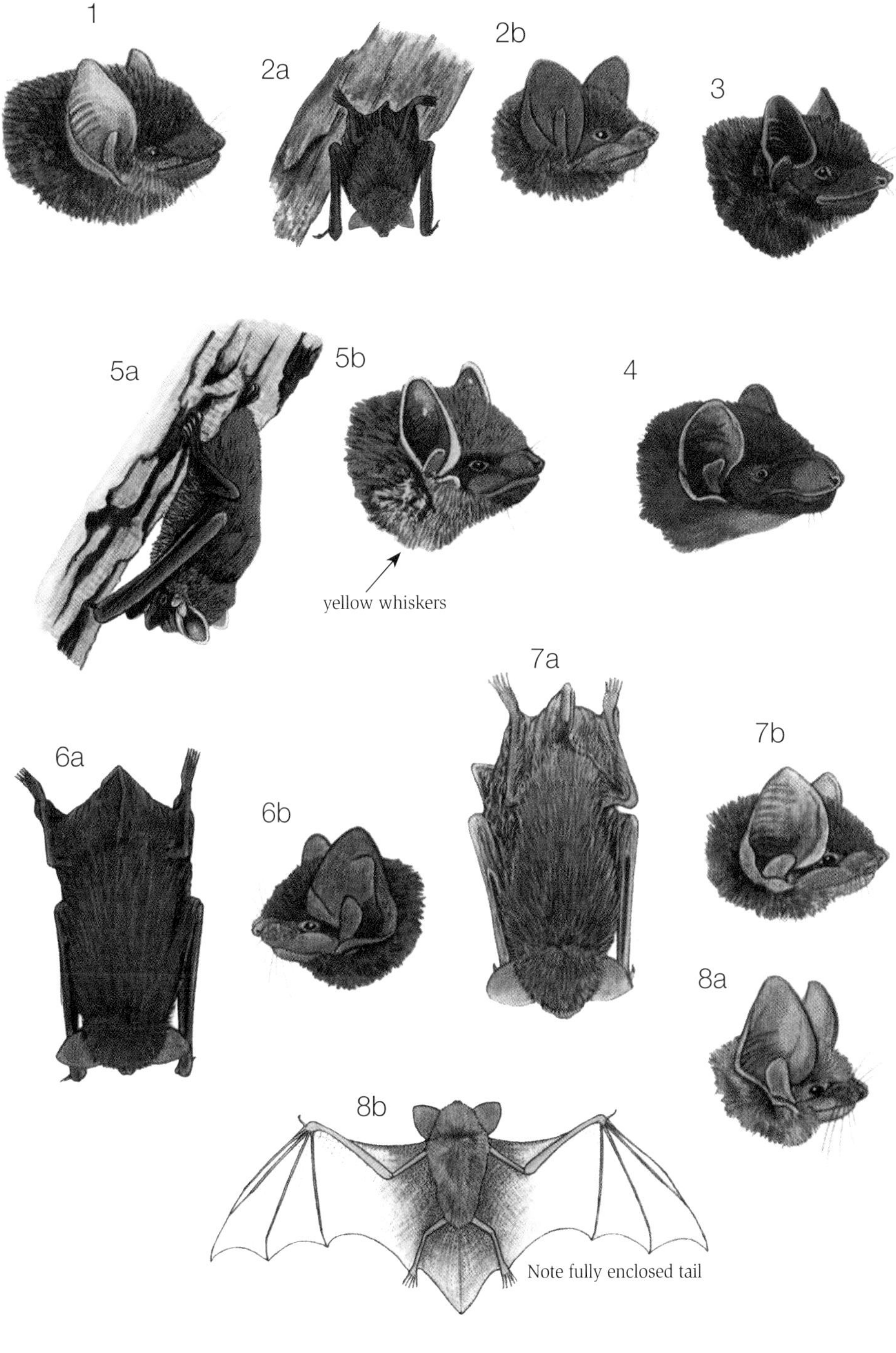
1
2a
2b
3
5a
5b
4
yellow whiskers
7a
6a
7b
6b
8a
8b
Note fully enclosed tail

VESPER BATS 2: *TYLONYCTERIS*, *GLISCHROPUS* AND *PHILETOR*

1 LESSER BAMBOO BAT *Tylonycteris pachypus* **FA 24–28, T 27–29, E 8–9, Wt 3.5–5 Common**
Locally common throughout Borneo, especially near clumps of bamboo. **ID:** Body and skull flattened, with large pads on thumbs and feet. Distinguished from *T. robustula* by smaller size and weight, which is always under 5g, whereas weight of *T. robustula* always exceeds 5g. **Habits:** Roosts in small groups in bamboo internodes, entering through small slits created by beetles. Frequently chooses small live bamboos, whilst *T. robustula* prefers larger, often dead stems. Both species may use the same roost at different times. **Range:** India to S China, south to Malaya, the Philippines, Sumatra, Java.

2 GREATER BAMBOO BAT *Tylonycteris robustula* **FA 26–30, T 29–36, E 11, Wt 6.5–8.5 Common**
Locally common from Kinabalu (to 1,000m) south to Kuching. No records as yet from Kalimantan. **ID:** Smooth, glossy, dark brown fur compared with reddish fluffy fur of *T. pachypus*. Forearm lengths of the 2 bamboo bats overlap but weights do not. Weight of *T. robustula* always exceeds 5g. **Habits:** See above. **Range:** S China south to Malaya, Sumatra, Java, Sulawesi, Borneo.

3 THICK-THUMBED PIPISTRELLE *Glischropus tylopus* **FA 26–32, T 32–39, E 8–11, Wt 3.5–4.8**
Common throughout Borneo, often near large bamboos. **ID:** Distinguished by pale or pinkish pads on thumbs and feet. *Hesperoptenus blanfordi* (p. 122) has dark pads. Bamboo bats also have dark thumb pads. **Habits:** Often aggressive when handled (Hall 2002). Found roosting in broken bamboos at Niah (Hall et al. 2002), and in a group of 12 in bamboos at Temburong, Brunei, Kofron (1994). May share roosts with *Tylonicteris* spp. In Malaya also roosts in rock crevices and new banana leaves. **Range:** Myanmar south to Malaya, the Philippines, Sumatra. **Borneo race**: *G. t. tylopus*.

4 ROHU'S BAT *Philetor brachypterus* **FA 30–36, T 30–38, E 13–16, Wt 8–13 Scarce**
[Narrow-winged Brown Bat] [New Guinea Brown Bat] Very widespread bat of varied habitats in different parts of the extensive range. Recorded from peat-swamp, grassland, disturbed virgin lowland and montane forest. Widespread in Borneo south to Niah in Sarawak. **ID:** Small, plain brown bat with large ears and narrow wings. Wings similar to those of *P. stenopterus* (p. 118), with a short fifth finger (p. 99). Distinguished by elaborate genitals: 'male has elongate penis with bristly pad near end of main shaft, followed by a narrow shaft supporting a broadened triangular structure; female has five separate pads around the vulva' (Francis 2008). **Habits:** Roosts in hollow trees or coconut palms (India). Feeds both at the forest edge and in the understorey of forest. At Niah recorded roosting in tree hollows 1–5m above the ground. **Range:** N India to Borneo and the Philippines, to New Guinea and the Pacific Islands.

BREEDING OF BAMBOO BATS has been studied by Medway & Marshall (1972) at Ulu Gombak (Malaya), and Hua et al. (2011, 2013) in S China. Bamboo bats produce 2 young (most bats only one).
Sperm storage Many female bats, including bamboo bats, can store male sperm for several months so that mating and giving birth are separated by variable time periods. This allows bat colonies to coordinate birthing during a favourable season independent of when they mated.
Seasonal birthing In Malaya both species gave birth during a 1-month period centred around mid-April.
Group size Medway examined 448 roosting groups from 78 diferent bamboo-bat roost sites (1,059 individuals) and found that bats were loyal neither to a roost site nor to roost companions. Males were more likely to be found alone and females in groups, especially during the birthing season. *T. pachypus* was most common, with an average group size of 4.9 and a maximum group size of 20, whilst the average group size of *T. robustula* was 3.5 and maximum group size was 32.
Roost choice *T. pachypus* tended to roost in bamboos with smaller slits down to 4.8mm wide, but both species occupied most roosts. The 2 species were only found together once.
Lesser Bamboo Bats in S China: Hua et al. analaysed the DNA of 662 Lesser Bamboo Bats from 54 separate bamboo internodes in 9 localities to 49km apart in S China. They found that females nearly always roosted in groups with their newborn offspring, normally in association with a single male or multiple adult males. Some males roosted alone or in small, all-male groups. 1. Males dispersed further than females (male-biased dispersal). 2. Females were more likely to roost with related females, but males had no preference for roosting with relatives, i.e. female philopatry. 3. Roost size varied at 1–27 bats. 4. Group membership was relatively stable across seasons. 5. About half (43.5%) of twins had different fathers. 6. Related females like half-sisters, sisters and cousins preferred to mate with the same male. 7. Related bats were found in bamboos to 3km apart, showing local dispersal.
Biased sex ratios Both Medway and Hua found that female adult bamboo bats were up to twice or more as common as males.

1

2

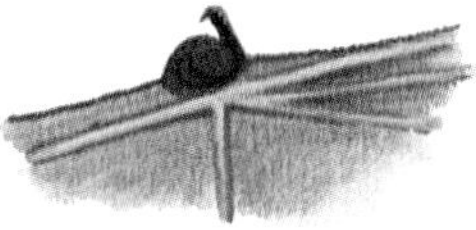

BAMBOO BATS *Tylonycteris tomesi* and *T. robustula* rely on hollow bamboo nodes to provide safe sleeping accommodation. Holes are accessed via narrow slits drilled by bamboo beetles *Lasiochila goryi*. Other Bornean bats often found roosting in bamboos include *Glischropus tylopus*, *Hesperotenus blanfordi* and *Kerivoula papilosa*. Because the last 3 listed bats do not have flattened bodies, they can only access old broken bamboo stems.

Snakes often inhabit bamboo clumps, but the slits are usually too thin to give snakes access to roosting bats. Illustrated is a **Paradise Tree Snake** *Chrysopelea paradisi* grabbing an emerging bamboo bat, recorded in Singapore by Chan Kwok Wai.

3a

3b

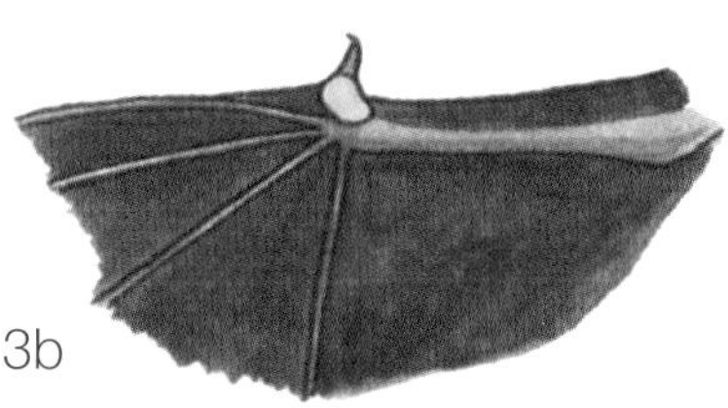

3c

4

VESPER BATS 3: *SCOTOPHILUS* AND *HESPEROTENUS*

1 SODY'S YELLOW HOUSE BAT *Scotophilus collinus* **FA 47–52, T 45–52, E 14–15, Wt 18–23 Common**
[*Scotophilus kuhlii*] One of the most common bats in towns on the E Asian mainland. Common in W Sabah, including Kota Kinabalu and Kota Belud, as well as S Tengah in S Kalimantan. UMS has 30 specimens from P Layangan, a small, rocky forested island opposite the mouth of the Papar River, and 15 from Jalan Saga, Likas, a coastal suburb of KK. **ID:** Ear has long, narrow tragus bent forwards. **Habits:** Often roosts in roofs of houses. In the Philippines recorded roosting in palm tents constructed from the leaves of *Livistonia rotundifolia* (Rickart et al. 1989). Most likely the tents are constructed by sympatric *Cynopterus* bats (p. 129). **Taxonomy:** The type was collected by Sody in Bali in 1936. Split by Kitchener et al. (1997). **Range:** Sri Lanka to Taiwan, south to Malaya, Singapore, the Philippines, Sumatra, Java, Bali. **Borneo race:** *S. k. castaneus*.

2 DORIA'S FALSE SEROTINE *Hesperoptenus doriae* **FA 38–41 Rare**
Collected once by the Italian botanist Odoardo Beccari in SW Sarawak, and named after his friend the Marques of Doria. **ID:** Fur dark brown. All false serotines have a short, broad, hatchet-shaped tragus, and are distinguished between species by the length of their forearm (FA). **Habits:** In Malaya a small group was found roosting under a palm leaf near a forest stream at Ulu Gombak. **Range:** Malaya, Borneo.

3 BLANDFORD'S FALSE SEROTINE *Hesperoptenus blanfordi* **FA 24–26.5, T 27–30, E 11, Wt 6.1–6.4**
Rare. In Malaya the most common false serotine, but in Borneo only recorded from the Witti Range and Sepilok in Sabah in virgin dipterocarp forest. **ID:** Distinguished by small size, shape of tragus and distinctive flat pads at bases of thumbs and soles of feet, indicating that it roosts in bamboos. Fur is entirely glossy dark reddish-brown or brown. **Habits:** In Malaya roosts in small colonies in the entrances of limestone caves in hill forest. At Krau usually mist-netted over rivers. **Range:** S Thailand, Malaya, Borneo.

4. TOMES' FALSE SEROTINE *Hesperoptenus tomesi* **FA 50–53, T 49–53, E 17–18, Wt 30–32g Rare**
[Large False Serotine] Recorded in E Sabah from Sandakan and Tabin, and Sarawak at Bukit Sarang and Gng Penrissen (Khan et al. 2008). In Malaya recorded from Taman Negara and Krau, but everywhere rare. **ID:** Fur is entirely blackish-brown. Distinguished by large size, shape of tragus and large teeth. **Habits:** Usually netted flying along forest streams. Relatively large size and large teeth (see photo) suggest that *H. tomesi* catches small fish or frogs as well as insects. **Range:** S Thailand, Malaya, Borneo.

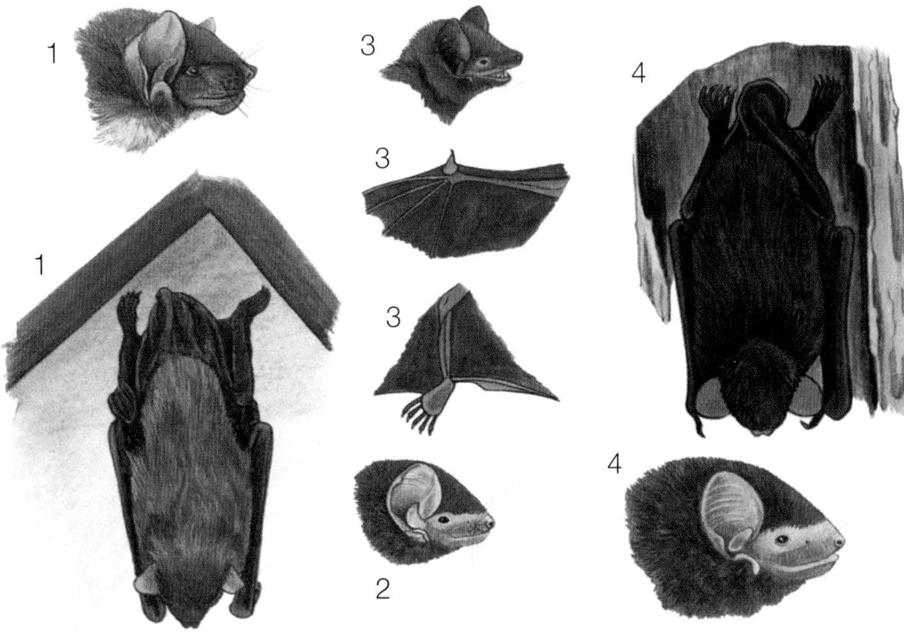

Tomes' False Serotine, Bukit Sarang. (Photo: Ch'ien C. Lee)

VESPER BATS 4: *MURINA*, TUBE-NOSED BATS

World: *c.* 30 spp. **Borneo:** 5 spp. in 2 genera. *Murina* are a subfamily of the Vespertilionidae confined to S and E Asia, east of Pakistan, north to Japan and south to Australia. Distinguished by tube-like nostrils that open at right angles (sideways) to the mouth. Ears are rounded, not pointed like those of *Kerivoula* bats. In 3 species the long, pointed tragus is notched as in *Phoniscus* bats (p. 129).
Cryptic species: Csorba et al. (2011) note that 8 new *Murina* species have recently been found in Asia and more are likely.
Habits: *Murina* bats specialize in gleaning stationary beetles and spiders off cluttered vegetation in the forest understorey. The tube-like nostrils may have evolved to avoid breathing in bombardier beetle toxins, or to sniff out these toxins when hunting for prey. The toxins may be sequestered to protect against predators (below).

1 GILDED TUBE-NOSED BAT *Murina rozendaali* **FA 31.5–33.5, T 35–41, E 13–15, Wt 4.3–4.8 Rare**
First described from Sepilok (Hill & Francis 1984) as a Borneo endemic known only from Poring, Gomantong and Tapadong in Sabah. Now known from Kubah, Bukit Kana and Gng Murud, Sarawak (Khan 2008), and the Sangkulirang karst, E Kalimantan (Suyanto 2007). At Krau (Malaya) found in very low densities **ID:** Upperparts patterned with yellow/golden tipped fur; underparts buffy with yellow tinge. *M. aenea* is smaller and has orange-brown upperparts and no yellow tinge to underparts. **Habits:** Trapped over streams in lowland dipterocarp forest. Kingston et al. (2009) note that some adult males have a large gland at the base of the penis, as well as additional glands that extend halfway down the tail and secrete a clear, pungent liquid, probably for sexual marking and possibly also defence (p. 160). **Range:** Malaya, Borneo.

2 BRONZED TUBE-NOSED BAT *Murina aenea* **FA 35–38, T 35–41, E 13.5–15.5, Wt 6–8.5 Scarce**
Widespread in Sabah with records from Sepilok, Segarong (Semporna) and the Crocker Range (1,200m). Also C Kalimantan (Struebig 2010). **ID:** Upper fur has orange-brown tips, not yellow/golden tips. Tragus notched at base. **Habits:** Has been caught in lowland dipterocarp forest and hill moss forest. **Range:** Malaya, Borneo.

3 LESSER TUBE-NOSED BAT *Murina suilla* **FA 28–31, T 26–35, E 10.5–13, Wt 2.5–5.5 Common**
Common in forested areas throughout Borneo, including coastal forest at Samunsam (Sarawak) and peat-swamp and kerangas forest at Sabangau and Tg Puting (C Kalimantan). **ID:** Smallest, plainest and most common *Murina* bat, with buffy to grey upperparts, greyish-white below. Distinguished from other *Murina* by size of FA. **Habits:** Turner (2011) reported that *M. suilla* became increasingly common following repeated logging at the SAFE project in Sabah. **Range:** Malaya, Sumatra, Java, Borneo.

4 ORANGE TUBE-NOSED BAT *Murina peninsularis* **FA 34–41, T 38–50, E 13–16, Wt 6.5–10 Common**
[*Murina cyclotis*] Locally common at Sepilok, Tabin and Gomantong (Sabah); Tasek Merimbun (Brunei); Gng Mulu (Sarawak) and C Kalimantan in the understorey of lowland forest **ID:** Distinguished from *M. aenea* by coat pattern. Interfemoral membrane covered in sparse, long red hairs. Tragus notched. Roosts in banana leaves. **Taxonomy:** Split by Soisook et al. (2013) from *M. cyclotis*. **Range:** Malaya, Sumatra, Java, Borneo.

5 HAIRY-WINGED BAT *Harpiocephalus harpia* **FA 48–52.5, Wt 19–25.5 Rare**
[*Harpiocephalus mordax*] Restricted to Sabah, with records from forest at Tawau and Sepilok. **ID:** Bright orange above, greyer below. Rounded ear with long-pointed notched tragus (p. 129). Wing and interfemoral membranes covered in short orange hairs. **Habits:** Bright orange fur is most likely a warning signal to possible predators of toxic flesh, the result of eating poisonous insects. **Taxonomy:** See Simmons (2005). **Range:** Myanmar south to Malaya, Sumatra, Java, Moluccas. **Borneo race:** *H. h. harpia*.

POISONOUS BEETLES OF BORNEO Borneo hosts more than 15,000 species of beetle. Many beetles protect themselves from predation with toxic chemicals, and advertise their toxicity with colourful aposematic danger-warning signals. One of the most toxic beetle groups, the bombardier beetles, is illustrated. *Murina* and *Phonicus* bats are probably specialist predators on poisonous beetles and spiders, and advertise the sequestered poisons with colourful fur. See p. 129 (*Phoniscus*); p.150 (Large Treeshrew); p. 160 (Slow Loris).

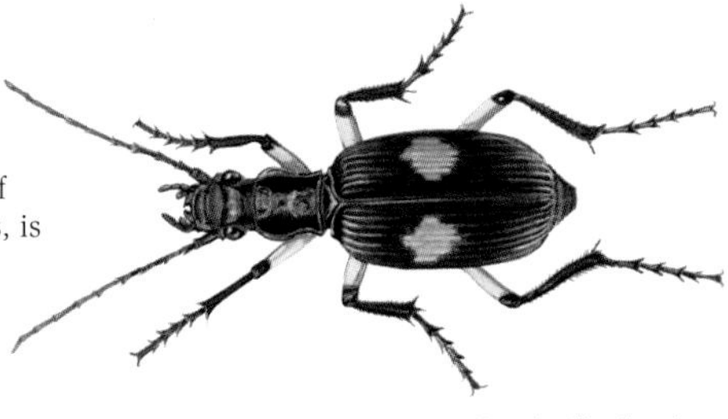

Bombadier beetle

1
2
3
4
5

VESPER BATS 5: *KERIVOULA*, WOOLLY BATS

World: 25 spp. **Borneo:** 10 spp in 2 genera, *Kerivoula* and *Phoniscus*. *Kerivoula* woolly bats are recognized by their distinctive, pointed, half-enclosed (funnel) ears with a large side panel. Compared with other small insectivorous bats, the tragus in the centre of the ear funnel is longer, straighter and more pointed. **Habits:** *Kerivoula* bats flutter slowly in dense foliage at low levels in the forest understorey. An additional Kerivoula *K. krauensis* has recently been recorded from Kalimantan, see Francis (2011).

1 SMALL WOOLLY BAT *Kerivoula intermedia* **FA 26.5–31, T 37–41, E 9–11.5, Wt 2.9–4.2** **Scarce**
Uncommon in both primary and secondary forest in the lowlands. The most common *Kerivoula* in heath forest at Tg Puting (Struebig 2006). **ID:** Distinguished from *K. minuta* by weight, as FA length overlaps. *K. minuta* always weighs under 2.5g, *K. intermedia* always more than 2.5g. **Range:** Malaya, Borneo.

2 LEAST WOOLLY BAT *Kerivoula minuta* **FA 25–29.5, T 8–10, Wt 1.9–2.5** **Locally common**
Locally common throughout the lowland forests of Borneo, including peat-swamp forest in Kalimantan. **ID:** Borneo's smallest bat. Very similar to *K. intermedia*, but always weighs less (above). **Habits:** Forages in the forest understorey in dense vegetation. **Range:** S Thailand, Malaya, Borneo.

3 HARDWICKE'S WOOLLY BAT *Kerivoula hardwickii* **FA 32–34, T 44–47, E 12–14, Wt 3.5–4.2**
Common throughout lowland forests. In peat-swamp forest at Tg Puting and Sabangau less common than *K. intermedia*. The most common insect bat at Tasek Merimbun in Brunei (Struebig 2008). **ID:** Same size as *K. intermedia*, but has larger ears and more speckled fur. Wings are semi-translucent but not as transparent as those of *K. pellucida*. **Habits:** Roosts in hollow trees, furled ginger leaves and *Nepenthes* pitchers, particularly *N. baramensis* (p. 70). **Taxonomy:** A specimen from 1,500m on Gng Kinabalu was larger (FA 36.5, Wt 5.2), with dark grey fur, possibly a new montane species (Payne et al. 1985). **Range:** Sri Lanka to S China, south to Malaya, the Philippines, Sumatra, Java, Sulawesi. **Borneo race:** *K. h. hardwickii.*

4 INDIAN WOOLLY BAT *Kerivoula lenis* **FA 37–41** **Scarce**
[Lenis Woolly Bat] Locally common throughout lowland Borneo, including heath forest at Tg Puting. **Taxonomy**: Not listed in Payne et al. (1985). Previously mistaken for larger *K. papiliosa* in Borneo. Can only be told apart by measurements. See Vanitharani et al. (2003). **Range:** India to Malaya and Borneo.

5 WHITEHEAD'S WOOLLY BAT *Kerivoula whiteheadi* **FA 28–29** **Scarce**
First collected by Whitehead in the Philippines (p. 207). Scarce bat usually found in poor soil or kerangas forest from Sabah south to C Sarawak. **ID:** Distinguished by distinctive speckled colouration; upperparts brown, fur with dark grey bases, underparts greyish-white. **Habits:** Group of *c.* 25 was roosting in dead leaves by a river (Payne et al. 1985). **Range:** S Thailand, Malaya, the Philippines. **Borneo race:** *K. w. pusilla.*

6 CLEAR-WINGED WOOLLY BAT *Kerivoula pellucida* **FA 29.5–32, T 39–53, E 14.5–17, Wt 3.5–4.8**
Locally common throughout Borneo, including kerangas and peat-swamp forest at Tg Puting and Sabangau in Kalimantan. **ID:** Distinguished by orange face, pale fur and transparent ears and wings. **Habits:** Has been found roosting in dead curled banana leaves. **Range:** Malaya, the Philippines, Sumatra, Java, Borneo.

7 PAPILLOSE WOOLLY BAT *Kerivoula papiliosa* **FA 38–49, T 49–56, E 14–17, Wt 6–13** **Common**
Most common *Kerivoula* in undisturbed lowland to lower montane forest throughout Borneo. Most common insect bat in primary forest at Sg Wain (Struebig 2006). **ID:** Largest *Kerivoula* bat. **Habits:** Roosts in hollow trees and bamboos in Malaya. **Taxonomy:** Some *K. papiliosa* collections from Borneo may represent *K. lenis, K. flora* or an undescribed cryptic species (Struebig 2008). Measurements of specimens at UNIMAS Sarawak by Hasan & Abdullah (2011) suggest that a smaller cryptic species similar to *K. papiliosa* occurs at Lambir and Similajau. **Range:** NE India to Malaya, Sumatra, Java and Sulawesi. **Borneo race:** *K. p. malayana.*

COUNTING *KERIVOLUA* BATS TO MEASURE FOREST DISTURBANCE Some *Kerivoula* bats, like *K. hardwickii*, become more common in disturbed and logged forest, whilst others, like *K. papiliosa*, become less common. Turner (2011) reported that *K. papillosa* became increasingly uncommon across a gradient of increasingly disturbed (repeatedly logged) forest at the SAFE project in Sabah. Because *K. papiliosa* is so sensitive to logging, Struebig et al. (2007) suggest that a standardized population count of *K. papilosa* in different areas could be used as an indicator (measure) of forest disturbance in Borneo. We also need to know if reduced populations result from the loss of roost sites or reductions in insect prey or other factors.

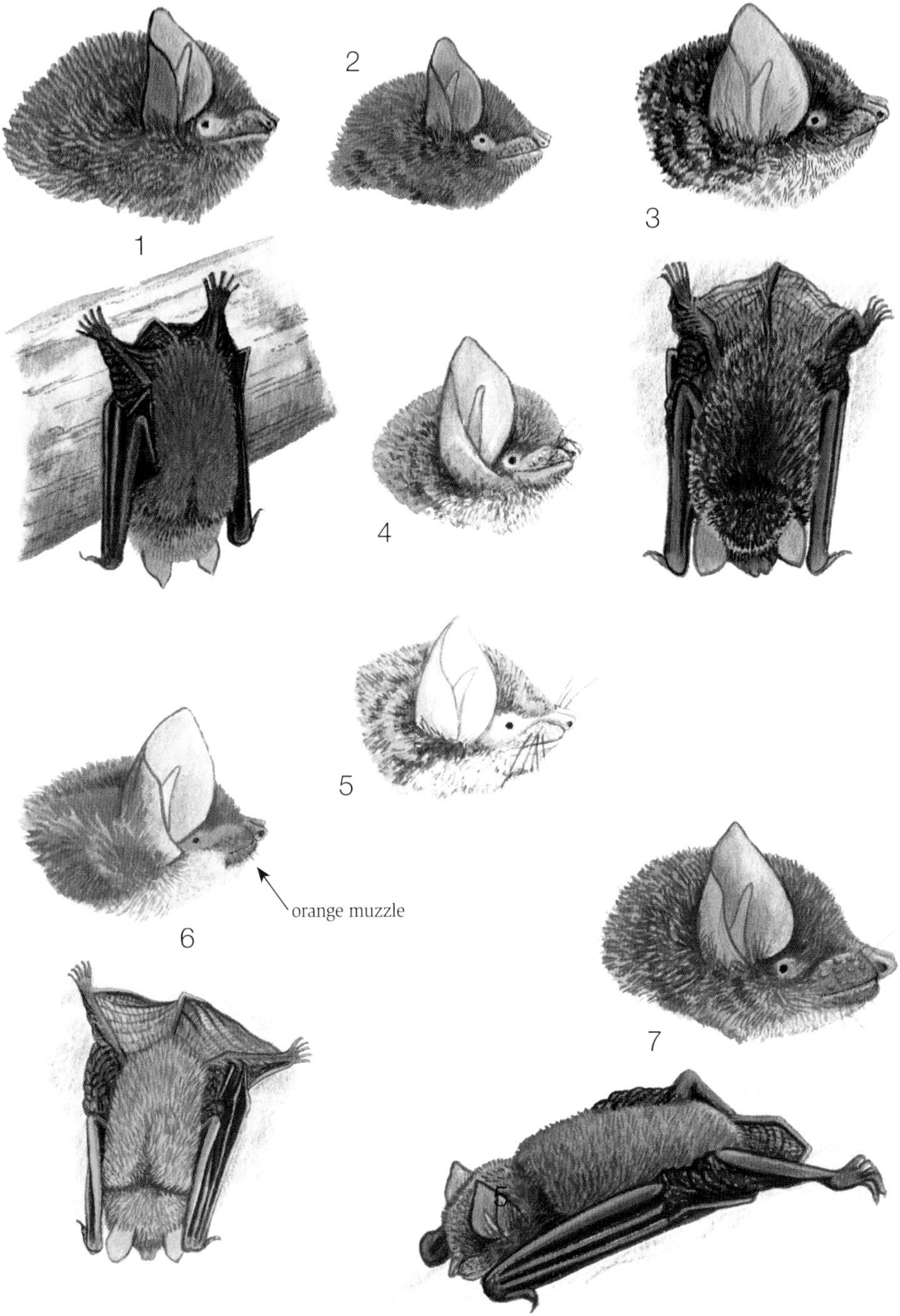
2
3
1
4
5
6
orange muzzle
7
5

VESPER BATS 6: *PHONISCUS*, WOOLLY BATS

Closely related and similar to *Kerivoula*, with the following differences. 1. The tragus of *Phoniscus* is white not grey as in *Kerivoula*. 2. There is a clear notch at the base of the tragus in *Phoniscus*, as illustrated. 3. The fur of *Phoniscus* is clearly banded in both species with pale tips. 4. Each upper incisor of the 2 *Phoniscus* is marked with 2 longitudinal grooves, whereas the upper incisors of *Kerivoula* are smooth. Both the Bornean *Phoniscus* species are rare throughout their world range, indicating a specialized ecology. In Malaya, Kingston et al. (2009) found that the 2 *Phoniscus* species were rare local residents in the primary forest understorey. Schulz & Wainer (1997) found that *P. papuensis* in N Australia roosted in suspended birds' nests after making a hole in the base, and up to 8 bats occupied 1 nest. Ninety per cent of the diet comprised web-building spiders. Small quantities of beetles, moths and flies were also eaten.

1 FROSTED GROOVE-TOOTHED BAT *Phoniscus jagorii* **FA 37–42.5, Wt 9–11g** **Rare**

[Peter's Trumpet-eared Bat] At least 4 records from throughout Borneo, usually in nutrient-poor forest such as kerangas or peat-swamp, but very rare. **ID:** Both species of *Phoniscus* have distinctive banded fur with at least 4 bands of black, brown, yellow and white, but always paler at the tips. *P. jagori* is larger, with more colourful fur than *P. atrox*. **Habits:** In Vietnam, Thong et al. (2006) caught *P. jagori* in a harp trap in disturbed forest near primary forest. It was highly manoeuvrable, often flying close to the ground. **Range:** Vietnam, Thailand, Malaya, the Philippines (Samar Island Type), Java, Bali, Sulawesi. **Borneo race:** *P. j. javanus*.

2 GILDED GROOVE-TOOTHED BAT *Phoniscus atrox* **FA 31–35.5, T 39, Wt 3–6.5g** **Rare**

Rare but more common than *P. jagori*. Recorded throughout Borneo in primary forest, including heath forest at Tg Puting. **ID:** Smaller version of *P. jagori*. Fur is banded like that of *P. jagori*, but generally paler. Distinguished by size, particularly the length of the forearm (FA), which does not overlap. **Habits:** At Krau, trapped in the understorey of lowland dipterocarp forest. In Thailand, Thong et al. (2006) caught this bat in a harp trap in orchards near primary forest. In Sumatra, 2 females were found in a broadbill's nest in daytime. At Krau, recorded roosting in an abandoned hanging bird's nest. All individuals handled had a distinctive acrid smell (Kingston 2009). **Range:** S Thailand, Malaya, Sumatra, Borneo.

ROOST CONSTRUCTION BY BATS IN BORNEO All 4 species of Bornean *Cynopterus* fruit bats are known to modify large palm, *Macaranga* and banana leaves, biting through the main leaf ribs or veins so that the leaf collapses into a cosy tent around the roosting bats. In addition, the tiny fruit bat *Balyonycteris maculata* excavates hollows under epiphytic ferns and gingers to construct a bell-shaped hollow (p. 93). In all these cases the construction is carried out by males to attract a female harem.

***Phoniscus* bat roosts** According to Schulz (1997), in Australia *P. papuenesis* makes an entrance hole in the bottom of a vacant hanging bird's nests before occupation. *Murina florium* has similar habits (Schultz 1998). As yet these are the only proven cases of insectivorous bat-nest manufacture or adaptation. In Borneo similar hanging nests are made by the broadbills (see below) and sunbirds.

CYNOPTERUS fruit bats construct harem tents by biting through the structural veins of large leaves such as those of bananas until they collapse (pp. 87 and 130).

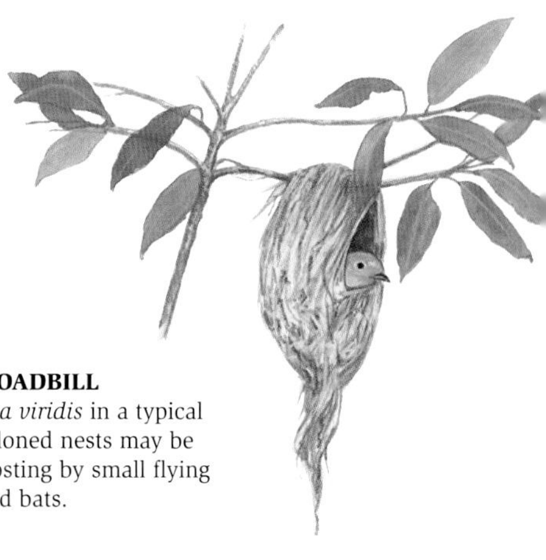

GREEN BROADBILL *Calyptomena viridis* in a typical nest. Abandoned nests may be used for roosting by small flying squirrels and bats.

1

NOTCHED TRAGUS At least 5 species of vespertilionid bat have a notched tragus as illustrated, including the 2 *Phoniscus* bats and 3 *Murina* bats (p. 124), indicating either convergent evolution or a closer taxonomic relationship than currently recognized.

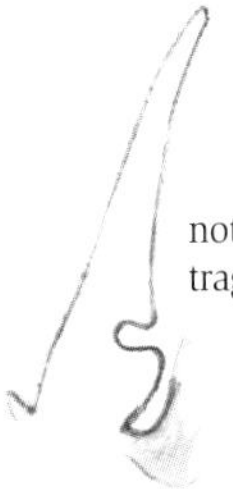

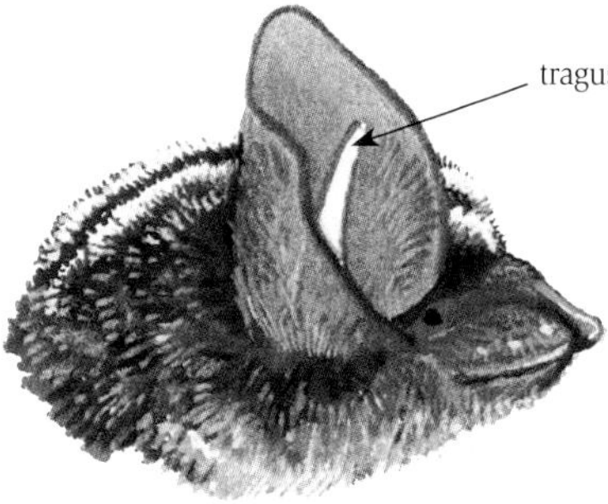

2

Curved Long-spined Spider *Macracantha arcuata* An uncommon large spider that builds an oval 'orb' web along the forest edge in Borneo. The spider is strikingly marked with aposematic danger signals, warning of a nasty taste to bird predators such as spiderhunters.

Toxic bats with gilded fur The most likely *Macracantha* predators are *Phonicus* bats, which sequester the poisons to protect themselves from predators. Based on their aposematic colouration, we can speculate that Borneo's toxic bats include *Kerivoula whiteheadii* (p. 126), *Murina rozendaali*, *M. aenea*, *Harpiocephalus harpia* (p.124) and *Arielulus cuprosus* (p. 118). (See also p. 352 re. Brunei).

VESPER BATS 7, *MYOTIS* 1

World: 100 spp. **SE Asia:** 15 spp. **Borneo:** 10 spp. The largest genus of vesper bats, found worldwide excluding Antarctica. Distinguished from *Kerivoula* bats by the tragus, which is bent forwards, and the shorter fur. In *Kerivoula* bats the tragus points straight up and the ears tend to be more enclosed (funnel shaped) than in *Myotis*. Some *Myotis* have large, often hairy feet and **trawl** for insects and fish over the surfaces of calm reservoirs and lagoons (next page). The wing attachment to the feet, which varies between different *Myotis* species, is a useful distinguishing feature. Some species can only be distinguished by forearm (FA) length, requiring measurement in the hand.

1 PETER'S MYOTIS *Myotis ater* FA 34.7–39.5, HF 8–9, Wt 6.5–8 Scarce

[Black Myotis] [*Selysius ater*] [*Myotis mystacillus nugax*] Widespread in Sabah. In Payne et al. (1985) confused with *M. muricola* and *M. gomantongensis*. **ID:** Feet small. Similar to *M. muricola* but significantly larger and darker on average. Upperparts dark grey-brown fur with blackish bases for a third the length of each hair. Underparts pale grey with brownish tinge on lower belly. Wing membrane attached at bases of toes. **Habits:** Roosts individually or in small colonies in caves. **Taxonomy:** See Francis & Hill (1998). **Range:** The Philippines, Sulawesi to New Guinea. **Borneo race:** *M. a. nugax*. The type is from Bundu Tuhan on Kinabalu.

2 HORSFIELD'S MYOTIS *Myotis horsfieldii* FA 35–38, HF 10–11, Wt 5–7.8 Locally common

[*Leuconoe horsfieldi*] Found in lowland localities in most areas, including cave roosts at Sukau, Madai and Tepadong in Sabah; Niah in Sarawak. **ID:** Upperparts grey-brown; underparts greyer. Ears large. Feet moderately large with wing membrane attached to side of foot at least 1mm from base of toes. **Habits:** Roosts in crevices or bell-holes in caves, usually close to large streams or rivers. Often feeds over large streams or rivers. **Range:** India to S China south to Malaya, Java, Bali, Sulawesi. **Borneo race:** *M. h. horsfieldii*.

3 ASIAN WHISKERED MYOTIS *Myotis muricola* FA 32–35.5, HF 6–7, Wt 4–5.5 Abundant

[*Selysius muricola*] [*Myotis mystacinus*] Very common bat throughout Borneo to 1,500m on Kinabalu.
ID: Feet small with wing membrane attached at bases of toes. Tragus slender, bent forwards and bluntly pointed (p. 99). Distinguished from *M. ater* by smaller size and paler fur. *M. siligorensis* has similar FA length, but is overall much smaller with red-brown fur. *M. ridleyi* has a shorter FA and darker fur. *Pipistrellus javanicus* (p. 118), has a blunt, more rounded tragus. **Habits:** Often roosts in young rolled-up banana leaves (see below). In Thailand roosts in caves. **Taxonomy:** Wiantoro (2011) suggests that the *M. muricola* east and west of Wallace's are different species based on measurements and DNA analysis. **Range:** E India to N Guinea. **Borneo race:** *M. m. muricola*.

4 RIDLEY'S MYOTIS *Myotis ridleyi* FA 27–32, Wt 4–6g Scarce

[*Selysius ridleyi*] Recorded from Sepilok, Tabin and the Witti Range in Sabah. **ID: Feet small** with wing membrane attached to side of foot. Distinguished by measurements – the short FA. **Habits:** Confined to lowland dipterocarp forest. At Tabin Wildlife Resort a colony of *c.* 30 bats has roosted under the first visitor cabin on the hill for many years. At Sepilok also recorded roosting under a forest hut. **Range:** Malaya, Borneo.

5 GOMANTONG MYOTIS *Myotis gomantongensis* FA 40–43, Wt 6.4–8.8 (Not illustrated) Endemic

Split by Francis & Hill (1998) from *M. ater*. Only recorded from Gomantong and Baturong Caves in E Sabah in small numbers. Probably also found in most major cave systems throughout Borneo. **ID:** Feet small. Upperparts dark brown with dark brown tips and blackish bases. Golden-brown patch in centre of belly. **Taxonomy:** See Francis & Hill (1998). **Range:** Endemic to Borneo.

BANANA LEAVES AND ROOSTING BATS

Banana trees are an important source of food (nectar and fruit pulp) for Borneo's fruit bats (pp. 73 and 81). Male ***Cynopterus*** fruit bats gnaw through the midribs of banana leaves so that they collapse, to make a sheltered harem tent (p. 129). Both small insect bats and the tiny Long-tongued Nectar Bat *Macroglossus minimus* roost in the rolled-up young leaves of forest bananas (p. 96). Bats that use banana-leaf roosts include *Kerivoula pellucida* (p. 127), *K. hardwickii* (p. 127), *Myotis muricola* (above) and *Glischropus tylophus* (p. 121). On Bukit Harun (Kayan Mentarang NP), Mohd Azlan Jayasilan et al. (2003) found that local villagers relished *M. muricola* as a delicacy and caught these tiny bats by bending over the top of the furled banana leaf before the bats could escape.

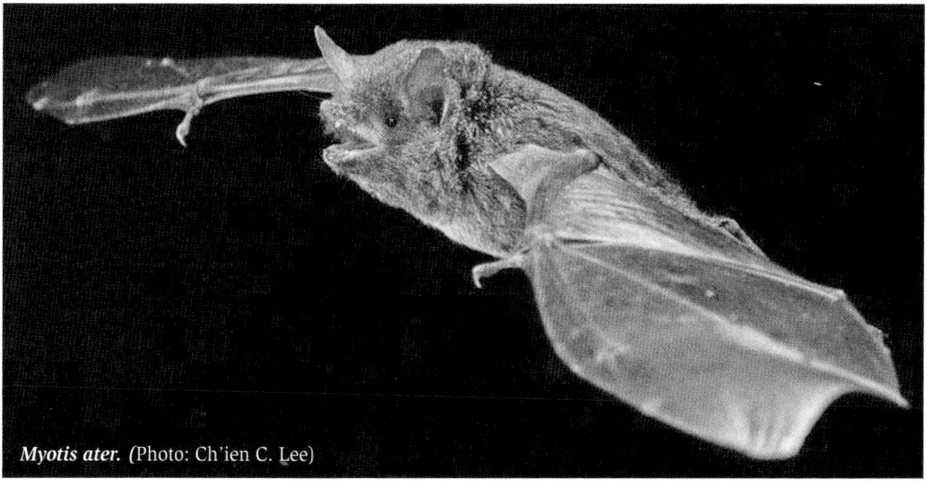

Myotis ater. (Photo: Ch'ien C. Lee)

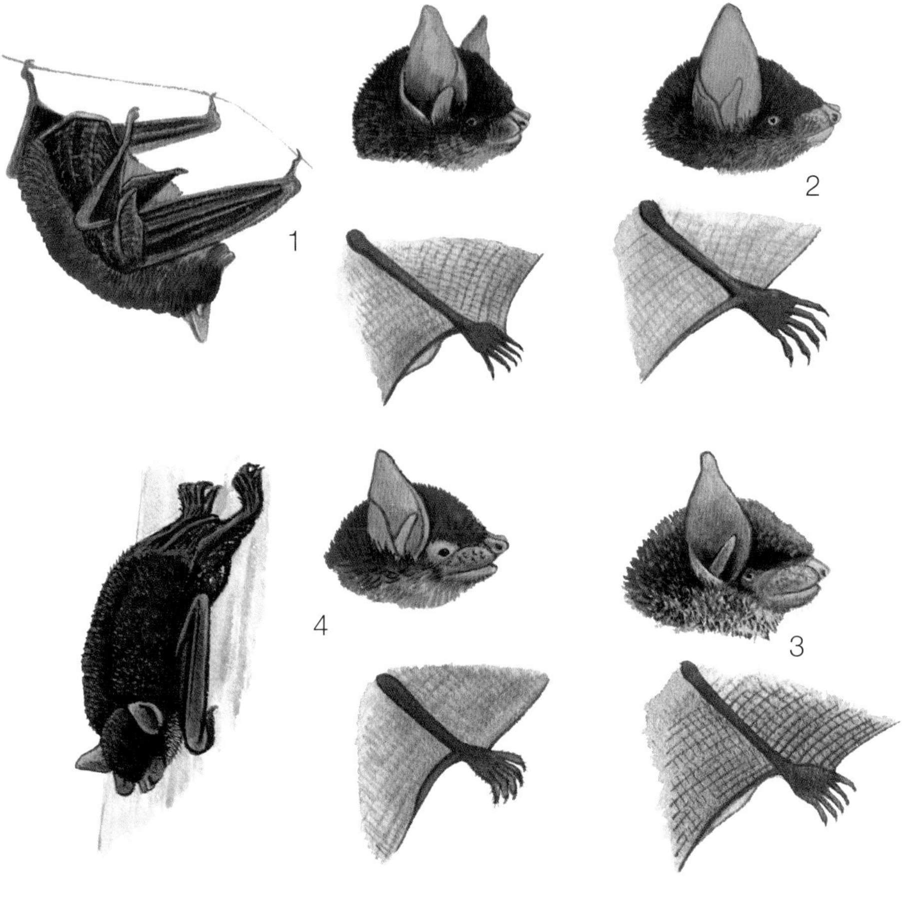

VESPER BATS 8: *MYOTIS* 2

1 GREY LARGE-FOOTED MYOTIS *Myotis adversus* **FA 39–40** **Rare**
[*Leuconoe adversus*] Known from 3 coastal sites, Sandakan Bay (Sabah), Bako (Sarawak) and P Karimata (W Kalimantan). **ID:** Large feet. Wing membrane is attached at ankle. *M. horsfieldi* has wing membrane attached to side of foot at least 1mm from bases of toes. Similar to *M. hasseltii*, which has shorter, more velvety fur. **Habits:** At Bako collected over a small stream near the beach (Khan 2008). In Australia the similar *M. macropus* trawls over lakes, catching fish and insects with its large claws. The fish are detected by surface ripples using sonar. **Taxonomy:** Khan (2008) suggests the Borneo race DNA differs enough to be split. **Range:** Malaya, Java, Sulawesi to Australia. **Borneo race:** *M. a. carimatae.*

2 BORNEAN WHISKERED MYOTIS *Myotis borneoensis* **FA 42–45, Wt 9–13.5** **Rare endemic**
[Large Brown Myotis *M. montivagus*] [*Selysius montivagus*] Rare Bornean endemic with a scattered distribution in the northern half of Borneo. Recorded from the Sepilok and Madai Caves in E Sabah, Grand Perfect Plantation, Bintulu, Sarawak (Wilson 2006), and the Sangkulirang Caves (Suyanto 2007) in E Kalimantan. **ID:** Small feet with wing membrane attached at bases of toes. Distinguished by longer FA. *M. macrotarus*, the only other large *Myotis*, has large feet. **Taxonomy:** Split from *M. montivagus* by Gorfol et al. (2013). **Habits:** Has been trapped flying along streams in tall forest. At Sangkulirang trapped in a cave.

3 HASSELT'S LARGE-FOOTED MYOTIS *Myotis hasseltii* **FA 38–43** **Rare**
[*Leuconoe hasseltii*] Widespread in Sarawak and S Borneo. No records from Sabah and Brunei. **ID:** Large feet with wing membrane attached at ankle. Fur is short and velvety. Fur appears silvery when torchlit in flight at night (Payne et al. 1985). *M. horsfieldii* has wing membrane attached to side of foot. **Habits:** In Malaya forages low over the sea, often near mangrove, frequently dipping its large feet into the water to grab food (Payne et al. 1985). **Range:** Sri Lanka east to Thailand, Malaya, Sumatra, Java. **Borneo race:** *M. h. macellus*.

4 SMALL-TOOTHED MYOTIS *Myotis siligorensis* **FA 30–33.5, Wt 2.3–2.6** **Rare**
[*Selysius siligorensis*] One collected from Ranau (Kinabalu). **ID: Small feet** with wing membrane attached to bases of toes. Tiny bat with a long forearm. Long ears that extend past end of nose when folded forwards. *M. ridieyi* has a shorter forearm but is larger and heavier. **Habits:** Roosts in cracks in rocks. **Range:** Nepal through southern China, south to Malaya, Borneo.

5 PALLID LARGE-FOOTED MYOTIS *Myotis macrotarsus* **FA 45–49, Wt 12–16** **Rare**
[*Leuconoe macrotarsus*] Caught roosting in caves on P Balembangan, at Madai, and near Semporna in Sabah; S Baram in Sarawak. **ID: Feet large** with wing attached at ankle. Wing membranes pale pinkish-grey. **Habits:** Roosts in small numbers in coastal caves. Trawls for fish and insects over calm waters. **Range:** The Philippines. **Borneo race:** *M. m. saba*.

CARNIVOROUS BATS OF BORNEO

Megaderma spasma (p. 111)	Recorded feeding on birds, small mammals and other bats
Hipposideros diadema (p. 107)	In Australia feeds on swiftlets in caves and small forest birds
Rousettus spinalatus (p. 91)	Alleged to feed on swiftlets and their nests in caves
Hesperptenus tomesi (p. 123)	Probably feeds on frogs along streams but no proof as yet

FISHING BATS OF BORNEO Borneo is a centre of diversity for fishing bats, with a possible 5 or more species as listed below. Note that freshwater rivers are breeding grounds for many insects, so bats trawling over rivers could be feeding on insects or fish, whilst bats trawling over the sea or saltwater lagoons are most likely to be catching fish.

Myotis adversus	Malaya to N Guinea	Campbell (2011)
Myotis horsfieldii	India to Sulawesi	Campbell (2011)
Myotis macrotarsus	Philippines, Borneo	Campbell (2011)
Myotis hasseltii	Sri Lanka to Java	Campbell (2011)
Hypsugo vordermanii	Borneo, Biliton	Conjecture

Campbell (2011) lists 16 world species of fishing bat with long legs and large feet that trawl for insects and fish over rivers and calm seas. Fishing bats are found in most of the world, including Europe (*Myotis capaccinii*), the Americas (5 species), Japan (*M. dactylus*) and Australia (*M. macropus*).

1
1
2
3
4
5

MOLOSSIDAE 1, WRINKLE-LIPPED BATS

1 FREE-TAILED BAT *Mops mops* **FA 43–46 Wt 28–35g** **Rare**

[*Tadarida mops*] Two specimens reported from an unspecified location in Sarawak (Payne et al. 1985). **ID:** Similar to *T. plicata* but with a longer forearm. Both species have heavily wrinkled upper lips, believed to be an adaption to deal with the 'spiky' legs of their beetle prey. Skulls of museum specimens are much heavier than those of *T. plicata*. **Habits:** In Malaya forages over the forest canopy and rivers, and roosts in tree hollows, often with *Cheiromeles torquatus*. **Range:** Malaya, Sumatra, Borneo.

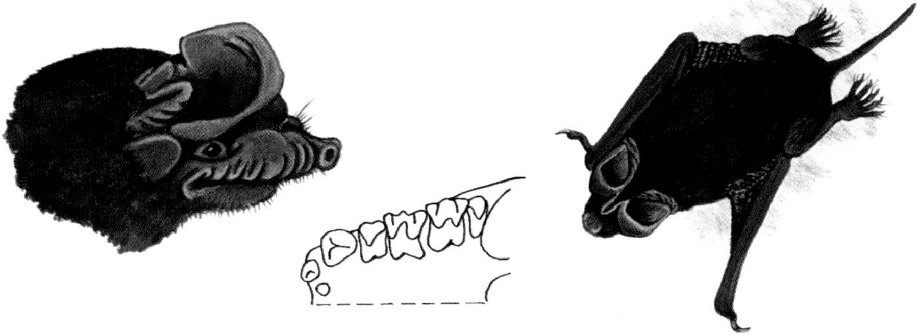

2 WRINKLE-LIPPED BAT *Tadarida plicata* **FA 40–43.5, Wt 10.5–18g** **Locally abundant**

[Guano Bat] [*Chaerephon plicata*] The most common bat of large caves, with colonies of several millions at Madai and Gomantong in Sabah, and Mulu in Sarawak. Has been collected near Kuching. **ID:** Similar *T. mops* is slightly larger with a much more massive skull. **Habits:** At the Bat Observatory Mulu (p. 372), a continuous stream of Wrinkle-lipped Bats emerges from holes in the limestone cliffs before dusk in smoke-like wisps, first hugging the forest canopy, then spiralling up to gain height. Not all the bats emerge each evening, and when rain is expected no bats may emerge. **Diet:** In Thailand, Leelaipaibul et al. (2005) found that *T. plicata* is a generalist forager on a wide range of insects, including migrant insects that fly at high altitude. The Khao Chong Pran Cave houses 2.6 million bats and is surrounded by rice fields. A quarter of the diet comprised *Sogatella* plant hoppers (Homoptera), which are a serious pest of the local rice fields. **Range:** Sri Lanka to S China, SE Asia, the Philippines, Sumatra, Java. **Borneo race:** *T. p. plicata*.

THE MYSTERY OF THE WRINKLE-LIPPED BAT AT NIAH

The Wrinkle-lipped Bat is the most common bat in Borneo's largest caves, with the Mulu and Gomantong populations estimated at several millions. The bones of Wrinkle-lipped Bats are the most common bat bones found in archaeological digs at Niah between 40,000 YBP and 1,280 YBP, after which they vanish. Wrinkle-lipped Bats are not found at Niah today. There is no evidence of a change in forest cover *c.* 1,280 YBP, so the collapse of the Niah population is probably due to excessive unsustainable hunting by humans for food. Today large bats are under severe hunting pressure throughout Sarawak and Kalimantan (pp. 84, 137 and 366).

Wallace's Hawk Eagle catching Wrinkle-lipped Bats at the Gomantong Caves (Photo: Cede Prudente).

BAT HAWK *Machaeramphus alcinus* Bat-roost caves at Niah, Mulu (Sarawak) and Gomantong (Sabah) are some of the best places in Borneo to look for large birds of prey, which wait near cave entrances for bats to emerge at dusk. Eagles and falcons often catch bats, but only the specialist Bat Hawk continues to hunt after dusk has fallen on moonlit nights. During the day Bat Hawks often roost on giant emergent *Koompasia* trees near the caves. *Koompasia* have pale bark and due to their height are easy to see at night above the canopy. It is believed that the pale bark has evolved to attract nesting nomadic Giant Honey Bees *Apis dorsata*, which also often forage for nectar at night. The bees defend *Koompasia* against leaf-eating langurs (p. 66).

MOLOSSIDAE 2: NAKED BAT

NAKED BAT *Cheiromeles torquatus* **FA 74–86, Wt 150–200** **Scarce**

[Bull Dog Bat] Recorded from scattered localities in the north and west, including P Banggi, Sandakan, Tabin and Tenom in Sabah, BSB in Brunei, Niah and the Mulu Caves. In caves near Kuching previously common but now absent (Hall et al. 2002). At Lanjak Entimau in Sarawak, reported as abundant by Han (2000), but the cave colony had vanished 10 years later (Roberta et al. 2010). At Mulu a small colony in the Deer Cave can be found from the bat earwigs *Arixenia easau* that forage on the cave floor underneath the roost. **ID:** Unmistakable. The world's heaviest insectivorous bat. A large 'naked bat' covered with very short hair so looks hairless. In flight recognized by large size, strong flight with shallow wingbeats and the audible clicking of its sonar as it searches for insects. Look out also for the large ears and the large, exposed tail. **Scent gland:** Both sexes have a scent gland in a pocket (gular pouch) under the throat that secretes a smelly oil described by Hose 'like the smell of burnt leather', and by Leong (2009) as 'a repulsive stench comparable to stale socks drenched in engine oil. While handling the bats, the oily exudate was smeared onto the fingers of the author, and the smell lingered for days, despite numerous washings.' The oil stops the skin drying out in flight. **Habits:** In Malaya roosts in large caves, old buildings or hollow trees, sometimes associated with *Mops mops* in large colonies (Kingston et al. 2009). Feeds in open areas above the canopy or over clearings and rivers. Naked Bats have a pouch under the armpit (axillary) where the wing-tip is tucked when roosting, climbing or feeding on the ground. **Breeding:** Nipples of female bats are in the pouch. Females produce a single young once a year, which is left behind at the roost whilst the females forage. **Diet:** Most often feeds above the canopy, but also feeds on the ground when food is abundant, for example on swarming flying ants or termites. At Mulu recorded foraging on the ground and on railings under strong lamps, which attract moths and other large insects. As this bat cannot take off from the ground it crawls backwards *c.* 2m up a nearby tree to take off. **Range:** S Thailand, Malaya, Palawan, Sumatra, Java. **Borneo race:** *C. t. torquatus*.

MUTUALISTIC ASSOCIATION WITH THE BAT EARWIG *ARIXENIA ESAU* This earwig was first described in 1909 from an individual found in the pouch of a Naked Bat that had been collected by Charles Hose (p. 242). When Lord Medway worked at the Niah Caves in 1957 for the Sarawak Museum, he observed that the earwigs were 'swarming on the bats themselves and the floors of caves, where they fed on guano, insect remains and even parasitized a Tenebrionid beetle with their heads under the elytrae, feeding on it while it still lived. Insects from the cave floor behave in the same way on a human hand. Clinging with their sharp curved claws, hard to shake off, they move jerkily around with near hysterical agitation; it is a very ticklish feeling. All ignored the skin on my palms, some found my metal watch strap an impassible barrier, and several began to feed on the soft sweaty skin between and on the back of my fingers. In feeding they pressed their mandibles to the skin, and, opening and closing them rapidly and continuously, scraped the skin surface and moved steadily forward. The direction of the movement was always upwards, and changed at once if the hand was turned. The sensation was not painful, but was very irritating – like the gentle beginning of a subtle torture – and since each "bite" was applied to a fresh place, would never break the skin, but would clearly scrape the surface clean.' (Medway 1958).

Wrinkle-lipped Bat *Tadarida plicata*, the most common Borneo cave bat (p. 134). By contrast, the Naked Bat, also Molossidae, is rare. It resembles *T. plicata* in flight but is twice the width and ten times the weight.

Illustration: Thomas Hardwicke (1830)

Naked Bat *Cheiromeles torquatus*
Samarakan (Batang Ai), Sarawak. (Photo: Ch'ien C. Lee)

DECLINE OF THE NAKED BAT Borneo's largest insectivorous bat is considered a tasty meal by many locals and there is archaeological evidence from the Niah Caves (Stimpson 2010) that this bat has been heavily hunted for tens of thousands of years. Medway (1958) estimated a population of 18,000 Naked Bats at Niah, which is now reduced to under a 1,000 (Hall et al. 2002). Medway describes how this bat is being hunted to extinction in most Sarawak and Kalimantan caves.
'The flesh is good eating, succulent and gamey. The local Sea Dayaks, relative newcomers to the district, without cave rights, relish the bats' flesh and sometimes collect them, using lamps or fires. By one method a bright light is put against the rock face at night on the bats' line of return flight from mouth to roost; some are attracted and stunned on collision with the rock. I accidentally caught four this way, at Lobang Tulang on an evening when 8,000 Naked Bats went out by this mouth. The other method employs a bonfire under the roost late at night, when all have returned. This, it is said, also attracts the bats which can be caught by sackfuls.' (adapted from Medway 1958).

SHREWS

SORICIDAE **World:** 385 spp. **Borneo:** 8 spp. Shrews are small, highly active, nocturnal, terrestrial insectivores. For mammal surveys shrews can be caught with pit-fall traps, made from half a plastic bottle with the wide end level with the ground. Most shrews have toxic flesh and dead shrews may be found on forest paths early in the morning dropped by a predator. Shrews probably sequester toxins from toxic insects (p. 124). Dead shrews should either be frozen or preserved in strong alcohol like brandy and taken to a museum along with a note giving your name, address, date, locality, habitat and altitude. Research by Esslytn and Setiawan indicates that cryptic shrews are waiting to be discovered in Borneo. See p. 387 re *Crocidura malayana*.

1 HOSE'S PIGMY SHREW *Suncus hosei* **HB 53, T 28 (48–56% of HB), Wt 2 g** **Scarce endemic**
[Savi's Pigmy Shrew] Locally common in virgin lowland dipterocarp forest to 800m in the Crocker Range (UKMS). Records include Sepilok, Belalong, Mulu and Lanjak Entimau. Type collected by Hose in forest on the Baram River (p. 242). **ID:** Tiny shrew with a relatively short tail. The world's smallest mammal, excluding bats. **Taxonomy:** Split by Hutterer (Wilson & Reeder 2005) from Savi's Pigmy Shrew common in Asia.

2 BLACK SHREW *Suncus ater* **HB 75, T 57 (76% of HB), Wt ?** **Rare Kinabalu endemic**
Collected once at Kiau Gap (Lumu-lumu), *c.* 1,700m asl, halfway along the road from Kinabalu Park headquarters to Timpohon Gate. **ID:** Small with dark, almost black upperparts. Tail has long dark hairs on tip. See teeth diagram. **Habits:** Unknown.

3 HOUSE SHREW *Suncus murinus* **HB 120, T 66 (50–64% of HB), Wt 23–147g** **Locally common**
[Indian Musk Shrew] Invasive species, locally common near houses and coastal villages throughout Borneo. **ID:** Tail narrows in size from base to end. Has a musk gland on flanks as illustrated. Males heavier than females. **Habits:** Originated in India and spread by boat around the shores of the Indian and Pacific Oceans. On P Maratua (E Kalimantan), locals claim that it arrived recently on a boat from Palu in Sulawesi and is now abundant at Kg Boheybukut. In Mauritius caused the extinction of rare lizards and insects on small islands. A favoured food was the invasive Giant African Snail *Achatina fulica*, also common in Borneo (Varnham et al. 2000). **Call:** Contact call is a very high-pitched squeak. **Range:** Many races from Africa to Pacific Islands.

4 BORNEAN SHREW *Crocidura foetida* **HB 82, T 77 (54–90% of HB), Wt ?** **Locally common endemic**
The most common lowland shrew throughout Borneo. On Kinabalu found in open areas and secondary forest to 1,500m, where it is replaced by the Kinabalu Shrew. **ID:** Body hair shorter than 4mm. See teeth diagram. **Habits:** Both this and the Kinabalu Shrew prefer similar open habitat but at different altitudes. **Taxonomy:** Split from SE Asian White-toothed Shrew *C. fuliginosa* by Ruedi (1995).

5 KINABALU SHREW *Crocidura baluensis* **HB 82,T 77 (54–90% of HB),Wt ?** **Locally common endemic**
Locally common in cloud forest on Kinabalu from the park headquarters to the tree line on Kinabalu. Also found in grassland in the Kelabit Highlands above 1,000m. **ID:** Body hair longer than 5mm. See teeth diagram. **Taxonomy:** Split from the SE Asian White-toothed Shrew *C. fuliginosa* by Corbet & Hill (1992).

6 SUNDA SHREW *Crocidura monticola* **HB 62, T 37, Wt 2.5g** **Rare**
Uncommon shrew of montane forest recorded from Kinabalu (1,500m), Gng Mulu and the Kelabit Highlands and Karangan (E Kalimantan). **ID:** Very small. Body entirely grey-brown. Tail has long pale hairs on first 1cm. **Range:** Sumatra, Java, Borneo.

7 BORNEAN WATER SHREW *Chimarrogale phaeura* **HB 100, T 82 (*c.* 82% of HB), Wt ?** **Endemic**
Scarce endemic found near mountain streams on Kinabalu at 460–1,700m and on Gng Trus Madi. Found in secondary forest at Kg Tumbalang, Kinabalu (Wells 2005). **ID:** Sides of feet covered with distinctive short, stiff hairs, whilst back has silver guard hairs. No external ears, only a hole in fur. **Taxonomy:** In Payne (1985) listed as a race of the Himalayan Water Shrew *C. himalayica* widespread on the Asian mainland, but see Hutterer, in Wilson & Reeder (2005).

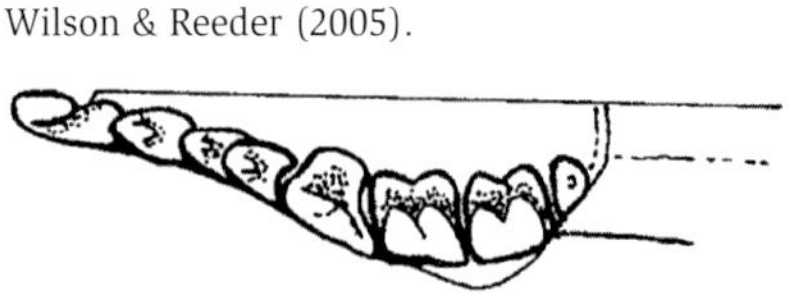

All *Crocidura* have 8 teeth in each upper row.

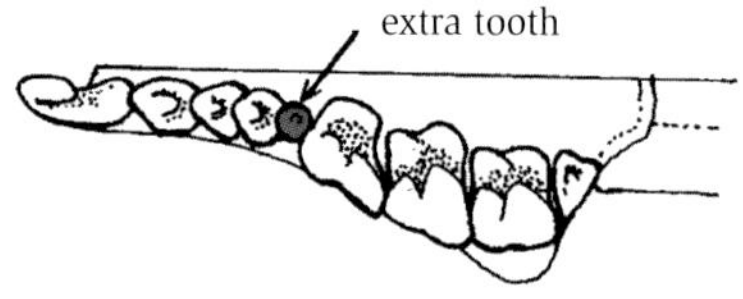

All *Suncus* have 9 teeth in each upper row.

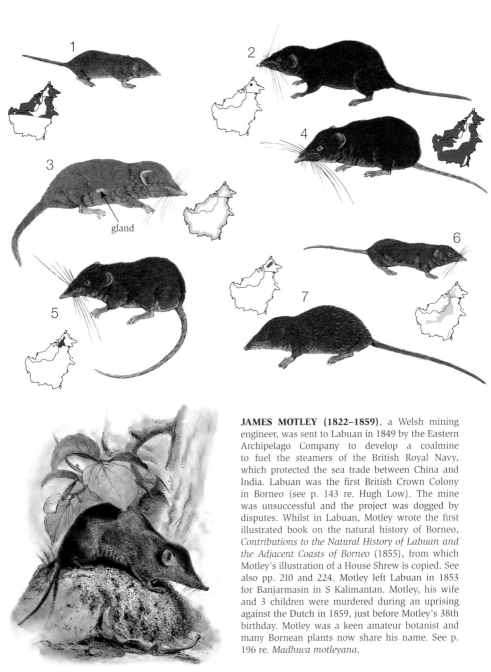

JAMES MOTLEY (1822–1859), a Welsh mining engineer, was sent to Labuan in 1849 by the Eastern Archipelago Company to develop a coalmine to fuel the steamers of the British Royal Navy, which protected the sea trade between China and India. Labuan was the first British Crown Colony in Borneo (see p. 143 re. Hugh Low). The mine was unsuccessful and the project was dogged by disputes. Whilst in Labuan, Motley wrote the first illustrated book on the natural history of Borneo, *Contributions to the Natural History of Labuan and the Adjacent Coasts of Borneo* (1855), from which Motley's illustration of a House Shrew is copied. See also pp. 210 and 224. Motley left Labuan in 1853 for Banjarmasin in S Kalimantan. Motley, his wife and 3 children were murdered during an uprising against the Dutch in 1859, just before Motley's 38th birthday. Motley was a keen amateur botanist and many Bornean plants now share his name. See p. 196 re. *Madhuca motleyana*.

House Shrew on Labuan 'Very common near streams in the jungle and often disturbed during day time. The specimen shown is a female, and was found with its male and young among rotten wood and dead leaves. When caught it bit savagely' (Motley 1855).

MOONRAT AND HYLOMYS

ERINACEIDAE **World** 43 spp. **Borneo** 2 spp. The Erinaceidae are primitive insectivores most closely related to shrews but generally larger. They include 16 spp of hedgehog found from Europe to Asia, but not Borneo.

MOONRAT *Echinosorex gymnurus* **HB 358, T 250, Wt 985** **Locally common**

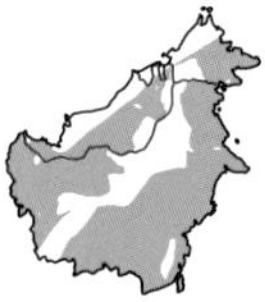

Malay: Haji Bulan or Tikus Bulan [Gymnure] Locally common, often in pairs foraging at night along small, muddy streams and damp areas in lowland primary and logged forest. There are no records for Kinabalu or for the peat-swamp forests in Sarawak. **ID:** Looks like a large white rat and has a terrible smell. Usually unafraid. Opens mouth in a snarl if it feels threatened. **Habits:** Nocturnal and terrestrial. Sleeps in burrows during the day. 'In captivity it is fond of its bathtub and gets right into it' (Banks 1931). **Diet:** In captivity favours frogs, fish and cockroaches (Banks 1931). In the wild prefers worms (Lim 1967). **Range:** S Thailand, Malaya, Sumatra, Borneo. **Borneo races** 1. *E. g. albus* E and S Borneo, including the Kelabit Highlands. 2. *E. g. candidus* in W Borneo from P. Labuan south to Kuching, with more black hairs in fur. One camera-trapped at Sabangau was all dark except for white throat and neck (Susan Cheyne, pers. comm.).

HYLOMYS *Hylomys suillus* **HB 130, T 22, Wt 60** **Locally common in mountains**

[Lesser Gymnure] Locally common in mountain mossy cloud forest on Kinabalu at 1,000–3,400m (Panar Laban) south to the Kelabit Highlands in NE Sarawak. In Malaya also found at lower altitudes in hill forest. **ID:** Note very short, distinctive tail. **Habits:** Often active during the day. Makes a sheltered nest out of leaves under rocks or logs. At Mesilau commonly forages in grassy banks and flowerbeds around the buildings. The normal habitat is the hollows covered in moss under tree roots in montane mossy forest (cloud forest) that first establishes between 900–1,000m on Kinabalu. **Range:** SW China south to SE Asia, Sumatra, Java, Borneo. **Borneo** *H. s. dorsalis.* Has indistinct darker dorsal stripe along back, missing in races on Asian continent.

THE NAMPUNGHER 'Today (9 February 1888), I obtained a curious insectivore – a species of Shrew in the bamboo traps. I have several times seen this little animal running about in the daytime, but up till now have failed to secure it. Its scientific name is *Hylomys suillus*. This animal looks more like a tiny pig than anything; its caudal appendage is the merest apology for a tail. It searches for its food amongst the roots and rocks. The Dusuns, besides eating this animal, are very amused at its want of tail, always laughing at the "Nampungher" and making the same remark, "Esok tikiu!" i. e. without a tail.' (Whitehead 1893, *The Exploration of Kinabalu*).

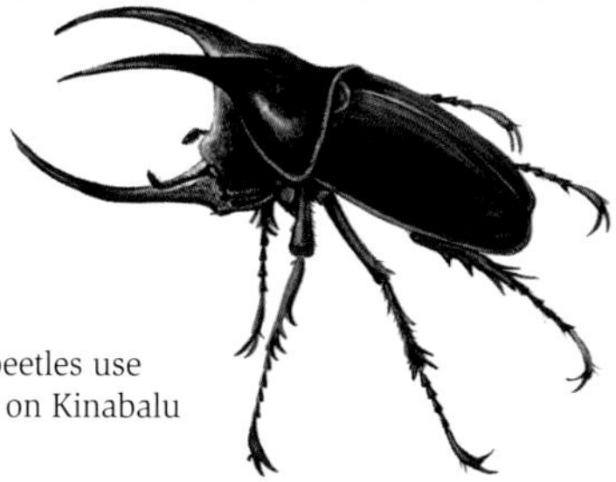

MALE ATLAS BEETLES *Chalcosoma moellenkampi* These beetles use their giant horns to fight rival males. Atlas Beetles are common on Kinabalu in the same habitat as *Hylomis.*

MAMMALS OF MOSSY CLOUD FOREST ON KINABALU Cloud forest is the stunted forest with moss covering the ground that on Kinabalu occurs at 900–3,300m. Whitehead's illustration opposite of an *Hylomis* shows the animal in characteristic cloud-forest habitat where moss covers the extended roots of trees, creating an extra storey to the forest floor, and providing numerous hiding and foraging niches for small rats, squirrels, treeshrews and shrews. On Kinabalu, typical ground mammals confined to mossy cloud forest include the Mountain Treeshrew (p. 146), Mountain Ground Squirrel (p. 212), and Hylomys. Typical cloud-forest rats include *Maxomys baeodon* (p. 236), *Sundamys infraluteus* and *Maxomys alticola* (p. 230). The only predator small and thin enough to follow its prey into its burrows under the moss is the Malay Weasel, which is relatively common in cloud forest to 2,000m (p. 252).

KINABATANGAN MOONRAT 'Being short of supplies we set one of the men to make a "pagar", or hedge formed of branches and leaves, with gaps at intervals, each gap being supplied with a noose or "jerat". These traps were visited twice daily, and sometimes yielded us a mousedeer, a partridge or a lovely fire-back pheasant; but, more often it was a civet cat, a huge monitor lizard or a sort of skunk that was trapped. Amongst other curious creatures caught in the traps was a Moonrat, a little white creature with a pig-like face and a bare, rat-like tail. I believe no specimen of this animal has ever been imported into England, for the reason that the smell they emit is insufferable, and hangs about for such a long time. It is so overpowering, that I have been once or twice awakened from a sound sleep owing to one of these animals having passed below the house.' (condensed from Ada Pryer 1894, describing an expedition up the Kinabatangan River in the 1880s.

Illustration by John Whitehead from *The Exploration of Kinabalu* (1893)

TUPAIIDAE **World** 18 spp. **Borneo** 9 spp., of which 7 are endemic, making Borneo the world centre of treeshrew diversity. The notes below refer to all tree shrews except the Pen-Tailed which has different habits.
Tupai, the Malay name, refers to both squirrels and treeshrews which look similar. However, the 2 groups are unrelated. Squirrels are rodents most closely related to rats, whilst treeshrews are most closely related to primates, bats and colugos.
ID Distinguished from squirrels by pale shoulder stripe, longer nose and more terrestrial (ground loving) habits. Alarmed treeshrews flick their tails upwards from the horizontal, whilst most squirrels flick their tails backwards from a curled position over the back (Emmons 2000).
Diet: Treeshrew teeth lack the very sharp front incisors of rodents, so treeshrews eat soft fruit and insects rather than gnawing on hard nuts as do squirrels and rats. The arboreal Lesser Treeshrew is the most frugivorous. Fruit fibre is spat out in wads as in fruit bats. Adult sexes are the same size, indicating competition for food.
Recalcitrant (soft) and orthodox (hard) seeds Seed-eating ground squirrels are rare in the Borneo lowlands, where they are replaced by abundant treeshrews that eat soft fruit such as figs. In dryer or colder areas on the Asian continent (and above 2000m on Kinabalu) where hard seeds predominate, ground squirrels outnumber treeshrews (pp. 212, 234).
Calls Treeshrews' distinctive alarm calls can be used for identification (Emmons 2000).
Breeding Treeshrews are unique among mammals in having what is known as an absentee maternal care system. 'Treeshrews normally sleep individually in loose nests of plant material in holes in the ground, tree hollows or old bird's nests. However before giving birth the female constructs a separate nest where the young are born. The mother then visits the nest only once every 2 days for a few minutes in order to feed the young with her own milk. Apart from these rare visits the mother goes nowhere near the nest presumably to avoid alerting predators. Once the young emerge from the nest the mother becomes a normal attentive mother helping the youngsters look for food of their own. The male appears to play no part in looking after the youngsters even though the male and female territories usually overlap and they are often seen together.' (Emmons 2000).
Mimicry The predatory Collared Mongoose with a shoulder stripe may mimic harmless treeshrews (p. 272). The information on treeshrews in this guide is largely derived from an 18-month study by Louise H. Emmons (Emmons 2000) at Poring and Danum, and Emmon's split of *Tupaia glis* is followed (p. 145).

PTILOCERIDAE

PEN-TAILED TREESHREW *Ptilocercus lowii* **HB 140, T 160, Wt 50** **Scarce**

[Low's Treeshrew, Feather-tailed Treeshrew] Uncommon, with a relict distribution. Recent records from Poring, Kinabalu (Wells), south to Kuching and Lanjak Entimau, but Emmons found it common at Danum. Recorded E Kalimantan at Bukit Soeharto (Yasuma) and Sg Wain in freshwater-swamp forest (Pak Agusdin). **ID:** 'The only nocturnal treeshrew. Most mammals' eyes shine red or orange in reflected light at night but Pen–tailed Treeshrew eyes reflect bright silver. The stunningly brilliant white eyeshine of *P. lowii* is the brightest I have observed in any mammal. Once recognised this brilliant eyeshine can readily be identified from a distance of tens of metres so that these "rare" animals were found instead to be common' (Emmons referring to Danum). Has a musky, shrew-like ordure (Davis 1962). **Habits:** Nocturnal and arboreal. Can run down tree trunks head-first. Lives in communal family nests in tree holes and spends the night actively foraging for insects on vertical tree trunks from the base to the canopy. **Diet:** In Malaya, Wiens (2008) found that Pen-tails spent long periods feeding on alcoholic palm nectar, but did not seem to suffer any negative effects from the alcohol (p. 52). In captivity Lim (1967) found that Pen-tails ate only insects and meat, not fruit. **Call:** Chirps with bird-like calls (Emmons 2000). **Taxonomy** An aberrant treeshrew recently reclassified into its own family, Ptilocercidae, with one species, in the order Scandentia (treeshrews). **Range:** S Thailand, Malaya, Sumatra, Bangka, Borneo including Labuan and Sirhassen (Serasan, South Natunas).

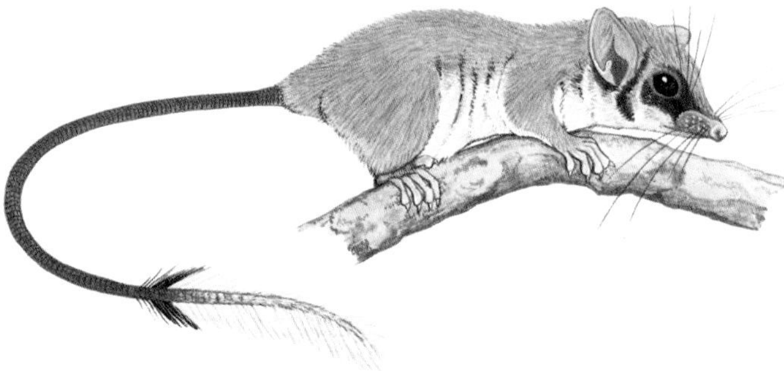

Illustration by Joseph Wolf of the type specimen of *Ptilocercus lowii* collected in Rajah James Brooke's bungalow on the bank of the Sarawak River at Kuching, and named by the zoologist J. E. Gray (1848) of the British Museum in honour of Hugh Low.

Pen-tailed Treeshrew sipping alcoholic nectar from a *Eugeissona* palm flower. Both the treeshrew and *Eugeissona* palms are locally common at Matang near Kuching (p. 52, palms, and p. 360, Matang).

HUGH LOW 1824–1905 At the age of 19, in 1844, Hugh Low was sent by his father, the owner of a plant nursery in Hackney, East London, to Singapore to collect living orchid plants for sale in London. In Singapore, James Brooke, the Rajah of Sarawak, invited Low to stay for two years in Kuching, described by Low in *Sarawak Notes During a Residence in that Country with H.H. the Rajah Brooke* (1848). Low's book contained the first list of Bornean mammals, including both wild dog and tapir. In 1848 Low was appointed colonial secretary of Labuan island, recently ceded to the British government by the Sultan of Brunei. In 1851 and twice in 1858, Low made the first botanical explorations of Kinabalu, detailed in Spencer St John's book (1863) *Life in the Forests of the Far East*. The two most significant geologic features of Kinabalu, Low's Peak (highest point) and Low's Gully are named after Low (p. 332). In addition, two Bornean mammals, *P. lowii* and *Sundasciurus lowii* (p. 200), carry Low's name. Low is best known for new plant discoveries, especially orchids and *Nepenthes* pitcher plants (p. 70). Low left Labuan in 1877, becoming the British Resident of Perak in West Malaysia for 12 years.

LESSER, SLENDER AND PLAIN TREESHREWS

1 LESSER TREESHREW *Tupaia minor* HB 128, T 160, Wt 51 — Common

Common resident of lowland primary and peat-swamp forest throughout Borneo. The most arboreal of the treeshrews, which means that it is seen more often than other treeshrews, although ground trapping catches more terrestrial treeshrews. See chart opposite. **ID:** By habits. Hunts for insects among lianas and leaf bunches in the middle storey of the forest and feeds on figs in the canopy. **Habits:** At Poring, Emmons found that Lesser Treeshrew often foraged for insects in association with Yellow-bellied Bulbul and Racket-tailed Drongo, which waited nearby to catch insects flushed by the activities of the treeshrew (see below). The population crashes immediately after logging, but recovers in vine-covered logged forest. *T. minor* is unable to survive in tree plantations. **Alarm call:** Soft peeping sound when slightly alarmed and loud chatter when strongly alarmed. **Range:** S Thailand, Malaya, Sumatra. **Borneo races** 1. *T. m. caedis*, NE Borneo (illustrated); 2. *T. m. minor* elsewhere, with a more prominent shoulder-stripe.

2 SLENDER TREESHREW *Tupaia gracilis* HB 141, T 180, Wt 72 — Scarce endemic

Scarce terrestrial resident of lowland and hilly primary and logged forest throughout most of lowland Borneo, but absent from SE Kalimantan. Least common of the Bornean treeshrews in Sabah (Wells 2005), with the largest home range. Survives in logged forest, but absent from tree plantations (Stuebing & Gassis 1989).
ID: Easily confused with Lesser Treeshrew but slimmer. 'This treeshrew is rarely found higher than 1.5m off the ground whilst Lesser spends most time above 1.5m. Most purported sightings of *T. gracilis* on the ground are likely to be cases of mistaken identity and to be Lesser Treeshrew instead' (Emmons 2000). **Alarm call:** Long, soft whines. **Diet:** Prefers caterpillars (butterfly and moth larvae) gleaned from the ground and the undersurfaces of leaves on low shrubs. Also eats crickets, cockroaches and ants. **Borneo races** 1. *T. g. gracilis*. Mainland Borneo (see map). 2. *T. edarata*, P Karimata only.

3 PLAIN TREESHREW *Tupaia longipes* HB 200, T 210, Wt 166 — Common endemic

[Common Treeshrew *T. glis* in Payne (1985), Bornean Treeshrew] From trapping records the second most common treeshrew in Sabah after *T. tana* (p. 150). Equally common in virgin and logged forest, and population increases in tree plantations with a dense understorey (Stuebing & Gassis 1989). Not found in cloud forest above 900m. **ID:** See p. 148. Size similar to Large Treeshrew but no back stripes. 'One of the most nervous and wary treeshrews difficult to see for more than fleeting moments. Rarely seen off the ground.' (Emmons 2000). **Alarm call:** Long, rasping whines or hoarse squawks. **Habits:** Strictly terrestrial. Forages on the ground and nests in holes in the ground. Preferred diet is ants and termites, and thrives in most habitats as ant populations do not fall in plantations. **Taxonomy:** Split from Malayan *T. glis* by Emmons (2000). **Borneo races** 1. *T. l. longipes*. Northern half of Borneo south to Sg Rajang and Sg Kayan. 2. *T. g. salatana*. Southern half of Borneo.

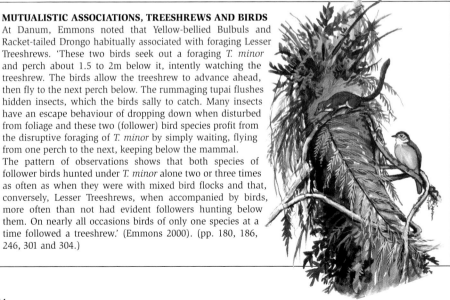

MUTUALISTIC ASSOCIATIONS, TREESHREWS AND BIRDS

At Danum, Emmons noted that Yellow-bellied Bulbuls and Racket-tailed Drongo habitually associated with foraging Lesser Treeshrews. 'These two birds seek out a foraging *T. minor* and perch about 1.5 to 2m below it, intently watching the treeshrew. The birds allow the treeshrew to advance ahead, then fly to the next perch below. The rummaging tupai flushes hidden insects, which the birds sally to catch. Many insects have an escape behaviour of dropping down when disturbed from foliage and these two (follower) bird species profit from the disruptive foraging of *T. minor* by simply waiting, flying from one perch to the next, keeping below the mammal.
The pattern of observations shows that both species of follower birds hunted under *T. minor* alone two or three times as often as when they were with mixed bird flocks and that, conversely, Lesser Treeshrews, when accompanied by birds, more often than not had evident followers hunting below them. On nearly all occasions birds of only one species at a time followed a treeshrew.' (Emmons 2000). (pp. 180, 186, 246, 301 and 304.)

COMPARATIVE ABUNDANCE OF TREESHREWS IN SABAH

Based on 40,552 trap days (Wells 2005). In primary (PF) and logged forest (LF)

Treeshrew species	Total	PF: 22,753 Trap Days	LF: 17,800 Trap Days	Home Range (Emmons)	Foraging (Emmons)
Pen-tailed, *P. lowii*	2	1	1	6.4ha	Tree trunks
Slender, *T. gracilis*	24	14	10	1.5ha	Shrubs, ground
Lesser, *T. minor*	76	28	48	9.1ha	Vines, trees
Plain, *T. longipes*	117	80	37	6.9ha	Ground
Large, *T. tana*	173	49	124	3.3ha	Digs ground
TOTALS	**392**	**172**	**220**		

MOUNTAIN, STRIPED AND SMOOTH-TAILED TREESHREWS

1 MOUNTAIN TREESHREW *Tupaia montana* **HB 200, T 178, Wt 148 Common montane endemic**
Abundant at ground level in the central chain of mountains from Kinabalu south to Gng Pueh in SW Sarawak. On Kinabalu found from about 900m to 3,170m (Paka Cave), but more common lower down, whilst Mt. Ground Squirrel increases with altitude to the tree line (p. 212). **ID:** Distinguished from Mt. Ground Squirrel by more pointed nose, faint shoulder-stripe and longer, less bushy tail. **Race:** *T. m. montana* (Sarawak mountains) has a faint dorsal stripe. **Alarm call:** Squawking sound. **Habits:** Forages among mossy logs and fallen branches to 1.5m from the ground, similar to Mt Ground Squirrel. **Diet:** Omnivorous. Eats more insects then Mt. Ground Squirrel, which prefers nuts and worms. Both species raid dustbins on Kinabalu. ***Nepenthes* pitcher plants:** On Kinabalu termites are not found above 1,900m (Gathorne Hardy 2002) and ants not above 2,300m (Bruhl et al. 1999); instead 3 species of large montane pitcher plant have evolved a mutualistic relationship with *T. montana*. The *Nepenthes* exude waxy pellets (Beccarian bodies) from the undersurface of the pitcher lid. Whilst feeding on the pellets *T. montana* defecates into the pitcher, providing scarce nitrogen fertilizer to the plant (p. 70). **Borneo races** 1. *T. m. baluensis* Kinabalu to Gng Pueh excluding localities occupied by 2. *T. m. montana* in C Sarawak, including Gng Dulit, Batu Song, Kalulong and Usun Apau.

CARNIVOROUS MOUNTAIN TREESHREWS ON KINABALU Mountain Wren-babblers *Napothera crassa* are common small ground birds that forage in family parties (up to 9) on the forest floor surrounding Kinabalu Park HQ (1,650m). Mountain Treeshrews often associate with foraging wren-babbler groups to benefit from insects disturbed by both parties. As part of a study into the breeding ecology of Kinabalu's birds, the University of Montana Bird Study Group (UMBSG) has mist-netted and ringed many of the resident birds around the park headquarters. In one year 11 Mountain Wren-babblers were attacked and killed by Mountain Treeshrews after becoming trapped in mist nets.

2 SMOOTH-TAILED TREESHREW *Dendrogale melanura* **HB 120, T 140 Rare montane endemic**
Uncommon montane arboreal treeshrew with a shrinking distribution. In Sarawak isolated populations are found on Gng Dulit, Gng Mulu and Gng Murud. In Sabah found on Kinabalu, Trus Madi and the Crocker Range. Coolidge et al. (1940) collected 19 skins on Kinabalu at 1,200–3,350m. Lim (1968) trapped three on tree branches at 1,300–1,650m. More recently, Nor (1996) trapped 375 *T. montana* but no *D. melanura* on Kinabalu at 700–3,300m. Possible explanations are that Dusun bamboo dead traps catch more arboreal mammals than ground-level wire cages or the population on Kinabalu has collapsed. **ID:** Distinguished by thin tail and arboreal habits. Distinguished from Jentink's Squirrel (p. 200) by lack of white facial markings and pointed muzzle. **Habits:** Usually seen in trees, not on the ground, whilst Mountain Treeshrew has opposite habits. Active both night and day (Griswold). **Taxonomy:** The closest relative is *D. murina* (Vietnam), showing a regional as well as a local, shrinking, relict distribution (p. 148).

3 STRIPED TREESHREW *Tupaia dorsalis* **HB 194, T 148 Local endemic**
Locally common throughout Brunei and Sarawak but in Sabah only found near the Kalimantan border (Davis 1962). Absent from S and C Kalimantan. **ID:** Frequently mistaken for Large Treeshrew. In the hand has; 1. less heavy build than *T. tana*, with a shorter muzzle; 2. claws on forefeet are not enlarged as in *T. tana*; 3. dorsal stripe extends full length of the back. Note that the extended rhinarium (nose skin) resembles *T. tana*, not other treeshrews (p. 148). Similar *T. picta* also has small front claws, but a normal rhinarium and a reddish tip to the tail. **Habits:** In Sabah only recorded from Kalabakan and Maliau Basin on the Kalimantan border. See Davis (1962), Wearne and Thorley (SAFE Project, 2015). At Lambir Nakagawa et al. (2006) found that Striped Treeshrew was common both in virgin forest and in the pioneer vegetation of regenerating swidden farms.

1

2

3

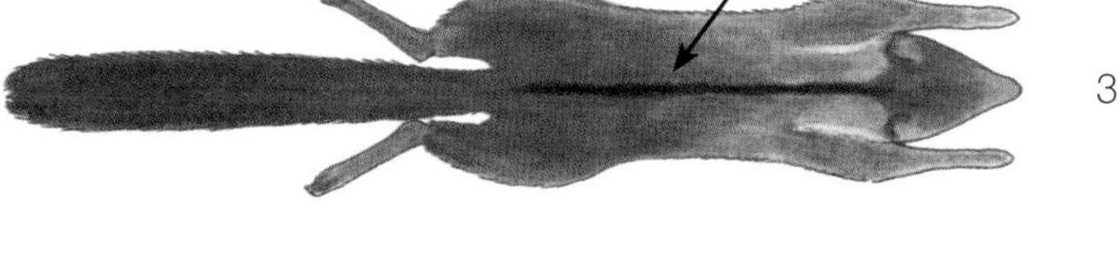

3

PAINTED AND SPLENDID TREESHREWS

1 PAINTED TREESHREW *Tupaia picta* HB 209, T 150, Wt? Scarce endemic

Ground-dwelling mystery treeshrew with two relict populations of different races. a. *T. p. picta* Locally common from Bintulu north to Belalong in Brunei where it was trapped next to river. (Dr Joe Charles). Recorded from Gng Dulit, Mulu to 1,000m in the Kelabit Highlands. Distinguished by clearly defined back stripe. b. *T. p. fusicor* Coastal E Kalimantan from Sangkulirang south to the Mahakam River. Black back stripe not clearly defined. Lacks red tip to tail (not illustrated). **ID:** Similar in size to *T. tana*. In the hand has normal treeshrew rhinarium, not the extended rhinarium of *T. tana* and *T. dorsalis* (Lyon 1913). Small front claws similar to those of *T. dorsalis*, not like large front claws of *T. tana*. **Habits:** 'This treeshrew is more common in the low country than in the mountains: it is usually found in dense forest and is particularly active in its movement' (Hose 1893).

Extended rhinarium (nose skin) characteristic of *Tuapia tana* (p. 150) and *T. dorsalis* (p. 146). Drawings from Lyon (1913).

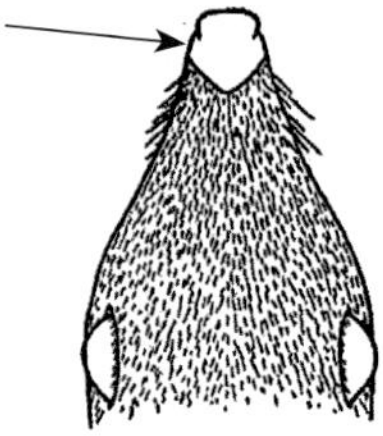

Normal rhinarium (nose skin) of all the other Bornean treeshrews, including *T. picta* and *T. splendidula*.

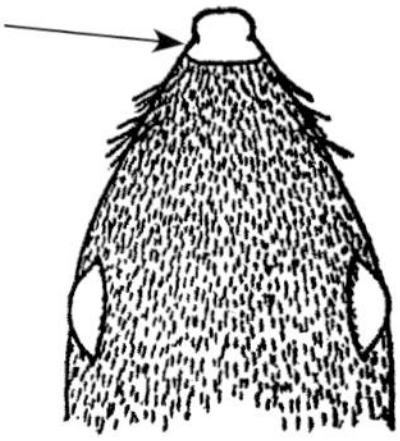

2 SPLENDID TREESHREW *Tupaia splendidula* HB 180, T 140, Wt? Scarce endemic

[Ruddy Treeshrew, Medway 1977, Payne 1985] Scarce terrestrial treeshrew confined to southern Kalimantan. The only large treeshrew in the peat-swamp forests of C Kalimantan at Sabangau and Tg Puting. **ID:** North of coastal peat-swamp in Kalimantan range overlaps with *T. tana*. Distinguished in the hand by the normal rhinarium and small front claws, compared with the extended rhinarium and large front claws of *T. tana*. The distribution maps show that this treeshrew has an allopatric (adjacent but not overlapping) distribution with *T. dorsalis* (p. 146), indicating that they compete ecologically. **Taxonomy:** South China Sea island races 1. *T. s. carimatae* Karimata. 2. *T. s. natunae* Bunguran besar. 3. *T. s. lucida* Pulau Laut, Natuna (see Lyon 1913).

RELICT DISTRIBUTIONS OF RATS AND TREESHREWS Distribution maps that show isolated populations of a previously common mammal indicate a shrinking range or relict distribution e.g. Painted and Splendid Treeshrews. The numerous races of *T. splendidula* on the islands of the South China Sea indicate that *T. splendidula* was the most common treeshrew of the Sunda basin before it was covered by rising sea levels some 10,000 years ago.

Most of Borneo's endemic mountain rats also show relict distributions, indicating that the mountains of Sumatra and Borneo were linked by corridors of cooler mountain forests, during colder periods in the past (pp. 14 and 16).

Species area relationships Smaller areas support fewer species, so once a population becomes isolated extinction accelerates (Allee Effect, p. 298). Due to genetic drift, small, isolated populations are also more likely to evolve into separate species, resulting in the high level of endemism in Borneo's montane mammals (pp. 168 and 386).

POPULATION COLLAPSE SMOOTH-TAILED TREESHREW AND RAPIT RAT
The apparent population collapse of the Smooth-tailed Treeshrew (p. 146) and Rapit Rat (p. 232) on Kinabalu in the last 50 years may not result from climate change, but derive from other factors, such as destruction of forest outside Kinabalu Park that was previously used as a refuge during droughts, *or* it may simply result from different trapping techniques. Early European explorers such as Everett, Hose, Whitehead and Griswold paid local Dusuns to trap mammals for them using traditional bamboo traps that killed the animals. These traps were usually set along artificial bamboo runways and branches, and would catch a different range of mammal species from those caught in wire-cage traps set on the ground.

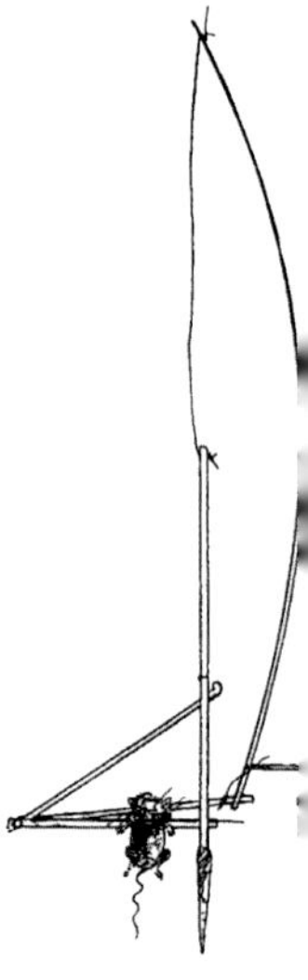

Dusun Rat Trap fror Whitehead (1893).

1

T. p. picta

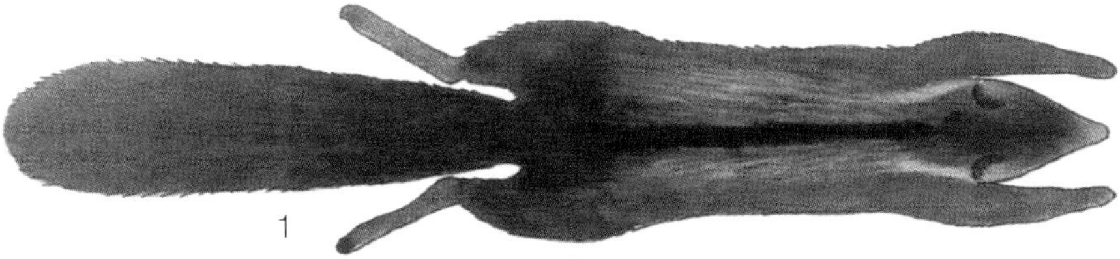

1

2

T. s. carimatae

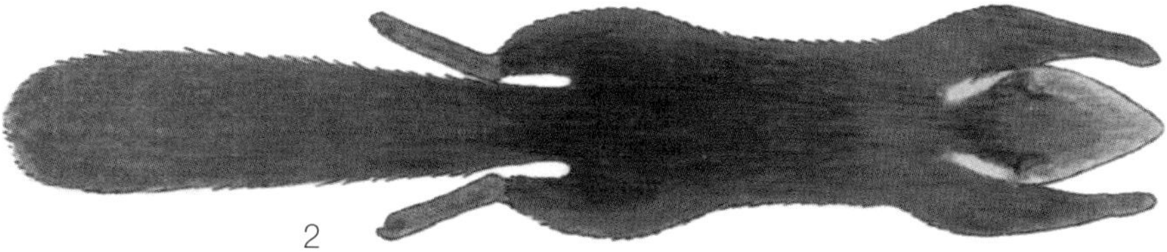

2

LARGE TREESHREW

LARGE TREESHREW *Tupaia tana* **HB 208, T 178, Wt 205g** **Common**

A common resident of lowland primary, logged and secondary forest throughout Borneo. Replaced by smaller Splendid Treeshrew (p.149) in Kalimantan peat-swamp forest. Above 900m, on Kinabalu replaced by Mountain Treeshrew. Very variable in size and colouration. Recorded weights are 130–300g. Non-breeding males and females are the same weight. **ID:** Overlaps with Striped, Splendid and Painted Treeshrews (pp. 147 and 149), from which it can only be distinguished by its extra-large front claws and distinctive rhinarium (bare skin on the nose) (p. 148). **Habits:** The largest and most terrestrial (ground-loving) treeshrew. Large Treeshrew populations often increase in logged and secondary forest. At night despite the terrestrial habits, adults occupy separate nests – normally a ball nest of leaves in a concealed hole or hollow usually 2–8m above the ground. **Alarm call:** Chattering at close range but at long distance, calls with several bird-like whistles sometimes followed by chatters (Emmons 2000). **Diet:** Generalist feeder on wide variety of insects and worms, which are obtained by searching under leaves and by digging shallow holes in soft ground. Also eats fallen soft fruit such as figs, and recorded as dispersing the tiny seeds of giant *Rafflesia* fruit. (p. 56). **Breeding:** Like other treeshrews has an unusual absentee maternal care breeding system (p. 142), combined with behavioural monogamy and dispersed pair living. **Range:** Sumatra. **Borneo.** Ten races occur in Borneo and the Natuna Islands of the S China Sea.

FEMALE CHOICE IN LARGE TREESHREWS A two-year Sabah study by Jason Munshi-South found that adult males and females associated with each other in monogamous pairs, in overlapping territories. Pairs travelled together but rarely spent the night in the same nest, and the male did not participate in rearing the young. Despite the strong pair bond between individual males and females, in 40% of births the male was not the father, and in several cases there was more than one father. Females wandered much more widely than males, and were more likely to be recent immigrants to an area than males. On a rare occasion males were seen to fight at a known territorial boundary. In most mammalian societies stronger, larger males compete with each other for multiple smaller females. It appears that in Large Treeshrews it is the females that make the choice over which male will father their young (Jason Munshi-South 2006).

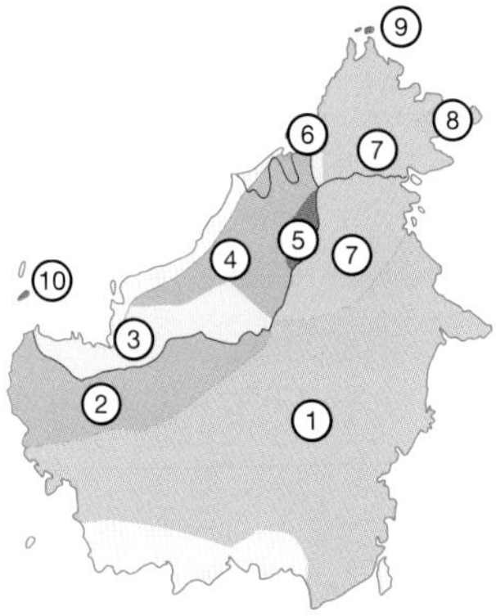

KEY

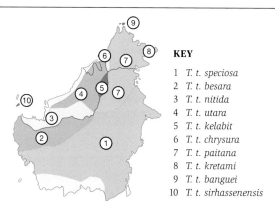

1 *T. t. speciosa*
2 *T. t. besara*
3 *T. t. nitida*
4 *T. t. utara*
5 *T. t. kelabit*
6 *T. t. chrysura*
7 *T. t. paitana*
8 *T. t. kretami*
9 *T. t. banguei*
10 *T. t. sirhassenensis*

DO SOME TREESHREWS HAVE POISONOUS FLESH? Locals report that the flesh of some animals is so noxious that it cannot be eaten. Some mammals are seasonally inedible, such as porcupines, Argus Pheasants and some treeshrews, due to eating toxic seeds or insects, whilst others are always inedible, for example weasel, Moonrat, Teledu, Binturong, mongooses, slow loris and all shrews. An animal with poisonous flesh needs to advertise this fact before it is caught and killed by a predator. The aposematic danger-warning colours of the coats of Splendid, Painted and some Large Treeshrews are almost certainly advertising the fact that the flesh is not edible. Emmons (2000) reported that Large Treeshrews ate a much wider variety of invertebrates that any of the other treeshrews she researched, including poisonous scorpions, toxic millipedes and several species of beetle known to produce defensive toxins. It is likely that the more colourful races of *T. tana* are advertising sequestered toxins that would make their flesh poisonous. If these toxins are sequestered, it is likely that the toxicity of the flesh will vary with the diet over time and space (pp. 124 and 272).

T. t. paitana

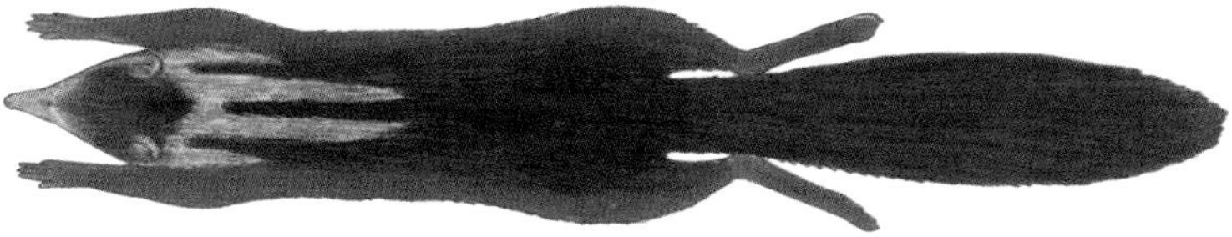

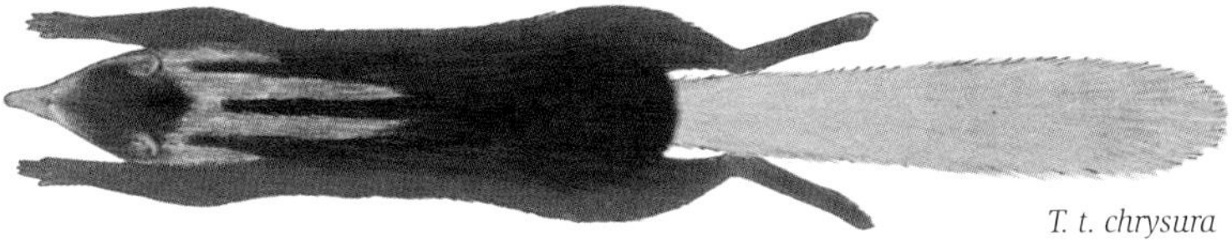

T. t. chrysura

T. t. nitida

PANGOLINS

MALAY: TENGGILING

PHOLIDOTA **World** 9 spp. **Asia** 4 spp. **Borneo** 2 spp., one long extinct. Pangolins originated in Africa, where they reach their highest diversity (4 species). All pangolins are specialist feeders on ants and termites, which have a major impact on tropical forest ecology. Pangolin populations worldwide are collapsing as a result of poaching to supply the traditional Chinese medicine market (TCM).

1 SUNDA PANGOLIN *Manis javanica* **HB 521, T 458 Wt 2.5–7kg** **Rare**

[Scaly Ant-eater] Previously common throughout Borneo in forest and cultivated areas from the peat-swamps of Sabangau to 1,700m on Kinabalu. Now on the verge of extinction due to poaching. **ID:** Unmistakable. Hard scales cover whole body except for nose and soft underbelly. **Habits:** Nocturnal and often arboreal. Sleeps during the day in tree hollows, amongst clumps of epiphytic ferns. One of a few Bornean mammals that thrive in secondary forest and cultivated areas. Until recently P. Gaya, opposite Kota Kinabalu, had a pangolin population, and pangolins were often seen at night on the rural roads around Kota Kinabalu. **Breeding:** Pangolins are believed to be slow breeders with a long gestation of 150–180 days followed by four months of maternal care. There is normally one young, which travels by clinging on to the mother's back. Males are thought to be larger than females and have larger home ranges. Captive males defecate and urinate in their water dish, indicating that they mark territories. On P. Tekong (Singapore), Lim & Ng (2008) reported home ranges as 43ha male and 7ha female. A female with baby used three different large tree holes for daytime sleep. **Diet:** In the wild, pangolins eat large quantities of ants, termites and a few invertebrates. Pangolins rip open the ground and tree nests of ants and termites with their long claws, and lick up the escaping insects with their long tongues. Observations by Lim show that pangolins prefer some ant and termite species over others. **Predators:** The only known predator is the Clouded Leopard. Pangolins can thrive in logged forest and oil palm, so it is obvious that the population is only limited by uncontrolled poaching, not habitat loss. **Captive diet:** Pangolins are kept successfully in captivity at Singapore Zoo, Taipei Zoo, San Diego Zoo and the CPCP at Cuc Phuong NP in Vietnam. The diet at Singapore Zoo includes mealworms, raw meat, boiled egg and vitamin supplements with added termite mound earth. Most rescued pangolins refuse food and should be given water and released as soon as possible. Pantel et al. (2009). **Range:** SE Asia, Sumatra, Java, **Borneo** including Buguran Besar (Natuna Islands).

Pangolins have a single baby that rides on the back of the mother until it becomes independent.

PANGOLINS AND TCM (traditional Chinese medicine) Chinese Pangolins *Manis pentadactyla* used to be common in S China but over-harvesting led to a collapse in the population of *M. pentadactyla* and suppliers began to look overseas for pangolins. All international trade in pangolins has been banned by CITES since 2,000 AD, however since the ban the illegal trade has actually increased.

Trade Figures Sabah Between 1912–1935 an average 2,300 pangolins were killed each year so their scales could be legally exported year from Sabah (Burgess 1961). However by 2009 the Sabah Wildlife Dept estimated that one exporter alone was illegally shipping the scales of over 1,000 pangolins per month.

Trade Figures Sarawak Legal exports of pangolin scales totaled 60 tons between 1958–1964 harvested from an estimated 50,000 pangolins – mainly smuggled from Kalimantan (Harrisson 1965). The pangolin is almost extinct in Sarawak.

Local uses Locals eat pangolins and use the scales for body armour, for deterring deer from entering rice fields and as charms against ghosts. **TCM uses** Scales are used externally for scratching itchy skin. Powdered scales are used internally as a circulation and blood tonic. De-scaled pangolins are boiled whole to make an expensive soup.

1

Sunda Pangolin scales have been found in Clouded Leopard scats. Pangolins have no other known predators in Borneo.

2

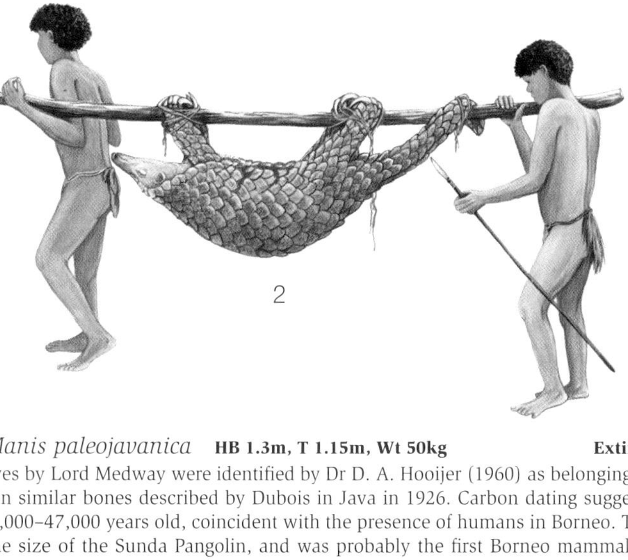

Remains of extinct Giant Pangolins, which weighed more than a man, have been found in Java and at the Niah Caves in Sarawak.

2 GIANT PANGOLIN *Manis paleojavanica* **HB 1.3m, T 1.15m, Wt 50kg** **Extinct**

Bones excavated at the Niah Caves by Lord Medway were identified by Dr D. A. Hooijer (1960) as belonging to a giant extinct pangolin based on similar bones described by Dubois in Java in 1926. Carbon dating suggests that the Niah bones are some 42,000–47,000 years old, coincident with the presence of humans in Borneo. The Giant Pangolin was 2.5 times the size of the Sunda Pangolin, and was probably the first Borneo mammal to become extinct after the arrival of humans (p. 20).

COLUGOS

MALAY: KUBONG

DERMOPTERA Until recently, zoologists agreed that there were two species of colugo in the world, the Kagwang *Cynocephalus volans* confined to Mindanao and nearby islands in the Philippines, and the Colugo found in Borneo and the Asian continent north to N Laos. Recent genetic research by Janecka et al. (2008) and Mason (2011), indicates that there is at least one and possibly several cryptic colugo species endemic to Borneo, as well as an endemic colugo on Sirhassen Island (Serasan, Natuna group) in the South China Sea. Colugos are most closely related to treeshrews and more distantly to primates. The current world distribution is relict – that is, colugos (like tarsiers) were much more widespread in the past than they are now (Marivaux et al. 2006).

BORNEAN COLUGO *Galeopterus borneanus* **HB 360, T 250, Wt 1.25–1.75kg Common endemic**

[Flying Lemur *Cynocephalus variegatus*] Common in primary and tall secondary forest and the edges of plantations including Poring at 900m, but not recorded at Kinabalu Park HQ at 1,650m. No records from peat-swamp forest at Sabangau, but common in coastal forest at Bako (Kuching), where the ecology has been studied by Nasir (2012). In Singapore, Lim (2007) recorded a density of 50 colugos per sq km (one per 2ha) in tall secondary forest surrounding Singapore Zoo. **ID:** In Borneo over 90% of colugos are greyish speckled with black markings, and the majority of these are female. The remaining 10% are more or less rufous or dark brown. In Borneo dark rufous colugos are always males, but females are sometimes light rufous (Banks 1931). Nasir estimated that 'grey females' are four times more common than males. Unlike flying squirrels Colugos lack a free tail (diagram, p. 216). **Habits:** Nocturnal. During the day colugos roost alone, hanging upside down from a shady branch, or clinging flat and motionless upright on a tree trunk, often with a youngster peeping from the mother's pouch. At Bako, Nasir found that roosting trees were chosen for rain protection and rarely coincided with feeding trees. Like flying squirrels the colugo glides, not flies. Glides up to 136m have been recorded with a loss of altitude of about 12m (Walker 1975). Colugos can change direction by up to 60 degrees during a flight (Lim 2007). The skin around the tail can be curled inwards to form a pouch for holding the young baby, and is folded backwards for defecation and urination. **Call:** The cry from young and old is a kind of harsh, grating squeak repeated several times, rather like the quacking of a very hoarse duck (Banks 1931). Fighting males produce a sound like the ripping of a thick piece of cardboard. Newly captured colugos produce a wailing sound (Lim 2007). Receptive females solicit the attention of males with squeaks (Dzulhelmi). **Diet:** A curious fact is that colugos have never been successfully kept in captivity. They are generalist leaf eaters, eating small amounts of leaves from many tree species each night, often in a regular nocturnal circuit. Colugos often scrape and lick the surfaces of branches, using comb teeth, and some 'scraping' sites are visited repeatedly. Lim (2007) notes that colugos often carry heavy parasite loads of nematodes in their guts. It is possible that these worms help detoxify leaf toxins and digest cellulose in a mutualistic relationship. Nor (1996) notes that a colugo kept as a pet on P Balambangan lived for six months on a diet of young fig leaves, and gave birth after 60 days in captivity. There are several records of colugos occasionally eating ants (Nasir 2012). **Breeding:** Males are smaller than females and fight other males over either territory or females (Lim 2007). Urine marking of tree trunks was seen at Bako (Nasir 2012). An unbalanced sex ratio of one male to four females suggests a Noyau breeding system with male territories overlapping several female territories (p. 158). Colugos breed year round, producing one young. Gestation has been estimated at 60–150 days, indicating that females may be able to delay implantation of the embryo. Males visit females with babies (Nasir 2012), and sometimes carry babies (Lim 2007). **Predators:** At Danum Valley BRL a guide, Paul, saw a Yellow-throated Marten chasing a Colugo from tree to tree. The marten ran along the ground whilst the Colugo glided from trunk to trunk. Eventually the exhausted colugo landed on the ground, where it was taken by the marten. At Danum large owls attack colugos lit up by tourist spotlights at night. Hawk-eagles pythons and Long-tailed Macaques (rarely) eat colugos. **Range:** Vietnam south to Malaya, Sumatra, Java, **Borneo**, including small islands, Balembangan, Banggi and Serasan, Bunguran, Aor and Subi (S China Sea).

COMB TEETH The curious comb-like lower teeth at the front of a colugo's mouth point forwards and are used for both scraping bark and grooming the fur.

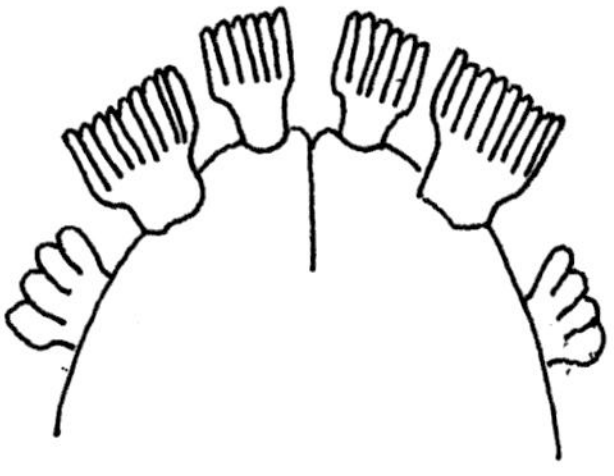

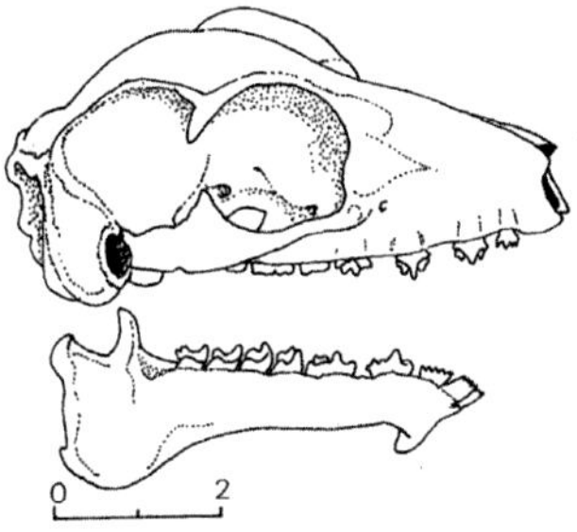

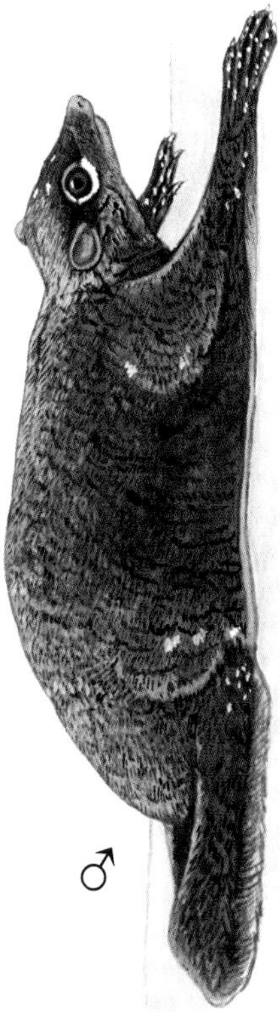

Rufous male colugo carrying an infant grey female during a glide.

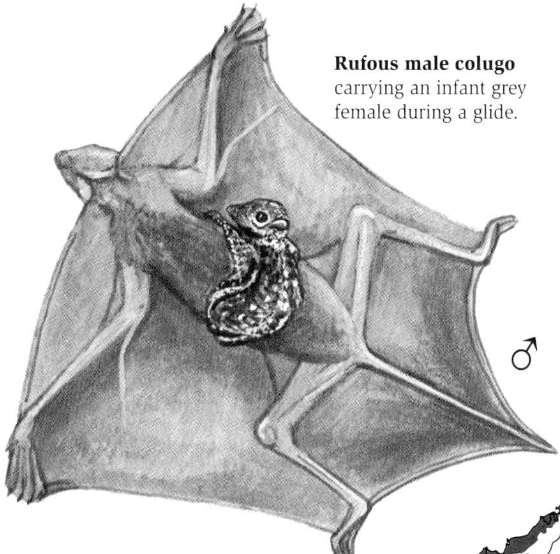

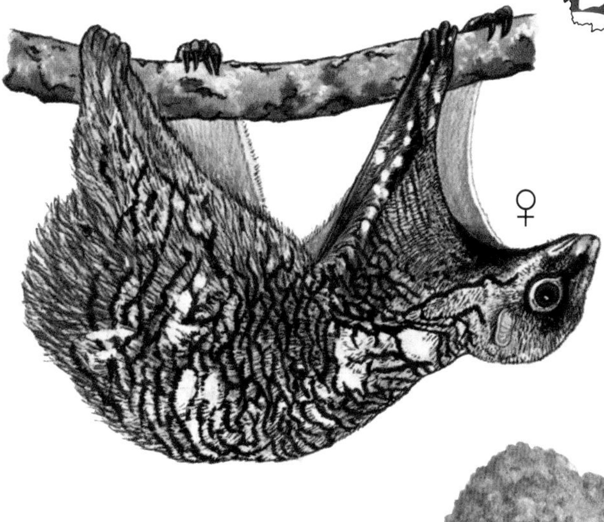

INTRODUCTION TO THE PRIMATES OF BORNEO

PRIMATES World: 446 spp. Borneo: 21 spp. 12 endemics. Primates evolved from small treeshrew like mammals but have diverged to include carnivores (tarsiers), omnivores (macaques, slow loris) leaf eating folivores (langurs) and fruit eating apes (orangutan and gibbon)with a wide variety of social systems and breeding strategies as described below

Endemics Payne et al (1985) listed 13 primates for Borneo of which 5 were endemics. This Field Guide lists 21 primate species for Borneo with 12 endemics following advances in DNA research.

BSC and PSC Zoologists are increasingly using DNA analysis and the **Phylogenetic Species Concept** (PSC) to replace the traditional **Biological Species Concept** (BSC) with the result that many races have been split into species. (p. 168)

BORNEAN PRIMATE SOCIAL AND BREEDING SYSTEMS

Noyau Adult males defend overlapping territories of several breeding females (Slow Loris, Tarsier).

Harem groups (polygyny) A single adult alpha male defends a group of breeding females and their young. Single males form all male groups. Lone rival males fight alpha males to take over the harem. After takeover, infants and new births are killed by the new alpha male rival. Pregnant females often leave at this stage. (Langurs, Proboscis). (p. 162). Males defend harems rather than fixed territories like gibbons and but male langurs make spacing calls early each morning to warn other groups of their presence.

Monogamous family Adult males and females live in lifelong pairs with their immediate young. Both sexes defend the feeding territory (Gibbons, p.184).

Promiscuous solitary Both males and females with young are normally solitary and socialize only for a short period whilst mating (Orangutans, p. 188).

Promiscuous group Non-territorial mixed sex groups led by an alpha male. Both adult sexes have multiple partners, but DNA tests show that alpha males father most group infants (Macaques, p.180).

Primate	Social System	Digestion	Preferred Diet	Preferred habitat
Tarsier	Noyau	Hindgut	Insects, bats, birds	Disturbed forest
Slow loris (5 spp.)	Noyau	Hindgut	Omnivorus esp. sap	Tall forest
Silvered Langur	Harem groups	Foregut	Leaves, unripe seeds	Coastal forest
Proboscis (a Langur)	Harem groups	Foregut	Leaves, unripe seeds	River bank
Grey langurs (4 spp.)	Harem groups	Foregut	Leaves, unripe seeds	Tall forest
Sarawak Langur	Harem groups	Foregut	Unripe seeds, leaves	Coastal forest
Red Langur	Harem groups	Foregut	Unripe seeds, leaves	Tall forest
Gibbons (4 spp.)	Monogamous family	Hindgut	Fruit, leaves	Tall forest
Orangutan	Promiscuous solitary	Hindgut	Fruit, leaves	Tall forest
Pig-tailed Macaque	Promiscuous group	Hindgut	Fruit, insects	Tall forest
L.-tailed Macaque	Promiscuous group	Hindgut	Omnivorous	Disturbed forest
Human	Monogamous/harem	Hindgut	Omnivorous	Ubiquitous

MIMICRY IN BORNEAN PRIMATES

Batesian mimicry was first described by Henry Bates in Brazilian butterflies in 1862. Many harmless S American butterflies (mimics) copy the wing patterns of poisonous butterflies (models) to protect themselves from bird attack.

Müllerian mimicry In 1878 Müller explained that many dangerous animals shared the same danger warning (aposematic) patterns to protect themselves from attack, e.g. poisonous snakes and insects are often banded black and yellow as a warning signal.

Mimicry rings are groups of Batesian and Müllerian mimics that share the same warning colours, some of which are false. Mimicry rings are abundant amongst birds, insects, reptiles and mammals (p. 26).

Colour groups Borneo's monkeys and apes can be split into two colour groups, those with:

a **Camouflage colours** Generally grey with pale underneath and darker above (counter-shading), including the gibbons, grey langurs and Long-tailed Macaque.

b **Advertising colours** (they want to be seen), include Red Langur, Orangutan, Pig-tailed Macaque and Proboscis Monkey. All those with advertising colours (apart from the Red Langur) are capable of defending themselves against a Clouded Leopard either individually (Orangutan) or by a strong male group leader. Red Langurs in E Sabah are often found in a pale white morph, probably a mimic of Pig-tailed Macaques. The Sarawak Langur also occurs in two morphs, one camouflaged and the other advertising (pp. 170 and 261).

NOTES ON PRIMATE DIETS

1 **Hindgut digesters** e.g. humans, use chewing, stomach acid and bacteria in the hind gut (long intestine) to break down easily digestible foods such as fruit but are unable to survive on indigestible cellulose rich leaves. Generally the longer the hind gut and the larger the caecum the higher the proportion of plant fiber in the diet.

2 **Foregut Digesters** e.g. langurs use multiple stomachs filled with friendly bacteria to break down (pre-digest) the cellulose in leaves before it enters the hind gut. This enables Langurs to eat the most abundant forest food (leaves) and explains why langurs are both the most speciose (8 spp.) and most common primates in forested areas.

3 **Coprophagy** Young langurs acquire friendly bacteria through coprophagy, by eating their parents faeces.

4 **Rumination** Non-primate foregut digesters such cattle also ruminate. Ruminants regurgitate previously swallowed food and re-masticate (chew) it a second time. Rumination was unknown in primates until Matsuda (2015) discovered that Proboscis regularly ruminated. (p.176).

6 **Salt Licks, Mineral Springs and Clay** Unripe fruit and leaves contain large amounts of toxic chemicals for protection against seed and leaf predators. Mammals which eat unripe fruit and seeds frequently visit salt springs and also eat clay. Salt is required to maintain the alkaline PH preferred by the cellulose digesting bacteria in the foregut whilst tiny clay particles chemically bond with many plant toxins thereby neutralising them. (p. 24).

7 **Poor Seed Dispersal by Foregut Digesters** Foregut digesters such as langurs have a very narrow gap between the forestomach(s) and the main stomach and can only swallow and defecate tiny seeds such as those of figs (p.76), Perepat (p. 185) and Laran (p. 224) which produce sugar free fruit with tiny seeds targeted at langur dispersal. Langurs also eat large amounts of unripe seeds and are thus primarily seed predators.

8 **Important Seed Dispersal by Hindgut Digesters** Frugivorous hindgut digesters e.g. (gibbons and orangutans) are extremely important long distance seed dispersers of large seeds by swallowing and defecation. See chart (p.37).

9 **Omnivorous Primates** such as the macaques, swallow tiny seeds, and either predate or spit larger seeds. They are therefore equally important as both seed predators and seed dispersers.

Red Langur mother with her cream-coloured infant. After the first three months infants start turning red. However, in some areas of Sabah a small proportion of Red Langurs remains cream for life.

ASYMMETRIC MIMICRY OF THE RED LANGUR

Apart from its long tail, the Red Langur looks almost like a cartoon caricature of an Orangutan. The fur is brighter and redder, and the hairlessface is even darker. Red Langurs and Orangutans have similar distributions, although the Red Langur is up to 10 times more common. The most likely explanation for this exaggerated similarity is that the Red Langur gains some benefit from being mistaken for an Orangutan, particularly reduced predation. The main threat to Red Langurs are Clouded Leopards. A Clouded Leopard could suffer serious injury and possible death in an attack on an adult Orangutan.

Classical mimicry theory (see opposite) states that the model (Orangutan) will always outnumber the mimic (Red Langur). However, classical theory is based on birds attacking butterflies, where the bird only risks a nasty taste. If a Clouded Leopard attacks an adult Orangutan it risks death. The risk reward/ratio (one meal in return for a high chance of death) is unbalanced or asymmetric. Thus the Red Langur gains a protective advantage by mimicking the Orangutan even though the Red Langur is more common.

Borneo and Sumatra The Red Langur is confined to Borneo whereas Orangutans are found both in Sumatra and Borneo.The reddish morphs of the Banded Langur *Presbytis melalophos* in Sumatra probably evolved to mimic Orangutans when they were more common in Sumatra.

TARSIIDAE **World:** 11 spp. **Borneo:** 1 sp. Tarsiers are small, nocturnal, carnivorous, primitive primates very distantly related to the primate ancestors of early humans. Tarsiers hunt for large insects in the understorey of the forest at night, using their long legs to leap from one vertical sapling to another. The name is derived from 'tarsus', or ankle bone, which in tarsiers is relatively longer than in other primates.

World range Tarsier fossils have been found from Europe to Asia and N America. The current relict range is restricted to S Sumatra, Borneo and S Philippines (Leyte, Bohol and Mindanao), with a centre of diversity in Sulawesi, where 9 mostly sympatric species occur. *T. spectrum* of lowland Sulawesi occurs in groups and is notably more sociable than *Cephalopachus bancanus*, where the adults are normally solitary.

WESTERN TARSIER *Cephalopachus bancanus* HB 30–40, T 35, Wt 150g

[Horsfield's Tarsier] Tarsiers are locally common in both primary and secondary lowland forests, but rarely seen because of their small size and stationary posture. Tarsier eyes glow dull reddish-orange when spotlighted at night but they quickly turn away from light so are difficult to see. There are two montane records: 1. 1,200m, Bukit Baka Raya, Kalimantan (Gorog/Sinaga 1999). 2. 1,100m, Bario, Kelabit Highlands. Locals may be reluctant to discuss or even admit seeing a tarsier, based on traditional headhunting beliefs that doing so could result in the loss of one's head. This is due to the tarsier's ability to rotate its head 180 degrees. The eyes themselves cannot move. **Density:** (Crompton 1987) estimated 12 per km^2 at Sepilok whilst (Niemitz 1979) estimated 80 per km^2 at Semengoh. Crompton recorded mist netting nine individuals within a 9ha Sepilok plot in 13 days**. ID:** Adults always forage and sleep alone. Listen for bird-like, twittering calls, loudest at dusk and dawn. Experienced observers can smell the territorial markings of males on trail-side saplings. Tarsiers can be found emerging from known roosts in dense vines just after dark. **Habits:** Nocturnal. Males are strictly territorial and scent-mark territories of 1.5–12.5ha with urine, epigastric (upper abdomen) and mouth secretions. Male territories usually overlap several smaller female territories. Tarsiers hunt by sight and hearing, leaping down from a vertical sapling perch to snatch prey on the ground. Tarsiers have curious round suction pads on the ends of their fingers to aid in gripping smooth, vertical saplings, as well as two grooming claws on each foot. When ready to mate females scent-mark and actively solicit copulation, which is quickly over, after which the pair separates. **Voice:** The most common call is a high pitched *tsit—tsit tsit*, often in concert (Crompton 1987). Also described as a *chick-chick-chick* call (Blackham). **Diet:** Primarily large insects. Tarsiers are often trapped in mist nets set for bats or owls at night. Also recorded feeding on frogs, roosting birds, small lizards, geckos, bats and *Maticora intestinalis*, a small, very poisonous snake (p. 26). Hearsay claims that tarsiers feed on the contents of *Nepenthes* pitchers remain unconfirmed (see opposite). **Range:** S Sumatra, **Borneo race:** *C. b. borneanus*. Also Serasan (Natuna Islands).

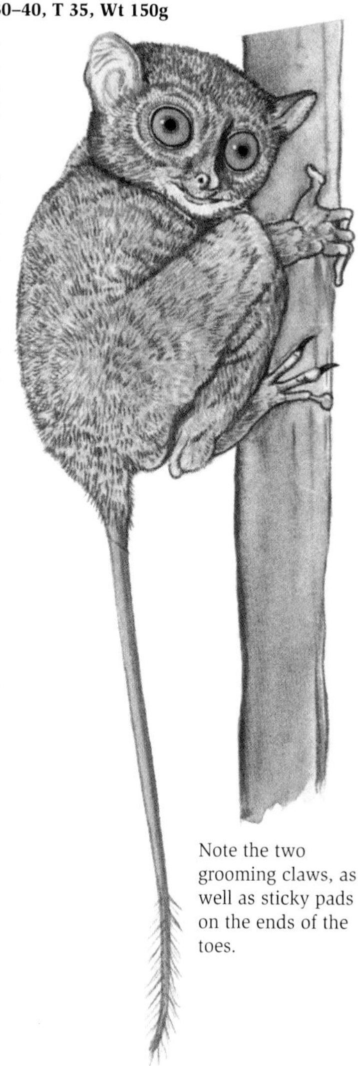

Note the two grooming claws, as well as sticky pads on the ends of the toes.

TARSIERS IN CAPTIVITY Tarsiers may be sold alive in local *tamus* (markets) for making *ubat* (medicine) for curing eye problems. Rescued tarsiers quickly become tame and take live insects from the hand within 24 hours. Tarsiers are easily stressed and ***must*** be provided with a dark nest box and drinking water before being released as soon as possible. On Bohol Island (S Philippines) there is a large Tarsier Centre with a colony of semi-wild breeding tarsiers.

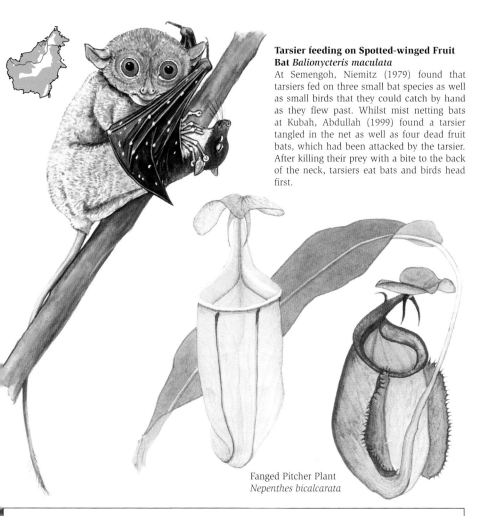

Tarsier feeding on Spotted-winged Fruit Bat ***Balionycteris maculata***

At Semengoh, Niemitz (1979) found that tarsiers fed on three small bat species as well as small birds that they could catch by hand as they flew past. Whilst mist netting bats at Kubah, Abdullah (1999) found a tarsier tangled in the net as well as four dead fruit bats, which had been attacked by the tarsier. After killing their prey with a bite to the back of the neck, tarsiers eat bats and birds head first.

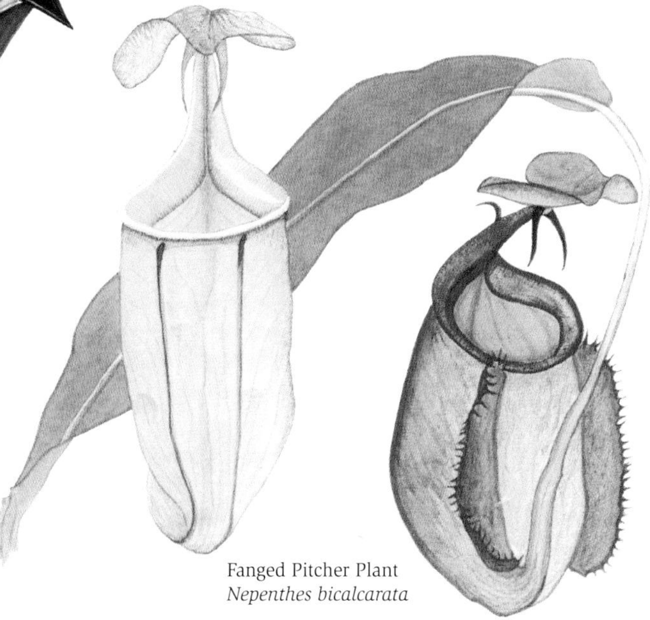

Fanged Pitcher Plant
Nepenthes bicalcarata

THE TARSIER AND THE FANGED PITCHER PLANT 'Now a word as to the walrus-tooth-like prickles or spurs which lie concealed under the kidney-shaped lid of the *Nepenthes* urns. There is found in Bornean forests in the locality where this fine pitcher-plant grows, a little animal called by the natives ***Tamperlilie***. This little creature is an insect-eater and knowing that the pitchers of *Nepenthes* so very frequently contain entrapped insects, visits them pretty regularly. In the case of *N. rafflesiana* the insects imprisoned in their unarmed urns are readily removed, but not so in the case of *N. bicalcarata* [Fanged Pitcher Plant], as the sharp spurs are so placed that the tarsier is sure to be pricked by them and pretty sharply too, if its head is placed under the lid for the purpose of inspecting the interior. I repeatedly saw this animal amongst plants of *N. bicalcarata* and shot one or two specimens and the fact of its frequenting *Nepenthes* in quest of insects is well-known to the more intelligent of the native forest hunters.' (condensed from Burbidge 1880). There may well be an element of truth to Burbidge's story, but Charles Clarke, who studied *N. bicalcarata* in the peat-swamps of Brunei in 1989–90, noted that it was more likely that the twin fangs were a form of insect trap, as nectar from the lid gathered on the tips of the fangs, and insects in search of nectar were likely to slip and fall into the digestive pitcher fluid below, where they provided essential nutrients for the *Nepenthes* (Clarke 1993) (p. 70).

LORISINAE **World** 7–10 spp. **Borneo** 5 spp. In this book we follow Munds & Nekaris et al. (2013), who split the slow loris found on mainland Borneo into four species, two of them endemic, based on differing facial markings. The Natuna Island (Bunguran Besar) slow loris was described as a new species, *Nycticebus natunae*, in 1906 by Lyon. Chasen (1935) lumped it as a race of Sunda Slow loris *N. coucang natunae*, but with darker fur below making five species for Borneo. DNA analysis and further ecological research is required to confirm the new taxonomy. [Local names: Kukang, Kongkang, Kera Duku]

1 **SUNDA SLOW LORIS *Nycticebus coucang*** Malaya, Sumatra, Natuna Islands.
2 **PHILIPPINE SLOW LORIS *Nycticebus menagensis*** Coastal N, W, E Borneo, Tawi Tawi (S Philippines).
3 **KAYAN SLOW LORIS *Nycticebus kayan*** Endemic to N, C and W Borneo.
4 **BORNEAN SLOW LORIS *Nycticebus borneanus*** Endemic to S Borneo, west of Barito River.
5 **BANKA SLOW LORIS *Nycticebus bancanus*** Banka and Biliton Islands, SE Sumatra and W Borneo north to Samunsam.

SLOW LORIS (BORNEO SPECIES) **HB 27–30cm, No tail, Wt Adults variable, Wt 265–800g** **Scarce**

Slow loris are widespread but scarce from the peat-swamp forests of Kalimantan to 1,500m in montane forest at Kinabalu Park HQ. **ID:** Nocturnal and arboreal, with bright orange-red eyeshine at night. Climbs slowly and deliberately from branch to branch in the canopy. Young are paler than adults, with longer fur. **Habits:** Slow loris ecology has been studied in Java and the Malay Peninsula, and to a limited extent in Borneo. Slow loris are the only Bornean primate with a wet nose (similar to a dog), indicating that scent is ecologically important. Both sexes mark food sources and territories with large amounts of urine. Male territories often overlap with one or more female territories, and males fight at territorial boundaries. Borneo population densities are low, e.g. 5 per km^2 (Munds 2013), less than one-tenth of densities recorded in Malaya (Wiens 2002). **Breeding:** Female receptive every 42 days. Normally one young with a long gestation of c.190 days. Data for *N. coucang* (Nekaris 2013). Usually found alone or mother and baby, but family groups are common in Borneo. **Call:** Whistle or chitter in conflicts. **Diet:** Omnivorous. Slow loris search for fruit, birds and insects at night in the canopy, but prefer sap and use comb teeth to scrape bark and incisors to gouge deep holes in tree trunks to feed on gums, sap and resins. Even poisonous 'rengas' sap (*Gluta*) is taken. Scraping sites may be visited regularly. Slow loris visit *Eugeissona* palms in Malaya to feed on alcoholic nectar (Wiens 2003) (p. 52). Slow loris eat poisonous insects and millipedes rejected by most mammals (Streicher et al. 2012). **Predators:** Banks (1949) noted that a civet refused to eat the head. Bock (1881) described the body fat as having an intolerable odour. Sun Bears reject the scent. Sumatran Orangutans (with a poor sense of smell) do eat slow loris (p. 190). **Conservation:** Often kept as unsuitable pets, leading to a local collapse in populations. See www.nocturama.org (Prof. Anna Nekaris, Little Fireface Project).

WHY ARE SLOW LORIS POISONOUS? Both sexes of all loris species have a gland inside their elbow (brachial gland), which sweats a clear oil. Loris often lick the gland when under stress, then lick their young all over or rub the mixed saliva and oil over their heads. Observations show that the liquid is toxic to leeches and ticks, and repels predators such as Sun Bears. The oil in the gland contains venom that is activated when combined with saliva. This venom is powerful enough to kill mice when injected, and cause severe allergic shock in humans, occasionally resulting in death. Nekaris et al. (2013) suggest that the poison has developed as a defence against both predation and attacks from rival slow loris during territorial breeding fights. If toxins are sequestered from poisonous saps and beetles, then toxin strength would vary with diet. A slow loris that ate toxic foods, signalled to predators and rival Slow Loris by urine smell, would have a competitive advantage.

DO SLOW LORIS MIMIC LARGE OWLS IN BORNEO? In 1905, John Still illustrated the face pattern and attitude of his frightened pet Slender Loris in Sri Lanka that mimicked a rearing Spectacled Cobra. Nekaris et al. (2013) suggested that when slow loris expanded their range from India into Sundaland 8 MYA, they took with them both their cobra-mimicking facial markings and their cobra-mimicking venom. The majority of predatory mammals in Borneo including slow loris show black-and-white, aposematic (danger-warning) facial markings (p. 26). In Borneo neither of the two cobra species is arboreal or shows the 'spectacles' seen on Indian cobras. (Stuebing et al. 2014). It is more plausible that the facial markings of slow loris in Borneo mimic the similar-sized Wood and Eagle Owls, a form of Müllerian mimicry (p. 157). Mimicry of different owl species in different areas, rather than speciation, may explain the varied facial markings of slow loris.

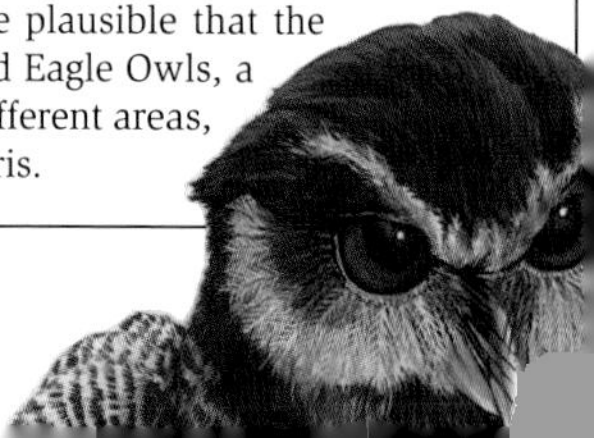

Sunda Slow Loris
N. coucang Malayan
Sumatra, Natuna
Islands

Philippine
Slow Loris
N. menagensis
N Borneo and
Tawi Tawi

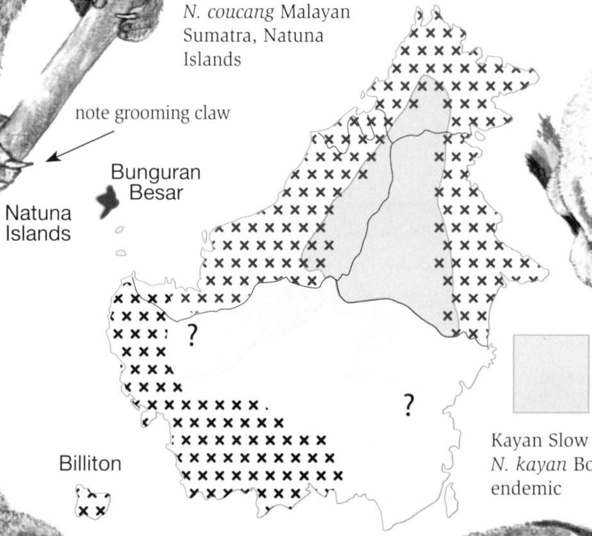

Kayan Slow Loris
N. kayan Borneo
endemic

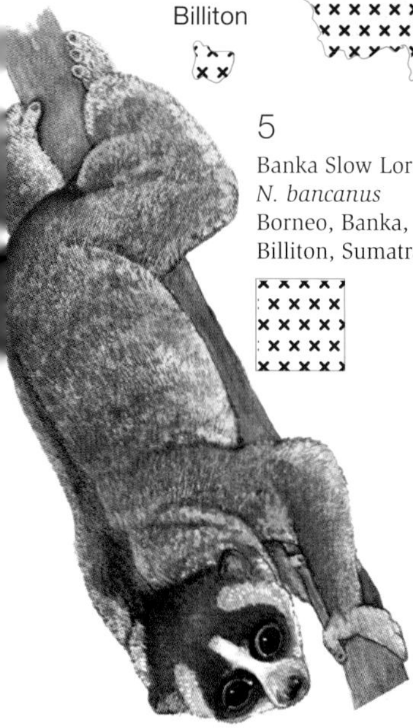

Banka Slow Loris
N. bancanus
Borneo, Banka,
Billiton, Sumatra

Bornean
Slow Loris
N. borneanus
Borneo
endemic

RED LANGUR *Presbytis rubicunda* **HB 51, T 72, Wt 5.5–7kg** **Common endemic**

[**Local**: Sabangau – Kelasi] [Red Leaf Monkey, Maroon Langur, Maroon Surili] The most common Bornean langur found from the peat-swamps of Sabangau in Kalimantan to 2,000m at Mesilau on Kinabalu. In many areas Red Langur overlaps with one of the four endemic grey langurs. **Grey langurs** are usually more common than Red Langurs in the mountains, e.g at Ulu Temburong, Kelabit Highlands, Kayan Mentarang and Betung Kerihun, whilst Red Langurs are more common in the lowlands except at Tabin in E Sabah. **Sarawak langurs** historically did not overlap in range with Red Langurs (see map) indicating they share a similar ecological niche (p. 170). **ID:** Males slightly bigger than females. Five races separated by rivers in the lowlands have been described, as well as a pale morph. Distinguished from Orangutans by brighter colours, smaller size, long tail and much more agile behaviour – leaping rapidly from tree to tree, not climbing. Distinguished from reddish morph of Silvered Langur with a pale face (p. 173) by the dark face. **Pale morph Red Langurs** that retain the juvenile white coat are common in Tawau Hills Park, where Orangutans are absent, probably indicating Batesian mimicry of a heavy aggressive male Pig-tailed Macaque (p. 348). **Call:** The male loud call is a rapid *Kek ha ha ha ha ha*. This territorial call is given just before dawn and can be heard from several hundred metres. Males also call when alarmed and lead the group a short distance away, after which the whole group freezes (Supriatna et al. 1986). **Diet:** During fruit masting Red Langurs eat unripe dipterocarp seeds. During the 'lean' inter-mast periods their preferred food is unripe legume beans and the young leaves of *Spatholobus* lianas (p. 68). Red Langurs visit salt licks and eat soil from termite mounds, but not as often as grey langurs. **Breeding**: Harem group led by an alpha male. Lone males form bachelor groups (p. 156).

Female Red Langur with pale morph infant.

DENSITY COMPENSATION BETWEEN GREY AND RED LANGURS

Density Compensation occurs in similar species when an increase in one population results in a decrease in the other as with the populations of grey and Red Langurs in Borneo. Possible reasons include:

1. The two species have high dietary overlap but with some small differences; for example, the Red Langur is reported to be more frugivorous than grey langurs.
2. The two langur types might suffer differential rates of predation in different areas. For instance, the Red Langur is brightly coloured and makes loud noises when threatened (characteristics of langurs that live in a high-predation environment), whilst grey langurs are cryptically camouflaged and freeze when threatened (characteristics of langurs in low-predation environment). See Nijman (2010), Nijman & Nekaris (2012).

Site	**Habitat**	**Red** km²	**Grey** km²	**Source**
Sepilok	Dipterocarp forest	19	low	Davies (1984)
Tabin	Lowland logged forest	5	19	Mitchell (1994)
Temburong	Hill diptercarp forest	15	28	Bennett et al. (1987)
L. Entimau	Hill diptercarp forest	5	7	Blough & Gombek (2000)
Sungai Wain	Dry dipterocarp forest	10	4	Bersacola (2012), Lhota (2005)
Barito Ulu	Dipterocarp/kerangas forest	8	low	McConkey et al. (2002)
Sabangau	Mixed swamp forest	18	0	Ehlers-Smith (2013)
Gng Palung	Peat swamp	2	0	Marshall (2008)
Gng Palung	Freshwater swamp	8	0	Marshall (2008)
Gng Palung	Alluvial bench	10	0	Marshall (2008)
Gng Palung	Lowland sandstone	6	0	Marshall (2008)
Gng Palung	Lowland granite	7	0	Marshall (2008)
Gng Palung	Upland granite	7	0	Marshall (2008)
Gng Palung	Montane	3	0	Marshall (2008)

Note differences in population density in different habitats at Gng Palung

P. r. ignita

P. r. chrysea

P. r. rubida

Pale Morph

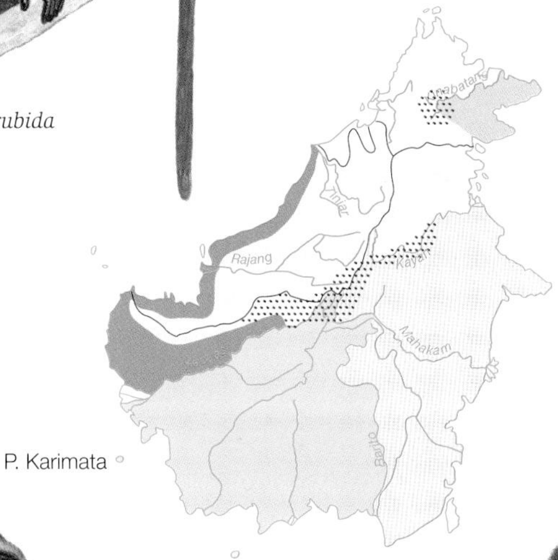

HISTORIC RANGE OF RED LANGUR
Presbytis rubicunda

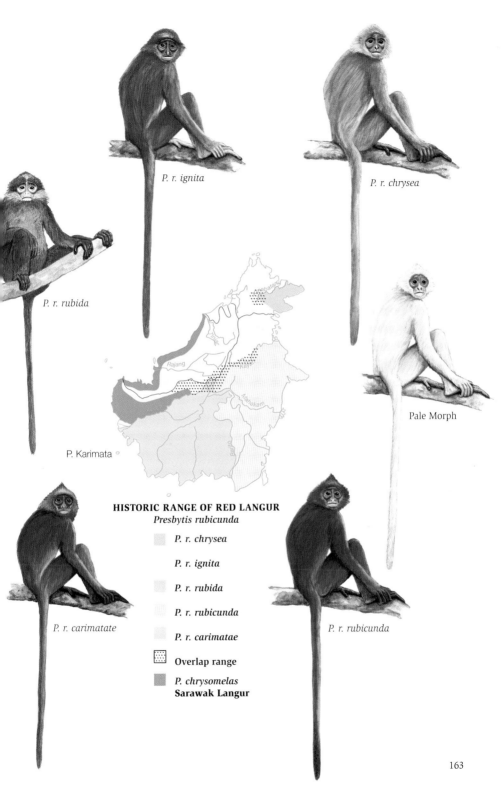

- ***P. r. chrysea***
- ***P. r. ignita***
- ***P. r. rubida***
- ***P. r. rubicunda***
- ***P. r. carimatae***
- **Overlap range**
- ***P. chrysomelas***
  Sarawak Langur

P. r. carimatate

P. r. rubicunda

GREY LANGURS 1 MALAY: LUTONG. KADAZAN: MONOSOP. KALIMANTAN: BERANGKAT

GREY *PRESBYTIS* LANGURS The 4 Borneo endemic grey langurs have largely allopatric (separate) distributions, overlapping (sympatric) at the margins. Apart from the Kalimantan Langur they were all described as races of Hose's Langur in Payne et at (2005) but split into separate endemic species by Groves & Roos in Mittermeier et at (2013) *Handbook of the Mammals of the World*. See p. 166 for Grey Langur Ecology.

1 HOSE'S GREY LANGUR *Presbytis hosei* **HB 520, T 750, Wt 5.5–7kg** **Rare Local endemic**

[Grey Leaf Monkey] Historical range is from Niah (Sarawak) north to W Kinabalu and west to the Kayan River in Kalimantan. **ID:** Adult sexes differ but immatures and elderly females resemble males leading to the mistaken description of two new species by Thomas (1889), *Semnopithecus hosei* (male) and *S. everetti* (female) causing much confusion. **Status:** Rare due to hunting. Almost extinct at Mulu and in SE Sabah. The only safe population is in Brunei at Ulu Tutong and Ulu Temburong where Bennett et at (1987) reported Hose's was more common than Red Langur with a group density of 3.25 km^2. With groups estimated at 8.5 this equates to a density of 28/km^2 the highest in Borneo, possibly related to the absence of orangutans in Brunei. See p. 332 re historical Kinabalu records. **Territorial Call:** A soft, woodpecker-like rattle lasting 2 to 5 seconds mostly heard from before dawn until c. 10.00 am. Rival males can be heard calling from the Belalong Canopy Walkway in Brunei. **Alarm Call:** A soft gruff **wooh uh uh uh** and variations thereof.

2 SABAH GREY LANGUR *Presbytis sabana* **HB 520, T 750, Wt 5.5–7kg** **Scarce Local endemic**

Widespread in E. Sabah, but much less common than Red Langur apart from Tabin where Sabah Langur is more common. Reports indicate some overlap with Hose's Langur in NE Kalimantan. **ID:** A striking black band across a pale pink face. Silvered Langur has a uniformly dark face. Females c.7% bigger than males. For the first four months infants are white with a black cross across the shoulders and down the back. **Territorial Call:** "Alpha males make a territorial call most mornings just before the dawn bird chorus at 6.00am. This call may also be used when encountering rival-groups and sometimes at night. The call is a gargling growl lasting 2–4 seconds at intervals of several minutes. It is audible at up to one km in pre-dawn silence and could be mistaken for a woodpecker drumming" (Mitchell 1994). **Male Alarm Call:** "A series of 3 or 4 quick guttural grunts, almost pig like, the sequence lasting about half a second" (Davis). **Female Alarm Call:** "High pitched rattled chucks" (Mitchell). **Habits:** "When a mixed group of Red and Sabah Langurs is alarmed, Red Langur make off at once in a series of crashing leaps whilst Sabah Langur may not flee until shot at" (Davis 1962). This habit common to all grey langurs makes them more vulnerable to hunting with guns than Red Langurs.

3 KUTAI GREY LANGUR *Presbytis canicrus* **HB 520, T 750, Wt 5.5–7kg** **Rare endemic**

[Sunda Island Leaf Monkey *P. aygula*],[Payne Hoses Langur *P. h. canicrus*], [Miller's Grizzled Surili] Recorded from the Mahakam River north to the Kayan River in coastal E Kalimantan. 'The commonest primate at Kutai with a density of 20 per km^2 and a group size of 8' (Rodman 1978). Now locally extinct due to hunting for bezoar stones. Recently recorded Wehea community forest north of Kutai where Loken (2011) found both Kutai and Red Langur were equally common at salt licks. **ID:** Has a dark face with a pair of white stripes forming a "U" below the nose. **Habits:** At Kutai the diet is 66% leaves and 28% unripe seeds (Rodman). Frequently visits salt licks. See p. 24. For a semi-biographical account of researching primates at Kutai before the park was destroyed by illegal logging, fire and coal mining see *The Wind Monkey* by Leo Berenstain (1992) **Call:** "Splash rattle the big male's gruff chugging call heralded the start of each long move" (Berenstain).

4 KALIMANTAN GREY LANGUR *Prebytis frontata* **HB 500, T 700, Wt 5.0–6.5kg.** **Scarce endemic**

[White-fronted Langur] The only grey langur in the hills of C Kalimantan and Sarawak south of the Sg Rajang. Absent from peatswamp forest. Extinct at Gng Palung. Overlaps with Hose's Grey Langur in Kayan Mentarang and previously with Kutai Langur at Kutai. At Sungai Wain less common than Red Langur. Lhota et at (2005) estimated one group per km^2. At Lanjak Entimau, half as common as Red Langur. Blough and Gombek (2000) estimate a park population of 13,400 and a density of 1.7 groups km^2, but in the adjacent hilly Betung Kerihun (Kalimantan) N. Soedjito found that *P. frontata* was very common and Red Langur was rare. Group size avg. was 3.63. **ID:** Has dark face with double white markings above the nose. **Habits:** Nijman (2012) observed that of all the grey langurs, the Kalimantan Langur has the dullest colours, is the quietest, lives in the smallest groups, makes the least noise when escaping danger, often freezing rather than fleeing and flees on the ground rather than through the trees, all anti-predator strategies. **Call:** Male makes typical grey langur territorial call before dawn and sometimes at night but rarely during the day (Nijman 2012, Lhota 2005).

Presbytis hosei

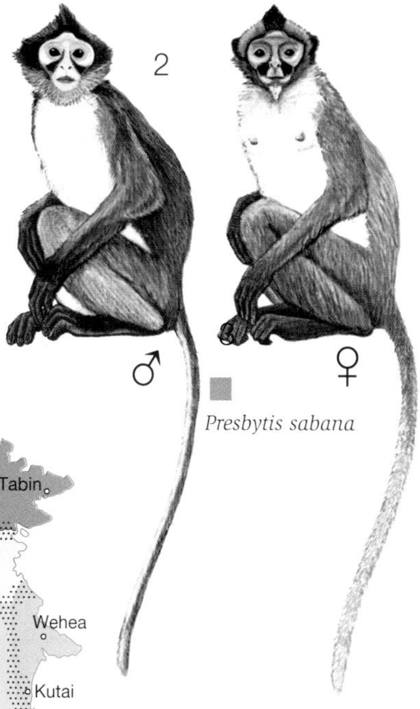

Presbytis sabana

HISTORICAL RANGE GREY LANGURS

Overlap range

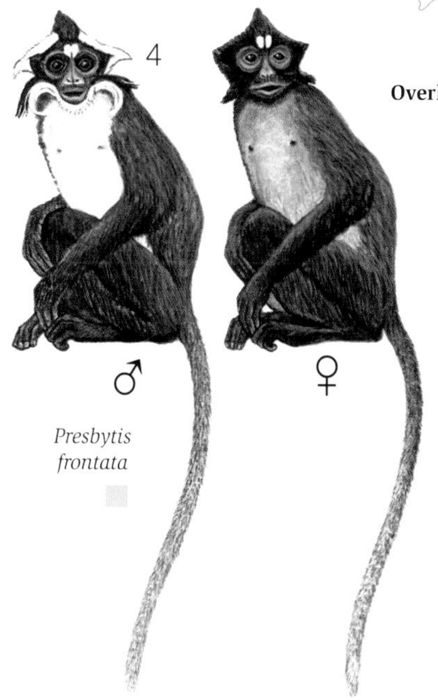

Presbytis frontata

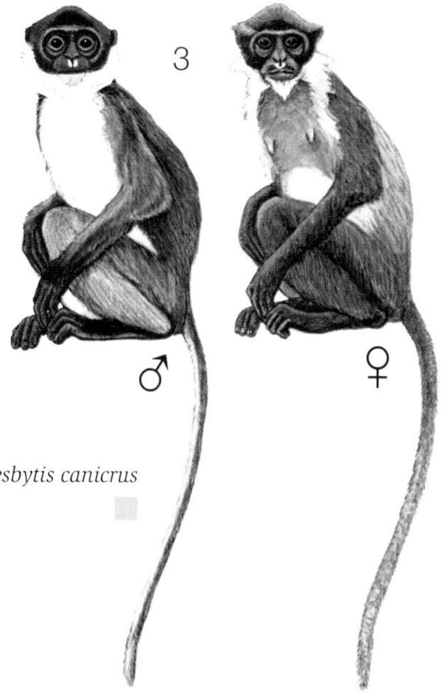

Presbytis canicrus

GREY LANGURS 2

GREY LANGUR ECOLOGY

Grey Langurs are less common in Borneo than Red Langurs with the exception of 3 sites, (1) Ulu Temburong (Brunei), (2) Tabin Wildlife Reserve (Sabah) and (3) Betung Kerihun (NW Kalimantan) where Grey Langurs are more common. Grey Langurs eat more leaves and less unripe seeds than Red Langurs and outcompete Red Langurs in habitats with less fruit. Grey Langurs are replaced in coastal forest by Silvered Langurs and do not occur in peatswamp. Grey Langur troops are strictly territorial and therefore cannot survive logging and poaching whilst Silvered Langur troops are non-territorial and can therefore survive in areas of poaching. This explains why Silvered Langurs survive whilst Grey Langurs have been hunted out in many areas.

Red Langurs are much bolder than Grey Langurs which appear to be exceptionally shy. On p. 157, I propose that Red Langurs benefit from mimicking the reddish coat colour of Orangutans which probably helps protect them from attacks by Clouded Leopards. In contrast Grey Langurs avoid attacks by hiding and are more likely to freeze than flee from danger. In comparison with Red Langurs, Grey Langur calls are softer and ventriloquial, difficult to trace back to source.

HOSE'S LANGUR AT ULU TEMBURONG, BRUNEI At Ulu Temburong Bennett et al (1987) estimated Hose's Langurs (3.25 groups per km^2) to be roughly twice as common as Red Langurs with groups ranging from 6–12 individuals. Red Langur density was estimated at 2.16 groups per km^2 but groups were smaller (avg. 6). Gibbons were also common 3.3 groups per km^2. In comparison with other sites in Borneo, Ulu Temburong has the highest density of langurs (43 per km^2) but this is still well below the avg. of 122 per km^2 in Malaya (Bennett 1987). The reason for the abundance at Ulu Temburong is probably the absence of Orangutans. The abundance of langurs in Malaya probably results from the abundance of leguminous trees in Malaya compared with Bornean forests dominated by dipterocarps. See pp 54–55 and 66–67.

SABAH LANGURS OF TABIN WILDLIFE RESERVE At Tabin, Davies & Payne (1987) estimated Sabah Langurs to be 4 x more common (4.25 groups km^2) than Red Langurs with an estimated Tabin population of c. 7,000 Hose's and 1,800 Red. Mitchell (1994) studied two troops of Sabah Langurs for 18 months in the forest around the Lipad Mud Volcano at Tabin. One troop occupied virgin forest around the mud volcano and the other occupied nearby logged forest. Both groups comprised 7–8 individuals led by an alpha male plus his harem and young. The troop in logged forest ranged over 45ha and ate more unripe fruit and seeds whilst the troop in virgin forest ranged over 35ha and ate more young leaves. **Diet:** There were 218 species of tree in Mitchell's study area but only 36 of these (16.5%) were used for food as well as 16 species of liana – mostly legumes. The forest was dominated by dipterocarps (70% of basal area) but young dipterocarp leaves made up only a tiny proportion of the diet. The dietary proportions of fruits, seeds and leaves varied monthly dependent upon availability. The two most popular food plants were the fruit and young leaves of Laran *Anthocephalus cadamba* p. 224 and the leaves of *Spatholobus* a common leguminous vine' pp. 68–69. See also p. 172.

BEZOARS: STONES OF DEATH

Bezoar stones, also known as Mustika Pearls or in Malay as Batu geliga, are hard, shiny, smooth mineral deposits about the size of a large marble found in the digestive organs of mammals. In Borneo bezoars are found in c 5% of the 4 species of grey langur. Bezoar stones have been traded from the forested interior of Borneo to China and Europe for at least the last 1,000 years. Bezoar stones were thought to have magical powers because the chemicals in some bezoars are capable of neutralizing arsenic poison. Today bezoars continue to be sold as good luck charms (p. 172).

Hunting for bezoars Historically bezoars were a scarce by-product of hunting for food. However Nijman (2005) describes how a coastal trader offering high prices for bezoars to villagers living next to Kayan Mentarang NP in NE Kalimantan resulted in the collapse of the local Hose's Langur population. In Kutai, once one of the finest forested parks in Borneo, the commercial hunting of *Presbytis langurs* for Batu geliga by immigrants working in Borneo's largest coal mine has wiped out the total population of Kutai and Kalimantan Langurs in the park (Setiawan, 2008).

Langur Langur Pangolin Porcupine

The alpha male Hose's Langur of the Belalong Canopy Walkway troop at Ulu Temburong in Brunei eating the unripe seeds of *Baccaurea bracteata* fruit. Gibbons swallow the sweet pulp of the ripe fruit and defecate the seeds but langurs eat only the unripe toxic seeds using specialized stomach bacteria to detoxify the poisons (p. 357). (Photo taken from the Belalong Canopy Walkway by Hans Hazebroek.)

NATUNA LANGUR (KEKAH) *Presbytis natunae* **HB 52, T 72** **Endemic to Bunguran Island**
Found only on Bunguran Besar, the largest Natuna island midway between Kota Kinabalu and Singapore in the S China Sea administered by Indonesia as part of the Riau Islands. **ID:** The only langur on Bunguran. Adults and young similar. **Call:** *Kek-Kah*, hence the local name. **Habits:** Everett, who visited in 1893, reported that 'these animals were common about the base of Mt Ranai, going in troops and they commit great depredations on the native gardens'. Bunguran was mostly covered in virgin primary forest until the 1980s, when it was heavily logged. Lammertink et al. (2003) found that Kekah was most common in the remaining patches of lowland primary forest, with a density of 2.3 groups per km^2, and 3.5 individuals per group. Kekah were present at lower densities in logged forest, hill forest, secondary forest and rubber gardens. **Conservation:** The largely Muslim population does not eat monkeys, and the main threat to the population is habitat destruction and hunting for the pet trade. Kekah are frequently kept as pets by locals and sold to Indonesian army personnel. Lammertink estimated the Kekah population as 30,000 (pre-logging), reduced to 10,000 (post logging). Bunguran Island is located next to the world's largest natural gas fields, currently being exploited by a consortium including Petronas, Pertamina and Elf. **Taxonomy:** First collected by Everett and described by Thomas and Hartert (1895) as the endemic *Semnopithecus natunae*, but **lumped** by Chasen (1940) as a race of Banded Langur. Later **split** by Groves (2001) as a Natuna endemic.

SPECIES/AREA RELATIONSHIPS Zoologists have long known that there is a **species/area relationship** (SAR) that applies both to islands and similar areas of habitat such as national parks. The larger the area, the more species and the greater the diversity. A large island or national park hosts not only greater numbers, but also more species of mammal, bird and plant than a smaller island. This relationship was clarified in 1963 when McArthur & Wilson published their Equilibrium Theory of Island Biogeography, which in simplified terms states: 1. Larger areas host more species than smaller areas. 2. Smaller islands have higher extinction rates and lower colonization rates. 3. Islands close to the mainland have higher immigration rates. 4. Eventually all islands reach an equilibrium (balance) between extinction and immigration, and the number of species stablizes.
In a 2008 paper Nijman & Meijaard listed the primate species resident on 215 SE Asian islands and confirmed that the largest islands had the greatest diversity. The result was the same whether the number of species was calculated using the Biological Species Concept (BSC), or the more recent Phylogenic Species Concept (PSC).

SPECIES/AREA RELATIONSHIPS – ISLANDS: Primates per Sundaland island

	Sundaland Total	Extra at LGM	Borneo	Sumatra	Malaya	Java	Palawan	Bunguran
Area km^2	2,000,000	612,113	743,380	443,066	131,598	53,588	14,650	1,605
Orangutan	2	0	1	1	0	0	0	0
Gibbons	9	0	4	3	3	1	0	0
Langurs	20	0	7	8	4	2	0	1
Macaques	3	0	2	2	3	1	1	1
Loris/Tarsier	5	0	2	2	2	1	0	1
Totals	**39**	**0**	**16**	**16**	**12**	**5**	**1**	**3**

Taxonomy based on *HBMW* (2013) 1. Mentawi Islands are not included. 2. Sundaland as per map opposite. 3. 'Malaya' denotes the Malay Peninsula, a bio-geographic term which includes a part of S. Thailand.

HOW TO DECIDE ON WHAT CONSTITUTES A SPECIES, BSC or PSC?
Definition of a species A genetically distinct unit that in the wild normally only breeds with its own species.
Problems with defining a species 1. Different species e.g. tigers and Lions, can produce hybrids in captivity. 2. Where wild mammal species are divided by islands or rivers, there is no way of telling if they will breed or not in the absence of these natural barriers.
Biological Species Concept (BSC) Traditional zoologists used morphology, bone shape, body size and coat colours to decide on what was a species, but often species occur in several morphs, like most Bornean langurs.
Phylogenetic Species Concept (PSC) Uses measurements of genetic differences in DNA and RNA to decide on species. However, species may be split based on as little as 2% in difference, or lumped even at a 5% difference. One problem is that measurements are often not standardized on the same part of the genome.
Conclusion Traditional zoologists tended to be either lumpers, like Chasen (1940), who combined related mammals into fewer species, or splitters, like Groves (2001), who divided many of Chasen's mammals into more species. Using DNA, we can now find the precise per cent genetic difference between two similar mammals. Based on standardized measurements scientists are likely to come to a consensus in future on the degree of genetic difference that constitutes a species (pp. 108 and 156.)

Natuna Langur (Kekah)
Presbytis natunae
Male, female and juveniles look the same, but some infants may have additional white markings on the face.

The Natuna Islands are located midway between Kota Kinabalu and Singapore

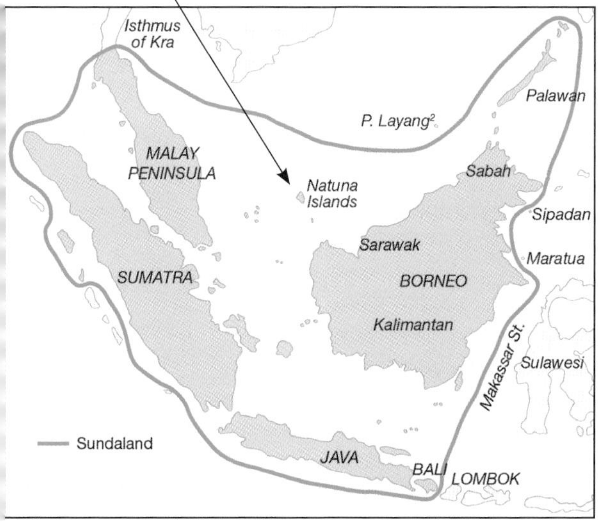

SARAWAK LANGUR *Presbytis chrysomelas* **HB 52, T 73, Wt 5.5–7kg Rare endemic W Sarawak** [Iban: Bijit, Lundu Dayak: Penyatat] [Payne: Banded Langur *Presbytis melalophos*, Brandon-Jones: Sarawak Surili, Bennett: Red-banded Langur, Groves et al, in *HBMW*: Cross-marked Langur, Bornean Banded Langur, Tricoloured Langur]. Once Sarawak's most common lowland leaf-eating monkey, the beautiful Sarawak Langur is now on the verge of extinction, with a population of under 300 individuals (Jason Hon), one of the most threatened primates in the world. (p. 368). **ID:** Very variable. Most individuals can be split into one of **two morphs**: black with a white or grey belly, and reddish with a pale belly and a 'black cross' along the arms and down the back. The young of all morphs are pale white/grey/reddish, with a 'black cross' along the back and across the arms. The black morph is dominant in W Kalimantan and at Samunsam, whilst the Maludam population is all reddish. Further north at Similajau, mixed groups occur. **Mimicry:** The black morph has a typical counter-shaded camouflage pattern, whilst the warning colours of the reddish morph probably mimic the Orangutan (pp. 156 and 162 for the explanation). **Habits:** In 1949 Banks, the curator of the Sarawak Museum (1925–45), wrote 'the commonest langur, found 6 or 7 at a time on mountains up to 1,000m, on hills, plains and occasionally estuarine swamps. A langur of primary forest having little contact with cultivation'. **Relict Populations** survive in three small areas of coastal forest in W Sarawak, with the majority in Samunsan/Tg Datu NP, where it has been researched by Bennett (1986, 1988, 1990), Rajanathan (1992), Jebron (2006) and Ampeng & Zain (2011). **Ecology:** At Samunsam, 3 leaf-eating primates co-exist sympatrically in a matrix of coastal forest, mangroves, riverine forest and mixed dipterocarp forest (MDF). Sarawak Langurs preferred young leaves in the MDF, Proboscis preferred riverine forest and Silvered Langurs preferred mangrove and coastal forest. All primates moved between different habitats dependent on the seasonal availability of young leaves and immature fruit. **Call:** 'A noisy staccato chuckle like that of a big squirrel. First 2 notes then a pause followed by a series of 3 or 4 more. The young make a querulous mewing cat like noise sometimes to be heard at night' (Banks 1931). Adult male loud call a staccato '*ke-ke-ke-ke-ke*' (Payne 1985). **Historical distribution:** Recorded north of the Kapuas River east to Gng Kenepai and Danau Sentarum, where the Dutch Scientific Expedition recorded both red and black morphs (Jentink 1897), north to the Baram River where Hose collected both red and black morphs from the same group (Hose 1893). There are no records from Brunei and Sabah. The record for Melalap, in Sabah, Groves (2001) is an error. **Current distribution:** Very scarce or extinct throughout the historical range with small populations at Samunsam, Maludam and Similajau, all in Sarawak. Other recent isolated records are from Niah (Tan 2001), and Danau Sentarum (Wadley 2006). The historical range of Sarawak Langur includes the lower slopes of the Betung Kerihun NP (now heavily hunted), and it is unlikely to occur in Lanjak Entimau.

SARAWAK LANGUR TAXONOMIC CONFUSION
Due to its very variable colouration the Sarawak Langur has been subject to much taxonomic confusion. Banks (1931) listed the Sarawak Langur as two Bornean endemics *Pygathrix cruciger* (red) and *P. chrysomelas* (black). Chasen's (1940) *Handlist of Malaysian Mammals* recorded black and red as two races of the Banded Langur of Malaya and Sumatra. This approach was followed by Medway (1978) and Payne et al. (1985). However, Liz Bennett, who studied both species in the wild, considers the Sarawak Langur different enough to be a separate species. This approach was followed by Groves & Roos (*HBMW* 2013), who call it the Cross-marked Langur *P. chrysomelas*, endemic to Borneo. Here we follow *HBMW* taxonomy, but treat it as one endemic species with multiple morphs rather than 3 subspecies. We also rename it the Sarawak Langur, as the distribution has always centred on Sarawak, and the continued survival of the Sarawak Langur depends entirely on the good will of the people of Sarawak and the future policies of the Sarawak government (p. 368).

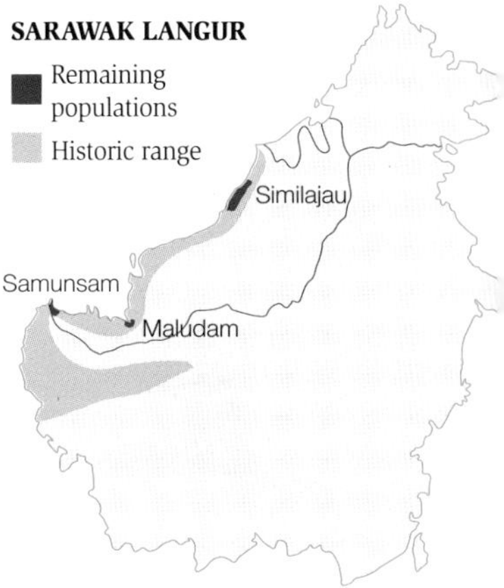

HISTORICAL RANGES OF RED AND SARAWAK LANGURS Historically these langurs had allopatric (non-overlapping) ranges, indicating that they are closely related and share a similar ecological niche (p. 163).

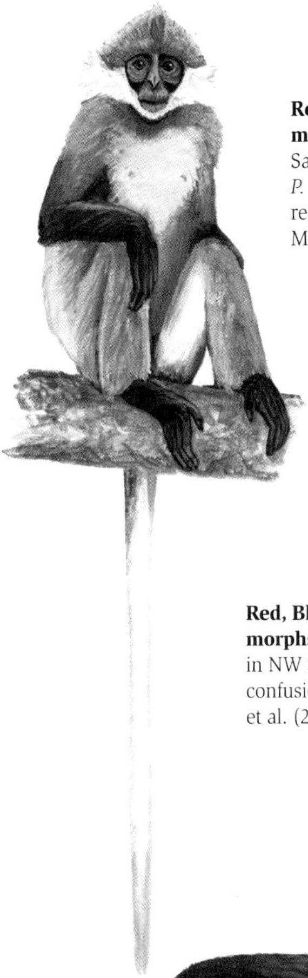

Red *cruciger* morph of Sarawak Langur *P. chrysomelas* resident at Maludam.

Red, Black and Intermediate morphs occur together at Similajau in NW Sarawak leading to much confusion in the past. See Duckworth et al. (2011).

Black *chryosmelas* morph of Sarawak Langur *P. chrysomelas* resident at Samunsam.

SILVERED LANGUR

MALAY: LUTONG KELABU

SILVERED LANGUR *Trachypithecus cristatus* **HB 478, T 680, Wt 4.0–6.5kg** **Locally common**
Locally common langur of coastal mangroves throughout Borneo, occasionally found far inland along large rivers. Recorded inland at Deramakot, Danum, Maliau Basin, Gng Mulu and 900m on Gng Dulit in NW Sarawak. The site of the Shell Complex at Miri is named after the Malay name of this langur, 'Lutong'. Best sites to see: Sabah Klias (W Sabah), Labuk Bay Resort (Sandakan), Sukau (Kinabatangan); Brunei Panaga Club (Seria), Kuala Tutong; Sarawak Permai Resort (Santubong), Bako; Kalimantan Kutai (E Kalimantan), Tg Puting, Sabangau (C Kalimantan). **ID:** Adult is dark grey all over mixed with greyish-white hairs, giving a 'silvered' appearance. Infant is bright orange for the first 3 months of life, gradually turning grey. Males are about 10–20% larger than females, which usually have white markings around the groin that are lacking in males. **Black morph:** Very dark, almost black populations occur, in SE Kalimantan (Abbot in Lyon 2011) and Serasan, Natunas (Everett). **Pale reddish morph** A pale white morph with a reddish-orange tinge to the fur has often been recorded from Deramakot, Danau Pitas (Kinabatangan) and Kutai. The proportion of pale morphs varies from group to group. Liz Bennett reports that a captive group of reddish morphs at the Bronx Zoo (New York) is slowly breeding back to the normal grey The persistence of this morph in the wild indicates that it confers a survival advantage, possibly by confusing predators such as Clouded Leopard that the langur may be an Orangutan or a Pig-tailed Macaque. **Distinguished from grey langurs** (p. 164) by plain dark grey face. All the grey langurs have some white markings on the face. Distinguish from Long-tailed Macaques (p.180) by triangular 'crest' on top of the head. **Habits:** Diurnal and mostly arboreal. The most common langur in mangrove forest. Often shares habitat with the Proboscis. **Call:** 'When a gun is fired this langur makes the forest resound with deep groaning hoots quite unlike its ordinary note, which may be described as *che-koh*' (Everett). **Diet:** Has the longest digestive gut of any langur. This allows it to digest leaves and seeds too toxic or tough for other langurs, perhaps one reason why it has survived whilst other langurs have vanished from many areas. Unlike Red Langur and grey langurs, not known to visit salt springs, presumably because of the salt contained in mangrove leaves. **Breeding:** Harem breeding as in other langurs and Proboscis Monkey (p. 174). At Kuala Selangor (Malaya) three troops studied by Medway (1970) bred year round. Average family group size at Samunsam in Sarawak 5–6. **Taxonomy:** Groves (2013) in *HBMW* split off the Malayan and Javan Silvered Langurs. **Range:** *T. cristatus* is found in Sumatra, the Riau Islands and Borneo with two races 1. *T. c. cristatus* throughout, apart from 2. *T. c. vigilans* confined to the small island of Serasan in the south Natuna Islands.

BEZOAR STONES AND PERSIMMON FRUIT Bezoar stones are commercially valuable stony deposits found in the digestive organs of langurs, porcupines and pangolins. In Borneo bezoars are most common in the four species of grey langur, but may occur in the other langurs, including Proboscis Monkey and Silvered Langur (p. 165). Research shows that the Silvered Langur is able to eat the most toxic leaves, whilst grey langurs follow a close second. It is believed that salt *Sodium chloride* aids friendly bacteria in the animal's stomach to digest cellulose and neutralize leaf toxins and bitter tannins. Most Silvered Langurs live in coastal forest and the mangrove leaves they eat have a high salt content, so they do not need to visit salt licks or mineral springs, whilst grey langurs that live in inland forests regularly visit mineral springs.

Origin of bezoars There are many myths concerning the origin of bezoars, but it is known that a diet of unripe persimmon fruit (*Diospyros virginiana* in the USA) is particularly likely to cause bezoars in humans. At least 80 species of wild persimmon (*Diospyros* species – Kayu malam or Kayu arang) occur in Bornean forests, where they are an important primate fruit. At Tabin, Mitchell (1994) found that Sabah Grey Langurs ate the young leaves and seeds of four species of *Diospyros*, and *Disopyros* was one of the top 10 langur food trees. Locals regard unripe persimmon fruit and seeds as highly toxic, and use them as a fish poison.

Borneo Persimmon *Diospyros borneensis* The fruit ripen pale green, indicating that the seeds are targeted at fruit bats or langurs for dispersal. *Diospyros* fruit are easily recognized by the 3–8 triangular calyx at the base of the fruit stalk.

Normal morph with three-month-old infant

Reddish morph with three-month-old infant. Note the pale face. Red Langurs have black faces.

Silvered Langur babies are bright orange for the first 3 months of their lives so they can be easily seen and protected from danger by the whole group. Young macaques are black and young Red Langurs are white for the same reason.

Normal morph with four-month-old infant.

RELIGION AND WILDLIFE IN BORNEO

Most coastal fishing communities around Borneo have been Muslims for at least 600 years following the arrival of Muslim traders from Yemen, who married locals and became the first rajahs of coastal Sultanates. In contrast, the majority of Borneo's inland tribes either remained animist or were converted to Christianity by western missionaries in the 20th century, as they refused to give up hunting wild pigs. In addition to pigs, Islam also prohibits the eating of monkeys and turtles. Today these religious differences mean that the wildlife of coastal areas populated by Muslim fisherfolk often survives whilst wildlife is scarce near to most inland villages.

PROBOSCIS MONKEY MALAY: MONYET BELANDA; INDONESIAN: BEKANTAN

COLOBINAE Proboscis Monkeys are closely related to the langurs and share the same leafy diet and specialized digestion (p.156). The closest relative is the relict Pig-tailed Langur (Simakobou) of the Mentawi Islands, W Sumatra.

PROBOSCIS MONKEY *Nasalis larvatus* **H & B 20–40cm, T 20–50cm, Wt Male 24kg, F 12kg Local**
Locally common in mangroves and river estuaries along the Borneo coast, but often absent due to hunting. Often wanders inland along rivers into the hills, and has been recorded at Danum Valley, Imbak Canyon and Maliau Basin (Sabah), Barito Ulu and the Kayan Mentarang NP in Kalimantan (Puri 2005). **ID:** Males are twice as large as females, with massive noses and prominent white rump-patches that continue down the tail. Females have smaller pointed noses and grey rumps and tails. Infants under 4 months old are covered in thin back hair. **Habits:** Proboscis Monkey populations are highest in undisturbed riverine forest adjacent to peat-swamp or mangrove forest. Along the Kinabatangan River, the monkeys forage inland and return each afternoon to roost in a different tall tree overlooking the river. Troops of langurs, macaques and Proboscis often roost in the same or nearby trees without aggression. Proboscis Monkey troops have feeding home ranges of 100–900ha, but they are non-territorial. Alpha males defend their harem females against rival males, but do not defend feeding territories. **Call:** The large male nose acts as a loudspeaker to amplify the alpha males' loud honking and roaring calls given in the evening at roosting sites. Calls are often accompanied by jumps and leaps to show off the alpha males' health. **Diet:** Typical langur diet of unripe seeds and young leaves. Unripe seeds are preferred, indicating that young leaves are a fallback food (p. 176). **Range:** Endemic to Borneo, including the island of P. Laut off the coast of SE Kalimantan. Not found on Banka and Biliton Islands between Borneo and Sumatra, suggesting a prehistoric catastrophic event eliminated Proboscis Monkeys from the mangrove habitat on the coast of SE Sumatra. An uncorroborated report by Motley (1855) records Proboscis Monkeys on the east coast of Sumatra in 1854 (p. 139).

PROBOSCIS MONKEY BREEDING Proboscis Monkeys live in harem groups dominated by an alpha male. Troops of to 32 have been recorded. Alpha males have exclusive breeding rights in the troop until the ageing male is defeated in a fight with a younger, stronger usurper, which may end in death. Young males leave the family group at around two years old to join all-male groups. They become sexually mature at 5–8 years old. Eventually, at around 10 years old, they become strong enough to challenge an alpha male and if successful, take over the breeding rights of the harem. After a takeover, females may move group, especially when they have young babies or are pregnant, presumably to protect their young from attack by the new alpha male. Males are much heavier than females. The reason for this is probably dual purpose – larger, stronger males will win in a fight for dominance, and only a large male has the size and strength to defend its troop against Clouded Leopard attacks. When facing danger or crossing rivers, alpha males always defend the rear. The enormous nose is believed to be a signal of a male's health both to other males and its own female harem. Dominant males usually exhibit a permanently erect bright red penis, and actively display their strength and vigour at roosting sites by leaping from tree to tree and calling.

PIG-TAILED LANGUR *Simias concolor* (Simakobou) of the isolated Mentawi Islands off the west coast of N Sumatra is the closest relative of the Proboscis Monkey. The relict distribution indicates that a common ancestor once populated most of SE Asia including Sundaland, but later became extinct. Today the Proboscis is confined to Borneo. A possible explanation was supplied by Meijaard (1994). who suggests that Proboscis were once common along Sundaland's coast, but were wiped out by a traumatic event such as rapidly rising sea levels, leaving a small relict population on an island refuge off the coast of Borneo. When conditions improved, the monkeys swam the channel to Borneo and spread around the coast, but as yet have not managed to swim to Sumatra or the intervening islands of Banka and Biliton. The most likely refuge island is suggested to be Pulau Laut, but it could easily have been Sebatik, Nunukan or Tarakan. Alternatively, Proboscis Monkeys may have survived in an inland riverine refuge, before returning to repopulate the Bornean coast.

INFANTICIDE BY ALPHA MALES According to Agoramoorthy (2013), the Proboscis Monkeys at Labuk Bay (Sandakan) in 2003 divided into 5 groups. One group was all male, the other 4 were harem groups, each dominated by a single alpha male. The overall sex ratio excluding infants was one male to 5 females. Singapore Zoo records indicate that male and female Proboscis Monkey births are roughly equal. It appears that males are five times more likely to die than females before adulthood. Possible reasons are: 1. Male infants suffer higher mortality than females. 2. All-male groups suffer higher predation. 3. Alpha males kill rival males to take over their troops. 4. Alpha males selectively kill male but not female infants.

Although all 4 factors may apply, explanation 4 seems most likely to explain the missing adult males. Agoramoorthy witnessed two deaths in 2002–3. The leader of an all-male group killed the alpha male of a harem group, and shortly afterwards killed an infant in the same group. The mother of the infant rapidly came into oestrus and mated with the new alpha male. The sex of the dead infant was unknown.

PROBOSCIS MONKEY 2: ECOLOGY

Diet At the Menanggul River near Sukau on the Kinabatangan, Matsuda (2009) followed a Proboscis Monkey harem troop led by a dominant alpha male for 13 months (2005–6). There were 5 breeding females in the group and 5–8 juveniles. Young leaves dominated the diet apart from during fruiting seasons, when both unripe and ripe seeds were preferred. Matsuda found that Proboscis Monkeys are generalist leaf and seed predators, eating small amounts of a large number (188 species) of plants. The monkeys also regularly ate the nests of an arboreal termite, *Microcerotermes distans*.

Seed dispersal Proboscis Monkeys predated the unripe seeds of *Ficus binnendijkii* (bird fig), but dispersed the ripe seeds of *F. globosa* (bat fig). They also dispersed the tiny, hard seeds of *Antidesma thwaitesianum* and *Nauclea subdita* (Rubiaceae), indicating that these are specialist langur-dispersed fruit. See Perepat illustration opposite. Boonratana (2003), who also studied the diet of Proboscis Monkeys along the Kinabatangan River, found that young leaves low in tannins and saponins were eaten, not mature leaves. Unripe seeds and fruit were preferred when available. Bennett & Rajahnathan (1990, 1992) at Samunsam found that Proboscis Monkeys prefer to feed in riverine floodplain forest, and use mangrove forest during lean periods when no trees are fruiting in the riverine forest. (p.156).

Predation by Clouded Leopards The most commonly observed predators of Proboscis Monkeys are Clouded Leopards. See Davis (1962), Matsuda (2009) and numerous anecdotal accounts. Saltwater Crocodiles, which are still common in many areas may kill more. At Tg Puting, Yeager (1985) noted that Proboscis use a number of anti-predator strategies that would otherwise seem unnecessary:

1 They often forage away from the river but always roost next to the river for escape by jumping into it.
2 Proboscis have partly webbed feet and are excellent swimmers, but never play in water.
3 When roosting they prefer trees along narrow rivers so they will not have far to swim.
4 Langurs and macaques often roost next to Proboscis Monkeys to gain safety in numbers.

When the Kinabatangan forest is flooded Proboscis Monkey troops roost inland away from the river bank (Matsuda 2009). Pythons and Water Monitors *Varanus salvatore* also attack Proboscis Monkeys.

RUMINATION BY PROBOSCIS MONKEYS
Rumination, also known as 'chewing the cud', is the regurgitation of foliage that has been swallowed and softened by bacterial digestion in the forestomach back into the mouth, so that it can be re-chewed into smaller pieces. Rumination is standard practice for forestomach digesters such as cows and deer, but had never been recorded for langurs until reported by Matsuda (2014). Matsuda only recorded rumination on 11 days out of 169, and reported that rumination speeded up digestion, allowing the Proboscis Monkeys to feed for longer during the day. (p.156)

Proboscis Monkey eats a Nipah Palm flower spathe at the mouth of the Kinabatangan River in E Sabah, as recorded by Boonratana (2003).

WHY REPTILES ARE THE TOP MAMMALIAN PREDATORS IN BORNEO Borneo hosts 6 large reptiles, including 4 crocodiles and 2 pythons, the most important large mammal predators in Borneo.

1 **Saltwater Crocodile *Crocodylus porosus*** Common, large crocodile, a notorious man-eater. To 6m.
2 **Tomistoma *Tomistoma schlegeli*** Most common crocodile in Kalimantan peat-swamps. To 5m.
3 **Frog-nosed Crocodile *Crocodylus raninus*** Rare endemic. Kalimantan north to Loagan Bunut.
4 **Siamese Crocodile *Crocodylus siamensis*** Rare, Mahakam Lakes, Kalimantan. To 4m.
5 **Borneo Blood Python *Python breitensteini*** Endemic. Abundant in oil palm. To 2m.
6 **Reticulated Python *Python reticulatus*** World's largest snake, common throughout. To 10m.

Large reptilian predators dominate the carnivorous food chain in Borneo because their slow, cold-blooded metabolism allows them to survive 3 or more months without food, whilst a tiger, Leopard or Clouded Leopard needs to eat every 3 days. Thus, during lean periods between forest mastings, when even generalist foragers such as pigs and Sun Bears die of starvation, these reptiles can wait it out. Bezuijen et al. (2005, 2013), Cox (1993), Bonke (2008), Frazier (2000), Stuebing et al. (2014).

PEREPAT (PEDADA) ***SONNERATIA***
Three species of *Sonneratia* are abundant trees of mangrove forest around the coast of Borneo. The distinctive fruit, capped with 5–7 triangular sepals, ripen to green and are eaten by locals as part of a sour salad known as *ulam*. The white fluffy flowers are pollinated by *Macroglossus* and *Eonycteris* nectar bats (p. 96). Both the leaves and the fruit are a favourite food of the Proboscis Monkey and Silvered Langur, which disperse the tiny seeds. *Sonneratia* are part of a group that produce sugar-free fruit with tiny seeds which evolved for langur dispersal including Laran (p. 224) and Bangkal *Nauclea orientalis*, a common tree of the Kinabatangan floodplain (Valentine Thiry and Oriana Bhasin).

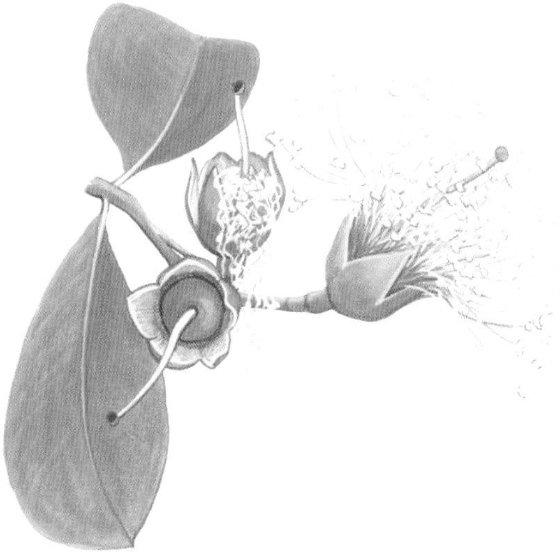

TOMISTOMA ***Tomistoma schlegeli*** seizing a Proboscis Monkey in a black-water river at Tg Puting in C Kalimantan. Also known as the False Gharial, the Tomistoma has a long, thin jaw filled with sharp teeth, evolved for catching fish. Yeager (1985) records 3 instances of Tomistoma killing primates, once a Long-tailed Macaque and twice a Proboscis Monkey. A large, 4m Tomistoma has also been recorded killing a man moving a raft of logs in the same area. In the black freshwater peat-swamp rivers of Tg Putting, the Tomistoma is more common than the Saltwater Crocodile, which is more common in brackish water closer to the sea.

PROBOSCIS MONKEY 3: CONSERVATION

Preferred habitat River-bank vegetation, but rivers have been the main highways of Borneo for thousands of years and as a result of persistent hunting Proboscis Monkeys retreated to fallback habitat in coastal mangroves, which are now severely threatened by development for industry, fish and prawn farms. Proboscis Monkeys are legally protected throughout Borneo, but hunting by non-Muslims continues to drive local populations towards extinction in Sarawak and Kalimantan.

Sabah Most of the mangrove forest in Sabah is protected as forest reserve, but is under heavy pressure for development. The estimated Sabah population totals 5,900 (Sha et al. 2011), with about 1,500 along the Kinabatangan River and 800 remaining in the Klias wetlands (they can be viewed on a day trip from Kota Kinabalu). See opposite for Labuk Bay.

Brunei Due to its oil wealth and conservation ethic, Brunei has resisted development and a healthy population of about 1,500 remains around Brunei Bay (can be viewed on easily arranged evening boat cruises).

Sarawak In 1988, Bennett estimated the Sarawak population as about 700, but the current population is probably under 500 due to hunting pressure. Sarawak sold most of its mangroves to Japan for pulping in the 1990s and the forests have not yet recovered. Banks (1931) reported that Proboscis Monkeys were common around Kuching, and they can still be seen on Kuching river cruises but appear to be terrified. There is a fully protected population of around 200 at Bako (Nasir 2012), but all other Sarawak populations remain at risk due to poaching.

Kalimantan MacKinnon (1987) estimated a Kalimantan population of some 250,000 Proboscis Monkeys. A more realistic estimate today is under 15,000. The largest secure population is at Tg Puting NP, which is probably in excess of 2,000. Lhota (2008) estimated the population around the rapidly developing Balikpapan Bay at 1,400, but most of this mangrove forest is unprotected. Smaller, severely fragmented populations in many areas of Kalimantan are hunted by non-Muslims (Dyaks), for example at the Mahakam Lakes and Danau Sentarum, and are headed for total extinction in the next 20–30 years. The very rough estimates for Kalimantan populations opposite are based on Meijaard & Nijman (2000).

PROBOSCIS MONKEY DENSITY IN DIFFERENT HABITATS

Site	Location	Pop. km^2	Forest Type	Source
Menanggul River	Kinabatangan, E Sabah	30	River floodplain	Matsuda (2009)
Samunsam	SW Sarawak coast	6	Riverine p. 170	Bennett et al (1988)
Natai Lengkus	Tg Puting, Kalimantan	63	Peat-swamp forest	Yeager (1989)

COULD PROBOSCIS MONKEYS BE REINTRODUCED IN PROTECTED AREAS?

Despite multiple attempts, only zoos in Singapore and Java, which have easy access to abundant supplies of local tree foliage, have managed to breed Proboscis Monkeys in captivity. Most captive Proboscis Monkeys die rapidly from stress and dietary problems. However, wild Proboscis Monkeys thrive in relatively small areas of protected coastal forest such as at Bako (Kuching) and Labuk Bay (Sandakan). At Labuk Bay supplementary feeding has led to an expanding population. There are many coastal areas in W Borneo where Proboscis Monkeys are absent and could be reintroduced, including the coastal mangrove forests north of Kota Kinabalu at the Nexus and Rasa Ria resorts.

A mature adult male Proboscis (Photo: Cede Prudente).

PROBOSCIS MONKEY POPULATIONS

	SABAH	
1	Kinabatangan	1,500
2	Segama	1,000
3	Klias	800
	Other	2,600
	BRUNEI	
4	Brunei Bay	1,500
	SARAWAK	
5	Bako	200
	Other	500
	KALIMANTAN	
6	Danau Sentarum	500
7	Sambas Paloh	500
8	Gng Palung	500
9	Kendawangan	1,000
10	Tg Puting	2,000
11	Barito river area	1,500
12	Balikpapan Bay	1,400
13	Mahakam lakes	500
14	Samarinda delta	500
15	Sebuku area	2,000
	Other	2,200
	BORNEO	**20,700**

BORNEO POPULATION ESTIMATES

Sabah	5,900	Sha (2008)
Brunei	1,500	Estimate
Sarawak	700	Bennett (1988)
Kalimantan	12,600	Estimate
Borneo	20,700	Estimate

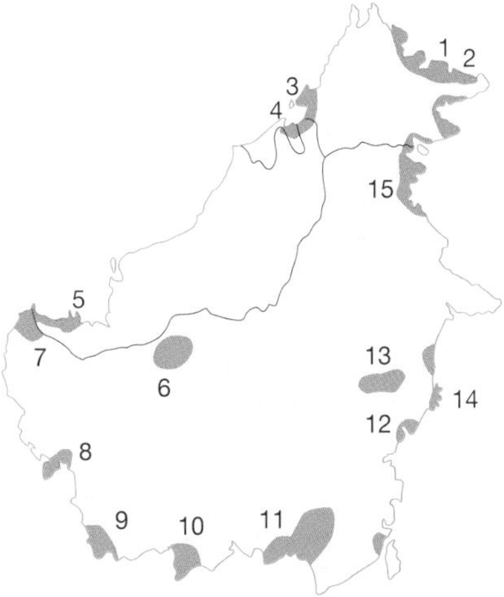

ABUK BAY PROBOSCIS MONKEY SANCTUARY (SANDAKAN) This comprises 162ha of coastal mangroves facing Labuk Bay, surrounded by 500ha of degraded coastal secondary forest reserve, in turn surrounded by an oil-palm plantation. When the original forest was converted to oil palm, the workers noticed that the Proboscis Monkeys were stealing food from their kitchen and so started feeding them on cucumbers, green beans and sugar-free flour pancakes. With the extra food the population of Proboscis Monkeys at Labuk Bay continues to expand year after year. Feeding takes place twice a day and attracts a variety of wildlife, including Silvered Langurs, Pied Hornbills, White-bellied Sea Eagles and Brahminy Kites, as well as tourists.

LONG-TAILED MACAQUE *Macaca fascicularis* **HB 435, T 550, M 5–7kg, F 3–4kg** **Common**
[Crab-eating Macaque] The most common monkey of disturbed and secondary forest in the lowlands to about 1,300m in the mountains. A small feral troop forages around the Gng Emas resort (1,800m) in the Crocker Range. In virgin dipterocarp forest, confined to the forest edge along rivers, for example at Danum Valley. Common on many small islands, including Gaya Island (KK), Pulau Tiga (W Sabah) and Maratua (NE Kalimantan). **ID:** Overlaps in size with Pig-tailed Macaques, but usually 30% smaller, more grey than brown. and with a longer straighter tail. Infants are covered in thin black hair for the first six weeks. **Habits:** The natural habitat is jungle river banks, but Long-tailed Macaques are now common around towns and on public beaches. Macaques often raid orchards and steal food from houses and tourists. **Predators:** At night on the Kinabatangan River, troops roost together in a tall riverside trees, presumably for protection against Clouded Leopards. Saltwater Crocodiles *Crocodylus porosus* frequently take Long-tailed Macaques from river banks (p. 176). **Diet:** The most omnivorous and flexible in diet of all the Bornean primates. Eats fruit, seeds, leaves, insects and small animals dependent on availability. Forages for crabs in mangroves and on beaches. Food is stored in cheek pouches for later consumption in a safe place. **Seed dispersal:** Corlett & Lucas (1990) found that seeds under 4mm width were swallowed and dispersed. Larger seeds were spat out, near the fruiting tree. **Call:** Warning call a series of explosive grunts, *kera kera*, higher pitched than call of the Berok. **Breeding:** Lives in groups of 5–80, which forage and roost together led by a large, dominant alpha male. Most troops contain a few subdominant males and a majority of breeding females and their young. Long-tailed Macaques groom each other more than any other primate in Borneo, showing strong social bonds. Males often switch groups or forage in small all-male groups. **Research:** Wheatley (1978), Aldrich-Blake (1980), Englehardt et al. (2006), Fooden (1995). **Range:** Tropical SE Asia from Bangladesh, north to S Vietnam and east to Timor. Common in the Philippines but not on Sulawesi. **Borneo race** *M. f. fascicularis.*

NUISANCE LONG-TAILED MACAQUES Before 1982, W Malaysia exported around 10,000 Long-tailed Macaques every year for the testing of drugs and cosmetics to be used on humans. Due to protests from animal rights groups, macaque exports were banned in 1982. However, increasing land development in W Malaysia has resulted in a population explosion of urban Long-tailed Macaques with no natural predators. Large numbers live on the fringes of cities, subsisting on food handouts and by raiding refuse dumps. In 2011 the W Malaysian authorities instructed state wildlife departments to cull an estimated 100,000 macaques a year, a target that was reportedly achieved in 2012 and 2013, and resulted in much adverse publicity. Current policies towards urban macaques are not publicized. In Borneo some non-Muslim locals still hunt and eat macaques. www.ippl.com

MARATUA MACAQUE The Maratua race of the Long-tailed Macaque is distinctly darker grey than the Long-tailed Macaques resident on mainland Borneo, and was described as a distinct race, *M. fascicularis tua*, by Kellogg in 1947. Pulau Maratua, (*c.* 2,376ha), 50km off the coast of NE Kalimantan, is zoologically important because it has never been connected to the Bornean mainland, even during periods of low sea level in the last 2.6 million years. The only non-flying mammals are two species of rat, a shrew and several troops of Long-tailed Macaques. Due to Maratua's relatively long isolation at least two species of resident bird, the Maratua Shama and the Maratua Bulbul, have evolved into endemic species (Chua, Sheldon et al. 2015). Fooden (1995) lists 10 different races of L.T. Macaque, including four similar dark, geographically isolated races from 'deep-water' islands: 1. the Nicobar Islands, 2. P. Simeulue and P. Lasia W Sumatra, 3. the Philippines and 4. Maratua. Fooden speculates that these isolated races are relicts (living fossils) of the original founder Long-tailed Macaques in SE Asia. Maratua is an atoll, the remnant of an extinct volcano, and the macaques probably arrived by 'rafting' (p. 40).

WHITE EYELIDS Many Bornean primates have pale markings around the eyes, but the two macaque species have additional prominent white eyelids, presumably to make it look as if their eyes are open when they are sleeping.

The drongo as the servant of the Kera 'The drongo is often called the servant of the Kera from its habit of following a troop of these monkeys. It does not accompany them out of altruism, but in order to catch the various small insects which the monkeys disturb as they jump from tree to tree.' (Hose 1929) (p.242)

MACAQUE SOCIAL SYSTEMS A study of wild Long-tailed Macaques at Ketambe in Sumatra (Englehardt et al. 2006) found that in a troop of 5 adult males and 8 adult females, the majority of infants were sired by 2 alpha males, one of which visited from a neighbouring troop. Females were fertile in 4 days of each ovulation cycle, and were escorted by a dominant male throughout the fertile period. Escorted females mated with an average of 2.7 partners, whilst unescorted females mated with an average of 5.2 partners. Despite multiple partners, 4 out of 6 infants born during the study were sired by alpha males.
Females mated more often with dominant males, but Englehardt's conclusion was that the reason that dominant males sired most of the infants was due to "post-mating events in the females' reproductive tracts", which may be due to one or more of the following:

1 Higher quality sperm of dominant males.
2 Females only mated with low-ranking males when they are infertile (false oestrus).
3 Females are able to select sperm after copulation in some way.

GREATER RAQUET-TAILED DRONGO
Dicrurus paradiseus
A common bird of the forest edge and forest gaps in Borneo.

PIG-TAILED MACAQUE *Macaca nemestrina* **HB 495, T 180, Wt M 7–9kg, F 4–6kg** **Common**
[Southern Pig-tailed Macaque] Locally common in forested areas, especially in hill forest and at the edge of oil palm and forest. **ID:** Generally larger and pale brown rather than grey, as compared with Long-tailed Macaque. The short, twisted, pig-like tail is distinctive. Hybrids between the two species have been recorded at Sepilok Orangutan Rehabilitation Centre, where both are abundant. According to local guides, these hybrids are social rejects and are probably infertile. **Habits:** Not as widespread or as flexible in habits as Long-tailed Macaque, which is more common in secondary and coastal forest. In undisturbed forest the habits of the two species are very different. Long-tailed Macaque forages in pioneer vegetation that fruits continuously along river banks, whilst Pig-tailed Macaque troops travel long distances on the ground feeding on scarce fruiting trees. Fruiting figs are likely found from barbet calls (Wong Siew Te). Usually flees from threats on the ground, unlike all other Bornean primates, which climb through the trees. **Call:** Warning call is a harsh grunt ending like the crack of a whip, hence the local name, Berok. **Diet:** Mainly fruit and insects, but including leaves and bark. According to Corner (1992), his botanical macaques were immune to rengas, the highly irritant sap of several trees in the Anacardiace (mango) family, but could not tolerate rhapides, the dangerous calcium oxalate crystal produced by some palms (p. 50). **Fruit:** At Pasoh (Malaya), Yasuda et al. (2005) camera-trapped mammals that fed on 49 species of fallen fruit. They found that of 13 terrestrial mammals Pig-tailed Macaque ate 90% of the fruit species, whilst wild pigs (*Sus scrofa*) only ate 30%. In many areas of Borneo where plantations abut forest, oil-palm fruits have replaced figs as a fallback food, leading to abnormally high non-nomadic populations of Pig-tailed Macaques. **Meat:** At the Segari Melintang FR in Malaya researchers found that P. T. Macaques habitually hunted rats in an oil-palm estate next to the forest. **Seed dispersal and predation:** Pig-tailed Macaques use their cheek pouches to store fruit temporarily before retiring to a safe spot to swallow the sweet flesh, whilst spitting out the toxic seeds (p. 65). Some small seeds, such as those of figs, are swallowed and defecated. Non-toxic large seeds such as those of dipterocarps, and oak acorns are predated during masts (p. 42). **Breeding:** Dominant male controls a troop of 15–40, including a harem of females along with a few non-breeding subordinate males. Lone males excluded from a troop may also be encountered. **Range:** S Thailand, Malaya, Sumatra, **Borneo race** *M. n. nemestrina*.

'NEDOK HUNTING' BY PENANS, IMITATING A TROOP OF PIG-TAILED MACAQUES
When their hunting dogs die of disease the Penans of the Lurah river valley in the Kayan Mentarang NP in NE Kalimantan hunt Bearded Pigs by imitating a travelling troop of Pig-tailed Macaques foraging for fallen fruit. The technique is successful because not only are the noises made by the Penan hunters disguised, but pigs and deer themselves use the sounds made by foraging Pig-tailed Macaques to find fruiting trees. 'A small hunting group moves through the forest at a steady pace calling from five to ten times a minute. The basic travelling call consists of four notes: the first is a high '**hoo**'. The second and third are a low and hummed '**mmm**' and the fourth is a '**hoo**' in mid range. As they walk hunters bend and release saplings along the trail. This walking and calling continues until a pig is detected. The hunter then squats low and calls a muted low chesty murmur '**mmmm**'. This is supposed to sound like a contented monkey feeding in the bushes. Eventually the pigs move to within a couple of metres of the hunter where they can be speared.' (adapted from Puri 2005).

MINYAK BEROK *XANTHOPHYLLUM* SP. (POLYGALACEACE)
Asia 100 spp. **Borneo** with 55 spp. (41 endemic) is the world centre of distribution. This is a genus of medium-sized trees (to 35m) common throughout the Bornean forests, with fruits targeted at primate dispersal. It is interesting because the fruit of most species contain many soft, edible seeds, surrounded by a sweet pulp, and the trees mast fruit in synchrony with dipterocarps (p. 54). The Malay name Minyak Berok means Berok Oil. Locals use the oil from the seeds for cooking (Burkill 1935). The largest fruit, *Xanthophyllum obscurum* (opposite), varies in size from 4 to 14cm in diameter, thereby encouraging a wide range of mammals, from Sun Bears to elephants, to swallow the fallen fruit and disperse the seeds. The seeds of fallen fruit are often missing as many mammals eat the seeds rather than the sweet flesh as illustrated.

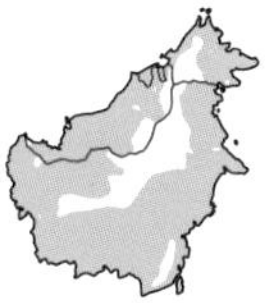

CORNER'S BOTANICAL MACAQUES Along the coast of the South China Sea there is a local tradition of training young male Pig-tailed Macaques to pick coconuts. Macaques wear a collar attached to a long lead controlled by the owner and pick up to 500 coconuts a day. Young males are the easiest to train, but older males become difficult and temperamental. Whilst writing his classic book *The Wayside Trees of Malaya* (1952), E. J. H. Corner trained a series of macaques to collect plant specimens from the tops of tall forest trees. The activities of Corner's macaques, Jambul, Puteh and Merah, are described in Corner's book *Botanical Monkeys* (1992). Training was not always easy. Merah died after eating palm fruits containing irritant crystals known as rhapides (p. 50). Macaques become extremely nervous at dusk and Corner was badly bitten on his hand by Puteh when taking him back to his cage one evening. In 1945, at the end of the Second World War, Corner left his job as assistant director at the Singapore Botanic Gardens, eventually becoming professor of tropical botany at Cambridge (Corner, J. K. 2013).

DOMINANT MALE PIG-TAILED MACAQUES
These 'stand guard' over their troop and can be aggressive to humans when they perceive a threat. Whilst females and young probably regularly fall prey to Clouded Leopards, a Clouded Leopard would be foolish to attack a large male. The pale morphs of Red Langurs in E Sabah probably gain a protective advantage from Clouded Leopards by being mistaken for Pig-tailed Macaques (p. 278).

GIBBONS

HYLOBATIDAE **World** 19 spp. (all Asian) **Borneo** 4 endemic spp. **HB 48cm (no tail), Wt 6** **Locally common**
The 4 endemic species of Bornean gibbon described below are the same size and of similar but variable colouration. They are allopatric (geographically separated), but hybridize readily where their ranges overlap. As far as is known, their habits and ecology are similar so these are described together below and on the next pages.
ID: Distinguished from the 2 macaques and grey langurs by the lack of a tail. May be recognized from a distance by the distinctive habit of 'brachiating' through the canopy by swinging from a branch using each arm alternately. Often walk upright along branches, unlike langurs and macaques.
Call: Gibbons are known locally as Wa Wa, or Wak Wak, from their early-morning territorial calls, a characteristic sound of Borneo's rainforest. The male calls first at 4.30–5 a.m., followed at dawn, after the first feed, by a 15-minute duet between male and female, usually finished by a short male call. The female call is loudest and longest. White-bearded and Müller's Gibbons have distinctively different calls, and hybrids can be recognized by the mixing of the different calls (see below). Gibbons also use a simple *hoo* as a social call between family members. Clarke et al. (2015) notes that Lar Gibbons (Thailand) used call variations to describe different predators. **Habits:** Diurnal. Gibbons prefer virgin tall forest, but can survive in degraded logged forest. Unlike macaques, they cannot survive in areas where hunting is regular (perhaps due to their fixed territories), and are absent from many of Borneo's parks where macaques are still common e.g. Matang, Lambir, Mulu, Crocker Range and Kinabalu. **Diet:** Fruit and some leaves. The most important primate dispersers of fruiting trees and lianas (see pp. 34 and 36). **Breeding:** Like humans, gibbons are monogamous, occasionally polygamous, and live in small family groups of an adult pair and their children. Young gibbons stay with their parents until they are 6–8 years old. Gibbons are the most strongly territorial large primate in Borneo (p. 156).
Territoriality: Gibbons occupy and defend their rainforest-canopy territories year round. Family territories average 40ha (see chart, p. 186). Males confront rival males and females confront rival females. Normally the female leads the family on a daily foraging round of the territorial boundaries.
Distribution in Borneo: Populations of the 4 endemic species are limited by the lower reaches of 4 of Borneo's largest rivers, as shown. In the headwaters the 4 species overlap and hybridize with fertile offspring.
1 Abbott's Gibbon *Hylobates abbotti* Borneo's rarest gibbon due to being hunted. The original range was from the Batang Lupar River (SW Sarawak) south to the Kapuas River in W Kalimantan. Small populations at Samunsam (Sarawak) and Danau Sentarum (W Kalimantan) are on the verge of extinction. The only viable population is in the trans-boundary Lanjak Entimau-Betuang Kerihun NP on the hilly border of Sarawak (Malaysia) and W Kalimantan (Indonesia), where this gibbon hybridizes with adjacent gibbon species.
2 North Borneo Gibbon *Hylobates funereus* In *HBMW* (2013) called East Bornean Gray Gibbon. The most common Borneo gibbon with the largest range south to the Batang Lupar River (SW Sarawak) and the Mahakam River (E Kalimantan). **Sabah** Hunted out of most of W Sabah, including the Crocker Range and Kinabalu, but still common at Sepilok, Kinabatangan, Tabin, Danum Valley and Tawau Hills in E Sabah. **Brunei** Common at Belalong (Ulu Temburong). **Sarawak** Rare. Extinct at Lambir, Similajau, Niah, Mulu.
3 White-bearded Gibbon *Hylobates alibarbis* Closely related to Agile Gibbon *Hylobates agilis* of Sumatra and N Malaya, with which it was once considered conspecific. In Borneo only found south of the Kapuas River (W Kalimantan) and west of the Barito River, which divides C and S Kalimantan. First recognized as a different species by the territorial call, which differs from Müller's Gibbon's in being shorter and less 'bubbly'.
4 Müller's Gibbon *Hylobates muelleri* Common in hill forests of NC and E Kalimantan. Small populations at Bukit Bangkirai and Sg Wain (Balikpapan). Female territorial call is longer and more bubbly than White-bearded Gibbon's.

GIBBON FAMILY TERRITORIES (Average 3.5–4 individuals per family)

Location	Ha	Density/km²	Habitat
Gng Palung	28	9–14	Lowland dipterocarp
Sabangau	47	4–7	Peat-swamp
Tg Puting	48	7–8	Peat-swamp
Kutai	36	9–15	Lowland dipterocarp
Kayan Mentarang	42	7–10	Hill forest
Temburong Tudal (1)	31	13	Hill forest
Temburong Belalong (2)	19	21	Lowland dipterocarp
Average	**36**	**11**	

(1) Bennett et al (1987) *A Wildlife Survey of Ulu Temburong*
(2) Cranbook & Edwards (1994) *A Tropical Rainforest*
The high density of gibbons at both sites in Ulu Temburong (Brunei) may be due to the absence of Orangutans.

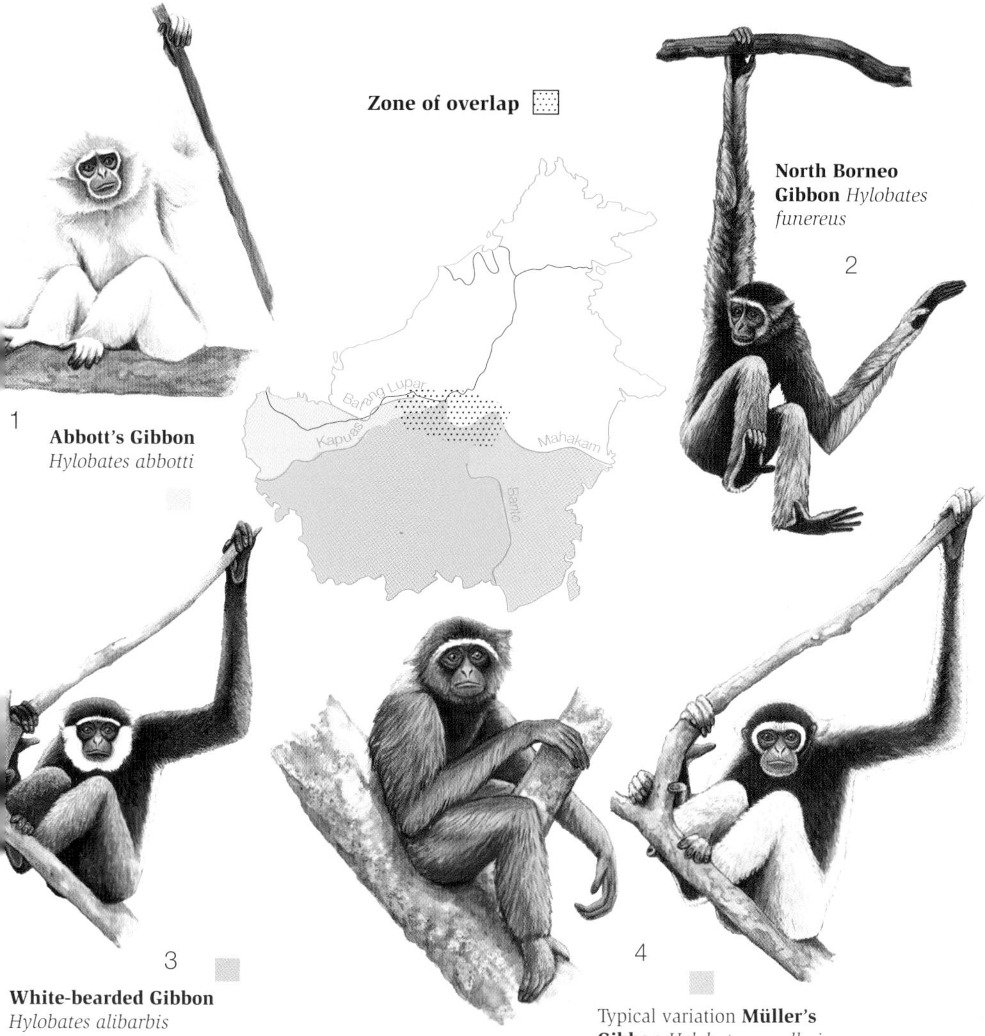

1 **Abbott's Gibbon** *Hylobates abbotti*

North Borneo Gibbon *Hylobates funereus* 2

3 **White-bearded Gibbon** *Hylobates alibarbis*

4 Typical variation **Müller's Gibbon** *Hylobates muelleri*

GIBBON TAXONOMY IN BORNEO Gibbon colouration is not only very variable but also pales with age, so it is difficult to distinguish between species on the basis of coat colour, although as pointed out by Lord Medway (1977), the predominant shade and colour pattern prevailing among the gibbons of any particular part of Borneo are predictable on geographic grounds. In the first edition of *Mammals of Borneo*, Medway (1965) listed a single gibbon, Sunda Island Gibbon *Hylobates moloch*, with 4 races for Borneo. Later studies of gibbon calls by Marshall & Marshall (1975, 1976) indicated that the gibbon found in SW Borneo was closely related to the SE Sumatran gibbon *H. agilis* based on call alone. In the 2nd edition of *Mammals of Borneo* (1977), Medway listed 2 gibbon species for Borneo, followed by Payne et al. (1985). Since 1976, the analysis of territorial calls indicates that White-bearded and Müller's Gibbons hybridize over a wide area in the headwaters of the Barito River (Mather 1992). More recently, based on DNA analysis and morphological differences, the world's leading gibbon experts, Chivers, Groves, Richardson, Roos and Whittaker, concluded in the *Handbook of the Mammals of the World* (2013) that there are 4 endemic gibbon species in Borneo with a distribution which mirrors that of the 4 gibbon races originally described by Lord Medway in 1965, and we are following that decision here.

GIBBONS 2: ECOLOGY

Gibbons are the second most common primate (after the langurs) in virgin dipterocarp forest, and the most important dispersers of primate fruit. A study at Sabangau (Mumford 2008) found that gibbons dispersed more plant species than Orangutans, and more seeds germinated. Note that Langurs predate rather than disperse most seeds – apart from the tiny seeds of specialist langur fruit such as Laran (p. 224). The loud territorial calls of gibbons and their refusal to leave their territories unoccupied during lean periods indicate that finding vacant habitat for young gibbons to establish their own territories at eight years old is a major problem.

WHY DO GIBBONS OUTNUMBER ORANGUTANS?
Orangutan density averages c. 2 per km^2, whilst gibbon density averages c. 9 per km^2 in lowland forest. Gibbons are c. 5 times as common as Orangutans, even though Orangutans are more flexible in their diet than gibbons, and eat more leaves, bark, unripe fruit and seeds. Gibbons are loyal to their home territory during lean seasons, whereas Orangutans have to travel long distances to find fruiting trees.

How do gibbons survive lean seasons on their territory where Orangutans cannot?
Both gibbons and Orangutans favour ripe primate fruit above all else, and eat figs and young leaves as a fallback food in lean periods. Gibbons are much lighter and travel much faster than Orangutans, using their long arms to brachiate, or swing, at high speed from tree to tree. This enables gibbons to exploit fruit crops on small trees or lianas that are unavailable to Orangutans.

The biomass of Orangutans is actually higher than that of gibbons
On average gibbons weigh 6kg, whereas Orangutans average c. 45kg (female) to 90kg (male). Thus the biomass of Orangutans avg. 135kg per km^2 is more than twice that of gibbons 54kg per km^2.

In summary, gibbons are more numerous because they are better able to harvest small fruit patches, but the biomass of Orangutans is higher because they are more flexible in diet and can store more fat than gibbons.

A large female N. Borneo gibbon, Kate, feeding on *Ficus punctata* figs at the Belalong Canopy Walkway in the Ulu Temburong National Park, Brunei. Figs provide essential fallback food for gibbons and allow families to remain on territory during lean seasons when nothing else is fruiting.
(Photo Hanyrol H. Ahmad Sah, resident researcher at the Ulu Ulu Resort)

Kate calling in the early morning to defend her family's forest canopy territory surrounding the Belalong Canopy Walkway in the Ulu Temburong National Park. Kate and her smaller, shyer partner William have recently had their first baby Wak-Wak. (Photo by Hans Hazebroek)
See also pp. 352, 356 and https://uluulublog.wordpress.com.

BORNEAN ORANGUTAN *Pongo pygmaeus* **Wt M 90kg, F 45kg** **Scarce Borneo endemic**

Before the arrival of humans, Orangutans occupied most of forested Borneo apart from the mountains. The Bornean Orangutan is an extreme lowland specialist with the highest populations in the lowest, flattest and wettest areas of forest, with a density in prime habitat averaging 2 per km^2 (Payne & Davies 2013). Orangutans can survive at lower densities in logged and degraded forest, if not hunted.

BORNEO'S ORANGUTANS The majority of Borneo's Orangutans live in Kalimantan (Indonesia), where the planned conversion of 49% of known Orangutan habitat in Kalimantan to oil palm or *Acacia mangium* wood-pulp plantations will displace (kill) one-third of the Bornean population, an estimated 20,000 plus Orangutans (Wich et al. 2012) (p. 32 and map, p. 193). **ID:** Can only be confused with the Red Langur, which has similar reddish hair but is smaller, far more agile and has a long tail. The Orangutan being an ape, closely related to humans, has no tail. **Diet:** Prefers fruit and seeds of all types when available. During lean periods when no trees are fruiting, survives initially on figs, then falls back to young leaves, shoots, bark (cambium), and the occasional bird, egg or small mammal. **Call:** Usually silent but dominant flanged breeding males make a long call to attract receptive females and warn off rival males. The long call can be heard for a kilometre and lasts up to 3 minutes. The call starts with bubbling sounds followed by groans, terminating in a loud roar. At Batang Ai, during an oak masting event, Ross (2009) heard 4 males calling at night from nests only 200m apart. Most calls are heard at dawn and dusk. However, Mackinnon (1974) in Sabah found that most calls were made midmorning. **Habits:** The Bornean Orangutan is by far the best-studied mammal in Borneo. Researchers have followed Orangutans through the Bornean jungle for hundreds of thousands of hours, documenting their every action. Orangutans are the world's largest tree-climbing mammals, but large males sometimes grow so heavy that they travel between fruiting trees on the ground. **Predators:** Clouded Leopards attack females and young, but would be unwise to attack an adult male. **Taxonomy:** The Sumatran Orangutan *Pongo abeli* is considered a separate species. The population of *c.* 6,000 is *c.* 10% of the Bornean population of *c.* 60,000. See below for differences.

SUMATRAN AND BORNEAN ORANGUTANS DNA analysis shows that Sumatran and Bornean Orangutans diverged some 400,000 years ago. Until 10,000 years ago Borneo and Sumatra were joined by land, but large rivers prevented the populations from mixing. Sumatra's rich volcanic soils host more fruit trees and less dipterocarps than Borneo's sandy soils. Sumatran Orangutans spend less time foraging and are more sociable than Bornean Orangutans, resulting in enhanced group learning and tool use. Sumatrans have longer, paler hair than Borneans, weigh slightly less and have paler faces with more prominent beards. Male cheek flanges are smaller. In zoos interbreeding is common and the offspring are fertile.

WHY ARE ORANGUTANS SEXUALLY DIMORPHIC? Orangutans are the most sexually dimorphic of all primates, that is with the greatest difference in size between males and females. Possible explanations:

1 **Female choice** Females prefer large males that can fight other males (Susanto, Knott et al. 2010).
2 **Defence against predators** Unlikely, because males do not defend females against predators.
3 **Partitioning of diet** Stronger males have access to foods unavailable to females – for example, males can crack *Mezzetia* seeds whereas females cannot. Heavier males wander long distances to finds large patches of food, whereas sedentary females occupy small home ranges of 3–8.5sq km. The answer is probably mostly point one and a bit of point three.

ORANGUTAN FOSSILS These have been found from S China south to Java. Javan fossils show that Orangutans arrived in Java some 100,000 years ago and became extinct around 20,000 years ago. Possible reasons for local extinctions: 1. Severe droughts during cold glacial maximums, which reduced rainforests to small refugia in Borneo and Sumatra (Arora 2010). 2. Competition with other primates on the Asian continent. 3. Hunting by humans. 4. Leopards arrived late in Asia and solitary Orangutans were unable to survive in areas with Leopards (p. 16).

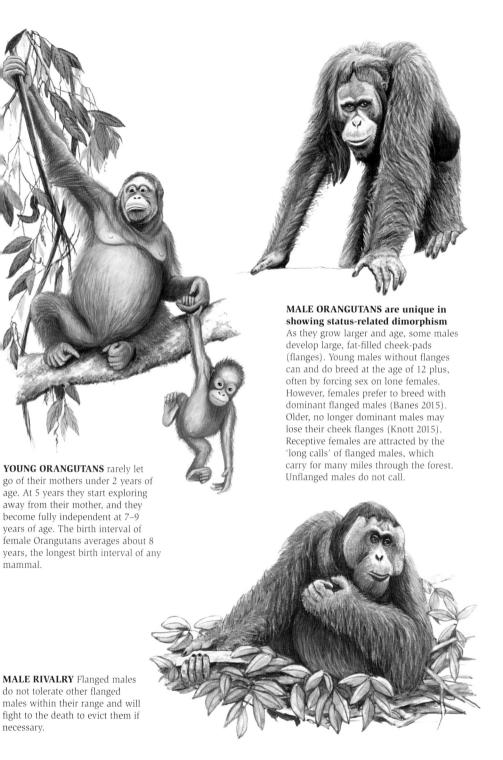

MALE ORANGUTANS are unique in showing status-related dimorphism As they grow larger and age, some males develop large, fat-filled cheek-pads (flanges). Young males without flanges can and do breed at the age of 12 plus, often by forcing sex on lone females. However, females prefer to breed with dominant flanged males (Banes 2015). Older, no longer dominant males may lose their cheek flanges (Knott 2015). Receptive females are attracted by the 'long calls' of flanged males, which carry for many miles through the forest. Unflanged males do not call.

YOUNG ORANGUTANS rarely let go of their mothers under 2 years of age. At 5 years they start exploring away from their mother, and they become fully independent at 7–9 years of age. The birth interval of female Orangutans averages about 8 years, the longest birth interval of any mammal.

MALE RIVALRY Flanged males do not tolerate other flanged males within their range and will fight to the death to evict them if necessary.

ORANGUTAN 2: ECOLOGY

COUNTING ORANGUTANS Orangutan density can be calculated by counting their nests. The most efficient way of doing this (using a helicopter) was discovered by chance by Mikaail Kavanagh in his wildlife survey of Lanjak Entimau in Sarawak. Adult Orangutans build a new sleeping nest every night. The number of nests sighted along a transect is counted and the population is estimated with a formula that allows for nest decay. (See Ancrenaz 2005, Kavanagh 1982, Payne 1988, Marshall 2008, Husson 2009.) Density calculations for different habitats are listed below:

Site	km^2	Habitat (Forest)	Source
Danum	1.0	Virgin forest	Davies & Payne
Kinabatangan Sabah	2.2	Degraded alluvial	Ancrenaz et al. (2004)
Deramakot FR Sabah	1.64	Lightly logged	Ancrenaz et al. (2005)
Tangkulap FR Sabah	0.84	Heavily logged	Ancrenaz et al. (2005)
Mawas, Tuanan, Kalimantan	4.3	Logged peat-swamp	Vogel (2012)
Sabangau, Kalimantan	1.82	Logged peat-swamp	Vogel (2012)
Rimba Raya (Tg Puting) peat-swamp	1.5	Lightly logged	Bolick (2012)

ORANGUTAN DIET At Danum, Kanamori (2010) found ripe primate fruit was the preferred diet. Fallback foods were figs and *Spatholobus* liana leaves (p. 68). At Kutai NP (E Kalimantan), Leighton (1992) found that Orangutans preferred to feed in large fruiting trees and ignored small food patches produced by lianas and small trees, that tannins and other toxins deter feeding and that energy content (sugars) rather than protein content of foods was more important. When available Orangutans chose the following foods in order of preference.

1	Ripe primate fruit	49%
2	Unripe seeds	17%
3	Ripe figs	9%
4	Leaves	7%

5	Unripe pulp	6%
6	Bark, palm hearts	6%
7	Unripe figs	5%
8	Flowers	1%

Notes: 1. The seeds of ripe primate fruit are swallowed and dispersed. 2. Unripe seeds are predated. Orangutans rarely ate the unripe seeds of primate fruit, indicating that they are toxic. See p. 36 regarding Argus Pheasant. The supply of ripe primate fruit and unripe seeds, fluctuated by more than 10 times during the two-year study. When primate fruit was available, figs, leaves and bark were not eaten, indicating that they are all 'fallback foods'.

ORANGUTANS AND *MEZZETIA* SEEDS

Mezzetias are tall forest trees to 40m in the Annonacea family, with a centre of distribution in Borneo [**Local**: Kepayang babi, Pisang Pisang besar]. *Mezzetia* fruit contain two oblong seeds with thick, woody shells protecting an oily, edible kernel. *Mezzetia* seeds have evolved to be dispersed by megafauna such as rhinoceros, but are predated by Orangutans, which crunch the shells to get at the kernel. At Sabangau Orangutans eat up to 1,000 *M. parviflora* seeds a day. Adult male Orangutans use their strong jaws to crack the seeds, but juveniles and females often fail (Cheyne et al. 2011). Seeds tested mechanically broke at a pressure of 6,000 newtons – equivalent to the weight of six humans (Lucas et al. 2005).

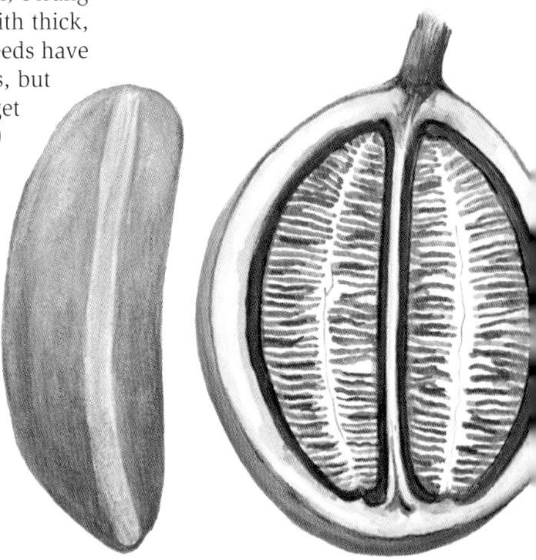

Mezzetia macrocarpa fruit are up to 7cm wide, which indicates they are targeted at rhino or elephant dispersal.

MALE AND FEMALE RESOURCE PARTITIONING
Male Orangutans wander over vast areas of forest looking for food. Due to their weight, which is double that of females, they can only survive by feeding on very large patches (large fruiting trees), whereas the smaller, more sedentary females can survive on smaller fruit patches and therefore range over much smaller areas. In ecological terms gibbons, female Orangutans and male Orangutans partition the available fruit patches by size, based on their own own size and agility.

ORANGUTAN FEEDING STRATEGIES
Orangutans prefer ripe primate fruit, but this is only abundant over a 3-month period about every 4 years during masting events (pp. 12 and 54). In between masts Orangutans feed on a vast range of fallback foods. At Gg Palung Knott (1998) found Orangutans consistently burnt fat (lost weight) during inter-mast periods, as they fed on suboptimal foods such as leaves and bark.

Habitat differences Ecologists have found that while lowland forest produces the most fruit, it also has the most pronounced masts and therefore the greatest variation in supply, while peat-swamp forest tends to produce an even supply of fruit throughout the year. Hill forest masts out of sequence with lowland forests, so Orangutan populations are likely to be highest where they can roam over large areas of varied habitat.

Meat eating Orangutans eat such a wide range of foods that it is not suprising that they occasionally catch and eat small mammals including rats, slow loris and gibbons. This has been recorded most often among Sumatran Orangutans (as illustrated) and is rare in Borneo.

Orangutan using a twig to extract *Neesia synandra* seeds
Neesia is a relative of the durian, which produces hornbill-dispersed seed surround by an edible aril, protected by irritant hairs. Sumatran Orangutans use twigs to extract and predate the seeds whilst avoiding the hairs.

TOOL-USING ORANGUTANS
Zookeepers and staff at rehabilitation centres regard Orangutans as their most highly intelligent inmates, able to copy human actions and predict when best to use deceitful behaviour. Use of tools in the wild, such as twigs to extract food, has been recorded most often in Sumatran Orangutans, which are more sociable than Bornean Orangutans and thus have more opportunities to learn new behaviours from others in the group.

ORANGUTAN 3: CONSERVATION

BEFORE THE ARRIVAL OF MAN IN BORNEO Orangutans almost certainly lived throughout the lowland forests. Meijaard et al (2010) suggests that original Orangutan density was at least 3 x higher than densities encountered today. 1,000 years ago Borneo's Orangutan population probably exceeded one million. The map opposite shows the current locations of the majority of Borneo's Orangutans with over two thirds in Kalimantan. Some 22% of the Kalimantan Orangutans live in fully protected forest, another 29% in forest reserves scheduled for logging (where Orangutans can survive if not hunted). 25% live in forest scheduled for conversion to oil palm and another 24% in unallocated land. Thus at least of one quarter (10,000) of Kalimantan's or a maximum of 49% (19,500 Orangutans) live in unprotected forest (Wich et al. 2012).

HUNTING ORANGUTANS FOR FOOD This has led to the complete absence of Orangutans from many areas of lowland Borneo including W Sabah, Brunei and NW Sarawak. Abundant remains of Orangutan have been found at the Niah caves in Sarawak where they are now absent. Today Orangutans remain most common in Borneo's peat-swamp forests, which were never inhabited by humans and therefore free from hunting pressure.

Hunting Orangutans for Profit From 1750 AD onwards the wealth generated by the Industrial Revolution in Europe led to a scientific renaissance. Both dead and live Orangutans fetched high prices from new zoos and museums throughout Europe. Between 1854–1856, A. R. Wallace shot 17 Orangutans at Simunjan near Kuching (p. 360). In 1867 the Italian botanist, Beccari, collected 26 Orangutans at Marop on the Batang Lupar also near Kuching. In 1878 the famous conservationist W. T. Hornaday collected 43 Orangutans also along the Simunjan river for the United States National Museum (Smithsonian). In 1893 hunters employed by the German zoologists Emil and Margaret Selenka collected 139 Orangutans from Mt Kenepai in W. Kalimantan. Today, Orangutans are rarely hunted for food or for pets in Borneo. Conversion of forest to oil palm is the main threat, and is most severe in Kalimantan and Sumatra (pp. 32 and 188).

ORANGUTAN REHABILITATION is often criticised for being a very expensive way to save a tiny number of Orangutans. In the whole history of rehabilitation in Borneo less than 500 Orangutans have been successfully returned to the wild, with some 800+ waiting in rehabilitation centres due to a lack of suitable forest.

Why Rehabilitation Centres are Essential for the Survival of the Orangutan The future success of Orangutan conservation in Borneo rightly rests in the hands of locals who were born, grew up and work in Borneo. Without the positive support of these Bornean locals all the efforts of foreign scientists and NGOs who pioneered many of the Orangutan conservation projects listed opposite, are doomed.

1 Orangutan rehabilitation centres attract over 100,000+ foreign wildlife tourists to Borneo each year. Tourists provide an income and jobs to many locals, who realize that Orangutans are more valuable alive than dead.
2 Rehabilitation centres are important educational sites for conservation education for both locals and tourists.
3 Rehabilitation centres protect very large areas of forest from illegal logging and land squatting.
4 Rehabilitation centres attract world-class zoologists and veterinarians who pass on their skills to locals.

Primates watching primates at Sepilok Orangutan Rehabilitation Centre.

Orangutan races	Population	Habitat km²	Density km²
P. abelii Sumatra	6,624	6,946	1.00
P. p. pygmaeus A	4,000	7,500	0.50
P. p. wurmbii B	35,000	46,250	0.75
P. p. morio C	4,825	10,750	0.45
P.p. morio D	11,000	17,450	0.60
World population	**61,449**	**88,896**	**0.70**

Data from Wich et al (2008 and 2012) & Meijaard et al (2010)

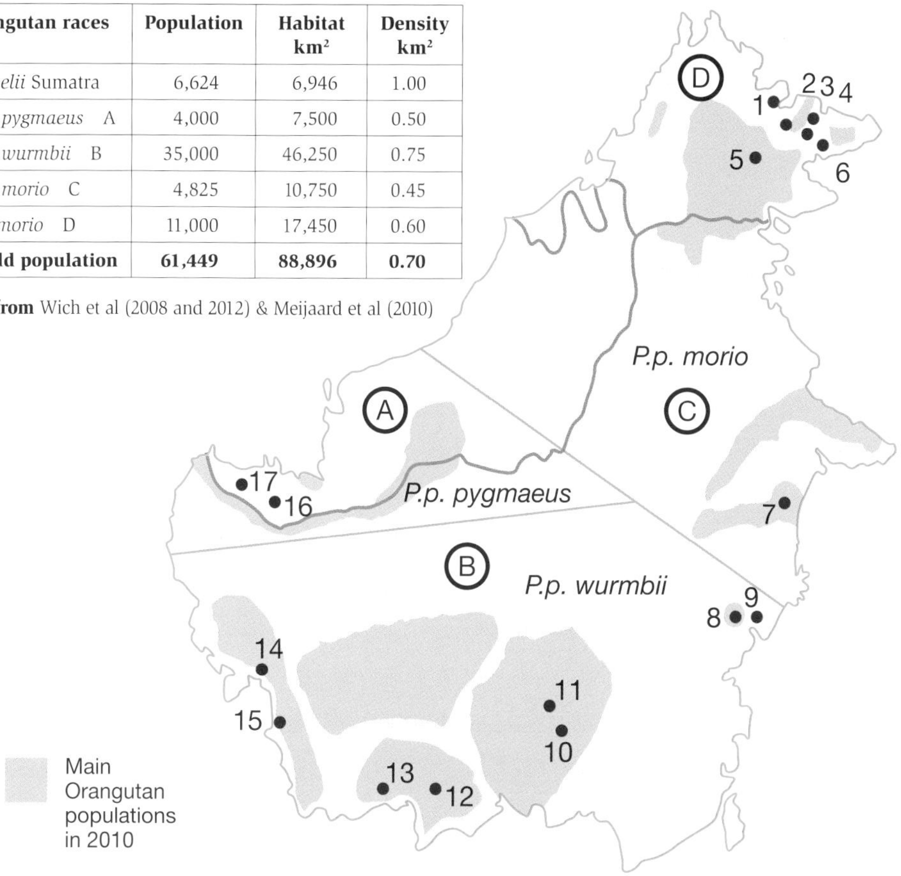

ORANGUTAN RESEARCH, REHABILITATION AND TOURIST SITES IN BORNEO (No. at each site)

1. SEPILOK Rehabilitation centre. Tourist site. www.orangutan-appeal.org.uk (30)
2. KINBATANGAN RIVER Wild population. Many tourist lodges. www.sabahtourism.com
3. DANAU GIRANG F. C. (KINABATANGAN) www.cardiff.ac.uk/biosi/facilities/danaugirangfieldcentre
4. HUTAN (KINABATANGAN) Conservation and research www.hutan.org.my
5. DANUM VALLEY Wild population. Tourist lodge. www.borneonaturetours.com & www.searrp.org
6. TABIN Wild population. Tourist lodge. www.tabinwildlife.com
7. KUTAI Wild population. www.borneotourgigant.com
8. SUNGAI WAIN Wild population. www.borneotourgigant.com
9. SAMBOJA LESTARI Rehabilitation centre. Tourist lodge. www.sambojalodge.com (200)
10. SABANGAU Wild Orangutan research. www.orangutantrop.com
11. NYARU MENTENG Rehabilitation centre. www.savetheorangutan.co.uk (600)
12. TG PUTING Tourist site. Tourist lodges. Feeding wild Orangutans. www.orangutan.org.uk (300)
13. LAMANDAU Rehabilitation and release site. www.orangutan.org.uk
14. GUNUNG PALUNG Wild Orangutan research. http://people.bu.edu/orang/
15. KETAPANG INTERNATIONAL ANIMAL RESCUE www.internationalanimalrescue.org (60)
16. SEMENGOH Rehabilitation and release. www.forestry.sarawak.gov.my (30)
17. MATANG Rehabilitation and release. Tourist cabins. www.orangutanproject.com (?)

SQUIRRELS

SCIURIDAE World: 285 spp. **Borneo:** 36 spp. **Endemics:** 14 spp., making Borneo the world centre of squirrel diversity. Squirrels are rodents adapted to living in trees. In comparison with rats their body fur is longer, and their tails are long and furry to aid balance when climbing. Like all rodents they have front teeth (incisors) adapted for constant gnawing, which continue to grow throughout their lives.
Diet All Borneo's squirrels are omnivorous. They eat a mixed diet of ripe and unripe fruit, leaves, seeds, insects, sap, bark and small animals, although different species prefer different foods and will always select preferred foods when they are available. For example, Prevost's Squirrel prefers ripe fruit to leaves, but will eat leaves when ripe fruit is unavailable. The Shrew-faced Ground Squirrel prefers insects and worms, but will eat fruit when insects are unavailable. **Seed predation** Most squirrels are seed predators as well as important seed dispersers (p. 44, seed predation; p. 60, oaks; p. 212, scatter-hoarding and p. 232, acorns).

Squirrel taxonomy Borneo's squirrels divide into three subfamilies based on DNA (Steppan et al. 2004).
Callosciuridae Most diurnal (day) squirrels apart from giant squirrels (origin SE Asia).
Sciurinae The diurnal Tufted Ground Squirrel and all the nocturnal flying squirrels (origin S America).
Ratufinae Two diurnal giant squirrels (origin S Asia).
According to den Tex et al. (2010), most speciation in Sundaland squirrels dates back to the Pliocene some 6–7 MYA, and not to more recent Pleistocene sea-level changes (pp. 14 and 200).

Squirrel ecology Borneo's Squirrels can be split into the day squirrels with 22 species (below), and the nocturnal flying squirrels with 14 species (p. 216). Day squirrels are active only during the day (diurnal). The majority build flimsy stick nests (dreys) for sleeping and breeding (p. 222). Day squirrels partition resources by size and diet and by foraging at different heights in the forest, from the ground to the canopy. They often join insect-hunting parties led by vocal birds (Phillipps 2014, p. 270).

Calls: The three most common day squirrels in Borneo, Plantain, Prevost's and Bornean Pigmy Squirrels (and possibly other species as well), all make a very high-pitched contact call, *SssK*, repeated intermittently throughout the day. In Malaya, Tamura & Yong (1993) found that 3 species of *Callosciurus* squirrel also made alarm calls that identified different predators and subsequently used different escape strategies for different predators. **Predators:** Snakes, hawk-eagles, serpent eagles and Yellow-throated Martens are believed to be the main predators. **Coat patterns and colours** are a mixture of camouflage, deceit and aposematic danger-warning patterns (pp. 27 and 202).

On Kinabalu. (Photo: Ch'ien C. Lee)

Bornean Mountain Ground Squirrel ***Dremomys everetti*** Ground squirrels are rare in Borneo apart from *D. everetti*, which is abundant in the Bornean mountains. The explanation for this is that most Bornean lowland forest trees have soft, rapidly germinating recalcitrant seeds. In the mountains, trees with hard, slow-germinating orthodox seeds, such as oaks, laurels and hollies, predominate and are both dispersed and predated by *D. everetti*. The reason why orthodox seeds are most common in cold, dry areas of the world and recalcitrant seeds are most common in tropical forests is probably related to fungal attack, which would be most rapid in hot, wet environments, and lowland tropical rainforest seeds need to germinate before they are overwhelmed (pp. 45, 212, 232, 234, 237).

KINABALU SQUIRREL *Callosciurus baluensis* **HB 240, T 245, Wt 370g** **Endemic**

Uncommon diurnal tree squirrel of Bornean mountains from Kinabalu south to Ulu Baleh in the hills of C Sarawak. Most records are from 1,000m to 1,980m (Gng Murud). On Kinabalu recorded down to 300m. Resident in forest around Kinabalu Park headquarters, but scarce. Banks shot a pair of these squirrels at 1,540m on Gng Mulu in 1934. Recorded from geographically isolated Gng Dulit (NW Sarawak). **ID:** Overlaps with similar-sized Prevost's Squirrel in mountains at 1,000–1,200m. Only likely to be confused with *C. p. caroli* in NW Sarawak (p. 197). Distinguished by distinct reddish tinge to leading edge of thigh and reddish fur on face. **Habits:** Unknown, but inhabits the world's most diverse oak and chestnut forests, so the ecology is probably linked (p. 60). **Taxonomy:** Payne (1985) lists the race *C. p. baramensis* for Sarawak with the speckling of the body extending to the tail, but this was not accepted by Thorington et al. (2012).

BARK-EATING SQUIRRELS OF BORNEO

Many small Bornean squirrels eat small flakes of bark as a major part of their diet. Only surface bark is eaten, not the sweet inner cambium favoured by Orangutans, deer and porcupines. Bark-eating squirrels include the 3 pigmy squirrels, plus Low's, Slender and Brooke's Squirrels. Large areas of surface bark are removed without damage to the tree. Whitten (1987) analyzed bark eaten by Low's Squirrel in Sumatra, but found no significant food value and very high levels of tannins. Seventeen out of 41 tree families present in the area were selected for bark eating, with the Euphorbiaceae and Fabaceae being most popular.

Surface barks are made up of three indigestible substances, cellulose, lignin and suberin, a waterproofing wax. Bark is also protected by bitter antibacterial tannins. Bark-eating squirrels often eat insects, but rarely fruit.

Possible explanation Bark-eating squirrels may be able to digest the waxy suberin. Perhaps some Bornean trees provide edible bark to encourage small squirrels to defend the trunk against wood-eating termites and wood-boring, longicorn beetles (p. 207).

Black-eared Pigmy Squirrel eating bark at Gng Penrissen near Kuching. Note that most of the surface bark on the trunk has been nibbled away (p. 360).

PREVOST'S SQUIRREL

PREVOST'S SQUIRREL *Callosciurus prevostii* **HB 238, T 233, Wt 373g Common**
The most common forest squirrel in most of Borneo. In the Kalimantan peat swamps, common at Tg Puting, but scarce at Sabangau and apparently absent from SE Kalimantan. Found in tall and secondary forests, and raids orchards close to forest, but not usually found in open countryside and plantations. "When the forest on Labuan was cleared, this squirrel adapted to coconut plantations" (Banks 1949). **ID:** All races have a rufous belly, but often richly coloured upperparts. Distinguish from Giant Squirrel by habit of resting along a branch, not with tail hanging down like Giant Squirrel (p. 210). Overlaps with Kinabalu Squirrel in N Borneo mountains 1,000–1,200m (p. 195). **Habits:** Diurnal and arboreal. Forages on tree trunks and foliage in mid to high canopy. Solitary and territorial. Rarely on the ground. **Diet:** Favoured diet is ripe fruit. Often eats canopy figs; unripe seeds, young leaves, bark and insects. **Call:** Warning call (for humans) is a very noisy, churring, rattling chatter not unlike that of some monkeys, similar to call of Giant Squirrel but in a much lower, less shrill key (Banks 1949). **Contact call:** Short, high-pitched hiss, Sssk. **Breeding:** Builds a loose nest of gnawed sticks lined with shredded bark and grasses. Normally 2–3 young. **Range:** Malaya, Sumatra, Borneo. The brightly coloured races in SW Borneo most resemble the races in Sumatra and the Malay Peninsula, indicating a series of repeat invasions from the Asian continent during the low sea levels of the Pleistocene ice ages.

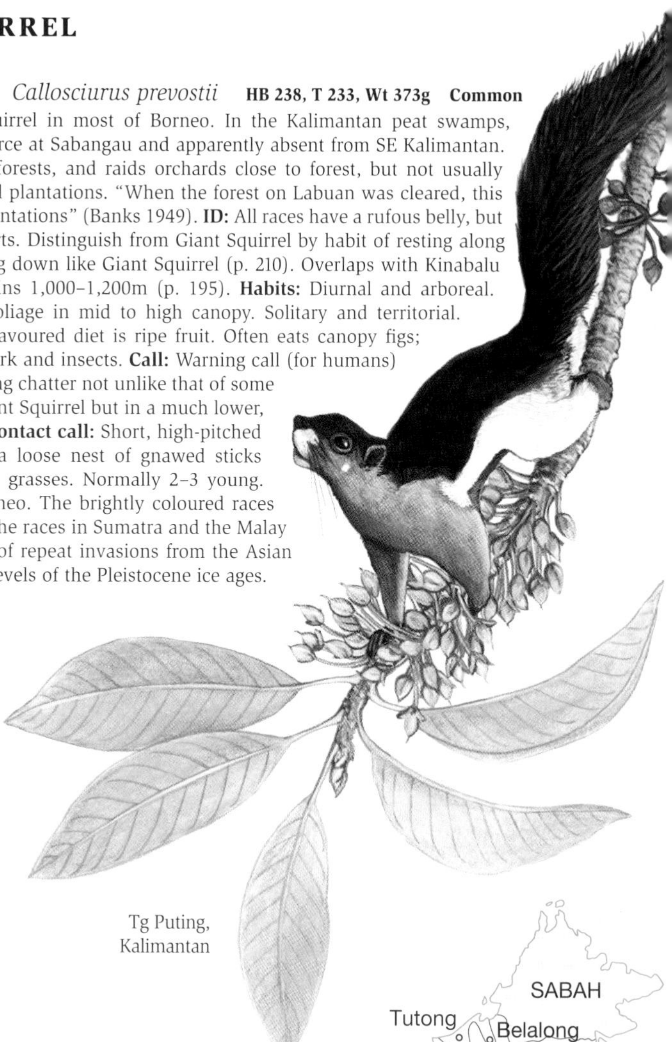

Tg Puting, Kalimantan

PREVOST'S SQUIRREL pollinating *Madhuca motleyana* at Tg Puting in Kalimantan. *Madhuca* (SAPOTACEA) (Local: Nyatoh) are one of the most common non-dipterocarp trees in Bornean lowland forests. Many *Madhuca* species have sweet, fleshy, edible flower petals and corollas shaped like berries to attract squirrels and primates which both eat and pollinate the flowers.

PREVOST'S SQUIRREL RACES
In the first edition of this *Field Guide* we mapped 13 different races of Prevost's Squirrel. However photographs from different locations in Borneo show that the differences are too variable to justify this taxonomy. Only the Sabah race *C. p. pluto* is sufficiently uniform over a large area to be considered a separate race or possible endemic. The map shows the locations of the squirrels illustrated opposite.

Sabah race *C.P. pluto*

Belalong, Brunei

Tutong, Brunei

Kubah, Sarawak

Penrissen, Sarawak

Batang Ai, Sarawak

HORSE-TAILED SQUIRREL *Sundasciurus hippurus* **HB 225, T 216, Wt 312g** **Scarce**

A Sundaland endemic confined to large areas of wet primary lowland and hill forest. Once considered abundant, but now regarded as patchy or rare. Recorded to 1,500m on Gng Dulit in NW Sarawak. Davis (1962) found Horse-tailed to be very common in the Sapagaya FR and Bettotan near Sandakan. Norhayati (2001) found Horse-tailed to be the most common squirrel in her study plots at Danum. Locally common in logged forest at SAFE in SE Sabah, Cussack (2011). According to Banks (1949) previously common throughout lowland Sarawak, with over 40 specimens in the Sarawak Museum. **Decline:** A possible explanation for the population decline is that this squirrel larder-hoards hard nuts in tree holes to survive lean seasons. Logging has removed old trees with holes and led to a population collapse. **ID:** Distinguish from Prevost's Squirrel by the white belly in Sabah and the absence of a white side stripe south of the Sabah border. **Habits:** A medium size tree squirrel which unlike all other Bornean squirrels, moves frequently between the canopy and the ground, probably collecting nuts which are larder hoarded both in the canopy and at ground level. **Diet:** A specialist feeder on very hard nuts of sub-canopy trees especially *Canarium* species (p. 214). Nuts are eaten unripe on the tree, and fallen ripe nuts are foraged on the ground. Scatter-hoarding has been recorded at Gng Palung by Blate et al. (2009) and at Kutai by Laman for *Maranthes corymbosa* (*Chrysobalancea*)(Prance 1989). Davis (1962) examined the stomach contents of 7 individuals taken in primary forest and found mainly pulpy fruit, and also an earthworm, a small insect and some fly larvae. **Call:** The most commonly heard call is CHEK! CHEK! ... chekchekchekchek (Payne 1985). A call I heard at the Belalong Canopy Walkway in Brunei was a steady tok tok tok tok, similar to the night call of a Long-tailed Nightjar. **Range:** S Thailand, Malaya, Sumatra, Borneo. **Taxonomy:** The map opposite shows the races listed in Payne et al. (1985). The most obvious difference between races is the change from a white to a red belly at the South Sabah Zoological Boundary and it is likely that the Sabah races will one day be split off as a Borneo endemic. See p. 350.

Horse-tailed Squirrel photographed at Sandakan by Cede Prudente.

CANARIUM NUTS

'The Horse-tailed Squirrel was seen most often in primary forest, but was also common in old logged forest around Sandakan Bay. It was not observed in clearings. All individuals, that I observed (14) were in the smaller trees of the second storey, not the huge trees that form the canopy. *Sundasciurus hippurus* appears to live in the lower middle story of the forest. On one occasion I observed three individuals feeding in a Kedondong Canarium tree. The fallen nuts each about 35mm long, each had a neat hole 8–10mm in diameter chiseled in the side through which the contents had been removed" (Davis 1962).
See p. 214.

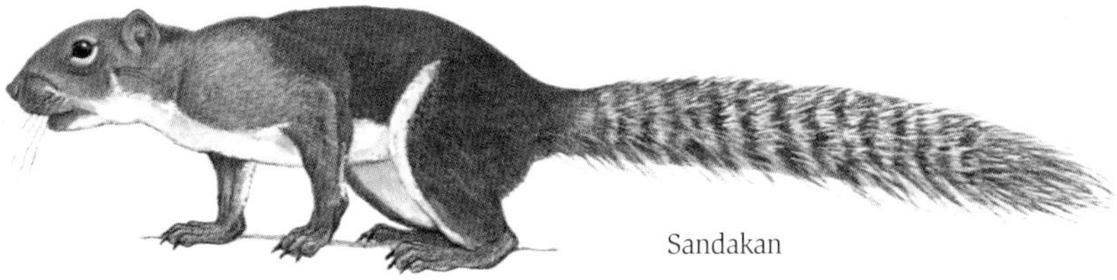

Sandakan

Tawau

Gng Palung

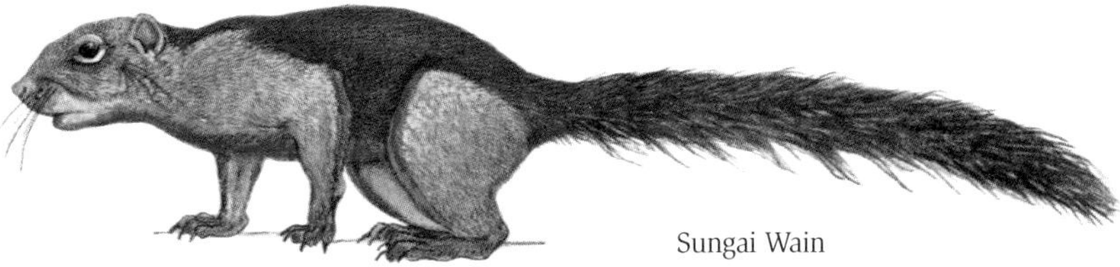

Sungai Wain

BORNEO RACES *Sundasciurus hippurus*

The map shows the races of *Sundasciurus hippurus* listed in Payne et al (1985). Above are illustrations based on photographs taken in four different locations in Borneo from north to south showing a clear difference between the Sabah squirrels (white bellies) and the squirrels south of the Sabah border with rufous to dark red bellies. Horse-taileds show brighter aposematic (danger warning) markings in Sabah whilst becoming camouflaged in Kalimantan. In contrast Prevost's Squirrel is camouflaged in Sabah but in Kalimantan develops brighter warning markings the further south you go. The reason is unknown but probably relates to differences in predator pressure. See p. 350 re the South Sabah Zoological boundary.

SMALL SUNDASCIURUS SQUIRRELS

1 BROOKE'S SQUIRREL *Sundasciurus brookei* **HB 17cm, T 14cm** **Montane endemic**
Common tree squirrel of primary forest in the hills and mountains of Borneo. One of a few Bornean mammals restricted to mid levels in the mountains, where it is found at 600–1,500m. Recorded from Langanan waterfall trail at Poring (Kinabalu), but not lower down. Recorded at 1,350m on Gng Harun in the Kayan Mentarang NP (Sebastian 2003). Not found south of Gng Penrissen near Kuching. **ID:** Distinguished from Low's Squirrel by longer ringed tail and grey not buffy or white underparts. Museum specimens have a reddish patch between the hind legs. **Habits:** Feeds mostly on surface tree bark. **Taxonomy:** The type was collected on Mt Dulit by Hose and named by Oldfield Thomas (1892) after Rajah Charles Brooke (p. 242).

2 JENTINK'S SQUIRREL *Sundasciurus jentinki* **HB 13cm, T 12cm** **Montane endemic**
Locally common small tree squirrel in montane forest at 1,000–3000m. **ID:** Distinguished by clear white markings on sides of nose, and around eyes and ears. **Habits:** Mostly active in the canopy. Often joins mixed feeding flocks of birds, squirrels and treeshrews in the mountains. Commonly encountered around rest huts and refuse bins on Kinabalu Summit trail along with *Dremomys everetti* (p. 213), which has a shorter, thicker tail and no white markings on the face. 'Hunts insects in the foliage of small trees' (Emmons re. Langanan ridge, Poring). **Borneo races:** 1. *S. j. jentinki*, south to C Sarawak. 2. *S. j. subsignanus*, mountains of Kalimantan.

3 LOW'S SQUIRREL *Sundasciurus lowi* **HB 14cm, T 9cm** **Common**
Common small tree squirrel of primary and secondary forest throughout the lowland forests of Borneo, foraging from the ground to the subcanopy. Also recorded on Kelabit Highlands to 1,400m. **ID:** In mountainous areas overlaps with Brooke's Squirrel, from which it is distinguished by a white rather than grey belly, and shorter, thicker, plain (not ringed), bushy tail. Pale hairs at bases of ears (illustrated) vary in prominence and may not be obvious. **Habits:** 'The commonest squirrel in all habitats. Similar habits to montane Brooke's Squirrel. Forages intensively for an unknown resource on the bark of large trees near the ground' (Emmons re. Poring). **Diet:** Feeds mainly on surface bark (p. 195). At Gng Palung recorded scatter-hoarding *Lithocarpus* acorns (Curran & Leighton 2000) (p. 232). **Breeding:** Nests made of woven plant fibres were found in palm branches at 2–3.5m above the ground. Also nests in tree hollows. Litter averages 2.3. **Call:** Series of bird-like *chiks* (Payne). **Taxonomy:** Named after Hugh Low (p. 142). **Range:** Malaya, Sumatra. **Borneo races:** 1. *S. l. banguyea* (P. Banggi). 2. *S. l. natunensis* (Bunguran Besar). 3. *S. lowii* (Borneo mainland).

4 SLENDER SQUIRREL *Sundasciurus tenuis* **HB 14cm, T 13cm** **Locally common S Borneo**
Locally common small tree squirrel in lowland and hill forest in Brunei, Sarawak and throughout Kalimantan apart from NE Kalimantan. Recorded at 1,650m on Gng Pueh near Kuching. In Sabah only known from Sipitang on the border with Sarawak. Forages from subcanopy to canopy. **Diet:** At Krau, Malaya, fed mostly on surface bark, including that of *Intsia palembanica* (Fabaceae). Also eats soft fruit and young leaves (MacKinnon 1978). **Habits:** Often seen in small family parties. **Range:** Malaya, Sumatra, Borneo.

SUNDASCIURUS TAXONOMY
A study of Sundaland *Sundasciurus* squirrel DNA by R. J. den Tex et al. (2010) came to two suprising conclusions.
1. Two montane races of *S. tenuis*, *S. t. tahan* (Malaya) and *S. t. altitudinus* (Sumatra) are more closely related to *S. jentinki* (Borneo mountains) than to *S. tenuis* of the lowlands.
2. Speciation in Sundaland *Sundasciurus* took place around 6–7 MYA, not during the more recent Pleistocene sea-level changes starting 2.6 MYA (p. 14).

Jentink's Squirrel at a rest stop on Kinabalu Summit Trail, 2,300m.

1
2
3
4

RED-BELLIED SQUIRRELS

1 PLANTAIN SQUIRREL *Callosciurus notatus* **HB 199, T 185, Wt 215g** **Abundant**

The most common squirrel in cultivated areas, secondary forest, coastal forest and islands, gardens and plantations. Only occurs in primary forest as a visitor from adjacent degraded forest. Tame individuals may hang around resorts waiting for food scraps. **ID:** Distinguished by pale rufous underparts and no white spot behind ear. **Habits:** Notorious pest of coconut plantations and orchards. The young coconut nut is damaged by being gnawed open before it ripens. Metal wrappers around coconut palm trunks are designed to stop this squirrel from climbing the trunk. Serious pest of cocoa and oil-palm plantations, where it is controlled by shooting. The only squirrel that can live in tree plantations such as oil palm, rubber and Albizzia. **Diet:** More flexible in diet than other squirrels. Feeds on fruit, nuts, bark, leaves and insects, in particular ants. **Ants and macarangas:** Several species of *Macaranga*, a pioneer shrub, have a mutualistic relationship with ants and both feed them with **Beccarian bodies** and house them in their hollow stems, so that they can defend the plant against leaf-eating insects such as moth and butterfly larvae. Both woodpeckers *Meiglyptes tristis* and Plantain Squirrels often attack these hollow stems to access the ant colonies inside. See Phillipps (2014) (p. 365) and Leo et al. (1999). **Calls:** Repetitive staccato barks in response to ground predators, a low chuckle in response to aerial predators, rattle sounds when a bird flew close overhead and squeaks when mobbing snakes (Tamura & Yong 1993 re. Malaya). **Range:** S Thailand, Malaya, Sumatra, Java. **Borneo races:** 1. *C. n. dilutus*, Sabah south to Kelabit Highlands and E Borneo. 2. *C. n. dulitensis*, Sarawak and Kalimantan. 3. *C. n. conipus*, coastal SE Borneo.

2 EAR-SPOT SQUIRREL *Callosciurus adamsi* **HB 175, T 160, Wt 135g** **Scarce endemic**

Scarce inhabitant of lowland primary forest in Sabah and Brunei south to Rajang River in C Sarawak. No Kalimantan records. In forest-edge resorts, for example at Sepilok, may overlap with Plantain Squirrel, but usually much less common. Payne records the maximum altitude as 900m in the Kelabit Highlands. **ID:** Slightly smaller than Plantain Squirrel, but otherwise similar. Distinguished by pale spot behind each ear. Distinguished from smaller but similar Sculptor Squirrel by blunt or flat nose (rostrum) of Sculptor Squirrel. Museum skins show that belly hairs are grey-tipped dull reddish, unlike those of Plantain Squirrel, which has entirely reddish underbelly hairs. **Habits:** Unknown.

Ear-spot Squirrel, Sepilok, Sandakan. Photo by Raja Stephenson.

Plantain Squirrel Labuk Bay, Sandakan.

Relative abundance of squirrels collected by Davis near Sandakan pre-logging (1962)

Plantain	**45**
Prevost's	**31**
Low's	**23**
Horse-tailed	**23**
Giant	**16**
Bornean Pigmy	**12**
Tufted Ground	**1**
Four-striped Ground	**1**
Ear-Spot	**1**

Plantain Squirrel
Permai Resort, Santubong, Kuching, feeding on pandan cake.

GREY-BELLIED CALLOSCIURUS TREE SQUIRRELS

1 SUNDA BLACK-BANDED SQUIRREL *Callosciurus nigrovittatus* **HB 205, T 187, Wt 220g Rare**
Common squirrel in the Malay Peninsula, Sumatra and Java, but either extremely rare or under-recorded in Borneo. A recent photograph by Ronald Orenstein taken at Gng Penrissen at the Kalimantan viewpoint (1,100m) in the hills near Kuching indicates that *C. nigrovittatus* is present in Borneo. There are possible reports from Kalimantan, where it appears to be widespread but much less common than Plantain Squirrel. **Habits:** At Krau Wildlife Reserve (Malay Peninsula) only a quarter as common as Plantain Squirrel. In the Malay Peninsula usually more common in disturbed forest than in virgin primary forest. **Range:** Thorington (2012) records that the nearest geographical location for *C. nigrovittatus* to Borneo is the small island of Kayu Ara (Saddle Island) in the Tambelan Islands, almost exactly midway between W Borneo and Singapore. See p. 210 re. Giant Squirrel in the Natuna Islands.

TAXONOMIC CONFUSION *Mammals of Borneo* (Medway 1977) listed *C. nigrovittatus* with three subspecies, *C. n. orestes* (Sarawak), *C. n. venutus* (Kinabalu and Trus Madi), and *C. n. atristriatus* (N bank Mahakam River, E Kalimantan). In *A Field Guide to the Mammals of Borneo* (1985), Payne et al. described the montane *C. orestes* as the only Black-banded Squirrel in Borneo, but noted the problems with three other records of *C. nigrovittatus*: 1. 6th mile Stapok Road, Kuching; 2. Mahakam River; 3. sight records from Kutai. The most likely explanation is that there is a relict population of Black-banded Squirrels in Borneo.

2 BORNEAN BLACK-BANDED SQUIRREL *Callosciurus orestes* **HB 136, T 137 Montane endemic**
Locally common endemic in the montane forests of N Borneo south to the Usun Apau Plateau in the hills of C Sarawak. Also recorded from Mt Dulit in NW Sarawak. The most common tree squirrel in the forest around Kinabalu Park headquarters, but not recorded above Timpohon Gate (1,866m) at the start of Kinabalu Summit Trail. **ID:** Looks like a small Plantain Squirrel, but with a grey not reddish belly, and white spots behind the ears. Note that *C. nigrovittatus* never has white spots behind the ears. **Habits:** Can often be found during the day foraging around the large refuse bins on the roadside about 100m below the Timpohon Gate in the company of Bornean Mountain Ground Squirrels and Mountain Treeshrews. **Diet:** Fruit, seeds and insects. Often feeds on ants on tree trunks. These form trails that extend from their underground nests to forage in the canopy. The ant trails are particularly common on oaks, which are abundant on Kinabalu, but the ecology has yet to be investigated (p. 60).

Bornean Black-banded Squirrel *C. orestes* on Kinabalu *c.* 1,800m. (Photo: Ch'ien C. Lee)

Sunda Black-banded Squirrel *C. nigrovittatus* at Gng Penrissen *c.* 1,100m asl near Kuching. (Photo: Ronald Orenstein)

SE ASIA: 6 spp. **BORNEO:** 3 spp., 2 endemic, making Borneo the world centre of pigmy squirrel diversity. These tiny squirrels feed on flakes of surface bark and small insects. Despite their abundance in Borneo, their ecology remains a mystery (p. 195).

1 BORNEAN PIGMY SQUIRREL *Exilisciurus exilis* **HB 73mm, T 48mm, Wt 17g Endemic** [Plain Pigmy Squirrel (Payne 1985)] [Least Pygmy Squirrel (Thorington 2012)]. Probably Borneo's most common forest squirrel found to 1,000m, in all lowland forests. Collected at 1,700m on Gng Pueh near Kuching. Competes with Emily's Pigmy Flying Squirrel (p. 217) for the title of the world's smallest squirrel. **Habits:** Feeds on bark and ants on trunks of large trees. Usually tame and unafraid. **Call:** Contact call is a high-pitched, sharp hiss, *tssK*. Also described as a long-drawn squeak (Banks). This call is made when the animal is quite still and usually hidden, so it is difficult to source the sound. The call is made all day but is most obvious during the mid-afternoon heat, when forest birds and insects are silent. Other Bornean squirrels make similar contact calls, including Plantain and Prevost's Squirrels, which I cannot differentiate.

2 BLACK-EARED PIGMY SQUIRREL *Nannosciurus melanotis* **HB 78, T 66, Wt 17g Local** Tiny, locally common squirrel of lowland and hill forests found in most of Sarawak and Kalimantan, but absent from Sabah apart from a single provisional record from the Maliau Basin (1988 expedition). Locally common at Gng Penrissen, Samunsam, Semengoh, Matang, Sg Wain, Sabangau. Outside Sabah range overlaps with that of Bornean Pigmy Squirrel, which is nearly always more common. Often quite tame and seen in family groups. **Call:** Distinctive irregular series of loud, high-pitched, piercing *chiks* or *cheeps* followed by a very high-pitched descending twitter that gradually dies out without an ending (Payne 1985). Frequently heard at Sabangau, but less common than *E. exilis*. **Range:** Sumatra, Java. **Borneo race:** *N. m. borneanus*.

3 WHITEHEAD'S PIGMY SQUIRREL *Exilisciurus whiteheadi* **HB 86, T 64, Wt 22g Endemic** [Tufted Pygmy Squirrel]. Locally common tiny squirrel of the Bornean mountains, 1,000–3,000m. On Kinabalu common at park headquarters (1,500m). On Mulu common at 2,000m. At Lanjak Entimau found at 300m. **ID:** Small squirrel with distinctive white ear-tufts seen on tree trunks in mountain forest. **Habits:** 'The pigmy squirrel with the long ear-tufts is common here, and I am often able to approach within a few yards of it. It travels over the trunks of the larger forest-trees somewhat after the manner of a woodpecker, the tail being pressed against the tree and the hind legs sprawled out on either side of the stomach on the bark, while the front legs and fore part of the body are kept well off the tree; in this way the little animal proceeds in short jerks over the large trunks, feeding on the bark, which is sometimes much gnawn away; the ears are generally held erect' (Whitehead 1893). **Diet:** Mainly insects, particularly ants, some bark, and a little fruit and vegetable matter (Lim et al. 1968). **Call:** A shrill whistle (Whitehead 1893).

Bornean Pigmy Squirrel *E. exilis*, Kinabatangan. (Photo: Ch'ien C. Lee)

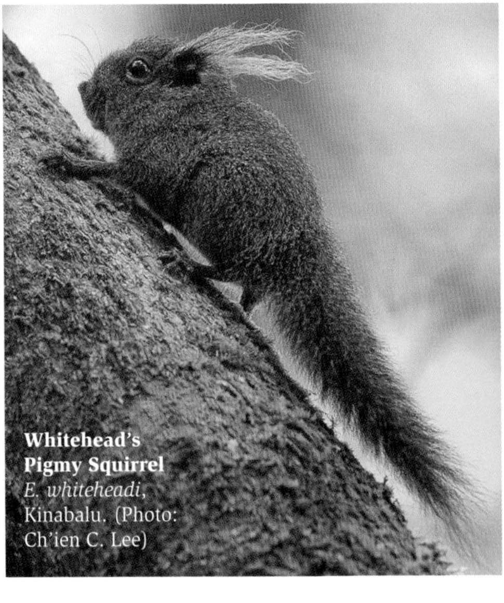

Whitehead's Pigmy Squirrel *E. whiteheadi*, Kinabalu. (Photo: Ch'ien C. Lee)

JOHN WHITEHEAD (1860–1899)
This English ornithologist is best known for collecting Kinabalu's most iconic birds, Whitehead's Broadbill, Trogon and Spiderhunter (Phillipps & Phillipps 2014). During two expeditions in 1887 and 1888, Whitehead made the first recorded ascent of Low's Peak on 11 February 1888, aided by his local guides Kabong and Kurow, the headmen of Kampong Kiau, a village on the western slopes (if you climb Kinabalu today your guide may also be from Kg Kiau). Although best known for the rare birds named after him and his friends, Whitehead also collected many mammals, including a rat, *Maxomys whiteheadi*, and a squirrel, *Exilisciurus whiteheadi*. Whitehead's Kinabalu diary and sketches were later transformed into a magnificent book, *The Exploration of Mount Kina-Balu* (1893). Some passages from the book are summarized in this field guide (p. 230).

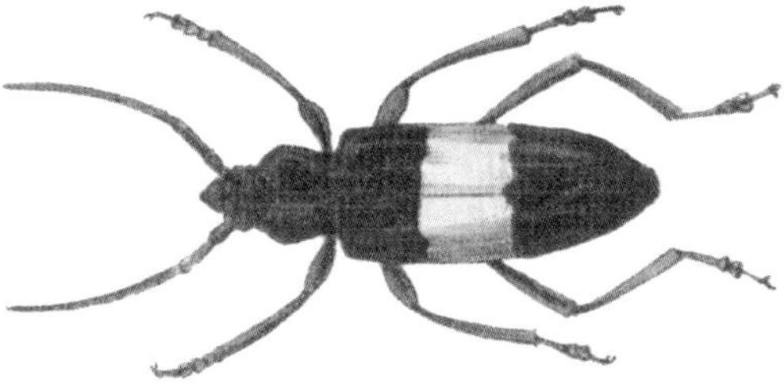

Moratichroma magnifica Bates (1889) listed by Whitehead as *Zonopterus magnificus* a Longicorn Beetle of the Ceramycidae, endemic to Borneo, collected by Whitehead on Kinabalu. Pigmy Squirrels are believed to feed on wood-boring longicorn beetles and their eggs thus protecting their host tree from attack. The tree rewards the squirrels with edible bark (p.195). Illustration by John Whitehead.

BORNEAN SCULPTOR SQUIRREL

SCULPTOR SQUIRREL *Glyphotes simus* **HB 120, T 100, Wt?** **Scarce endemic**

Rare squirrel endemic to Borneo, with unusual sculpted incisor teeth that appear to have evolved for scraping the central veins on the undersides of large fig leaves, so that the squirrel can feed on the latex. **ID:** Can only be confused with the Ear-spot Squirrel *Callosciurus adamsi*, which also has white spots behind the ears, black-and-white side-stripes and a red belly. Sculptor squirrel distinguished by the blunt nose, different habits and smaller (two-thirds) size. **Habits:** Anecdotal reports are that the Sculptor Squirrel travels in nomadic parties to feed on the latex of the newly flushed leaves of large fig trees. Examination of the fallen leaves shows that the central vein underneath has been scraped on both sides. Locals say that the squirrels are eating the latex. An alternative explanation is that the squirrels are eating the exudates (Beccarian bodies) produced by many fig trees on the undersides of the leaves to reward ants that defend the leaves against folivores (leaf-eating insects). The squirrel may be eating both. **Range:** Confined to hills and mountains of Borneo from Kinabalu south to Long Bawan in C Borneo at altitudes of 285–1,800m. Several older records are from the Tenompok Pass (when it was forested), not far from Kinabalu Park headquarters. Common at Maliau Basin (see below). Recorded from Gng Harun at 1,800m at northern end of Kayan Mentarang NP in NE Kalimantan (Sebastian 2003), south to Pa Raye (Long Bawan), also in Kayan Mentarang NP. Recent unusual record from SAFE project at Kalabakan in SE Sabah, in logged forest at about 285m (Cusack 2011).

SCULPTOR SQUIRREL INCISORS
'The skull is globular with an exceptionally short, broad and deep rostrum. The lower incisors are worn into broad flat chisel-shaped blades, the inner corners more worn than the outer so that viewed from the front the teeth present a shallow "V" shape.' (Hill 1959).

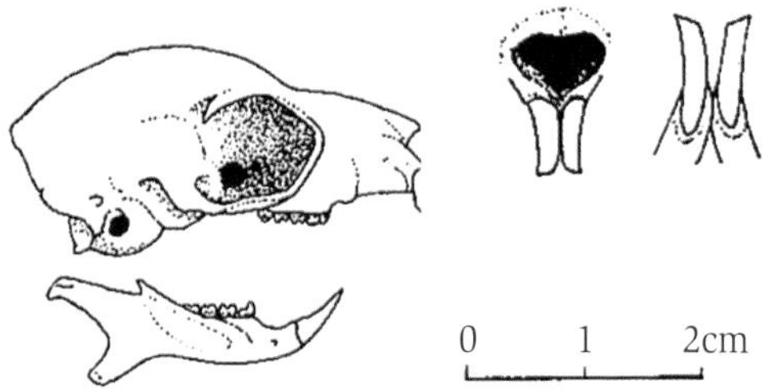

ANECDOTAL EVIDENCE OF LATEX EATING BY SCULPTOR SQUIRREL

1 'Seems to feed on the latex of a wild fig called Bongan (Lundaye). Feeds in large numbers up in the leaves, the tree seems alive with them. Large numbers are sometimes shot with a sumpitan (blowpipe) at one tree, but one must take plenty of ammunition.' Local names, Murut: Antila or Tulaki; Lundaye: Labo Maa (Jim Comber, see below).

2 'In 1988, I joined an expedition to the Maliau Basin, during which a large group of researchers was flown in by Air Force helicopter. One memory is of observing a group of six or so of one of the world's weirdest squirrels, unique to Borneo, known as the Red-bellied Sculptor Squirrel (*Glyphotes simus*). This little squirrel has two lower incisor teeth that have a concave front surface and splay outwards in a V shape. I watched them at eye-level, across a narrow, deep valley, as they hung upside down from the outermost twigs of a large strangling fig, high above the ground, running their odd little teeth along the central vein on the underside of the fig leaves.' (condensed from *Wild Sabah*, Junaidi Payne, 2010).

3 Both the fig tree and the small squirrel that feeds on the latex in the leaves are well known to the Kadazan hill-rice farmers living in the Crocker Range (Linus Gokusing, Kipandi).

JIM COMBER (1929–2005) This orchid fanatic authored three important books on the orchids of SE Asia, including *Orchids of Java* (1990) and *Orchids of Sumatra* (2001). In 1960–71 Comber was the manager of Sapong Rubber Estate near Tenom, at the southern end of the Crocker Range in Sabah. He spent much of his free time exploring the Crocker Range forests for rare orchids with his local Murut and Lundaye friends, during a period when wildlife was still relatively abundant. His unpublished mammal notes are referred to several times in this book (see p. 244, porcupines; p. 250, Marten and p. 254, Ferret Badger).

Sculptor Squirrel ***Glyphotes simus*** feeding on the latex of ***Ficus stupenda***, a giant strangling fig tree common in hill and montane forest in N Borneo as described by Kadazan swidden farmers in the Crocker Range.

Party of Sculptor Squirrels feeding on the Beccarian bodies produced on he undersides of the heart-shaped leaves of *Ficus deltoidea*, a mmon epiphytic fig throughout Borneo.

GIANT SQUIRREL *Ratufa affinis* HB 350, T 407, Wt 1.2kg **Common**

[Cream coloured Giant Squirrel] The largest tree squirrel in Borneo, found in tall forest from the peat-swamps of Kalimantan to 1,500m on Kinabalu. **ID:** Colours are very variable even between individuals in the same area, including a pale morph (possibly increasing with age) that occurs throughout Borneo. When feeding, sits across a branch with the long tail hanging down. Prevost's Squirrel always feeds sitting along a branch. **Call:** The loud call is a short, harsh rattle. Also a distinctive soft call, a series of hgip hgip hgip. (Payne et al 1985). 'The usual note is a harsh loud chatter, strikingly similar to the chatter of a magpie. We have also seen it making a sort of repeated croak which seemed to shake its whole frame and gave the tail a peculiar swinging motion' (Motley). **Habits:** Diurnal and arboreal, usually emerging from the nest well after dawn and retiring for the night before dusk (Payne). 'This squirrel is very abundant on Labuan rarely if ever descending to the ground and can run head first down the smooth trunk of a very high tree. They are often gregarious, as many as 20 feeding together. The males and females associate in pairs throughout the year. When made into soup they are excellent.' (Motley 1855) (p. 141). **Breeding:** Builds a large stick nest from twigs far out on the branches of a tall tree. The nest is loosely built and easily falls apart, an anti-predator strategy (p. 222). 'We shot a pregnant female containing 3 young and her mate continued to haunt the spot for several days, making a moaning noise.' (Motley 1855). **Range:** S. Thailand, Malaya, Sumatra, Borneo. Extinct in Singapore. Absent from Java. **Taxonomy:** Thorington et al (2012) list 4 mainland Borneo races. Sabah squirrels tend to be darker but the variation is such that I am unable to distinguish distinct races. See the illustrations opposite painted from individual photos showing locations.

Ratufa bicolor eating *Ficus variegata* figs. Note that in Malaya *Ratufa affinis* does not eat figs but does eat figs in Borneo.

BLACK GIANT SQUIRREL

Ratufa bicolor **HB 335, T 400, Wt 0.98kg**

P. Lingung, Natuna Islands

The most common giant squirrel in the seasonally dry climates of the Malay Peninsula and Thailand. Less common in the wetter rainforests further south. Present in seasonally dry Java where *R. affinis* is absent. In the Borneo Province (p. 15) confined to the tiny island of Lingung (Lagong) c. 25km^2. just off the south coast of Bunguran Besar in the Natuna Islands. Technically therefore *Ratufa bicolor* is included in the list of Bornean mammals. **Diet:** In Malaya Lambert (1990) found that *Ratufa bicolor* ate the fruit of 10 species of fig whilst *Ratufa affinis* did not eat figs. In Borneo *Ratufa affinis* often eats figs indicating that *Ratufa affinis* in Borneo may be a separate species. **Range:** N India south to Malaya, Sumatra and Java. P. Lingung (Natunas) **Race:** *R. b. angusticeps*. Map p. 386.

FRUIT *v.* SEED EATERS AND CLIMATE CHANGE

Borneo's hot and wet climate benefits fruit-eating mammals whilst cooler (montane) or dryer (more seasonal) climates benefit seed eaters. In hot wet climates, seeds tend to germinate rapidly (recalcitrant seeds) to avoid fungal decay. In seasonal or cooler climates hard seeds can be stored indefinitely (orthodox seeds).

Climate Change During the Pleistocene the Borneo climate varied repeatedly between cool and dry and hot and wet, alternately benefitting fruit eaters and seed eaters. A study by Yaakob (2005) in Malaya indicated that *R. affinis* ate less seeds (25%) compared to 38% seeds in the diet of *R. bicolor*. This enabled *R. affinis* to out-compete *R. bicolor* in wetter climates such as Borneo whilst *R. bicolor* outcompeted *R. affinis* in dryer Java. See pp. 14, 44–45, 46–47, 232 and 234.

Sandakan, Sabah

Danum, Sabah

Ulu Temburong, Brunei

Kuala Balai, Brunei

Gng Palung, W Kalimantan

Gng Palung

GROUND SQUIRRELS

1 BORNEAN MOUNTAIN GROUND SQUIRREL *Dremomys everetti* **HB 175, T 111, Wt 130**
Locally abundant endemic ground squirrel confined to the Bornean mountains from Kinabalu south to Gng Penrissen and Gng Pueh near Kuching. On Kinabalu found between 980m (start of mossy forest) to treeline at 3,400m. **ID:** Often confused with Mountain Treeshrew, which has a more pointed muzzle and longer, thinner tail (p. 146). On Kinabalu not found above Paka Cave at 3,150m. **Habits:** Diurnal and terrestrial, but can climb trees. **Diet:** Includes insects, earthworms, berries and nuts. Scavenges around dustbins on summit trail and for food scraps at Panar Laban Mountain Rest House on Kinabalu.

SQUIRREL AND TREESHREW FOOD, ANTS, TERMITES AND HARD NUTS Ants are the most successful form of animal life on planet Earth (E. O. Wilson). They reach their highest diversity in the tropical rainforests of Borneo, with 524 species found at Poring alone (Brühl et al. 1998). Ants and termites are a primary source of food for many Bornean mammals, including pangolins, squirrels and treeshrews. Termites are absent above 1,900m on Kinabalu (Gathorne Hardy 2002), whilst ants are not found above 2,300m (Bruhl et al. 1999), where they are replaced by abundant earthworms. Hard nuts replace soft recalcitrant lowland seeds in the mountains (p. 142). This probably accounts for differences in the distribution of Mountain Treeshrews and Bornean Mountain Ground Squirrels on Kinabalu (p. 194).

2 FOUR-STRIPED GROUND SQUIRREL *Lariscus hosei* **HB 181, T 126, Wt 180 Rare endemic**
Rare ground squirrel with relict distribution mainly in the mountains of N Borneo, but with several lowland records. Sabah records include Kinabalu (1,530m), Poring (600m), Sandakan, Danum, Tawau Hills. **ID:** Four narrow black stripes on back, the central two stripes separated from each other by a reddish-buff line, the two outer black stripes separated from the central two by pale white or buff line. Underparts orange. Overall much darker than Three-striped Ground Squirrel. The two species do not overlap in range. **Habits:** Diurnal and terrestrial. All records are from undisturbed primary forest. **Range:** From Kinabalu south to Gng Dulit, Bt Kalulong, Gng Batu Song and the Kelabit highlands in the hills of N Sarawak. There are no records as yet from Kayan Mentarang in NE Kalimantan.

3 THREE-STRIPED GROUND SQUIRREL *Lariscus insignis* **HB 200, T 130, Wt 175g**
Locally common terrestrial and diurnal forest squirrel of Kalimantan and S Sarawak north to the Baram River. No records for Sabah and Brunei. Common at Lanjak Entimau (Sarawak) and Sg Wain and Gng Palung, but no records from peat-swamp forest in Kalimantan. **ID:** Three wide dark stripes along back. Underparts pale white. **Habits:** In Sarawak, not uncommon in lowlands; usually single, seen running over fallen tree trunks (Banks). **Diet:** Seed predator and scatter-hoarder. At Pasoh (Malaya), as common as Plantain Squirrel when trapped with oil-palm fruit as a bait (see below). At Sg Wain (E Kalimantan) came to bait of maize. **Range:** Malaya, Sumatra, Java. **Borneo race:** *L. i. diversus.*

SCATTER-HOARDING BY THREE-STRIPED GROUND SQUIRREL AT PASOH
At Pasoh, a 2,500ha lowland dipterocarp forest reserve in W Malaysia, Yasuda (2000) found that *L. insignis* was a fallen fruit generalist. It was photographed feeding on over 50% of available fruits, including *Dipterocarpus* seeds, *Lithocarpus* acorns, *Canarium littorale* seeds and oily fruit such as *Alangium ebennaceum* and *Elaeocarpus stipularis*. In experiments with oil-palm fruit, it buried excess fruit at a depth of about 1cm in the ground, about 15m from the source. Some of these caches were retrieved the same day. At least three species of rat, *Leopoldamys sabanus* and *Maxomys* brown and spiny rats, also scatter-hoarded oil-palm bait by hiding the fruit under leaves.

4 SHREW-FACED GROUND SQUIRREL *Rhinosciurus laticaudatus* **HB 214, T 150, Wt 221 Rare.**
In Borneo a rare ground squirrel with a relict patchy distribution. Sabah records include Benoni (Papar) and Betotan (Sandakan). Kalimantan records include Pontianak, Gng Palung and Sabangau, where it is locally common (Schep 2014). Has been collected on both Bunguran Besar and Serasan in the Natuna Islands (Chasen 1985). **ID:** May be mistaken for Large Treeshrew by the pointed nose (p. 151), but lacks the treeshrew's stripes and plain tail. Tail is shorter and more bushy, and often held upwards with fluffed-out hairs when the squirrel is active (Payne 1985). **Habits:** 'In the old days very common around Kuching but felling the jungle has driven it away and in five years only one specimen has been taken' (Banks 1931). **Diet:** Feeds on worms, ants and termites in primary forest. At Pasoh in Malaya large numbers were trapped with oil-palm fruit as bait (Miura). Also ate 20% of fallen fruit (Yasuda 2005). **Range:** Malaya, Sumatra, Bunguran Besar. **Borneo race:** *R. l. laticaudatus.*

1
2
3
4

TUFTED GROUND SQUIRREL *Rheithrosciurus macrotis* **HB 442, T 320, Wt 1.25kg** **Endemic**

[Groove-toothed Squirrel – refers to the fact that the front incisors have vertical grooves, resulting in a serrated cutting edge for sawing through very hard nut shells]. The world's most magnificent squirrel is rare in most of forested Borneo from Gng Palung (W Kalimantan) to park headquarters at 1,500m on Kinabalu. There are no records from peat-swamp forest. Most common in hill forest but rarely seen repeatedly in the same locality, indicating that it is nomadic and follows fruiting patches of trees with hard nuts such as *Lithocarpus* oaks from valley to valley (p. 60). With the fragmentation of Borneo's forests, it is nomadic mammals that are in greatest danger of extinction (p. 42). **ID:** The enormous bushy tail, probably developed to confuse predators both as to the size and the shape of the squirrel, is held curled over the back or straight out, never hanging down like the tail of the arboreal Giant Squirrel (p. 210). **Habits:** Seen equally often in fruiting trees and on the ground. Like the Binturong and Pig-tailed Macaque, probably travels between fruiting trees on the ground rather than through the canopy. **Diet:** Recorded feeding on mangoes in Brunei hill forest (Bennett et al. 1987). According to Banks (1978) 'I was told it visited cultivation, feeding on bananas and particularly on maize, holding the corn cob in between its front legs, the tail curled over the back and that it would stand its ground and not just run away.' At Gng Palung fed on thick-shelled *Canarium* and *Mezzetia leptopoda* seeds (Marshall) (p. 190). **A killer squirrel?** A local report that the Tufted Ground Squirrel hunts muntjac for its blood (Meijaard et al. 2014) almost certainly results from confusion with the similar sized Yellow-throated Marten (p. 250). **Borneo records, Sabah:** Crocker Range, Kinabalu Park headquarters, Poring, Danum, Sepilok, Tabin, Tawau Hills, Maliau. **Brunei:** Ulu Temburong. **Sarawak:** Pulong Tau, Gng Penrissen, Usun Apau. **W Kalimantan:** Gng Palung, Gng Kenepai (Kapuas). **C Kalimantan:** Murung Raya, Bawan. **E Kalimantan:** Sg Wain, 'Common in Kayan Mentarang. Said to resist blow-dart poison and thus difficult to catch. The meat is said to be nutritious' (Puri 2005). Yasuma (1994) had no records for E Kalimantan.

KEDONDONG
Canrium pilosum
The oily fruit (3 x 1.5cm) are swallowed whole by hornbills and Sun Bears, and the seeds are dropped. Tufted Ground Squirrels predate both the unripe seeds on the tree and the ripe seeds on the ground, sawing through the hard shells with their strong, serrated teeth.

KEDONDONG: OILY FRUIT AND NUTS Burseraceae, World: 550 spp. **Borneo** *c.* 60 spp. The Burseraceae are a family of tall (to 45m) tropical forest trees most common in the Americas. They can be recognized by a strong, resinous smell to all parts. Fruit comprise a single, very hard, triangular nut covered with oily flesh. Both pulp and nut of several species, such as *Dacroydes rostrata* (dabai) and *Canarium odontophyllum* (pili nut), are eaten by humans but avoided by Orangutans (Leighton 1992 re. Kutai). The size of the largest fruit, *Canarium decumanum* (8.5 x 6cm) indicates rhino dispersal.

Predation of *Canarium* seeds Tufted Ground Squirrels predate *Canarium* seeds and at Gng Palung often foraged in or under fruiting *Canarium* trees. In contrast, Prevost's Squirrel is a pulp thief of Burseraceae, nibbling the oily pulp whilst dropping the nut near the tree (Becker et al. 1985).

Primary dispersal of *Canarium* seeds At Barito Ulu, McConkey (1999) found that Sun Bears gorged on ripe *C. pilosum* fruit. Beneath one tree McConkey found 21 Sun Bear scats containing 1,515 seeds. In Thailand Kitamura et al. (2006) found that the ripe fruit of *C. euphyllum* (fruit size 3–4.6cm x 1.7–2.8cm) were dispersed by hornbills and imperial pigeons. Fallen fruit were dispersed by mousedeer, muntjac and Sambar deer. Both hornbills and deer swallowed the fruit whole and regurgitated the stones.

Secondary dispersal of *Canarium* seeds Fallen *Canarium* seeds are so hard that they are avoided by *Maxomys* rats, the most important seed predators in Bornean forests (Blate 1998). Fallen seeds provide a specialist diet for scatter-hoarding rodents including ground squirrels, Horse-tailed Squirrel and porcupines, which both predate and disperse hard nuts (pp. 212 and 232).

AN UNDESCRIBED montane race of *Rheithrosciurus macrotis* with more grey in the fur has been recorded from mountain forest in the Maliau Basin (Sabah) and Pulong Tau (NW Sarawak).

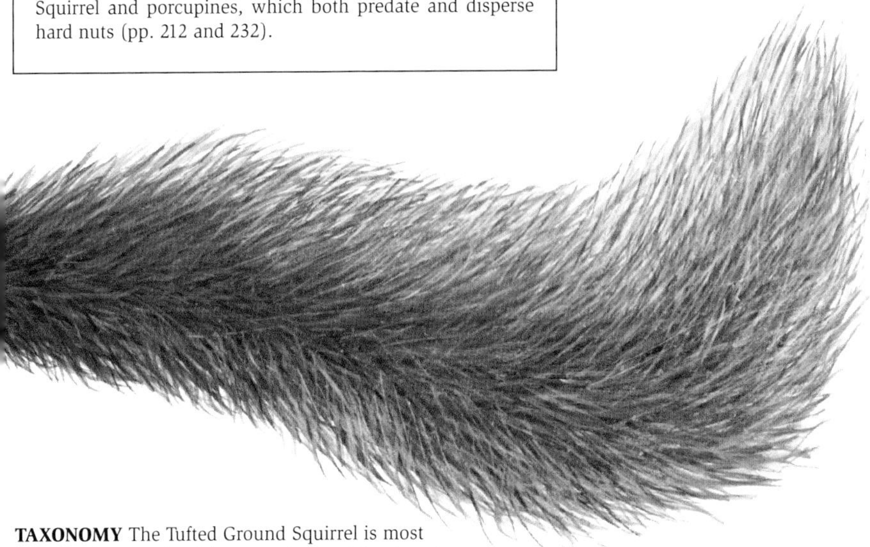

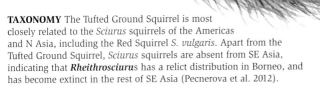

TAXONOMY The Tufted Ground Squirrel is most closely related to the *Sciurus* squirrels of the Americas and N Asia, including the Red Squirrel *S. vulgaris*. Apart from the Tufted Ground Squirrel, *Sciurus* squirrels are absent from SE Asia, indicating that ***Rheithrosciurus*** has a relict distribution in Borneo, and has become extinct in the rest of SE Asia (Pecnerova et al. 2012).

FLYING SQUIRRELS: INTRODUCTION

PETAURISTINAE **World:** 49 spp. **Borneo**, with 14 spp., is the world centre of flying squirrel diversity. **Flying squirrels** are wrongly named, because they glide not fly, using flaps of skin between their legs called a patagium to travel long distances (more than 150m) between trees at night. Unlike colugos (p. 154), which also glide, the long tail is free hanging. **Breeding:** Unlike day squirrels, which build their own nests (dreys), flying squirrels nest in tree holes and normally rear 1–3 young (p. 222). As in colugos, females are slightly larger than males, presumably because they need to carry young during the glide. **Ecology:** All flying squirrels are nocturnal. They emerge from their tree-hole day roosts at dusk and forage through the night for leaves, fruit, seeds and insects in varying proportions. **Diet:** In Malaya, Muul & Lim (1978) found that the largest flying squirrels (like langurs) ate mostly leaves, whilst the smallest flying squirrels ate seeds and fruit. The two *Hylopetes* species had the most generalist diet, eating fruit, seeds, insects and leaves. **Calls:** Most flying squirrel calls are as yet unknown, but see p. 222. **Logging:** Muul & Lim (1978) found that some flying squirrels increased in disturbed forest, whilst others declined. See species accounts. Logging normally results in a reduction of nesting holes, which adversely affects many mammals including some bats, some treeshrews and flying squirrels (p. 32). **Apparent rarity:** Muul and Lim (1978) note that of 100,000 mammals trapped by the Institute for Medical Research (IMR) in Malaya, only a dozen were flying squirrels. However, when forest in Johore was being converted to oil palm the IMR managed to collect 2,000 flying squirrels from tree holes in two years. **Absence of research:** Recent advances in technology such as endoscopic cameras and radio tracking have made it possible to study flying squirrel ecology for the first time, but the challenge has yet to be taken up in Borneo. As a result flying squirrel distribution maps are often blank.

Identification problems Young flying squirrels taken from nests are almost impossible to identify, and even adult small to medium-sized flying squirrels are difficult to distinguish in the hand. Pigmy flying squirrels always have flat, white-tipped tails.

Scale All illustrations opposite are 70% life size.

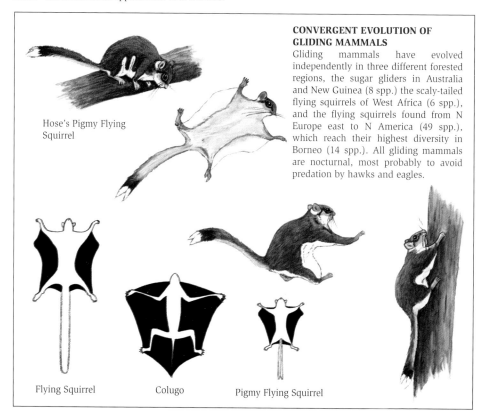

Hose's Pigmy Flying Squirrel

CONVERGENT EVOLUTION OF GLIDING MAMMALS

Gliding mammals have evolved independently in three different forested regions, the sugar gliders in Australia and New Guinea (8 spp.) the scaly-tailed flying squirrels of West Africa (6 spp.), and the flying squirrels found from N Europe east to N America (49 spp.), which reach their highest diversity in Borneo (14 spp.). All gliding mammals are nocturnal, most probably to avoid predation by hawks and eagles.

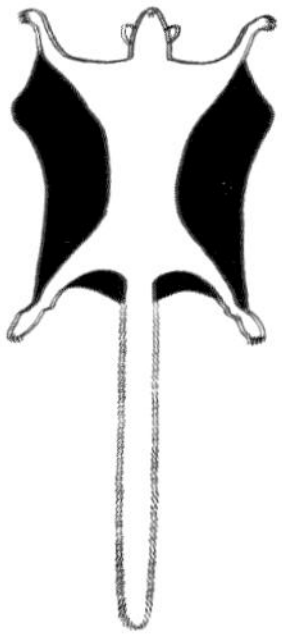

Flying Squirrel

Colugo

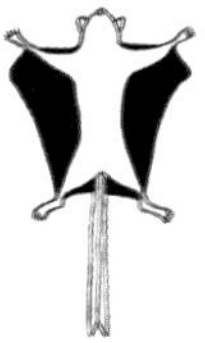

Pigmy Flying Squirrel

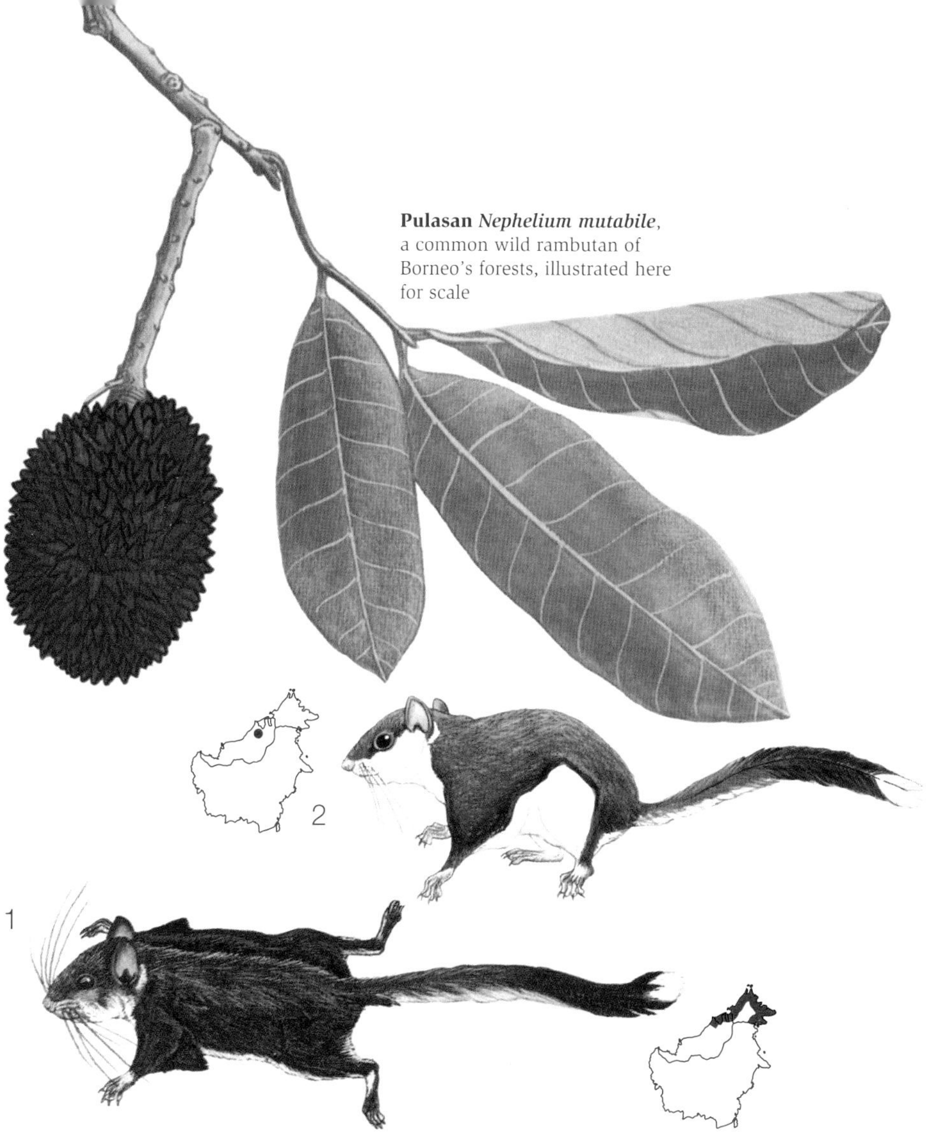

Pulasan *Nephelium mutabile*, a common wild rambutan of Borneo's forests, illustrated here for scale

PIGMY FLYING SQUIRRELS

1 HOSE'S PIGMY FLYING SQUIRREL *Petaurillus hosei* HB 84, T 91, Wt 31g Rare endemic

Rare tiny endemic flying squirrel found in lowland forests, including records from Sepilok, Tasek Merimbun (Brunei) and Sarawak south to the Niah Caves. **ID:** Very small with a white tip to the tail and long, pointed ears. Possibly conspecific with Selangor Pigmy Flying Squirrel *P. kinlochi*, known only from Selangor in Peninsular Malaysia. **Habits:** Nocturnal. Four individuals were found in a nest hole about 6m above the ground in a dead tree at the edge of tall dipterocarp forest at Sg Toyut in the Baram district by Hose, hence the name (p. 242).

2 EMILY'S PIGMY FLYING SQUIRREL *Petaurillus emiliae* HB 70, T 64, Wt 13.5g Rare endemic

[Lesser Pigmy Flying Squirrel] Competes with Bornean Pigmy Squirrel (p. 206) for the title of the world's smallest squirrel. Known only from pair collected by Charles Hose near Marudi on the Baram River in 1901. **ID:** Similar to *P. hosei*, but 15% smaller, and cheeks entirely buffy-white without grey below the eyes. Possibly conspecific with *P. hosei*.

PETINOMYS AND PTEROMYSCUS MEDIUM FLYING SQUIRRELS

1 TEMMINCK'S FLYING SQUIRREL *Petinomys setosus* **HB 116, T 104, Wt 40g** **Common**
[White-bellied Flying Squirrel in Lekagul 1977) Widespread in lowlands and hills of Sabah south to Kuching in Sarawak, in both virgin and secondary forests but rarely seen. **ID:** Small with no orange tinge on bases of body hairs. **Habits:** One record of nest hole, 19mm wide, in tree trunk at 0.5m above the ground (Malaya). **Diet:** Seeds and fruit. Captives placed hard-shelled nuts in their water dish for a few days before attempting to eat them (Muul & Lim 1978). **Range:** Myanmar south to Sumatra. **Borneo race:** *P. s. setosus.*

2 VORDERMANN'S FLYING SQUIRREL *Petinomys vordermanni* **HB 98, T 100, Wt 36g** **Rare**
In Malaya, Muul & Lim (1978) found this squirrel most common in orchards and rubber plantations, and not in virgin forest. In Borneo only two records, at Tasek Merimbun (Brunei-lowland peat-swamp forest) and Sg Boh (E Kalimantan, hill forest). **ID:** Patagium has buff margin, but is only half the size of Horsfield's Flying Squirrel. Orange cheeks. Black fur around each eye. Tufts of whiskers at base of each ear. **Habits:** Nest holes recorded at 0.3–6m above the ground. **Range:** Malaya, Belitung. **Borneo race:** *P. v. vordermanni.*

3 SMOKY FLYING SQUIRREL *Pteromyscus pulverulentus* **HB 235, T 222, Wt 252g** **Scarce**
Locally common in undisturbed lowland and hill forest. At Poring (Kinabalu 600–900m) the most common flying squirrel caught from tree holes along the Langanan waterfall trail. Also recorded from Marudi, Gng Dulit and west of the Batang Lupar in SW Sarawak. No Kalimantan records. **ID:** Distinguished from Black Flying Squirrel by white, not grey, underparts and smaller size. **Habits:** Seven tree-hole nests found at Poring over 2 weeks were all 3–4 m above the ground. In Malaya, Muul and Lim (1974) found breeding year round, but only a small per cent bred at any one time, perhaps indicating shortage of nesting holes. **Range:** S Thailand, Malaya. **Borneo race:** *P. p. borneanus.*

4 WHISKERED FLYING SQUIRREL *Petinomys genibarbis* **HB 171, T 180, Wt 89g** **Scarce**
In Malaya a scarce resident of orchards and secondary forests. In Borneo widespread but scarce in secondary and hill forests, including Lanjak Entimau and in peat-swamp forest at Sabangau. **ID:** Has a pronounced wart, about 5mm in diameter and bearing a tuft of long black whiskers, on each cheek (Jackson 2012). This and the golden-pinkish rump are distinctive. Patagium has a white margin. **Habits:** In Malaya a captive uttered soft whistling sounds when alarmed and ate **rambutan** fruit in preference to all other food (Medway 1969). **Range:** Malaya, Sumatra, Java. **Borneo race:** *P. g. borneoensis.*

5 HAGEN'S FLYING SQUIRREL *Petinomys hageni* **HB 280, T 230** **(Not illustrated) Rare**
Collected once near Pontianak, W Kalimantan. The skin has been lost. **ID:** Sumatran form has broad band of reddish-brown between and around eyes, extending to ears. Long, stiff hairs behind and in front of ears. Tail thickly haired; blackish-red above buffy with blackish-red hair-tips below (Payne et al. 1985). **Habits:** Unknown. **Range:** Sumatra. **Borneo race:** *P. h. ouwensi.*

CAN FLYING SQUIRRELS FLY?
Adams (1978) recorded that a Red-cheeked Flying Squirrel managed to gain a metre in height by flapping during a 6m glide. Thorington et al. (2012) note that this is the only recorded instance of a flying squirrel actually flying. The most likely explanation is that all gliding mammals in Borneo fly in a 'J' curve so that they can land head up. The glide starts almost flat, but towards the end the squirrel increases the slope angle to increase the speed and uses the extra speed to land head up on a tree trunk (pp. 154, 216)

Spotted Giant Flying Squirrel

1

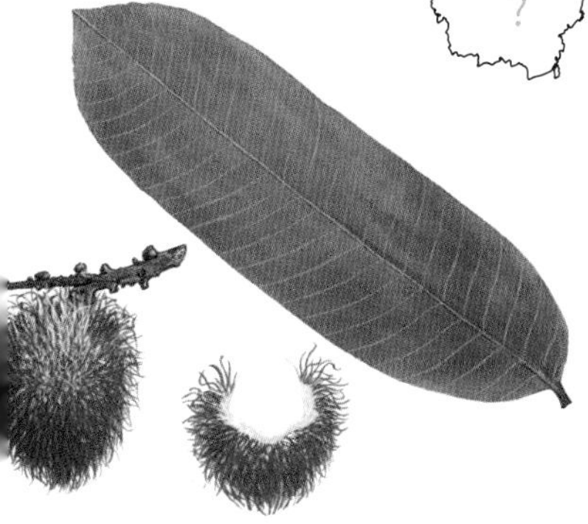

Rambutan ***Nepthelium rambutan-ake***
The Whiskered Flying Squirrel is a pulp thief of this popular primate-dispersed fruit.

2

3

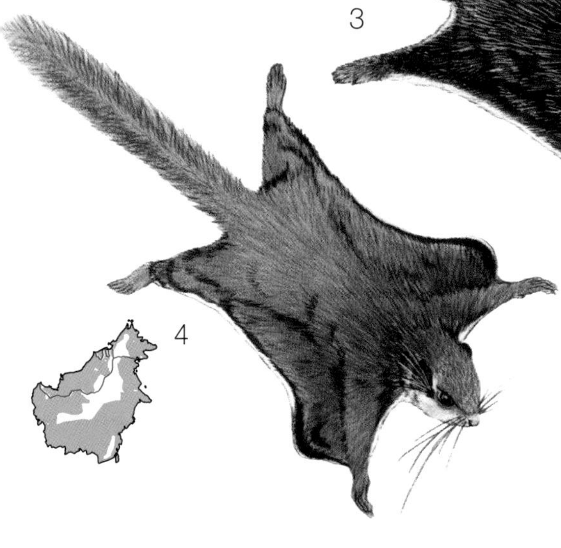

4

HYLOPETES AND IOMYS MEDIUM FLYING SQUIRRELS

1 HORSFIELD'S FLYING SQUIRREL *Iomys horsfieldi* **HB 194, T 181, Wt 188 Locally common**
[Javanese Flying Squirrel] One of the two most common small flying squirrels in Borneo, with wide altitude range from Sepilok to 1,800m on Kinabalu, found in both virgin and secondary forests. In Sarawak less common in lowland forest than Red-cheeked (Banks 1949). Lim (1968) found this squirrel to be very common in primary forest at Bundu Tuhan (1,300m) on Kinabalu. Seen gliding at night in forest around park headquarters. One Kalimantan record only (see below). **ID:** Distinguished from similar *Hylopetes* flying squirrels, which all have pale white/cream margin of the gliding wing, by the orange margin. **Habits:** In Malaya often competes for figs with *Cynopterus* bats (Muul & Lim 1978). **Call:** Alarm calls of both are nearly identical, a sort of 2-note bugling (Muul & Lim 1978). In Singapore the loud call sounds like the bark of a small dog (Nick Baker). **Breeding:** Litter to 4, but average of 2. **Diet:** Six stomachs were filled with fruit, also black ants and bark (Lim et al. 1968). **Range:** Malaya, Sumatra, Java. Common in Singapore. **Borneo race:** *I. h. thomsoni.*

NESTING FLYING SQUIRRELS "This squirrel was one of a pair that had a nest of leaves about 28cm in diameter, in the top of a small sapling, about 6m from the ground. They both flew out on the tree being shaken, the male going to a large tree trunk, where he was shot. The other was lost sight of" (W. L. Abbott 1908, re. a male *I. horsfieldi* collected at Batu Jurong, SW Borneo, nr Gng Palung in June 1908). **Note:** Records of flying squirrels in nests probably refer to old birds' nests taken over by the flying squirrels, rather than nests built by the squirrels (pp. 154, 222).

2 RED-CHEEKED FLYING SQUIRREL *Hylopetes spadiceus* **HB 155, T 143, Wt 78g Common**
One of the two most common small flying squirrels (including Horsfield's Flying Squirrel) in Borneo. The most common flying squirrel in lowland Sarawak (Banks 1949). These two species are the only flying squirrels that survive in Singapore, where they can live in secondary forests (Chua et al. 2013). In E Kalimantan recorded north of Kayan River only (Yasuma 1994). **ID:** Margin of gliding wing white; cheeks and base of tail with distinct orange tinge. Distinguished from *H. platyurus* by larger size and more extensive yellowish tinge on cheeks and base of tail. Juveniles dark grey above, white below. **Habits:** In Malaya and Singapore nest holes are often low down and nest entrance is plugged with a tight ball of grass when the squirrels are inside during the day and unblocked during the night (Nick Baker, Chua et al. 2013). Everett collected three individuals from a tree hole on Bunguran Besar, Natunas. **Range:** Myanmar south to Malaya, Sumatra, Java. **Borneo race:** *H. s. everetti.*

3 JENTINK'S FLYING SQUIRREL *Hylopetes platyurus* **HB 123, T 111, Wt 43 Scarce montane**
[Grey-cheeked Flying Squirrel *H. lepidus*] One of two flying squirrels confined to the mountains (p. 224). On Kinabalu found at 1,370–1,500m and in the Kelabit Highlands at 900–1,070m. **ID:** Margin of gliding wing white. Cheeks and base of tail grey. **Diet:** In Malaya *H. lepidus* eats seeds, fruit, leaves and insects (Muul and Lim 1978). **Breeding:** Three young found in a nest (possibly built by a bird) at Kinabalu Park headquarters by Andy Boyce may have been this species. In Malaya *H. Lepidus* breeds at very long intervals with gaps of up to 17 months, litter 1–3, average 2 (Muul & Lim, 1974). **Taxonomy:** In Payne (1985) listed as Grey-cheeked Flying Squirrel *H. lepidus*. Split by Rasmussen et al. (2008) and Thorington et al. (2012). Muul & Lim (1971) record this squirrel as common in secondary forest, farms and orchards in the Malay Peninsula, but not in primary or hill forest, indicating that *H. platyurus* in Borneo is ecologically distinct and is probably a Borneo endemic. **Range:** Malaya, Sumatra, Borneo.

Horsfield's Flying Squirrel at 1,100m at Fraser's Hill, Malaya, part of group of around 20 feeding on fruiting oak trees (p. 60). (Photo: Nick Baker)

Rambutan ***Nepthelium rabutan-ake***, a common primate fruit, to show scale

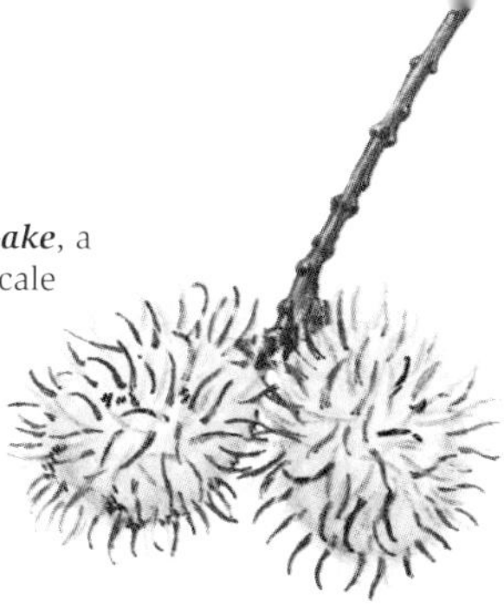

AEROMYS LARGE FLYING SQUIRRELS

1 BLACK FLYING SQUIRREL *Aeromys tephromelas* **HB 381, T 435, Wt 1,137g** **Scarce**

Widespread throughout the lowland forests of Borneo, but scarce. In Kalimantan recorded from Sg Wain and Gng Palung, where Red Giant Flying Squirrel is also present, and Sabangau peat-swamp forest in Kalimantan, where Red Giant Flying Squirrel is absent. **ID:** Large black or dark brown flying squirrel with a grey belly, unlike the much smaller Whiskered, which has white belly. Photographs of the Sepilok individuals show hairless pink ears and nose. An individual photographed at Gerik in Malaya has black tufted ears. **Diet:** Studies by Muul & Lim (1978) indicate a generalist diet of seeds, fruit and leaves, whilst giant flying squirrels eat mostly leaves. **Habits:** Nocturnal. At Sepilok lives in forest near the canopy walkway with the Red Giant Flying Squirrel, where it is less common and much shyer, emerging only after dark. Common at Tabin, where it has been recorded feeding in oil palm. **Taxonomy:** A reddish race has been recorded from Samarinda in E Kalimtan (Thorington et al. 2012). **Note:** Most likely this is an erythristic (red) morph rather than a separate race. **Distribution:** Malaya, Sumatra. **Borneo race:** *A. t. phaeomelas.*

Black Flying Squirrel, Sepilok
A much-photographed pair occupy a tree hole close to and level with the canopy walkway at Sepilok. Red Giant Flying Squirrels are more numerous in the area. Red Giants start emerging just before dusk, but the Black Flying Squirrels do not emerge until well after dusk, about half an hour later than the Red Giants. (Photo: Cosmo Phillipps)

2 THOMAS'S FLYING SQUIRREL *Aeromys thomasi* **HB 390, T 385, Wt 1,435g Local endemic**

Locally common in many forested areas of Borneo, including Sg Wain and Gng Palung, but not Sabangau in Kalimantan. Anecdotal reports indicate that *A. thomasi* is more common than Red Giant Flying Squirrel in hill forests and less common in the lowlands. On Kinabalu, Lim (1968) collected two in forest at 1,600m near the park headquarters, where Spotted Giant Flying Squirrel is usually more common. **ID:** Large, plain red flying squirrel with no black tail-tip. **Habits:** At Danum more common than Red Giant Flying Squirrel, frequently seen on night drives in tall forest, whereas Red Giant Flying Squirrel is more common in disturbed forest or along the forest edge. At Tabin less common than both Black and Red Giant Flying Squirrels (Nick Acheson). **Diet:** Two individuals collected by Lim (1968) on Kinabalu had only fruit in their stomachs, whereas the stomachs of Red Giant Flying Squirrels are normally filled with leaves. The dentition indicates a mixed diet of fruit and leaves (Muul & Lim 1978).

WHERE SQUIRRELS SLEEP: DREYS AND TREE HOLES As far as is known all 22 species of day-active squirrel in Borneo make nests known as **dreys** out of dense bundles of leaves and twigs, which they use for sleeping in at night, whilst the 14 species of nocturnal 'flying' squirrel all sleep in tree holes during the day. Both behaviours are probably a tactic to avoid predation by snakes, which can climb vertical tree trunks as long as the bark is rough and are most active at night, when they often investigate tree holes. Flying squirrels leave their roosting holes unoccupied at night so a snake finds nothing. If a snake attacks a sleeping day squirrel at night, the squirrel will be warned by rustling leaves and can easily exit from the drey due to the loose construction. A problem with tree holes is that there is often no rear safety exit.

1

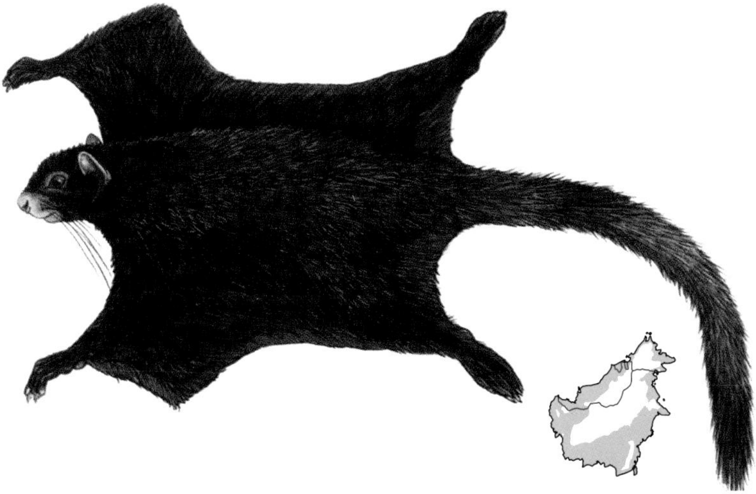

2

MYSTERY MAMMAL

In December 2005 Stephan Wulffraat of the WWF Indonesia Program released a camera-trap photo of a mystery mammal taken two years earlier near the Lalut Birai Field Station in the Kayan Mentarang NP (p. 384). The discovery of a possible new carnivore species for Borneo hit the headlines around the world. After the fuss had died down, a paper by Meijaard, Kitchener & Smeenk (2006) in the *Mammal Review* suggested (correctly) that the mystery mammal was actually a Thomas's Flying Squirrel in an unusual situation, that is it was at ground level, not high in a tree.

(Camera-trap photo: Andris Salo and Amat Uti, WWF Lalut Birai Field Station 700m asl, April 2003)

1 SPOTTED GIANT FLYING SQUIRREL *Petaurista elegans* **HB 352, T 352, Wt 1,040g Montane**
Replaces Red Giant Flying Squirrel in N Borneo mountains, 1,000–2,000m. Resident in forest around Kinabalu Park headquarters at 1,500m and at Mesilau at 2,000m. Common in Crocker Range south to Gng Dulit in N Sarawak. **ID:** Similar to Red Giant Flying Squirrel, but has all-black tail and white spots on back and head. Juveniles have variable pelage with fewer spots (Payne 1985). **Habits:** Nocturnal and arboreal. In the Himalayas occurs to 4,000m, often in rhododendron scrub and on cliffs (McNeeley 1977). In Malaya found at 225–1,300m (Medway 1969). **Range:** Himalayas south to Sumatra, Java. **Borneo race:** *P. e. banksi.*

2 RED GIANT FLYING SQUIRREL *Petaurista petaurista* **HB 400, T 418, Wt 1,985g**
Largest and most common flying squirrel found in all types of forest throughout lowland Borneo, to 900m on Kinabalu. Survives in cultivated areas near forest where there are large trees with suitable nest holes. **Habits:** At Sepilok several families occupy nest holes high up in trees surrounding the RDC canopy walkway. Adults start emerging just before dusk, gliding between the trunks of tall dipterocarps in the area. **Diet:** Eats more leaves than other squirrels, but also eats fruit and seeds, especially Laran (see below) and Binuang *Octomeles sumatrana* (p. 83). **Call:** When threatened a surprisingly fierce growl, and will strike with one or other of clawed fore-feet rather than bite (Banks 1949). **Breeding:** 'These animals are very common on Labuan, though as they move only in the evening, they are not often seen. They live and breed in hollow trees, often at a great height from the ground. If taken young they become as tame as kittens. In felling a large old tree at Tg Kubong, a whole family, male, female and two young ones, was caught. The young ones were very thickly furred and the hair on the tail much longer than the adults; their colour was dull ashy grey and they looked so unlike their parents that had we not caught them together we should have fancied them another species.' (adapted from Motley 1855, p. 140). At Sepilok large nest boxes erected for hornbills near the canopy walkway were rapidly occupied by families of these squirrels, indicating that nest-hole availability may limit populations in logged forest. **Range:** Sri Lanka, to S China, south to Sumatra, Java. Extinct in Singapore. **Borneo races:** 1. *P. p. rajah*, E Sarawak and Sabah, except range of 2. *P. p. nigrescens* (dark tail), Sandakan south to the Kinabatangan. 3. *P. p. lumholtzi*, NC and E Kalimantan. 4. *P. p. nitidula* (smaller), Natuna Islands.

LARAN ***ANTHOCEPHALUS (NEOLAMARCKIA) CADAMBA***
This is a common tree of the forest edge and river banks, sometimes planted in forest-tree plantations. Laran trees have pagoda-shaped *Terminalia*-type branching characteristic of fruit-bat pollinated or dispersed trees (p. 81). Laran and many other locally abundant trees in the Rubiaceae family, including *Nauclea*, *Neonauclea* and *Mitragyna*, produce round pompom flowers pollinated by bats and squirrels, which ripen into hard, round, yellow-green fruit with tiny seeds. These sugar-free fruit target leaf-eating folivores for dispersal, including langurs, Proboscis Monkeys and large flying squirrels (p. 176).

1

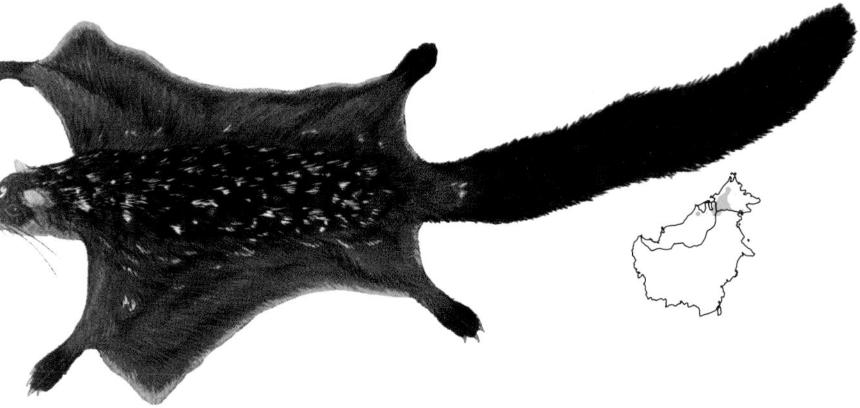

2

2

RATS: INTRODUCTION AND COMMENSAL RATS

MURIDAE **World:** *c.* 710 + spp. in 150 genera. **Borneo:** 27 spp. in 10 genera.
Commensal rats: (living in association with humans) are most likely the first mammals you will encounter in Borneo.
Invasive rats: 500 years ago Borneo was mostly covered with unbroken forest. The replacement of forest with farms and plantations has allowed some Asian rats with generalist habits to invade Borneo.
Forest rats: Most of Borneo's rats are forest dwellers, often with very specialized diets and lifestyles.
Breeding: Rats breed rapidly and populations may 'explode' when food is readily available (p. 228).
Zoonoses: Commensal rats act as vectors (carriers) of human diseases such as plague, typhus and leptospirosis.
Weights and sizes are averages based on Payne et al. (1985). Individual rats may vary by up to 20%.
Detailed data on Malayan rats (many of which occur in Borneo) can be found in Medway (1982).

1 NORWAY RAT *Rattus norvegicus* **HB 214, T 200 (less than HB), Wt 275g** **Abundant in towns**
[Brown Rat] Commensal large rat abundant in most towns, occasionally found in gardens and farms. Originally from N China, now considered a major pest by humans worldwide. Domesticated white Norway Rats are kept as pets, and large numbers are sacrificed in medical experiments to benefit humans. **ID**: 12 nipples. Large brown rat. **Habits:** Usually nocturnal and mainly terrestrial, but can climb. Most common near refuse or livestock such as chickens. Nests in piles of refuse, but can dig large burrows under buildings. Omnivorous and often aggressive. **Range:** Worldwide near human habitation.

2 POLYNESIAN RAT *Rattus exulans* **HB 116, T 139 (c. 110% of body), Wt 60g** **Abundant**
Commensal small rat in towns, gardens and cultivated areas. Found throughout Borneo including Labuan, and to 1,650m on Kinabalu. **ID**: 8 nipples. Small rat with rough fur and hard spines. **Habits:** Unlike other commensal rats builds a woven nest of grass. **Range:** SE Asia to the Pacific Islands.

3 ASIAN HOUSE RAT *Rattus tanezumi* **HB 170, T 171 (105% of HB), Wt 150g** **Locally common**
Invasive rat found in towns and villages, but also on plantations and farms. Recorded to 1,700m on Kinabalu, in oil palm at Tawau and in logged and secondary forest at the SAFE project in Sabah (Cussack 2012, Loveridge 2013). **ID:** 10 nipples. Smaller than Norway Rat, with greyish fur. **Habits:** Smaller, less aggressive and more arboreal than Norway Rat. Abidin et al. (2014) researched Black-winged Kites nesting in young oil palm with a ground cover of leguminous Kudzu vine (*Pueraria lobata*) near Lahad Datu (Sabah). Most common prey was *R. exulans* followed by *R. tanezumi diardii*, with a few *R. whiteheadi* and one *Crocidura fulginosa* (p. 140). **Taxonomy:** Closely related to Black Rat *R. rattus*, but split by Musser. See Wilson and Reeder (2005). The Black Rat is not officially recorded for Borneo, but there may be small populations around ports and docks. **Range:** Found throughout SE Asia. **Borneo race:** *R. t. diardii.*

4 RICEFIELD MOUSE *Mus caroli* **HB 76, T 78, Wt 14g** **Not confirmed**
The individual illustrated was caught at Kg Kaingaran, 700m (Gng Trus Madi in Sabah), but then eaten by a cat, so identification could not be confirmed. **ID**: 10 nipples. Small. Upperparts brownish-grey. Underparts whitish. Tail dark above, pale below. **Habits:** Elsewhere found in rice fields and grassland, unlike *M. casteneus*, which occurs near houses. **Range:** SE Asia, Taiwan, Sumatra and Java.

5 ASIAN HOUSE MOUSE *Mus castaneus* **HB 73, T 82, Wt 14g** **Locally common**
Commensal small rat in many coastal towns. **ID**: 10 nipples. Small. Entirely grey-brown. Underparts only slightly paler than upperparts. Tail all dark brown. **Habits:** Runs very fast, then stops. Difficult to trap; usually brought in by cats. **Range:** Widespread in E Asia.

RATS AS RICEFIELD PESTS
'Dusuns especially the Tambunan group are expert mouse catchers, and a long line of them will go through the padi fields with bamboo flares at night, catching the rodents in their hands with extraordinary dexterity, or killing them with sticks as they try to escape.' (Rutter (1929).

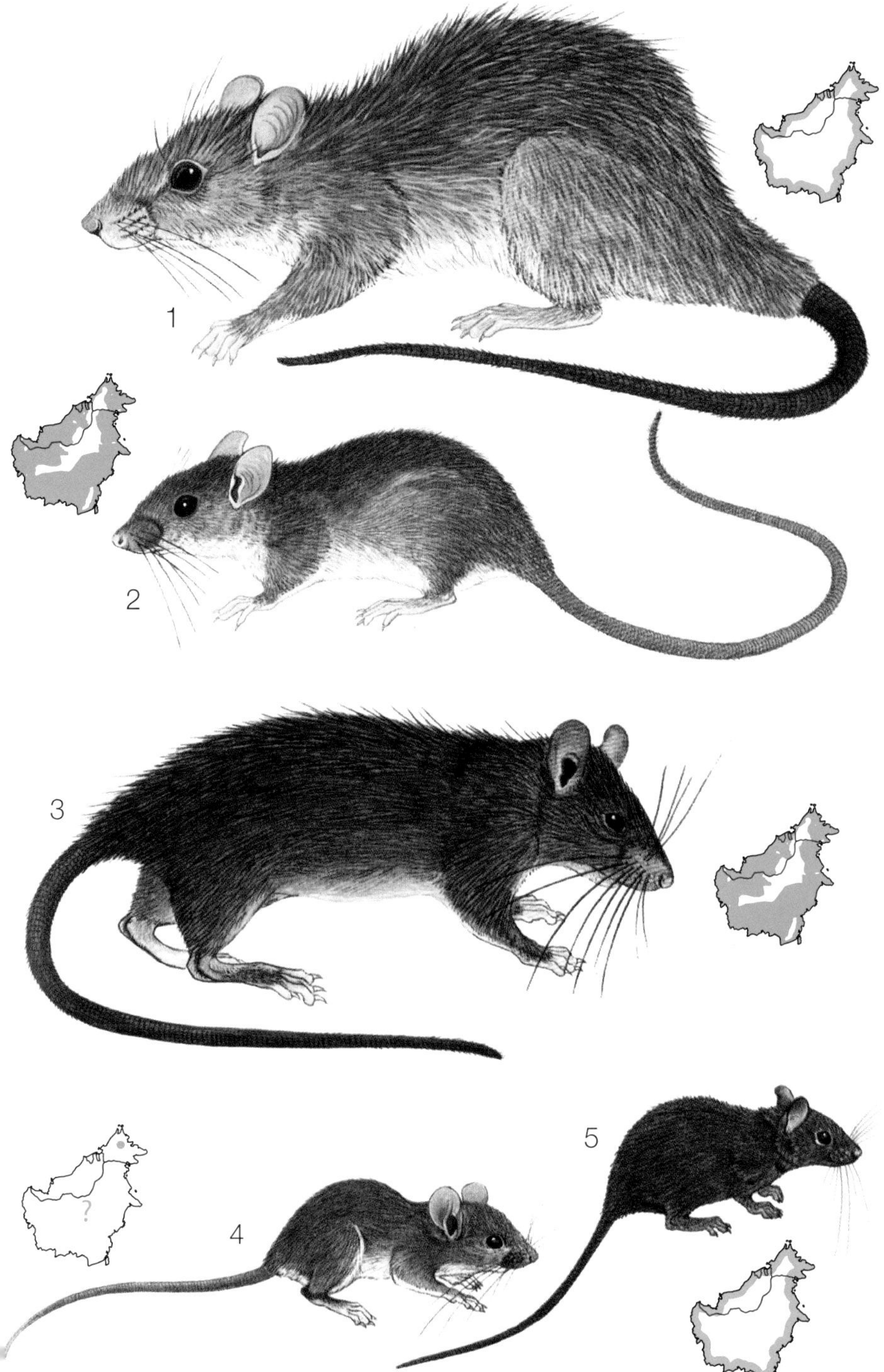
1
2
3
4
5

DARK-TAILED RATS

Dark-tailed rats are common ground rats of forest and farms, with long (over 100% of HB), dark tails.

1 TIOMAN RAT *Rattus tiomanicus* **HB 164, T 150 (75–120% of HB), Wt 102** **Abundant**
[Malaysian Wood Rat] Tioman Rats are often the most common rats in secondary forest and oil-palm plantations, and usually the most common rats on small islands such as Gaya Island opposite Kota Kinabalu, and the tiny island of Keraman near Labuan (UKMS). Recorded at 1,650m (park headquarters) on Kinabalu. **ID**: 10 nipples. Underparts greyish with buffy-white hair-tips. **Habits:** Nocturnal and terrestrial, but may climb small trees. **Range:** Malaya, Sumatra, Java and many small islands. **Borneo races:** 1. *R. t. sabae*, northern half of Borneo. 2. *R. t. jalorensis*, most of S Borneo. 3. *R. t. banguei*, Pulau Banggi and P. Malawali. 4. *R. t.* mara, Pulau Maratua, NE Kalimantan.

2 TIOMAN RAT *Rattus tiomanicus* **Race:** ***jalorensis***
The race of *R. tiomanicus* found in S Borneo. **ID:** Underparts white, not grey, with brown-tipped hairs.

3 RICEFIELD RAT *Rattus argentiventer* **HB 175, T 161 (*c.*100% of HB), Wt 133** **Locally common**
Often the most common rat in rice fields, grassland and cultivation, but absent from some areas. **ID**: 12 nipples. Underparts entirely silvery-grey, often with a dark streak along the middle. Young individuals have a distinctive orange-coloured tuft in front of each ear. **Habits:** Omnivorous. Usually burrows and nests in the ground. Serious pest of rice. **Range:** Invasive species from Asia scattered throughout Borneo.

4 MÜLLER'S RAT *Sundamys muelleri* **HB 212, T 234 (*c.* 110–120% of HB), Wt 232g** **Common**
[Müller's Giant Sunda Rat] Common large rat of forest edge and secondary forest from peat-swamp forest at Sabangau to 1,650m on Kinabalu. Often foraging along stream and river banks. The most common rat in damp limestone caves. **ID**: 8 nipples. Large dark rat with rough fur that has long black guard hairs but no spines. Fur underside varies from white to pale grey to rufous, and is soft and dense with no spines. Tail is all dark brown, unlike tails of *Maxomys* rats. Line between upperfur and underfur is not sharply defined as in Sabah Rat (p. 238). **Habits:** Mostly nocturnal and terrestrial, but can climb. Omnivorous. **Range:** S Thailand south to Malaya, Sumatra and Palawan. **Borneo races:** 1. *S. m. borneanus*, mainland. 2. *S. m. otiosus*, P. Banggi and P. Balembangan. 3. *S. m. sebucus*, P. Sebuku.

RODENT POPULATION CYCLES In captivity Norway Rats breed at 90 days and produce up to 12 young every 30 days thereafter. In theory a single breeding pair with abundant food can increase to more than 500,000 in two years. After forest masting the populations of some rats may temporarily increase (pp. 13 and 55), but when the food runs out hordes of rats may descend on local crops. In Asia rat plagues are particularly common after bamboo masting events (p. 49). Predators on rats such as Leopard Cats also breed continuously when rats are abundant, so both the rodents and their predators are subject to extreme population cycles in masting or seasonal habitats (see Elton 1924). In Borneo population fluctuations apply especially to dipterocarp seed predators such as Bearded Pig and Rajah Maxomys. (see p. 13; p. 55, dipterocarp masting; p. 234, *Maxomys* rats, and p. 301, Bearded Pigs. As predators of Bearded Pigs, Clouded Leopard populations are also predicted to fluctuate widely (p.278).
At Danum, Emmons (2000) reported that following a massive dipterocarp masting Sept–Nov (1990) the population of Red Spiny Maxomys and Sabah Rat increased slightly, whilst the population of Rajah Maxomys increased by more than 10 times and continued at high level for more than 7 months.
Carrying capacity and lean periods Emmons's extended observations illustrate the errors made by other researchers who estimate mammal population densities in one-off studies of dipterocarp forest without recording local masting (fruiting) periods. **Oil palm:** This is a steady state fruit producer, so populations of oil-palm fruit eating mammals and their predators, such as macaques and Clouded Leopards, living in the oil-palm/forest ecotone are likely to be relatively stable. In Borneo accurate mammalian density data can only be obtained from studies lasting at least 10 years, including two major mastings and the intervening lean period. Note: No such Borneo studies have yet been carried out, so all mammalian density figures quoted in this guide must be regarded with caution (p. 32).

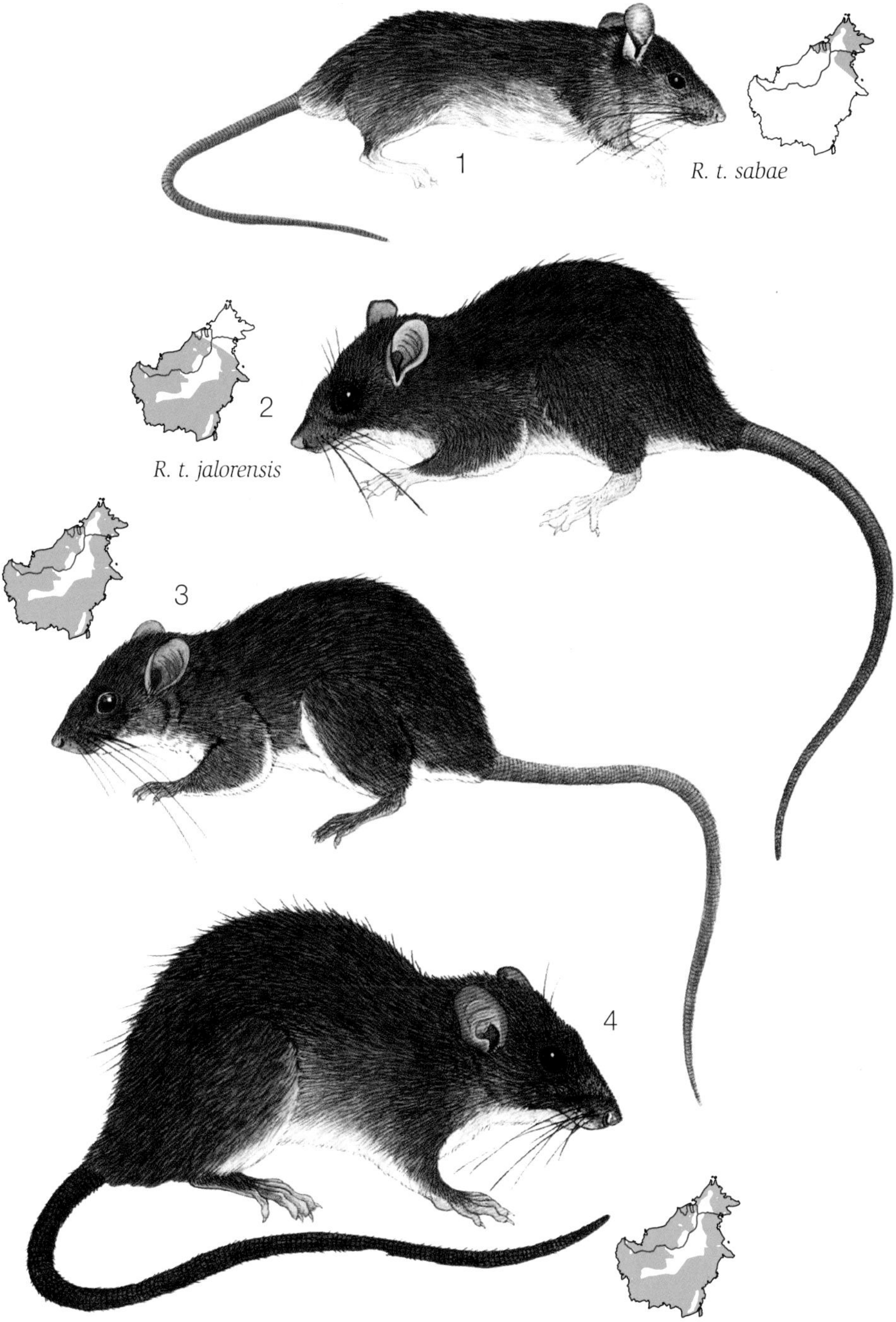
1
R. t. sabae
2
R. t. jalorensis
3
4

ENDEMIC MOUNTAIN RATS

1 KINABALU RAT *Rattus baluensis* **HB 170, T 175, Wt 108** **Abundant Kinabalu endemic**
[Summit Rat] The most common mammal on the higher slopes of Kinabalu. Mainly nocturnal but frequently active in late afternoon. Scavenges refuse around the Laban Rata rest huts. Recorded from park headquarters, 1,560m to the tree line at 3,360m, but most common in berry-bearing *Leptospermum* and *Schima* scrub above 2,200m. **ID:** Distinguished by long, fluffy black hair. 10 nipples. Tail uniform dark brown. Underparts grey-buff. **Habits:** 'The commonest mammal on Kinabalu is undoubtedly the Kinabalu Rat. This rat was quite tame, running about our shelter and over the men's bodies at night. We caught numbers in the Dusun traps round about the camp. The Kiau Dusuns have a path right up to the granite slopes. These paths are made by the Kiau Dusuns for the express purpose of setting their bamboo rat-traps, which are placed a few yards apart, along the paths to nearly 9000 feet. The frequented runs of the small mammalia, such as rats, squirrels, mice, are easily discernible on the soft moss-covered ground.' (Whitehead 1893). **Taxonomy:** In Payne (1985) listed as conspecific with *R. korinchi*, found on Gng Kerinci (Sumatra). Split by Musser (1986). The closest relative is the Tioman Rat.

2 BORNEO GIANT RAT *Sundamys infraluteus* **HB 260, T 302 (*c.* 120% HB), Wt 420g** **Endemic**
[Mountain Giant Rat] Borneo's largest rat inhabits a limited altitudinal range (920–2,350m) on Kinabalu and a few other mountains, including Trus Madi, Gng Lumaku at 1,365m, Gng Mulu at 1,850, Bkt Retak Brunei and Gng Harun in NE Kalimantan, showing an uneven relict distribution (p. 14). **ID:** Distinguished by size and 6 nipples. Upperparts dark brown, underparts grey with a strong orange tinge. Tail entirely dark brown. **Habits:** On Kinabalu, Md Nor (1996) found Borneo Giant Rats locally common from park headquarters up to Kamborangoh, which corresponds to mossy cloud forest dominated by oaks. The species preferred coconut and peanut butter bait (not banana), indicating a dietary preference for nuts rather than fruit. Giant rats are probably specialist feeders on *Lithocarpus* acorns (pp. 60 and 232). **Taxonomy:** In Payne (1985) listed as conspecific with *R. atchinensis*, found only in the Sumatran mountains. Split by Cranbrook et al (2014).

WHITEHEAD'S DIARY, 22 MARCH 1888 'Today a Dusun brought me in a gigantic rat but in a very decomposed state and full of maggots, but the cold in my head is so bad that my sense of smell has completely gone, and to that science may be grateful for the addition of "Mankulum" to the genus *Mus*. Two very large Kinabalu rats which I discovered *Leopoldamys sabanus* the "Barud" of the Dusuns and *Sundamys infraluteus*, the Mankulum are occasionally caught, and afford these people quite a meal. Rats are often split and fixed on bamboo frames, then smoked and stuck over the fireplaces in the houses until required.' (adapted from Whitehead 1893).

3 MOUNTAIN MAXOMYS *Maxomys alticola* **HB 158, T 154, Wt ?** **Rare endemic**
Uncommon rat endemic to the higher slopes of Kinabalu (1,070–3,360m) and Gng Trus Madi. **ID:** 8 nipples. Body covered in sharp spines above and below. Underparts whitish, no yellow tinge. Tail dark above, pale below. **Habits:** Diet is largely insects. Nor (1996) failed to trap this rat in his Kinabalu survey involving 3,780 trap nights and 824 captures. Junaini (1986) in a previous smaller survey only recorded this rat once at Carson's Camp (2,700m). Whitehead found this rat was most common among tall trees on Kinabalu.

WHITEHEAD'S DIARY, 13 MARCH 1888 'Today we have explored the forest above our camp (above Kiau on Kinabalu). This is easy work, as the Dusun have made rat trapping paths in all directions.
18 March 1888 Kabong (the headman of Kiau) called and has set over one hundred bamboo rat-traps in the forest. As we are living here, he says we can collect the rats, skin them (for the skins) and save the flesh for him to take away when he calls, which is about every other day. Kabong has given me nineteen Dusun names of nineteen species of rats and squirrels with which he is acquainted on these mountains. The pigmy squirrel he calls "Mantok", the common rat "Tikus tahiti" the house mouse "Tikus-walli" and a shrew "Gansouri". Rats are very numerous in Borneo, quite a plague at times; the Dusuns, however, eat rats so the rodents do not have it quite all their own way.
2 April 1888 Kabong called today; he brings us some rather alarming news: he says that all the available male population of Kiau are going headhunting to attack a village near Tuaran four days distant.
4 April 1888 Kabong came this evening: his news is that the party of headhunters were unable to go on the expedition, as soon after starting they met a mouse coming from the wrong direction; this was a bad omen so the expedition returned.' **Note:** John Whitehead, an English ornithologist, made the first recorded ascent of the summit of Kinabalu on 11 February 1888 (p. 207).

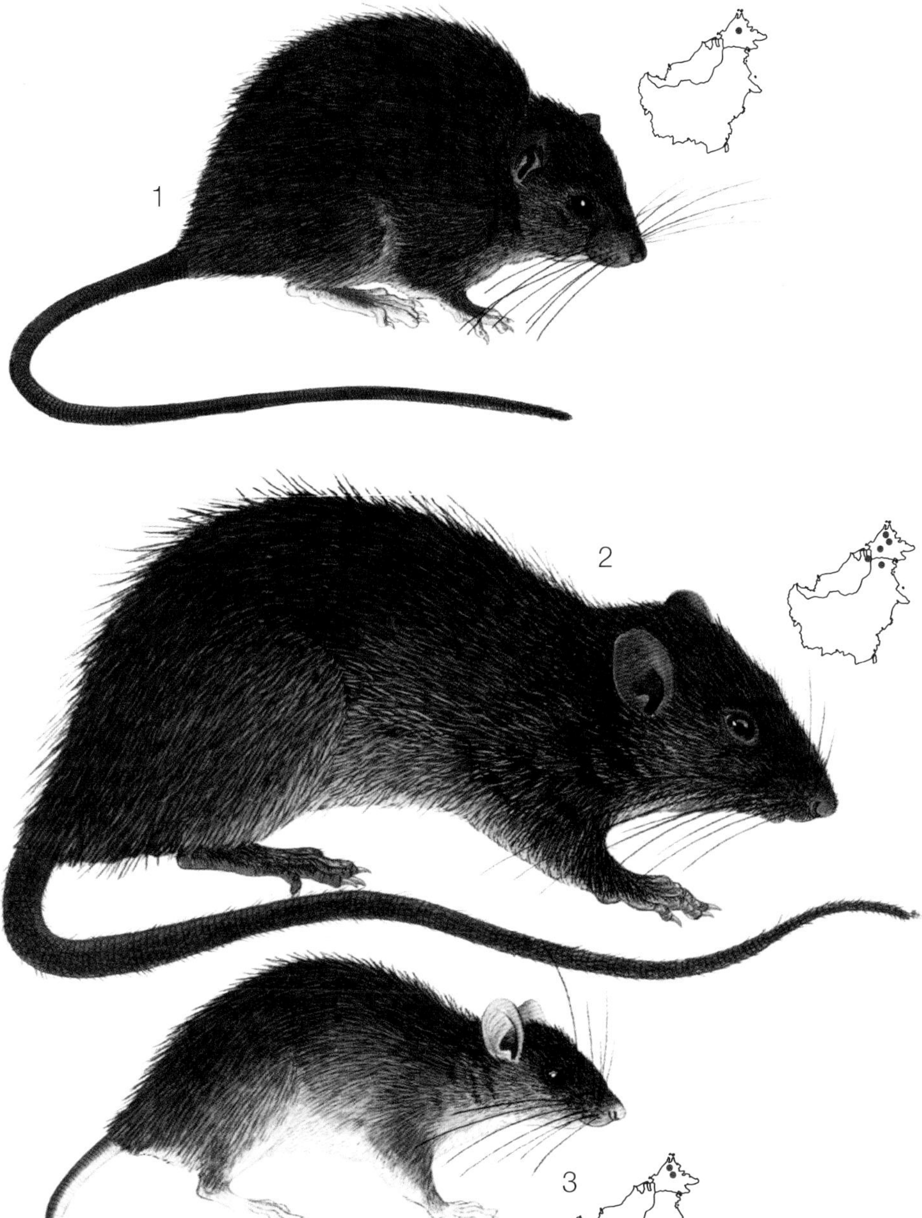
1
2
3

RELICT TREE RATS

1 GREY TREE RAT *Lenothrix canus* HB 193, T 232, Wt 150 **Rare**

Locally common arboreal rat in the forests and plantations of Malaya, but rare in Borneo. Recorded from 6 widely separated locations: 1. Matang near Kuching, 2. Sepilok, 3. Poring 600–900m in the Kinabalu Park, 4. Gng Palung (Blundell 1996, confirmed by Gorog in Musser & Carleton 2005), 5. Tawau Hills, 6. Kuala Belalong Brunei (Yasuma 1997). **ID:** 8 nipples. No spines in fur, which is thick and soft. Distinctive tail two-thirds black with a white tip. **Habits:** Nocturnal. In Malaya recorded feeding on alcoholic palm nectar (p. 53). At Poring trapped both on the ground and in the canopy, but more common in the canopy (Lakim 1998).**Range:** The type is from Pulau Tuangku (NW Sumatra) the only Sumatran record, Malaya, **Borneo race:** *L. c. malaisia*.

2 RAPIT RAT *Niviventer rapit* HB 143, T 197 (c. 140% of HB), Wt 60 **Rare endemic**

[Long-tailed Mountain Rat, Payne 1985] [Montane Bornean Niviventer, Musser & Carleton 2005]. Medium-sized rare arboreal tree rat with a relict distribution and an obviously shrinking range. On Kinabalu recorded from Poring 600m to tree line at 3,360m, but Nor (1996) failed to find it in 3,780 trap nights at all levels. In the last 20 years over 50,000 trap nights all over Sabah have failed to capture this rat. See Lakim (1998), Emmons (2000), Yasuma (2003), Wells (2005), Cussack (2011) and Loveridge (2012). Old Sarawak records include Mulu (1,200m), Kelabit Highlands rice fields (1,100m), Lawas and Niah. Scattered recent records include Maliau Basin (Gasis & A. H. Ahmad 1996), Gng Murud (Tuen et al. 2003), Sg Bloh, Lanjak Entimau (Roberta et al. 2010) and Bukit Baka (Kalimantan), where Rapit was common at 1,340–1,420m (Gorog et al. 2004), Bkt Retak Brunei (Yasuma 1997). **ID:** 8 nipples. Dark reddish-brown fur on sides of body, relatively long tail that is hairy at the tip and hard spines in the fur. Tail may be all dark, or dark above and pale below. Long-tailed Giant Rat (Sabah Rat) *Leopoldamys sabanus* has no tuft at the end of the tail and has soft, not hard spines. **Habits:** 'In Jan. 1984 whilst trapping rats to illustrate for *A Field Guide to the Mammals of Borneo* (1985) we found this rat to be locally common at Poring. One afternoon I watched a Rapit moving her babies one by one from a hole in a low horizontal bamboo to a higher hole in the large bamboo grove on the top of Poring Hill. Her action appeared to be triggered by the presence of a 1.8m Copperhead Rat Snake *Coelognathus radiatus*. The babies were gripped by the loose skin on the back of the neck just as a cat holds a kitten.' (Karen Phillipps). **Taxonomy:** Named by Bonhote (1903) after the Kiau Dusun name based on a Kinabalu skin collected by Everett in 1892. In Payne et al. (1985) listed as conspecific with *N. cameroni* (Malaya) and *N. fraternus* of the Sumatran mountains, but split by Musser (1986).

STONE OAKS AND RODENTS ON KINABALU ***Lithocarpus*, World:** 300 spp. **Borneo:** 61 spp. **Kinabalu:** 38 spp. Borneo and Kinabalu in particular are the world centre of diversity for *Lithocarpus* (stone oaks), a genus in the Fagaceae (p. 60). Kinabalu is also a world centre of diversity for rats, with 22 species (8 endemic) and squirrels, with 20 species (11 endemic). A genetic analysis of *Lithocarpus* indicates the continuous presence of tropical rainforest in SE Asia over the last 40 million years, the mountains of Borneo acting as refugia during periods of climate stress (Cannon 2003). Rodent and *Lithocarpus* diversity on Kinabalu results from millions of years of co-evolution. *Lithocarpus* acorns have hard, fleshy cupules surrounding a very hard, stony nut (seed). The cupule and nut attract mammalian dispersers in a two-stage process. Large mammals such as pigs, deer and rhinos swallow the whole fruit and defecate the 'bare' nut, which in turn is collected and hoarded by rodents using the convenient carrying handles on the smooth nut. (See p. 42, scatter-hoarding; p. 60, oaks and chestnuts, and p. 212, ground squirrels).

Cross sections of 3 common *Lithocarpus* fruit.
L to R: *L. palungensis, L. lucidus, L. pulcher.*
Scale: 50% life size

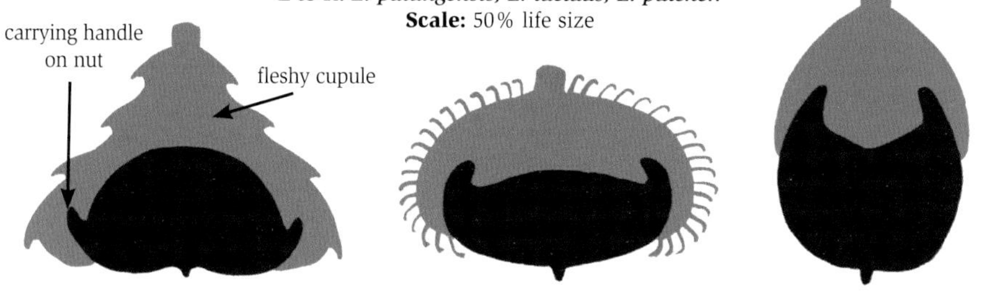

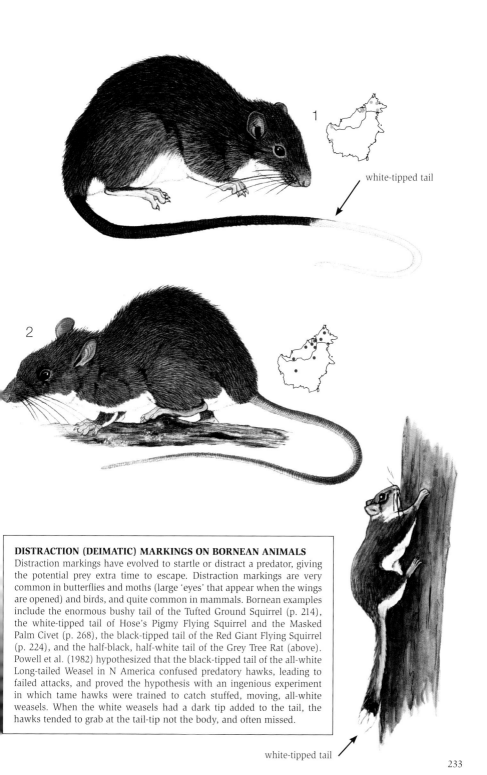

DISTRACTION (DEIMATIC) MARKINGS ON BORNEAN ANIMALS
Distraction markings have evolved to startle or distract a predator, giving the potential prey extra time to escape. Distraction markings are very common in butterflies and moths (large 'eyes' that appear when the wings are opened) and birds, and quite common in mammals. Bornean examples include the enormous bushy tail of the Tufted Ground Squirrel (p. 214), the white-tipped tail of Hose's Pigmy Flying Squirrel and the Masked Palm Civet (p. 268), the black-tipped tail of the Red Giant Flying Squirrel (p. 224), and the half-black, half-white tail of the Grey Tree Rat (above). Powell et al. (1982) hypothesized that the black-tipped tail of the all-white Long-tailed Weasel in N America confused predatory hawks, leading to failed attacks, and proved the hypothesis with an ingenious experiment in which tame hawks were trained to catch stuffed, moving, all-white weasels. When the white weasels had a dark tip added to the tail, the hawks tended to grab at the tail-tip not the body, and often missed.

LARGE MAXOMYS SPINY RATS

Borneo hosts 7 species of *Maxomys* forest rats, all with the following distinctive features:
1. Tails are bi-coloured, dark above and pale below. 2. Always 8 nipples. 3. Always sharp spines all over.
All species are predominantly terrestrial, breed in ground burrows and are reluctant climbers of trees. Males are normally 20% larger and heavier than females. Four sympatric Maxomys rats, two small (*M. whiteheadii* and *M. tajuddinii*) and two large (*M. surifer* and *M. rajah*) are the most common rats in both primary and secondary forests, but vary greatly (in both space and time) in relative abundance, possibly due to differing responses to masting events. Three other *Maxomys* rats are scarce relicts. (See p. 14 and next page.)

1 RED SPINY MAXOMYS *Maxomys surifer* **HB 195, T 200 (longer than HB), Wt 156g** **Common**

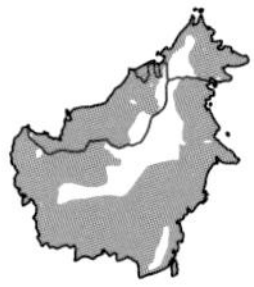

[Red Spiny Rat] Common forest rat found throughout Borneo, to 1,680m on Kinabalu. Wells (2005) found that both *M. surifer* and *M. rajah* preferred logged forest to virgin forest in Sabah, and that *M. rajah* was one-third more common than *M. surifer,* particularly in logged forest – but see below. Bernard (2002) found *M. surifer* the most abundant rat at Tabin, equally common in logged and virgin forest. **ID:** Adult underparts usually with 'collar' and inner sides of thighs the same colour as upperparts. **Habits:** Population in most areas is relatively stable, unlike that of *M. rajah*, which increases rapidly during and after masting, indicating a different ecology. In Malaya a larder hoarder of hard nuts (Medway 1978). **Range:** Vietnam, Thailand, south to Malaya, Sumatra, Java. **Borneo races:** 1. *R. s. bandahara.* 2. *M. s. panglima*, P. Banggi, P. Balembangan and P. Malawali. 3. *M. s.* perflavus, P. Laut. 4. *M. s. ubecus*, P. Sebuku. 5. *M. s. carimatae,* P. Karimata Besar.

2 RAJAH MAXOMYS *Maxomys rajah* **HB 188, T 179 (slightly shorter than HB), Wt 156g** **Common**

[Brown Spiny Rat in Payne 1985) Common forest rat throughout Borneo including peat-swamp at Sabangau. Often more common in logged or secondary forest than virgin forest. **ID:** Similar to *M. surifer* in average size but browner. Adults have a streak on the underparts, not a collar. White on inner side of thigh normally extends unbroken to feet. See illustration. **Habits:** Observations by Emmons at Danum, and Nakagawa at Lambir, indicate that that *M. rajah* populations are characterized by population explosions triggered by mass forest fruiting (a lifestyle strategy similar to that of Bearded Pigs), which benefits this rat when vacant territory is available (see pp. 13, 278 and 302). **Range:** S Thailand, Malaya, Sumatra. **Borneo races:** 1. *M. r. rajah.* 2. *M. r. hidongis*, P. Natuna Besar.

3 TAJUDDIN'S MAXOMYS *Maxomys tajuddini* **HB 106, T 114 (longer than HB), Wt 60g** **Common**

Common small rat found throughout Borneo, recently split from Whitehead's Rat (see below). **ID:** Similar to Whitehead's Maxomys (p. 236), but usually slightly heavier and larger. Distinguished by sharply defined line between cream belly and rufous upperparts. Unlike in Whitehead's Rat, tail is always the same length or longer than HB. **Habits:** This cryptic species overlaps with Whitehead's Rat throughout Borneo, including at P. Balambangan (Sabah), Kubah (Sarawak) and E Kalimantan dipterocarp and peat-swamp forest. **Taxonomy:** Split by Setiawan (2010) and Setiawan et al. (2012) based on morphology and DNA, and named in honour of Dr Mohd Tajuddin Abdullah, professor of zoology at UMS, Sarawak. **Range:** Malaya, Sumatra, Borneo.

RECALCITRANT AND ORTHODOX SEEDS – HOW PLANTS ADAPT TO CLIMATE CHANGE
Pollen analysis shows that during glacial maximums (cold periods), montane oak/laurel forest occurred at sea level (Niah Caves) replacing dipterocarp forest. Thus the altitude of montane forest in Borneo is controlled by temperature, not by soils. Both ants and termites decline with altitude on Kinabalu (p. 212). Not surprisingly, small mammals that eat ants and termites also decline with altitude on Kinabalu, but what stops dipterocarps from growing above 900m, and why are oaks, laurels and hollies more common in the mountains than in the lowlands? One important factor is the type of seed and its intended disperser. **Recalcitrant seeds:** The majority of rainforest tree seeds have a high water content and germinate rapidly, whereas the majority of tree seeds in seasonally cold or dry climates and on tropical mountains produce **orthodox seeds**, which have a low water content and remain dormant almost indefinitely in cold, dry conditions. On Kinabalu the proportion of trees with orthodox seeds increases with altitude. A possible reason is that hard seeds are more efficiently dispersed by larder-hoarding rodents than wind-dispersed dipterocarps, and lowland seeds require rapid germination to avoid fungal attack. (See p. 54, dipterocarps; p. 60, oaks; p. 194, fungal attacks on seeds and p. 42, scatter-hoarding.)

Young *Maxomys* rat Young rats look very different from adults and cannot be identified to species level.

1

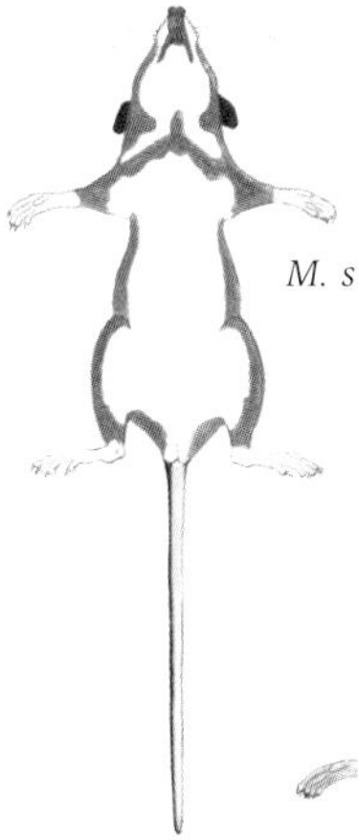

M. surifer

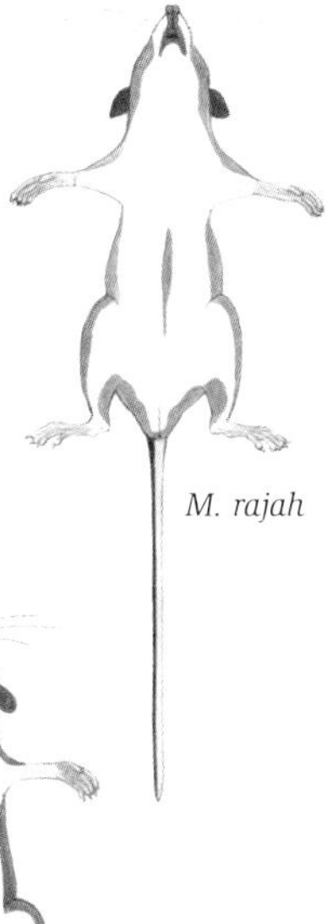

M. rajah

2

3

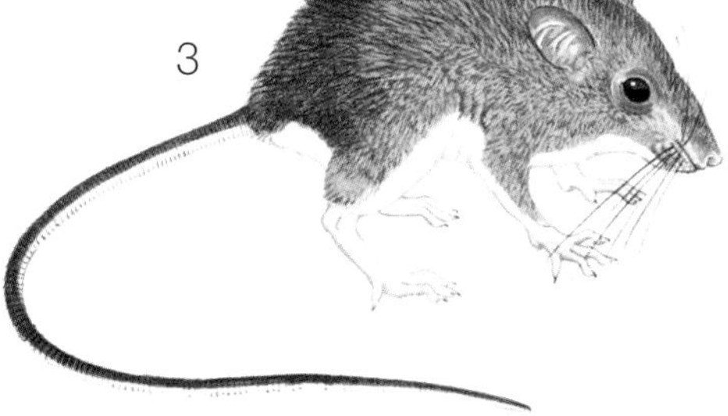

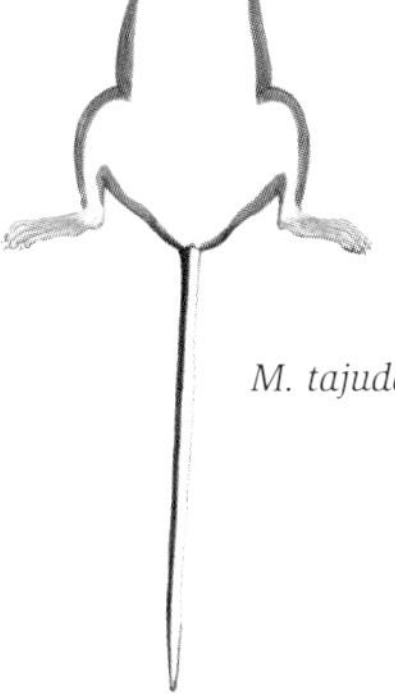

M. tajuddini

SMALL MAXOMYS SPINY RATS

1 CHESTNUT-BELLIED MAXOMYS *Maxomys ochraceiventer* **HB 156, T 152, Wt? Endemic**
Scarce rat of the hill forests of N Borneo south to Gng Pueh near Kuching on the west coast and the upper Mahakam (Sg Belayan) on the east coast. On Kinabalu uncommon at Poring at 700m, but locally common at Poring Miabau (1,200m). On the Kinabalu summit trail recorded to 1,700m, where it is rare. **ID:** Very spiny both above and below. Underparts have a yellow-orange tinge compared with whitish underparts of *M. alticola* (p. 231). *M. whiteheadi* is smaller and less spiny underneath. **Habits:** Habitat spans both hill dipterocarp and mossy oak laurel forest, so the ecology is likely to be unusual. **Borneo races:** 1. *M. o. ochraceiventer*, Sabah south to Kuching. 2. *M. o. perasper*, E Kalimantan.

2 WHITEHEAD'S MAXOMYS *Maxomys whiteheadi* **HB 101, T 101 (less than HB), Wt 57g Common**
Both the most common and smallest *Maxomys* found in rice fields, plantations and forest throughout Borneo and to 2,100m on Kinabalu. The most common rat in oil-palm plantations at Tabin. **ID:** Smallest *Maxomys*. Entire body very spiny; underparts buffy. See Tajuddin's Maxomys (p. 234). Polynesian Rat *Rattus exulans* has dark tail longer than body (p. 226). **Habits:** Diet is mainly insects including ants. In Sabah, Wells (2005) found that this rat was twice as common in logged forests as in virgin forest. **Range:** S Thailand, Malaya, Sumatra. **Borneo races:** 1. *M. w. whiteheadi*, mainland. 2. *M. w. piratae*, P. Banggi, P. Malawali, P. Balembangan.

3 BAEODON MAXOMYS *Maxomys baeodon* **HB 133, T 126 (shorter than HB), Wt 65g Rare endemic**
Small spiny Maxomys with very patchy distribution restricted to N Borneo including Kinabalu at 900–1400m, Danum, Sepilok; Maliau Basin, Ulu Senegang in the Crocker Range and the Kelabit Highlands above 1,200m in NE Sarawak, obviously a relict distribution. **ID:** Small and spiny. Underparts pale orange or pink with grey underfur. **Habits:** Unknown.

THE HUMP, OR MID-ELEVATION EFFECT ON TROPICAL MOUNTAINS
Trapping records indicate that squirrels and rats are more diverse (more species) between Kinabalu Park headquarters and the Timpohon Gate (1,563–1,866m) than anywhere else in Borneo. Md Nor (1996) found that mammal diversity recorded by previous zoologists peaked at 1,400m, whilst in his own survey diversity peaked at 1,700m. On a graph of altitude against diversity this appears as a distinct 'hump' between 900m–1,800m.

Cloud forest (mossy forest) On wet tropical mountains cloud forest replaces tall lowland forest between 900–1,800m. Moss covers the ground and tree trunks. The soil becomes acidic and peaty, and fallen leaves fail to rot. Trees become stunted and their roots are elevated above the soil, creating numerous hiding and foraging places for small mammals (see illustration by Whitehead, p. 141).

Cloud forest mammals Giant squirrels, pangolins, Malay Weasel and Bearded Pigs are able to survive in cloud forest, but most lowland mammals do not cross into cloud forest, and most cloud-forest mammals, such as Mountain Treeshrew and *Hylomis*, cannot survive in lowland forest. On Kinabalu, cloud forest appears at different altitudes in different areas, affecting exposed ridges first and narrow valleys and gullies last. This creates a patchwork transition zone (900–1,800m) where strips of cloud forest on ridges are interwoven with strips of lowland forest in the valleys, so that both lowland and cloud-forest mammals are found at the same altitude in different habitats. It is this overlap that creates the 'diversity hump' in graphs.

The Hump also applies to birds, insects and plants . See Grytnes et al (2008).

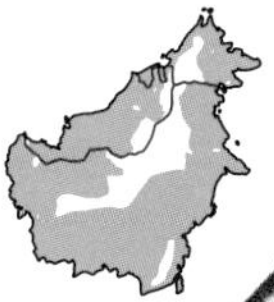

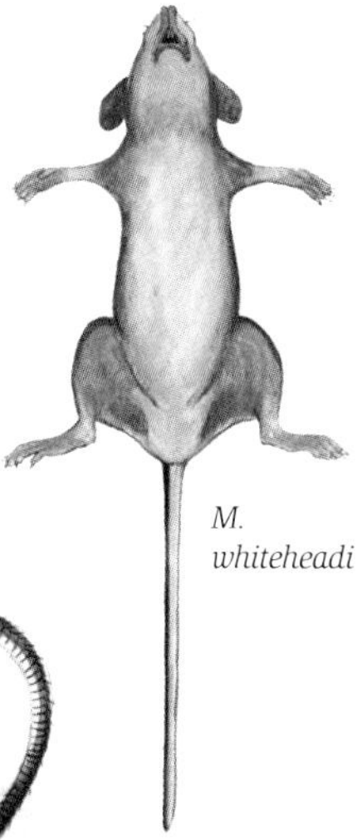

SECONDARY DISPERSAL OF ANACHRONISTIC FRUIT BY LARGE RODENTS

Bawang Hutan *Scorodocarpus borneensis* (Olacaceae) [**Malay**: forest onion] is a tall lowland forest tree to 40m. The whole tree including the fruit smells of onions, and both the leaves and the seeds are eaten by locals as a relish (*ulam*). The large, 5cm-diameter seed is protected by a hard shell covered with a thin flesh smelling of garlic. The size and smell, and the fact that this is a common drift seed which does not grow in beach forest, indicates that Bawang Hutan is an anachronistic fruit that evolved for primary dispersal by megafauna such as rhinoceroses and elephants. Bawang Hutan is a typical orthodox seed with an average germination delay of 518 days (Ng 2014). The ribbed shell assists large rodents to grip the seed and act as secondary dispersers. Payne (1982) found a Bornean Porcupine burrow on Gng Madalon (Sabah) with large quantities of the discarded remains of *Scorodocarpus* seeds scattered nearby. Illustration above shows a small spiny rat, *Maxomys baedon*, unable to remove the seed due to the large size. See also illustrations of Belian *Eusideroxylon* seeds with a similar ridged gripping design to aid secondary dispersal by porcupines (pp. 42 and 245).

LOWLAND TREE RATS

1 SABAH GIANT RAT *Leopoldamys sabanus* HB 244, T 365 (min. 135% of HB), Wt 391 Common

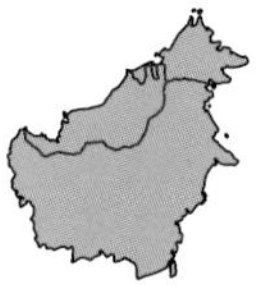

[Long-tailed Giant Rat] Borneo's longest rat, very common in lowland and hill forests to 3,100m (Paka Cave) on Kinabalu. The most common rat in the oak forest surrounding Kinabalu Park headquarters. **ID:** Extremely long tail and sharply defined, creamy-white underparts. Tail usually dark, sometimes blotched whitish. Rapit Rat *Niviventer rapit* has stiffer spines and tufted tail-tip. Müller's Rat has relatively shorter tail and poorly defined margin between upper and lower body. As illustrated opposite, above 1,700m on Gng Kinabalu this rat is larger and duller, with a blackish back and face. **Habits:** Nocturnal. In primary forest in Sabah, Wells (2007) found that it was the second most common rat after Dark-tailed Tree Rat. Also common in logged forest and secondary forest. Often climbs trees, but most often trapped on the ground. **Taxonomy:** First collected by Whitehead on Kinabalu and named by Oldfield Thomas (1887) after Sabah, where it was first discovered. **Range:** SE Asia south to Malaya, Sumatra, Java. **Borneo race:** *L. s. sabanus.*

2 DARK-TAILED TREE RAT *Niviventer cremoriventer* HB 133, T 181 (min. 125% of HB), Wt 77

Abundant. Small tree rat of all types of forest throughout Borneo, found to 1,650m (park headquarters) on Kinabalu. **ID:** Proportionately long tail with hairy tip. Whole body covered in stiff spines and long black guard hairs. The only rat with hairy-tipped tail apart from *N. rapit*. **Habits:** Eats mainly fruit. Nocturnal. The most common forest rat in virgin primary forest throughout Borneo. Also found in smaller numbers in logged and secondary forests. The most arboreal forest rat, but also active on the ground. The only Bornean rat known to construct its own free-hanging tree nest out of plant fibres. **Range:** Myanmar south to Malaya Sumatra, Java. **Borneo races:** 1. *N. c. kina*, throughout. 2. *N. c. malawali*, P. Banggi, P. Balembangan and P. Malawali.

NEST SITES OF FOREST RATS IN BORNEO

In a study of the nesting sites used by small mammals, Wells et al. (2006) used spool-and-line and radio tracking to discover 83 nests of small mammals at six Sabah sites in both logged and unlogged forest, including Poring, Danum Valley and Tawau Hills.

Habits Terrestrial (T) Arboreal (A)	Nest Below Ground	Nest Above Ground
Sabah Giant Rat (T)	20	4
Rajah Maxomys (T)	21	2
Red Spiny Maxomys (T)	12	1
Dark-tailed Tree Rat (A)	2	4
Low's Squirrel (T)	1	4
Plain Treeshrew (T)	0	2
Large Treeshrew (T)	1	6
TOTALS	57	23

The underground nests constructed by terrestrial *Maxomys* rats were usually 2m long and often had two entrances, allowing escape from predators. The entrance holes were covered with leaves when not in use. The Sabah Giant Rat, which is mainly terrestrial but also forages in the canopy, used primarily underground nests. Only the arboreal Dark-tailed Tree Rat twice wove hanging nests out of fibres and leaves as illustrated.

Dark-tailed Tree Rat ***Niviventer cremoriventer*** in nest.

1a

Found above 1,700m on Kinabalu.

1b

Common throughout Borneo apart from higher levels on Kinabalu.

2

CHIROPODOMYS SUNDA (PENCIL-TAILED) TREE MICE

World: 6 spp. **Borneo:** 4 spp., of which 1 sp., *C. gliroides*, is widespread in SE Asia, whilst the other three are Borneo endemics with relict distributions. Tree mice are distinguished from the Ranee Mouse by their shorter, more hairy tails. As in the Ranee Mouse, the big toe (hallux) is opposable. The thumb (pollux) has a large nail (not claws). Females have 4 nipples. In captivity these tree mice are omnivorous, but in the wild they are probably predators of small seeds, especially figs. **Taxonomy:** Medway (1977) listed 3 species for Borneo, followed by Payne et al. (1985), but both Nowak (1999) and Carleton & Musser (2005) list 4 species if the Natuna Islands are included with Borneo.

1 LARGE SUNDA TREE MOUSE *Chiropodomys major* **HB 104, T 127, Wt 40g** **Local endemic**

Largest, most common tree mouse but generally scarce. Recorded on Kinabalu to 1,500m, Sepilok and Kuching. **ID:** Underparts white. **Habits:** Nocturnal and arboreal but sometimes nests at or close to the ground in places such as tree holes and holes in stumps. Males approximately 5% bigger and heavier than females. At Poring, Wells found that this tree mouse was the most common canopy-dwelling mammal foraging largely in the canopy but coming to the ground for nesting (see below and Wells et al. 2004).

LARGE SUNDA TREE MOUSE AT PORING IN KINABALU PARK

A 5-month cage-trapping project at Poring (800–900m asl) in the Kinabalu Park by Wells et al. (2004) caught 40 individuals 275 times. However, 15 months later at the same sites, an 8-month trapping project failed to record a single tree mouse. A possible explanation is that these tree mice are locally nomadic specialist predators on tiny fig seeds (p. 242). Male ranges average 3,000m^2 and smaller females ranges average 1600m^2. Male and female ranges overlapped, so Large Sunda Tree Mice are not territorial. Tree mice were trapped twice on the ground but were most common in the subcanopy, where dense branching and vines made travel between adjacent trees easier. Four nesting sites were found by using a spool and line. One nesting site was in a tree hole 4m from the ground, two were under a log and tree roots, and a fourth was 5m up in a stump.

2 GREY-BELLIED SUNDA TREE MOUSE *Chiropodomys muroides* **HB 73, T 88** **Rare endemic**

Rarest of the tree mice. Recorded only from Kinabalu (1,100m) and Long Petak on the Sg Telen in NE Kalimantan. **ID:** Distinguished from other tree mice by different colouring, reddish-brown above and grey below. Distinguished from Ranee Mouse by shorter, hairy tail with tuft at the end. **Habits:** Unknown.

3 BORNEAN SUNDA TREE MOUSE *Chiropodomys pusillus* **HB 75, T 88, Wt 22g** **Rare endemic**

Borneo records are from the mountains, including Kinabalu to 1,220m, Mulu, Gng Dulit and the Kelabit uplands in Sarawak; also Riam in C Kalimantan. **ID:** Distinguished from Grey-bellied Tree Mouse by different colouring, and from other Bornean tree mice by small size. **Habits:** Possibly a bamboo specialist like *C. gliroides*.

4 COMMON SUNDA TREE MOUSE *Chiropodomys gliroides* **HB 90, T 113, Wt 29g** **Natuna Island**

Most common and widespread Sunda tree mouse outside Borneo, but not found on Bornean mainland, where it is replaced by *C. puisillus*. **Habits:** In Malaya a bamboo specialist (see opposite). **Range:** NE India east to S China, south to Malaya, Sumatra, Java, Bali, Natuna Island (Bunguran Besar), (p. 386).

SMALL MAMMALS OF PORING CANOPY

Total 6,445 trap nights. Banana bait. (Wells et al. 2004)

Chiropodomys major	275	*S. hippurus*	2	*Hylopetes spadiceus*	1
N. cremoriventer	52	*Sundasciurus brookei*	2	*L. sabanus*	1
Tupaia minor	24	*Nycticebus coucang*	2	*Ptilocercus lowii*	1
Lenothrix canus	15	*Callosciurus notatus*	1		

Note: Results refer to catches not individuals, which were often trapped multiple times Apr–Aug 2001.

1

2

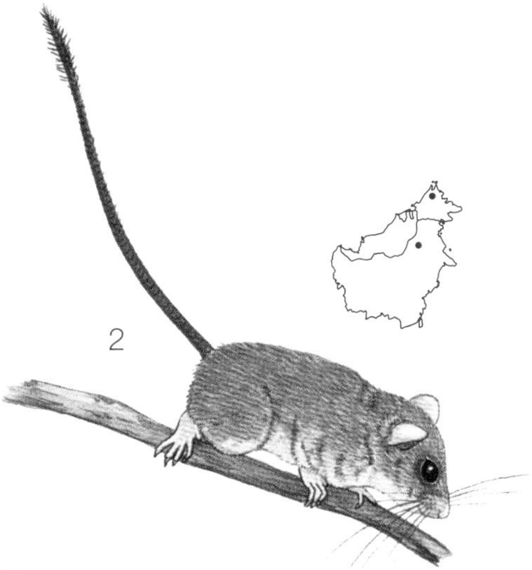

3

4

BREEDING OF COMMON SUNDA TREE MOUSE
A 1948 trapping programme by Harrison & Traub (1950) found that *C. gliroides* was locally abundant in the bamboo groves along the Pahang Road in the Ulu Gombak FR near Kuala Lumpur (Malaya). '*Chiropodomys* lives in bamboos and nests inside the stem. The nest is made of leaves arranged at the bottom of an internodal cavity and the exit hole is made near the top of this or a nearby internode. Holes through the nodes join a series of internodes into a long tunnel. The four nipples are in the groin area and a mother with young was observed to run and climb rapidly with the young holding fast to the nipples. In cages as many as possible will crowd together in a huddled mass.' Harrison (1955) reported litters of 1–3 with an average of 2.2. Medway (1967) investigated breeding by two captive pairs. Oestrus took place at 7-plus day intervals, and gestation averaged 21 days. Breeding occurred as soon as the young were weaned and independent and continued throughout the year, but was most common in Sept–May.

EMMON'S TREE RAT AND RANEE MOUSE

1 EMMON'S TREE-RAT *Pithecheirops otion* **HB 113, T 117, Wt 36g** **Rare endemic**

The first new endemic mammal genus for Borneo for many years was discovered by Louise H. Emmons, an American zoologist, near the Danum Valley Field Centre on 21 September 1991. It was in a cage trap set for treeshrews on a large stump 1.5m high in dense, viny roadside secondary brush along an old logging road about 600m from primary forest. To date this single record of a juvenile male is the only known record. The measurements are given above – adults are likely to be larger and heavier. **ID:** Small tree mouse with a distinctive, entirely smooth, semi-prehensile tail apart from about the first 2cm, which is covered with short, soft fur as illustrated. In contrast, all Sunda tree mice (p. 240) have tail tufts. The Ranee Mouse has very short, stiff hairs covering the long, thin tail. **Habits:** Unknown. The closely related *Pithecheir parvus* (Malaya) is nocturnal and largely arboreal, and has been reported from both virgin and disturbed forest (Francis 2008). **Taxonomy:** Externally *P. otion* is similar to two species of little-known woolly tree rat, *Pithecheir melanurus* (Java) and *P. parvus* (Malaya). Emmons (1993) described *P. otion* as belonging to a new genus, *Pithecheirops*, based on skull differences with *Pithecheir*, in particular the smaller ear bones (auditory bullae).

2 LESSER RANEE MOUSE *Haeromys pusillus* **HB 54, T 97** **(Not illustrated) Rare**

Recorded from Kinabalu, Sarawak, E and SW Kalimantan (Carleton & Musser 2005). **ID:** Small arboreal mouse with a very long tail. The tail is covered with almost invisible, short, stiff hairs, unlike the tail of *P. otion*, which is smooth, and the tails of Sunda tree mice, which are sparsely furred with a tuft at the far end. As in the Sunda tree mice the big toe (hallux) is opposable, so that vines can be gripped as with a fist, an aid to climbing. *Haeromys* females have 6 nipples. **Range:** Borneo, Palawan.

3 RANEE MOUSE *Haeromys margarettae* **HB 77, T 134** **Rare endemic**

H. margarettae was first collected from Gng Penrissen near Kuching. Other records are from Bintulu (Ch'ien. Lee) and Sandakan. **ID:** Indistinguishable from *H. pusillus* except by larger size. **Habits:** At Sepilok trapped in a pitfall trap in the ground at the edge of primary forest (Payne 1985). '*Haeromys* build globular nests in tree holes. Animals observed in Sulawesi ate only small seeds mostly from figs' (Musser 1979). **Nomenclature:** The type was collected by A. H. Everett at Gng Penrissen and named after Margaret Brooke, the wife of the second white Rajah of Sarawak, Charles Brooke, by Oldfield Thomas of the British Museum (1893), with the following dedication: 'I have taken the liberty of naming this beautiful little species, which looks as if it would make a most enchanting pet, in honor of Her Highness the Ranee of Sarawak, a lady whose interest in the zoology of that country is scarcely inferior to that of her husband the Rajah.' **Taxonomy:** Payne et al. (1985) suggest that there may be only one species of Ranee Mouse that is very variable in size, but Thomas (1893), Chasen (1940), Medway (1977) and Carleton & Musser (2005) all recognize two species from Borneo.

CHARLES HOSE (1863–1929) worked in Sarawak for the second Rajah, Charles Brooke (1884–1909). For most of his career, Hose was in charge of the Baram district based at Marudi. From here he managed to climb Mt Dulit, but never visited the Kelabit Highlands. Hose and his zoologist brother Ernest sent many specimens to the British Museum for identification by Oldfield Thomas (mammals) and Sharpe (birds). Endemic mammals named after Hose include Hose's Shrew (p. 140), Hose's Langur (p. 164), Hose's Palm Civet, (p. 270), Hose's Pigmy Flying Squirrel (p. 216), Four-striped Ground Squirrel (p. 212) and Hose's Dolphin (p. 320). Hose was the author of the first comprehensive book on Borneo's mammals, *A Descriptive Account of the Mammals of Borneo* (1893), illustrated on the frontispiece with Hose's Shrew *Crocidura hosei* and the rare Ranee Mouse *Haeromys margarettae*, collected by Hose's friend A. H. Everett on Gng Penrissen near Kuching.

1

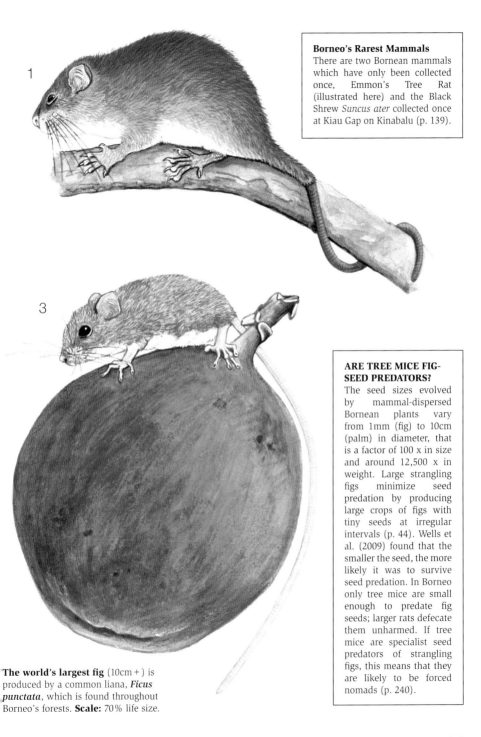

Borneo's Rarest Mammals
There are two Bornean mammals which have only been collected once, Emmon's Tree Rat (illustrated here) and the Black Shrew *Suncus ater* collected once at Kiau Gap on Kinabalu (p. 139).

3

The world's largest fig (10cm+) is produced by a common liana, ***Ficus punctata***, which is found throughout Borneo's forests. **Scale:** 70% life size.

ARE TREE MICE FIG-SEED PREDATORS?
The seed sizes evolved by mammal-dispersed Bornean plants vary from 1mm (fig) to 10cm (palm) in diameter, that is a factor of 100 x in size and around 12,500 x in weight. Large strangling figs minimize seed predation by producing large crops of figs with tiny seeds at irregular intervals (p. 44). Wells et al. (2009) found that the smaller the seed, the more likely it was to survive seed predation. In Borneo only tree mice are small enough to predate fig seeds; larger rats defecate them unharmed. If tree mice are specialist seed predators of strangling figs, this means that they are likely to be forced nomads (p. 240).

OLD WORLD PORCUPINES

HYSTRICIDAE World: 12 spp. **Borneo:** 3 spp., 1 endemic. Porcupines are giant rats (rodents) with hair that has evolved into large, sharp defensive spines. They live in small family groups, emerging after dusk from their large burrow systems. At Lanjak Entimau, Mohd Azlan (2013) found that the Malayan Porcupine was active from 6 p.m. to 5 a.m., whilst the Bornean Porcupine was active from 8 p.m. to 7 a.m. Dung is deposited in a communal 'latrine' near the burrow. Like all rodents' teeth, porcupine teeth grow continuously throughout their lives, so porcupines need to gnaw constantly on wood and bones. Unlike the 17 species of New World porcupines, Erethizontidae, Borneo's porcupines rarely climb trees. Porcupines visit the furthest depths of limestone caves to scavenge fallen bats and swiftlets. Paleontologists examining the bones and teeth of ancient animals lament that key identification features are often missing due to porcupine gnawing. **Diet:** Porcupines are the most omnivorous of Borneo's mammals, able to eat almost anything remotely edible, including animal remains, fruit, bark, bamboo shoots, bones and ivory. They are known to eat toxic seeds such as those of *Dysoxylum acutangulum* (at Pasoh, Miura 1997), and toxic roots like those of *Derris trifoliata* (tuba – used locally as a fish poison and insecticide). Porcupines raid farms (p. 49) to dig up cultivated tapioca, keladi and yam tubers, and are a serious pest of oil palms, eating both the young palm shoots and the fruit. **Breeding:** Porcupines breed continuously as long as food is available. The normal litter is 1. Male porcupines nibble away the sharpest spines on the back of the female before mating. **Defence:** Porcupines are hunted by humans for both bezoar stones and meat (p. 164). When threatened the two larger porcupines rattle their hollow tail quills and reverse into an intruder. The quills have backwards-pointing barbs like arrowheads, making them difficult to remove.

1 MALAYAN PORCUPINE *Hystrix brachyura* **HB 610, T 113** **Least common porcupine**
[Common Porcupine]. The least common of the 3 Bornean porcupines, but found throughout Borneo in forested areas to 900m – for example, at Lambir a camera survey by Mohd Azlan (2006) obtained 52 photos of Bornean Porcupine, 9 of Long-tailed Porcupine and only 2 of Malayan Porcupine. In Kalimantan often more common than Bornean. At Bukit Bakitap (C Kalimantan), Tim van Berkel camera trapped 1 Bornean, 7 Malayan and 1 Long-tailed Porcupine. Recorded for Gng Palung, Tg Puting and Sabangau, where Bornean Porcupine is scarce/absent. **ID:** Distinguished by long, black-and-white quills. Overall colouration is black and white, not brown and white. **Range:** S Thailand, Malaya, Sumatra. **Borneo race:** *H. b. longicauda*, scarce throughout.

2 BORNEAN PORCUPINE *Thecurus crassispinis* **HB 608, T 112** **Locally common endemic**
[Thick-spined Porcupine] The most common large porcupine in N Borneo, but not found in S Sarawak and scarce in most of Kalimantan. Recorded at 1,200m (Kelabit Highlands). The most common porcupine in E Kalimantan (Yasuma 1994). **ID:** Same size as Malayan Porcupine, but overall colouration is a mottled brown rather than contrasting black and white. Quills are shorter and black-and-white quill pattern is much duller. **Habits:** Recorded larder-hoarding *Scorodocarpus borneensis* seeds at Gng Madalon, Sabah (Payne 1982) (p. 237). According to Jim Comber 'I shot a porcupine in the foothills of Trus Madi which did not die immediately. It shot out a lot of large spines, mostly from the tail area for about 3–4 metres. The people who were with me (Lun Dayeh) knew this was going to happen and warned me in advance not to approach too close until it was dead. We then ate it because we were all hungry.'

3 LONG-TAILED PORCUPINE *Trichys fasciculata* **HB 406, T 196** **Most common porcupine**
[*Trichys lipura*] Common in both forest and cultivation to 900m on Kinabalu, but no records for peat-swamp forest in Kalimantan. **ID:** Looks like a large spiny rat with a small brush on the end of its scaly tail. **Habits:** At Sepilok, where it is locally common, recorded 'larder-hoarding' the hard, woody seeds of belian in its burrow (see opposite). According to Whitehead (1893), 'On Kinabalu a peculiar porcupine-rat which Dusuns call ***Licis*** was caught in the bamboo traps. The skin of this rat is most tender, almost dropping to pieces in one's hands while skinning it. The peculiar delicate skin is the same on all spinous rats, their hides being more tender than a Goatsucker's (nightjar) skin.' **Range:** S Thailand, Malaya, Sumatra. **Borneo race:** *T. f. lipura*.

TAXONOMIC CONFUSION Unlike the two larger porcupines, the Long-tailed Porcupine runs from danger, relying on a loosely attached tail to fool predators that attack the tail, which detaches, enabling the porcupine to escape. The fact that the tail is often missing led to much taxonomic confusion in the past, with two species described, *Trichys lipura* and *T. guentheri*.

1

2

3

LARDER-HOARDING

Porcupines are seed predators of large, hard orthodox seeds with delayed germination, but also disperse these seeds by carrying them back to their burrows for later consumption, a habit known as larder-hoarding. Hoarded seeds include Bawang Hutan *Scorodocarpus borneensis* (p. 237), Belian *Eusideroxlyon zwageri* (p. 37), and *Entada* beans (p. 68). During transport a porcupine may drop the seed, or the seed may germinate later during storage. Porcupines are therefore (like rats and squirrels) seed dispersers as well as seed predators. The presence of large anachronistic fruit with hard seeds throughout Borneo's forests is almost certainly due to primary dispersal by large mammals, followed by secondary dispersal by porcupines and large rats (p. 42).

SUN BEAR

MALAY: BERUANG MADU (HONEY BEAR)

URSIDAE World: 8 spp. **Borneo:** 1 sp. All bears (apart from the carnivorous Polar Bear) are omnivorous, feeding on a varied diet of fruit, insects, honey and small animals. Despite being the world's smallest bear, the Sun Bear has a fierce reputation in Borneo as a result of occasional attacks on humans. Sun Bears disperse many forest fruits. Females are smaller and around two-thirds the weight of males.

BORNEAN SUN BEAR *Helarctos malayanus* **HB 1,145, T 60, Wt 20–65kg** **Scarce**

Sun Bears inhabit both primary and logged forest from the peat-swamps of Sabangau to more than 2,000m on Kinabalu, but populations are much reduced by habitat loss and hunting. A small wild population remains at Sepilok. At the Danum Valley Field Centre (Sabah) Sun Bears occasionally raid dustbins. Sun Bears living in forest next to oil palm plantations occasionally eat fallen fruits but do not destroy the 'cabbage' of young palms, as opposed to certain other wildlife species.

Habits: Normally solitary, apart from mothers with a cub. At Danum, Wong (2002) and Sg Wain (Fredriksson 2012) found that Sun Bears had overlapping home ranges (average 7–15km^2) with exclusive core areas. Sun Bears are naturally active by day, but in areas with human disturbance, they enter plantations at night (Nomura 2004, Fredriksson 2005). Sun Bears may make tree nests to forage in trees with large fruit crop or to sleep for the night. These nests are poorly constructed and closer to the trunk than Orangutan nests (Payne 1985), but most bears in good forest sleep on logs. During extreme fruit low periods [after the mast] Fredriksson et al. (2006) at Sg Wain and Wong (2005) at Danum found that both Bearded Pigs and Sun Bears were reduced to starvation. A weakened adult Sun Bear was eaten by a python (Fredriksson 2004).

Breeding Sun Bears become sexually active at 3–4 years old, and cubs are born all year round. Gestation is *c.* 100 days. Cubs (usually single) stay with their mother until *c.* 3 years old. Mothers are fiercely protective of their cubs.

Call When breeding, or at times of displacement [habitat loss], roaring is frequently heard, which may be confused with that of male Orangutans; also, less commonly, short barks emitted when startled, similar to those of a muntjak or rhinoceros (Payne 1985).

ID Look for prominent claw scratches on tree trunks and excavations for bees' nests in large trees to indicate Sun Bear presence. Sun Bears with *erythrism* (dark reddish fur) occasionally occur.

Diet Omnivorous. Sun Bears use their powerful jaws to rip open tree trunks for the nests of stingless honey bees and use their strong claws to excavate logs for beetle grubs and termite mounds. Sun Bears climb fruiting trees to feed in the canopy, but most often feed on fallen fruit. Hard seeds, up to 4.5cm in size, can be swallowed and dispersed. Oil-rich seeds such as acorns are crushed and predated. At Barito Ulu, C Kalimantan, McConkey (1999) found 21 scats containing 1,515 seeds of *Canarium pilosum* below a fruiting tree (p. 215). At Sg Wain, Fredriksson found that during a fruit mast Sun Bears fed primarily on fruit with more than 115 species documented in the Sun Bear diet, but reverted to a diet of termites and other insects during lean periods between masting. Figs are a staple food.

Range Eastern India, mainland SW Asia, south to Malaya, Sumatra. **Borneo race:** *H. m. euryspilus* has a smaller skull. See Lyon (2011), Pocock (1941) and Meijaard (2004).

THE MOST DANGEROUS MAMMAL IN BORNEO? 'I was planning a visit to the hilly regions between the headwaters of the Busang River and the upper Barito. Few natives, if any, have entered that region which is described as very mountainous. But all who were approached on the subject, absolutely declined to take part in an expedition to that country, because they would be killed by an animal called Nundun, which is very numerous there. They might be able to tackle one, they said, but as soon as you encounter one there are hundreds more coming for you, and there is nothing else to do but run for your life. Those regions are shunned by all natives. Nundun would appear to be a kind of bear which perhaps in fruit seasons gathers in great numbers and which is ferocious. Nundun is said to run faster than a dog, is killed with the sumpitan (blow-pipe) at 20–30 metres distance and is eaten. Both the lieutenant and I having so many rifles, we were much inclined to defy the terrors of the Nundun, but desirable as this expedition may have been, it had to be given up because of the formidable difficulties in getting native assistants.' Condensed from *Through Central Borneo* (1913–1917), Carl Lumholtz.

When threatened a Sun Bear rears up, exposing a large, pale crescent 'sun' on its chest as a danger warning (p. 27).

Sun Bears excavating rotten branches and logs for termites, beetle larvae, scorpions, millipedes and ants attract the attentions of a Bornean Crested Fireback Pheasant and a Bornean Ground-cuckoo that feed on the same prey. Sun Bears swallow and disperse seeds up to 4.5cm in width. By contrast, pheasants are seed predators, using their grit-filled gizzards to grind up the seeds of fallen fruit.

SUN BEAR ECOLOGY

WHAT LIMITS SUN BEAR POPULATIONS? Sun Bears have few natural enemies. Even pythons, crocodiles and Clouded Leopards would be foolish to attack an adult Sun Bear. The bear's populations today are limited by the conversion of forest to oil palm and poaching. In the past populations were limited by the carrying capacity of their habitat. Sun Bears' preferred diet is fruit and insects. In Borneo a frugivore's food supply varies dramatically between rare mast fruiting periods followed by a long intermast lean period (p. 12).

Do figs provide fallback foods for Sun Bears? Borneo's strangling figs fruit randomly out of sequence with masting, thus providing fallback foods to many animals during lean periods (p. 76). However, both Gabriella Fredriksson and Wong Siew Te found that forest figs failed to fruit for long periods following El Niño droughts, possibly due to extinction of fig-wasp pollinators caused by the drought. See Harrison (2000) re. Lambir. The result was that Sun Bears and Bearded Pigs starved during the lean period and ate insects to survive.

SUN BEARS AS PESTS OF PALMS Palms native to Borneo are heavily protected by sharp spines or toxic sap for defence against elephants and Sun Bears, but non-native coconut and oil palms have no such protection (p. 50). The American zoologist W. L. Abbot describes Sun Bear attacks on a coconut plantation at Pamukang Bay in SE Kalimantan. 'Bears seem to be pretty common wherever there is a plantation of coconuts. Some of the trees are said to be dead or dying as a result of their depredations. The bears climb up and eat the "heart" out of the palm. In a small grove of about ninety trees, near Tanjong Pamukang the bears had destroyed about half the trees. It was full moon during my stay there, so the owners said it was no use to watch for bears, as they only came out on dark nights. The Dutch authorities took away all the guns about a year ago, so now the animals have it all their own way.' (Lyon 1911). Sun Bears feeding on fallen oil palm fruits are rarely seen as a pest as they do not destroy the oil palm shoots, as opposed to coconut palms.

CAN SUN BEARS BE REHABILITATED? Sun Bears are hunted both for their gall bladders, used in traditional Chinese medicine, and for food. When a mother is shot the cub is kept as an entertaining pet until it outgrows its welcome. Hunting and keeping Sun Bears as pets is illegal in Borneo and habituated pets are often confiscated and kept in 1 of the few Sun Bear rehabilitation centres in Borneo.

Problems with rehabilitation Unlike rehabilitated Orangutans, which can be returned successfully to the wild, habituated Sun Bears are too dangerous to return to forest visited by humans, such as Kinabalu Park and Mulu. Remote vacant habitat is already occupied by Sun Bears that would be negatively affected by additional releases. Thus most captive Sun Bears are unlikely ever to be returned to the wild.

BORNEAN SUN BEAR CONSERVATION CENTRE • BSBCC •

Sun Bears are expert tree climbers (Photo: Nick Garbutt; www.nickgarbutt.com).

SUN BEAR EDUCATION AND REHABILITATION CENTRES

Bornean Sun Bear Conservation Centre Sepilok, Sabah (30 + bears) www.bsbcc.org.my

Matang Wildlife Centre Kuching, Sarawak (5 + bears) www.sarawakforestry.com and www.projectorangutan.com

BOS Samboja Lestari, Balikpapan, E Kalimantan (50 + bears) www.sambojalodge.com

KWPLH Sun Bear Education and Conservation Centre Balikpapan, E Kalimantan (7 + bears) www.beruangmadu.org

BOS Palangkaraya Central Kalimantan (10 + bears) http://orangutan.or.id

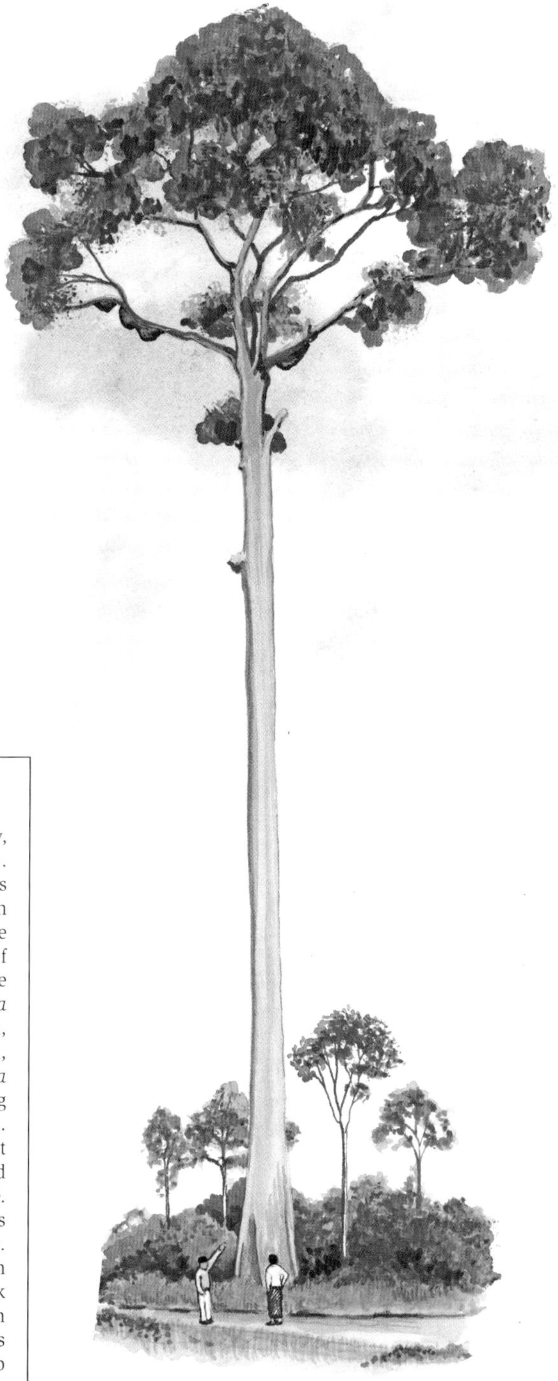

GIANT BEES, *KOOMPASIA* TREES AND SUN BEARS

Borneo is the world centre of honey-bee diversity, with 5 out of 8 world species (Koeniger 2010). One of these bees, *Apis dorsata* (the world's largest honey bee), builds giant combs often grouped with other combs in large colonies. The most preferred sites are the open branches of giant *Koompasia* trees common throughout the Bornean forests. You can see giant *Koompasia* trees next to the canopy walkway at Sepilok, along the access roads to Tabin and Danum, and Gng Penrissen near Kuching. *Apis dorsata* colonies are nomadic, following flowering patches of forest from one valley to another (p. 42), but why do the bees favour *Koompasia*? It is likely that the relationship is mutualistic and that *Koompasia* has evolved to attract the bee. Like many legumes (p. 67), the young leaves of *Koompasia* are a favourite food of langurs. The vicious nesting bees deter langurs from eating the leaves. The smooth, pale grey trunk can be easily seen at night by the bees, which often forage nocturnally, and the tall trunk is too smooth for honey-loving Sun Bears to climb (p. 66).

MARTENS, WEASELS, OTTERS AND BADGERS

MUSTELIDAE **World:** 59 spp. **Borneo:** 7 spp. The mustelidae are a varied group of generally small, carnivorous mammals with diverse habits, found from Europe to Africa, Asia and the Americas.

YELLOW-THROATED MARTEN *Martes flavigula* **HB 435, T 343, Wt 1.4kg** **Scarce**

This is the most common weasel you are likely to see in Borneo, but it is nowhere common. It is found in all forested areas from the coast to 1,700m on Kinabalu. At Kinabalu Park headquarters, it is less common than the Malay Weasel. It has been recorded throughout Sarawak, including Samunsam and the Kelabit Highlands. It is scarce in E Kalimantan (Yasuma 1994), Puri (2005). In peat-swamp forest at Sabangau only 4/27 camera stations captured the species, and of these 4, only 2 had repeat visits (Cheyne et al. 2013).

ID: Large weasel with distinctive yellow throat and tail held erect like a question mark, usually seen in pairs or small family groups. Both this and the Malay Weasel do not run rapidly along the ground like a mongoose with the tail held low, but move in distinctive leaps, 'awkward hops' or 'stop-start bounding'.

Call: Series of soft, rapid *chuks* (Payne 1985).

Habits: Active during the day and rarely at night. A pair used to live under the Tabin Wildlife Resort restaurant when it was first established. Emmons (2000), when researching treeshrew ecology at Poring and Danum in Sabah, found that Yellow-throated Martens were the most common diurnal (daytime) carnivores. 'These large muscular martens hunt swiftly, sometimes travelling in pairs or triplets. They sniff intently as they ferret along the ground investigating every treefall, or climb up and down over the boles of large trees. Martens range through high canopy or the viny sub-canopy, leaping with agility from branch to branch. Their behaviour makes them especially likely to encounter treeshrew nestlings hidden in exposed leaf nests or vulnerable hollows.' A pair was seen mating in the crown of a tall dipterocarp tree (A. Lamb). At Deramakot (Sabah), I watched a fruiting *Ficus sundaica* from dawn, but hornbills and a flock of mynas refused to land due to an active Yellow-throated Marten that chased the feeding birds.

Diet: Omnivorous. Climbs into the canopy to feed on fruit, birds and squirrels. Reputed to be fond of honey and raid bees' nests. At Danum chased a colugo, eventually catching it on the ground (p. 154).

Range: N India to E Siberia south to Malaya, Sumatra, Java. **Borneo race:** *M. f. saba.*

A KELABIT FOLKTALE ABOUT MARTENS AND GIBBONS

The Kelabits are a tribe that lives in the remote Kelabit Highlands plateau adjacent to Gng Murud and the mountains of Pulong Tau National Park in the NE corner of Sarawak.

'Many hundreds of years ago before there were hunting dogs there lived a man whose name was Saluyah who settled on the Kelabit plateau. Unfortunately, due to settling in a new place, Saluyah found much disturbance towards his crops from wild pigs, sambar deer, barking deer, mousedeer, monkeys and other wild animals.

Saluyah held a discussion with his people on how to get rid of these pests. They finally agreed to catch some Yellow-throated Martins (*ngala*) to rear them and use them like we now use dogs. They reared *ngala* in great numbers and found them very useful, even attacking and killing the largest animal that came to forage among their crops.

This strategy was so successful that soon Saluyah feared there would be no animals left in the jungle. So Saluyah called another meeting to seek another animal that could work like the *ngala* without being so destructive to life. In the end the people agreed that they should get the gibbon because it made a loud sound, *wak wak,* enough to scare away all the animals; and thereafter the pests never came to the fields again to do damage.' (Kelabit folk tale as told to Tom Harrisson, *Sarawak Museum Journal*, 1966). **Note:** This folk tale is entirely plausible. The closely related Polecat has been domesticated as the Ferret *Mustela furo* and used for hunting rabbits and rats in Europe. Domesticated otters are used for fishing in the Sunderbans of Bangladesh.

YELLOW-THROATED MARTENS HUNTING IN PACKS There are a number of anecdotal reports of martens hunting deer and pigs in family packs, a strategy rarely reported outside Borneo.

1 'Martens are mostly arboreal, generally to be seen high up in the tops of the tallest trees but apparently descend to the ground at times when they are reputed to attack both pigs and deer, fastening on to either the eye or underneath the belly and even causing their death by sucking their blood.' (Banks 1931).

2 'Martens hunt other animals, payau, kijang, pig etc. in packs of 3 or 4. Reputed to jump on a kijang's back and bite at the hind legs until the kijang is exhausted.' (Jim Comber 1960).

3 'The Marten is a fierce hunter which will bring down a sambar buck weighing 90kg by persistence and hanging on to the testicles. Often hunts in pairs and said by the Kelabits to work in family groups.' (Harrisson 1966).

4 'Amongst the Orang Sungai of the Segama River the Marten is well known to attack deer and pigs in pairs or family groups biting at the tendons on the hind legs and clinging on to the back until the animal is exhausted and collapses. This is something I have observed twice myself.' Palin (guide at Tabin Wildlife Resort).

See Pierce et al. (2014) for Asian records.

Kuala Belait Road, Brunei, May 2013. (Photo: Folkert Hindriks)

MALAY WEASEL

MALAY WEASEL *Mustela nudipes* **HB 315, T 218, Wt ?** **Rare**

Recorded throughout Borneo, from the peat-swamps of Sabangau to 2,000m at Mesilau on Kinabalu, but rarely seen. Locally common in mossy cloud forest above 1,000m from Kinabalu south to Kalimantan. Seen both within and outside the forest at Kinabalu Park headquarters (1,500m) and Mesilau (2,000m). In lowland forest it is always less common than the Yellow-throated Marten, but in the mountains this pattern is reversed. More common in oil palm than forest at Danum (Ross et at. 2013).

ID Fur varies from pale yellow to bright orange, usually offset by white head and white tip to tail. Can only be mistaken for the even rarer 'orange morph' of the Collared Mongoose (p. 273). As both move very fast, a flash of orange could easily cause confusion. However, the Collared Mongoose runs fast with the tail level with the ground, whilst the Malay Weasel leaps rather than runs, usually with a raised tail. See Holden/Meijaard (2012), Ross et al. (2012) and Brodie/Giordano (2012).

Habits Diurnal. Usually alone and on the ground, often investigating small holes, moving rapidly in a distinctive bounding zigzag pattern. Banks (1931) noted that the feet are webbed halfway along the digits, 'suggesting mildly aquatic habits'. Although one was killed when swimming across the Ulu Mahakam River, Duckworth et al. (2006) concluded that there was no evidence that it associated with rivers or swamps.

Often described as unafraid 'On my way back down from the Timpohon Gate to Kinabalu Park HQ in the rain a Malay Weasel came at me from the side of the road and tried to climb my leg. It didn't seem aggressive, but I wasn't ready to test my luck, creating a weasel baffling buffer with my umbrella. This boisterous character stayed around for ten minutes, taking ginger leaps over the forest floor, disappearing into holes, re-appearing several metres away, slithering up saplings, and crossing the road several times without looking. All within a few feet. Obviously busy hunting, it periodically investigated my tentative squeaks to see if I could get his or her attention. Neither of us cared that we were soaked.' (Brendan McGarry 2011).

Diet 'One morning at Danum I was astonished by the sight of a bright orange Malay Weasel climbing up to 4m to forage diligently in a dense vine canopy. It hunted around intently among the vines, descended to the ground, and then climbed another vine to repeat the process. The weasel may have been searching for birds' nests but with this behaviour could discover above ground nestling treeshrews.' (Emmons 2000). The Malay Weasel has been described as a chicken thief, but is probably attracted by the rats attracted to chicken feed, rather than the chickens themselves. In 1970, I acquired a Malay Weasel that had been trapped in a hen coop at Tamparuli, Sabah. It escaped and lived happily in our overgrown coastal garden at Tg Aru for several years, catching rats in piles of brushwood. Its presence could be detected by a strong musky odour. On Kinabalu recorded feeding on a skink and at Danum BRL on a small snake.

Range Malaya, Sumatra. **Borneo race:** Monotypic.

APOSEMATIC MARKINGS AND MIMICRY 'This is a small and very furry stoat with the usual offensive smell of its kind. It is nowhere common. One I saw walked around the forest floor like a giant hairy caterpillar, the yellow fur puffed out all round the body as a sort of warning to wantons. It had a decided smell of ammonia to back up this warning.' (Banks 1980). The bright contrasting colours, the bold behaviour, and the strong smell of the Malay Weasel are explicit danger-warning (aposematic) signs shared with a number of other Bornean mammals. The imitation of the weasel's appearance by a rare morph of the Collared Mongoose is a form of Müllerian mimicry, which may also include some races of the Large Treeshrew with brightly coloured tails (p. 150, treeshrew; p. 273, mongoose).

This Malay Weasel emerged from under a pile of building materials at the Borneo Rainforest Lodge, Danum Valley. Malay Weasels are sometimes recorded on the fringes of urban areas and near rural buildings, most probably hunting for rats. (Photo: George Hong.)

Malay Weasels are generally rare but are always more common than Yellow-throated Martens in the mountains, in oil palm and on the edge of towns, all areas where rats are abundant, indicating that Malay Weasels target rats for food. Photo above by Ross & Hearn (Crocker Range). Photo below by Cede Prudente in logged lowland forest in Sabah.

SUNDA SKUNK AND FERRET-BADGER

MEPHITIDAE **World:** 12 spp. **Sundaland:** 2 spp. **Borneo:** 1 sp. Previously commonly known as the Stink Badger, *Mydaus javanensis* is a skunk not a badger. Skunks are restricted to the Americas apart from the 2 Asian skunks, the Sunda Skunk and Palawan Skunk endemic to Palawan.

1 SUNDA SKUNK (TELEDU) *Mydaus javanensis* **HB 445, T 36, Wt?** **Locally common**

[Malay Badger] [Sunda Stink Badger] Locally common, for example at Papar, Deramakot, Sepilok, Kelabit Highlands, Long Ketok (E Kalimantan), but absent from other areas, such as Kinabalu, S Sarawak and peat-swamp forests in Kalimantan. Found in both primary and secondary forest and the edges of cultivation up to 1,100m in the Kelabit Highlands. However, at SAFE, Fitzmaurice (2015) found that Teledu declined in logged forest. **ID:** Variable-width white stripe on back. Short tail under which are two anal glands that squirt a foul liquid. **Scent:** 'Many many times the teledu has discovered its proximity to us by its extremely disagreeable and peculiar odour. So powerful indeed is this that natives, attempting to catch these animals, often fall down insensible if struck by the discharge from their anal battery. Even at the distance of half a mile and more the stink, as I must call it, permeates the atmosphere so thickly that it is plainly discernible by taste.' (Forbes 1879). **Habits:** Nocturnal and terrestrial. In logged forest at Deramakot, camera trapping by Wilting et al. (2010) found that the Teledu was less common (107 records) than the Malay Civet (326 records) and Island Palm Civet (225 records). **Call:** Makes a noise resembling that of a dog just before it begins to bark; when moving about keeps up a snuffling or low grunting noise, something like a pig (Bock 1881). **Range:** Sumatra, Java, Bunguran Besar, (Natuna Islands). **Borneo race:** *M. j. lucifer.*

TELEDU SKINS USED AS SITTING MATS Lonnberg & Mjoberg (1925) noted that 'in most Kelabit houses flat skunk skins, very much stretched in order to make large sitting mats, were found'. Banks (1931) added that 'the Kelabit dogs find the entrance to these teledu burrows and the smallest dogs will eagerly enter and bay the quarry underground while the men dig furiously down from above with the aid of sharpened sticks. Kelabits eat the animal and value its skin for sale to down country people, who mix the shavings with water and drink them as a cure for fever or rheumatism.' The value of Teledu skins as mats in long houses is that they are the only animal skins that the local dogs refuse to eat.

MUSTELIDAE **World:** 57 spp. **Borneo:** 7 spp. Carnivorous mammals that include the otters, badgers, weasels, martens and ferrets. Most Bornean species are uncommon and shy, and are rarely seen.

2 BORNEAN FERRET-BADGER *Melogale everetti* **HB 314, T 137, Wt?** **Endemic**

[Kinabalu Ferret Badger] [*Melogale orientalis*]. Uncommon resident of hill and montane cloud forest at *c.* 300–3,000m on Kinabalu and the Crocker Range. A Kinabatangan record (Boonratana 2010) is probably an error. Based on 24,506 camera trap nights Vickers and Evans (2016) recorded 470 Sunda Skunks but no Ferret-badgers. Bones found at the Niah Caves in Sarawak (Cranbrook 2000) indicate that Bornean Ferret-badgers were once widespread in the lowlands. **ID:** Distinguished from the Teledu by bushy tail. **Habits:** Mostly nocturnal and terrestrial. In the Crocker Range, Jim Comber (p. 208) noted that the ferret-badger often lives in Long-tailed Porcupine holes. 'Hunting dogs often find the occupied holes and refuse to leave the area until the "Simbong" is dug out by their Murut masters.' Griswold (Coolidge 1940) saw one at the Paka Cave (Kinabalu) in the early morning. 'It moved like a weasel in and out of the shrubbery; lost for one minute only to appear running along to some log and then into a thicket. They are quite tenacious of life.' **Diet:** Earthworms, lizards, birds and rats (Payne 1985). A nocturnal visitor to the rubbish bins below Timpohon Gate on Kinabalu 1,850m. **Taxonomy:** Split by Long (1992) from *M. personata*, which occurs in India west to Vietnam, south to Java.

1

TELEDU IN S KALIMANTAN

'In Amontai, Barabai and Biraijan (in the foothills of the Meratus Mountains, S Kalimantan), where the elevation does not exceed 30m, Saats are as common as rats. Under the tail are two small glands containing a fluid, which the animal discharges when irritated. The odour emitted by this fluid is very pungent and disagreeable, and is retained long after death. These animals are never seen in the daytime, when they rest in burrows in the ground. It was only at night-time that the Bukkits and Malays succeeded in capturing me a specimen or two, by watching the holes of their retreat, and capturing them as they emerged after dusk in search of food. Their food consists of worms and larvae. They have from three to four young at a time.' (Bock 1881).

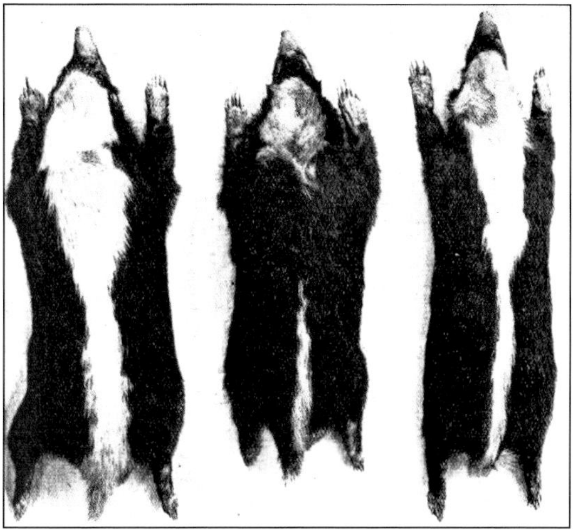

Three Teledu skins collected by Mjöberg in the Kelabit Highlands showing the very variable width of the white dorsal stripe.

2

LUTRINAE World: 13 spp. **Borneo:** 4 spp. Two Bornean otters, the Small-clawed and the Smooth, are social, living in family groups and often seen, whilst the Eurasian and Hairy-nosed Otters are rare and solitary, with only the mother and her cubs associating for a year after birth. Otters are normally crepuscular or diurnal, but near habitation they are usually secretive and nocturnal, revealed by their whistles at night. All otters are expert swimmers and feed on fish and other aquatic prey along coasts, in swamps, rivers and streams to 1,700m on Kinabalu. Otters may dig holes in river banks or use tree-root dens for sleeping or protecting their young. Multiple dens are used within a group home range. Small-clawed Otters move their cubs daily between different dens. Otters use **spraints** to mark their feeding sites within a home range.

Diet: The 4 Bornean otters are sympatric (occur together) along forested lowland rivers, but specialize in different prey in different habitats. The Smooth Otter hunts large fish in family groups (average 5) along large rivers and around the coast. The Small-clawed Otter feeds on crabs and shrimps caught with the front paws in small family groups (average 5) from the coast to the hills. The solitary Hairy-nosed Otter catches small fish in forest rivers and peat-swamps. Otters are hated by Bornean fishermen and fish farmers for 'stealing' fish. In Bangladesh domesticated Smooth Otters are used to drive fish into nets.

Breeding: Otters average 63 days' gestation and breed continuously when food is available. Females are slightly smaller than males. In social otters, only the alpha pair breeds and the whole family cares for the young. Litters of 1–2 cubs (to 5) are normal. Otters are independent at 1 year and sexually mature at 2 years.

Calls: All otters use a variety of whistles, chirps and danger squeals to communicate. Social otters will aid a family member calling in distress.

1 HAIRY-NOSED OTTER *Lutra sumatrana* **HT 1–1.2m, Wt 5–8kg** **Rare**

Found in peat-swamp and lowland forest rivers. Highest record is 1,200m, Pa Umor, Kelabit Highlands (Davis 1958). Recent records from Deramakot FR in Sabah and Brunei. Usually solitary. Groups likely to be maximum of 3 (mother and 2 cubs). In Thailand, Kanchanasaka (2007) found it fed on small fish and water snakes. **ID:** Similar head profile to Eurasian Otter, distinguished by hairy nose (rhinarium); from the other otters by flat head, and from Smooth Otter by rounded not triangular tail. Coat darker brown than in other otters, with well-defined pale markings on throat and lower jaw. **Range:** Cambodia south to Thailand, Malaya, Sumatra, Borneo.

2 SMOOTH OTTER *Lutrogale perspicillata* **HT 1–1.3m, T 42cm, Wt 7–11kg** **Locally common**

[Smooth-coated Otter] The second most common and largest otter – the size of a dog. Found along both large and small rivers, for example at Kinabatangan, Tabin, and often fishes along the coast, for instance at Santubong near Kuching and Gaya Island (KK). **ID:** Distinguished by large size, social habits and slightly domed skull. Tail is a flattish triangle in cross-section. Male has an external penis unlike other otters. **Habits:** At Tabin, Lesser Fish Eagles follow groups of Smooth Otters to try and steal their fish. On the Kinabatangan Leona Wai found monitor lizard skin in a scat. **Range:** Iraq to Sumatra and Borneo.

3 EURASIAN OTTER *Lutra lutra*, race *barang* **HT 1–1.2m, Wt 5–8kg** **Rare**

A mystery otter. Payne (1985) reports 2 possible skins from the Kelabit Highlands. A pair was photographed by Jon Johnston (Humbolt California State University) near the Danum Valley FC (Segama River) in July 2014. **ID:** Flat skull (head) similar to the Hairy-nosed Otter's. The 2 species can only be reliably distinguished by the hairy nose of the Hairy-nosed Otter compared with the bare dark-skin nose of the Eurasian Otter. **Range:** Europe across N Asia to Japan south to Thailand, Malaya, Sumatra, Borneo.

4 SMALL-CLAWED OTTER *Aonyx cinerea*

HT 65cm, Wt 2.5–4kg **Common**

Common, small, cat-sized otter. Cubs born with claws that later drop off, leaving 5 finger 'hands' used to catch shrimps and molluscs. Closely related to Smooth Otter. **ID:** Recognizable by small size, social habits (groups of up to 12, average 5) and short, rounded head. **Habits:** At Danum BRL a family group travels daily downriver each morning, returning upriver each afternoon. **Range:** India east to Palawan, Borneo, Java, Bali.

4

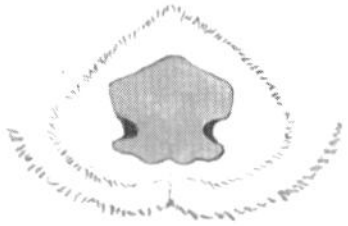

smooth rhinarium

1
airy rhinarium
tail cross-section
2
nooth rhinarium
tail cross-section
3
ooth rhinarium
tail cross-section

OTTER ECOLOGY

Resource partitioning by three sympatric otters in Thailand Otters appear to have boundless energy when playing and hunting, so they eat large amounts of food. Kruuk (2012) estimates that *Lutra lutra* in the UK eat 15–20% of their body weight each day. Assuming a family of 5 Smooth Otters weighed around 45kg, the otter group would eat *c.* 7kg of fish per day. Otters thus need many kilometres of productive river to survive. SE Asia is unique in that in some of its river systems there are at least 3 (possibly 4) sympatric otter species hunting for food along the same river. How do they partition the food resources? Studies on the Huay Kha Khaeng River in hill forest in NW Thailand (Kruuk et al. 1994) found that:

Smooth Otters preferred the lower reaches and the river mouth where the river was wider, the water slower and the pools deeper. Smooth Otters fed on large fish, which were chased cooperatively by group members.

Eurasian Otters preferred the narrow, fast-flowing river head waters. Eurasian Otters are solitary. Their flat skull allows them to catch fish in narrow crevices that are unavailable to Smooth Otters.

Small-clawed Otters feed on molluscs, crabs and shrimps so do not compete directly with the other otters.

In East Sabah all 4 Bornean otters have been recorded in similar forest rivers. Small-clawed and Smooth are relatively common and often seen, whilst Eurasian and Hairy-nosed are both very rare. It may be that the social otters dominate prime habitat, whilst the 2 solitary otters are forced into marginal habitat.

OTTERS IN THE UPPER SEGAMA 'Fish eaters such as monitor lizards, fish eagles and darters were all regarded as pests by the Dusuns, but none incurred the hatred that was reserved for Rongon, the otter. Possibly the Dusuns' hatred was justified, but I had to admit that of all the riverine fauna, otters were my favourite. One day when I accompanied Pingas on a trip up the Bole River in search of durian fruit, we rounded a bend and saw a family of otters cavorting beside the river on the far shore. Slowly the otters, an adult and four playful cubs, worked their way down the beach. Their progress was slowed by a non-stop game of tag among the youngsters. When they were nearly level with us they sneaked into the river and played hide-and-seek in the brown water. One cub climbed out on our bank and stood high on his hind legs, whistling to his family. He was no more than five yards from us and I could feel Pingas itching, for action. Our cub dashed back to the river, slid gracefully in, swam rapidly across, and was soon racing after the rest of the family. We broke our cover and I asked Pingas if that had not been an exciting experience. "Yes," replied the unrepentant Dusun; "if I had had a stone I could have killed him."' (John Mackinnon 1975, Borneo.)

Spraints and resource marking Otters have a keen sense of smell, but it is used for monitoring other otters, not fishing. Both sexes of all ages use anal glands to deposit a strong-smelling secretion on their faeces (spraints). Spraints (often including fish scales) are deposited along otter-foraging routes on prominent sites such as river rocks. Both otters and zoologists can identify individual otters and their sexual status from their spraints. Researchers use DNA and otters use smell. Kruuk (2012) suggests that spraints are used for resource marking to inform other otters that the locality has been 'fished out'. The 2 social otters, Smooth and Small-clawed, deposit both individual and communal spraints. A group may deposit spraints simultaneously, then roll in the deposit afterwards as a method of establishing a group identity. Like dogs, Smooth, Eurasian and Small-clawed Otters have bare-skin noses known as a rhinarium. In dogs this area secretes a mucus that is licked by the dog to carry scent particles from the nose surface to scent receptors in the mouth. The rhinarium of the Hairy-nosed Otter is covered in hair, not bare skin. This indicates an (unknown) difference in ecology from the closely related and morphologically similar Eurasian Otter.

Pet **Small-clawed Otters** from the Kudat mangroves (thanks to Terry Mills).

Hairy-nosed Otter. Note that head profile and eye placement exactly match Eurasian Otter. Camera trap at Deramakot, Azlan & Wilting, CONSACON.

Smooth Otters. Note domed head and eye placement. Kinabatangan. (Photo: Ch'ien C. Lee)

Eurasian Otters. Head profile matches Hairy-nosed Otter. Danum DVFC. (Photo: Jon Johnston)

LINSANG

PRIONODONTIDAE **World:** 2 spp. **Borneo:** 1 sp. Listed by Hose (1893) as a cat, *Felis gracilis*, the linsangs were later classified with the Viverridae (civets), but today they are considered to be so different that they are now placed in their own family, **Prionodontidae**. The African Linsang of tropical W Africa remains in the Viverridae. Unlike the majority of the civets, which are omnivorous, the linsangs are exclusively carnivorous with very sharp teeth. The claws can be fully retracted like a cat's, and are unlike the claws of civets, which are only partially retractable. Linsang are one of a select few mammals, including pangolins and tarsiers, that are equally common in virgin primary forest and tall secondary forest – although the Banded Linsang itself is rare.

BANDED LINSANG *Prionodon linsang* **HB 380, T 328, Wt 700g** **Rare**

Inhabits primary and secondary forests throughout Borneo, from the peat-swamps of Sabangau to 1,800m on Kinabalu, but very rarely seen. Neither Puri (2005) nor Yasuma (1994) have any records from E Kalimantan.

ID: The size of a small cat or large squirrel with a long, banded tail. The varied dark coat markings are variously described as black or dark chocolate-brown, with a background that is white, pale yellow, buff or orange. Individuals can be recognized from photographs.

Habits: Nocturnal and mainly arboreal. Hunts for sleeping birds in the canopy at night. At Gng Penrissen in hill forest near Kuching, seen hunting for worms on the golf course at night (Yeo Siew Teck). The only linsang I have ever seen had been trapped in tall secondary forest near Kg Moyog (600m asl) in the Crocker Range. Regularly seen at Poring (Wells, Emmons). The highest camera-trap density was obtained in the upper reaches of the Seruyan River, C Kalimantan, in the Sari Bumi Kusuma logging concession, where Samejima et al. (2012) obtained 20 camera-trap images in 17,974 trap nights. **Range:** Myanmar, S. Thailand Malaya, Sumatra, Java. **Borneo race:** Monotypic.

BORNEAN MAMMALS WITH BLACK AND WHITE DANGER MARKINGS Many Bornean mammals have aposematic (danger-warning) markings on their heads and faces, for example the black-and-white stripes on slow loris, Ferret-badger, civets, grey langurs and Clouded Leopard, but only a few Bornean mammals advertise their presence with aposematic patterns covering their whole body and the Banded Linsang is one of them. Others include the Malay Civet and Teledu (both black and white), Moonrat (all white), Bornean Orangutan and Red Langur (red), and Malay Weasel (all orange). Traditional theories of mimicry were based on observations of butterflies, which are the flying billboards of the insect world.

Batesian mimicry takes place when an edible butterfly (the mimic) copies the colour patterns and often the behaviour of a poisonous or nasty-tasting butterfly – the model.

Müllerian mimicry takes place when poisonous or dangerous insects share the same aposematic patterns, for example wasps and bees with black-and-yellow stripes.

Mimicry rings are groups of both weak and dangerous animals that share the same aposematic patterns. The animals in a mimicry ring may be very dangerous, slightly dangerous or not at all dangerous, in which case the aposematic patterns are just a bluff.

The importance of numbers in mimicry Zoologists previously thought that in Batesian mimicry the model must be more common than the mimic, otherwise the predator (the target) will not learn fast enough to make the mimicry worthwhile for the mimic. In butterflies the risk to the target (bird) is only a nasty taste, so young birds catch both nasty and harmless butterflies. The bird learns over time to avoid *all* butterflies with aposematic markings. However, it seems likely that many target animals are born with an inbuilt genetic ability to recognize aposematic patterns as being dangerous. This inherited ability is almost certainly backed up by the ability to learn by experience. If this hypothesis is correct, the importance of numbers does not apply. Any animal that displays aposematic markings enjoys some degree of protection from attack (p. 157).

Both the porcupine and the Malay Civet eat poisonous seeds and may develop seasonally toxic flesh.

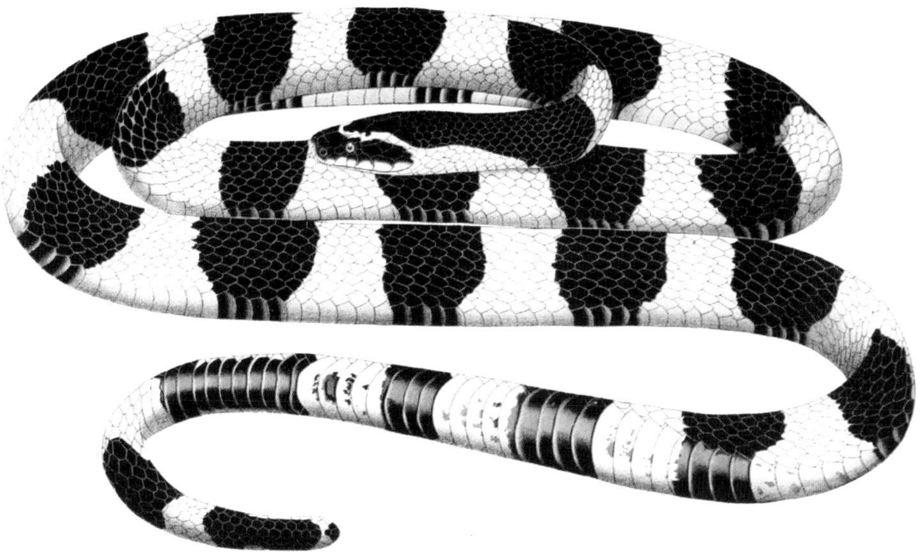

The BANDED KRAIT ***Bungarus fasciatus*** is the main cause of human snakebite fatalities in Borneo. According to Banks (1978), his captive Banded Linsang, which slept hunched up with the banded tail curled over the head between the ears, mimicked both the colour and the pattern of a coiled Banded Krait. The Banded Krait is a predator on other snakes, mostly at night. *Gonysoma* racer snakes systematically investigate tree holes for prey during the day and would be very wary of attacking a sleeping Banded Krait. Painting by R. Soedirman, in Ouwens & Kieweit de Jonge (1916).

The Giant Pill Millipede shows evidence of Müllerian mimicry (p. 266).

INTRODUCTION TO CIVETS

VIVERRIDAE World: 38 spp. **Malaya:** 10 spp. **Borneo:** 9 spp. Civets are a fully nocturnal subfamily of the carnivores that evolved in the wet tropics of SE Asia, later spreading to the dryer regions of India, Africa and S Europe, for example the Genet. Of all the carnivores the civets eat the most fruit. The palm civets in particular favour palm nectar, palm fruit and figs for food. See opposite.

Communication by scent More than most mammals, civets use scent rather than voice to communicate. All the Bornean civets with one exception possess specialist glands located around the anus (perianal). These glands produce a waxy substance known as civet or civetone, which acts as a fixative to additional hormonal scents produced by each civet. Civets 'scent mark' feeding trees, branches and logs. The Island Palm Civet leaves its scent-marked dung in the open on forest paths and walkways. The Malay Civet also leaves dung piles (civetries) in prominent locations. It is no coincidence that the only Bornean civet without a scent gland, the male Striped Palm Civet, is also the most vocal. In dense tropical vegetation civets use scent not calls to advertise their species, location, age, sex and breeding status.

Defence by scent At least 2 civets, the Masked Palm Civet and Island Palm Civet, can project a foul-smelling spray from the anal area for defence against predators.

Civet breeding All civets are solitary and are only seen together when courting or bringing up young, which is exclusively the mothers' responsibility. Radio-tracking studies show that feeding ranges are stable but often overlap with conspecifics. Civets tend to avoid each other when not courting and do not aggressively defend territorial boundaries. Scent marking is effectively a form of passive territorial defence. The most frugivorous civets, the Striped Palm Civet and Binturong, gather in fruiting fig trees, although individuals do not interact. These 2 civet species have very large home ranges as most canopy fig trees are thinly scattered and fruit unpredictably in Bornean forests.

PALM CIVETS AND TODDY CATS

The 3 palm civets are important seed dispersers in Borneo especially for first stage reforestation of forest gaps and degraded forest. The teeth are adapted for a soft fruit diet and they are not known to predate seeds. At Tabin, Nakashima (2010) reported Island Palm Civets dispersed 19 species of pioneer plants. Faeces were deposited non-randomly in open areas, landslides, tree falls and along roads. Pioneer plant seeds only grow in full sun. Thus Island Palm Civets unknowingly farm their future food supply.

Palms and Civets In India (as in Borneo) locals tap the flower spikes of large palms for palm wine or toddy. Palm civets often steal the toddy and are known as Toddy Cats. In Java, Bartels (1964) reported Island Palm Civets ate at least 35 species of pioneer forest fruit including 6 figs and 8 palms. Civets ate palm fruits with toxic raphides in the pulp that would be lethal to seed predators. Thus palm civets have a strong mutualistic relationship with many palm species assisting both pollination and seed dispersal.

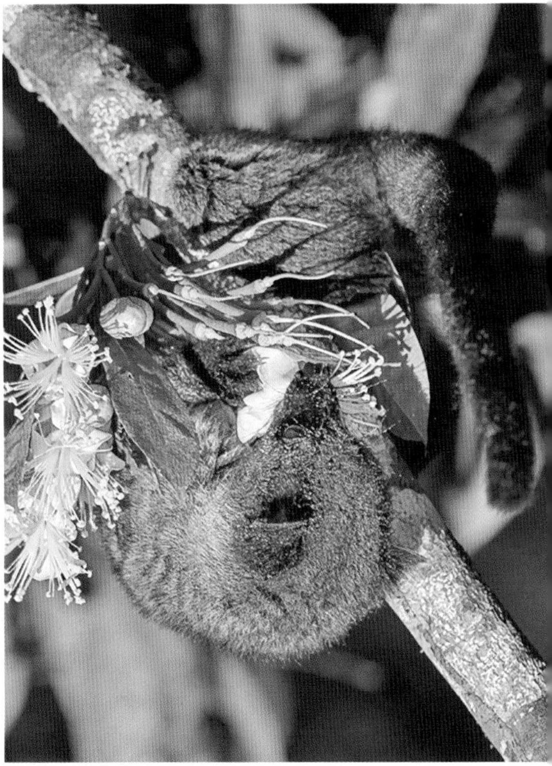

Bornean Striped Palm Civet feeding on the nectar of durian flowers at Danum Valley Field Centre in Sabah. (Photo Chien C. Lee)

A family of endemic Bornean Striped Palm Civets emerge at dawn from a hole in a large epiphyte clump next to the Bulalong Canopy Walkway, Temburong, Brunei (p. 357). (Photo Zdeněk Mačát)

1 BORNEAN STRIPED PALM CIVET *Arctogalidia stigmatica* **HB 480, T 550, Wt 1.6–5kg Endemic**
[Malay: Musang akar (Vine Civet)]. [Small-toothed Palm Civet] Locally common in tall forest throughout Borneo, from the peat-swamp forests of Sabangau to 1,500m on Kinabalu. Unlike the Island Palm Civet (IPC), rarely seen on the ground or camera-trapped. Both species overlap at the forest edge, e.g. at Tabin, where Nakabayashi et al (2014) sighted IPC 3 x more often than the Striped Palm Civet when walking night transects. Due to arboreal habits rarely recorded in camera-trap surveys or trapped in standard traps, the population is probably underestimated. **ID:** Similar to IPC but larger, with tail distinctly longer than body. Distinguished from IPC by uniformly dark face, although 70% of individuals have a longitudinal white stripe on nose, Veron et al (2015). Three faint stripes or spot lines along back. In the hand has 2 pairs of nipples, not 3 as in IPC. Most individuals are dark brown or dark grey but light grey and yellow golden-brown variations are known. Some Bornean individuals also have very pale skin inside the ears. When the ears are pointed forward at night, these pale patches could easily be mistaken for large eyes. **Habits:** Mostly nocturnal. Usually alone but may feed in the same tree as conspecifics without aggression. IPC is always solitary (apart from mother and baby), and usually aggressive to conspecifics. At Poring, Lakim (1994) trapped 9 individuals on the 266m canopy walkway in 6 months (10,000 trap nights). Unlike IPC, only female has an anal scent gland. This indicates that this civet is non-territorial and ranges widely to find fruiting trees. Radio tracking by Nakabayashi found that the home range was 79ha, half the area of a Binturong and similar to the area of a male IPC. The tail is prehensile, used to steady the body when feeding but not strong enough to use as a fifth limb as with pangolin and Binturong. **Call:** The most vocal of the palm civets, calling constantly at night when breeding. In Singapore Chua et al. (2012) reported that the closely related Three-striped Palm Civet was 'Highly vocal – calling incessantly – a loud chirping call *chirrp chirrp* – sounding like a Slender Squirrel (p. 200) but much louder'. **Diet:** Omnivorous; often eats green bat figs, including *Ficus variegata*, *F. septica* and *F. lepicarpa* (p. 78). A captive ate bananas, birds, bats and a snake, but refused to eat a Pied Hornbill due to the smell (Banks 1931). At Danum, Miyabi Nakabaysahi recorded this civet eating unripe fruits of *Ficus variegata* and *Fagraea cuspidata*, as well as the sap of Laran (p. 224) and durian nectar. Figs are pulped (not swallowed) and the fibre wad spat as with fruit bats. **Taxonomy:** Split by Veron et al. (2015) from Three-striped Palm Civet based on DNA (see below).

2 THREE-STRIPED PALM CIVET *Arctogalidia trivirgata* **Race:** *A. t. inornata* **(Not illustrated)**
Studies by Veron et al. (2015) found that Three-striped Palm Civet specimens from Borneo differed by 5.7% in DNA from the Three-striped Palm Civets found elsewhere in Asia and the Borneo species deserved to be split off as *Arctogalidia stigmatica* (see above). However, Three-striped Pam Civets, race: *A. t. inornata*, collected from P. Bunguran Besar (Natuna Islands) have DNA closer to the race on the Malay Peninsula and Sumatra. They are also smaller and darker and with no back stripes. **Range:** NE India to S China, Thailand, Malaya, Singapore, Sumatra, Java, Bunguran Besar (map, p. 168).

3 ISLAND PALM CIVET *Paradoxurus philippinensis* **HB 450, T 370, Wt 2–3kg Common**
[*P. hermaphrodites*] **Malay:** Musang pulut (Sticky Rice Civet), [Common Palm Civet], [Toddy Cat]. The most common civet in lowland forested areas but rare in the hills. Collected in Kelabit Highlands (1,100m). Often visits farms and orchards near forest and reported to steal chickens. **ID:** As in Bornean Striped Palm Civet, colour varies from rusty-brown to dark grey, but most have spots on flanks and pale band on face below ears. E Sabah specimens are darker than W Bornean ones (Payne 1985). At Deramakot 14% of Island Palm Civets had a white or yellow tail-tip (Wilting 2010), previously regarded a distinguishing feature of the Masked Palm Civet. **Habits:** Usually nocturnal but at Sabangau reported as being active by day. An excellent tree climber but less arboreal than the Bornean Striped Palm Civet. Often seen on the ground. Yasuma (1994) notes that this civet is the most common road kill between Balikpapan and Samarinda, E Kalimantan. At Tabin, Nakashima et al (2013) radio-tracked 12 Island Palm Civets and calculated (95% MCP) that male ranges averaged 73ha, more than twice the size of female ranges, which averaged 24 ha. **Diet:** See p. 262. Often eats oil-palm fruit. In Singapore urbanized Island Palm Civets eat squirrels and rats.In Borneo eats rodents, millipedes, crabs, insects, birds, snails and flowers as well as fruit, Nakashima et al (2010). **Taxonomy:** Patou et al. (2010), using DNA and tooth morphology, split the Common Palm Civet *P. hermaphrodites* into 3 species: 1. Asian continent north of the Isthmus of Kra, 2. Malaya, Sumatra and Java, 3. Borneo and the Philippines, including a relict race in the Mentawi islands (W Sumatra) – illustrating the complexity of Sundaland zoogeography. Future taxonomic changes are likely. See Veron et al. (2014). **Range:** Mentawi Islands (W Sumatra), Phillippine Islands, Borneo.

1

3

CIVET COFFEE OR KOPI MUSANG is the name for coffee beans that have been collected from the faeces of palm civets. Coffee that grows naturally as an understorey shrub in African forests was originally introduced to Java in 1819 by the Dutch, who established plantations on the slopes of Javan and Sumatran volcanoes. The planters noted that thieving nocturnal palm civets ate only perfectly ripe coffee fruits, and laid their bean-rich faeces on estate paths overnight. Locals claimed that civet coffee was less bitter and had a better flavour than hand-picked coffee beans. Civet-defecated coffee beans fetch premium prices in Java, where they are known as Kopi Luwak. In the last 30 years the rise of international coffee-shop chains such as Starbucks and Costa Coffee has increased demand for Kopi Musang. Many coffee gardens in Indonesia and the Philippines hand-pick coffee beans and feed them to captive palm civets to obtain Kopi Musang. Palm-civet researchers note that wild civets only eat perfectly ripe fruit. Feeding hand-picked fruit to captive civets appears to defeat the object of the exercise, although gullible consumers are unlikely to taste the difference. Coffee is grown as a smallholder crop throughout the hills of Borneo, but there is as yet no local demand for Kopi Musang.

MALAY CIVET AND OTTER CIVET

1 MALAY CIVET (TANGALUNG) *Viverra tangalunga* **HB 640, T 320, Wt 3–5kg** **Common**

Local: Tangalung. **Malay:** Musang jebat (scent). Common terrestrial forest civet found throughout the lowlands and hills of Borneo, up to 1,100m in the Kelabit Highlands (Sarawak). Like the Banded Civet runs rather than climbs from danger. Less common than Banded Civet in virgin forest but more common in logged forest. The population declines after logging, but does not collapse like the Banded Civet. Due to its boldness the most often seen civet in Borneo. Many wildlife lodges feed an habituated tangalung. **ID:** The warning coloration may indicate poisonous flesh. See p. 260. **Habits:** Nocturnal and terrestrial. Wanders the forest floor at night hunting for small animals and scavenging. The smell of cooking in the forest often attracts a Tangalung. **Territories:** Malay Civets have been radio-tracked at Ulu Segama FR by Colon (Dec. 1995–June 1997). Civets were solitary but individual ranges overlapped and averaged just over 110 ha. At Mulu an individual ranged just under 100ha (McDonald & Wise 1979 RGS Expedition). Mathai points out that this is the only Bornean civet which deposits its faeces multiple times in the same location. **Diet:** Omnivorous but with a preference for poisonous millipedes and centipedes (Colon & Sugau 2012). McConkey (2004) found that Tangalungs ate the seeds of toxic primate fruits defecated by gibbons. This preference for poisonous food indicates that the poisons may be sequestered and taint the flesh, which may account for the Tangalung's boldness. See pp. 34 and 261. Cranbrook (2016) notes that Tangalung bones were much less common than palm civet bones in the middens left by humans in the Niah caves even though Tangalung is easier to catch. Also eats large insects, worms, rats, fallen bats and ground birds up to the size of a pheasant. Regarded by locals as a chicken thief. **Range:** Malaya, Sumatra, Borneo. Also Sulawesi, Buton and Palawan where captive Tangalungs were probably introduced to produce civetone for perfume but later escaped.

CIVET PERFUMES At least 3 civet species produce a commercially valuable scent, **civetone**, from their perianal glands, including the African, Small Indian and Malay Civets. The gland exudes a highly odorous, oily wax that can be scraped out with a small spoon, or the whole gland can be removed from dead civets and dried for sale.

Civetone has been used as an ingredient in perfumes, traditional Ayurvedic medicines and as an aphrodisiac for at least 2,000 years. It is harvested commercially in Ethiopia and India from civets kept in small cages, and continues to be used in some very expensive perfumes. In Borneo dried glands removed from hunted Malay Civets were traded with China until recently. In contrast the glands of palm civets have no commercial value. Artificial civetone synthesized from palm oil is available commercially for use as a camera-trap lure to encourage mammals to linger near the camera (p. 270).

Toxic Giant Pill Millipedes in the family *Zephroniidae* are a favourite food of the Tangalung.

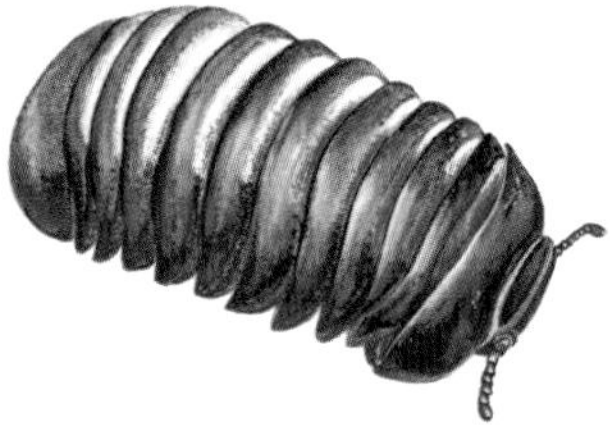

2 OTTER CIVET *Cynogale bennettii* **HB 628, T 162, Wt 3.5–5.6kg** **Rare aquatic cive**

[**Malay:** Padi Baru, from the smell of freshly harvested padi (unhusked rice)]. Globally rare aquatic civet confined to the vicinity of forested lowland rivers and swamps. Veron (2006) found that there were more specimens from Borneo (40) in museums than anywhere else in the range, but even in Borneo it is the rarest civet. Recorded from Sepilok, Deramakot, Danum, Kinabatangan and Tabin in Sabah, Tasek Merimbun in Brunei, the Kelabi Highlands, Ulu Baram, Ulu Rajang and Mukah in Sarawak, and Bukit Soeharto, Gng Palung and Sabangau in Kalimantan. ID: A distinctive odd shape like a small pig with a very broad, flat muzzle and dull colouring. The feet are partially webbed, an adaption to an aquatic habitat. Habits: Camera trapping at Way Kambas in Sumatra showed that Otter Civets were active during the day and even showed one climbing a tree, but most records indicate that they are terrestrial and usually nocturnal. Diet: Unlike the Flat-headed Cat (p. 285), which occupies the same habitat, the Otter Civet can close its nostrils and ears with flaps and is thus fully adapted to hunting under water like an otter. The nostrils are placed at the top of the muzzle like those of a crocodile, enabling thi civet to approach prey on the bank unawares. Like an otter this civet has abundant long whiskers. Range: S Thailand, Malaya, Sumatra, Borneo.

1

Note the
very long
widespread
whiskers

2

Peat-swamp forest at Sabangau. Photo: Susan Cheyne/Ou Trop.

MASKED PALM CIVET AND BINTURONG

1 MASKED PALM CIVET *Paguma larvata* **HB 590, T 580, Wt 3–5kg** **Scarce**

Malay: Musang lamri (fox). [Himalayan Palm Civet] Resident in primary forest throughout N Borneo, but absent from most of S Borneo. Very scarce in lowland forest; more common in hills and mountains to 2,150m on Kinabalu. At Tabin and Danum the least common palm civet, but the most common at Imbak Canyon (Matsubayashi 2011). **Sarawak:** A recent record from degraded forest at Bintulu (Belden et al. 2014). At Gng Murud Kechil second in abundance to Hose's Civet in mountain forest (Mathai 2010). In Kalimantan recorded from Bukit Soeharto and Sg Wain (Balikpapan) and Gng Palung, but not from peat-swamp forest.
ID: Distinguished by large size and plain black and rufous fur. Often (but not always) has distinctive pale tip to tail. **Note:** At Deramakot, Wilting found that 14% of Island Palm Civets had white- or yellow-tipped tails. Pale face mask is usually larger and more uniform than in Island Palm Civet, and there are 2 pairs of nipples, not 3. **Habits:** Nocturnal. May sleep high up in trees. On Gng Tambayukon, Kinabalu, a mother and baby occupied a hole at the base of a tree next to a mountain stream at 1,800m. In India this civet is reported to eject a foul-smelling liquid when disturbed, like a skunk (Prater). In Thailand a male Masked Palm Civet had a home range of 590ha compared with 110–340ha for Common Palm Civet (Grassman 1998). **Call:** Mournful cry at night is often mistakenly thought to be the sound of human ghosts wandering the forest (Puri 2005). **Note:** This observation may refer to a male breeding Striped Palm Civet, which is the only palm civet known to call (p. 264). **Diet:** In Thailand, Grassman found that both the Masked and Common Palm Civets were omnivorous, and switched diets rather than range when food was seasonally scarce. Figs made up a large proportion of their diets (24%), especially when other food was scarce. In Hong Kong reported to feed on nectar of leguminous *Mucuna* liana flowers, which are normally bat pollinated (Lau 2012). A reported chicken thief. **Range:** Widest global range of any palm civet. N Pakistan to S China, Japan (introduced), Taiwan, south to Thailand, Malaya, Sumatra. **Borneo race:** *P. l ogilbyi.*

2 BINTURONG *Arctictis binturong* **HB 780, T 670, Wt 6–10kg** **Scarce**

[Bearcat] Uncommon, large, very hairy black civet usually seen in fruiting strangling fig trees. Confined to primary forest throughout Borneo, from the peat-swamps of Kalimantan to Kinabalu Park headquarters (1,500m). One of a few Bornean animals, such as the pangolin (p. 152), with a muscled prehensile tail that can be twisted around branches to aid tree climbing and feeding. Binturongs are occasionally kept as native pets. **ID:** Edges of ears are rimmed in white and have prominent hairy tufts. Head and face may be silvery-grey, especially in young animals. Unlike the other highly agile arboreal palm civets, the Binturong climbs slowly and deliberately, and uses its long, tapering tail as an anchor whilst feeding. **Call:** In captivity very vocal, uttering high-pitched whines and howls and a rasping growl (Medway 1983, re. Malaya). **Habits:** At Danum an individual female was active from 3 p.m. until dawn. It rested close to the fruiting fig where it fed, and had a home range of 133 ha (95% MCP) (Nakabayashi 2015). Rests by lying along a branch with the legs hanging down on either side. Both sexes have scent glands under tail and on heel of hind feet, which are used to scent mark branches. In Thailand radio-tracked Binturongs had overlapping ranges that averaged 620ha, with a mean range overlap of 35% (Grassman 2005). Usually solitary, but more than one Binturong may feed in the same fig tree without aggression. Penans say the flesh is inedible due to the smell (Puri 2005). **Diet:** Omnivorous and raids chicken coops, but prefers figs. Reports of fishing Binturong (Ogilvie 1958) are probably mistaken otters. Banks (1931) notes that Binturong often steal ripe bananas from bunches hanging from the verandahs of isolated forest huts. **Taxonomy:** The Palawan Binturong race ***A. b. whitei*** may be split. **Range:** Thailand, Malaya, Sumatra, Java, Palawan. **Borneo race:** *A. b. pageli.*

BINTURONGS' FAVOURITE FOODS are the figs of canopy-level strangling fig trees, which produce large fruit crops at random intervals ripening over 1 week (Nakabayashi 2015). Binturongs feed in the same fig tree until the crop is finished, then travel on the ground to another fruiting fig. They prefer large figs and do not discriminate between bat, bird and primate figs. Fruiting strangling figs are probably detected by listening to the calls of barbets, which are fig-eating specialists (Wong Siew Te).

Yellow-crowned Barbet feeding on *Ficus sundaica*, the most common, large strangling fig in lowland forests.

Masked Palm Civet resting during the day in a fruiting *Ficus brunneoaurata*, an endemic secondary forest fig found in the hills and mountains here at Paya Maga, N Sarawak. Note white-tipped tail. (Photo: Ch'ien C. Lee)

HOSE'S CIVET AND BANDED CIVET

1 HOSE'S CIVET *Hemigalus hosei* **HB 500, T 318, Wt 2–3kg** **Rare endemic**

Malay: Musang hitam pudar (Grey Civet) Mysterious endemic civet confined to hills and mountains from Kinabalu south to C Kalimantan. Altitude records range from 325 to 1,700m. On Kinabalu, rare with records from Poring (700m) and a few skins at 1,200–1,300m. Records include Danum, the Crocker Range and Maliau Basin and Imbak Canyon. The type was collected on isolated Mt Dulit by Hose in 1891 (p. 242). Most common in NW Sarawak in forest surrounding Gng Murud and the Kelabit Highlands, where it is most common at 1,500m and rarely found below 900m asl (Mathai et al. 2010). In Kalimantan recorded from Ulu Seruyan (Schwaner Mountains at 325m) in a logging concession (Samejima & Semiadi 2012). Suprisingly, no records from the Kayan Mentarang NP just over the border from Gng Murud. Claimed sightings from the Kinabatangan are probably mistakes (Jennings et al. 2012). **ID:** Closely related to the Banded Civet and a similar size and shape, but with no markings on the plain grey or brownish back. Long, very wide muzzle, long whiskers and hairs between the toes. **Habits:** Camera trapping by Mathai (2010) in the Samling Sela'an Linau logging FMU in the upper Baram River found that Hose's was the second most common civet after the Malay Civet and more common than the Masked Palm Civet. 'All 14 images were from unlogged forest and all but one from montane forests with low hunting pressure far from logging roads. The one exception was at 731m in logged forest fragmented by swiddens.' Camera-trapping records were spread through the night, showing that Hose's Civet is crepuscular and nocturnal. **Diet:** An individual trapped on Bukit Retak in Brunei and kept in captivity for 10 weeks by Yasuma (2004) preferred fish to meat and declined to eat fruit. The counter-shading colouration indicates that Hose's Civet might search hill streams for small fish, crustaceans and frogs. Faeces were deposited in water and Yasuma notes that 'the faeces smelt sufficiently strong to irritate everyone else in my house', indicating that the faeces are probably used for '**resource marking**', like otter spraints (p. 258).

2 BANDED CIVET *Hemigalus derbyanus* **HB 530, T 330, Wt 2–3kg** **Uncommon and threatened**

Outside Borneo, the Banded Civet is considered rare. The first zoologists to collect extensively in Borneo, for example Chasen & Kloss (1927), and Davis (1962), found that it was the most common civet in areas of extensive undisturbed primary forest. In Borneo it is still the most common civet in the few remaining areas of lowland virgin forest, but the population collapses in logged forest, and it cannot survive in secondary forest or cultivation. In the Kelabit Highlands it overlaps in altitude with the similar montane Hose's Civet. As the Banded Civet is so sensitive to forest disturbance the population is threatened by logging throughout Borneo. At Tabin in the forest around the mud volcano (Nakabayashi) and in the Danum Valley Conservation Area (Ross & Hearn) it is still the most common forest civet. Not recorded from peat-swamp forest at Sabangau, but there is an old record from coastal S Kalimantan in an area that is now deforested. In logged forest at Deramakot, Wilting (2010) found that in camera traps the Banded Civet was less common than the Malay and Island Palm Civets, but more common than the Otter Civet and Linsang. **ID:** The distinctive bands on the back can only be confused with the Linsang, which is much smaller, rarer and rarely seen on the ground. The Linsang's tail is fully banded, whereas that of the Banded Civet is only half banded at the base. Background fur colour can vary from bright red/orange to yellow in Sabah, to pale grey in Sarawak. **Habits:** Nocturnal and terrestrial. Unlike the Malay Civet, very shy. Can climb trees but usually runs from danger. May sleep in low tree holes. **Call:** In captivity recorded hissing, spitting, whining and growling. **Diet:** Feeds in the understorey of primary forest on the ground, largely on earthworms and ants (Davis1962). Recorded diet includes frogs, a freshwater crab and a rat. As in Hose's Civet the feet have hairs between the foot pads to sense prey movement on the ground. **Range:** S Myanmar, S Thailand, Malaya, Sumatra. **Borneo race:** *H. d. boiei.*

HOSES'S CIVET AND SMALL CARNIVORE PROJECT (HOSCAP Borneo) is a Sarawak-based research and conservation project founded by wildlife ecologist, John Mathai, to study the wildlife of the Se'la'an Linau Forest Management Unit (FMU) in the mountainous headwaters (ulu) of the Baram River in the Kelabit Highlands of NE Sarawak. Camera trapping by Mathai and his colleagues revealed the highest reported number of Hose's Civet encounters anywhere in Borneo together with detections of Clouded Leopard, Marbled Cat and the endemic Bay Cat. Two other rare endemics, the giant Tufted Ground Squirrel and Bulwer's Pheasant were also commonly detected, often at higher altitudes. Access: The Kelabit Highlands are one of the most scenic areas of Borneo. Flights to Long Lellang depart from Miri and a variety of study trips can be arranged via a local NGO, the Society of Wilderness Sarawak (SOW Sarawak).
See www. hoscap-borneo.org/

Camera trap photo by HOSCAP Borneo.

MONGOOSES

HERPESTIDAE **World:** **34** spp. **Borneo:** 2 spp. In India and many parts of Africa mongooses are known to attack and kill poisonous snakes such as cobras, a behaviour not yet observed in Borneo. The two mongooses found in Borneo are usually solitary, unlike many African mongooses such as the Meerkat, which forage in groups. Both Bornean mongoose species are absent from Kinabalu.

1 SHORT-TAILED MONGOOSE *Urva brachyurus* **HB 412, T 228 (< 55% of HB), Wt 1–1.5kg**

About twice as common as the Collared Mongoose, which is scarce. Found throughout Borneo, with the same range as the Collared Mongoose. Collected at 1,500m in the S Crocker Range. **ID:** Throat pale brown, not yellow-orange like Collared Mongoose's. Tail shorter and bushier. **Habits:** 'A wild one I saw was running in and out among the stones on the bank of a stream. The stomach of this one was crammed full of cockroaches. It is said to be partially aquatic and to fluff itself out when molested until all its hairs stand on end. It is certainly a good climber. In captivity the Dumbang (Iban name) has one of the best claims to be Borneo's "Speed King". Occasionally it walks, even runs at times but mostly gallops, but to see it shooting in and out of holes and sliding round corners gives one an impression of passing shadows.' (Adapted from Banks 1931). Unlike the Collared Mongoose, often found in oil-palm estates. **Call:** Two kept together kept up a continuous cackling that when angry changed to explosive spits (Banks 1931). **Taxonomy:** In Payne (1985) Hose's Mongoose was listed for Borneo based on a single collection by Hose in 1893. *H. hosei* is considered a synonym of *H. brachyurus*, for example in Corbet & Hill 1992 and Patou et al. 2009. It is illustrated opposite as a pale morph of the Short-tailed Mongoose. **Taxonomy:** Palawan race was split from *U. brachyurus* on DNA by Veron et al. (2015). **Range:** Malaya, Sumatra. **Borneo race:** *Herpestes brachyurus* now *Urva brachyurus rajah.*

ROBERT W. SHELFORD (1872–1912) was the curator of the Sarawak Museum for 7 years (1897–1905). He was an acute observer of nature and a keen entomologist, and his book, ***A Naturalist in Borneo* (1916)**, is an unrecognized classic. Shelford was a world expert both on insect mimicry and on cockroaches *Blattodea*, which are both diverse and abundant in Borneo, with more than 200 species recorded (George Beccaloni). In Borneo cockroaches are found in caves, in the leaf litter on the ground and high in the canopy hiding amongst epiphytes. Illustration shows *Sundablatta pulcherrima*, an unusual diurnal Borneo endemic with aposematic markings, suggesting that this cockroach might be nasty to eat. The type was collected by Shelford in 1906 near Kuching.

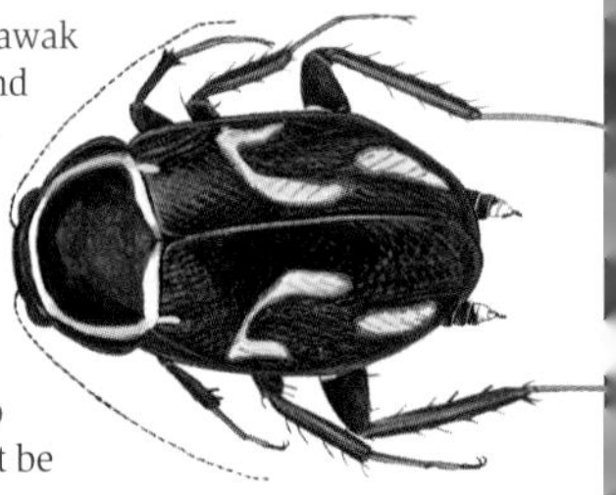

2 COLLARED MONGOOSE *Urva semitorquata* **HB 430, T 280 (60% of HB), Wt 1–1.5kg** **Scarce**

[*Herpestes semitorquata*] Least common of the two Bornean mongooses. Scarce inhabitant of lowland forest, plantations and cultivation, recorded throughout the lowlands of Borneo from Sabangau to 1,200m on Gng Dulit. **ID:** Pale yellow-orange throat. More or less obvious pale yellow stripe behind ear similar to stripes on necks of some treeshrews, such as *Tupaia tana* and *T. dorsalis.* **Habits:** Camera trapping by Wilting (2010) showed that the Collared Mongoose was active 24 hours a day, whilst the Short-tailed was only active during the day or crepuscular. **Diet:** 'The only other mammals that foraged somewhat like treeshrews in the same habitat were the two diurnal mongooses which meandered through the forest, nosing the ground, frequently digging into it for prey. These are likely to compete with large treeshrew for invertebrates hidden under the surface leaf litter. Unlike large treeshrews, I saw these mongooses enthusiastically digging quite deep holes in the clay below the litter, but I never saw what they pursued.' (Emmons 2000). Puri (2005) notes that Penan hunters of the Kayan Mentarang NP claim that mongooses associate with Bearded Pigs, so that seeing a mongoose indicates that pigs are nearby. **Range:** Sumatra (rare). **Borneo race:** *U. s. semitorquatus.*

APOSEMATIC MARKINGS OF THE COLLARED MONGOOSE The mimicry of a Malay Weasel by a rare morph of the Collared Mongoose (Ross, Hearn et al. 2012) is a rare form of Müllerian mimicry. It is even more curious that the normal Collared Mongoose appears to mimic a treeshrew with a white shoulder-stripe, possibly to fool potential prey. The Penan Benalui of Kayan Mentarang do not eat mongooses because of the bad smell of the flesh (Puri 2005). This is probably the result of a diet of poisonous millipedes, beetles and cockroaches (p. 124, poisonous beetles; p. 129, poisonous spiders; p. 150, toxic treeshrews).

1

1

Pale morph

2

2

Red morph

Reddish morph Five out of 86 Collared Mongooses camera-trapped by Ross & Hearn were bright orange, most likely mimicking the Malay Weasel.

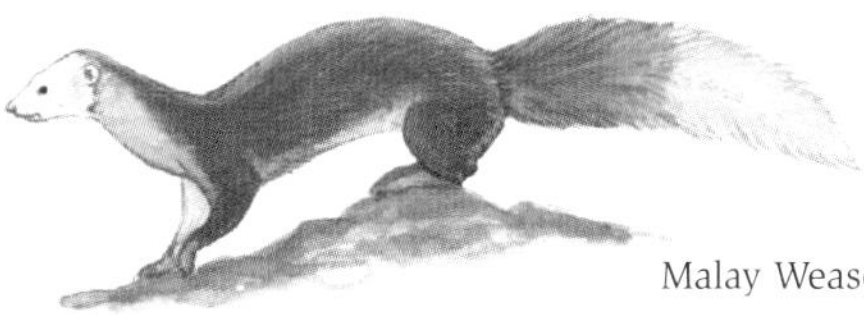

Malay Weasel

FELIDAE **World:** 37 spp. **Borneo:** 5 spp. with 1 endemic, the Bornean Bay Cat. Apart from the Leopard Cat, all Bornean cats are scarce forest dwellers ranging in size from a small domestic cat (Flat-headed Cat) to the size of a large dog (Clouded Leopard). Bornean cats are all solitary. The Bay and Marbled Cats are most active by day, whilst the Clouded Leopard, Leopard Cat and Flat-headed Cat are nocturnal or crepuscular. **Diet:** All cats are carnivorous (meat or fish eating), powerful hunters with sharp teeth and retractable claws designed for catching, holding and eating their prey. Their claws are retractable so they do not blunt as happens in dogs. **Breeding** Cats average 90 days gestation with the ability to have large litters. In seasonal climates, populations rapidly increase when food is abundant later collapsing during the following lean season.

Appearance Cats' coats combine both camouflage and aposematic patterns. This is best seen on Clouded Leopards, where the clouds mimic the appearance of leaf bunches seen from below, whilst the prominent neck-stripes warn of serious danger. The Clouded Leopard, Marbled Cat and Leopard Cat have white spots on the backs of the ears. As in some squirrels, these may have evolved to mimic a pair of eyes on the back of the head to deter attacks from the rear.

Scent Unlike dogs, most cats hunt by sight not by scent, the Clouded Leopard seems to be an exception. See pg. 276. Male cats mix scent from anal glands with urine, which is sprayed on territorial boundaries to advertise their presence to both other males and receptive females.

Calls Cats use a variety of mews and purrs to communicate. Caterwauling sounds made by breeding cats have not been recorded in Bornean wild cats. Clouded Leopard males make long, deep moaning calls when breeding.

Borneo's missing cats Three Sundaland cats, the Asian Leopard, tiger and Fishing Cat, are absent from Borneo, probably due to extinction. The tiger most likely became extinct in Borneo within the last 500 years (pp.18 and 370).

Comparative Abundance of Borneo's Wild Cats Camera-trap surveys show that only the Leopard Cat is common. Clouded Leopards and Marbled Cats are very scarce and the other 2 cats are very rare. Note that sampling bias likely over-estimates populations of Clouded Leopard (large size) and under-estimates Marbled Cat (arboreal habits), Bay Cat (does not use trails) and Flat-headed Cat (confined to river banks and swamps).

CAT SPECIES	(1) D'kot	(2) Danum	(3) Danum	(4) Tabin	(5) Tabin	(6) K'bakan	(7) S'bgu	Totals
Leopard Cat	192	757	22	7	15	23	21	1037
Clouded Leopard	20	210	5	5	0	15	22	277
Marbled Cat	2	19	2	2	0	9	3	37
Bay Cat	2	7	2	2	0	8	0	21
Flat-headed Cat	4	0	0	0	0	1	7	12

(1) Deramakot (logged): Mohamed et al (2009), (2) Malua (logged): Ross et al (2007) (3) Danum (virgin): Ross et al (2007), (4) Tabin (logged): Bernard et al (2012), (5) Tabin(oil palm): Bernard et al (2012), (6) Kalabakan (logged): Wearne et al (2013), (7) Sabangau (peat-swamp): Cheyne & Macdonald (2011).

Important Note: Further research indicates that Marbled Cats are more common than Clouded Leopards in virgin forest but decline in logged forest, whilst Clouded Leopard populations benefit from logging. See the species accounts.

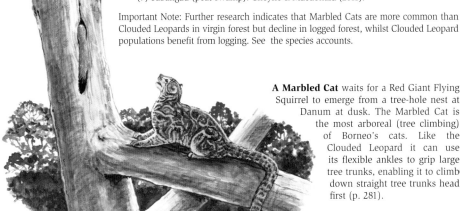

A Marbled Cat waits for a Red Giant Flying Squirrel to emerge from a tree-hole nest at Danum at dusk. The Marbled Cat is the most arboreal (tree climbing) of Borneo's cats. Like the Clouded Leopard it can use its flexible ankles to grip large tree trunks, enabling it to climb down straight tree trunks head first (p. 281).

Bornean Clouded Leopard
Neofelis diardi
Rare shy inhabitant of primary and logged forest. Rests in trees during the day. Hunts on the ground at night. The size of a large dog. Males are *c.* twice the weight of females (p. 276).

Marbled Cat ***Pardofelis marmorata***
Uncommon. Usually seen in tall forest trees at night, but on the ground during the day. Size of a large domestic cat with an enormous long, furry tail (p. 280).

Leopard Cat ***Prionailurus bengalensis*** Most common wild cat. Active at night on the ground in disturbed forest and along edges of oil-palm plantations. Size of a local domestic cat. Distinguished by heavy spotting on a yellow-orange background (p. 286).

Bornean Bay Cat ***Catopuma badia***
Rare inhabitant of the primary forest floor most active during the day. Size of a small dog, with a plain coat varying from orange to grey (p. 282).

Flat-headed Cat ***Prionailurus planiceps***
Smallest Bornean wild cat. Size of a small domestic cat. Rare inhabitant of river banks and swamps. Strictly nocturnal. Distinguished by plain grey-brown coat, short tail and distinctive face markings (p. 284).

CLOUDED LEOPARD

BORNEAN CLOUDED LEOPARD *Neofelis diardi borneensis* **Scarce**

Female: HB 87cm, T 77cm, W 11kg; Male: HB 104cm, T 79cm, W. 24kg (see Najera et al 2017) The largest wild cat in Borneo, thinly spread in forested areas from coastal mangroves to 1,800m on Mt Dulit. The rarest and least known of the world's 6 big cats. Although protected by law, poaching (normally incidental to pig hunting) has made the Clouded Leopard both scarce and shy. Clouded Leopard preferred prey, Bearded Pigs are most abundant at the ecotone between forest and oil palm, but this is also where most hunting takes place. A camera-trap survey by Jedediah Brodie in Pulong Tau (NE Sarawak) showed that Clouded Leopards did not occur within one day's walk from human settlements.

ID Males are larger and twice the weight of females indicating major differences in prey and hunting strategies between the sexes (p. 278). Both very pale and melanistic (black) individuals occur. The grey background fur of young animals tends to pale with age.

Habits Surveys show that Clouded Leopard density increases after logging due an increase in favoured prey, including pigs and sambar deer. Clouded Leopards hunt at night and rest high on a tree branch or cliff during the day. Captive males frequently kill females when mating with a bite to the back of the neck.

Range Clouded Leopards do not hold exclusive territories and both sexes have overlapping ranges with males ranging much further than females (Hearn and Ross: Females est. 21 km^2 and males 45 km^2).

Prey partitioning between males and females Based on camera traps placed randomly in logged forest Wearne et al (2013) found that larger males preferred to use game trails and logging roads, whilst smaller females avoided trails, possibly to avoid attacks by males. It is also likely that males and females partition prey resources with males targeting large pigs on ridge top pig trails and logging roads, whilst the lighter females target smaller primates in the canopy where there is no competition or danger from males.

Diet A large variety of prey including porcupines, pangolins and otters have been recorded. Particular favourites are Bearded Pigs and Proboscis Monkeys. Young Orangutans are attacked but adults are usually left alone. Most large cats kill by gripping the throat of the prey. Clouded Leopards use their giant canine teeth to cut the spinal cord on the back of the neck leaving a pair of distinctive punctures on their prey (see Puri 2005). There are no confirmed attacks on humans.

Taxonomy A recent split from the Clouded Leopard of mainland Asia *Neofelis nebulosa*. See Buckley Beason et al (2006) Kitchener et al (2006), and Wilting et al (2007).

Range Extinct in Java. Confined to Sumatra and Borneo, with guesstimated 'normal' populations of: Sabah (750), Brunei: (150), Sarawak: (100), Kalimantan: (2000). Borneo total: (3,000). Following forest masting and successful pig breeding, local Clouded Leopard populations are likely to double temporarily before returning to a 'lean season' norm. Borneo race: *N.d borneensis*, Sumatran race: *N.d diardi*.

WHERE TO SEE CLOUDED LEOPARDS Clouded Leopards are seen regularly by tourists at only 5 sites, Deramakot, Danum BRL, Danum DVFC, Tabin and the Kinabatangan River, all in E Sabah.

Deramakot FMU Currently the top site in Borneo, p. 338.

Kinabatangan River Clouded Leopards have been seen hunting Proboscis Monkeys many times but are generally shy due to poaching. A long-term Clouded Leopard satellite tracking study led by Benoit Goosens is based at the Danau Girang Field Centre, p. 342.

Tabin Willdlife Reserve Clouded Leopards are resident in the forest near the Tabin Resort but quite shy. A pig kill was found cached on the first floor of the Lipad mud volcano tower by Wilting, p. 344.

Danum BRL Guides report that Clouded Leopards appear roughly once a month near the Lodge, at which time all the resident mouse deer and pheasants vanish. Due to the lack of poaching tourists are usually ignored.

Danum DVFC Clouded Leopards are regularly seen in the adjacent logged forest on night drives, p. 346.

Flehmen Response Clouded Leopards are nearly always photographed with their lower jaw hanging down. This maximizes the airflow over scent sensors in the Jacobson's organ (vomeronasal organ) at the back of the mouth, known as the flehmen response, indicating that unlike most wild cats Clouded Leopards mainly use scent, not sight, to detect their prey (Joanna Ross).

Adult male Clouded Leopard on the Tomanggong Road, Tabin at 4.30 a.m., 10 Oct 2010. This large adult male had a swollen paw (rear right-hand side) and was limping. Note also the open mouth.

Young male Clouded Leopard (with his mother) on the Danum Borneo Rainforest Lodge access road, 9 p.m., 28 Oct 2011. Young Clouded Leopards usually have greyish background fur that lightens with age. Note the open mouth. (Photo: Cosmo Phillipps)

CLOUDED LEOPARD ECOLOGY

The extreme sexual dimorphism between male and female Clouded Leopards results in different foraging ecology. Males walk very long distances along pig trails repeatedly covering the same ground whilst females either actively avoid game trails and hunt cross country or spend a lot of time in trees waiting to surprise primates. Males and females probably feed largely on different prey, males on larger pigs and deer and females on primates and small ground mammals. The similar results from different habitats indicate that sexual dimorphism rather than habitat differences lead to resource partitioning. See camera trap results below.

Clouded Leopards Sabangau 2009–2011 (1)

Trap days 35,129	Captures	Ind. Captures	Captures multiple X
Males	61	5	12
Females	3	1	3
Cubs	0	0	0
All	64	6	

Clouded Leopards Sabah 2007–2013 (2)

Trap days 46,865	Captures	Ind. Captures	Captures multiple X
Males	470	34	14
Females	58	26	2
Cubs	4	4	1
All	532	64	

(1) Cheyne et al (2013) Population Ecology of *Neofelis diardi.*
(2) Hearn et al (2017) Responses of Sunda clouded leopard population density to anthropogenic disturbance.

Logging benefits Clouded Leopard populations only when poaching is controlled

'Logging' and 'logged forest' are catch-all words for many different practices. Generally the longer the period since logging the greater the benefit to Clouded Leopard prey. Both camera trapping and anecdotal reports indicate that when dipterocarp forest is logged in small coups on a sustainable 30+ year cycle the mosaic of new growth in the forest benefits browsers such as pigs and sambar deer. Provided that poaching is controlled. Clouded Leopards benefit from an increase in prey species. However, unsustainable logging practices and uncontrolled hunting have serious adverse effects on all wildlife including Clouded Leopards.

One might expect that if logging only benefits large prey species, male Clouded Leopards would benefit more from logging than females, but this hypothesis has yet to be researched.

Site	Primary Habitat	Poaching	CL Density/100 km²
Crocker Range NP	Virgin hill forest	High	1.39
Kinabatangan	Thin strip of virgin lowland forest	High	1.54
Danum Valley	Virgin lowland forest	None	1.73
Tawau Hills	Virgin lowland and hill forest	Low	2.23
Tabin Wildlife Reserve	Regenerating logged forest 20 yrs +	Low	2.66
Ulu Segama FR	Regenerating logged forest 20 yrs +	Very low	3.10

Hearn et al (2017) Responses of Sunda clouded leopard population density to anthropogenic disturbance.

Male Clouded Leopards weigh twice as much as females, occupy very large ranges and walk long distances at night following the same routes along logging roads and ridge tops to target Bearded Pigs which use the same game trails.

Female Clouded Leopards are half the weight of males, occupy smaller ranges, are much less likely than males to be camera trapped and re-trapped and are often seen in trees whilst males are mostly encountered on pig trails on the ground. It is likely that females are more sedentary than males and target the local primate troops by hiding and waiting in the canopy. This makes sense because females are too small to kill large adult pigs whilst adult male Clouded Leopards are too heavy to chase primates through the canopy. Photo shows an exhausted female resting after an unsuccessful chase after a gibbon family at Danum BRL (Photo Sam Woods, Tropical Birding).

Extinction of tiger and leopard in Borneo

In the Malay Peninsula 3 large cats co-exist in Taman Negara, the tiger, leopard and Asian clouded leopard. Borneo almost certainly hosted 3 large cats during a dryer colder climate in the past (pp. 18–19).

Why does Borneo now have only one large cat? Over the last 10,000 years as Borneo became wetter and tall dipterocarp forest replaced dry grassland, both grazing animals and their large feline predators were starved out. Only Clouded Leopards are small and agile enough to catch canopy primates. Canopy primates provide a fall back food for Clouded Leopards during lean seasons between masting episodes in dipterocarp forest.

THE ECOLOGY OF FEAR At Sepilok (Sabah) the Clouded Leopard is locally extinct but hunting by humans for pigs along the oil palm/forest ecotone is commonplace.

Ross et al (2013) found that at Sepilok pigs were most active at night whilst in areas where Clouded Leopards are common and hunters are absent Bearded Pigs were most active during the day. Female pigs with young were almost exclusively diurnal in these locations.

Female Clouded Leopards target gibbons, macaques, proboscis and langurs. These primates roost communally and move their roosting sites every night probably to avoid 'sit and wait' Clouded Leopard predation.

MARBLED CAT *Pardofelis marmorata* HB 658, T 736, W 2.5–5kg Rare forest cat

Found throughout forested Borneo up to 1,780m on Kinabalu (Paul Carter 2016). At Sabangau peat swamp camera traps recorded 22 Clouded Leopard captures but only 3 Marbled Cat captures (Cheyne et al 2011).

ID Size of a large domestic cat with a very long, very thick, furry tail, which is always longer than body. Less than half the weight of a female Clouded Leopard. In comparison the fur is not as distinctly marked and the head is marked with stripes not spots. Fur colour varies from reddish to grey brown and occasionally black.

Diet Lim (2001) in Malaya found that 2 shot specimens had eaten a tree squirrel, a Long-tailed Porcupine, a Leopard Cat and a partridge. One collected by Davis (1962) near Sandakan had caught a rat on the ground. At Danum seen waiting for a flying squirrel to emerge from its hole. Only rarely enters oil palm to hunt rats.

Habits from camera traps Camera trapping by Ross & Hearn found that the Marbled Cat is the least nocturnal Bornean wild cat most often recorded between dawn and midday on the ground. The density is highest in virgin forest and falls in logged forest.

Habits from observation According to Danum BRL guides Marbled Cats are usually seen in trees at night and are more common than Clouded Leopard which are seen on the ground at night. A possible explanation is as follows; 1. We know from observations that the Marbled Cat is the most arboreal Bornean cat. 2. In virgin forest Marbled Cats probably specialize in catching flying squirrels emerging from tree holes at night (illus. p 274). A shortage of squirrel holes means that vacant holes are soon reoccupied. Marbled Cats probably visit all the squirrel holes in their range on a regular circuit. Travelling to new squirrel holes (during the day) would be fastest on the ground. Logging large trees reduces squirrel holes and therefore both the squirrel and Marbled Cat populations.

Range N. India south to Malaya, Sumatra. Borneo race *F. m. marmorata*.

Relative Abundance of Marbled Cat compared with Clouded Leopard

Camera trapping by Hearn and Ross in different forested sites in central Sabah showed that Marbled Cats (MC) were most common in virgin lowland forest at Danum where they were twice as common as Clouded Leopards (CL). In logged forest at Ulu Segama, Marbled Cats were only half as common as Clouded Leopards. Thus logging appears to benefit Clouded Leopards but has a negative effect on Marbled Cats, whilst poaching is negative for both. RA = No. of trap nights required for individual captures. High numbers = least common.

Site	Forest	Poaching	Trap days	CL	RA	MC	RA
Sepilok	Virgin small area	High	2054	0	0	0	0
Kinabatangan	Thin strip virgin	High	4340	5	868	3	1446
Malua	Logged	Very high	3869	6	645	3	1290
Crocker	Virgin hill	High	4059	8	507	5	811
Tawau	Virgin hill	Low	17397	12	1450	28	621
Tabin	Logged	Low	6462	9	718	13	497
Ulu Segama	Logged	Very low	2847	11	258	6	474
Danum	Virgin lowland	None	5837	9	648	17	343
Totals			**46,865**	**60**		**75**	

Source: Hearn & Ross (2016) The First Estimates of Marbled Cat Population Density from Bornean Primary and Selectively Logged Forest. All records refer to identified individuals.

Marbled Cat hunting for rats at night in oil palm at Tabin. (Photo: Cosmo Phillipps.)

Marbled Cat climbing down tree trunk head first whilst a Black Flying Squirrel looks on from the safety of a tree hole. The relatively enormous tail of the Marbled Cat indicates that it is a specialist hunter of canopy mammals at night, and large flying squirrels probably make up a large part of Marbled Cat diet in virgin forest.

In Borneo only Clouded Leopards and Marbled Cats can climb down bare tree trunks head first, due to the highly elastic tendons in their hips and ankles (supinatory ability). This allows them to flatten their bodies against tree trunks and use their claws to grip the curve of a trunk.

BAY CAT *Catopuma badia* **HB 660, T 400, Wt 3–5kg** **Rare endemic**

[*Felis badia*] Borneo's rarest and least known wild cat is endemic to Borneo, with scattered records from throughout the lowland forests up to 1,460m at Pulong Tau in the Kelabit Highlands of Sarawak, Brodie and Giordano (2009). An unusual sight record in 1970 of a Bay Cat on the Kiau View Trail at Kinabalu Park headquarters (1,650m) is probably related to a period of rapid forest destruction in the Bundu Tuhan Valley below, which forced locally resident mammals to retreat to unsuitable habitat higher up Kinabalu. Most records in Sarawak are from banks of rivers, from the coast to the hills (see below). A camera-trap survey of peat-swamp forest at Sabangau, comprising 5,777 trap nights that resulted in 22 Clouded Leopard, 21 Leopard Cat, 7 Flat-headed Cat and Marbled Cat records, failed to photograph the Bay Cat (Cheyne & Macdonald 2011). Camera trapping at Sg. Ingei in Brunei found Bay Cats locally common.

ID Most Bay Cats are roughly the size and colour of a local hunting dog, but with a much longer, straight tail that is held low rather than upright like that of a dog. Dark melanistic morph Bay Cats have also been recorded.

Habits The extreme rarity of this cat indicates that it travels the forest floor of large areas of primary forest and is probably non-territorial. The most likely predator would be the Clouded Leopard.

Diet Most camera-trap photos were taken in the early morning before 11 a.m. and this cat has never been seen in a tree, which indicates that it hunts for medium to small terrestrial birds and mammals. The relatively small size of the Bay Cat allows it to creep into the tunnels in thick undergrowth used by ruminating (resting) mousedeer, which would be inaccessible to Clouded Leopards.

Taxonomy Closely related to much larger Golden Cat of continental Asia, not found in Borneo.

IS THE BAY CAT MOST COMMON IN LOGGED FOREST? At the heavily disturbed Kalabakan FR in SE Sabah, Wearne et al. (2013) obtained 8 camera-trap captures of Bay Cats compared with 15 for the Clouded Leopard and 9 for the Marbled Cat – the most dense Bay Cat population ever found in Borneo. Wearne hypothesized that this was due to the random placement of camera traps. In most camera-trap surveys the cameras are placed next to game tracks, logging trails and salt licks, the optimum sites for detecting large mammals. It appears that either the Bay Cat avoids game trails through fear of encountering Clouded Leopards, or more likely it travels 'cross country', avoiding game trails like the mousedeer and ground birds that probably comprise most of its prey.

Lesser Mousedeer chased by a Bay Cat running to a river Mousedeer are expert swimmers and head downhill towards the nearest river when threatened. They can stay submerged for up to 5 minutes and swim long distances underwater. See Puri 2005 and Meijaard et al. (2010). The plain counter-shaded colouring of the Bay Cat matches that of mousedeer exactly. It would not be surprising to find that the Bay Cat specializes in hunting mousedeer and frequently ends up chasing them into rivers and catching them in the water, although this has yet to be recorded. Note the Bay Cat's curious tail, which is flat beneath like an otter's tail and counter-shaded like the body of a fish. Camera trapping at Tabin showed that the early morning crepuscular activity pattern of Lesser Mousedeer coincides almost exactly with the activity pattern of the Bay Cat.

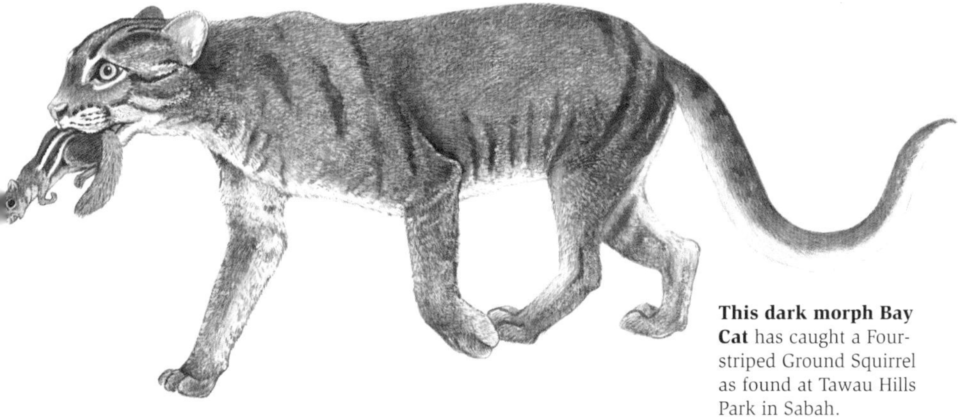

This dark morph Bay Cat has caught a Four-striped Ground Squirrel as found at Tawau Hills Park in Sabah.

Bay Cat illustration by Joseph Wolf of the type specimen collected near Kuching. The Bay Cat was first described by J. E. Gray in the *Proceedings of the Zoological Society of London* in 1874 from a skin collected by A. R. Wallace from the Batang Lupar river near Kuching on his expedition to collect Orangutans and other animals in Sarawak in Nov 1854–Jan 1856. It is possible that Sarawak's capital city was originally named after this rare wild cat. When the description was published, Wallace was already internationally famous as the author of the best natural history travel book ever written, *The Malay Archipelago* (1869), and as a joint discoverer with Darwin of the theory of evolution by natural selection, first published as *The Origin of Species* in 1859.

FLAT-HEADED CAT *Felis planiceps* **HB 475, T 150, Wt 1.5–2.5kg** **Rare in lowland wetlands**

Small, rare aquatic cat found throughout the forested lowlands of Borneo, most commonly near swamps and rivers. The only sites in Borneo where it is regularly seen at night are on the banks of the Menanggul River, a small tributary of the Kinabatangan River in E Sabah, and along the banks of the Maludam River in SW Sarawak. In camera-trap surveys the least common Bornean cat, probably due to habitat bias as most cameras are placed on forest trails not river banks (see below).

Under-recorded in Kalimantan where no camera-trap surveys have targeted the Mahakam Lakes and Danau Sentarum, both areas known to host this cat. Lyon (1911), listing Abbot's collections from coastal SW Borneo, records 5 Flat-headed Cats from Sg Sempang and Kendawangan, but only 2 Leopard Cats. Wilting et al. (2010) analysed 70 records from Borneo, including 27 museum specimens, and found that the preferred habitat was lowland forest adjacent to large rivers and freshwater lakes. In Sabah recorded along river banks of the forested interior, for example at Danum and Tabin, and in forest swamps at Deramakot. Historical records show that the Flat-headed Cat used to be common around Kuching. There is a recent record of one trapped in a *bubu* fish trap at Buntal near Kuching.

ID Easily confused with similar-sized local domestic grey tabby cats, which may also have a short, stubby tail, although the coat is plain grey-brown, not blotchy like a local tabby's. In fact, some of the cats seen in coastal Malay fishing villages look so similar to Flat-headed Cats that it would not be surprising to find that they shared a recent ancestor. Distinguished by prominent white-and-brown facial markings. Males and females are the same size and weight.

Habits Nocturnal and terrestrial. Along the Kinabatangan and Maludam Rivers normally seen sitting on the river bank at night. A Flat-headed Cat trapped and released at Maludam slid into the water, dived and swam 25m across the river (Gumal et al. 2010). Yasuma (1994) recorded that a captive taken at Bukit Soeharto, E Kalimantan, preferred fish to flesh and sometimes sat in a water tub for half an hour doing nothing. Muul & Lim (1970) note that 'A captive kitten played in a basin of water for hours and submerged his head to seize pieces of fish. He often "washed" objects in water like a raccoon. He pounced on live frogs in the cage, snarled and always carried them at least two meters away from where they were placed. This suggests that in the wild slippery live fish and frogs would not be able to escape back into the water.'

Diet According to Banks (1931) 'this cat is fond of fish having sometimes been caught in a *bubu* or conical fish trap into which it may have got by accident or in attempt at an easy meal'. In 1970, I saw one that had been trapped attempting to steal chickens in a logging camp at Kimanis, W Sabah. This forest has now been converted to oil palm. Bock (1881) records 'these cats are exceedingly common at Biraijan (Negara River basin, S Kalimantan) and like the Malay Civet and Common Palm Civet are unwelcome guests in the village on account of their poultry killing propensities'.

Range S Thailand, Malaya, Sumatra. **Borneo:** Probably holds most of the world population (Wilting 2010).

CAMERA TRAPPING has revolutionized our knowledge of mammal distributions in Borneo. The data can be used in many ways, e.g. looking for correlations between Clouded Leopards and their prey, deer and pigs. Results, however, need to be treated with caution.

Location Bias Cameras set at 1m height along forest tracks will under-record arboreal mammals (primates, Striped Palm Civets, female Clouded Leopards) and mammals that don't use tracks (Bay Cat, mousedeer and also female Clouded Leopards).

Habitat Bias To avoid flooding, camera traps are not set along river banks and so otters and Otter Civets, and Flat-headed Cats are under-recorded.

Size Bias Large mammals, such as pigs, are more likely to trigger the sensor than a rat.

Auto-correlation happens when the same animal appears repeatedly in multiple photographs. Only a few mammals, e.g. Clouded Leopard, can be identified by individual markings but then 2 cameras are needed one for each side of the mammal to avoid double counting.

Statistical Problems Many studies lack good data because of poor layout or few cameras.

Repeat trapping and Temporal Problems Mammal populations vary over time, so only repeat projects based on the same grid can provide reliable population density estimates.

Seasonal Problems In Borneo, seasons are both annual and multi-annual with gaps up to 6 years (p. 12). Only very long-term projects can provide accurate density data.

Other Problems Cameras are often stolen by poachers or flattened by elephants!

See Ancrenaz et al. (2012), Wearne et al. (2013) and Gardner (2014).

Giant River Toads ***Phrynoidis juxtaspera*** secrete a toxic milky poison from the glands on their necks when threatened, thus protecting themselves from attacks by Flat-headed Cats, which hunt for frogs along river banks at night. Female toads can grow to 21cm, almost half the size of the cat.

Flat-headed Cat camera-trapped at Tangkulap forest reserve March 2009 by Mohamed and Wilting IZW, SFD, SWD. Note the second camera + flash in the background, so that both sides of the mammal can be photographed simultaneously to distinguish mammals with distinctive markings e.g. Clouded Leopards.

BORNEAN LEOPARD CAT **MALAY: KUCHING BATU (ROCK CAT)**

BORNEAN LEOPARD CAT *Prionailurus javanensis borneoensis* (Brongersma 1936)

HB 415, T 220, Wt 2.5kg **Common**

Borneo's most common wild cat, found throughout the lowlands and hills in most habitats. One of several mammals that benefits from logging. Camera-trap records from Danum and Ulu Segama FR (Ross & Hearn) show that the Leopard Cat was rare in virgin primary forest, but in the adjacent logged forest it was very common. In some areas where forest adjoins oil palm, for instance at Tabin, it may be locally abundant. Has been seen swimming across the Kinabatangan River (Cede Prudente). Occasionally recorded as road kill in cultivated areas.

ID The size of a local domestic cat but with longer legs. Covered all over with small black blotches on an orange-yellow to tawny background.

Habits Nocturnal and usually terrestrial. May sleep in trees during the day, but does not hunt in trees like the Marbled Cat and Clouded Leopard. A sit-and-wait predator. In captivity highly strung, with both adults and young reputed to be very fierce and untamable. A captive at the Lok Kawi Zoo interbred successfully with a domestic cat. In primary forest at Bukit Soeharto near Balikpapan in E Kalimantan, Yasuma (1994) found that Marbled Cat was seen more often but the Leopard Cat was trapped more often.

Diet Rajaratnam et al. (2007) examined 72 Leopard Cat scats found on the gravel road at Tabin that runs between the logged forest and oil-palm plantation. Ninety per cent of the scats contained remains of rats, principally Whitehead's Maxomys, but also included 4 other rat species. In addition the remains of 2 squirrels, 1 treeshrew, 4 birds, 6 lizards, 3 snakes and 5 frogs were found. From trapping records, Whitehead's Maxomys was the most common rat found in the oil palm – so Leopard Cats appear to be unselective in diet. Prey up to the size of a mousedeer has been recorded. According to Hose (1893), 'This pretty little cat is very fond of stealing fowls, going into villages and taking chickens from beneath the houses.' **Range:** Sumatra, Borneo, Java. Race *P. j. borneoensis* is endemic to Borneo. See Kitchener et al (2017).

WHITEHEAD'S MAXOMYS ***Maxomys whiteheadi*** is the most common rat in oil-palm plantations at Tabin. At night Leopard Cats cross over from the forest to sit and wait inside the oil palm for rats to pass by. Leopard Cats do not live inside oil-palm plantations because of a lack of secure sleeping sites. By providing secure cat-roosting boxes inside oil-palm plantations, plantation owners could possibly reduce losses to rats.

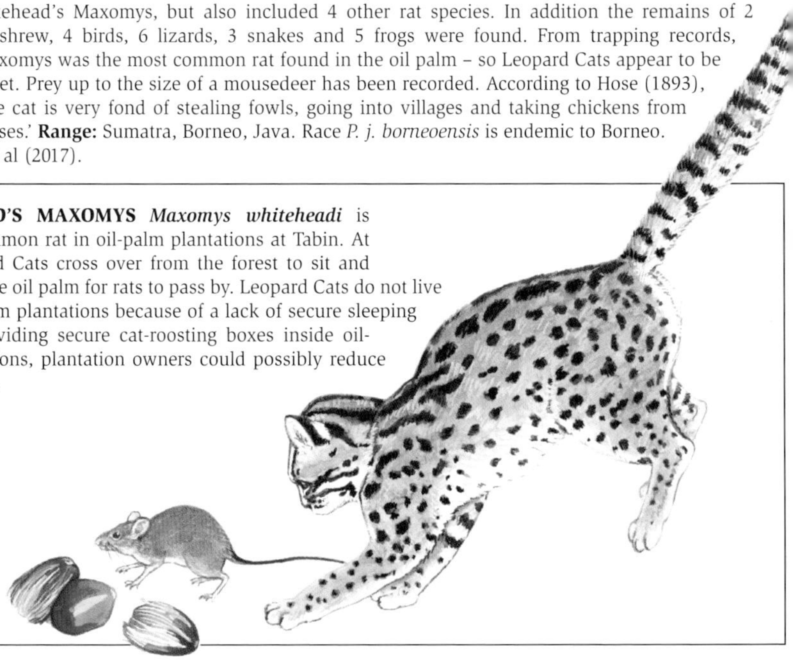

RADIO TRACKING LEOPARD CATS IN BORNEO Two separate studies have radio collared and tracked Leopard Cats in Borneo. 1. Ross & Hearn (2010) radio-collared 9 Leopard Cats in logged forest in the Ulu Segama FR. Home ranges averaged around 3km^2 but 2 male cats moved 25km to an oil-palm estate, although one of them later returned to its original home range. Of the 9 cats, 5 died during the study. Two were killed in traffic accidents and 2 by pythons. 2. Rajaratnam et al. (2007) caught and collared 10 leopard cats in logged forest at Tabin and in the adjacent oil-palm estate. Home ranges also averaged *c.* 3km^2. The collared Leopard Cats preferred to feed in the oil palm even though the density of rats in the adjacent logged forest was almost three times higher. Rajaratnam suggests that Leopard Cats may prefer to hunt in oil-palm plantations despite smaller numbers of rats because the habitat is more open with fewer places for the rats to hide.

Kinabatangan. (Photo: Nick Garbutt; www.nickgarbutt.com)

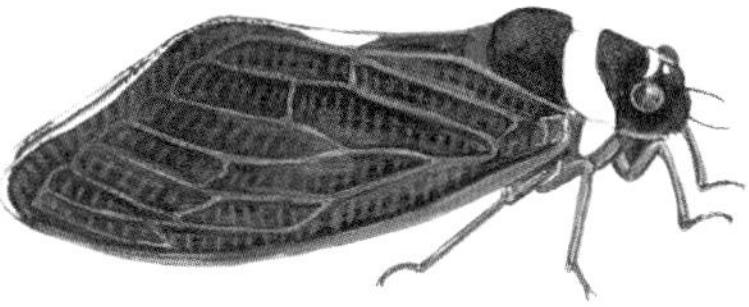

TACUA SPECIOSA (8cm length) is one of several very large cicadas found in Borneo. *Tacua* feed on plant sap and are found from the coast to 2,100m in the mountains. Cicadas often attract attention because of the buzzing calls used by males to lure females, and make a tasty meal for a hungry cat. *T. speciosa* is also found in Sumatra, Java and the Malay Peninsula. See p. 347 where the Six O'Clock Cicada *Pomponia merula* is illustrated.

ELEPHANTIDAE **World:** 3 spp. **Africa:** 2 spp. **Asia:** 1 sp., possibly 2.

BORNEAN PIGMY ELEPHANT *Elephas maximus borneensis* **SH 2.6m, Wt 2,500kg** **Local**

[Asian Elephant, Indian Elephant]. Alfred et al. (2010) estimated the Borneo population as 2,040, all in Sabah, including *c.* 30 nomads that regularly travel into NE Kalimantan (see below). The abundance of elephant-dispersed fruits in Bornean forests indicates that elephants were once common in lowland forests (pp. 38, 291). **ID:** Compared with African Elephants, Asian Elephants are smaller, with smaller ears, a rounded, humped back, a longer tail and 1 'finger' at the end of the trunk, not 2. In most African Elephants both sexes have tusks, whereas only male Asian Elephants have tusks. Bornean elephants are smaller than the elephants found in Sri Lanka and India, but the same size as Malayan and Sumatran elephants (Cranbrook et al. 2007, Nurzahafarina et al. 2008). Therefore Malayan, Sumatran and Bornean Elephants are separate races of what may in future be described as a Sunda Pigmy Elephant. **Habits:** Elephants live in small family groups of 3–9 led by an experienced female 'matriarch'. Groups may join larger groups temporarily. Young males are excluded from the family group when they become sexually active at around 13 years old. Like rhinos and Bearded Pigs, elephants make mud wallows for cooling and to protect themselves against biting flies. **Home range:** Family groups are restricted to flat land, which can be walked by group infants. However, lone adult males often travel in hill forest. Oliver (1978) found home range to be 59–167km^2 (Malaya). Alfred et al. (2012) radio tracked 5 Sabah groups and found home ranges to be 250–400km^2. **Diet:** Due to their bulky, high-fibre diet, elephants must eat almost continuously for up to 18 hours a day. Preferred foods are grasses and bamboos, some palms and soft pioneer vegetation such as *Macarangas* and *Musa*, but they prefer fruit when available. Elephants need access to water daily and visit mineral licks (p. 24). **Call:** Groans, bellows and trumpeting. It is believed Asian Elephants can use low-frequency rumbles (infrasound) to communicate over several kilometres. **Breeding:** Gestation is *c.* 22 months. In captivity life span exceeds 70 years. **Taxonomy:** Fernando et al. (2003), using DNA analysis, concluded that Bornean Elephants were more similar to Sumatran and Malayan Elephants than other Asian Elephants, but because they had been genetically separated from both for *c.* 300,000 years they varied enough to be considered a separate race, *E. m. borneensis.* **Asian Elephant range:** Sri Lanka, India east to S China, south to Thailand. **Sunda Pigmy Elephant range:** Malaya, Sumatra, Java (extinct), Borneo.

THE ELEPHANTS OF SEBUKU, NE KALIMANTAN Surveys by Suyitno & Wulffraat in 2007 and 2012 found that *c.* 30 elephants regularly cross the border from SE Sabah (Kalabakan) into NE Kalimantan via 2 narrow river valleys, the Ulu Agison and Ulu Sibuda, to visit large salt licks and feed on the river-bank vegetation. Matriach-led groups with infants used well-established 'elephant trails' along the valley bottom, whilst solitary males climbed steep slopes between valleys. Several large mud wallows used by elephants were found away from rivers. Solitary males raided farms and small oil-palm plantations, whilst family groups kept to the forest. Preferred foods included young bamboo shoots, and palms including *Arenga undulatifolia* and rattan palm hearts (p. 50). Suyitno notes that when eating the shoots and leaves of a common fern, *Blechnum orientale*, elephants are careful not to harm the fern stem. The elephants incorporated bamboo-clump sites into their routes. With banana clumps the whole inner stem is eaten, but elephants only ever ate small amounts of gingers. Grasses and sedges were also eaten. Wild sugar cane *Saccharum spontaneum*, common along muddy river banks in Borneo, was strongly favoured. *Artocarpus* fruit and leaves were also popular, and the intact seeds were often found in the elephants' dung (p. 74). The carcass of a Bearded Pig killed by a lone elephant in a dispute over fallen *Artocarpus* fruit was found. Mangosteen fruits (p. 376) were popular, but figs (p. 76) were eaten less often. Locals reported elephants swallowed durian fruit whole after wrapping them in leaves (p. 62).

ARE ELEPHANTS AND RHINOS ECOSYSTEM ENGINEERS IN BORNEO? African **Savannah Elephants** living on grassy plains destroy invading tree saplings and help maintain preferred grassland for feeding. Likewise smaller **Forest Elephants** disperse their favoured forest fruit seeds along preferred trails, thereby 'farming the forest'. In Borneo the ecology is not so simple.

Palms Wild palm populations are lowest in E Sabah because elephants destroy the palms by eating the bud, thus destroying preferred habitat (Marsh & Greer 1992). Banks (1982), however, pointed out that because wild sago palms (*Eugeissona* sp.) are rare in E Sabah, this meant that there was no fallback food (sago) for humans, resulting in few humans and much wildlife. **Rhinos** In contrast, rhino-dispersed palms flourish in Sarawak (where elephants have long been absent). Ironically, by dispersing the seeds of wild sago palms thoughout the hills of Sarawak, rhinos provided a fallback food to Penan hunters and swidden farmers, which led to the total extinction of the rhinoceros in Sarawak by hunting (pp. 50, 52 and 297).

Photo above: www.nickgarbutt.com. It is believed that Sunda elephants have longer tails than other elephants so that young elephants can grip their mother's tail when climbing muddy river banks.
Photo below: Calvin Ng. A female matriarch with two young males, probably her sons, on the banks of the Kinabatangan River, East Sabah.

BORNEAN ELEPHANT ECOLOGY

There are two major advantages to being the largest mammal in the forest. Firstly, elephants are safe from attack by large carnivores such as tigers (recently extinct in Borneo, p. 18). Secondly, they can digest fibrous plants low in nutrients in their enormous stomachs. A disadvantage of large size is that elephants need to eat constantly, enforcing a nomadic lifestyle. In Sabah as elsewhere in Asia, wild elephants travel constantly, reappearing at the same sites at regular long intervals. After trashing the local bananas and grasses, they move on so that the plant life has time to recover. **Elephants as ecosystems engineers** Elephants are one of several Bornean animals able to modify their habitat for their own long-term benefit. They achieve this in two ways, by destroying young trees along river banks before they shade out their favoured grass, and by swallowing, defecating and dispersing the seeds of their favoured fruit trees. (Campos-Arceiz et al. 2008, 2011 and 2012, but see p. 288.)

CAN ELEPHANTS AND OIL PALM CO-EXIST?
In areas where oil palm is planted next to forest containing elephants, such as at Tabin and along the Kinabatangan River, elephants are a serious pest of young palms. They eat the growing bud thus killing the palm. A herd of elephants can destroy many hectares of young palms overnight. Once the oil palm reaches elephant height and starts fruiting at 7 years old, however, the palm is safe. When mature oil-palm fruit bunches are harvested the leaves surrounding the fruit are cut. Elephants eat these cut fronds and do no damage to the mature palm. Thus elephants and mature oil palms can co-exist successfully as long as young palms are protected with electric fencing. It should be possible to design the layout of an oil-palm estate so that elephants are allowed to wander in areas of mature palm, whilst areas of young palms are temporarily secured against elephants.

CASSOWARIES AND ELEPHANTS: What do they have in common? New Guinea, the world's largest tropical forested island (786,000km^2 v Borneo's 743,000km^2) has similar botanical diversity to Borneo – some 15,000 plants, many shared or closely related. Both islands were joined to continents until 10,000 years ago, Borneo to Asia and New Guinea to Australia. Both possess a very diverse bird life, but New Guinea has no large native mammals. In Borneo very large seeds are dispersed by elephants, rhinoceroses and Sun Bears. In New Guinea large seeds are dispersed by 3 species of flightless cassowary. These birds swallow Borassus palm fruit up to 10cm in width, and defecate seeds up to 4cm in width. (Baker & Dransfield 2006, Pangau-Adam & Muhlenberg 2014, see opposite.)

The terrestrial seed predator role occupied by wild pigs, porcupines and rats in Borneo is filled in New Guinea by giant ground pigeons and flightless scrub turkeys. New Guinea's flightless birds fill exactly the same size-related seed dispersal and predation guilds that occur in Bornean mammals. This is no strange coincidence, but a clear demonstration of how competition between plants for scarce animal seed dispersers drives the evolution of tree diversity in both Borneo and New Guinea. Similarly, competition to disperse plants by Borneo's mammals and New Guinea's birds drives the evolution of animal diversity in both Borneo and New Guinea (pp. 37 and 47).

ELEPHANTS AND SEED DISPERSAL Obligate elephant-dispersed fruit are fruit so large that they can only be swallowed by elephants, like the 2 largest mangoes illustrated on p. 58. Illustrated opposite are 2 other examples of obligate elephant fruit currently growing wild in the forests of Borneo, mostly in areas where elephants have become extinct, evidence of a vanished megafauna.

PANGI OR KEPAYANG ***Pangium edule***

Football fruit The Flacourtiacea plant family contains a number of trees with large fruit, including several species of *Hydnocarpus*. However, Pangi fruit are the largest, growing to more than 12cm in width. When ripe the smell of the edible soft flesh has been likened to the durian's. Unlike the durian the fruit does not dehisce (split) when ripe, indicating that the Pangi has evolved to be swallowed whole by elephants. The numerous hard seeds contain cyanide and are highly toxic to humans, but can be heat treated and washed to remove the toxins and ground up to make a delicious oily paste, *keluak*.

BINDANG, BORNEO BORASSUS PALM ***Borassodendron borneense.*** [Bandang or Bendang (Kalimantan)]. Locally common endemic forest fan palm to 12m with large fruit over 10cm in width, containing 3 seeds each over 4cm in width. The ripe fruit smells like peaches (Dransfield). In Africa and India related palms are elephant dispersed (Ridley 1930), and it is likely that *B. borneense* owes the current distribution in lowland forests to elephant dispersal. **Brunei sites:** Batu Apoi, Temburong, Lamunin, Ladan Hills, Tutong. **Sarawak sites:** Lambir and Bintulu. In Kalimantan locally abundant throughout lowland NC Kalimantan and E Kalimantan. (Rodman 1978, Rijksen & Meijaard 1999, Dransfield 1972.) Another locally common endemic palm, *Pholidocarpus majadum*, is also probably elephant dispersed (p. 341).

ELEPHANT CONSERVATION

THE ORIGIN OF AND FUTURE FOR BORNEAN ELEPHANTS

Human–elephant conflict Male elephants in musth can be extremely dangerous and result in occasional death or injury in Sabah, but far more elephants are killed in Borneo by humans every year than humans killed by elephants. The main cause of death is poison sprayed on young oil palms. Poisoning elephants is illegal in Sabah but prosecutions are rare. Electric fences can be used to protect young palms but poison is cheaper.

Elephants can survive and thrive in logged forest Virgin dipterocarp forest provides little food for elephants, which prefer to graze along river banks or the forest edge. Following logging, pioneer plants such as climbing bamboos, leguminous vines, and fleshy herbs and shrubs grow along logging roads, providing abundant elephant fodder. In hill forest, logging roads provide access to elephant family groups that cannot climb the steep slopes. Anecdotal evidence is that well-managed production forest as at Deramakot FMU (Sabah) can support more elephants than virgin forest. If this is correct and if production forests are not converted to oil palm, the elephant is likely to be safe in Sabah (p. 338).

ELEPHANT POPULATIONS

Elephant Species Most taxonomists currently recognise 3 species of elephants, 2 species confined to Africa, 1. African Savannah Elephant *Loxodonta africana* (400,000), 2. African Forest Elephant *Loxodonta cyclotis* (200,000) and the Asian Elephant formerly found from Iran to S China and south to Java, *Elephas maximus* (21,000).

Sunda Pigmy Elephants Future taxonomists may split the Asian Elephants into 2 species 1. Indian Elephant (15,000) and 2. Sunda Pigmy Elephants with 3 sub-species, 1. Sumatra (2,600), 2. Borneo (2,000), 3. Malaya (1,400), 4. Java (Extinct).

COUNTING ELEPHANTS VIA THEIR DUNG PILES, 'BOLI' In the dense forests of Borneo elephants are difficult to count, so when he was tasked with estimating the Sabah elephant population, zoologist Ramesh Boonratana used a mathematical formula to count elephants by counting the boli they left behind: elephants per km^2 = Boli per km^2 x Dung Decomposition rate divided by 13.2 (the average number of times an elephant drops boli per day). By establishing a 'boli garden' at the Danum Valley Field Centre, Boonratana found that in the shady Borneo forest elephant boli lasted an average of 153.85 days. (In dryer areas such as Thailand boli may last an extra 10 days or so.) By walking forest transects and counting elephant boli, Boonratana estimated elephant density in suitable habitat at Tabin and in the logged forest reserves surrounding Danum as 0.27–0.29km^2. Note that hilly areas far away from rivers are likely to hold much lower populations – so these figures cannot be used for all Sabah's forests. (See Boonratana 1997.)

DID BORNEAN ELEPHANTS ORIGINATE IN JAVA? The small population of Bornean elephants confined to E Sabah has led to much speculation about their origin. DNA analysis by Fernando et al. (2003) has shown that Bornean elephants diverged from Sumatran elephants around 300,000 years ago. A history of the Sulu sultanate on the island on Jolo (map, p. 15) records that 2 elephants from the Rajah of Java were presented to Sulu in around 1395 (Salleeby 1908). An English trader who visited Jolo in 1814 reported that feral elephants originally from Banjarmasin (S Borneo) were hunted by the Sulus (Hunt 1837), but by 1848 they were gone (Keppel 1853). Further unsubstantiated reports claimed that Jolo's unwanted elephants had been dumped on the Sabah coast, resulting in the current Bornean population.
A Javan origin: In a very detailed and comprehensive paper, 3 of Borneo's leading zoologists, Cranbrook, Payne and Leh (2008), argue that despite the 5 pieces of fossilized elephant found in Borneo to date, it is most likely that Bornean elephants are derived from the feral Jolo elephants, which probably originated in Java. Because the Javan elephant is extinct, DNA can neither prove nor disprove the theory, but Cranbrook et al's conclusion is debatable. Until 10,000 years ago, Borneo was joined to Java by land and shared the same mammals for most of the last million years. The evidence from anachronistic fruit (p. 38) is that elephants were once common along lowland river valleys throughout Borneo, but have been reduced to a small relict population, initially by climate change and latterly by human hunting. Due to hunting pressure elephants only survived in the unpopulated lowland forests of E Sabah (p. 288).

Stogodon trignocephalus (extinct)

Panthera palaeojavanica (extinct)

Elephas maximus borneensis

Elephas hyeudridicus (extinct)

THE EXTINCT ELEPHANTS OF SUNDALAND The ancestor of all elephants originated in Africa, later splitting into numerous species, including the European Mammoth and the American Gomphothere. During the Pleistocene (p. 14), Sundaland was a centre of large mammal diversity, including elephants, rhinoceroses and hippopotamuses. Based on Javan fossils dating to 1,800,0000–40,000 years ago, Sundaland hosted at least 5 species of elephant, all now extinct (Hooijer 1955).

Absence of evidence is not evidence of absence Neither the sedimentary geology nor the wet climate help to preserve fossils in Borneo. Large mammal fossils at Niah (Sarawak) and the Madai Caves (Sabah) (p. 366) are rare compared with Javan fossil sites preserved by a relatively dry climate and volcanic ash. During glacial maximums when Borneo was part of Sundaland, these Javan mammals must also have inhabited the Kalimantan lowlands. The absence of Bornean fossils is not evidence of absence.

Fossils from caves Most mammal fossils in Borneo have been found in caves, carried there for consumption by hunters. Large mammals were probably a small part of early human diets and would have been butchered away from the caves. In Borneo porcupines often enter caves and eat bones, teeth and tusks. These are the most likely explanations as to why the fossil remains of elephants are so rare in Borneo.

RHINOCEROTIDAE World: 5 spp. **Africa:** 2 spp. **Asia:** 3 spp. **Borneo:** 1 sp. The rhinoceroses are members of the order Perissodactyla, which also includes the tapirs (p. 18). In Africa 2 rhino species are sympatric but do not compete ecologically. The Black Rhino is a 'browser' feeding on leaves and twigs, whilst the White Rhino is a 'grazer' feeding on grasses. In Asia the 3 rhino species also partition resources. The Indian Rhino is a grazer, whilst both the Javan and Sumatran Rhinos are browsers. **Fossil rhinos:** Fossil remains show that rhinoceroses have a relict distribution. Over the last million years Asia alone has hosted at least 8 rhinoceros species, 5 of which have become extinct (Louys et al. 2007). www.savingrhinos.org.

1 SUMATRAN RHINOCEROS *Dicerorhinus sumatrensis* **H 1–1.4m, Wt 500–800kg Rare**
[Asian Two-horned Rhinoceros] The world's smallest, hairiest rhino. **Diet:** Generalist feeder on foliage of over 100 species of small tree and understorey shrub. Pushes over saplings with feet and cuts off branches with sharp teeth. According to Dr Zainal of BORA, rhinos prefer the leaves of pioneer trees and vines, especially *Ficus* (p. 76), *Artocarpus* (p. 74), *Spatholobus* (p. 68) and *Macarangas*, and eat fruit when available. Rhinos are especially fond of both the figs and leaves of common secondary forest *Ficus fulva* and *F. aurata*, indicating that fig leaves act as bait for seed dispersal. **Call:** 'When feeding the rhino squeals to itself with pleasure and can be heard some way off. When wallowing it snorts and blows. When suspicious it gives a loud snort, breathes heavily through the nose and finally when really alarmed lets out a squeal' (Banks 1978). **Breeding:** Males occupy large territories overlapping with other males. These territories are marked with dung piles, by spraying of urine and by foot dragging to scent mark scrapes with scent excreted from foot glands. Gestation is 16 months. **Status:** In Borneo only 2 + ? wild rhinos remain at Kutai in E Kalimantan (camera trapped by WWF Indonesia). See p. 299 for captive breeding. **Taxonomy:** Groves (1967) used measurements to list the Bornean *D. sumatrensis* as a separate race, *D. s. harrissoni*, but Amato et al. (1995), using DNA, found that *D. sumatrensis* from Malaya, Sumatra and Borneo were closely related, and recommended that all captive rhinos should be combined for breeding – which has not yet been implemented. **Range:** Extinct apart from 2 wild rhinos and 3 captives in Borneo, and *c.* 100 rhinos in scattered populations in Sumatra.

2 JAVAN RHINOCEROS *Rhinoceros sondaicus* **H 1.6–1.8m, Wt 1,400–2,000kg Extinct Borneo**
[Lesser One-horned Rhinoceros] Fossils from the Niah Caves in Sarawak and Madai Caves in Sabah indicate that Javan Rhinos occurred in Borneo until relatively recently. The Javan Rhino has only 1 horn instead of 2 (Sumatran Rhino), and its neck area is protected with an additional fold of thick skin, presumably against attacks by tigers. Substantially larger than the Sumatran Rhino, so much less mobile in hills and mountains. Gestation period *c.* 16 months. **Status:** Vietnamese population became extinct in 2011. Once so common that it was shot as a pest on Javan tea plantations. An estimated 50 Javan Rhinos remain in the 1,206km^2 Ujung Kulong NP on Java's western tip (map, p. 14).

RESOURCE PARTITIONING BY JAVAN AND SUMATRAN RHINOS Historical accounts indicate that Javan and Sumatran Rhinos share a similar diet and habits, but the smaller Sumatran Rhino is more agile and can 'burrow' through very dense vegetation and climb very steep slopes. According to Talbot (1960), the most frequented Sumatran Rhino paths were stream beds. Next were game trails, ruts in the mud to 1m deep. Rhinos also wandered cross-country. Muddy, vine-covered slopes too steep for men to climb were ascended with ease. Sumatran Rhinos are able to cross swift rivers to 1.5m deep with slippery rounded rocks for a bottom. Thus the Sumatran Rhino was able to survive competition with the Javan Rhino by being a slope specialist retreating to remote mountains, whilst the larger, slower Javan Rhino was hunted to extinction in the lowlands.

3 INDIAN RHINOCEROS *Rhinoceros unicornis* **H 1.6–1.8m, Wt 1,600–2,200kg Extinct Borneo**
[Greater One-horned Rhinoceros]. Large rhinoceros with an estimated world population of *c.* 3,000. Fossils from Thailand, Vietnam and Kedong Brubus in Java indicate that it was once a common inhabitant of Sundaland river floodplains probably including Borneo. Today, Indian Rhinoceroses are confined to river floodplains at the base of the Himalayas, with the largest population in Kaziranga, Nepal. **Diet:** Mainly grass but including sapling leaves and fruit. **Breeding:** Gestation 16 months. Solitary males are significantly larger than females and defend home ranges that overlap with several females, using their sharp lower incisors to fight and often kill rival males. **Habits:** At Chitwan NP, Nepal, Dinerstein (2003) found that rhinos dispersed 38 species of plant in their dung. Both males and females defecate into communal dung piles or latrines to indicate their presence. Both sexes also spray urine to mark their trails. On the fertile alluvial floodplain at Chitwan, rhino density reached 1 rhino per 18ha, and the rhinos had a major impact on local plant ecology both by grazing saplings and by seed dispersal (p. 296).

1

2

3

SUMATRAN RHINO ECOLOGY

SUMATRAN RHINOCEROS AND SEED DISPERSAL The existence of anachronistic rhino-dispersed fruit (p. 38) indicates that Sumatran Rhinos were once abundant in Bornean forest, living at a relatively high density. A forest area the size of Tabin (1,200km^2) would probably have supported 50–100 rhinos, and the whole forest would have been criss-crossed with their trails, wallows and dung piles. While Sumatran Rhinos are mainly browsers on pioneer woody shrubs and lianas, they eat fruit whenever possible, especially mangoes.

Rhino-targeted fruit As explained on p. 37, trees compete to evolve seeds for dispersal by large mammals. The Seed Size Chart shows that for fruit 4–6cm wide there is a vacant disperser slot that only fits the profile of rhino dispersal. Note that many of the plants in the lists that follow are most common in hill forest or along ridges where rhinoceroses would have been common and elephants rarely found.

Fruit seeds dispersed by Sumatran Rhinos from observations *Artocarpus* (p. 74), *Cassia nodosa* mangoes (p. 58), *Entada* bean pods (p. 68), *Parkia* beans (p. 67), *Mezzetia* (p. 190), wild *Citrus*, *Diospyrus* (p. 172), Laran (p. 224) *Canarium* (p. 214), wild mangosteen (p. 376), wild rambutan (p. 216), most figs (p. 76), *Calophyllum* sp., *Payena* sp., *Pouteria* sp., *Baccaurea* sp. References: Abdullah 1985, Lee et al. 1993, Zainuddin et al. 1990, Flynn 1981, Metcalf 1961, Strickland 1967, Strien 1986, Dr Zainal (BORA), Junaidi Payne (pers. comm.).

Fruit with the morphology and ecology that fit the profile for specialist rhino-dispersed seeds Many species of palm, including *Eugeissona utilis* and *E. tristis* (p. 52), at least 20 species of mango (p. 58), at least 2 species of Annonacaea, including *Mezzetia parvifolia* and *Monocarpia kalimantensis*, 2 species of oak, *Lithocarpus turnbinatus* and *L. keningauensis* (p. 60), at least 3 species of the Lauracea, including *Eusideroxylon zwageri* and *E. malangangai*, 18 species of *Barringtonia* (Leythidaceae) and at least 2 species of dipterocarp, including *Vatica resak* (p. 38).

Secondary dispersal by water Sumatran Rhinos prefer to defecate in streams and watercourses (Strien 1986). Many rhino-dispersed fruit are secondarily dispersed by water. Thus preferred rhino fruit would have been some of the first trees to colonize land exposed by falling sea levels during the Pleistocene (p. 38). Stream defecation may also be a means of marking the river valley as a territory (Dr Zainal of BORA).

Ecosystem engineering by rhinos Rhinos traditionally followed the same forest trails year after year, eventually making deep, sunken paths in the forest. Rhinos push over saplings with their feet and prune off the top leaves. The shrub then regrows these leaves, which are again harvested by the rhinos. Similarly, dung piles along trails eventually produce groves of fruit trees favoured by rhinos. Thus rhinos **farmed** their forest trails for maximum productivity, and their loss will irretrievably alter Borneo's rainforest ecology.

***MALLOTUS NUDIFLORUS* – AN ANACHRONISTIC RHINO-DISPERED FRUIT** Research in Chitwan NP (Nepal) by Dinerstein & Wemmer (1988) found that the Indian Rhino is the primary dispersal agent for the large (to 4.5cm wide), hard, bitter fruit of *Mallotus nudiflorus* (*Trewia nudiflora*), Euphorbiaceae. In Nepal *M. nudiflorus* is only dispersed by rhinos, deer and cattle, but not by bats, monkeys or birds. Typically, *M. nudiflorus* trees fruit in June–Oct each year in floodplain forest along the Rapti River, leaving carpets of ripe fruit on the forest floor. Indian Rhinos eat hundreds of these fruit every day, which remain in their gut for up to 7 days. The rhinos deposit their dung in large 'communal latrines' on the grassy river floodplain. Some seeds sprout and grow in the manure. When the river floods, seeds in the latrines float downstream, colonizing any new land created by the flood. Thus the river disperses the seeds downstream whilst the rhino disperses the seeds upstream and away from the river. *M. nudiflorus* is a common floodplain tree of the more seasonal forests of S Borneo, Sumatra and Java, indicating dispersal by Sundaland, Javan and Indian rhinos in the past.

Belian seed dispersal: Trees with an equivalent ecology confined to wet forest in Borneo and Sumatra are the 2 Belian species *Eusideroxylon zwageri* and *E. malangangai*, which have fruit so large that they can only be swallowed whole by elephants and rhinos. As *E. zwageri* is common along rivers in hill forest, it is likely that the Sumatran Rhino was an important disperser of Belian seeds in the past (pp. 38, 244).

Mother and baby Sumatran Rhinoceros ***Dicerorhinus sumatrensis*** feeding on wild mango fruit *Mangifera lagenifera* in the forested hills of Borneo, whilst a pair of Bulwer's Pheasants forages for insects in a dung pile. Many Bornean forest trees, including *M. lagenifera*, fruit rarely but simultaneously at long intervals (masting), which triggers breeding in many Bornean birds and mammals (p. 12).

SUMATRAN RHINO CONSERVATION

THE ALLEE EFFECT is a term used to describe 'Positive Density Dependence', that is a situation where a population of animals or plants grows faster at higher densities, in contrast to NDD, or 'Negative Density Dependence', where a population grows slower if the density is too high. Most animal and plant species are subject to both NDD and Allee Effects. For example, the seeds of Bornean rainforest trees are more likely to be predated the closer they are to the parent tree (NDD), but thinly spread tree species are less likely to be pollinated (Allee Effect). Thus there is an Optimum Density (OD) for most populations at which both survivorship and population growth are highest. With long-living trees in large, stable environments such as virgin Borneo rainforest, tree-species densities will eventually stabilize around the OD. The OD varies between species, but is unlikely to be random as claimed by mathematical ecologists like Hubbell (2001), (pp. 32, 46).

Optimum Density of Sumatran Rhinos Zoologists believe that the Bornean rhino population has been below the **optimum density** for several hundred years, resulting in low reproduction. Potential mates had difficulty meeting, accelerating a population collapse. The solution agreed in Sabah in 2007 has been to capture all remaining wild rhinos and bring them together to one site to manage each individual so as to maximise its potential contribution to producing baby rhinos. The site chosen was Tabin Wildlife Reserve, and the programme is managed by Borneo Rhino Alliance (BORA) under supervision of Sabah Wildlife Department. The tragedy is that this policy came too late within Malaysia, where there appear to be no more wild rhinos, and Indonesia has a different policy. The situation is now so desperate that some Sumatran rhino experts believe that the only way to prevent extinction is to manage all remaining Sumatran rhinos as a single population, using advanced reproductive technologies to boost births.

COLLAPSE OF THE SUMATRAN RHINOCEROS POPULATION IN SABAH Soon after Sandakan was founded, Ada Pryer (1893) reported Sumatran Rhinoceros visiting their garden at night. On a visit to Lamag on the Kinabatangan, the Pryers dined on rhinoceros steak. The last rhino on the Kinabalu Summit Trail was reported in 1924 (Enriquez 1927). The Royal Society Expedition in 1961 found the last evidence of rhinos on Kinabalu on the Eastern Ridge at 3,000m. When the Danum Valley Field Centre was established in 1985, there were active rhino wallows within 2km of the research buildings, but recent camera traps show that there are no remaining rhinos at Danum. Today there are only 3 Sumatran Rhinos left in Sabah, all in captivity at the BORA compound at Tabin.

WORLD POPULATION OF SUMATRAN RHINOS (2015)

Rhinos	Sumatra	Sabah	Kalimantan	Cincinnati Zoo
Wild	*c*. 40	0	2 at Kutai?	0
Captive	4	3	0	0

39 Sumatran Rhinos have died in captivity in the last 30 years due to ignorance of the correct husbandry. However, the breeding of 3 calves at the Cincinnati Zoo beginning in 2001 indicates that this problem has been solved. Recently, a Cincinnati-born rhino, Andalas, fathered a calf, Andatu (2013), at the Way Kambas breeding centre in Sumatra. See Rabinowitz 1995 and Ahmad, Payne & Zainuddin 2013.

THE LAST SUMATRAN RHINOCEROS ON GNG MULU? In 1931, Edwards Banks, the curator of the Sarawak Museum, wrote 'there can at the moment be no fear of the rhinoceros becoming scarce for as many as 36 trophies were brought into Belaga (Upper Rejang River) in two years, not long ago, and I have met men who have claimed to have shot over 30 in the course of their lifetime'. Soon after these foolishly optimistic words were written it became obvious that the rhinoceros was extinct in most of Sarawak.

Gng Mulu, the last rhino refuge in Sarawak. The tourist trail to the summit of Gng Mulu was originally established by local Berawan rhino hunters. The first European to climb Gng Mulu in 1932, Edward Shackleton, was guided by Tama Lilong, who had previously killed a rhino on nearby Gng Tamachu. Rhino trails are easily recognized because they follow ridge tops with frequent mud wallows. Shackleton's party encountered numerous old hunting shelters along the Mulu summit trail. When Banks himself climbed Mulu in 1934, he found fresh rhino tracks on the summit trail at 2,000m. In 1939, Banks went trophy hunting for a rhino in the Paya Maga mountains in the north-east corner of Sarawak on the Sabah border but found none. According to Liz Bennett, David Labang found Sumatran Rhino tracks on the border with Kalimantan in 1987. This is the last official record from Sarawak.

Captive Sumatran Rhino at Sepilok. (Photo:www. nickgarbutt.com)

Borneo Rhino Alliance (BORA; www.borneorhinoalliance.org) is a Sabah-based NGO that evolved from a predecessor NGO, SOS Rhino, in a last-ditch attempt to save the Sumatran Rhino from extinction in Borneo. BORA cares for three rhinos at Tabin while government is building the facilities to hold Tam (Kretam), an old male captured in 2008, Puntung, a female captured in 2011 and Iman, a female captured in 2014. Whilst Tam is keen to breed, both females have severe cysts and tumours in their reproductive tracts (a consequence of not breeding, in turn due to no wild males within their home ranges) making a natural successful pregnancy impossible. Had the Tabin programme been started as envisaged in 1984, it might have been possible to save the Sumatran Rhino through a well-established collaborative global programme.

RHINOCEROS WALLOWS The Sumatran Rhino feeds at night and during the coolest times of day in the early morning and late afternoon, and spends the heat of the day in a cool mud wallow. Illustration shows the last Sumatran Rhinoceros on Gng Mulu, *c.*1934, enjoying a final mud wallow on the Mulu Summit Trail before being killed for its horns, to be used in traditional Chinese medicine. Gunung Api is in the background.

SUIDAE World: 18 spp. **Borneo:** 2 spp. Pigs are omnivorous generalists that can live almost anywhere there is sufficient food, but prefer the safety of the forest understorey. They reach their highest diversity in Africa, with 5 species. In the Americas their ecological niche is occupied by 3 species of peccary. In Asia no location has more than 2 pig species, and in most areas only a single species (Eurasian Wild Boar *Sus scrofa*) survives.

BEARDED PIG *Sus barbatus* **Male: HB 145, Wt 60–200kg, Female: HB 135cm, Wt 45–120kg**

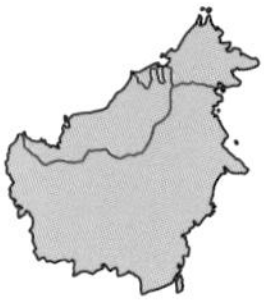

Locally common where forest adjoins oil palm, but hunted out in most settled areas. Pig hunting has provided a staple meat supply for Borneo's interior tribes for over 40,000 years. Bearded Pigs undergo extreme population fluctuations, but the ecology is not yet fully understood. (See Meijaard 2000, 2003 and 2015.) **ID:** Young, blackish Bearded Pigs are easily mistaken for feral domesticated pigs, but adult Bearded Pigs are larger and paler. **Domesticated piglets with stripes** are sometimes seen in forest edge kampongs and domesticated pigs sometimes run wild, so some hybridization is likely. Piglets lose their stripes at 3 months and turn grey/black, becoming paler and whiter as they age, so that old pigs may look all white. The male's upper incisors develop into a pair of large tusks used for slashing upwards in defence. **Diet:** Bearded Pigs are seed predators on oak acorns, chestnuts and dipterocarps. To avoid predation, these trees fruit rarely and then in unison (masting) on average every 4 years (pp. 10, 11, 44, 54 and 60), so Bearded Pigs have evolved to survive in an environment of a rare feast followed by a long famine. Bearded Pigs may starve during the intermast lean period. Fallback foods are believed to be earthworms and beetle larvae (grubs). Pigs also eat large amounts of vegetation, including grass, the primitive fern *Selaginella* and a common herb, *Syndrella* (rumput babi). Bearded Pigs often scavenge dead animals. When the geologist in the Bre-X gold-mining fraud jumped from a helicopter over C Kalimantan in 1997 his body was eaten by Bearded Pigs. For this reason the interior tribes of Borneo do not bury their dead but use platforms (Ibans), holes in cliffs (Orang Sungai) or large ceramic **gusi** jars (Dusun) to dispose of the deceased. **Range:** Malaya, Sumatra, Sibutu and Tawi Tawi (S Philippines). **Borneo race:** *S. b. barbartus*. On Palawan the wild pig is related to *S. barbatus*, but on Balabac it is closer to *S. scrofa*. Recorded swimming 45km between P Sibutu and mainland Borneo (Meijaard 2000).

EURASIAN WILD BOAR *Sus scrofa* **HB 140, T 25, Wt 75–200kg Bunguran Besar (Natunas)**

The most common wild pig throughout Europe and Asia, including the Malay Peninsula and Sumatra. In the Borneo province confined to Bunguran Besar, the largest Natuna Island (p. 386). *S. scrofa* is the ancestor of the domesticated pig, which in Australia and the USA has become a feral pest. There are no known viable populations of feral *S. scrofa* in Borneo, but this may yet happen with the spread of oil palm.

ABSENCE OF *SUS SCROFA* FROM MAINLAND BORNEO It is remarkable that only the Bearded Pig survives on Borneo, whilst Java and Sumatra host two wild pigs (Meijaard 1994).
Competitive exclusion It is likely that *S. scrofa* was once present on Borneo but became extinct. In Malaya and Sumatra, where both species occur, the Bearded Pig is in steep decline, whilst *S. scrofa* is increasingly abundant as land is converted from forest to plantations. Possibly, in lean periods *S. barbatus* can utilize a fallback food in virgin forest unavailable to *S. scrofa*, and vice versa in more open edge habitats.

	ISLAND	**Area km²**	***Sus* sp. 1**	***Sus* sp. 2**	**Total spp.**
WILD	Borneo	743,380	*S. barbatus*	None	1
PIGS	Sumatra	443,066	*S. barbatus*	*S. scrofa*	2
OF	Java	53,588	*S. scrofa*	*S. verrucosus*	2
SUNDALAND	Palawan	14,650	*S. barbatus*	None	1
	Bunguran	1,720	*S. scrofa*	None	1
	Balabac	527	*S. philippensis*	None	1

EURASIAN WILD BOAR *Sus scrofa* is the single species of wild pig found on Bunguran Besar (p. 386) in the Natuna Group. For most of the last 2.6 million years, Bunguran Besar has been a mountain surrounded by the forested lowlands of the Sunda Basin, and many mammals once present on Bunguran Besar, like the Bearded Pig, must have become extinct (p. 173) each time sea level rises turned the mountain into an island.

BREEDING
When food is abundant Bearded Pigs can breed twice a year with a litter of up to 12 each time, resulting in a population explosion.

MASS MIGRATIONS OF BEARDED PIGS The Penan Benalui claim that Bearded Pigs mate when the forest starts flowering. The sow gives birth 90 days later at first fruit fall (Puri 2005). The fruit bonanza continues for 2–4 months. At 6 months the young piglets feed themselves and the sow mates again – potentially producing 2 litters of 12 piglets in 1 year, resulting in rapid population growth.
Bearded Pigs migrate annually between patches of forest flowering in different areas of interior hill forests (see Puri 2005 and Dove 1983). Logging and forest fragmentation have reduced these annual movements.
Pig population explosions take place on rare occasions when one dipterocarp masting immediately follows another or by the masting of oaks, chestnuts or bamboos in adjacent hill forest as happened in the Upper Baram of Sarawak in 1983. As documented by Caldecott (1985 and 1988), a mass migration of over 800,000 Bearded Pigs resulted. This lasted from 1983 to 1984, and started and ended in the hill oak forests between Sarawak and Kalimantan. A previous mass migration also followed a double dipterocarp mast in 1959.

PYTHONS AND BEARDED PIGS
Pythons both eat and are eaten by Bearded Pigs. Pigs eat small pythons but large pythons swallow deer, pigs and even the occasional human. Two python species occur in Borneo, the **Blood Python** (to 2m) and the **Reticulated Python**, which can grow to 10m – the longest snake in the world. Pythons are common both in forest and around farms. After a large meal these snakes can hardly move and there are many local tales of hunters finding a swollen immobile python. The normal local response (by non-Muslims) is to execute the python and collect both predator and prey for consumption back at the kampong. Young pythons often inhabit the loft spaces in rural dwellings, where they are tolerated for their rat-catching activities. Outgrowing their food supply, they then start emerging at night to feed on chickens, and at this stage they are caught and eaten or taken to the market for sale (p. 176).

RETICULATED PYTHON killing a large Bearded Pig on a Kinabatangan River bank (see Osa Johnson 1966).

BEARDED PIG ECOLOGY

The Bearded Pig is by far the most important mammal in Bornean forests in terms of biomass and ecology, yet no comprehensive study has ever been carried out. This is partly due to the fact that Islam is the predominant religion throughout much of Borneo, and Muslims consider pigs and pig meat to be unclean (p. 173).

Prehistory Bearded Pigs provided most of the meat for humans living in the Niah Caves over the last 40,000 years. No Eurasian Wild Boar (*Sus scrofa*) remains have been found at the Niah Caves. Remains of domesticated pigs first appear *c.* 4,000–3,000 years ago (Cucci et al. 2009).

Subsistence hunting of the Bearded Pig Until recently hunted pigs provided most of the meat consumed by most Bornean interior tribes. Puri (2005) describes the subsistence hunting of the Bearded Pig in the 200,000ha Lurah River valley in the Kayan Mentarang NP (NE Kalimantan) by the Penan Benalui. Hunted pig meat was supplemented with wild palm sago, forest greens, fish, forest fruits and cultivated hill rice, tapioca, sweet potato roots and leaves. On most days around 10% of the adult population was out hunting. Over 21 months 707 pigs were killed, the majority by hunting with dogs. In 6 of these months under 10 pigs were killed each month. However, over 50 were killed each month in the 6 peak migration months. During migrations some meat was abandoned as storage was impossible (no freezers). Nearly all hunting was carried out within a day's walk of *c.* 8,000ha of mixed forest surrounding the village of Long Peliran, comprising 36 Penan (mainly hunter gatherers) and 77 Kenyah (mainly swidden farmers). Puri also recorded the kills of 33 Sambar, 10 muntjac, 9 civets, 9 primates, 6 porcupines and 3 Sun Bears in the same period.

Annual local pig migration patterns Puri recorded annual pig migrations from Aug 1990–Dec 1992. Forest flowering coincided with pig rutting in February. Pregnant sows started migrating through the area in May. Mast fruiting in August coincided with migrating sows with many young piglets. Pig families, often 'led' by an old boar, moved by day over a broad front along traditional routes, returning in reduced numbers 5 months later in December. The hilly topography 'funnelled' the pigs into well-known river crossings, where Penan hunters speared the pigs from the bank and waiting boats. Not all pigs migrated and a few lone males remained after the migrating pigs had left the valley.

Bearded Pig seed predation and seed dispersal Adult male Bearded Pigs use their powerful jaws to crush large, hard seeds such as those of *Eugeissona utilis* (p. 38). However, females and juveniles cannot crush hard seeds (Puri 2005). Wong Siew Te at Danum found few intact seeds in pig faeces. Only tiny seeds like those of *Ficus*, *Fagraea* and *Melastoma*, and the slim, flat seeds of Cucurbitacea (forest melons and cucumbers), survived. At Pasoh (Malaya), Yasuda (2005) found that abundant wild pigs *S. scrofa* only ate 30% of the fallen fruit. The highly toxic seeds of primate fruit like those of *Dysoxylum acutangulum* were eaten by Long-tailed Porcupines, not by pigs (p. 36).

PIGS AS ECOSYSTEM ENGINEERS
Pigs churn up the ground, damaging saplings but also burying seeds such as acorns. Heydon (1997) found that at Pasoh in Malaya pigs were able to break saplings to 3cm in diameter and used up to 136 saplings to make 1 nest. Pigs dig large mud wallows that act as nesting sites for forest kingfishers and frogs, transport hubs for leeches, and watering holes for other mammals and ground birds during droughts. At Gng Palung, due to seed predation by pigs dipterocarps showed no seedling recruitment at all over a 10-year period. The local pig population was only satiated with dipterocarp fruit when masting took place on a regional not a local scale (Curran et al. 1999). Thus major droughts that trigger masting over very large areas were necessary for the successful reproduction of dipterocarps at Gng Palung.

Female Bearded Pigs build breeding nests out of tree saplings, often on dry ridge tops, in which to give birth. Abandoned nests may be tick infested.

Bearded Pigs and Bornean Ground-Cuckoos. When disturbing soil searching for worms, pigs attract pheasants, partridges and ground-cuckoos, which also feed on insects and invertebrates, and provide additional eyes and ears to guard against predators. Penans claim that mongooses also associate with Bearded Pigs (p. 272).

BANTENG AND WATER BUFFALO LOCAL: TEMBADAU AND KEREBAU

BOVIDAE World: 143 spp. **Borneo:** 1 wild bovid, plus domesticated cattle, goats and buffaloes. Bovidae are ruminants with multiple stomachs that use bacteria for digesting grass. Domesticated bovids are the main source of red meat (beef) and milk products eaten by humans. All bovids have horns that grow throughout their lives. Bovids are dispersers of grasses and tropical leguminous beans including *Cassia* and *Accacia*. At Kota Belud (Sabah), domestic cattle disperse the introduced Central American Rain Tree *Samea saman* (p. 66).

1 BORNEAN BANTENG *Bos javanicus* SH 120–170cm, Wt 400–900kg Scarce

[Local: Tembadau] Previously common throughout Borneo along grassy river banks and in abandoned swidden (hill rice) farms in the interior, but now scarce due to poaching. Hedges & Meijaard (1999) found Banteng heavily hunted in the Kayan Mentarang grasslands in NE Kalimantan. Small populations survive elsewhere in Kalimantan. Almost extinct in Sarawak and Brunei. Widely scattered small herds at Danum, Deramakot, Kalumba, Maliau, Malua, Tabin, and Sipitang in Sabah. **ID:** Distinguished from domestic cattle by white rump and white stockings. Females are smaller than males and brown rather than black. **Aposematic markings:** White stockings are probably a warning to snakes in dense grassland. Insides of ears are pink and point forwards when a Banteng is threatened, giving the appearance in the gloom of large eyes on an enormous head. White rump markings may help the herd stay together in the dark. **Habits:** Small herds are most active at dawn and rest during the heat of the day. Sabah Banteng often feed along logging roads at night. **Diet:** Prefers grass to browse (leaves), but eats both. Whitehead recorded Banteng on the Klias Peninsula beaches in search of sea salt, and Banteng often visit salt licks. **Seed dispersal:** Matsubayashi et al. (2007) found that Banteng at Deramakot dispersed grass and bamboo seeds to 3mm in width, as well as the invasive grass *Paspalum conjugatum* and the sensitive plant *Mimosa pudica*. **Breeding:** Natural herds consist of an alpha male together with up to 18 females and young. Solitary males have been excluded from a herd. **Research:** A Sabah survey by Penny Gardner, students from Cardiff University, the Danau Girang Field Centre (Benoit Goosens) and the Sabah Wildlife Department estimated that under 500 Banteng remain in Sabah, where they are frequently poached (see Gardner 2014). **Range:** Three races: 1. *B. j. birmanicus* in continental SE Asia but extinct in Malaya, 2. *B. j. javanicus* in Java only, 3. *B. j. lowii* confined to Borneo.

BANTENG IN AUSTRALIA The largest population of wild Banteng in the world roams free in the Garig Gunak Barlu NP in the Coburg Peninsula near Darwin in N Australia. Around 20 tame Banteng were abandoned in 1849 and the population is now *c.* 10,000 genetically pure animals. The Coburg Banteng are hunted for sport (under licence) and for subsistence by the local aboriginal tribe. Domesticated Banteng (**Bali Cattle**) are common in Kalimantan and wander freely at the forest edge, leading to the possibility of wild hybrids. Adult male Bali Cattle are normally brown rather than black.

HUNTING BANTENG ON THE LIMBANG RIVER In 1858, the British Consul in Brunei, Spencer St John, made an expedition from Brunei Bay up the Limbang River to Gng Murud, passing Mulu on the way. St John and his men boated and walked the outward journey, but constructed precarious bamboo rafts for their return. St John records that they frequently saw Banteng grazing on the river bank. He describes the Banteng as fierce and dangerous and explains how the locals succeeded in the hunt. 'A Bisaya chief with whom I was acquainted killed three Tembadau in the following manner. He was well acquainted with their feeding grounds, and when the young moon gave just sufficient light to discern objects, he allowed his small canoe to drift down the stream near the shore. When he heard the sound of grazing he prepared his spear, and as he passed the wild bull he would hurl it at it, and then pull away out of danger; next morning he would land at the spot and track the wounded beast, and easily slay it when faint from loss of blood.' (St John, S., 1862, *Life in the Forests of the Far East*). **Note:** A few Banteng survive in Mulu NP on the Brunei border, an ideal reintroduction site (p. 353).

2 WILD WATER BUFFALO *Bubalus arnee* SH 150–190cm, Wt 700–1,200kg Extinct in Borneo

[Local: Kerebau] The domesticated water buffalo *Bubalus bubalus*, which is used for ploughing rice fields and pulling loads throughout Borneo, is descended from the Wild Water Buffalo, probably a common inhabitant of the swampy Sunda Basin during the Pleistocene (p. 14). Hose (1893) reported herds of up to 50 in the Miri River swamps, and Banks (1931) found them common around the mouth of the Baram River, Tg Sirik and Ulu Mukah. Banks also describes domesticated buffalo cows breeding with wild bulls. Whether the Wild Water Buffalo in Borneo became extinct from hunting or by interbreeding can only be revealed by genetic research. **Current range:** India east to Thailand and Cambodia.

2 **Domesticated Water Buffalo** ***Bubalus domesticus*** Photographed at Kota Belud. **Migrant Cattle Egrets** ***Bubulcus ibis*** breed in Japan and spend the cold northern winters in Borneo, feeding on the leeches, ticks and flies that pester domesticated cattle and buffaloes. Of the 6 species of egret found in Borneo, only the Cattle Egret feeds on insects, while the rest feed on fish and frogs.

MOUSEDEER OR CEVROTAINS

MALAY: KANCIL

TRAGULIDAE World: 10 spp. **Africa:** 1 sp. **Asia**: 9 spp. **Borneo:** 2 spp. The Tragulidae are the world's smallest deer, with an ancient history dating back 50 million years. Borneo's 2 species are roughly the size of a rabbit, the Lesser being two-thirds the size of the Greater. Both species are common in the understorey of lowland primary forest and forest gaps, becoming scarce in the hills, and have similar habits, described below. Both Mousedeer are most active at dusk and dawn, with Lesser more active in daytime and Greater at night.
ID: The 2 Bornean mousedeer are told apart by differences in size and by throat patterns. **Greater** have 5 white stripes on the throat, whilst **Lesser** have 3. Sideways on Lesser has a single unbroken white throat line, while with Greater the line is broken.
Diet: Mousedeer have 4 chambered ruminant stomachs and are therefore able to digest leaves, but feed mainly on fruit, with fallen figs acting as a staple or fallback food (Heydon & Bulloh 1997).
Seed dispersal: Fallen fruit are gathered and held in large cheek pouches. A mousedeer retires to a dense thicket and regurgitates the seeds (A. Lamb re. durians). At Pasoh, Malaya, Yasuda et al. (2005) recorded Lesser Mousedeer dispersing the 3cm-wide seeds of *Canarium littorale* and *Terminalia citrina*. Dipterocarp seeds (*Shorea maxima*) were predated.
Predators: At night mousedeer often rest (ruminate) with legs folded under on paths and river banks, where they are spotlighted and shot by hunters. Mousedeer are important prey for wild cats. Mousedeer typically flee towards rivers when hunted and swim underwater for long distances to escape (Puri 2005), (p. 282).
Breeding: Male mousedeer have large canines (downwards pointing small tusks) used in fighting other males, but it appears that they fight over females rather than territory. Females are marked by the male with scent glands located under the throat. Females usually mate within a few hours of giving birth.
Contact calls: Variety of soft squeaks and low whistles. A hunting technique used to attract mousedeer is to tap lightly on dry leaves with a stick. According to Tubb (1966), this mimics the sound made by female Lesser Mousedeer, which drum vigorously on the ground with both hind feet together to attract males. Up to 7 bouts of drumming have been recorded, with 8 beats in each bout. Both species drum (Meijaard 2011).

1 LESSER MOUSEDEER *Tragulus kanchil* **HB 450, T 72, Wt 2.25kg** **Common**

Usually less common than Greater but more common at Sepilok. Matsubayashi (2006) calculated home range at *c.* 5ha for males and *c.* 4ha for females. Females and males overlapped home ranges, but no males overlapped. At Danum, Lesser density was 30 per km^2 and 54.4km^2 for Greater (Heydon & Bulloh 1997). **Range:** SW China to Sumatra, Borneo. At Tabin Lesser preferred secondary forest and Greater preferred virgin forest.

2 GREATER MOUSEDEER *Tragulus napu* **HB 550, T 80, Wt 4.25kg** **Common**

The two mousedeer species are sympatric, with the Greater found to 1,200m in the Kelabit Highlands, whilst the Lesser has been recorded to 600m. At Danum, Ahmad (1993) found that males and females had home ranges of *c.* 7.5ha. **Range:** Vietnam south to Sumatra and Borneo. Also on Balabac Island in the S Philippines.

Resource Partitioning by Muntjac and Mousedeer
Mousedeer and muntjac are both common in the forest understorey throughout Sundaland. Research by Farida et al. (2003) on P. Nusakambangan (S Java) found that the diets of mousedeer and muntjac did not overlap. A total of 34 plant species were eaten, but mousedeer ate 90% fruit and 10% leaves, whilst muntjac ate 90% leaves (browse) and 10% fruit. Mousedeer ate 14 species of fruit, including those of gingers, figs, bean pods and palm fruit, whilst muntjac ate the leaves of 20 plants, including figs, macaranga and clerodendrum. When both species ate the same plant, like *Grewia laevigata*, mousedeer ate the fruit whilst muntjac ate the leaves. Occasionally, mousedeer ate leaves and muntjac ate fruit like those of *Canarium littorale*, 7cm long x 3cm widebut see above. **Note:** There is a single species each of mousedeer and muntjac in Java, compared with 2 of each in Borneo, so the ecological parallel may not be exact.

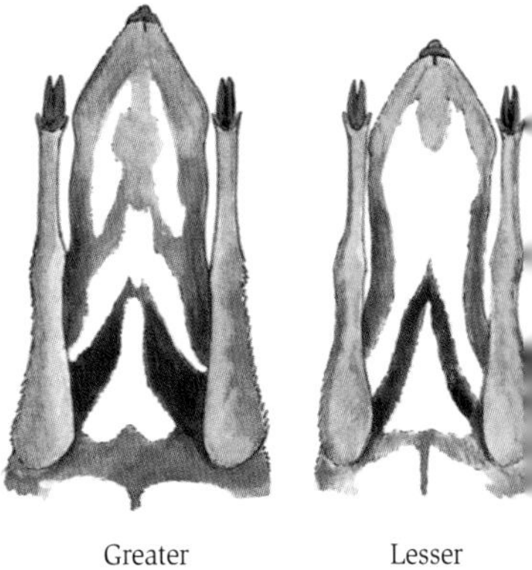

1

CLERODENDRUM Borneo has 22 species of *Clerodendrum* shrub or small tree in the Lamiaceae plant family, typically with prominent red or white flowers. [Malay: Bunga Pawang or Pangil Pangil] According to Burkill (1935), *Clerodendrum* were traditionally regarded as the most powerful magical plants in the Malay Peninsula, used by medicine men, 'Pawangs', to call up 'pangil pangil' forest spirits. In Borneo, *C. paniculatum* (illustrated) is an important plant in many Iban religious ceremonies (Christensen 2002). *Clerodendrum* leaves and flowers are regarded by many locals in Borneo as 'magical' bait when trapping mousedeer, and it maybe that this is the origin of the belief in *Clerodendrum*'s spiritual powers. Two other plants commonly used to attract mousedeer to traps are the fruit and leaves of *Sapium baccata* [Balakata baccata] and *Anisophyllea disticha* (Corner 1952).

Mousedeer Taxonomy and Niche Separation

On the larger Sunda Islands, Borneo and Sumatra plus Malaya, there are 2 mousedeer species, but on nearly all the smaller islands including Java, there is only 1 species, of variable colouration, mid-size between the Lesser and Greater. For example, Nor (1996) described the mousedeer of Balambangan and Banggi Islands, N Sabah, as the Greater, even though it is mid-size between the 2 species, and DNA tests show it to be closer to the Lesser (Meijaard 2011).

In 1910, Miller listed 41 species of mousedeer, most of them endemic to a single small Sundaland island. More sensibly, Chasen (1940) reduced the Sunda Islands mousedeer to 2 species of 54 races, but whether the single species on each small island is the Greater or Lesser seems to be a mystery. Mousedeer probably partition resources by fruit size and only larger islands provide enough fruit to support both sizes.

2

Pagoda Flower *Clerodendrum paniculatum* is a common forest-edge shrub in Borneo also planted in gardens. The shrub often shows a browse line (missing lower leaves) due to predation by deer.

CERVIDAE World: 53 spp. **Borneo:** 3 spp., including the Sambar and 2 muntjac spp. In most deer the males only develop antlers, which are replaced annually. Male Bornean Muntjac is an exception.

SAMBAR DEER *Cervus unicolor* **HB 180cm, T 24cm, SH 100cm, Wt 200kg** **Common**

Locally common, often on the fringe of cultivation where not hunted. Many interior tribes believe that eating Sambar meat will make the consumer timid so it is off the menu for most men. At Danum BRL, Sambar graze on the grassy river bank in the late afternoon, but normally they rest by day and feed at night.

ID Sambar are the largest deer in Borneo and can be recognized by size. Adult males grow large antlers that are shed and regrown each year.

Call The local name in Sabah, Payau, refers to the call. 'The only call I have ever heard from stags and hinds sounds like "piaow". It carries a long way and can only too easily be imitated by blowing on the edge of a leaf held sideways on between the thumbs – so that they can be shot' (Banks 1978).

Diet All Bornean deer eat the same foods, that is leaves (browse), grass, fallen fruit, bark, flowers and fungi, but in very different proportions. Sambar prefer grass and frequently visit salt licks. Muntjac prefer leaves and also visit salt licks. Mousedeer prefer fruit and rarely visit salt licks. At Deramakot, Onoguchi (2007) found that female Sambar visit salt licks more than males and more frequently when breeding, possibly for extra calcium. Sambar frequently raid crops near the forest, including young rubber trees and hill rice.

Breeding Sambar occur in small herds led by a powerful adult (alpha) male, who fights rival males to gain control over females (hinds). Young males and failed rivals are excluded from the herd.

Range Sri Lanka north to S China, the Philippines, Sumatra and Borneo. Feral in New Zealand and Australia.

> **A Traditional Sambar Hunt in Sarawak** 'A bend in the river is selected where the deer are known to lie hid. A *jarieng* or net is stretched across the narrow neck of land. The hunters then divide, some to watch the net, others to drive the deer towards it. The drivers simultaneously yell and shout with all their might and bark like dogs to rouse the game. The startled deer spring from their coverts and bounding towards the forest encounter the net and get entangled in its meshes. Before they have time to extricate themselves they are speared by the hunters.' (Hugh Brooke Low, in Roth 1896), (p. 48).

A Sore Spot on the Throat is unique to all Sambar Deer and is especially prominent during breeding. The spot exudes a milky hormone that is rubbed on tree trunks, and the spot may bleed. The spot normally only appears on wild deer, not captives.

♀

A family of Blue-headed Pittas removing leeches from a resting female Sambar Deer.
Deer that spend long periods resting and ruminating risk losing blood to leeches and ticks. Deer can self-groom most parts of their bodies apart from the neck. At Tabin, Sambar Deer smear the toxic sap of *Allocasia* leaves on their necks to repel ticks and leeches (p. 24).

Mutualistic relationships where birds groom large mammals to rid them of blood-sucking insects are well known, for example Jackdaws and Red Deer in the UK, oxpeckers and large mammals in Africa, mynas and cattle in India, and Cattle Egrets and Water Buffaloes in Borneo. We hypothesize here that at least 1 of Borneo's 10 species of brightly coloured pitta are specialized **leech birds** that groom resting deer and pigs to rid them of leeches and ticks. The bright colours of pittas may be a way of advertising their services. The Malay name for a pitta is '**burung pacat**', or leech bird.

SEED DISPERSAL All deer eat large amounts of fruit when it is available. They regurgitate large seeds rather than defecating them. Tiny mousedeer swallow and defecate tiny fig and ginger seeds, but can regurgitate seeds to 2.8cm in width, whilst Sambar regurgitate seeds to 4.5cm wide. Thus forest deer provide local dispersal for all but the largest rhino and elephant fruit (p. 36).

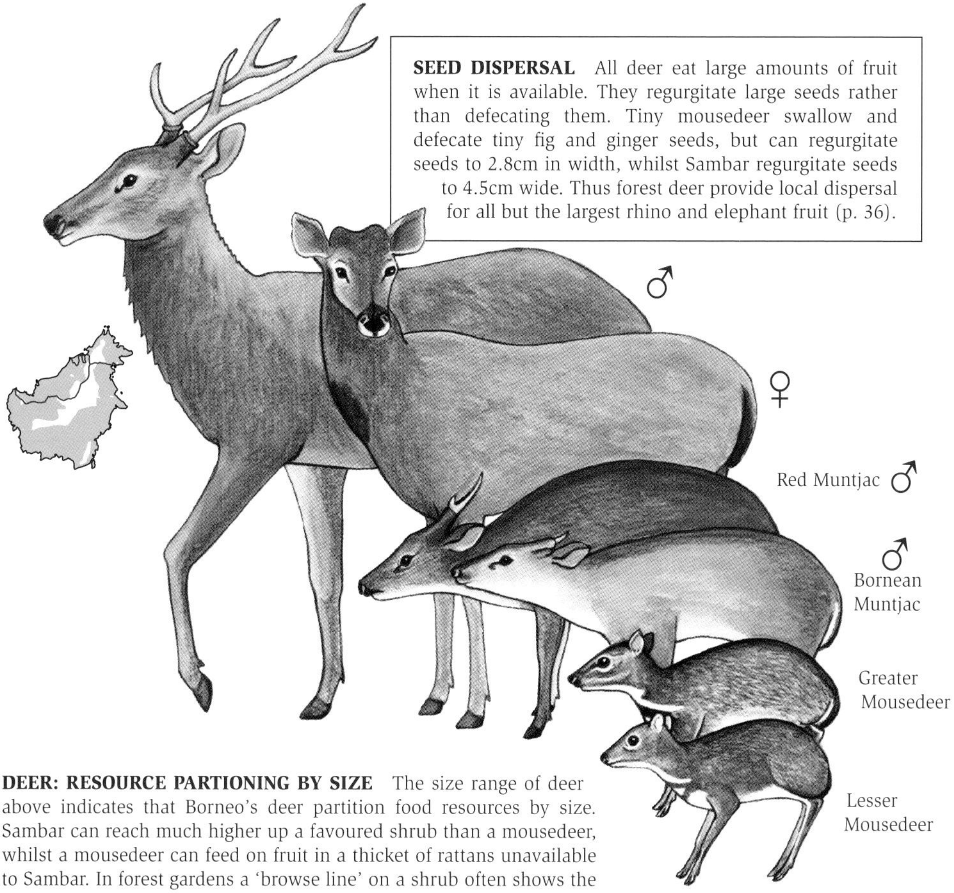

DEER: RESOURCE PARTIONING BY SIZE The size range of deer above indicates that Borneo's deer partition food resources by size. Sambar can reach much higher up a favoured shrub than a mousedeer, whilst a mousedeer can feed on fruit in a thicket of rattans unavailable to Sambar. In forest gardens a 'browse line' on a shrub often shows the maximum height a deer was able to reach.

IMPORTANCE OF SCENT IN THE FOREST More than in any other environment on Earth, mammals use both scent and their sense of smell to survive in Borneo's rainforest.

Mammals that mark home ranges and territories with scents include rhinos, wild cats, deer, slow loris, tarsier and treeshrews. Normally a scent gland will be rubbed on a prominent tree trunk or branch at regular intervals, leaving behind information about the sexual status of the owner, so that conspecific individuals are warned off or attracted to a potential mate. Rhinos and bears leave similar information in piles of dung.

Otters and civets are believed to mark feeding pools (otters, p. 256) and fruit trees (civets, p. 262) to advertise their 'resource ownership' of feeding sites that they visit on a regular basis. Due to heavy daily rain, these scent markings need to be renewed regularly.

Mammals use unpleasant or musky scents to advertise toxic flesh, for example shrews (p. 118), Moonrat (p. 140), slow loris (p. 138), Malay Weasel (p. 160), Teledu (p. 252), Binturong (p. 254) and mongooses (p. 267).

Clouded Leopard Borneo's apex predator detects prey mostly by scent rather than sight or sound, and in turn advertises its own presence and sexual status by neck rubbing and urine spraying (p. 278).

Ripe fruit such as durians, cempedaks and wild mangoes use powerful smells to attract deer, bears, rhinos and elephants from over a kilometre distance to disperse their fruit before the seeds are attacked by mould or predated by rats and porcupines. Rats and squirrels use scent to find nuts they have scatter-hoarded.

Humans Punan hunters claim that they can smell Bearded Pigs from over 100m distance, but their kill rate is higher when they use trained dogs to search the forest for the scent of wild pigs (Puri 2005).

MUNTJACS **World:** 9 spp., all Asian. **Borneo:** 2 spp., 1 endemic. Muntjacs are small forest deer about the size of a large goat with a curved back and backwards pointing antlers. They rarely wander outside the forest and are most active during the day, but also bark at night.

ID: Mature males have large canine teeth used for fighting rival males. These teeth are loose and may be heard rattling in their sockets (Payne 1985). The tail, white underneath, is raised when alarmed. The skulls have distinctive large pits in front of the eyes, which hold glands used for scent marking tree trunks. **Diet:** Both munjac species prefer leaves to grass and eat fruit when available. Muntjac predate dipterocarp seeds, but swallow and regurgitate many fruit seeds. In Thailand, Brodie et al. (2009) found muntjac were better seed dispersers than gibbons because they defecated seeds in secondary forest gaps. Muntjac are frequent visitors to forest salt licks. Muntjac and Sambar populations benefit from logging due to the increase in young foliage on pioneer plants such as leguminous vines (p. 68). **Habits:** Penan hunters train their dogs to search for prey uphill because preferred prey (pigs) escape downhill in front of the hunters. Dogs are trained not to chase muntjac because they escape uphill (Puri 2005). In Malaya Ruffino et al. (2010) found that Clouded Leopards had a crepuscular activity pattern which matched that of Muntjac their main prey. **Breeding:** Often seen in pairs. Males are believed to defend large home ranges. Females are receptive (oestrous) immediately after birth. Fawns are spotted for the first 2 months. **Call:** Both males and females call with a short sharp bark every few minutes when sexually receptive. Muntjac also bark in alarm. Young fawns with their mother and males following a receptive female use a mewing contact call that can be imitated by hunters.

1 BORNEAN YELLOW MUNTJAC *Muntiacus atherodes* **HB 85cm, S >50cm, Wt 16–20kg**
More common than the Red Muntjac in lowland areas, but less common in the hills. **Range:** Endemic to Borneo.

2 RED MUNTJAC or BARKING DEER *Muntiacus muntjak* **HB 100cm, S 50cm +, Wt 20–28kg**
Red Muntjac have been recorded at over 3,000m on Kinabalu and on the summit of Mulu (2,376m), whilst the Bornean is more common in the lowlands. The 2 species are sympatric (occur together), and where one is common the other appears to be scarce, indicating ecological overlap and competitive exclusion. At Deramakot (lowland Sabah), the Bornean Muntjac is 5 times more common than the Red (Onoguchi & Matsubayashi). At Danum, Heydon & Bulloh (1997) estimated Bornean's density as 5km2 and Red's as 1 per km^2. However, in 12-year logged forest the overall population was lower and the density of both was equal at *c.* 2 per km^2. At Sabangau in peat-swamp forest, the Bornean is uncommon and the Red is absent. **Range:** Sri Lanka east to Java.

CALLING IN A BORNEAN MUNTJAC 1. 'At that moment there was a high-pitched, chattering, rattling noise to our right. "Kijang!" whispered Leon. He eased his shotgun off his shoulder and into position across his knees. Breaking off a leaf, he held it between thumb and forefinger of each hand and sucked it, hard. The kijang answered at once; Leon and the deer called to each other, back and forth. Leon, as befitted his character, sounded like a very vigorous kijang indeed, which is perhaps why the deer, suddenly stopped, and then, no doubt, retreated. Leon sucked his leaf to tatters, and still there was no answer—but equally there was no bark of alarm. "Leon," I whispered, "The kijang just can't compete. He's left all the mating to you." "Ah, my friend," sighed Leon, "Perhaps he have a wife in a pink sarong?' (Redmond O'Hanlon 1984, *Into the Heart of Borneo*).
2. 'The Barking Deer at Mulu was more often heard than seen. The sound produced by blowing across a leaf or blade of grass is a well known trick for attracting it, although it is not a bit like a deer's bark. Our men tried this often but I never saw one fall for the trick' (Hanbury-Tenison 1980, *Mulu*).

Muntjak Mango ***Irvingia malayana*** [Malay: Pauh Kijang]. [Sabah Dusun: Tenghilan - the name of a small town on the road from Kota Kinabalu to Kota Belud where there used to be a large tree]. This tall forest tree (to 60m) with very hard wood often remains in cultivated areas long after the forest has been felled. The fruit, which ripen to green/yellow, are similar to a small, fibrous mango and are popular with muntjac deer, which swallow the fruit and regurgitate the seed, and Sun Bears, which swallow the fruit and defecate the seeds. In Thailand and Cambodia, *Irvingia* is relatively common and much favoured by elephants. Villagers collect the 'cleaned' seeds intact from forest elephant dung, then roast them in their hard shells before eating. In Borneo, *Irvingia* often grows on hillsides and ridge tops, indicating that it was probably dispersed by rhinoceroses in the past, as well as by muntjac. (Fruit: 3.7cm x 3.3cm, seed: 3cm x 2.3cm, Kitamura 2007.) At Pasoh (Malaya), Yasuda (2005) found that due to the absence of elephants, rhinos and muntjac, fallen Muntjac Mangoes lay rotting on the ground; with the absence of their normal dispersers, they had become anachronistic fruit (p. 38).

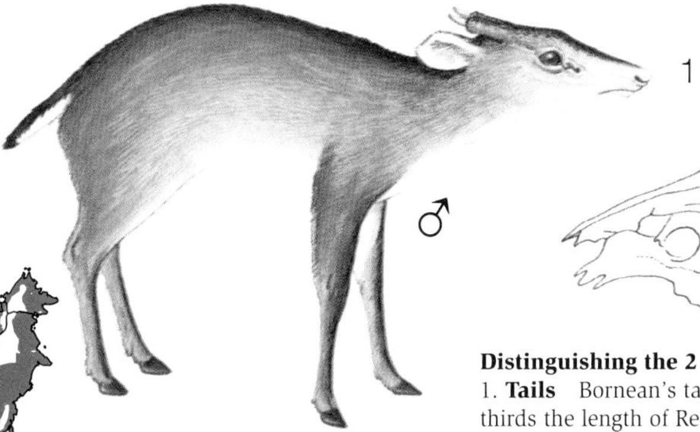

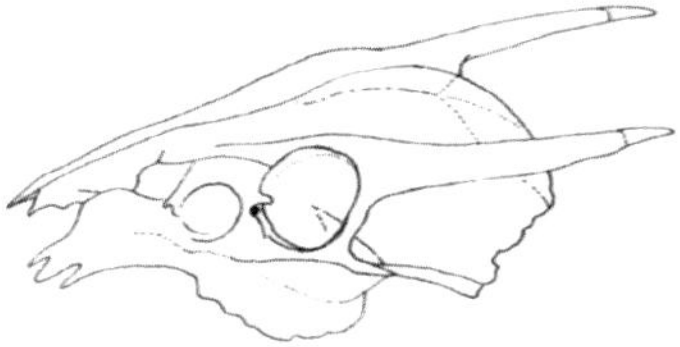

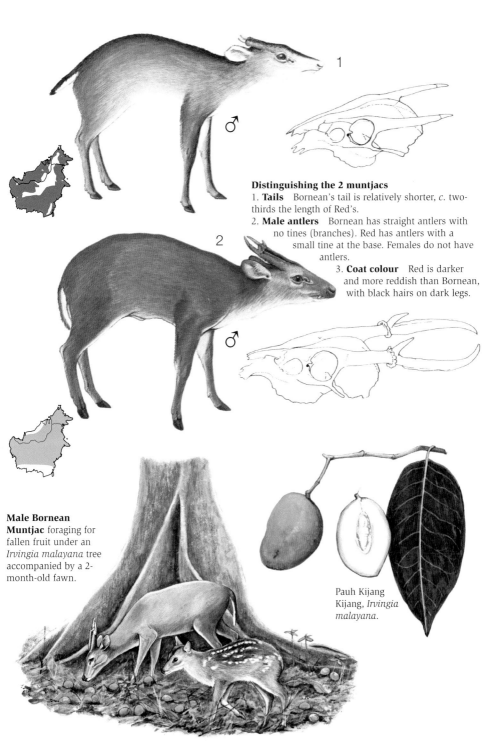

Distinguishing the 2 muntjacs

1. **Tails** Bornean's tail is relatively shorter, *c.* two-thirds the length of Red's.
2. **Male antlers** Bornean has straight antlers with no tines (branches). Red has antlers with a small tine at the base. Females do not have antlers.
3. **Coat colour** Red is darker and more reddish than Bornean, with black hairs on dark legs.

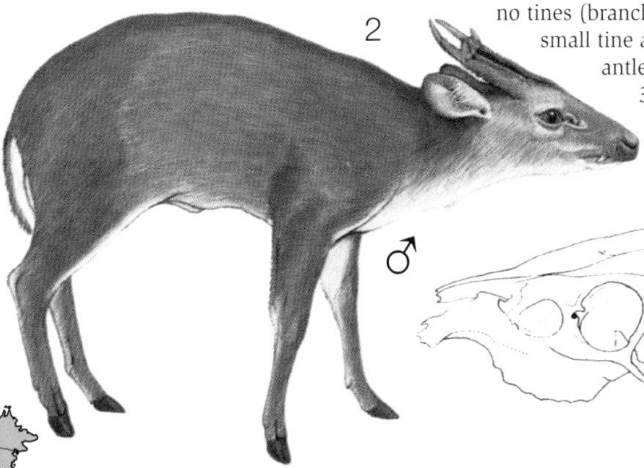

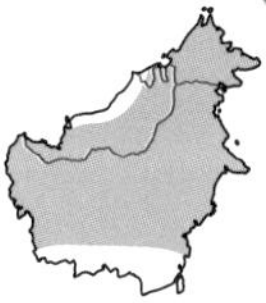

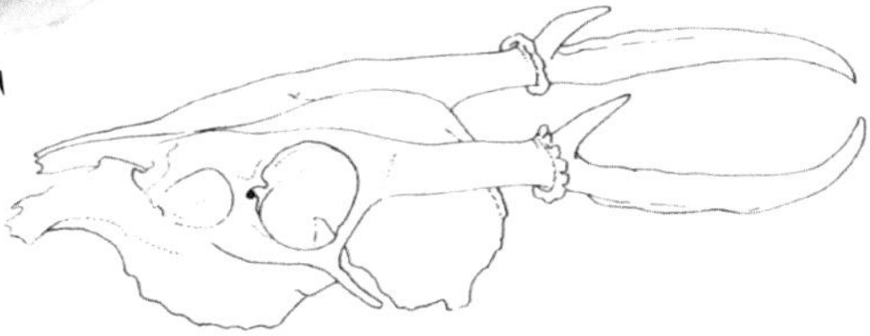

Male Bornean Muntjac foraging for fallen fruit under an *Irvingia malayana* tree accompanied by a 2-month-old fawn.

Pauh Kijang Kijang, *Irvingia malayana*.

DUGONGS

MALAY: DUYONG

DUGONGS are the only herbivorous sea mammals. The related herbvirous **manatees** prefer fresh water and are only found in the rivers and associated coastal waters of the tropical Atlantic, including the Amazon River north to Florida and W African rivers. The range of the Dugong and manatees does not overlap. The mammal most closely related to Dugongs, the giant Steller's Sea Cow, was hunted to extinction in the waters between N Japan and Alaska in around 1768 by Russian fur traders.

DUGONG *Dugong dugong* **L 2.7–3.3m, Wt 300–400kg** **Rare**

Once common in warm, shallow seas from the Pacific Islands to the Red Sea, but now hunted to extinction in most areas. The only viable population left along the coast of W Borneo is in Brunei Bay (p. 320).

ID: Breathes through the nostrils on top of its head and rarely shows the body above the sea's surface, so unlike dolphins the presence of Dugongs is difficult to detect from a boat. Underwater, Dugongs are easily distinguished from dolphins by the lack of a fin on the back and the large, hairy flat muzzle. Dugongs feed on whole seagrass plants, leaving characteristic long feeding trenches in the sand around 15cm wide.

Habits: Along the Great Barrier Reef (Australia), Dugongs live in large, nomadic herds that travel thousands of kilometres each year to graze seagrass beds along shallow coasts. In Borneo, Dugongs occur in small groups probably based on maternal relationships and are only locally nomadic.

Diet: Dugongs feed on several species of seagrass that grow in clear coastal waters rarely more than 10m deep. There are extensive beds of seagrass in many coastal areas of Borneo, harvested by Green Turtles but unoccupied by Dugongs. Like Green Turtles, Dugongs feed with the tides by day or night, but where hunters are present they tend to feed at night, resting in deeper water during the day.

Breeding: Dugongs become sexually mature at *c.* 10 years old and can live to over 70 years. Multiple males have been seen competing to mate with a reproductive female and there is no pair bond. Females give birth every 3–5 years and feed their young on milk. Due to their very slow reproduction rate, Dugongs take many years to recover from losses due to hunting. Small calves often ride on their mothers' backs.

Predation: Although some Muslim fishermen do not eat Dugong meat it sells readily to Chinese buyers. Dugong meat was often sold in the Sandakan fish market until the 1960s, and the decline of the Dugong around Borneo is mainly due to hunting. Additionally, Dugongs are often trapped in fishing nets or long-fence fish traps known as **keelongs**. Dugongs are also injured or killed by speedboat propellers.

Range: E Africa and the Red Sea east to the Pacific Islands and N Australia.

BAJAU FISHERMEN AND DUGONGS The Bajaus were called Sea Gypsies, or Orang Laut, by early authors as they were born, lived and died on their small wooden sailing boats, or **Lepa.** In Sabah, Bajaus, or Samal, are one of the largest ethnic groups, with a population exceeding 0.5 million. The majority of Bajaus now live ashore, but many continue to work as fishermen. Bajau Laut have collected sea slugs (trepang) and pearl shell for export to China for at least the last 500 years. Traditional Bajau Laut forage for marine food, including clams, octopuses, lobsters and fish, by diving in shallow coastal waters within the sunlit zone to 15m depth, where both seagrass beds and corals can grow. Dugongs forage in the same habitat. Dugongs have been hunted by Bajau fishermen with harpoons around the coast of Borneo for thousands of years. Their meat is considered a delicacy, the ground-up bones are used for Bajau medicine, and the tusks are used as fancy cigarette holders by Bajau dandies. Captured Dugongs usually 'weep' and the collected tears are considered to make potent Bajau love charms. In recent years the advent of powerful diesel-engine 'pump boats' and the use of fish bombs to kill Dugongs have exterminated Dugongs from most areas of suitable habitat. See Rajamani 2006, 2010, 2013.

DUGONG TUSKS

All Dugongs have the ability to grow tusks, but they normally only grow on males when they reach maturity at around 10 years old. Tusks are used by males competing to mate with receptive females.

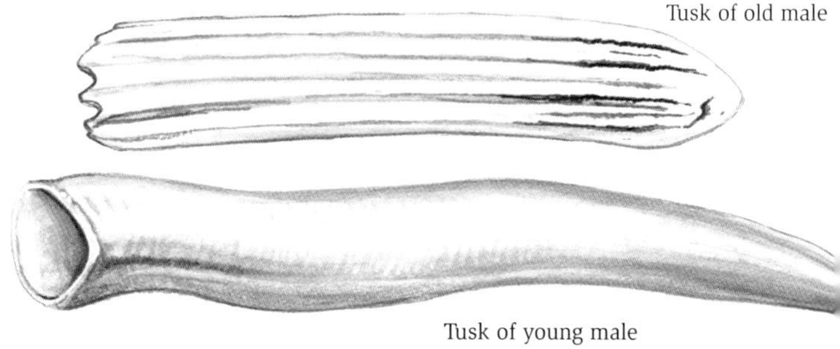

Tusk of old male

Tusk of young male

DUGONGS OF MANTANANI ISLAND Local children playing with a tame Dugong on Mantanani Island, W Sabah. This lonely Dugong entertained both tourists and locals for several years but vanished in 2007. Photo taken 2005. In the background on the left is Mantanani Kechil and on the right is Lungisan (Lingisan), where thousands of frigate birds roost on some nights. Lungisan also has a sea cave used for nesting by the rare Grey-rumped Swiftlet *Aerodramus inexpectatus*, subspecies *A. i. germani*, which builds an edible white nest.

A SEAGRASS DIET Both Green Turtles and Dugongs feed on seagrass of several species that are abundant in shallow coastal areas. Turtles and Dugongs feed on seagrass in different ways. Green Turtles crop only the stalks, whereas Dugongs pull the whole plant out of the sand, leaving a distinctive 15cm-wide trench behind them as they feed. It takes several months for the trench to be recolonized by new seagrass. This means that Dugongs need to be semi-nomadic, often travelling long distances between seagrass beds. Green Turtles can feed in much shallower water than Dugongs and are not eaten by Muslim fishermen, so they are much more common than Dugongs.

DOLPHINS, PORPOISES AND WHALES 1

PHOCOENIDAE (1 sp.) The one porpoise found around Borneo is described below.
DELPHINIDAE (18 spp.) All dolphins including the Killer Whale have rows of peg-like teeth in both upper and lower jaws, distinct dorsal fins and usually the jaw is extended into a beak. [Malay: Lumba lumba]
KOGIIDAE (2 spp. p. 316) Like Sperm Whale but much smaller with a blunt head. Teeth only on lower jaw.
ZIPHIIDAE (4 spp., p. 318) Identify stranded specimens from unusual jaws and teeth.
PHYSETERIDAE (1 sp., p. 335) Sperm Whale. Very large with blunt head. Teeth only in the lower jaw.
BALAENOPTERIDAE (2 spp., p. 335) Very large baleen whales. Malay: Paus
USEFUL WEBSITES: 1. http://archive.fieldmuseum.org/philippine_mammals. 2. www.balyena.org. 3. www.whalestrandingindonesia.com. 4. SEAWiMMS http://www.tmsi.nus.edu.sg/mmr. 5. www.ykrasi.org.

The 4 Most Common coastal marine mammals in order of abundance are 1. Irrawaddy Dolphin (p. 322), 2. Finless Porpoise, 3. Indo-Pacific Bottlenose Dolphin (p. 316) and 4. Indo-Pacific Hump-backed Dolphin. The most common deep-water dolphin is the Spinner Dolphin (p.320). All other marine mammals are rare. Hump-backed and Irrawaddy Dolphins are usually found in river estuaries and the latter also in bays.

1 FINLESS PORPOISE (PHOCOENIDAE) *Neophocaena phocaenoides* **Length 1.6–1.9m** **Common**

The second most common marine mammal around Borneo, not as common as Irrawaddy Dolphin and more often found away from river estuaries. **ID:** Pale grey with small round head. Distinguished from all dolphins by the lack of a dorsal fin. **Habits:** Often in playful groups of up to 10. In Balikpapan Bay Kreb (2011) found that Irrawaddy Dolphin was most common inside the mangrove-lined bay but Indo-Pacific Bottle-nosed Dolphin and Finless Porpoise were most common outside the bay. **Range:** Coastal waters from the Persian Gulf east to China, north to Korea and south to the north coasts of Sumatra and Java. Found all round the Borneo coast but not east of Borneo.

2 ROUGH-TOOTHED DOLPHIN *Steno bredanensis* **Length 1.8–2.8 m.** **Rare**

Only 3 sightings in 2 years in the Sulu Sea (Dolar 2006). A skull picked up on a Brunei beach in 1989 (Beasley & Jefferson 1997). 7 Philippine strandings (Aragones et al.). A rare visitor to the Sulawesi Sea (Budiono & Kreb 2015). **ID:** No distinct junction between head and beak unlike all other beaked dolphins. **Habits:** A deep-water dolphin, often in large mixed pods. **Range:** Worldwide in tropical and subtropical seas.

Dolphin abundance in the Sulu Sea a 4,000m deep basin with an area of 250,000 km^2 north of Sabah. Estimated population data from Dolar et al. (2006) surveys in 1994 and 1995. Map (p. 14).

1	Spinner Dolphin (p. 320)	33,272	5	Bottle-nose Dolphin (p. 316)	3,489
2	Spotted Dolphin (p. 320)	16,413	6	Risso's Dolphin (p. 316)	1,682
3	Hose's Dolphin (p. 320)	10,914	7	Melon-headed Whale (p. 316)	875
4	Short-finned Pilot Whale (p.318)	7,292	8	Dwarf Sperm Whale (p. 316)	381

Dolphins per km searched in the Derawan Islands Park (12,700 km^2) (Budiono & Kreb, 2008, 2015)

1	Spinner Dolphin (large)	Resident	1.50	9	Risso's Dolphin	Rare visitor
2	Spinner Dolphin (small)	Resident	0.64	10	L. B. Common Dolphin	Rare visitor
3	Spotted Dolphin	Resident	1.16	11	Pigmy Killer Whale	Rare visitor
4	Common Bottle-nose D.	Resident	0.38	12	S. Finned Pilot Whale	Rare visitor
5	Melon-headed Whale	Resident	0.30	13	Striped Dolphin	Rare visitor
6	Indo-P Bottle-nosed D.	Resident	0.30	14	Rough-toothed Dolphin	Rare visitor
7	Hose's Dolphin	Resident	0.90	15	Cuiver's Beaked Whale	Rare visitor
8	False Killer Whale	Oct only	0.01			

3 INDO-PACIFIC HUMPBACK DOLPHIN *Sousa chinensis* **L > 2.8m** **Scarce**

[*Sousa borneensis*] The 4th most common dolphin of shallow coastal waters around Borneo, most common in river estuaries. **ID:** Young dolphins are dark grey, sub-adults are spotted and adults are white or pink. **Habits:** Hunts for fish in small pods usually close to coastal mangroves. Fishes in shallow muddy water (less than 2m) with head down and tail straight up (Kreb & Budiyono). Larger and stronger than the other coastal dolphins. They can break fishing nets and are rarely trapped. **Range:** Coast of Myanmar north to Hong Kong and coastal Borneo and the Philippines.

1

2

3a

3b

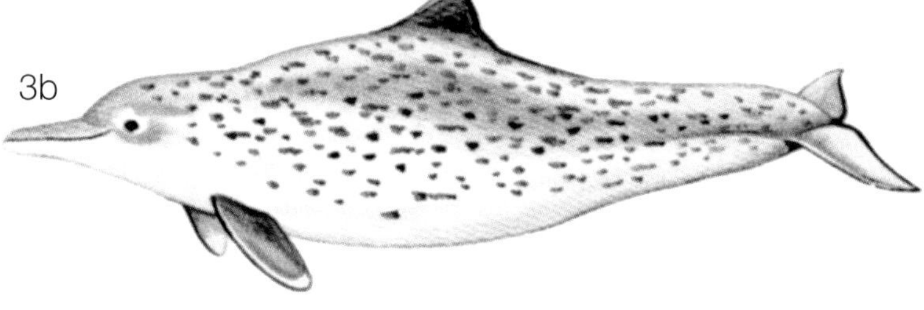

3c

DOLPHIN AND WHALE WATCHING IN E KALIMANTAN The best site to see dolphins around Borneo is the narrow strait between P. Maratua and P. Kakaban in the Derawan Islands. The best site to see whales is close to the southern shore of the Mangkalihat Peninsula (Sangkulirang Peninsula) between the Pulau Miang and Tg Mangkalihat between Nov and May when Fin Whales are present each year. Budiono and Kreb (2015).

DOLPHINS 2

1 PIGMY SPERM WHALE *Kogia breviceps* **L 2.7–3.4m** **Rare**
Two strandings: Kuching1958 and Derawan Islands 2015. 3 Philippine strandings (Aragones et al. 2010). **ID:** Only the lower jaw is toothed. Can only be confused with *K. simus,* which is smaller and with a larger dorsal fin. **Habits:** Often rests or swims slowly on the surface but rarely seen at sea. Dives in deep water to 300m for squid. Usually single, often stranded, especially mother and calf. **Range:** Worldwide in both temperate and tropical waters.

2 DWARF SPERM WHALE *Kogia simus* **L 2.1–2.7m** **Scarce**
The 8th commonest dolphin in the very deep Sulu Sea but much more common in the shallower Tanon Strait with a preference for water of av. 255m depth (Dolar 2006). No records S China Sea. In Aug 2015 a group of 4 near Maratua were very inquisitive around our stationary boat (Kreb). **ID:** Very similar to *K. breviceps* but smaller, with a larger dorsal fin. Both *Kogia* species have a white crescent mark behind the eye mimicking the appearance of a shark. **Habits:** Similar to *K. breviceps*. **Range:** Worldwide in tropical and temperate seas.

3 PIGMY KILLER WHALE *Feresa attenuata* **L 2.2–2.7m** **Scarce**
Generally uncommon in Philippine waters but locally common in the shallow seas north of Mindanao (Dolar 2006). Prone to mass strandings. A female stranded at Tg Aru beach on 10 Jan 2012 was returned to the sea at STAR Resort. Regularly seen south of the Mangkalihat Peninsula in groups of 13–25 individuals (Kreb & Budiono 2012). **ID:** Dark above with irregular patches of white on the belly, chin and lips. Relatively large dorsal tail fin. Flippers with rounded tips. Melon-headed Whale, flippers are more pointed. **Habits:** Sometimes in very large groups attacking other dolphins and whales. **Range:** Worldwide in tropical and subtropical seas.

4 MELON-HEADED WHALE *Peponocephala electra* **L 2.2–2.7m** **Locally common**
The 7th commonest dolphin in the deep water Sulu Sea but rare in the shallow S China Sea. Resident in the Sulawesi Sea and Makassar Strait (Budiono & Kreb, 2012 & 2015). Recorded offshore Similajau NP Sarawak where the placement of 1,500 concrete reef-balls by James Bali of the Beacon Project has resulted in abundant marine life. **ID:** Distinguish from Pigmy Killer Whale by more pointed flippers and more rounded head. Two regular white patches below. **Habits:** Prone to mass strandings. Often in large mixed herds. On 4 occasions seen in mixed groups with Hose's dolphin (Budiono & Kreb). Logs (rests) on the surface in large groups like Pilot Whales. Feeds on squid. **Range:** Worldwide in tropical and sub-tropical seas.

5 RISSO'S DOLPHIN *Grampus griseus* **TL 3.6–4m** **Scarce**
Frequently sighted along the W Borneo coast. See Harrisson (1974) Payne et al. (1985) and Elkin (1992). A rare visitor to the Derawan Islands and coastal waters south of the Mangkalihat Peninsula (Budiono & Kreb, 2012, 2015). **ID:** The distinctive domed head has a single groove down the middle. The grey body is usually covered in numerous scars more common in males probably the result of fighting. No teeth in the upper jaw. **Habits:** In the Sulu Sea prefers areas with steep marine slopes between 200-400m deep (Dolar 2006.) **Diet:** Feeds mainly on squid, but also fish; often in groups. **Range:** Worldwide in tropical and temperate seas.

6 COMMON BOTTLENOSE DOLPHIN *Tursiops truncatus* **L > 3.9m** **Locally common**
The world's best known dolphin (Flipper). Often confused in the past with the very similar *T. aduncus* but believed to prefer colder, deeper water. Most likely to be recorded in the Sulu Sea where it is the 5th most common dolphin (Dolar 2006) and in the deep Makassar Strait of E Borneo including the Derawan Islands and coastal E Kalimantan. A resident pod occupies the deep channel between Maratua and Kakaban islands. **ID:** See below. **Range:** Worldwide in tropical and temperate seas.

7 INDO-PACIFIC BOTTLENOSE DOLPHIN *Tursiops aduncus* **L > 3.9m** **Common**
The 3rd most common coastal dolphin around Borneo. Most common near coral reefs off sandy shores. Resident around the Derawan Islands but less common than *T. truncatus*. More common in coastal E Kalimantan (Budiono & Kreb, 2012 and 2015). **Habits:** Usually in small pods. Up to 34 recorded in the area south of Tanjung Mangkalihat Peninsula. Relatively tame and often bow-rides boats and follows fishing trawlers in the hope of sharing the catch. **ID:** Typically with a white tip to the beak. Compared with *T. truncatus* has a slimmer body with a longer slimmer beak, which is slightly tilted upwards. The belly is sometimes covered with spots and has a darker upper cape. Dorsal fins often full of notches and cuts. **Range:** Coastal tropical waters from E Africa to SE Asia.

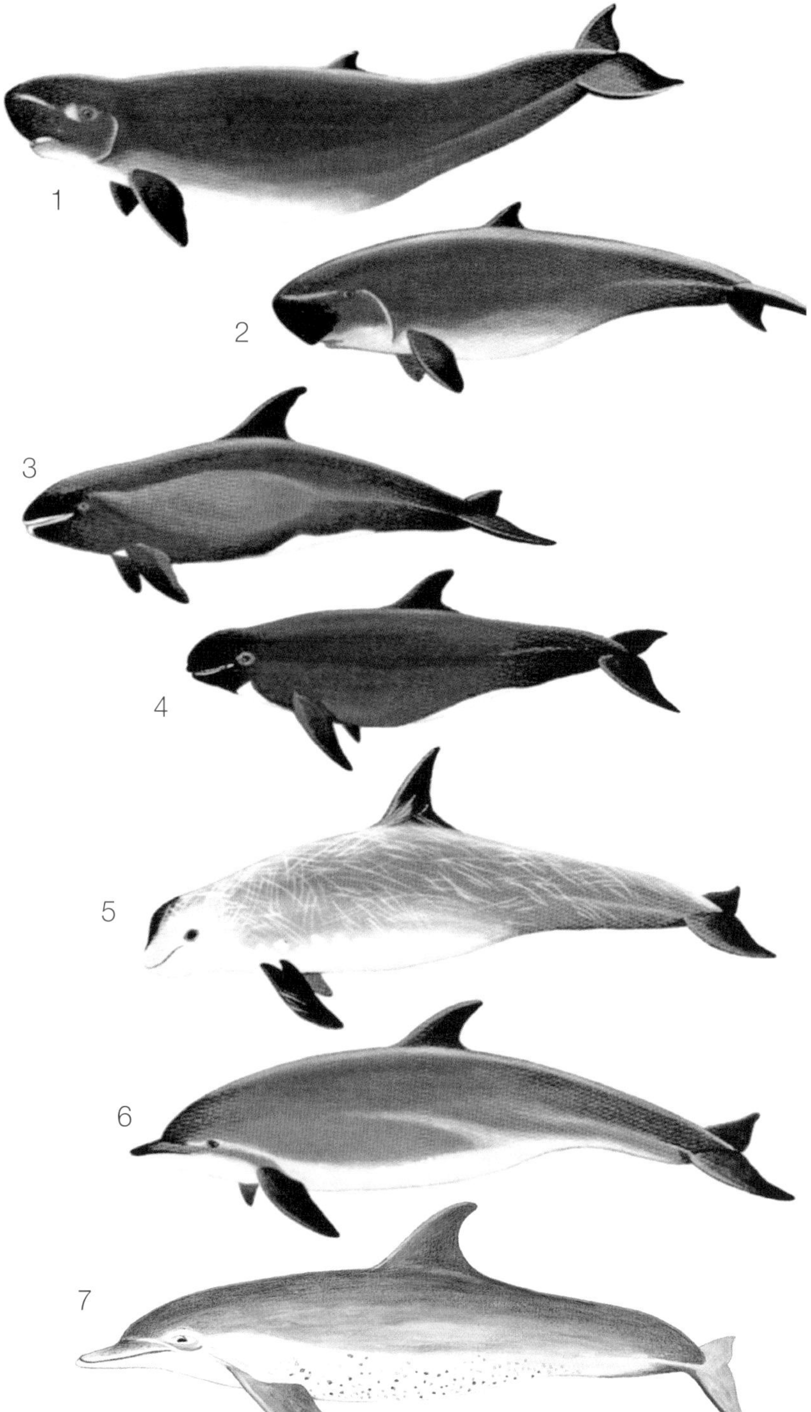
1
2
3
4
5
6
7

DOLPHINS 3 AND KILLER WHALE

1 KILLER WHALE *Orcinus orca* **Male: L >9.5m** **Rare**
Occasionally recorded in deep water around Layang Layang in the Spratley Islands, and in the Sulawesi Sea off Sipadan. One stranding at Miri, Sarawak. Rare in the Sulu Sea. **ID:** Unmistakable. Variable pattern of black and white on body with large, triangular dorsal fin. Usually in small pods. **Range:** Worldwide.

2 FALSE KILLER WHALE *Pseudorca crassidens* **L >6.1m** **Rare**
Rare away from deep ocean waters. Dolar (2015) notes a few Philippine records including the Sulu Sea. A seasonal visitor to the Derawan Islands in Oct. Recorded in Mar, May, Dec. south of the Mangkalihat Peninsula (Budiono & Kreb, 2012 and 2015). **ID:** Black above with pale markings below. Distinguish by the overhanging bulbous head and a hump on the leading edge of the flipper. **Habits:** A deep-water dolphin often in mixed species groups. May attack other dolphins and whales. **Range:** Tropical and temperate seas.

3 SHORT-FINNED PILOT WHALE *Globicephala macrorhynchuss* **L >6m** **Locally common**
Groups regularly sighted off the W Borneo coast but not common. The 4th most common dolphin in the deep waters of the Sulu Sea (Dolar 2006). One stranded at Likas Bay, Kota Kinabalu Mar 2015 had died from ingesting plastic. **ID:** Dark above with pale markings below. Distinguished by long, slender, sickle-shaped flippers. **Habits:** Usually in mixed dolphin groups. Groups often log (rest on the sea surface). Feed on squid in deep water. **Range:** Worldwide in tropical and temperate waters. Often stranded:

BEAKED WHALES (ZIPHIIDAE) L *c.* >12m, World: 21 spp. **Borneo waters:** 3 spp. Male lower jaws have one to several large teeth that can be used to distinguish stranded whales. Female has tiny teeth. Bodies often covered with long, pale scars. At sea look out for the large dolphins with oversize lower jaws. Males have a short tusk jutting out from the side of the jaw. Beaked whales dive very deep to catch squid.

4 CUIVIER'S BEAKED WHALE *Ziphius cavirostris* **L >9m** **Rare**
[Goose-beaked Whale] The most commonly recorded beaked whale worldwide. Dolar (2015) reports 3 records from the S Philippines. A rare visitor to the Derawan Islands (Budiono & Kreb 2015). **Range:** Deep seas worldwide except the cold polar seas. One stranded Kuching (2015).

5 BLAINVILLE'S (DENSE) BEAKED WHALE *Mesoplodon densirostris* **L >4.6m** **Rare**
A 3.8m female was stranded at Panaga, Brunei (Bachara et al. 2015). **ID:** Body is covered with longitudinal grooves like a sperm whale. **Habits:** Usually in offshore and deep waters. Seen alone or in groups up to 7. A single male associates with a 'harem' of females that stay separate from the group of subadults. The 'harems' tend to occur in more productive waters over the continental shelf, whereas the subadults tend to occur in inshore waters (Jefferson et al., 2008). In the Philippines, sightings of this species were often in deep waters close to shore (Dolar 2015). **Range:** Worldwide in tropical and temperate seas.

6 GINKGO-TOOTHED BEAKED WHALE *Mesoplodon ginkgodens* **L >5m (Not illustrated)**
Recorded from the Malacca strait north to Taiwan and Japan. **ID:** Distinguished by two ginkgo leaf-shaped teeth in the lower jaw. No Borneo records.

7 LONGMAN'S BEAKED WHALE *Indopacetus pacificus* **L >9m** **(Not illustrated)**
[Tropical Bottlenosed Whale, Indo-Pacific Beaked Whale]. A rare large plain beaked whale, widespread but rare. Dolar (2015) reports one stranding and two sightings from S Philippines. One stranding Malaya (Mead 1989). **Range:** Indian and Pacific Oceans

STRANDED WHALES AND DOLPHINS are usually ill. Necropsies often show stranded dolphins have swallowed waste plastic. Exceptions are groups of highly social species, e.g. Pilot Whales, Melon-headed Whales and Pigmy Killer Whales, where healthy individuals follow the distress calls of an injured dolphin and also get stranded. In these cases it may be possible to refloat the healthy individuals. If a dead dolphin is in good condition, the body should be frozen for later dissection. If in poor condition, the body can be buried above high tide mark in a strong net and the 'cleaned' bones recovered after *c.* 3 weeks and deposited with the local museum. Report Kalimantan strandings to http://www.whalestrandingindonesia.com. Elsewhere report the stranding asap to your local newspaper, university, museum or wildlife department. If possible take photos with a ruler of the top, bottom and each side of the body. Open the beak and take photos of jaws and teeth.

1

2

3

4

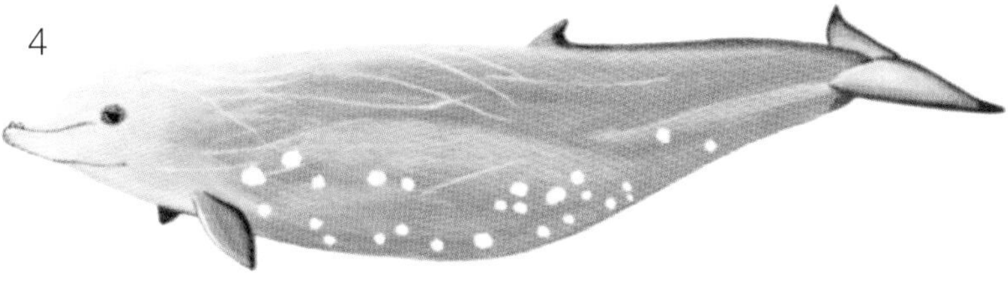

5

DOLPHINS 4

1 HOSE'S DOLPHIN *Lagenodelphis hosei* **L 2.3–2.7m** **Locally common**
[Fraser's or Short-snout Dolphin] A tropical deep-water dolphin most common in seas more than 700m deep. The 3rd most common dolphin in the Sulu Sea. 84% of observations were in mixed herds with Pilot Whales (Dolar 2006). Commonly observed in the Derawan Islands marine park in groups of 30-210 individuals. Often mixes with Melon-headed whales. Observed mating off N Maratua (Budiono & Kreb 2015).The type specimen was collected by Ernest Hose (p. 242) on the beach at Lutong near Miri in NW. Sarawak. See Fraser (1956), Harrisson (1957). **ID:** Short beak. **Habits:** Often feeds at night. **Range:** Worldwide in tropical seas.

2 SPINNER DOLPHIN *Stenella longirostris* **L 1.29–2.2m** **Common**
'By far the most numerous dolphin in the deep waters off NW Sabah especially around Ardasier Reef in the Spratley Islands where I have seen many hundreds of these usually in pods of 12 to 50. During the day, highly aerial spinning and leaping, but most fishing is at night taking full advantage of the flying fish and squid attracted by the lights of our boats' (Martin Wiles, professional fishing guide). **Habits:** The most common dolphin off N Bali where 35–100 dolphin-watching boats take tourists out daily from the village of Lovina (Mustika 2011). Fishes at night around offshore oil and gas platforms for fish attracted by the lights. Elkin (1992) has a photo of a stranded dolphin in Brunei. In the Sulu Sea usually associates with Spotted Dolphin. **Taxonomy:** Two sub-species are recorded for Borneo, *S. l. longirostris* (larger and more common) and *S. l. roseiventris* (smaller and prefers shallower water). Dolar (2006) found that *S. l. longirostris* was the most common dolphin in the Sulu Sea and *S. l. roseiventris* was rare. *S. l. roseiventris* is more common in the shallow S China Sea. In the Derawan Islands, both races occur year-round. Groups vary between 10 and 120 indviduals with up to 650 indivduals for *S. l. longirostris* (Budiyono and Kreb) **Range:** Worldwide tropical seas.

3 STRIPED DOLPHIN *Stenella coeruleoalba* **L 1.8–2.7m** **Rare**
Confined to deep waters off the continental shelf. Not recorded for the shallow southern S China Sea. There are sight records from further north in deeper waters (Dolar 2015). Recorded south of the Mangkalihat Peninsula. **ID:** By the obvious body stripes. **Habits:** Active in large groups usually in deep water. **Range:** Worldwide in tropical to temperate seas.

4 PANTROPICAL SPOTTED DOLPHIN *Stenella attenuata* **L >2.5m** **Locally common**
[Spotted or Bridled Dolphin] The 2nd most common dolphin in the deep water Sulu and Sulawesi Sea off E Kalimantan but uncommon in the S China Sea. A recent record of a pod of 4 adults and an infant off shore Bintulu (James Bali, Beacon Project). **ID:** By variable spotting and long narrow beak often with white tip and lips. Bottlenose Dolphin has a thicker beak and is plainer. **Habits:** Often associates with Spinner Dolphins and less frequently with Hose's and Bottlenose Dolphins. **Range:** Pacific and Indian Oceans.

5 LONG-BEAKED COMMON DOLPHIN *Delphinus capensis* **L 1.9–2.5m** **Rare**
Rare along the W Coast of Borneo. No Philippine records (Dolar 2015). However Smith et al. (1997) list this dolphin as the 2nd most common dolphin off the Vietnam coast with 17 skulls found in 9 different whale temples. **ID:** Distinguished from Spinner Dolphin by a saddle patch. **Habits:** Normally confined to shallow coastal waters. **Taxonomy:** Previously considered conspecific with Common Dolphin *D. delphis* which replaces *D. capensis* in colder coastal waters at higher latitudes.

6 A third species **Tropical Common Dolphin** *D. tropicalis* with an exceptionally long beak was photographed by Budiono & Kreb (2015) near the Derawan Islands, E Kalimantan. *D. tropicalis* is considered a race of *D. capensis* by Jefferson and Waerebeek (2002). **Range:** Scattered distribution in tropical coastal waters from E Africa to California.

UNSUSTAINABLE HARVESTING OF MARINE MAMMALS IN COASTAL BORNEO
As described by Jaaman et al. (2009) and Jaaman (2010), fishermen in Sabah and Sarawak regard marine mammals as 'fish' to be caught and eaten. Between Mar 1997 and Dec 2004 Jaaman carried out structured interviews with over 1,111 fishermen and reported estimated annual catches as below. Coastal Irrawaddy and Humpback Dolphins frequently help coastal fishermen to herd fish into nets in anticipation of sharing the catch and are not usually targeted or eaten by fisherman because it is considered bad luck but all other dolphins and the Dugong are caught and eaten.

Estimated annual catch	Dolphins	Dugongs
Sabah	306	479
Sarawak	221	14
East Malaysia total	**527**	**493**

1

2

3

4

5

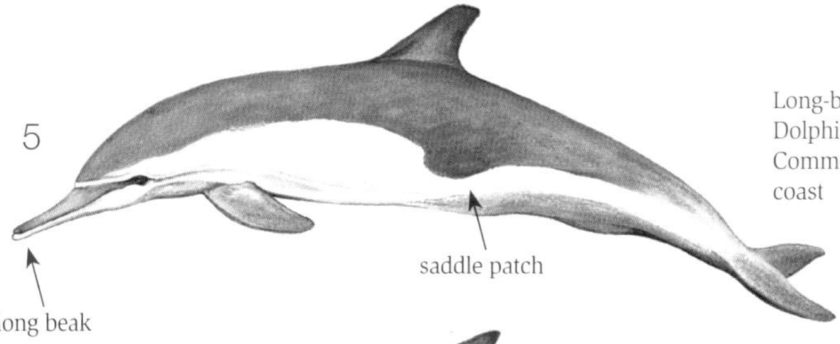

Long-beaked Common Dolphin *D. capensis*
Common, Vietnam coast

6

Tropical Common Dolphin *D. tropicalis*
One record Derawan Islands

IRRAWADDY DOLPHIN *Orcaella brevirostris* **L 2–2.5m** **Locally common**

The most common shallow-water coastal dolphin found around Borneo, usually in sheltered bays and river estuaries with brackish water. Locally common at Santubong and Buntal Bays near Kuching. Occasionally seen as far up river as Kuching. Also recorded off the coast at Similajau NP north of Bintulu. Previously common in the seas around the Tunku Abdul Rahman Park opposite Kota Kinabalu. Locally common in the Kinabatangan and Segama River estuaries and Cowie Bay, Tawau, E Sabah (Teoh 2012). In W Kalimantan recorded from Kapuas river estuary. On the east coast recorded from Balikpapan Bay (resident population *c.* 70), Sangkulirang Bay and the estuaries of the Mahakam, Berau and Sesayap Rivers. Dolphins will migrate upstream the Sesayap following saltwater intrusion into the river during the dry season (Kreb).

Mahakam River A distinctive pale grey, population of *c.* 90 fresh-water dolphins is found in the Mahakam River some 180km upstream from Samarinda E Kalimantan (Kreb et al., 2010, Kreb & Noor, 2012. See below.)

ID Coastal dolphins are dark grey. Mahakam dolphins are light grey. The dorsal fin is small and rounded.

Habits Fishes in muddy waters in groups by using sonar. Leaps occasionally, sometimes spy hops. Often follows fishing boats and fishes co-operatively with local fishermen by herding schools of fish towards their nets in the expectation of being rewarded with part of the catch. **Taxonomy:** The Mahakam River Dolphin is a possible future split from the coastal Irrawaddy Dolphin. The Australian/New Guinea form has recently been split as a new species *O. heinsohnii* [Snubfin Dolphin]. **Range:** Coastal India to SE Asia and throughout Indonesia. The only Philippine population of *c.* 70 dolphins live in the Malampaya sound NW Palawan where deaths due to gill-net fishing appear to exceed reproduction (Whitty 2013).

CAN THE MAHAKAM RIVER DOLPHIN BE SAVED FROM EXTINCTION? Most of the small isolated population of *c.* 90 Irrawaddy Dolphins survives along a 180 km stretch of the Mahakam River. Since 2009 when a core fish-spawning area was converted to oil-palm plantations, most sightings are in the Central Kutai district. Here, they mostly occur near river junctions and tributaries such as Muara Kaman, Kedang Kepala, Belayan, Pela and Muara Muntai. At medium- to high-water levels they may roam around in Semayang and Melintang Lakes. Known mortality has varied between 3 and 5 over the last few years with the majority of deaths due to dolphins being trapped in gill nets. Dolphins have also been killed to a minor extent by boat strikes, electro-fishing and hunting. Birth rates are estimated at 5 calves a year, so the population is on the edge of extinction. Water quality in the Mahakam River is deteriorating due to land clearance for oil palm, increasing traffic from coal mining barges and the spilling of poisonous mining effluent through ground water or transport loading into the river. Dolphins used to inhabit Jempang Lake but due to siltation from logging, Jempang is now too shallow for the dolphins (Danielle Kreb).

A local NGO Yaysan Konservasi RASI (Conservation Foundation for Rare Aquatic Species of Indonesia) has been heavily involved in both studying dolphin ecology and promoting a variety of strategies to reduce the dolphin death rate. A proposal to preserve existing riparian swamp forest and wetlands habitat of 52,000ha together with a management plan for zonation has been accepted by the local communities and is now in process of legalization by the local governments. However, unless the death rate can be drastically reduced, extinction of this rare dolphin is inevitable. (See Kreb & Noor (2012) and www.ykrasi.org).

Irrawaddy Dolphin drowned in a gill net Mahakam River. (Photo: Ivan Yusfi Noor)

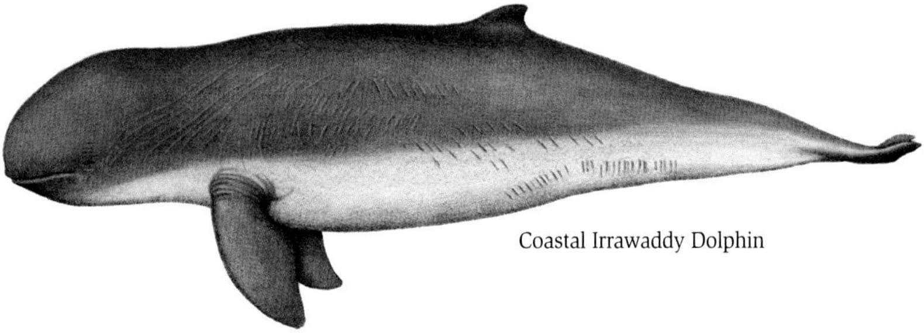

Coastal Irrawaddy Dolphin

Mahakam Irrawaddy Dolphin

Female Irrawaddy Dolphin mating in the Mahakam River. (Photo: Budiyono & Kreb)

BALAENOPTERIDAE Baleen whales are rare in Borneo waters due to the mostly shallow, warm, fish-poo seas under 200m deep that surround Borneo. An exception is the 2,000m deep Makassar trench that runs between Sulawesi and E Borneo, where whale sightings are regular. There are no confirmed records for Blue and Sei Whales. All baleen whale records are believed to refer to either Bryde's Whale or Fin Whales o possibly the mysterious small Omura's Whale. Most of the baleen whales are huge with tiny dorsal (back) fins towards the rear end of the body. Baleen whales have no teeth, and feed by using the baleen plates in thei mouth like a sieve to filter small fish and prawns from large volumes of swallowed sea water.

1 BLUE WHALE *Balaenoptera musculus* **L 22–30.5m**

A 13m baleen whale skeleton in the Labuan Marine Museum was originally stranded in Malacca in June 189 and resided at Raffles Museum, Singapore, from 1907–1974. Listed as an Indian Fin Whale (Blue Whale). In 2006 a 24m Pygmy Blue Whale *Balaenoptera musculus brevicauda* stranded off Gaya Island Kota Kinabalu. The skeleton is in the Sabah Museum. See Ponnampalam (2012).

2 FIN WHALE *Balaenoptera physalus* **L 18–27m**

De Boer (2000) Reported 3 Fin Whales sighted just north of Borneo near the Balabac Strait, possibly Omura' Whale. Budiyono and Kreb report Fin Whales in excess of 20m in length seen daily between Sandaran and T Mangkalihat, E Kalimantan Nov–May each year. Sightings include a mother and calf pair and 4 individual feeding on krill, 500m apart (Budiyono and Kreb 2011, 2015).

3 SEI WHALE *Balaenoptera borealis* **L 12–21m No records**

4 BRYDE'S WHALE *Balaenoptera bryde* **L 12–24m** **Scarc**

The most common whale in the southern S China Sea. Regularly sighted off shore W Borneo. **ID**: 3 prominent ridges on top of head. Other large baleen whales have only one ridge on the head. **Habits:** Feeds on schooling fish, often at depth. Previously hunted at Camiguin and Pamilacan Islands in the Philippines (Reeves, 2002) Elkin (1992) reports small groups (total 10 individuals) swimming north past Brunei in Apr/May 1991 **Strandings:** Sarawak 1909 (Pusa) 1956, 1957, 2013 (Kuching); Brunei Muara (2003); Sabah 1999 (Gaya Island), 2012 (Kuala Penyu), 2012 (Pulau Mengalum), 2014 (Banggi). Note: Old strandings might be either *B. bryde* or *B. omurai*, depending on size.

All illustrations thanks to SEAWIMMS
www.tmsi.nus.edu.sg/mmrl

5 OMURA'S WHALE *Balaenoptera omurai* **L 9–11m** **Rare**
[*B. edeni*] One stranded Pahang east coast Malaya in 2008 (Ponnampalam 2012). **ID:** Looks like a small Fin Whale. Distinguished from Fin Whale by smaller size. Has a single longitudinal ridge on the head as with most baleen whales, not 3 ridges as with Bryde's Whale. Both *B. omurai* and *B. physalus* have an irregular white patch on the right side of the lower jaw. **Range:** E Indian Ocean east to the Solomon Islands.

6 HUMPBACK WHALE *Megaptera novaeangliae* **L 11–16m** **Rare**
Single sight records off Sarawak (Harrisson 1958), Sabah (Slijper et al 1964) and Tawau (Jaaman, 2010). **ID:** Long, irregularly shaped flippers, white below and partly white above. Tail raised high out of the water on deep dives, like Sperm Whale. **Range:** Worldwide. Rare but widespread in Indonesia (Mustika et al 2009). 60 + breeding whales are present every northern winter around the Babuyan Islands, N Philippines. Kreb (2011) reported a mother and calf in both 2009 and 2010 (Jun–Sep) offshore Bontang, E Kalimantan. The calf was killed by bomb fishers.

7 SPERM WHALE (PHYSETERIDAE) *Physeter macrocephalus* **L 10–18m** **Scarce**
The whale most likely to be seen in the deep water of the northern S China Sea and the deep water (Makassar Trench) between Borneo and Sulawesi. Sperm whales have 'tanks' of 'spermacetti' oil in their large, square foreheads used to focus sonar for catching prey and for buoyancy. Only the lower jaw has teeth, which slot into sockets in the upper jaw. **Habits:** Feeds on large squid at depths up to 1,000 m. **Range:** Worldwide. **Borneo:** One stranded near Kuching (1995), Beasley Jefferson (1997). A sight record in the Balabac strait off N Borneo (De Boer 2000). Numerous strandings indicate that the Makassar Trench is a trans-equator migration route for Sperm Whales. Strandings include Pandanan Island (2001), Boheydulang Island (1998), Maratua (2001,2002, 2004, 2006) and on the E Kalimantan coast (1997, 2007). Kreb (pers. comm. 2015) reports individuals, pairs and a small group of 4 medium-sized, possibly juvenile males (10–12m) near the Mangkalihat Peninsula. Regularly sighted at Layang Layang in the S China Sea (Jaaman 2010). Common in the Sulawesi Sea but rare in the Sulu Sea (Dolar 2015).

SABAH 1: OVERVIEW

Sabah is the second largest state in Malaysia and retains substantial populations of Bornean Orangutans, Banteng and Pigmy Elephants due to a combination of good governance, and well-managed forestry and wildlife departments. Sabah also leads the way in sustainable low-impact logging techniques for producing FSC certified timber. Approximately 50% of Sabah is planned to be permanently retained as forest with 30% totally protected.

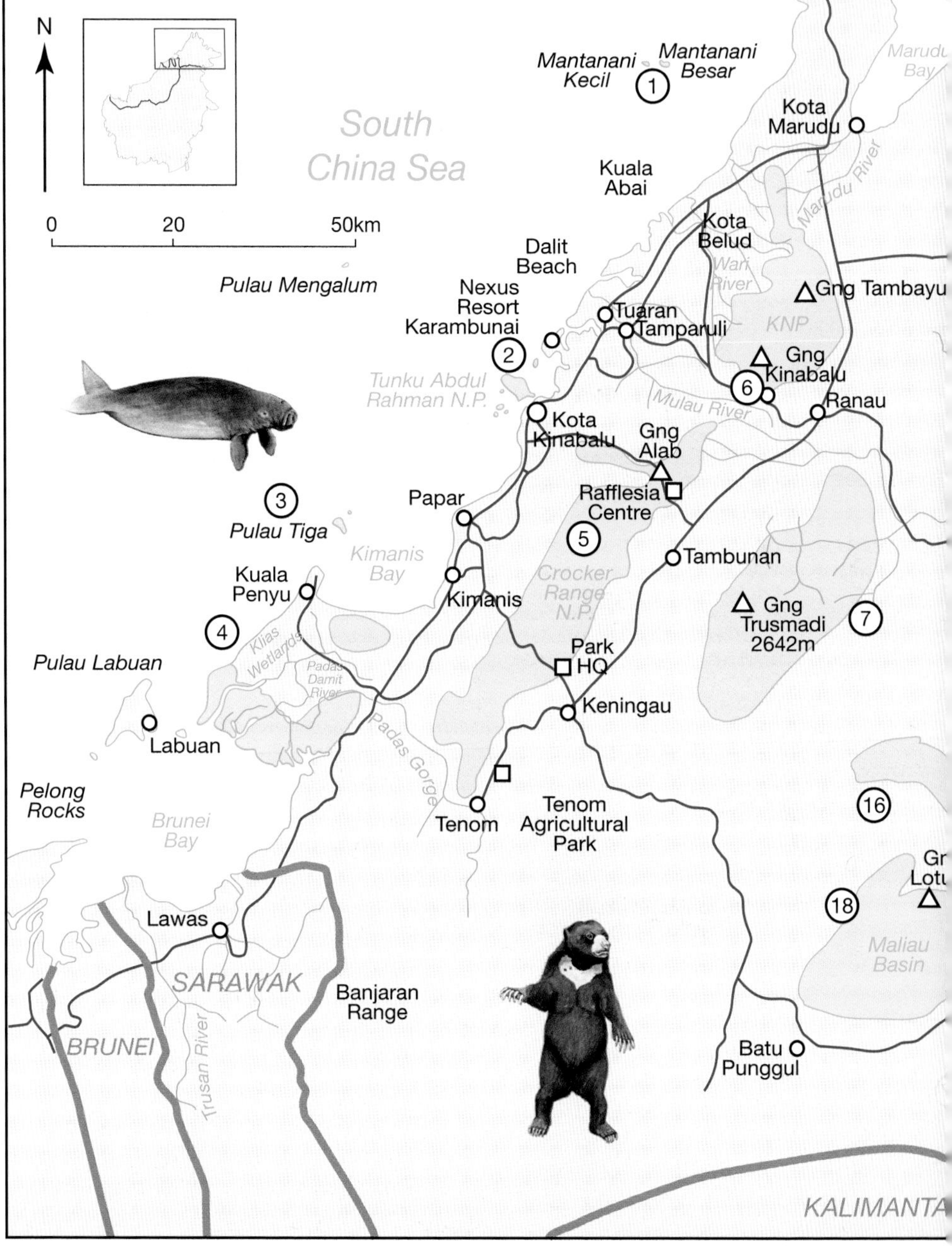

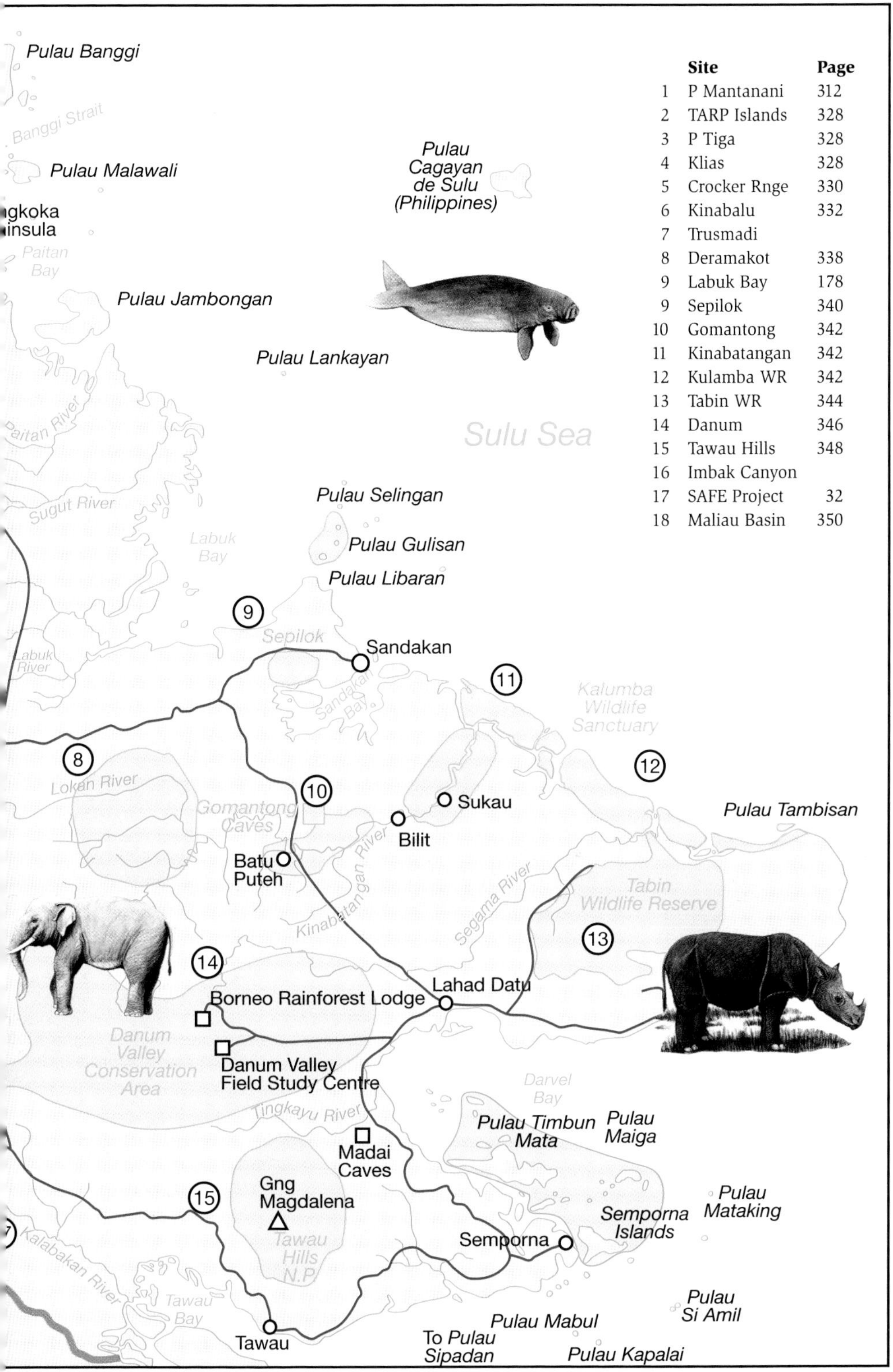

	Site	Page
1	P Mantanani	312
2	TARP Islands	328
3	P Tiga	328
4	Klias	328
5	Crocker Rnge	330
6	Kinabalu	332
7	Trusmadi	
8	Deramakot	338
9	Labuk Bay	178
9	Sepilok	340
10	Gomantong	342
11	Kinabatangan	342
12	Kulamba WR	342
13	Tabin WR	344
14	Danum	346
15	Tawau Hills	348
16	Imbak Canyon	
17	SAFE Project	32
18	Maliau Basin	350

SABAH 2: DAY TRIPS FROM KOTA KINABALU (KK)

TUNKU ABDUL RAHMAN PARK (TARP) (5°59´N, 116°00´E) 30 minutes by boat from KK
TARP consists of 4 small islands – Manukan, Sulug, Mamutik and Sapi, and one large island, Gaya.

Manukan This has park cabins that can be booked for overnight stays. A good trail circles the island. Look out for tame megapodes the size of chickens that lay eggs communally in a rotting mound of sand and leaves.

Sulug Most remote and least visited island, with a sinister reputation. Previously the site of a Suluk fishing village destroyed in a massacre during the Second World War (1944).

Mamutik Smallest island, with shelters and toilets, and good snorkelling.

Sapi Small island connected to Gaya at low tide. At weekends full of day visitors pestered by Long-tailed Macaques.

Gaya Largest island (1,465ha); was connected to the mainland 10,000 years ago. The interior retains the typical plants of Borneo's coastal forest, including 16 species of giant dipterocarp. The most common, *Dipterocarpus grandiflorus* (p. 54), dominates the Gaya skyline. Around the coast are patches of mangrove, along with fine examples of *Barringtonia* Association trees along the sandy beaches (p. 40). **Birds:** Overhead, look for the White-bellied Sea Eagle and Brahminy Kite. Forest birds include the Buffy Fish Owl, Pied and Green Imperial Pigeons, Pied Hornbills, Hill Myna and the Sabah endemic, the White-crowned Shama, renowned for its beautiful song. **Mammals:** Bearded Pigs common and often seen around the resorts; Long-tailed Macaque common; pangolin previously common (p. 152), Smooth Otter resident family groups (shy); Proboscis Monkey scarce resident of the Gaya mangroves. **Accommodation on Gaya:** Choice of three luxury resorts. Gayana, Bunga Raya and Gaya Island Resort are located on beaches on the north side of Gaya.

THE MARINE ECOLOGY RESEARCH CENTRE (MERC) next to the Guyana Resort on Gaya combines tourism with conservation, including fish breeding and rearing for food, coral-reef rehabilitation and Giant Clam breeding for restocking of the local reefs, which have been depleted by shell and food collectors. Easily visited on a day trip from KK. www.merc-guyana.com.

KLIAS PENINSULA AND PULAU TIGA (05°21´N, 115°35´E) 2-hour drive south of KK
Klias is the largest area of mangrove, fresh and brackish water swamp forest in W Sabah. Day tours from KK take ecotourists to view Proboscis Monkeys, Silvered Langurs and fireflies *Photinus pyralis* in the evening along the many small rivers. Banteng used to be common on the Klias Penisula and would make an ideal reintroduction project, because of abundant suitable habitat. The Tg Nosong-Menumbok ridge has 8 mud volcanoes. Boats for P Tiga leave from Kuala Penyu, and the Labuan car ferry leaves from Menumbok.

Pulau Tiga Small island formed from 3 mud volcanoes, with some of Sabah's finest coastal and island forests and three resorts. P. Tiga has never been connected to the mainland, so there are no squirrels, but there are many Tioman Rats (p. 228), which featured as food in a TV programme called *Survivor Island*. The Bearded Pigs vanished during a drought (p. 13). Long-tailed Macaques are common, but a large colony of flying foxes (p. 84) has vanished. The adjacent small Snake Island (P Kalampunian Besar) attracts breeding sea snakes during the calm season, Mar–June, which are predated by the resident pair of breeding White-bellied Sea Eagles.

Tanjong Nosong (05°38´N, 115°36´E) Rocky cliffs at the NW edge of the Klias Peninsula host nesting terns and reef egrets in Mar–June.

Binsulok Forest Reserve (12,106ha) backs a beautiful beach with a mini resort. The forest was logged and damaged in the 1998 fires. Rare kerangas birds Hook-billed Bulbul and Grey-breasted Babbler are present.

Sitompok Lake Brackish-water lake surrounded by mangrove close to Kuala Penyu. There are old records of Darter and Purple Heron breeding colonies in the area.

Klias and Garama Rivers, and Padas Damit FR (9,027ha) The fine riverine forest along the banks of the Klias and Garama Rivers is the best place to see Proboscis Monkeys and Silvered Leaf Monkeys in W Sabah. At least 10 groups of Proboscis Monkeys live along the Gramma. Small resorts provide overnight stays.

Padang Teratak 100ha of swampy, buffalo-grazing grassland that hosts numerous migrant ducks, bitterns, herons and egrets in wet winter months when the padang floods.

Weston and Klias FR (05°10´N, 115°25´E) 3,630ha of fire-damaged peat-swamp forest north of Weston. Smooth Otters, flying foxes and crocodiles are regularly sighted along the Api Api and Bukau Rivers. and in the nearby mangroves. The protected mangroves on the south side of the Klias Peninsula front onto Brunei Bay, the richest fishing ground in W Sabah, with Irrawaddy and Humpbacked Dolphins regularly encountered, and large beds of sea grass that attract Dugongs and Green Turtles.

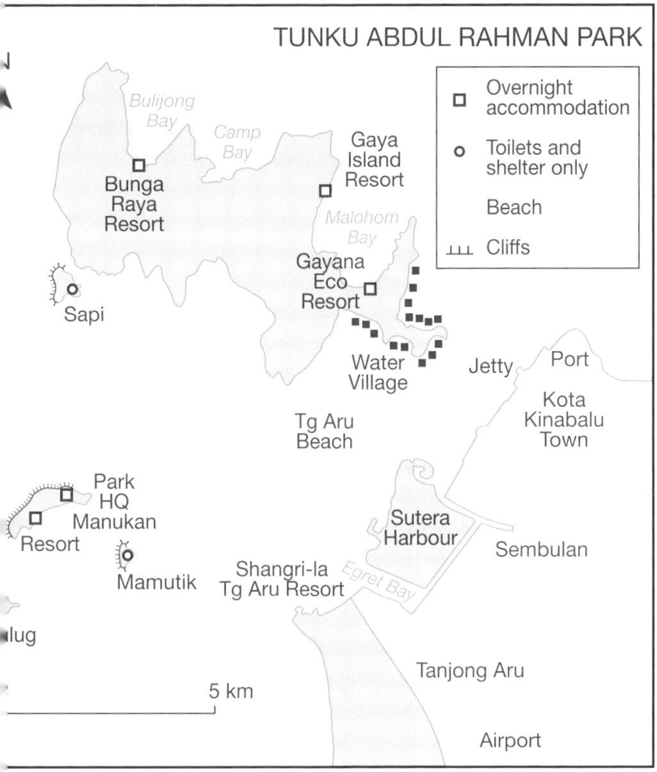

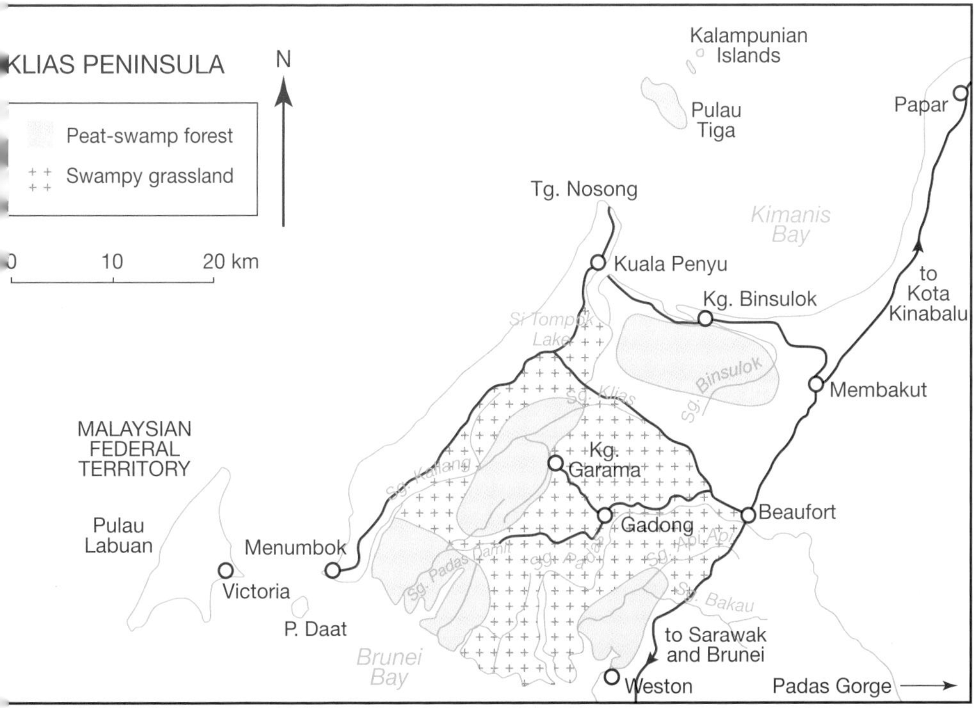

Tunku Abdul Rahman or *Bapa Malaysia* (Father of Malaysia) (1903–1990) was the popular and internationally respected Malaysian politician who served as the first Chief Minister of the Federation of Malaya from 1955 to 1957, before becoming Malaya's first Prime Minister after independence in 1957. Tunku Abdul Rahman was Prime Minister when Sabah and Sarawak joined the Federation of Malaysia in 1963. He retired in 1970.

SABAH 3: CROCKER RANGE PARK

CROCKER RANGE PARK (1,400 km²) The Crocker Range is the main dividing range between E and W Sabah, and isolates the fertile wet-rice fields of the Tambunan/Keningau/Tenom valley from the west coast. Until 1970, Tambunan was only accessible via a railway from KK to Tenom through the Padas Gorge, but 2 very steep roads now cross the Crocker Range. There is bookable park accommodation on both roads and also at 3 other sites in the Crocker Range. www.sabahtourism.com, www.sabahparks.org.my

A THE KK-TAMBUNAN ROAD runs due east of Kota Kinabalu.

Kipandi (730m) A 1-hour drive from KK is a privately run butterfly and orchid centre with a small insect museum, a butterfly garden with breeding local butterflies, and Borneo's best collection of native orchids and hoyas, as well as many other flowering plants. The local botanists and entomologists who staff Kipandi can organize day trips or specialized tours on request.

Gng Alab (1,964m) and Gng Minduk Sirung (2,050m) A 1½-hour drive from Kota Kinabalu is the highest point on the Crocker Range. You can drive up to Park Cabins at 1,850m, then up to Gng Alab's radio station at 1,964m. The highest point, Gng Minduk Sirung, is a stiff walk from the visitor cabins, and from here there is a steep trail down to the Mahua Waterfall. To access the park cabins turn left at the Gng Emas restaurant on the KK-Tambunan Road for a steep drive taking about 20 minutes. The weather is usually cool; it is often misty or raining by midday. Gng Emas has a troop of feral Long-tailed Macaques that forage nearby. A colony of rare endemic Bornean Swiftlets used to nest under the restaurant roof before their droppings resulted in eviction.

Rafflesia Centre (1,310m) This is on the far side of Crocker Range around a 2-hour drive from Kota Kinabalu. If you are lucky there might be a rare giant *Rafflesia pricei* flowering on one of the very steep surrounding slopes. **Birds:** The Rafflesia Centre is a favoured site for mid-level montane birds such as the Bornean Ibon, Long-Tailed Broadbill, Bornean Bulbul, Bornean Leafbird and Whitehead's Spiderhunter, which can be difficult to find on Kinabalu. Look out for rare squirrels *Sciurus brookei* and *Glyphotes simus*.

Mahua Waterfall (1,200m) A 3-hour drive from Kota Kinabalu, this has a long bird list including Whitehead's Trogon and Whitehead's Broadbill. A steep path runs between Gng Alab and the waterfall.

B INOBONG (200m) A 45-minute drive from Kota Kinabalu. You can rent self-catering cabins at Innobong, which is also the start of the **Salt Trail**, the name for a historical trail used by the local Kadazan Dusun rice farmers to trade between the previously isolated Tambunan Valley and the west coast. Buffalo, rice and forest products from Tambunan were exchanged for salt, cloth and iron tools from coastal towns. Today the salt trail is a strenuous 2-day trek that crosses the Crocker Range. Guides can be booked through Sabah Parks.

C KIMANIS–KENINGAU ROAD Crosses the Crocker Range 50km south of KK. High Point 1,400m.

When this road was first built it was possible to see Orangutans and gibbons from the roadside. There is more forest along this very steep road, and you will see more wildlife than on the northern route.

Crocker Range Park HQ (1,000m) A 2½-hour drive from Kota Kinabalu. Visitor cabins available for rent. Well known to birdwatchers for the Banded Pittas, Bornean Falconets and Honey Guides that live locally. The Ferret Badger and Hose's Civet have been recorded locally. *Rafflesia keithii* flowers infrequently near the headquarters reception building (p. 56).

CONFLICT OVER LAND IN THE CROCKER RANGE The forested slopes of the Crocker Range have long been the traditional hunting grounds of the Kadazan-Dusuns, who still cultivate hill rice in slash-and-burn swiddens on the lower slopes (p. 48). Until the 1950s, wildlife was abundant, but the availability of shotguns after the Second World War has eliminated most large mammals within a day's walk of human habitation. Because the Crocker Range is only 15km across and is easily accessed by hunters living on the park boundary, there is *no* safe area in the Crocker Range for large mammals. Local hunters primarily seek wild pigs, but also target pangolins for scales, and porcupines and langurs for their bezoar stones. Hornbills, eagles, Orangutans and gibbons are killed if encountered. Sabah Parks staff are thinly spread and often live in the same kampongs as the poachers, which makes enforcement difficult. Because no one 'owns' the wildlife, a villager who would never steal his neighbour's buffalo thinks nothing of shooting a forest gibbon for the pot. Population growth puts increasing pressure on the park boundaries. Hamilton & Jepson (2015) suggest a possible solution could be co-management with local villagers, combined with systematic **Ethical Analysis**, a decision-making procedure developed in hospitals to negotiate ethical solutions. Currently no one benefits – the forest is emptied of wildlife and wildlife tourism suffers – the real long-term losers are the locals (p. 368).

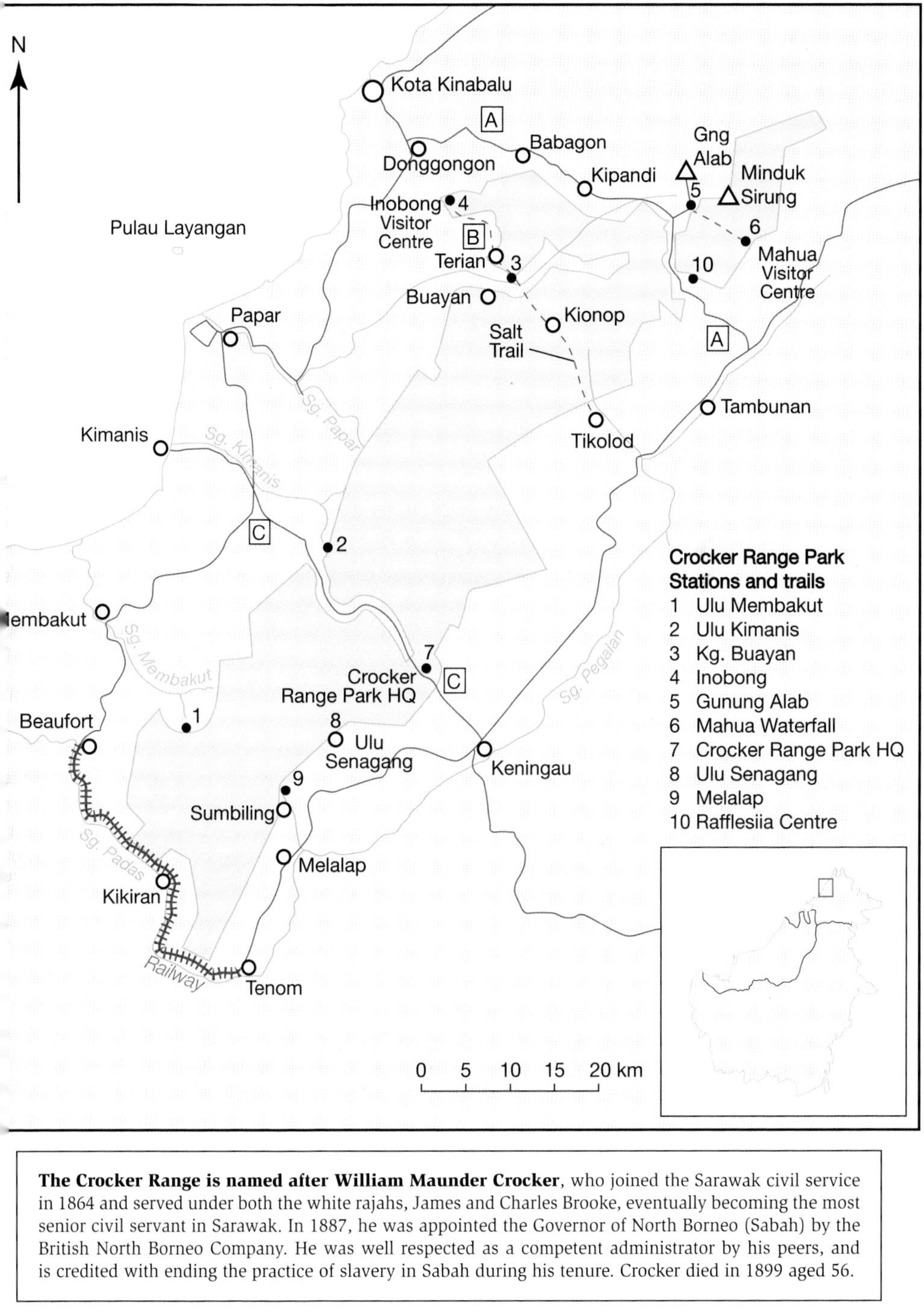

The Crocker Range is named after William Maunder Crocker, who joined the Sarawak civil service in 1864 and served under both the white rajahs, James and Charles Brooke, eventually becoming the most senior civil servant in Sarawak. In 1887, he was appointed the Governor of North Borneo (Sabah) by the British North Borneo Company. He was well respected as a competent administrator by his peers, and is credited with ending the practice of slavery in Sabah during his tenure. Crocker died in 1899 aged 56.

SABAH 4: KINABALU INTRODUCTION 1

KINABALU PARK HQ (6°00′35″N, 116°32′26″E) 1,600m 2-hour drive from Kota Kinabalu. A wide range of accommodation surrounded by pristine mountain forest with an excellent trail system. Best location to see Borneo's magnificent endemic montane birds (p. 334). The slopes of Kinabalu above 1,000m host the greatest diversity of rodents per unit area in the world (p. 236). In the forest around Kinabalu HQ look for 5 species of endemic squirrel, the Kinabalu Squirrel (p. 195), Black-banded Squirrel (p. 204), Whitehead's Pigmy Squirrel (p. 206), Brooke's Squirrel (p. 200) and Sculptor Squirrel (p. 208). The large refuse bins next to the main road, 100m below the Timpohon Gate, attract endemic Mountain Ground Squirrels (p. 212) and Mountain Treeshrews (p. 146) during the day, and a variety of rats and an occasional Ferret Badger at night (p. 254).

KINABALU SUMMIT TRAIL (6°04′28″N, 116°33′45″E) 1,500m rising to 4,100m From Timpohon Gate, a strenuous climb of around 5 hours takes you to the rest huts at Panar Laban, and a further climb of 3 hours (the following day) will see you reach the summit. Forest ranges from mossy montane to rhododendron scrub and bare rock higher up. Look for the endemic Jentink's Squirrel (p. 200) around rest-stop bins. You may be visited by the locally abundant Kinabalu Rat (p. 230) in your sleeping bag at night. During heavy rain look for the pink Giant Kinabalu Leeech *Mimobdella buettikoferi*, which emerges from its burrow to chase grey Giant Kinabalu Earthworms *Pheretima darnleiensis* across the Summit Trail (2,000–3,000m).

KINABALU MESILAU RESORT (5°59′55″N, 116°35′16″E) 2,000m 45-minute drive from headquarters. Of interest to botanists because of magnificent pitcher plant-festooned cliffs, but little visited because of limited trails. Look for *Hylomis* (p. 138), often seen foraging in the flowerbeds. The Malay Weasel and Spotted Giant Flying Squirrels are locally common. Mountain Treeshrew (by day) and Kinabalu Rat (by night) feed on the giant pitchers of *Nepenthes rajah* growing on the nearby cliffs (p. 70). **Note:** Cliff entry restricted – guide required.

KINABALU PORING HOT SPRINGS (6° 03′N, 116° 42′E) 550m rising to 1, 200m 90-minute drive from Kinabalu park headquarters. Excellent hill and submontane forest with a very long bird-list. Now overrun with noisy day trippers visiting the hot springs, butterfly garden, canopy walkway, and native orchid centre. A very large variety of mammals has been recorded at Poring along the **Langanan Waterfall Trail**, including wild Orangutans, Sun Bears, Clouded Leopards, Hose's Civet, Linsang and Sabah Langur, but due to poaching wildlife is now very scarce. A path passes a mini bat cave with Glossy Swiftlet nests en route. Colugos often seen around the hot springs at night. Mammal studies include treeshrews (Emmons 2000), small mammals (Wells 2006, 2009, p. 243) and canopy mammals (Lakim 1994).

JOHN WHITEHEAD AND THE MAMMALS OF KINABALU PARK

On his two expeditions to Kinabalu in 1887–8, Whitehead found that the local Kiau Dusuns had already cleared most of the forest up to 1,000m for swidden rice farming, and used established paths up to the tree line to trap small mammals. Whitehead collected 21 spp of mammals on Kinabalu, of which 3 squirrels, 4 rats and 1 treeshrew were new to science (p. 207).

Hose's Langur on Kinabalu 'To-day Buntar shot three large grey monkeys, which we gave to the Dusuns on condition that they skinned them for us. The skins, unfortunately, were destroyed by the blowflies. This monkey was a new species and has been re-discovered since on the Baram River and named, after its discoverer, Hose's Langur. The following day Kuro (the headman of Kiau) came and prepared one for me. He was such an adept with the skull that it struck me that he had prepared a few human ones in his day. He tells us that in Kiau there are over fifty heads, which have been taken from the various tribes around. Kuro made a hearty meal of monkey soup, and before he had finished his day's work his face was splashed with soup and gore: These Dusuns are very keen after monkeys, and would eat an orangutan.' (Whitehead 1893, *The Exploration of Kinabalu*).

Orangutans Whitehead never saw an Orangutan although they were well known to local Dusuns. In 1937, Griswold reported that he saw an Orangutan near the current location of park headquarters. Griswold's hunters collected both Hose's and Red Langurs on the western slopes of Kinabalu, but described both langurs as rare (Allen & Coolidge 1941). Small populations of Orangutan and both Red and Grey Sabah Langurs may survive on the remote eastern slopes of Kinabalu and on Gng Tambuyukon.

KINABALU EARTHQUAKE

Early in the morning of 5 June 2015, a severe earthquake (6.0 Richter Scale) caused massive landslides and rock falls on Kinabalu, killing 18 people. This was the first large earthquake in Kinabalu's known history. Kinabalu continues to grow in height by about 0.8cm per annum.

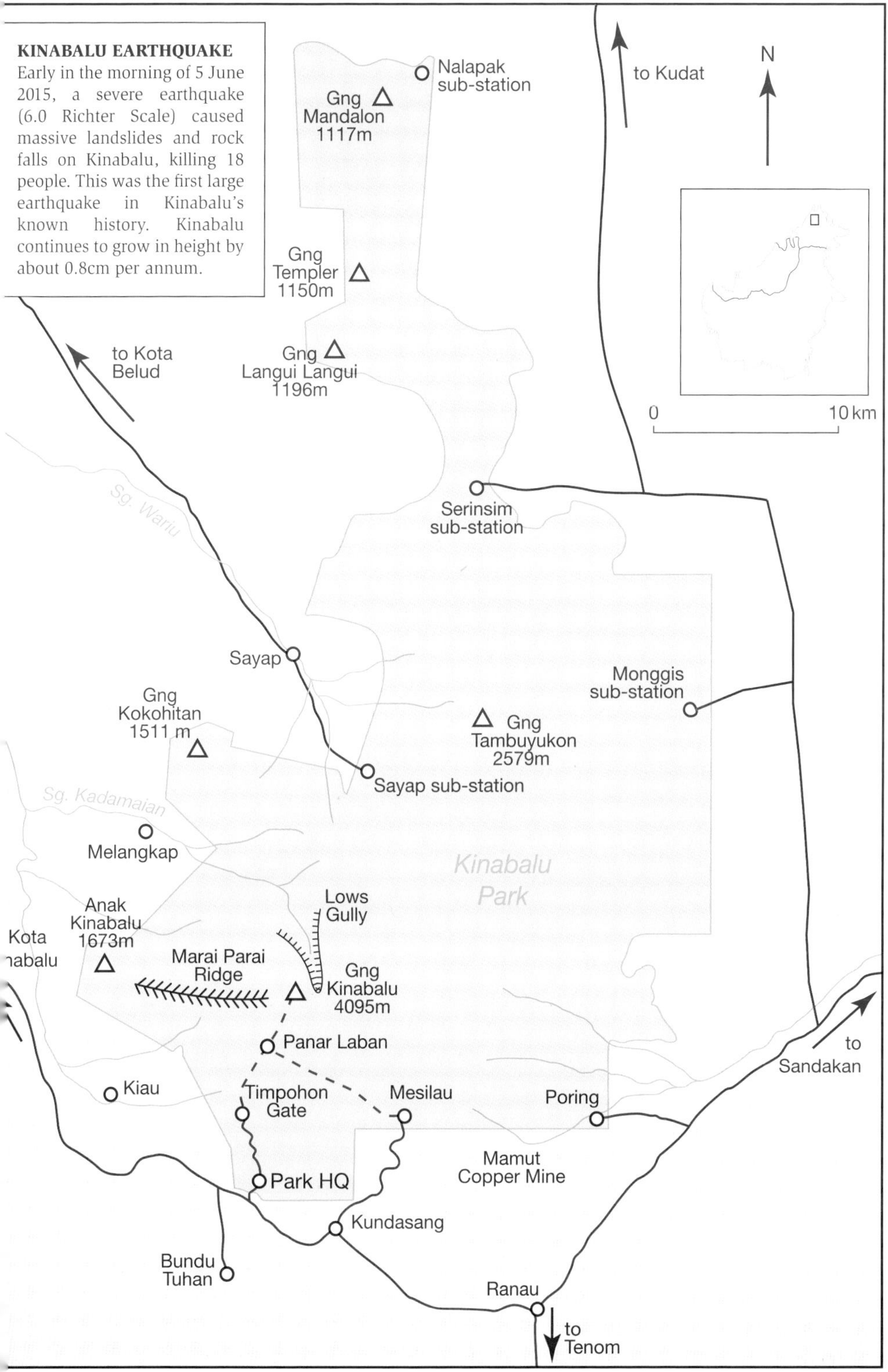

SABAH 5: SOME COMMON BIRDS OF KINABALU PARK HEADQUARTERS

Bornean Treepie
Dendrocitta cinerascens

Ashy Drongo
Dicrurus leucophaeus

Chestnut-hooded Laughing Thrush
Rhinocichla treacheri

Whitehead's Broadbill
Calyptomena whiteheadi

Whitehead's Spiderhunter
Arachnothera juliae

Whitehead's Trogon
Harpactes whiteheadi

WHITEHEAD AND THE BIRDS OF KINABALU John Whitehead, an English ornithologist, read extensively about Borneo before he left England for Borneo in 1884. Two books he read described botanical expeditions to Kinabalu: firstly, Spenser St John (1862), *Life in the Forests of the Far East*, which described 2 expeditions to Kinabalu with Hugh Low in 1858 (p. 143). Whitehead's reading also included *The Gardens of the Sun* by plant collector F. W. Burbidge (1880). Whitehead was fully aware that no ornithologist had yet collected birds on Kinabalu, and it was obvious that if the plant life on Kinabalu was so striking, the birds were likely to be equally unique. Whitehead's meticulous planning and dogged determination paid off handsomely. He added 59 bird species to the Borneo list and was the first to collect nearly all of Borneo's endemic montane birds. He made the first recorded ascent of Low's Peak, the highest point on Kinabalu, in 1888, but is best known for discovering Whitehead's Broadbill, Whitehead's Trogon and Whitehead's Spiderhunter, 3 of Borneo's most iconic birds (see also pp. 207 and 230).

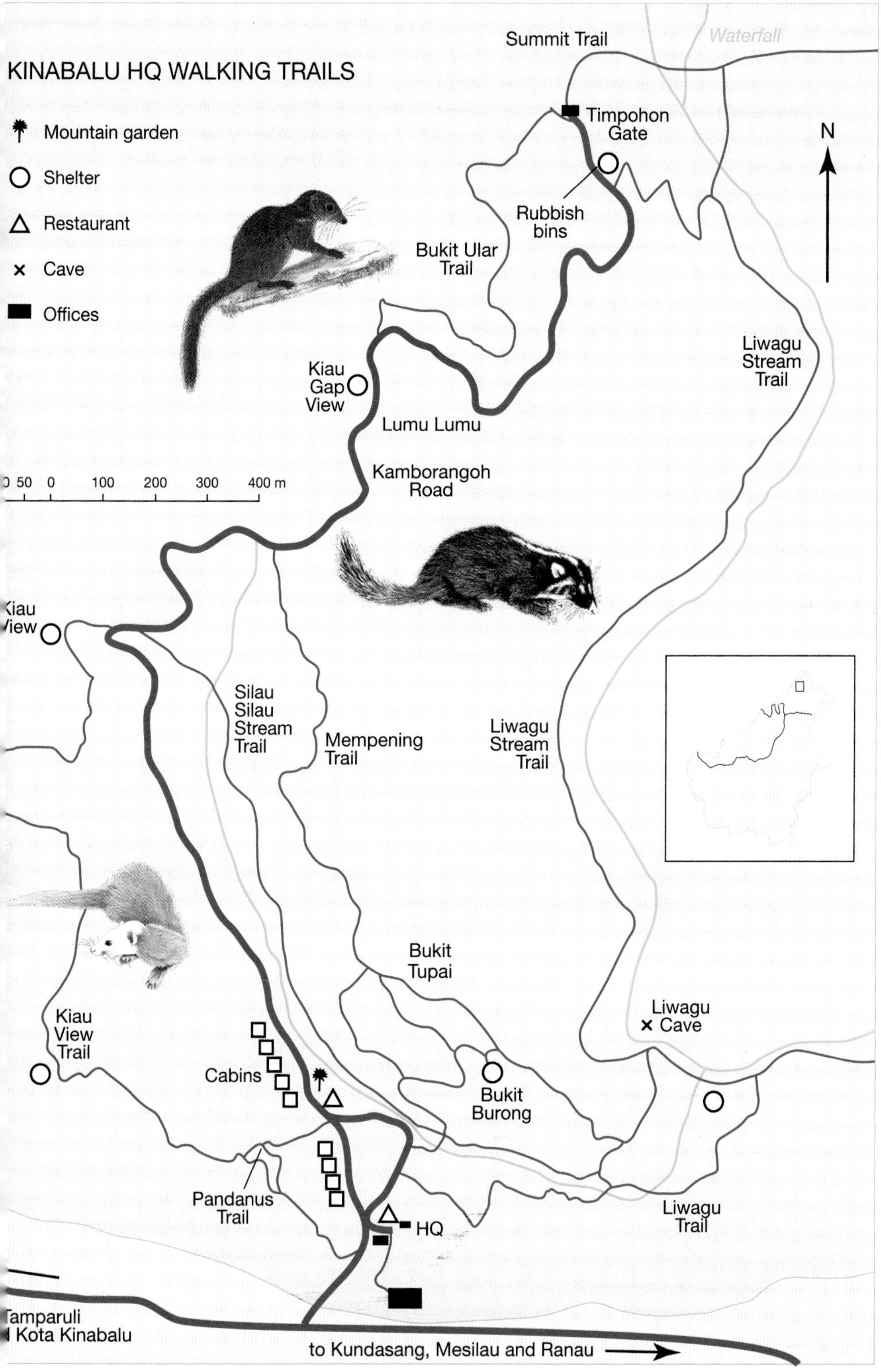

KINABALU HQ WALKING TRAILS
Mountain garden
Shelter
Restaurant
Cave
Offices
N
50 0 100 200 300 400 m
Summit Trail
Waterfall
Timpohon Gate
Rubbish bins
Bukit Ular Trail
Kiau Gap View
Lumu Lumu
Kamborangoh Road
Liwagu Stream Trail
Kiau View
Silau Silau Stream Trail
Mempening Trail
Liwagu Stream Trail
Bukit Tupai
Liwagu Cave
Kiau View Trail
Cabins
Bukit Burong
Pandanus Trail
HQ
Liwagu Trail
Tamparuli
Kota Kinabalu
to Kundasang, Mesilau and Ranau

SABAH 6: GRAHIC INDEX TO THE MAMMALS AND BIRDS OF THE KINABALU SUMMIT TRAIL

★ Endemic

Wreathed Hornbill
Mountain Black-eye *
Island Thrush
ountain
f-Warbler
Friendly Bush-Warbler *
Tawny-breasted Parrotfinch
Golden-naped Barbet *
Bornean Stubtail *
Mountain Wren Babbler *
Bornean Whistling-Thrush *
Grey-throated Babbler
Mountain Treeshew, p.146 *
Jentink's Squirrel, p.200 *

SABAH 7: DERAMAKOT FOREST MANAGEMENT UNIT

DERAMAKOT FMU (5°13′N, 117°35′E) 55,083ha, altitude 30–330m ASL Camera-trapping and wildlife surveys by Wilting (2010), Samejima et al. (2012), Matusbayashi, Mohd-Azlan and others show that Deramakot is one of the richest sites for wildlife in Borneo, despite repeated selective logging since 1956. The reserve is flat and swampy along the Kinabatangan River, with hills in the north, drained by the Sg Deramakot.

Deramakot is surrounded by 6,500km² of production and protected forest, part of the Sabah Foundation forests. Nearly 50% (4,500) of Sabah's Orangutans occur in these forests (Ancrenaz et al. 2005). Provided the Sabah Foundation concession continues to be logged sustainably and not converted to oil-palm or tree plantations, it will become the most important wildlife refuge in Borneo (see below).

Wildlife Deramakot alone hosts *c.* 700 Orangutans. The swampy SW corner next to the Kinabatangan River is rich in rare aquatic mammals, including the Hairy-nosed Otter, Flat-headed Cat and Otter Civet.

Cats Deramakot is one of a few sites in Borneo where all 5 Bornean cat species have been recorded. **Primates:** Orangutans and gibbons are common. The Red Langur is scarce and the Sabah Grey Langur is rare (see below). Banteng are present, and elephants use logging roads throughout.

Poaching pressure is low because there are only 5 small Muslim fishing villages along the Kinabatangan River and many of the villagers work in the FMU. **Access:** Deramakot can be reached by boat up the Kinabatangan from Batu Puteh (4 hours), or by 4-wheel drive vehicle on a logging road from Sandakan (3 hours). Visits can only be booked through local tour companies. The visitor cabins are self catering and you will need a 4WD vehicle and a local guide.

DERMAKOT IS A MODEL FMU (Forest Management Unit), one of 137 in Sabah dedicated to the sustainable long-term commercial production of timber. Following assistance from the German Agency for Technical Cooperation in 1995, Deramakot was split into 135 compartments, with 1–3 compartments to be logged every year on a sustainable basis, using Reduced Impact Logging (RIL). Deramakot is run by the Sabah Forest Department as a best-practice model, an example to the management of other FMUs in Sabah on how to obtain FSC status. Twenty-one per cent of Deramakot is permanently unlogged because of steep hillsides or because the area is one of 17 compartments (total 3,473ha) set aside for conservation.

Sustainable logging and the FSC To be certified as sustainable timber by the Forest Stewardship Council (FSC), production forest must be managed both for long-term (sustainable) timber production and to preserve biodiversity. However, these 2 aims are not entirely compatible. Whilst logging benefits some mammals, it causes problems to others. For example, the removal of large trees eliminates the nesting holes used by flying squirrels and hornbills, and liana cutting (a common practice allowing young trees to grow faster) destroys the most important source of food (leguminous beans and leaves) eaten by langurs (p. 68).

Survival of mammals in logged forest Research has shown that many Bornean mammals can survive and even thrive in responsibly logged forest. Removal of the largest dipterocarp trees and the construction of logging roads opens up gaps where wildlife-friendly secondary forest trees such as *Macaranga* and Laran (p. 224) flourish. Extra light increases the population of bananas, gingers and *Alocasia*, which provide much nectar and fruit for small birds and mammals (p. 72). Elephants, Banteng, Sambar, rats, macaques and Leopard Cats benefit from logging. **After logging, mammal populations often increase but species diversity falls**. Populations of virgin-forest specialists, including most civets, langurs and flying squirrels, crash when forest is logged (p. 28). Calculating the adverse effects of logging on wildlife in Borneo is confused by poaching. Logging roads open up previously inaccessible forest to hunters using spotlights at night. During logging, timber-camp workers are the main culprits. After the workers leave, sports hunters use the logging roads to drive in from nearby kampongs.

MINERAL SPRINGS AT DERAMAKOT Spread out along the banks of the Deramakot River, 11 small, clear pools of water with a high sodium (salt) and calcium content have been found. In their *Faunal Survey of Sabah* (1982), Davis & Payne found that large mammals such as elephants, rhinos and Banteng were usually associated with salt licks or mineral springs. Where mineral springs were absent, so were large mammals. Mineral springs are found throughout Borneo, particularly in the hilly interior, for example in the Kelabit Highlands (Sarawak), at Kayan Mentarang (NE Kalimantan), in the upper reaches of the Segama (Malua) and Kinabatangan Rivers, and at Tabin (Sabah). Camera trapping at Deramakot's mineral springs (Matsubayashi et al. 2006, 2011, 2014) found that Sambar were the most common visitors, followed by pigs, Lesser Mousedeer, Teledu and Orangutan. Female Sambar visited more than males, and more frequently when pregnant. A total of 23 larger mammals visited the springs, including elephants and Banteng, omnivores such as porcupines, civets and Sun Bear, and carnivores such as Clouded Leopards, Leopard Cats and Yellow-throated Martens.

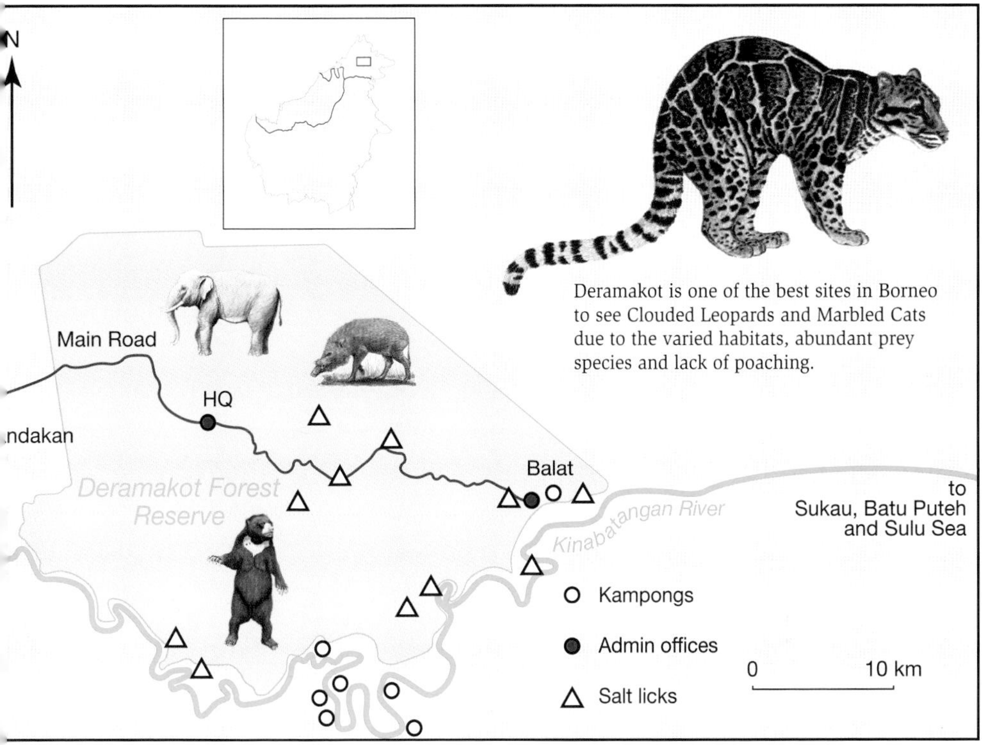

Mother and infant Orangutans drinking salty water from a mineral spring at Deramakot. Orangutans are the fifth most common visitor to Deramakot's salt springs. Both sexes of all ages are frequent visitors. (Camera trap photo from Matusbayashi and Lagan 2014)

SABAH 8: SEPILOK AND LABUK BAY, SANDAKAN

Sepilok is the centre of both wildlife and forest research in Sabah including a 6,000ha pristine forest reserve, an excellent herbarium, the Rainforest Discovery Centre, Orangutan and Sun Bear Rehabilitation Centres. The forest is rich in wildlife including gibbons and slow loris. Davies (1984) found the highest density of Red Langurs in Borneo at Sepilok (p. 162), while Crompton found an extraordinarily high density of tarsiers (p. 158). www.forest.sabah.gov.my

Access 8-hour drive from Kota Kinabalu or 45 minutes by air from KK to Sandakan, then 30 minutes by taxi.

Accommodation Sepilok has a large range of reasonably priced accommodation, from hostels to 4-star lodges. Visitors are strongly advised to stay at Sepilok, not in a hotel in Sandakan, due to daily traffic jams.

Rainforest Discovery Centre (RDC) This includes a cafe, numerous well-marked forest trails and an excellent small botanical garden. The canopy walkway is world renowned for the quality bird watching, including the frequently sighted endemic Bornean Bristlehead. The RDC hosts many wildlife-related events, including the annual Borneo Bird Festival and bird watching. Night walks when staff are available.

RDC Canopy Walkway This is the best place in Borneo to see both the Black and Red Giant Flying Squirrels, which emerge at dusk from their tree holes, gliding from one large tree trunk to another. You may also see semi-wild Orangutans, gibbons and Red Langurs, and both Long-tailed and Pig-tailed Macaques, as well as Giant and Prevost's Squirrels. www.forest.sabah.gov.my/rdc

Orangutan Rehabilitation Centre Sepilok was the original rehabilitation and release site for young Orangutans orphaned by forest conversion in Sabah. The forest at Sepilok has reached Orangutan carrying capacity and rehabilitated Orangutans are now released at Tabin. However, several generations of related habituated Orangutans arrive daily at the Sepilok feeding platform to feed on fruit and milk at 10 a.m. and 3 p.m., watched by more than 100,000 visitors every year. www.sabahtourism.com

The Sun Bear Centre was founded by Wong Siew Te, a Sun Bear researcher, to rehabilitate Sun Bears kept as illegal pets. This well-run site houses around 30 bears in a forest setting. Wild males from the surrounding Sepilok forest have been known to break into the centre to mate with receptive females. www.bsbcc.org.my

Walk to the Mangroves A 2-hour walk through the Sepilok forest that arrives at an information centre on the edge of Sandakan Bay is an excellent introduction to rainforest life. Book a boat for the return journey.

Labuk Bay Proboscis Sanctuary This is a 30-minute drive from Sepiloik. Best visited on a day trip from Sepilok, this privately owned tourist site comprises mangrove forest surrounded by oil palm. Provides accommodation and the opportunity to view the feeding of habituated Proboscis Monkeys, Silvered Langurs, Pied Hornbills, otters and sea eagles. A mangrove boardwalk provides bird-watching access to Collared and Ruddy Kingfishers, Mangrove Whistler, Mangrove Blue Flycatcher and the rare Black-hooded Oriole. (pp.174 and 179.) www.proboscis.cc

Lesser Mousedeer are more common at Sepilok than Greater possibly due to the local extinction of Clouded Leopard and Marbled Cat (Photo Hans Hazebroek).

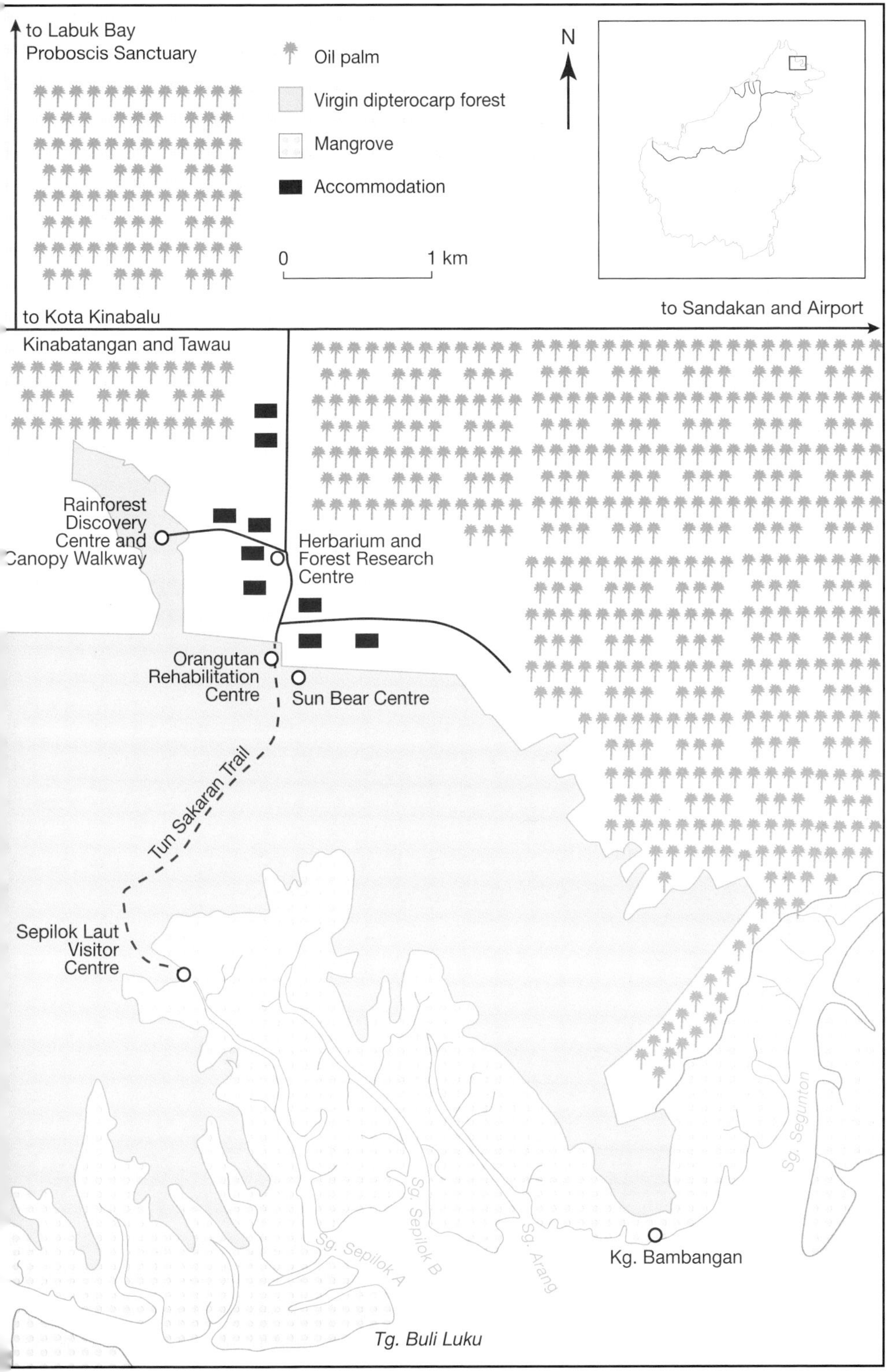

to Labuk Bay
Proboscis Sanctuary
Oil palm
Virgin dipterocarp forest
Mangrove
Accommodation
0
1 km
N
to Kota Kinabalu
Kinabatangan and Tawau
to Sandakan and Airport
Rainforest
Discovery
Centre and
Canopy Walkway
Herbarium and
Forest Research
Centre
Orangutan
Rehabilitation
Centre
Sun Bear Centre
Tun Sakaran Trail
Sepilok Laut
Visitor
Centre
Sg. Sepilok A
Sg. Sepilok B
Sg. Arang
Sg. Segunton
Kg. Bambangan
Tg. Buli Luku

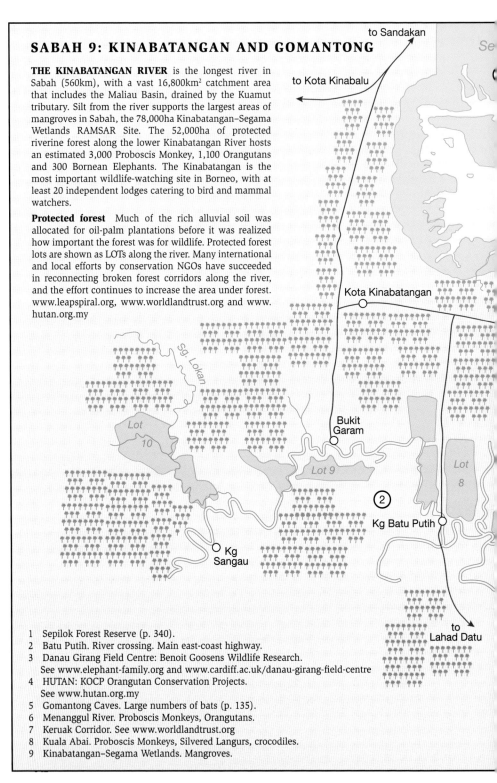

SABAH 9: KINABATANGAN AND GOMANTONG

THE KINABATANGAN RIVER is the longest river in Sabah (560km), with a vast 16,800km^2 catchment area that includes the Maliau Basin, drained by the Kuamut tributary. Silt from the river supports the largest areas of mangroves in Sabah, the 78,000ha Kinabatangan–Segama Wetlands RAMSAR Site. The 52,000ha of protected riverine forest along the lower Kinabatangan River hosts an estimated 3,000 Proboscis Monkey, 1,100 Orangutans and 300 Bornean Elephants. The Kinabatangan is the most important wildlife-watching site in Borneo, with at least 20 independent lodges catering to bird and mammal watchers.

Protected forest Much of the rich alluvial soil was allocated for oil-palm plantations before it was realized how important the forest was for wildlife. Protected forest lots are shown as LOTs along the river. Many international and local efforts by conservation NGOs have succeeded in reconnecting broken forest corridors along the river, and the effort continues to increase the area under forest. www.leapspiral.org, www.worldlandtrust.org and www.hutan.org.my

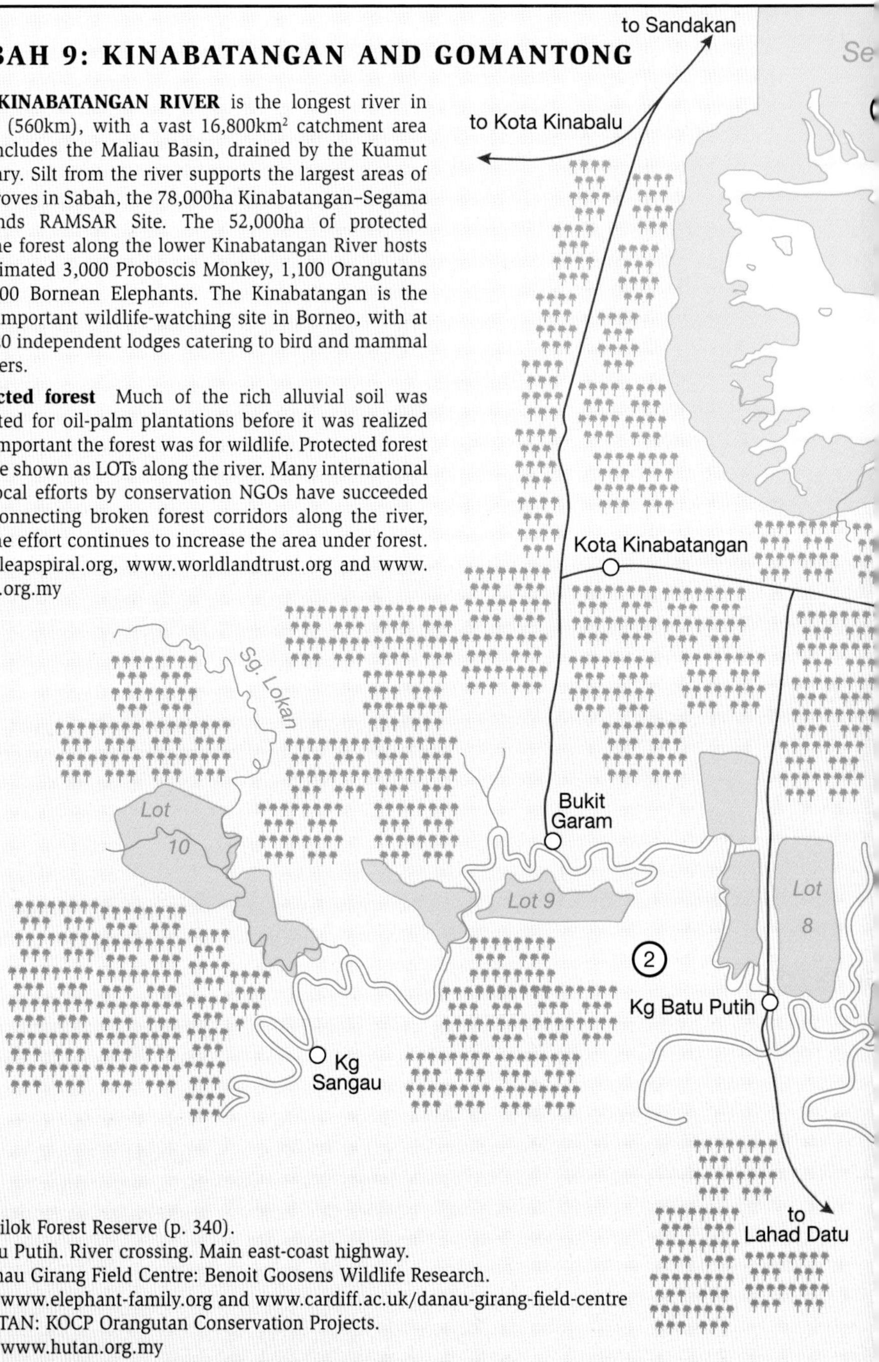

1 Sepilok Forest Reserve (p. 340).
2 Batu Putih. River crossing. Main east-coast highway.
3 Danau Girang Field Centre: Benoit Goosens Wildlife Research. See www.elephant-family.org and www.cardiff.ac.uk/danau-girang-field-centre
4 HUTAN: KOCP Orangutan Conservation Projects. See www.hutan.org.my
5 Gomantong Caves. Large numbers of bats (p. 135).
6 Menanggul River. Proboscis Monkeys, Orangutans.
7 Keruak Corridor. See www.worldlandtrust.org
8 Kuala Abai. Proboscis Monkeys, Silvered Langurs, crocodiles.
9 Kinabatangan–Segama Wetlands. Mangroves.

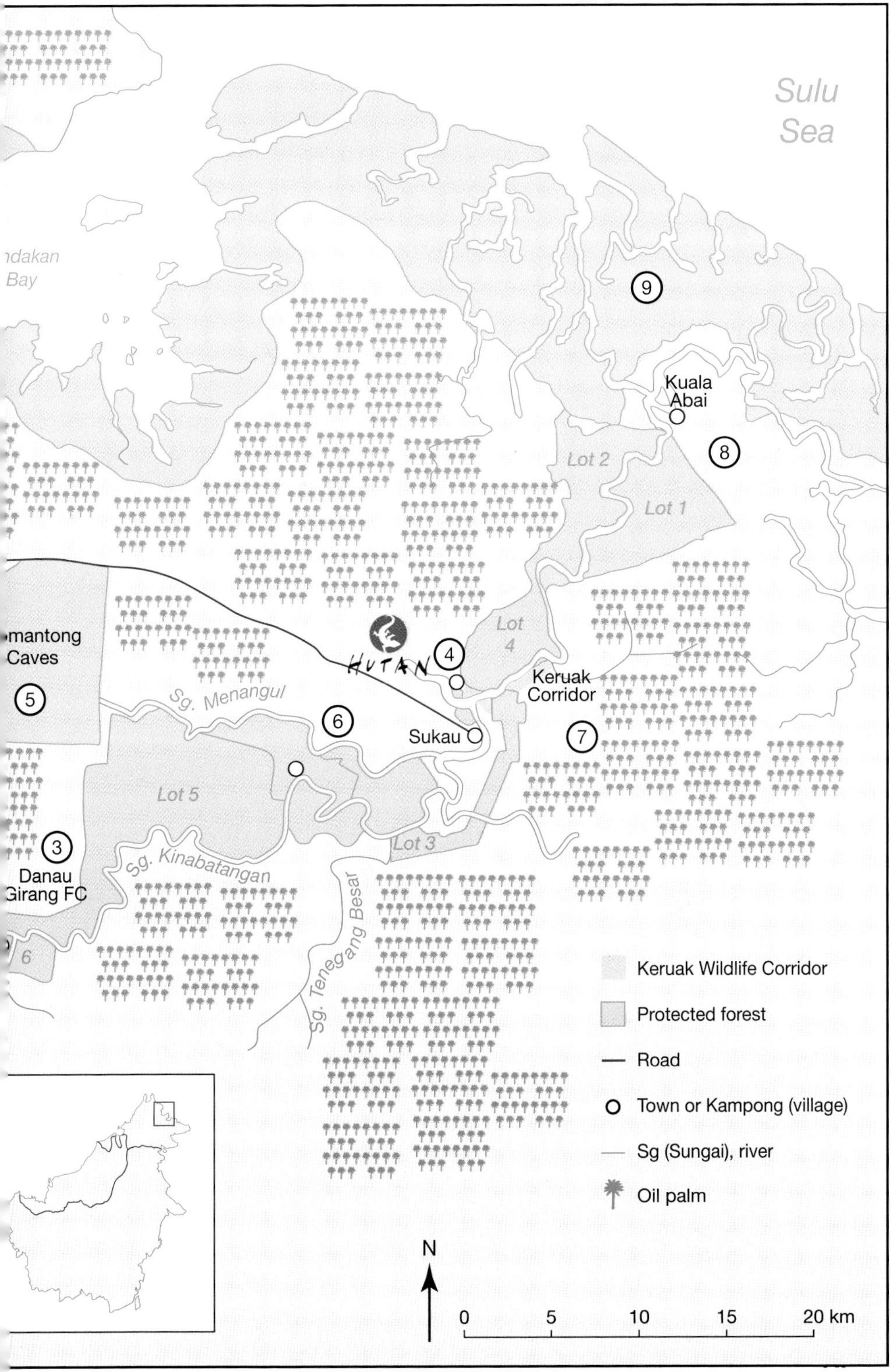
Sulu
Sea
ndakan
Bay
9
Kuala
Abai
8
Lot 2
Lot 1
Lot
4
mantong
Caves
5
HUTAN
4
Keruak
Corridor
Sg. Menangul
6
Sukau
7
Lot 5
3
Danau
Girang FC
Sg. Kinabatangan
Lot 3
Sg. Tenegang Besar
6
Keruak Wildlife Corridor
Protected forest
Road
Town or Kampong (village)
Sg (Sungai), river
Oil palm
N
0
5
10
15
20 km

SABAH 10: TABIN WILDLIFE RESERVE (TWR)

TABIN WR (5°10′N, 118°45′E) 1,200 km² Tabin is one of the best sites in Borneo to easily see a large variety of wildlife, including birds and rare mammals both large and small. Tabin WR was established after most of what was known as the Silabukan Forest Reserve had been logged. The only unlogged forest in 1984 was a 'core area' of 86 km² and the 100ha of forest surrounding the mud volcano. Altitude ranges from 120m at Lipad to 571m at Gng Hattam. There are extensive caves in a limestone hill in the north. NE Tabin is connected by a forested corridor to the Kinabatangan Segama Kulamba RAMSAR site (p. 343).

Access 2-hour drive from the small town of Lahad Datu over a rough dirt road. Lahad Datu is 1 hour by plane from Kota Kinabalu and a 3-hour drive from Sandakan.

Accommodation The cabins of the TWR overlook the Tabin River. From the resort you can take walks along the nearby trails or night drives along the Tomanggong Road that divides the forest from an oil-palm estate. Researchers stay in the nearby Sabah Wildlife Department (SWD) staff quarters.

Mud volcanoes There are 2 large mud volcanoes at Tabin, one in the remote central core area, and the Lipad mud volcano 3km from the TWR, which has a canopy tower for viewing visiting wildlife. Overnight stays are possible. Wilting (2007) reported that a Clouded Leopard dragged a pig carcass onto the first storey of the tower. The surrounding forest is rich in fig trees, and hornbills are often seen in the early morning.

Sumatran Rhinoceros The Borneo Rhino Alliance (BORA) rhino-breeding compound is situated in the TWR, although it is not yet open to the public. It houses the last 3 Sumatran Rhinos left in Sabah, Tam, a young male, Putung, a middle-aged female, and Iman, a female captured in 2014 (p. 298).

Elephants Dawson (1992) estimated *c.* 300 elephants at Tabin. A steadily increasing population frequently visits the TWR area. Elephants enter oil-palm plantations to feed on leaf fronds that have been cut during fruit harvesting (p. 290). Elephant-related human deaths are very unusual in Borneo, but in 2014 a young Australian tourist followed a single male elephant on foot, taking flash photographs, and was killed when the elephant attacked her. Single-tusked males with a damp cheek-patch (in musth) are especially dangerous.

Cats All five Bornean cats have been recorded. The Clouded Leopard and Marbled Cat are seen regularly. The Leopard Cat is often seen sitting on the edge of the oil-palm estate waiting for passing rats.

Otters Both Smooth and Small-clawed Otters hunt in groups along the Tabin River. Lesser Fish Eagles chase the Smooth Otters for their fish. Darters, 3 kingfisher spp. and the Flat-headed Cat also live along the river.

Sun Bears Normua et al. (2004) radio-tracked 4 Sun Bears near the TWR and found that they spent the day in the forest, but entered the oil-palm estate to feed on palm buds and oil-palm fruit at night (p. 248).

Primates Tabin is the release site for Orangutans rehabilitated at Sepilok and they are seen regularly. Dr Zainal of BORA reports that a mother Orangutan with baby was attacked by a Clouded Leopard next to the rhino paddock. The mother was found dead and the baby died later. Gibbon territories surround the Tabin Wildlife Resort and gibbons often feed in the many fig trees that grow around the cabins. This is the only accessible tourist site in Borneo where grey Sabah Langurs can be easily seen. (p. 166). Long-tailed Macaques feed along the river and a large troop of Pig-tailed Macaques feeds in the oil palm.

Birds All eight hornbills have been recorded at Tabin, many feeding on oil-palm fruit. Giant, Black-crowned and Blue-headed Pittas share overlapping territories in the forest around the mud volcano, which at night is the hunting ground of Large and Sundan Frogmouths. Large owls (at night) and eagles (by day) are often seen along the Tomanggong Road waiting for rats and snakes to cross between the forest and the oil palm.

Why Tabin is one of best sites for viewing wildlife in Borneo

1 Tabin is managed by the Sabah Wildlife Department for wildlife, not for timber production.
2 Tabin is one of the largest protected forest areas in Borneo (pp. 14 and 168, Species Area Relationships).
3 Logging has produced pioneer plants eaten by Sambar, elephants and Banteng.
4 Tabin is surrounded by well-managed oil-palm estates so that poaching is relatively easy to control.
5 Oil palms fruit continuously, providing fallback food during lean periods between forest masting.
6 Oil-palm fruit are eaten by pigs, Sun Bears, macaques, civets, squirrels, porcupines, bats and rats.
7 The abundance of rats and macaques attracts Clouded Leopards, and Marbled, Leopard and Bay Cats.
8 The mud volcanoes attract elephants, Banteng, wild pig, Sambar, muntjac and mousedeer (p. 24).

HUNTING AND POACHING The abundant wildlife at Tabin, where poaching is under control, proves that poaching is a major threat to wildlife. Poaching is particularly prevalent in logging concessions where the loggers hunt for the pot, followed by sports and commercial hunters from nearby towns and kampongs, who gain easy access to the forest via newly created logging roads. Once the large mammals and birds have been killed, forest fragmentation and roads cut off migration routes from source populations, resulting in rapid local extinction of all large wildlife. See p. 371, Source and Sink habitats.

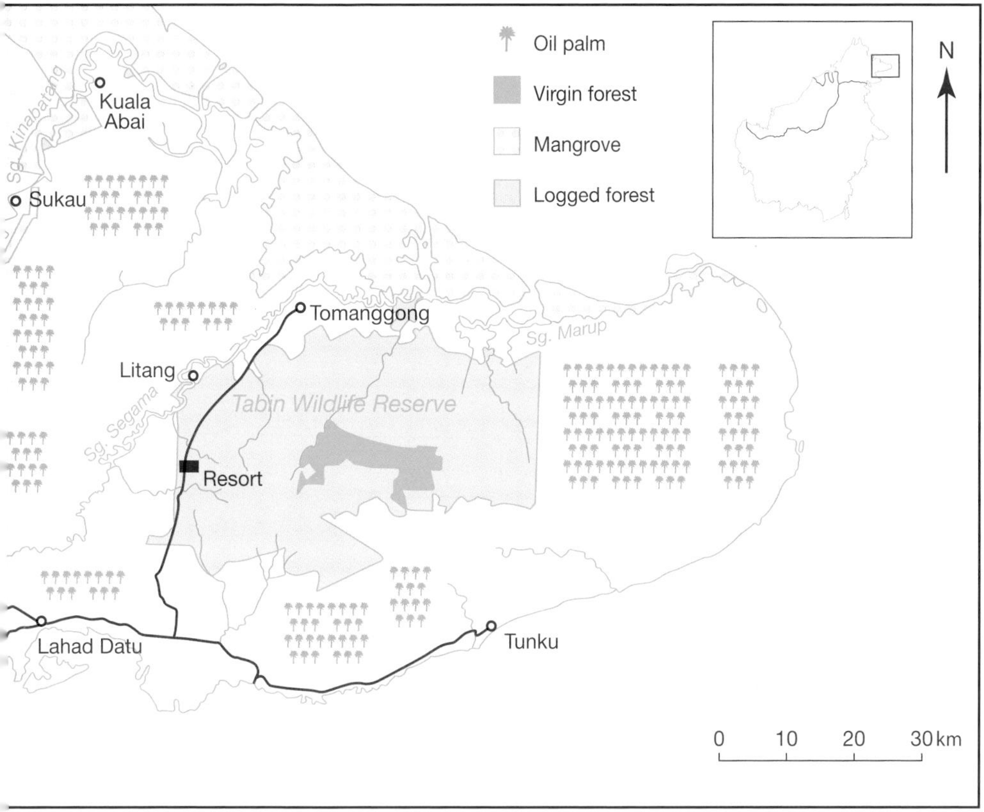

Adult Elephants eating salty mud at the Lipad Mud Volcano Tabin, while young elephants frolic in the mud. See pp. 24 and 339. (Photo: Lawrence Chin, TWR.)

SABAH 11: DANUM VALLEY

DANUM VALLEY CONSERVATION AREA (4°49′N, 117°28′E) Core area of virgin lowland and hill forest ($438km^2$) surrounded by a matrix of about 10,000km2 of both production and protected forest. Highest point is Gng Danum at 1,093m. For an insight into the forest before logging started (in the 1970s), read both of John MacKinnon's classic books, *In Search of the Red Ape* (1974) and *Borneo* (1978), about his Orangutan research (1968–9) at Kuala Bole, a tributary of the Segama, now fully protected forest once again.
Access 2½-hour drive from Lahad Datu, which is 1 hour by plane from Kota Kinabalu.
Accommodation Tourists are welcomed at the 5-star Borneo Rainforest Lodge (BRL), whilst students and bona fide researchers can apply to stay at the (much less expensive) Danum Valley Research Centre (DVFC). Both sites are situated in virgin lowland dipterocarp forest overlooking the river. Both are excellent for wildlife, with extensive, well-marked trails. At BRL a canopy walkway gives views of hornbills and gibbons, whilst DVFC has a scary tree tower but no canopy walkway.
Otters Two otter species, the Small Clawed and Smooth, are often seen travelling in groups along the river. In June 2014, Jon Johnston photographed the Eurasian Otter *Lutra lutra* in the Segama River at DVFC. The Hairy-nosed Otter occurs at Deramakot (35km away), so Danum probably hosts 4 sympatric otters (p. 256).
Elephants Elephant are often seen, with estimated density of 0.28 km^2. Boonratana (1997), p. 290.
Rhinoceros Ahmad et al. (1995) reported 5 active rhino wallows 1km from DVFC. Rhinos are now extinct at Danum (p. 294) due to poaching when surrounding forested areas were being logged.
Wild cats All 5 Bornean species have been recorded. Clouded Leopards appear roughly once a month around BRL, when they may be seen on night drives and occasionally during the day (p. 276).
Primates All the N Borneo primates have been recorded. The Red Langur is much more common than the Sabah Grey Langur. Orangutans are often seen during fig fruiting. Gibbon territories surround the accommodation at both BRL and DVFC (p. 186).
Research DVFC is the most important rainforest research centre in SE Asia. Starting in 1984, DVFC with the support of Yayasan Sabah, local universities and the Royal Society, has hosted hundreds of researchers into rainforest ecology. Danum is the ideal site for scientists to quantify the effect of logging on animal populations in comparison with the surrounding logged forest. For a recent overview see Hazebroek et al. (2012).

LEECHES If you go mammal watching in Borneo you will inevitably be bitten by a leech. According to Smythies (1959), the leeches (Hirudinae) of Borneo can be divided into four types. 1. **Giant leeches** found only in the mountains. These include the 30cm Giant Kinabalu Leech *Gastromobdella monticola* (p.332). 2. **Buffalo leeches** the size of a pen found in wet rice fields. 3. **Thread leeches** in clear mountain streams (also found in salt springs at Deramakot, Matsubayashi 2014), which enter the noses and mouths of drinking mammals. To avoid thread leeches, locals make leaf cups to drink from streams. 4. **Striped tiger leeches** (3 *Haemadipsa* species), common in damp forest where large mammals are abundant. Leeches breathe through the skin, and pigs and rhinos protect themselves from land leeches by wallowing in thick mud. Humans tend to use one of two alternative methods: a. wearing jungle boots and leech-proof socks sprayed with Deet; b. wearing sandals barefooted and checking the feet every 5 minutes. Neither method is fully effective because leeches can also grab on to you from twigs overhanging trails and vanish until blood stains your shirt.

Sounds of the forest: a typical 24-hour soundscape at Danum Valley in the heart of Borneo

5.30 a.m. Start of the bird dawn chorus. Listen for the rich chuckling of the Straw-headed Bulbul from the river, a bubbling White-crowned Shama from the forest edge and the repetitive *chonk chonk chonk* of the Striped Tit Babbler from riverside vegetation. A male North Borneo Gibbon provides your early-morning call.
6.15 a.m. Male and female gibbon duet with *whoops* for 20 minutes (p. 184).
8 a.m. Rhinoceros Hornbill flies in to feed on a fruiting fig tree. Listen for the *whoosh whoosh whoosh* of the wings and the amazing cackling call. Male Orangutan long calls, *whoooah*, are made day and night (p. 188).
10 a.m.–2 p.m. Barbets call *took took took* from fruiting fig trees in the distance, babblers and pittas slow whistle from the forest undergrowth and bulbuls chirp musically from the canopy (p. 268).
2–4 p.m. During the heat of the day birds fall silent. Listen for the sharp *tssk* contact call of a hidden squirrel and the hoarse hicupping *wuk wuk wuk* of a giant Tokay Gecko hidden in the roof void.
4–5.30 p.m. Heavy afternoon rain drowns out all forest sounds.
5.30 p.m. The Six O'Clock Cicada opens the dusk chorus with an eerie buzzing whine that waxes and wanes.
6 p.m. A displaying Eared Nightjar calls *tok-tadow, tok-tadow* in flight over the river bank.
6.30 p.m. Male mole crickets start stridulating from the forest floor, whilst male leaf hopper crickets and katydids stridulate from vegetation. The forest reaches a peak cacophony of sound that slowly reduces as the night chorus settles in. On wet nights frogs *croak, wark* and *peep* all night until dawn.

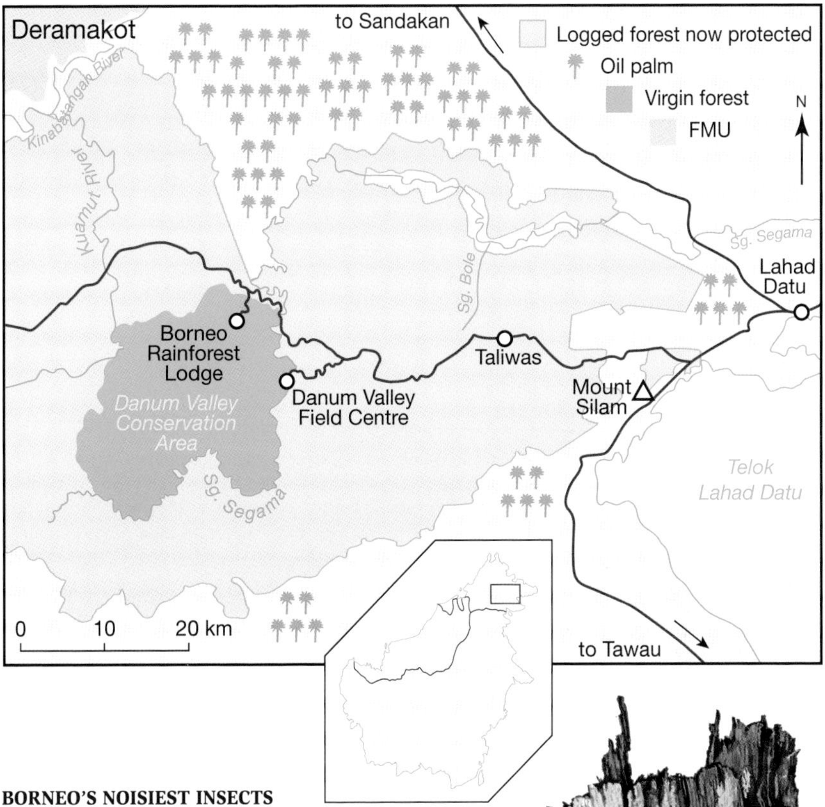

BORNEO'S NOISIEST INSECTS
(all insects 70% life size)

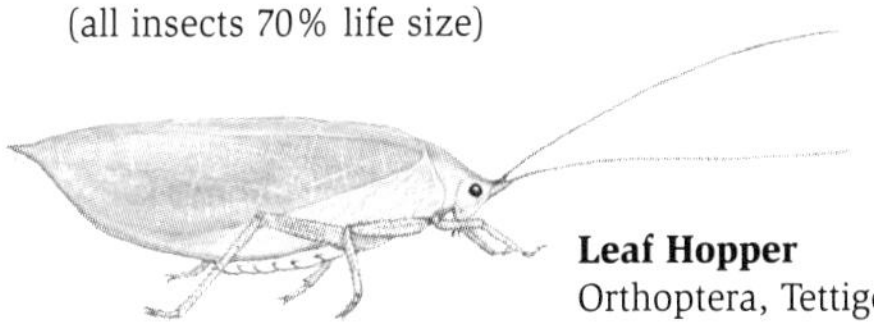

Leaf Hopper
Orthoptera, Tettigoniidae

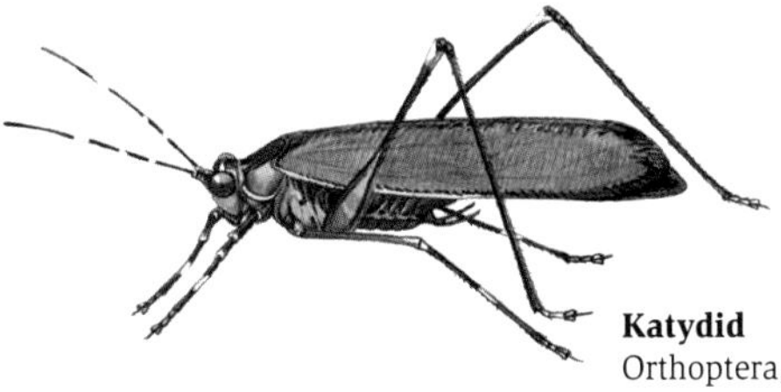

Katydid
Orthoptera, Tettigoniidae

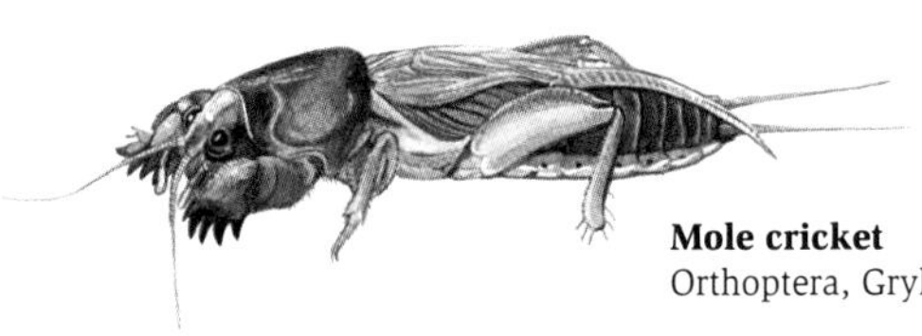

Mole cricket
Orthoptera, Gryllotalpidae

Six O'Clock Cicada
Pomponia merula
Riang Riang
Pukui Enam

SABAH 12: TAWAU HILLS PARK

TAWAU HILLS PARK (4°22´33 N, 117°59´02 E) 280km^2 of watershed catchment forest 20km from Tawau town, ranging from giant lowland dipterocarps to stunted montane moss forest at the summit of Gng Magdalena (1,310m). Tawau Hills Park (TWHP) is a little-known jewel amongst Sabah's Parks, and with better trails and a canopy walkway it could become one of Borneo's premier wildlife-watching destinations. The high conservation value of THWP lies in its rich volcanic soils, rare in Borneo, and its shared northern boundary with 510km^2 Ulu Kalumpang Forest Reserve, which was previously logged but is now fully protected. On the southern boundary lie the hills of the 30km^2 Andrassy FR, where a geothermal power plant with a projected output of 40 megawatts is currently being built. TWHP has some of the finest virgin lowland forest left in Sabah, including 4 of the world's tallest rainforest trees, the Yellow Meranti *Shorea faguetiana* (88.33m), Mengaris *Koompassia excelsa* (85.76m), *Shorea argentifolia* (84.85m) and *S. superba* (84.41m) (pp. 54 and 66).

Access 25-minute taxi drive from Tawau town or 30 minutes from Tawau Airport.

Park facilities Cabins, hostel, restaurant and small shop. Forest trails run north to a large hot spring and the summits of the 3 extinct volcanoes in the forested interior. The route to the highest peak, Gng Magdalena, is not currently open. The trek to the summit of Gng Lucia requires an overnight stay in a self-catering cabin. The walk to Gng Maria takes about 3 hours one way with a large hot spring about a 1-hour walk along the trail.

Where to stay Park headquarters is preferred, but Tawau town has many good (expensive) hotels and is close enough to taxi in. Alternatively, Balung Estate Resort, a 20-minute drive from Tawau Airport on the eastern edge of TWHP, has lodges near the scenic Balung River and cultivates a range of exotic crops.

Birds The rich bird life of TWHP is typical of lowland dipterocarp forest. In 1956, a British Museum expedition climbed Gng Magdalena in the hope of finding rare montane endemics similar to the relicts found on Mt Dulit in NW Sarawak, but discovered only flocks of Bornean Ibons (Banks 1982). This may be because the Tawau Hills volcanoes last erupted *c.* 27,000 years ago, wiping out any relict montane Pleistocene birds.

Mammals The rare Sabah endemic Four-striped Ground Squirrel is reputed to be locally common (pp. 212 and 282). Sabah Grey Langurs are rare, but Red Langurs are common, with a high proportion of white morphs. Orangutans are very scarce in the Tawau Hills, and a survey of the Kalumpang FR found a density of only 0.42/km^2, with a total population of just 183, despite the rich forest.

White Morph of Red Langur at Tawau Hills

Throughout Borneo, the Red Langur is usually most common where Orangutans are common, whilst grey langurs are most common where Orangutans are absent. For the possible reason, see p. 156. Unusually, at Tawau Hills, Red Langurs are common, whilst Orangutans are rare. However, Tawau Hills Red Langurs have a high proportion of white morphs, which have possibly evolved to confuse predatory Clouded Leopards into mistaking them for aggressive Pig-tailed Macaques. (Photo: Wong Tsu Shi.)

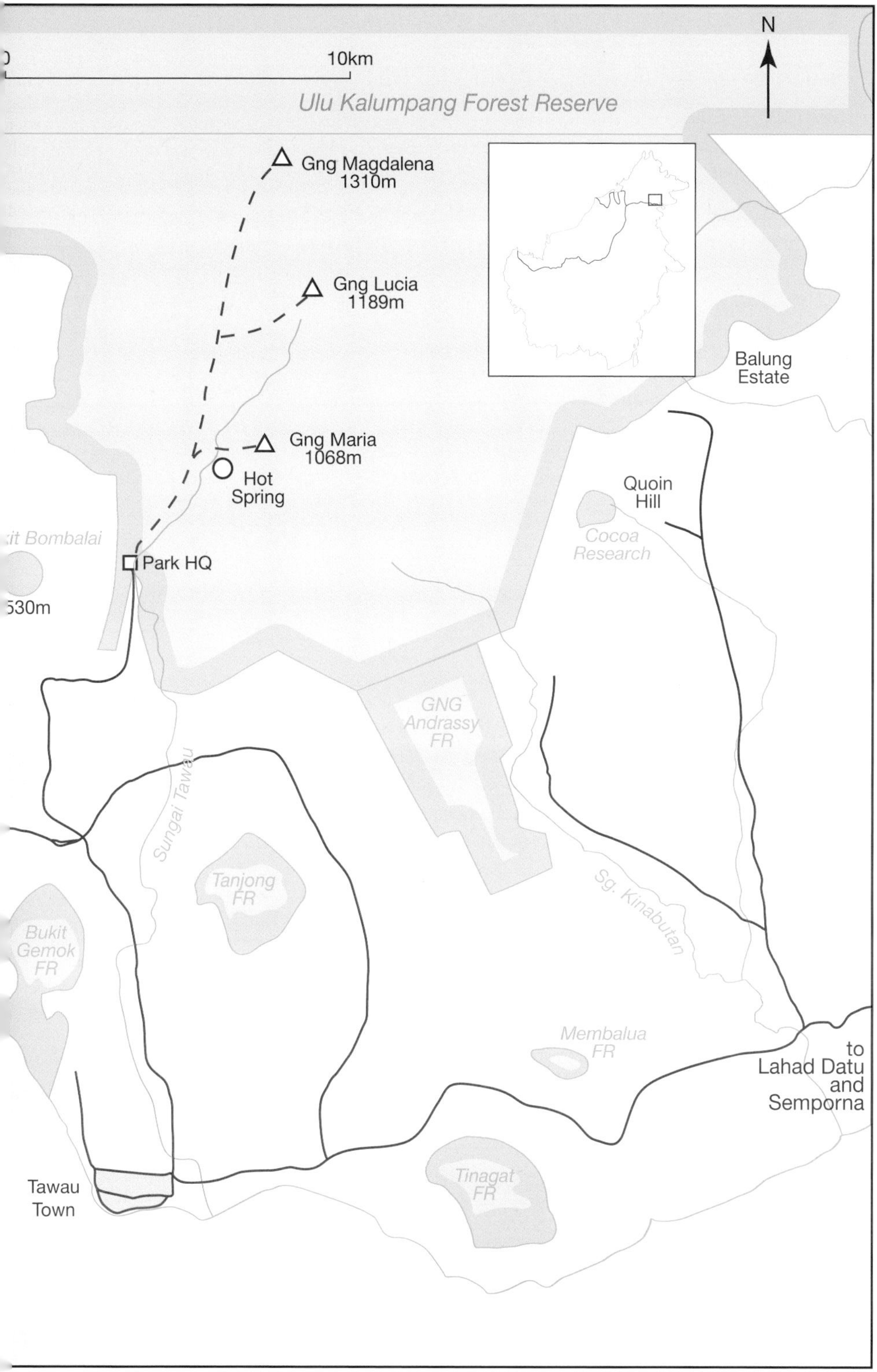
N
0
10km
Ulu Kalumpang Forest Reserve
Gng Magdalena
1310m
Gng Lucia
1189m
Balung
Estate
Gng Maria
1068m
Hot
Spring
Quoin
Hill
Cocoa
Research
kit Bombalai
Park HQ
530m
GNG
Andrassy
FR
Sungai Tawau
Tanjong
FR
Sg. Kinabutan
Bukit
Gemok
FR
Membalua
FR
to
Lahad Datu
and
Semporna
Tinagat
FR
Tawau
Town

SABAH 13: MALIAU BASIN

MALIAU BASIN 588 km^2 of pristine hill forest in South-central Sabah. Altitude varies from 300m to 1,600m at summit of Gng Lutong. Maliau is the Murut name for staircase due to the multiple stepped waterfalls at Maliau Basin.

Access 4-hour drive from Tawau or 8-hour drive from Kota Kinabalu.

Accommodation Researchers and long-term visitors stay at the administrative headquarters in the Maliau Basin Studies Centre (MBSC), where there is a variety of accommodation including a hostel. Most visitors are wildlife trekkers who spend 3–5 days walking a circuit from one 'trekking camp' to another. There are 4 trekking camps, Belian, Ginseng, Nepenthes and Agathis, roughly a 1-day walk apart with more or less basic hostel or tent-type accommodation. From the camps it is possible to take side treks to visit a variety of scenic waterfalls. The trekking is tough and involves some very steep climbs. Treks are best arranged through travel agencies, which can book porters and guides as required. Near the MBSC there is an observation tower and a canopy walkway allowing spectacular views over the surrounding forest.

Geology The Maliau Basin is shaped like a volcanic crater, but there is no geologic evidence that it results from either volcanism or meteorite impact (Hazebroek et al. 2004). There is a large seam of coal in the basin, but plans to mine the coal were abandoned when the Maliau Basin was fully protected in 1997.

Plants Due to the altitude range and variety of slopes and soils, Maliau has one of the most diverse floras in Sabah, including lowland dipterocarp forest, hill *Agathis* forest and large areas of stunted kerangas forest on poor sandy soils. At higher levels, patches of fruiting oak forest attract Bearded Pigs, Orangutans; Sambar deer and Proboscis Monkeys during masting.

Primates All of N Borneo's primates have been recorded from Maliau but are generally scarce, apart from the Red Langur, which is much more common than the Grey Sabah Langur.

Wild Cats All 5 Bornean wild cats have been recorded from Maliau. Brodie & Giordano (2012) camera trapped 4 Clouded Leopards in the southern conservation area for an estimated density of 0.8/100km^2.

Civets Brodie & Giordano (2012) camera trapped all Bornean civets except the Otter Civet. The Malay Civet was most common and the Masked Palm and rare Hose's Civet were more common than the Island Palm Civet.

Squirrels The scarce grey mountain race of the Tufted Ground Squirrel has been recorded (p. 214). Parties of the rare Sculptor Squirrel were seen feeding on a large strangling fig tree near Nepenthes Camp (p. 208).

Elephants Prefer the buffer zone of logged forest outside the basin. They only occasionally enter the basin.

Banteng Most common in the logged buffer zone, but sometimes found in the basin. Very shy due to poaching in the buffer zone and along the rivers where Banteng like to graze. Only active at night.

Rats 4 uncommon endemic rats, *Niviventer rapit*, *Maxomys baedon*, *M. ochraceiventer* and *Haeromys margarettae*, have been trapped higher up.

Birds Maliau is the best place in Borneo to find the endemic Bulwer's Pheasant, which can be heard calling *bek-kia bek-kia* when the oaks are masting. Flocks of rare Waterfall Swifts that breed in nests built behind waterfalls have been recorded, although no nests have been found.

SOUTH SABAH ZOOLOGICAL BOUNDARY (SSZB) The SSZB is the most important zoological boundary in Borneo. It almost exactly matches the political border between Sabah in the north and Sarawak and Kalimantan in the south along a line stretching from Tawau to Lawas. Lowland mammals and birds often split into different species or subspecies (races) north and south of the SSZB. See below.

Why the SSZB exists Only lowland (not montane) animals divide along the SSZB. The probable reasons are physical restrictions preventing north–south movement: 1. A narrow coastal strip north of the Lawas River in W Sabah and 2. Geologically recent volcanic lava fields near Tawau in E Sabah. 3. Wet rainforest refugia in N Borneo during cold dry periods (glacial maximums) may also have played a part (p. 14).

Maliau and the SSZB Blue-winged Leafbird, Black-eared Pigmy Squirrel and Striped Tree Shrew have been reported from Maliau, which is just north of the Sabah/Kalimantan border.

LOWLAND BIRDS	
North of the SSZB	**South of the SSZB**
White-crowned Shama	White-rumped Shama
Black-Crowned Pitta	Garnet Pitta
Bornean Falconet	Black-thighed Falconet
	Blue-winged Leafbird

LOWLAND MAMMALS	
North of the SSZB	**South of the SSZB**
Four-striped Ground Sq.	Three-striped Ground Sq.
	Slender Squirrel
	Black-eared Pigmy Sq.
	Striped Treeshrew
	Painted Treeshrew

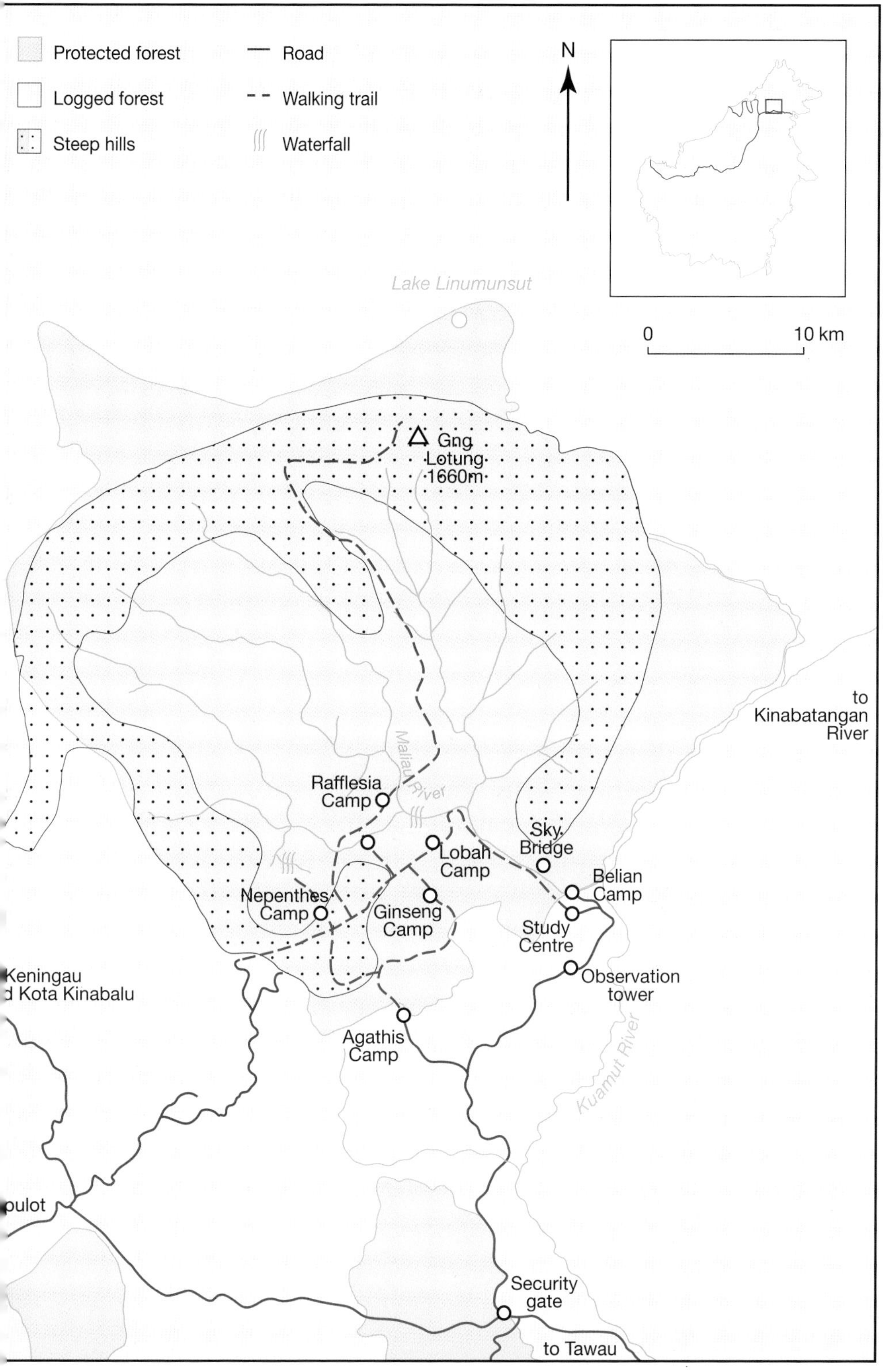
Protected forest
Logged forest
Steep hills
Road
Walking trail
Waterfall
N
0
10 km
Lake Linumunsut
Gng Lotung 1660m
Maliau River
Rafflesia Camp
Sky Bridge
Lobah Camp
Belian Camp
Nepenthes Camp
Ginseng Camp
Study Centre
Observation tower
Agathis Camp
Kuamut River
to Kinabatangan River
Keningau
d Kota Kinabalu
pulot
Security gate
to Tawau

BRUNEI 1: OVERVIEW

Thanks to the wisdom and conservationist philosophy of the current Sultan of Brunei and his father, Brunei contains the only large area of intact forest left on the west coast of Borneo. It is a green emerald, the majority of which remains virgin forest, surrounded by millions of hectares of oil-palm plantations and logged forest over the border in Sabah and Sarawak. See Google Earth for an overview.

1 **Temburong and the Ulu Temburong National Park** p. 356.

2 **Bandar Sei Begawan, Brunei Bay and Brunei Muara** See p. 354

3 **Seri Kenangan beach (Pantai Tutong) and Kuala Tutong** 10km of pristine sandy beach, lined with *Casuarina* trees backed by the Tutong River.

4 **Tasek Merimbun Park (4°36´N, 114° 41´E)** 1½ hours by car from BSB. Brunei's largest freshwater lake, surrounded by 78km² peat-swamp forest. Known for rare crocodiles and unusual bats.

5 **Sungai Liang Forest Recreation Park** provides easy access to the **Andulau Forest Reserve** about a 1½-hour drive from BSB. Lowland forest. Nature trails, canopy walkway. Forestry Centre popular with visitors.

6 **Panaga Camp, Seria (4°35´N, 114°15´E)** Private residential complex of 300ha for Shell employees, including houses and gardens next to the beach, with large old trees. Pied Hornbills, Silvered Langurs.

7 **Belait Peat Swamp Forest** Access via Badas Road and Kuala Balai Road. One of the finest fragments of threatened peat-swamp forest on the west coast of Borneo.

8 **Bukit Teraja Labi Hills and Mulu View Ridge** Follow Labi Road. Some nice forest with good paths for climbing Bukit Teraja. A recent PNHS survey reported Red Langurs.

9 **Sungei Ingei** Forest along the Belait River close to the Sarawak border and Mulu Park. Camera trapping by University of Brunei Darussalam researchers found healthy populations of Bay Cats and Clouded Leopards including a melanistic (black) Clouded Leopard.

Kate, a North Borneo Gibbon, feeds her first-born baby Wak-Wak next to the Belalong Canopy Walkway in the Ulu Temburong National Park. See pp. 184–187 and p. 356.
(Photo Hanyrol H. Ahmad Sah, resident researcher at the Ulu Ulu Resort)

BRUNEI DARUSSALAM	Hectares
Kerangas forest	3,000
Montane forest	7,200
Freshwater swamp forest	13,000
Mangrove forest	19,000
Peat-swamp forest	98,000
Mixed dipterocarp forest	190,000
Urban areas and cultivation	196,800
Total land area	527,000
Total sea area	50,000
Brunei Darussalam area	**577,000**

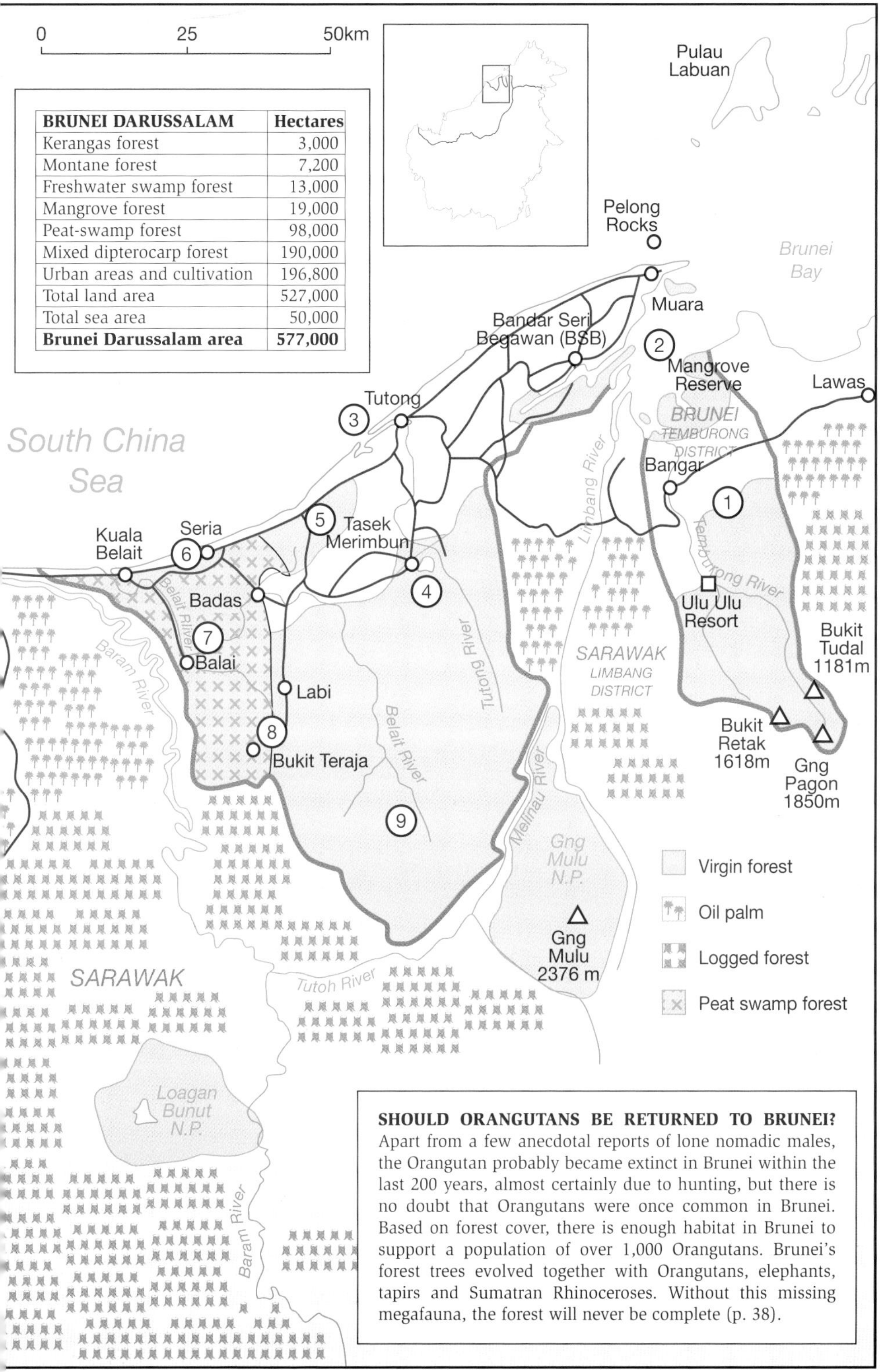

SHOULD ORANGUTANS BE RETURNED TO BRUNEI?
Apart from a few anecdotal reports of lone nomadic males, the Orangutan probably became extinct in Brunei within the last 200 years, almost certainly due to hunting, but there is no doubt that Orangutans were once common in Brunei. Based on forest cover, there is enough habitat in Brunei to support a population of over 1,000 Orangutans. Brunei's forest trees evolved together with Orangutans, elephants, tapirs and Sumatran Rhinoceroses. Without this missing megafauna, the forest will never be complete (p. 38).

BRUNEI 2: BRUNEI RIVER AND BRUNEI BAY

The 18,500ha of mangroves along the Brunei River and around its mouth (Muara) are the largest protected mangrove area on the west coast of Borneo, providing a rich breeding ground and nursery for young fish, prawns and mussels. Brunei Bay, including coastal Lawas (Sarawak) and Klias (Sabah), contains the largest area of seagrass beds in W Borneo, feeding grounds for the last Dugongs of W Borneo. Smooth and Small-clawed Otters, Bearded Pig and Saltwater Crocodiles are common but shy on the islands in the bay. Migrant waterbirds from Russia, China and Japan, including terns, egrets, herons, kingfishers and waders fleeing the northern winter, are common in September–April. Fish-eating birds of prey, including the migrant Osprey and resident Brahminy Kite and White-bellied Sea Eagle, often soar above Kg Ayer water village. Large monitor lizards slither along muddy banks. The mangroves also provide a safe haven for a large population of Proboscis Monkeys and the less common Silvered Langur, which eat the leaves of several common mangroves trees, including *Sonneratia* (p. 177). Dawn or late-afternoon tours are easily arranged with the taxi boats on the BSB waterfront.

1 Jerudong Country Club Luxury private members club with enormous grounds on the sea front.

2 Empire Golf and Country Club 35 minutes by car from BSB. Opulent sea-front hotel and resort with golf-course gardens and lakes. Look for migrant Red-throated Pipits and Yellow Wagtails on the lawns, and Blue Rock Thrush on the buildings, September–April.

3 Pulau Punyit Opposite the Empire Resort is a small island surrounded by a rocky reef of about 8ha. The forest on Pulau Punyit is dominated by 2 species of fig, *Ficus globosa* and *F. delosyce*, brought to the island by roosting fruit bats and Pied Imperial Pigeons.

4 Berakas Forest Reserve 348ha of kerangas forest growing at the back of Berakas beach. Long-tailed Macaques pester picknickers. Look for rare Asian migrant birds arriving on southwards migration in September–November each year, especially after storms. Many Asian migrant birds make their first landing in Brunei because it is the nearest land from their departure point in South Vietnam.

5 Meragang Beach 20 minutes by car from BSB. Sandy beach popular with locals.

6 Pelong Rocks Small group of rocky islands surrounded by a reef near the entrance to the Brunei River. Reef Egrets, and Bridled, Black-naped and Roseate Terns breed here during 'calm season', Apr–Jul. A large colony of Black-bearded Tomb Bats roosts in a small sea cave. See Wong & Hj. Ibrahim (1996).

7 Pulau Pelompong Originally a sand-spit, now an island forested with *Casuarina* and fig trees.

8 Serasa Beach and sandspit 25 minutes by car from BSB. Migrant birds feed in *Casuarina*, Sep–Mar. The beach at the far end is good for both mangrove and anachronistic drift seeds (p. 38).

9 Tasek Lama Park 10-minute walk from centre of BSB. Secondary forest with various trails, and a reservoir. Over 80 bird species recorded. Long-tailed Macaques common; occasional Proboscis Monkeys.

10 Kampung Ayer and the Brunei River Hire a water taxi from the river jetty for an early-morning or late-afternoon wildlife tour. Watch Whiskered and White-winged Black River Terns fishing.

11 Pulau Beremban Popular site for Proboscis Monkey-watching on the Brunei River.

12 Pulau Siarau Flying fox roosting and breeding island.

13 Pulau Selirong Large 2,566ha mangrove island on the Sarawak border (Lawas). A 45-minute boat trip from Muara. Excellent mangrove nature reserve, with a 2-km walkway and observation tower.

BATS OF BRUNEI BAY Many of Borneo's coastal trees, including several species of mangrove, have bat-pollinated flowers, including *Sonneratia* (p. 177), Nibong (p. 82) and Nipah Palms (p. 40). Nectar bats that favour *Sonneratia* include the Long-tongued Fruit Bat and Cave Nectar Bat *Eonycteris spelea*.
Flying foxes use mangroves for day roosts and for camps for their large breeding congregations (p. 85). Flying fox camps used to be common throughout Borneo, but due to hunting flying foxes are now rare.
Pulau Siarau is the last known large flying fox camp on the west coast of Borneo.
Flying foxes are locally nomadic and fly long distances inland at night to find flowering or fruiting patches of forest, as different areas of forest flower and fruit at different times (p. 42). It is believed that flying foxes favour mangroves for roosting for several reasons: a. mangroves surrounded by sea water are safe from most bat predators, like pythons; b. many mangrove and coastal trees flower year round, providing a steady supply of fruit and nectar to hungry bats. See pp. 40, 80 and 82. Evening flights of flying foxes used to be a common sight around the coast of Borneo, for example from Gaya Island over Kota Kinabalu, but due to hunting they are now rare except around Brunei Bay. Many non-Muslim Borneans hunt flying foxes because they are considered good eating (p. 173).

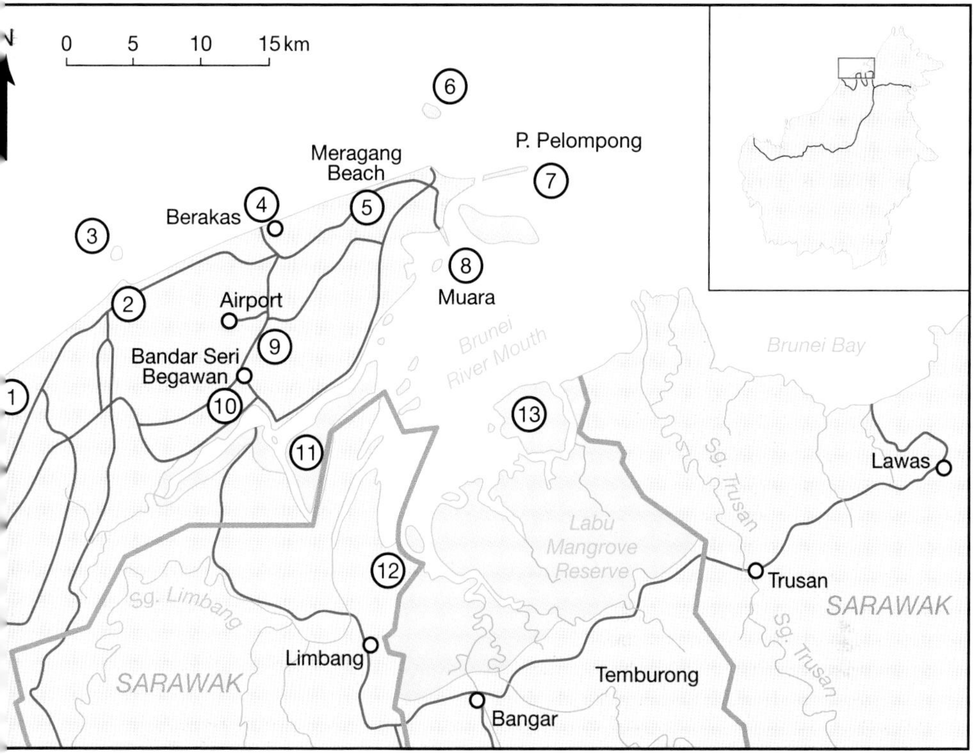

Flying Fox *Pteropus vampyrus* feeding on the nectar of Binuang *Octomeles sumatrana* flowers at Tabin. (Photo: Lawrence Chin TWR)

BRUNEI 3: ULU TEMBURONG AND THE BELALONG CANOPY WALKWAY

ULU TEMBURONG NATIONAL PARK (488 km^2) Brunei's northern enclave, squeezed between the ecologically devastated Limbang and Lawas areas of N Sarawak, is known as Temburong. The hilly interior (Ulu) of Temburong contains the largest area of intact rainforest remaining on the west coast of Borneo.

Access The main Sarawak-Sabah road passes through the town of Bangar in Temburong. However, a speedboat from Bandar Seri Begawan (BSB) to Bangar takes only 40 minutes. Crocodiles are often seen en route along the mangrove-lined channels of Brunei Bay. A road bridge across Brunei Bay is under construction.

Bukit Patoi A recreational forest park is a 10-minute drive from Bangar. Allow at least 3 hours for the return walk to the summit (290m) up a steep path. The reward is a clear view to the coast of Brunei and often good views of locally resident Rufous-bellied Hawk Eagles and Sunda Honey Buzzards.

Ulu Ulu Resort A 30-minute drive from Bangar takes you to the Temburong River jetty at Batang Duri (Thorn Rock) giving access to a number of popular local resorts and youth hostels. A 45-minute speedboat journey up the Temburong River ends at the river junction (kuala) with the Belalong River on the northern edge of the Ulu Temburong NP. The luxury Ulu Ulu Resort is located on the east bank of the Temburong River, whilst the Belalong Field Centre used by visiting scientists is on a forested hillside 200m away on the opposite bank. www.uluuluresort.com

Belalong Canopy walkway A 40-minute walk from the Ulu Ulu Resort up a steep hill is the highest tree-top canopy walkway in Borneo with spectacular views over Temburong's pristine forests. When one of the 12 different fig species is fruiting you are guaranteed eye-level views of gibbons and hornbills.

This is also the best site in Borneo to see Hose's Langurs. The males make a soft call similar to a woodpecker rattle which can be heard every morning from the Canopy Walkway, however the langurs are usually shyer than the gibbons and are seen less often.

The Temburong NP has the most dense population of gibbons and langurs in Borneo – possibly due to the absence of Orangutans. At dawn from the Belalong Canopy Walkway it is possible to hear six different gibbon families calling to defend their territories. The resident Canopy Walkway gibbon family currently comprises a very large bold female, Kate. Kate's smaller shyer partner, William (above), and a baby Wak-Wak was born in May 2017. Kate is shown with her baby on p. 352. In gibbon families typically the female is the largest and take a lead role in territorial defence and early morning territorial calls (pp. 186–187).

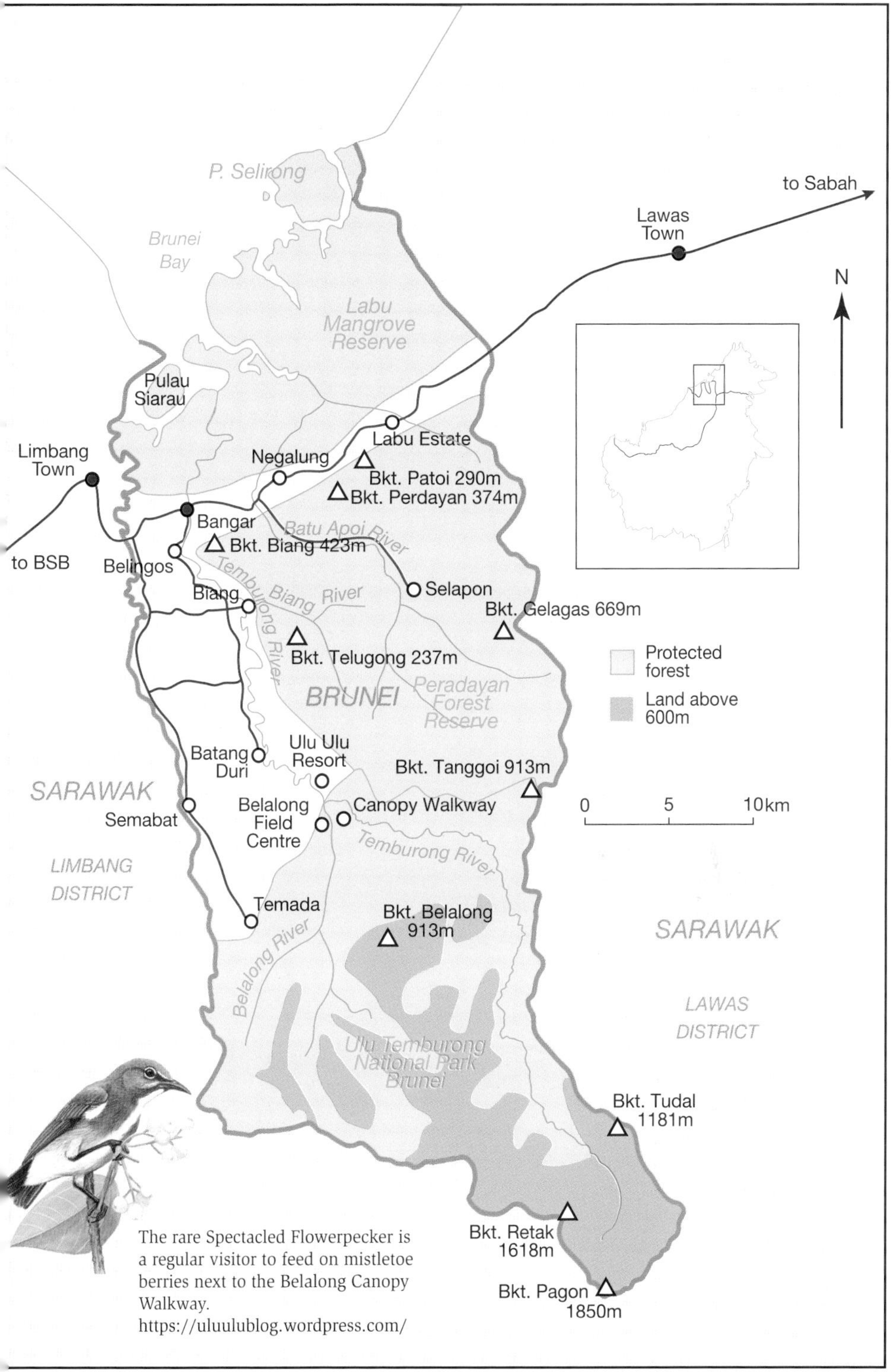

The rare Spectacled Flowerpecker is a regular visitor to feed on mistletoe berries next to the Belalong Canopy Walkway.
https://uluulublog.wordpress.com/

SARAWAK 1: OVERVIEW

Sarawak is both the largest and the richest state in Malaysia, but has probably suffered the greatest loss of wildlife of any state in Borneo (or Malaysia) over the last 50 years. **There are no protected areas of lowland forest in Sarawak either large enough or secure enough to conserve the natural diversity of Borneo's plants and mammals.** See p. 368, Lambir NP. Three previously common endemic Borneo primates, the Sarawak Langur (p. 170), Hose's Langur (p. 164) and Abbot's Gibbon (p. 184), are on the verge of extinction in Sarawak, and the surviving populations of the Proboscis Monkey and Banteng are not sustainable. The abundant populations of swiftlets and bats at Niah have collapsed and those at Mulu are threatened (p. 372).

	SITE	km²
1	Lambir Hills (p. 368)	70
2	Gng Mulu (p. 370)	856
3	Niah (p. 366)	31
4	Loagan Bunut	107
5	Kelabit Highlands	
6	Pulong Tau	698
7	Usun Apau	494
8	Similajau (p. 360)	221
9	P Bruit and Tg Sirik	99
10	Sedilu Samarahan	63
11	Ulu Sebuyau	18
12	Maludam (p. 360)	431
13	Samunsam (p. 170)	228
14	Tg Datu (p. 360)	14

	SITE	km²
15	Kuching Wetlands (p. 360)	66
16	Bako (p. 362)	27
17	Damai Beach/Santubong (p. 360)	14
18	Semengoh (p. 360)	7
19	Gng Penrissen (p. 360)	
20	Bungoh Range	81
21	Kubah & Gng Serapi (p. 360)	22
22	Gng Gading (p. 360)	42
23	Batang Ai (p. 364)	240
24	Lanjak Entimau (p. 364)	1,840

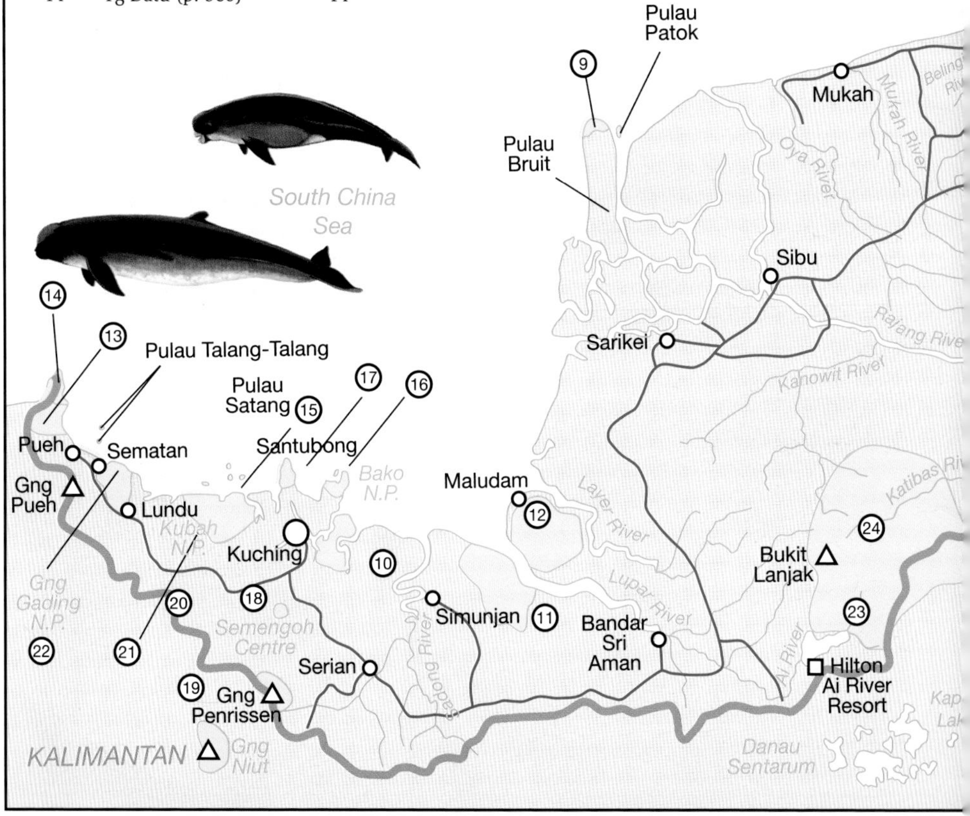

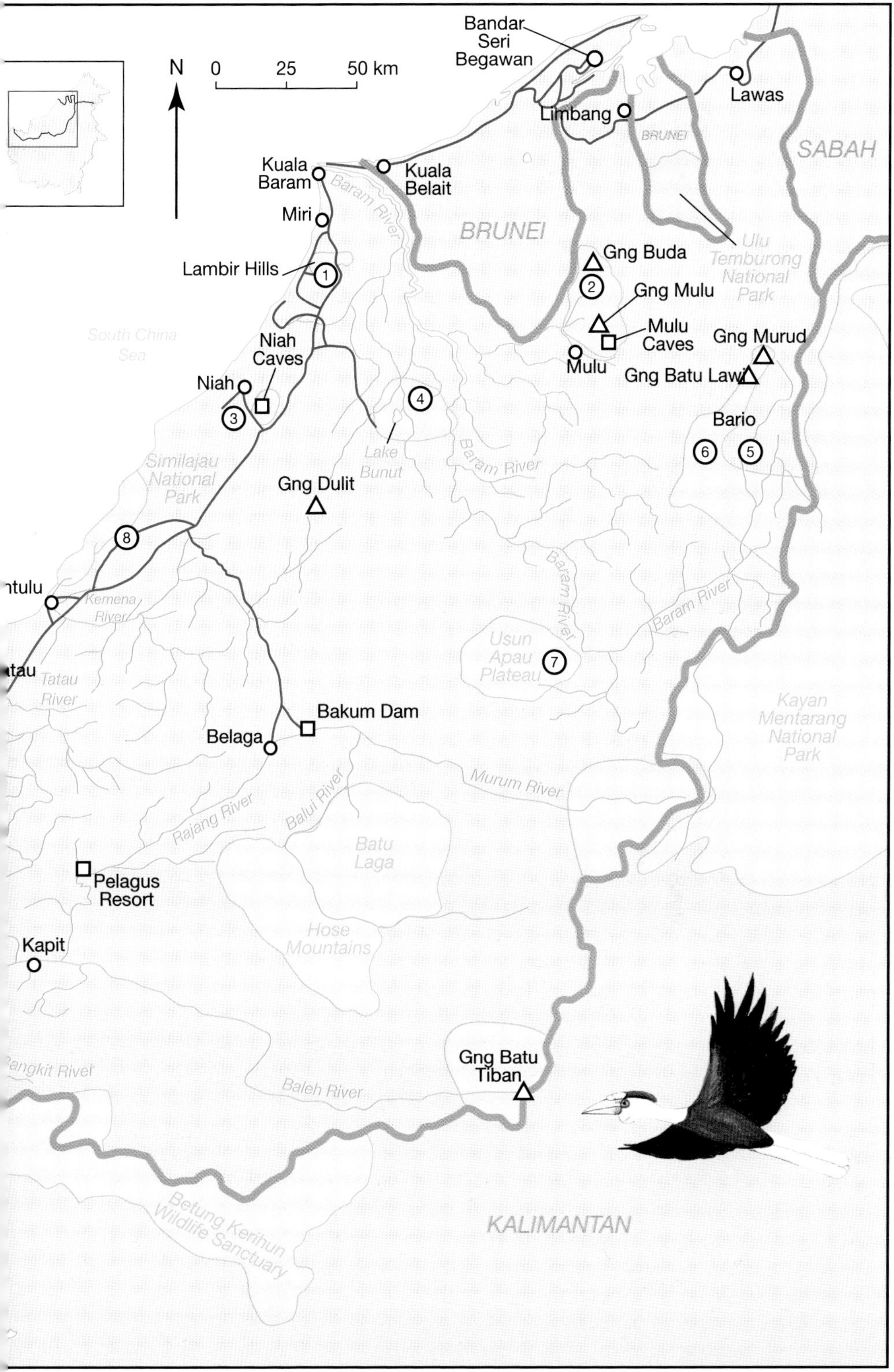
N
0
25
50 km
Bandar Seri Begawan
Lawas
Limbang
BRUNEI
SABAH
Kuala Baram
Kuala Belait
Baram River
Miri
BRUNEI
Ulu Temburong National Park
Lambir Hills
1
Gng Buda
2
Gng Mulu
Mulu Caves
Mulu
Gng Murud
Gng Batu Lawi
South China Sea
Niah Caves
Niah
3
4
Lake Bunut
Baram River
Bario
6
5
Similajau National Park
Gng Dulit
8
Kemena River
Baram River
Baram River
Usun Apau Plateau
7
Tatau River
Kayan Mentarang National Park
Bakum Dam
Belaga
Murum River
Rajang River
Balui River
Batu Laga
Pelagus Resort
Hose Mountains
Kapit
Gng Batu Tiban
Baleh River
Betung Kerihun Wildlife Sanctuary
KALIMANTAN

SARAWAK 2: KUCHING AREA

All the sites listed below (apart from Similajau and Batang Ai) can be visited on a day trip from Kuching.

1 Similajau National Park 221km² North of Bintulu town. A 40km scenic strip of sandy beaches and mangroves backed by coastal dipterocarp and kerangas forest. Accommodation includes chalets, hostel, canteen at park headquarters. Good trails and boat trips. Turtle hatchery. Small populations of Sarawak Langur (mainly black morph) and gibbons may survive. The park abuts the main Kuching to Miri road and suffers heavily from poaching.

2 Maludam NP 431km² Access via boat from the Malay fishing village at the mouth of the Maludam River. The largest area of peat-swamp forest left in Sarawak. Contains the world's only viable population of the Sarawak Langur (red morph), (p. 170). Extreme shyness indicates continued poaching. Small populations of Proboscis Monkey and Silvered Langur. Flat-headed Cat locally common (p. 284).

3 Bako National Park 27km² 45-minute drive from Kuching plus 25 minutes by boat (p. 362).

4 Damai beach, Permai and Santubong 45-minute drive west of Kuching. Sandy beach, mud flats, mangroves, golf courses and virgin primary forest. Accommodation at beach resorts or forest lodges at Permai. From Damai hire boats to cruise the Kuching mangroves (see below), or visit Pulau Satang Besar, the only island with public access. Allow 5 hours for the return walk to the summit of Gng Santubong (810m). Spectacular views, but fitness is essential. Silvered Langurs, Smooth Otters, Proboscis Monkeys.

5 Kuching Wetlands NP Look for crocodiles, Proboscis Monkeys and Silvered Langurs. Dolphin-watching tours in Santubong and Buntal bays can be booked in Kuching.

6 Kubah National Park (Gng Serapi) 22km² 40-minute drive from Kuching. Contains Matang Wildlife Centre mini zoo of rescued wildlife. Mixed hilly primary forest rising to summit of Gng Serapi (911m). Many birds. Occasional Black Hornbill and Argus Pheasant. www.orangutanproject.com

7 Gng Gading National Park 41km² 2-hour drive from Kuching, or 10 minutes from Lundu town. Highest point is Gng Gading (900m). Famous as a giant *Rafflesia* flower site. Good forest birding along steep, hilly trails. Hostel and chalets provide accommodation.

8 Samunsam Wildlife Sanctuary 228km² No tourist access. In theory one of Sarawak's finest parks, with varied vegetation and topography from coastal mangrove to hill forest up to 1,200m at Gng Pueh (Poi). Studies by Rajaratnam, Gombek & Bennett in the 1990s found substantial populations of 3 endemic primates, including the Proboscis Monkey, Sarawak Langur (black morph) and extremely rare Abbott's Gibbon. Reports are that poaching has reduced populations, which urgently need to be resurveyed.

9 Tanjung Datu NP 13km² 40 minutes by boat from Sematan when seas are calm (Apr–Sep). Small coastal park on westernmost tip of Borneo on the Kalimantan border. Mixed virgin dipterocarp forest, pristine beaches and coral reefs. Nesting turtles. Stay at Sematan Beach Resort 120km (2 hours) drive from Kuching.

10 Satang and Talang Islands National Park 45-minute drive from Kuching, plus 30 minutes by speedboat to Satang Besar. Four small forested islands off the SW coast of Sarawak provide protection for nesting sea turtles and Pied Imperial Pigeons. Book tour in Kuching.

11 Semengoh Nature Reserve 6.5km² 30-minute drive from Kuching. Orangutan Rehabilitation Centre set in lowland primary dipterocarp forest. Watch Orangutans being fed. Good birding.

12 Gng Penrissen Access via the Borneo Highlands Resort, 60km (1½-hour drive). Interesting forest with rare squirrels and bats. Gng Penrissen (1,326m) is part of the Kling Klang range of low mountains on the Kalimantan border that include the extinct volcano of Gng Niut (1,701m) in W Kalimantan visible from the Kalimantan viewpoint.

13 Lanjak Entimau Wildlife Sanctuary and Batang Ai p. 364.

PYTHON ATTACKING PIGLET AT SANTUBONG 'Mr. Ernest Hose was an eyewitness of a scene close to his house at Santubong. Hearing a tremendous noise of wild pigs grunting, snorting and squealing, he ran out to see what was the reason, and presently came on a large Python that had seized a young pig and was endeavouring to crush it. The snake was surrounded by a number of full-grown swine, which were goring it with their tusks and trampling on it; so resolute was their attack that the Python was compelled to relinquish its hold of the loudly protesting young pig, when the herd, catching sight of Mr. Hose, hastily made off, the young one, apparently little the worse for its adventure, trotting away with its companions. Mr. Hose examined the snake, and found it to be so slashed and mangled that it was unable to crawl away from the scene of battle.' (Shelford, 1912). See pp. 176 (reptiles), 272 (Shelford), 302 (python and pig).

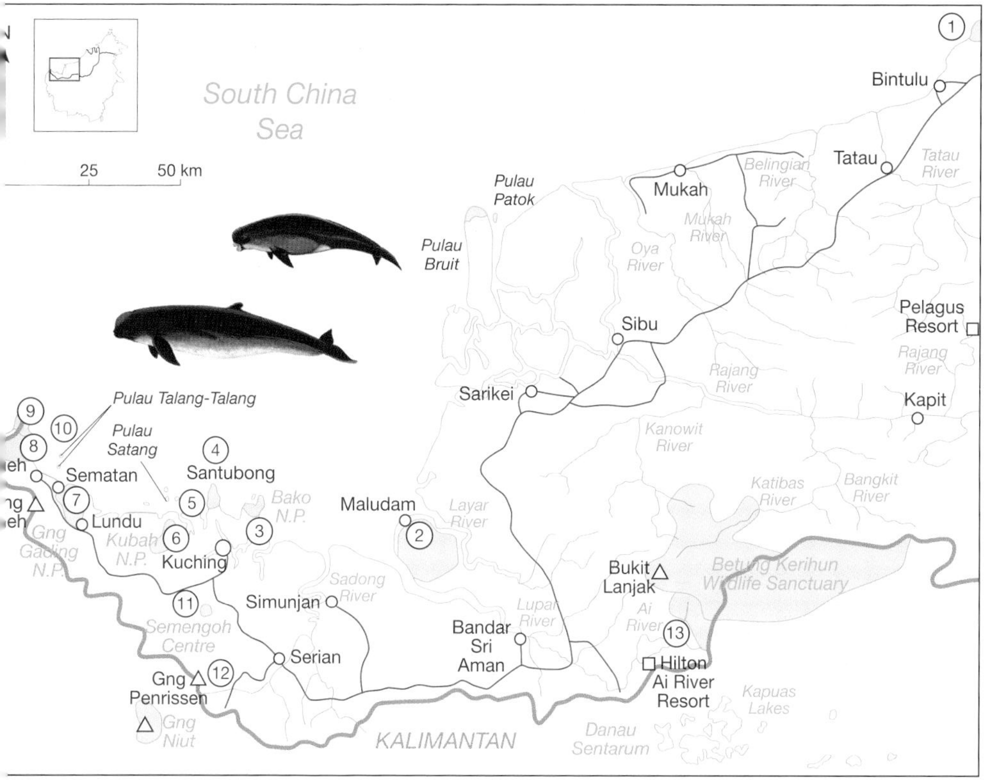

Family groups of Smooth Otters frequently fish in Santubong Bay at high tide amongst the rocks near the Permai Resort. Some group members act as 'drivers', driving the fish towards waiting 'catchers' (p.256). (Photo: Graeme Guy taken in Penang)

SARAWAK 3: BAKO

BAKO NATIONAL PARK (1°41' N, 110°17 E) 27km² One of the best places in Borneo to see habituated (tame) populations of Proboscis Monkeys, Silvered Langurs, Long-tailed Macaques, Bearded Pigs and Colugos. Clouded Leopards and Flat-headed Cats have been reported. The varied topography of sandstone cliffs, beaches, damp valleys and a dry rocky plateau results in diverse vegetation, including mangroves, coastal palms, dipterocarp and kerangas forest. Bako makes an excellent day trip from Kuching, or even better book a cabin for an overnight stay so you can explore the heath forest on the plateau in the cool of the morning.

Access 45-minute drive from Kuching plus 25-minute boat ride.

Accommodation Chalets, hostel and canteen at headquarters.

Plateau Plants The stunted kerangas, or heath forest, on the Bako plateau is rich in plants hard to find elsewhere, including *Nepenthes*, which trap insects in their pitchers (p. 70) and *Hydnophytum* ant plants, which obtain additional nutrients by housing ants in large chambers to harvest their waste products. The low open canopy supports a wide variety of parasitic mistletoe *Loranthus* and *Viscum* species that are normally too high to photograph. Note that there is no shade on the plateau, so visitors should start early and return by 11 a.m.

Dolphins Three species of dolphin are often seen in Buntal Bay, including the Finless Porpoise, Humpbacked Dolphin and Irrawaddy Dolphin. Dolphin-watching tours can be booked in Kuching (p. 314).

Bats Khan (2007) lists 34 species of bat for Bako, the most common being *Hipposideros cervinus* (p. 108), an insect-eating bat of the forest understorey, but also including the rare fishing bat *Myotis adversus* (p. 132).

Primates Estimated primate populations at Bako NP in (2007) were Proboscis Monkey 198; Silvered Langur 30 and Long-tailed Macaque 235 (see Nasir 2012). The healthy primate population at Bako indicates how common they were in the past all around the coast of Borneo. The main reason for their current absence from most of coastal Sarawak is poaching for food. Bako receives more than 50,000 foreign visitors a year, and it is their presence and tourism's contribution to the economy that keeps these primates safe (p. 192).

Otters Both Small-clawed and Smooth Otters are common at Bako, in the mangroves along Buntal Bay and the rocky coast around the Santubong Peninsula. Both species are 'social otters' normally found in large family groups, but otters forage over very large areas so seeing them is down to chance (p. 256).

COLUGOS AT BAKO There is a resident population of Colugos around the park headquarters building, and Bako is probably the best place to see Colugos in Borneo. Nasir (2012) found that roosting Colugos were easiest to find in the dry seasons, Aug–Oct and Mar–June, when they roost openly in the trees surrounding Bako headquarters. Bako is one of the wettest areas of Borneo, with rainfall averaging 4m per annum, and during wet months Colugos roost in trees with dense vegetation such as *Ilex cymosa* (Borneo holly) and *Garcinia hombroniana* (Kandis laut) for protection against the rain. This makes Colugos more difficult to find in wet months. At night they eat the young leaves of 10 different trees growing around the park headquarters, including *Buchanania arborescens* (Otak udang), *Ficus microcarpa* (Jejawi, or Ara), *Vitex pubescens* (Leban), *Syzygium* sp. (Ubah) and *Campnosperma* sp. (Terentang), (p.154).

PALMS OF BAKO The coastal forests of W Sarawak are a palm diversity hotspot – 20,000 years ago these palms were an abundant component of the Sundaland basin forests stretching all the way to Singapore (pp. 46, 50 and 368). The 5 most common palms of Bako and their most likely animal dispersers are as follows.

1 LIRAN *Pholidocarpus majadum* Tall forest endemic fan palm. Very large fruit dispersed by elephants (picture, p. 340).

2 SAL *Johannesteijsmannia altifrons* Trunkless palm with giant leaves in shady forests. Knobbly fruit dispersed by rodents.

3 BERTAM *Eugeissonia insignis* Trunkless wild sago palm. Large oblong fruit dispersed by rhinos (p. 52).

4 NIPAH *Nypa fruticans* Abundant along muddy coasts and estuaries, with large, floating seeds dispersed by sea (p. 51).

5 NIBUNG *Oncosperma tigillarium* Clumps of tall, spiny trunks abundant along landward edge of mangrove. Seeds dispersed by hornbills, imperial pigeons and flying foxes (p. 83).

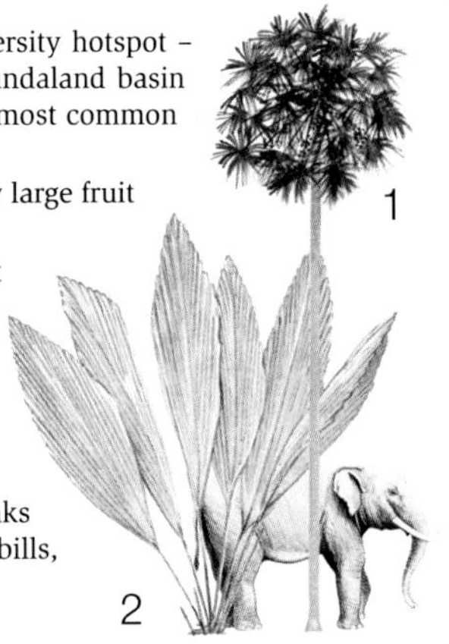

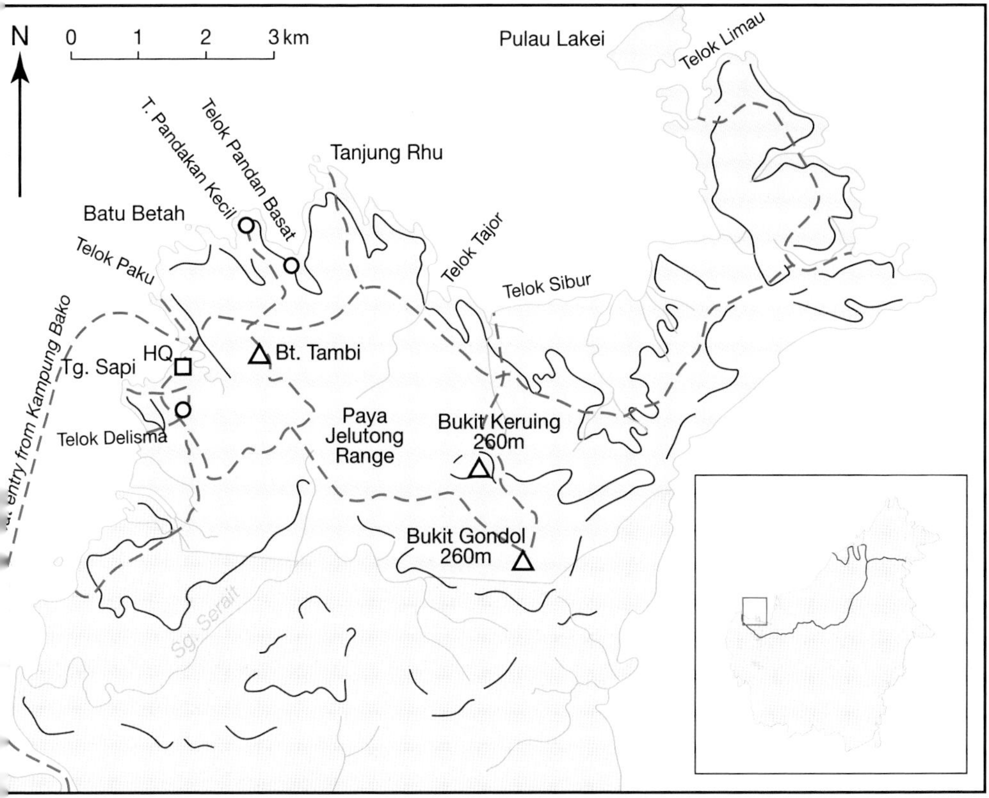

A troop of Silvered Langurs at Bako
Silvered Langurs are still common in protected areas around the Borneo coast (p. 173), whilst Sarawak Langurs (p. 171) are almost extinct. (Photo: Ch'ien C. Lee)

SARAWAK 4: BATANG AI AND LANJAK ENTIMAU KALIMANTAN: BETUNG KERIHUN

On the border of S Sarawak and W Kalimantan lie 3 adjoining national parks that together comprise the second largest area of protected hill forest in Borneo (c.10,000km²) after Kayan Mentarang (p. 384). These 3 parks, known collectively as a Trans-boundary Connected Area (TBCA), are described separately below, although the wildlife in them is obviously similar. The park topography is extremely rugged, with numerous peaks separated by steep, narrow valleys. Long, narrow Betung Kerihun with Dayak swidden settlements to the south and logged forest to the north suffers from serious poaching. There is potential to extend Lanjak Entimau on the Sarawak side to include the heavily logged forest north of the Kalimantan border.

BATANG AI NATIONAL PARK (1°20′ N, 112°10′ E) 270km² Watershed protection forest for the 84km² lake and hydroelectric dam that supplies electricity to Kuching.

Access and accommodation 4-hour drive from Kuching plus 10 minutes by boat to the Hilton Batang Ai Resort on the edge of the reservoir. A further 50-minute boat ride takes you to park headquarters. The northern end of Batang Ai adjoins the southern boundary of Lanjak Entimau, which is not open to tourism, although bona fide scientific researchers are welcomed by the Sarawak Forestry Department. Numerous trails and boat trips possible. Batang Ai is one of a few sites in Sarawak where viable populations of Orangutans, gibbons and hornbills still exist. www.sarawakforestry.com

LANJAK ENTIMAU WILDLIFE SANCTUARY (LEWS) (1°37′ N, 112°11′ E) 1,688km² Lanjak Entimau is named after the 2 highest peaks, Bukit Lanjak at 1,285m and Bukit Entimau at 975m. A management plan for Lanjak Entimau written by Kavanagh et al. (1982) found that in the Katibas Valley both gibbons and Red Langurs were abundant. The White-fronted Langur was rare. Orangutans were widespread but with a population reduced by hunting. Long-tailed and Pig-tailed Macaques were present in low densities. The Sumatran Rhino, last reported in 1965, is extinct. The varied hill-forest habitats host a variety of rare rodents including all 3 Pigmy Squirrels, the Giant Tufted Ground Squirrel and the Three-striped Ground Squirrel. Roberta et al. (2010) reported the rare Rapit Rat was abundant at Sg Bloh and Sg Menyarin in June 2008. Salt licks are present in many areas. Visitors to the salt licks include Orangutans, Sambar, Muntjac, wild pigs and Red Langurs (Ampeng et al. 2008). Deer are heavily hunted (legally) at salt licks in the park (Hazebroek 2000).

BETUNG KERIHUN NATIONAL PARK (BKNP) 8,000km² Adjacent to Lanjak Entimau on the Indonesian (south) side of the Sarawak/Kalimantan border.

Access The park is divided into 4 sections, each section being the headwaters (Ulu) of one of 4 tributaries of Borneo's longest river, the Kapuas (1,143km). The nearest large town is Putussibau on the Kapuas, around a 15-hour drive or 2½ hours by plane from Pontianak. From Putussibau, Betung Kerihun can be entered by boat up one of the 4 rivers. **Accommodation:** Limited, but home stays can be arranged through the park headquarters in Putussibau. http://betungkerihun.dephut.go.id.

Orangutans The TBCA contains an estimated 4,000 Orangutans of the rarest subspecies, *Pongo pygmaeus pygmaeus*, a small remnant of Sarawak's once large population. This population is split roughly as follows: LEWS 1,400, Batang Ai 300 and BKNP 2,300. The adjacent Orangutan population in the Danum Sentarum lakes area south of the TBCA is heading for extinction due to forest fragmentation, hunting, and forest fires.

Langurs The TBCA contains large populations of langurs. Blough & Gombek (2000) estimated the LEWS populations at 28,000 Red Langurs and 13,000 White-fronted Langurs. However, in the more mountainous BRNP, Soedijito et al. (1998) found that White-fronted Langurs were abundant, but Red Langurs were rare.

Gibbons The ITTO/SFD (1996) survey estimated the LEWS population at 24,000. Kavanagh et al. (1982) noted that the gibbons have the typical bubbling call of the N Bornean Gibbon, but that the coat colour is so varied that the population does not obviously fit any one accepted subspecies. Gibbons cannot swim and gibbon species evolve due to separation by rivers, but hybridize in the adjacent headwaters of these rivers (p. 184).

Pheasants Camera trapping by Modh-Azlan et al. (2013) found that after mousedeer (132 records), the Argus Pheasant was the second most common (71 records), three times more common than the Crested Fireback and 35 times more common than the Crestless Fireback. Kavanagh (1982) reported that 'the Iban of Ulu Engkari consider Bulwer's Pheasant quite common and that it is found in both secondary and primary forest' (see p. 36 for an hypothesis as to how pheasants might benefit from the presence of gibbons in Borneo).

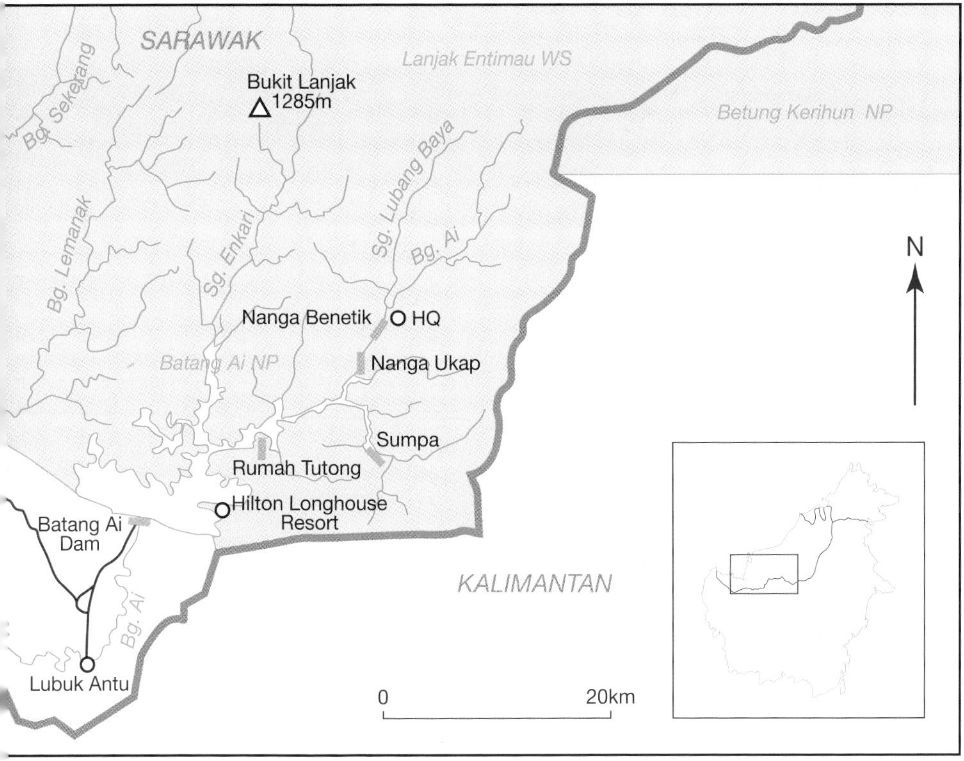
SARAWAK
Lanjak Entimau WS
Betung Kerihun NP
Bukit Lanjak
1285m
Bg. Sekerang
Bg. Lemanak
Sg. Enkari
Sg. Lubang Baya
Bg. Ai
Nanga Benetik
HQ
Nanga Ukap
Batang Ai NP
Sumpa
Rumah Tutong
Hilton Longhouse Resort
Batang Ai Dam
Bg. Ai
Lubuk Antu
KALIMANTAN
N
0
20km

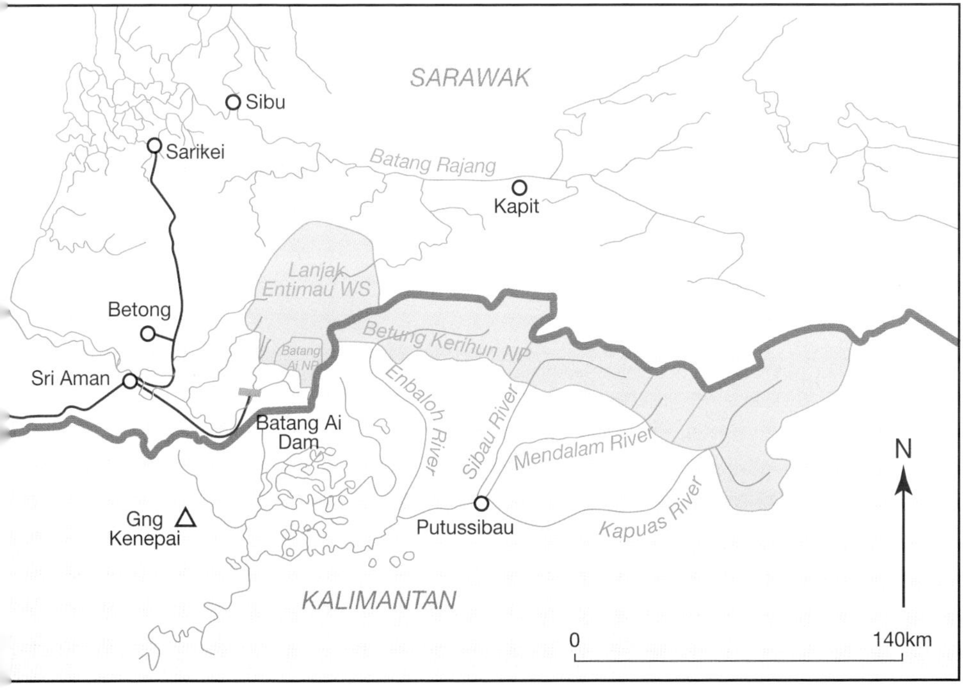
SARAWAK
Sibu
Sarikei
Batang Rajang
Kapit
Lanjak Entimau WS
Betong
Betung Kerihun NP
Batang Ai NP
Sri Aman
Enbaloh River
Sibau River
Batang Ai Dam
Mendalam River
Gng Kenepai
Putussibau
Kapuas River
KALIMANTAN
N
0
140km

SARAWAK 5: NIAH CAVES

NIAH CAVES (3°50´N, 113°45´E) 31km² Lowland forest surrounding a massive limestone hill, Gng Subis (494m), riddled with small caves. An adjacent smaller hill, Bukit Bekajang, contains large caves with evidence of human habitation dating back to more than 45,000 years. In 1958, Tom and Barbara Harrisson found the oldest modern human skull in Asia here, dating back to about 38,000 years ago. (p. 20, arrival of humans).

Access and accommodation 2-hour drive from Miri to Niah Park headquarters, where there is both private and park accommodation. Cross the river by boat to access a 4-km boardwalk through tall riverside forest to Bukit Bekajang to view the spectacular Great Cave and other smaller caves. Alternatively, climb Bukit Kasut. The tough climb (6 hours return) is rewarded with spectacular views to the coast 15km distant.

Birds Less than 10% of the original 3 million Black-nest Swiftlets now remain due to overharvesting of nests and the conversion of surrounding forests to oil-palm plantations. Visit the caves at dusk or dawn to see active avian predators Wallace's Hawk Eagle, Brahminy Kite, Bat Hawk, Eagle Owl and Buffy Fish Owl.

Mammals Once surrounded by diverse lowland forest, Niah is now a small island in a sea of oil palm. Mammals are scarce due to hunting and habitat degradation. Orangutans were once common at Niah, but they were already extinct by 1850, when the first European explorers arrived. Hose's Langur and Sarawak Langur (black morph) were previously abundant at Niah but are now locally extinct; only Long-tailed Macaques remain. The caves host large populations of smaller bats. Most larger bats have been hunted to extinction (p. 136).

EXTINCT MAMMALS OF THE NIAH CAVES Archaeological excavations at Niah were initiated by Tom Harrisson of the Sarawak Museum in 1954 and continued intermittently up to 1965. Zuraina Majid made further investigations in the 1970s. A comprehensive re-survey (2000–2004) led by Graham Barker of the McDonald Institute at the University of Cambridge has led to some surprising conclusions (see below). Harrisson had the assistance of the young Lord Medway (now the 5th Earl of Cranbrook, SE Asia's leading zoologist emeritus), and much of what we know about Borneo's prehistoric mammals and their hunting by humans is the result of Cranbrook's original work at Niah and elsewhere, published in numerous papers. See Barker et al. 2013 and Piper et al (2013) for an overview.

MODERN HUMANS began visiting Niah some 45,000 years ago during a cold, dry period, when Borneo was joined by land to mainland Asia (p. 14), to feed on the large bat population. Bone remnants indicate that early humans also hunted large numbers of Bearded Pigs, Orangutans, langurs and macaques. Less common are the bones of Banteng, deer, pythons, monitor lizards, pheasants and hornbills. Bone-arrow tips indicate that primates were hunted with bows and arrows, not blowpipes, which developed later in Borneo (p. 22).

Agriculture begins in Borneo Around 6,000 years ago, humans started rice cultivation at nearby Loagan Bunut, and taro *Colocasia esculenta* and yams *Dioscorea alata* were being cultivated at Niah (Hunt et al. 2007). It is believed that at this time mongoloid (straight-haired) Austronesians had not reached Borneo, so this is evidence of a Negrito hunter-gatherer society with basic agriculture, which extended from the Malay Peninsula through Borneo to New Guinea. This upsets the 'Bellwood model' in which non-farming hunter-gatherer (curly-haired) negritos are displaced by (straight-haired) mongoloid farmers who invaded from the north around 3,000–4,000 years ago (see Bellwood 1997).

EXTINCT	MAMMALS OF THE NIAH CAVES	LIKELY REASON
Orangutan	Abundant 40 KYA. Now extinct in N Sarawak and Brunei.	Hunting by humans
Elephant	Single tooth. Now extinct most of Borneo.	Hunting by humans
Sumatran Rhino	Present in Sarawak until 1960s. Now extinct in most of Borneo.	Hunting by humans
Javan Rhino	Extinct for at least 200 years in Borneo (p. 18).	Hunting by humans
Ferret Badger	Usually montane. Present at Niah during cold periods (p. 254).	Climate change
Tiger	Extinct in the last 500 years (pp. 18 and 370)?	Climate change?
Tapir	Extinct in the last 500 years (p. 18)?	Climate change?
Giant Pangolin	Extinct for 20,000 years (p. 152)?	Hunting by humans
Wrinkled Bat	Once abundant. Locally extinct for *c.* 750 years (p. 134).	Hunting by humans

KYA: Thousands of years before present.

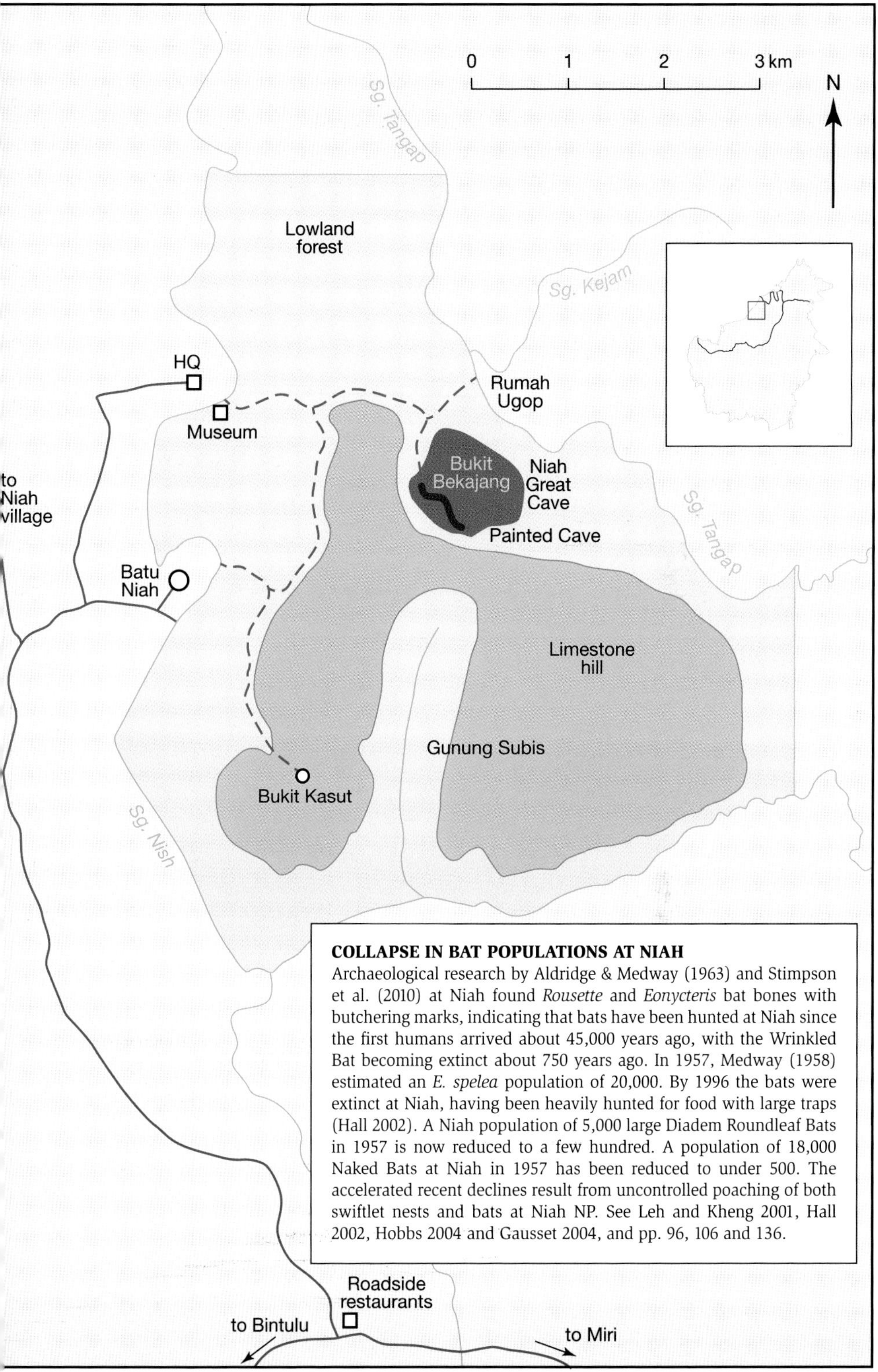

COLLAPSE IN BAT POPULATIONS AT NIAH

Archaeological research by Aldridge & Medway (1963) and Stimpson et al. (2010) at Niah found *Rousette* and *Eonycteris* bat bones with butchering marks, indicating that bats have been hunted at Niah since the first humans arrived about 45,000 years ago, with the Wrinkled Bat becoming extinct about 750 years ago. In 1957, Medway (1958) estimated an *E. spelea* population of 20,000. By 1996 the bats were extinct at Niah, having been heavily hunted for food with large traps (Hall 2002). A Niah population of 5,000 large Diadem Roundleaf Bats in 1957 is now reduced to a few hundred. A population of 18,000 Naked Bats at Niah in 1957 has been reduced to under 500. The accelerated recent declines result from uncontrolled poaching of both swiftlet nests and bats at Niah NP. See Leh and Kheng 2001, Hall 2002, Hobbs 2004 and Gausset 2004, and pp. 96, 106 and 136.

SARAWAK 6: LAMBIR

LAMBIR HILLS PARK (Lambir Benut) (4°15´N, 114°00´E) 70km² Lambir is a forest jewel in N Sarawak, the most important patch of virgin coastal forest left in Sarawak. It has lost most of its large mammals to poaching in recent years, but is still worth a visit because of the easily accessible, diverse plants – the richest forest in all of Asia after Kinabalu. Lambir's tall mixed dipterocarp forest grows on flat lowland clay to steep sandstone slopes rising to Bukit Lambir (465m). Stunted kerangas forest grows on the ridges.

Access 30-minute drive south of Miri in N Sarawak. Miri has a good range of accommodation, but it is best to stay overnight in chalets at park headquarters. Lambir has been the subject of much scientific research.

What to see and do 1. Climb Bukit Lambir, 6.3km (5-hour trek each way), to look for *Nepenthes* pitcher plants and hill casuarina *Gymnostoma nobile* forest. 2. Climb Bukit Pantu, 2.9km (2-hour trek each way), to look for wild sago palms (p. 52). 3. Walk the well-marked trails and swim in one of 8 waterfall pools. 4. Climb the canopy tree tower to look for fruiting fig trees and fig-loving barbets and fairy bluebirds.

THE DIVERSE FLORA OF LAMBIR – a clue to the vanished mammals of Sundaland Lambir's varied topography and soils are partly responsible for the very diverse flora. The most important reason, however, is that Lambir is a tiny relic of the vast lowland Sundaland forests that 20,000 years ago covered the Sundaland basin between Borneo, Java, Sumatra and the Malay Peninsula. Glacial meltwater drowned most of Sundaland's forests under the South China Sea about 10,000 years ago, turning Borneo into an island (p. 14). Conversion of the surrounding forest to agriculture has isolated Lambir even further. Lambir's fruit trees are an anachronistic remnant of the much larger and even more diverse Sundaland basin ecosystem (pp. 14 and 46). Today Lambir's surviving anachronistic trees provide a window into the past, to understand Sundaland's extinct giant megafauna of tapirs, hippos, rhinos and elephants (p. 19).

The Riau Pocket Refugia The Sundaland connection was first pointed out by botanist E. J. H. Corner (1960), who showed that many of W Borneo's rare trees, like the dipterocarp *Dryobalanops aromatica*, were shared with the east coast of the Malay Peninsula and the Riau Islands south of Singapore. Corner named this area the 'Riouw (Riau) Pocket' (map, p. 14). Lambir acted as a refuge for plants and mammals during the 1.6 million years of the Pleistocene, when Lambir remained above sea level (Hazebroek 2000).

Figs: 77 fig species have been recorded, including 27 species of strangler (see Harrison 2001, 2003 and 2005). Only 2,080 out of 470,000 trees in the 52ha plot are figs (less than 0.5%), yet figs are more important for wildlife than any Bornean plant family (p. 76). **Dipterocarps:** 94 species of these giant timber trees, which dominate Lambir's forests, have been recorded. See Peter Ashton (2005) on why Lambir was chosen for protection. **Palms:** Dransfield listed 67 palms for Lambir, including both wild sago palm *Eugeissona utilis*, found on the ridges, and Bornean borassus palm *Borassodendron borneense*, found in the valleys. Wild sago palms probably evolved to be dispersed by rhinos and borassus by elephants – evidence that these megafauna were once abundant at Lambir (pp. 38, 46, 290 and 296).

Collapse in large mammal and bird populations at Lambir Surveys in 1984–2011 show an almost complete loss of the large mammal fauna at Lambir, including gibbons, Sarawak Langurs, Hose's Langurs, Sun Bears, Clouded Leopards, Red Giant Flying Squirrels, Sambar and flying foxes (Harrison et al. 2011). Shanahan & Debiski (2002) note that in 1999 Lambir hosted 6 species of hornbill, but today 5 out of 6 of them are extinct. An estimated 20,000 forest durians of the 9 durian species dispersed by hornbills grow at Lambir. These durian trees will eventually also become extinct.

The 52ha Smithsonian Forest Dynamics Plot at Lambir was established in 1991 as part of a global programme by the CTFS of the Smithsonian Tropical Research Institute (USA) to compare tropical forest ecology worldwide. Every 5 years every tree in the plot more than 1cm in diameter at breast height (DBH) is counted, measured and recorded. Similar plots exist at Pasoh (W Malaysia), Bukit Timah (Singapore) and in many other tropical forests. Tree diversity at Lambir is only exceeded by Yasuni in Peru. In the Lambir plot 470,000 trees of 1,200 species were counted and identified (Harrison et al. 2013). Lambir's global importance has been studied by numerous local and international scientists from Britain, the USA and Japan. See Roubik et al. (2005).

Loss of primates and hornbills – an ecological disaster at Lambir Numerous studies show that a large majority of tropical forest tree species is animal dispersed, for example 84% at Pasoh (Sun et al. 2007). The loss of animal dispersers is already affecting Lambir's trees (Harrison et al. 2013). The forest at Lambir is large enough to support a population of 15 rhinos, at least 100 Orangutans, and hundreds of langurs and gibbons, all important seed dispersers. The loss of these dispersers will inevitably precipitate a collapse in tree diversity at Lambir, an ecological disaster for a globally important site.

A Wreathed Hornbill swallows the oily red aril-covered seed of *Durio acutifolius* near the summit of Bukit Lambir before these hornbills were poached into extinction at Lambir. The large seed will usually be regurgitated far from the parent tree (p. 62).

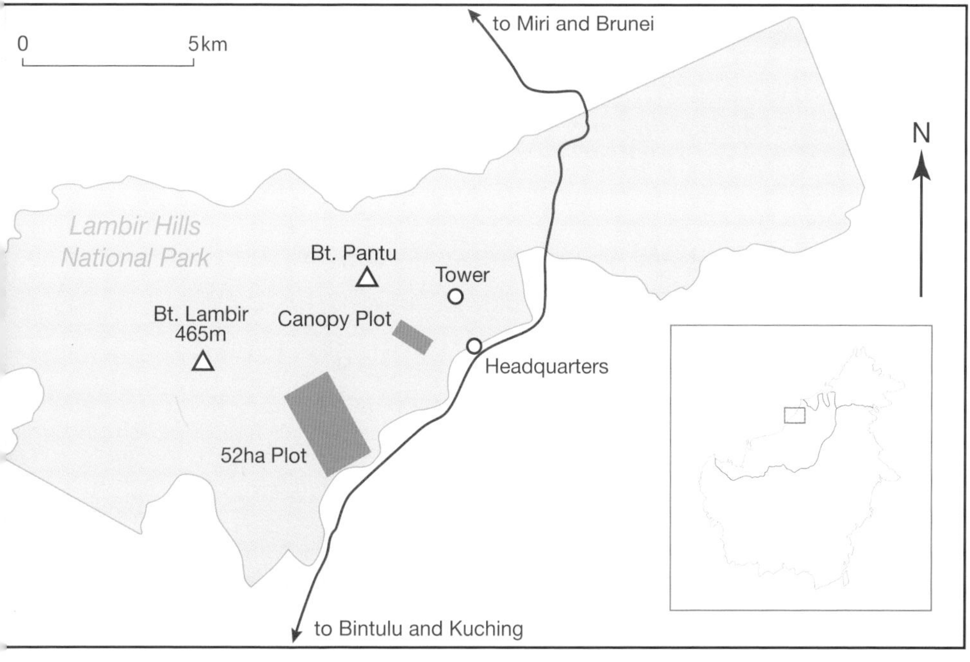

SARAWAK 7: MULU

GUNUNG MULU (4°02´N, 114°54E) 528km² Mulu contains Sarawak's second highest mountain (Gng Mulu, 2,376m), stunning limestone cliffs and karst scenery, some of the world's largest caves, many excellent guided jungle walks, cave explorations and overnight treks. The floodplain forest between the lowland Melinau River and the mountains contains some of Borneo's finest trees, including Belian (Borneo Ironwood *Eusideroxylon zwageri*), which is abundant around Mulu park headquarters, evidence (together with several old wallows) that rhinos were once locally common (pp. 38 and 299). Banteng, once common are on the verge of extinction (p. 304). If you are interested in bats and cave fauna, Mulu is the most accessible site in Borneo (p. 372).

Access Traditionally the park was reached by river boat, a 1-day journey from Miri. Today most visitors arrive by plane either from Miri (daily flights) or Kota Kinabalu (3 flights per week) on 2–7-night packages.
A variety of accommodation is available both inside and just outside the park. The chalets and hostel next to park headquarters are best for wildlife, www.mulupark.com The luxury Royal Mulu Resort built on a scenic bend of the Melinau River outside the park is good for squirrels. Bats and swiftlets roost under the resort.

Birds Mulu has a long bird list, but finding montane birds requires an arduous 3-day trek to the summit of Mulu. Wreathed Hornbills can be seen flying above Deer Cave, and Black Hornbills are common around Park HQ. The Mulu caves host large numbers of Mossy-nest, some Black-nest and a few White-nest Swiftlets. Bat Hawks are frequently seen at dusk near Deer Cave.

The entrance to Deer Cave (Gua Payau) from the Bat Observatory at Mulu
In the past Sambar frequently entered Deer Cave to feed on bat guano and bat bones to obtain mineral salts and calcium. Subsistence hunting by locals is permitted in Mulu, and Sambar are now locally extinct at Deer Cave.

THE LAST TIGERS IN BORNEO Due to the number of local tiger legends, it is likely that the Mulu mountains were one of the last strongholds of the now-extinct Bornean Tiger. Spencer St John, the British Consul in Brunei, heard many tiger stories on his expedition from Brunei up the Limbang River to Gng Murud in 1858. 'The highest peak beyond the houses, above 5,500 feet, is called Lobang Rimau, "The Tigers' Cave", about which they tell this story: that formerly a tiger killed a woman; the people turned out, and gave chase; the tigers, eight in number, took refuge in a cave near the peak, when the hunters lit a fire at the entrance, and smoked them to death. Since then there have been no tigers, but the place has been called "Tigers' Cave" to this day; and it is worth noticing that the Muruts of Padas have a great dread of ascending to the summit of some of their highest mountains, on account of the tigers which still, they say, lurk in the deepest recesses of the forest.' (St John 1862). Tigers' Cave can be viewed from Camp 5. See also p. 18.

HUNTING IN SARAWAK AND THE TRAGEDY OF THE COMMONS Although most large animals, such as Orangutans, are protected in Sarawak in most areas, there is no enforcement and hunting continues until the mammal population is extinct (see Lambir, p. 368). In addition to uncontrolled poaching, subsistence hunting of pigs and deer by locals is allowed in some of Sarawak's parks. However, no ecological studies on the impact of subsistence hunting have ever been carried out. Subsistence hunting by Penans for food in very large areas of protected forest by traditional methods is sustainable. Current levels of 'sport hunting' by locals in small parks such as Mulu and Lambir are not sustainable and have led to the local extinction of both protected and unprotected mammals from most of Sarawak. No one eventually benefits from this failure of governance and proper management planning. By wiping out their own food supply, local subsidence hunters lose out. Tourism loses out because most visitors want to see large mammals, and the ecosystem eventually suffers catastrophic failure because mutualistic relationships between plants and mammals are broken. The economic theory dealing with the over-exploitation of 'free' resources such as wildlife, air pollution (haze), or overfishing is known as the Economics of Externalities, or in popular terms The Tragedy of the Commons.

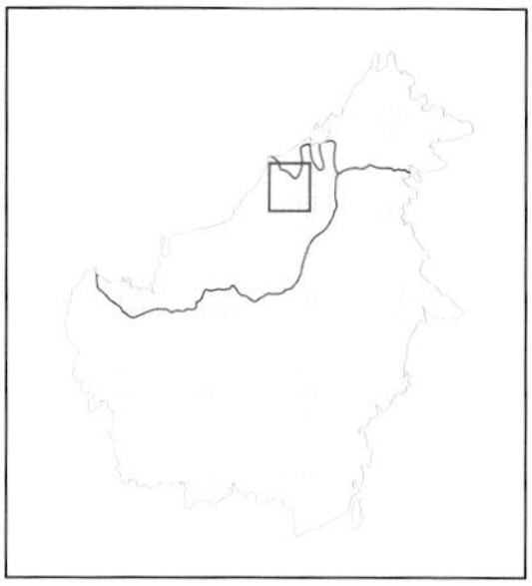

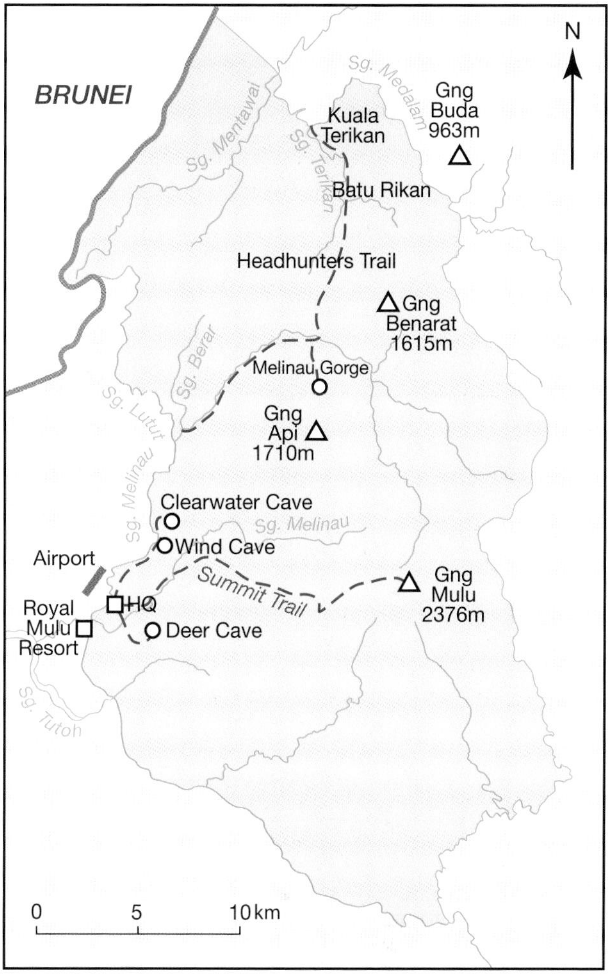

SUSTAINABLE HUNTING BY THE PENAN OF MULU IN 1982
'The Penan spoke of hunting monkeys in a most sophisticated manner. They seemed to know the size and membership of each langur group and claimed to select their victims carefully. They killed young males in preference to females, and had cropping programmes that would meet with the approval of any modern wildlife manager. In the area 20 years ago, food seemed to be in abundance. Today, by contrast, the Penan spoke of a shortage of monkeys, of a danger of having to kill too many of the breeding stock, problems out of which their concern for thoughtful harvesting grew.' Adapted from Macdonald (1982).

SOURCE AND SINK HABITATS For all mammals, some habitats are better than others. In ideal habitats (source habitats), breeding mammals produce a surplus population that is then forced to expand into suboptimal habitats (sink habitats), where the population dies out unless it is constantly replenished from the source. In Borneo, areas protected from hunting and poaching are typical source habitats, whilst areas where hunting is allowed or poaching is rife are typical sink habitats. If hunting is allowed in source habitats such as Sarawak's parks, mammals have nowhere safe to breed and the whole population is doomed to extinction. Banteng were once common along the river floodplains at Mulu, but are now almost extinct due to hunting. In hindsight it was an error to allow uncontrolled hunting inside source habitats such as Mulu. In other parts of the world many countries successfully manage protected areas with restricted hunting rights, as for the Banteng population in Australia (p. 304).

SARAWAK 8: MULU BATS

BATS OF MULU The Mulu limestone karst massif extends over 304km², one of the largest areas of karst in Borneo. Mulu's caves provide roosts for many millions of bats of 28 species (the Borneo bat total is 96 species, of which 44 are obligate cave dwellers). How does this vast population of bats find enough food in the forests surrounding Mulu? Four food-foraging strategies used by Bornean bats are described below.

1 Cave-dwelling, long-distance foragers Most of Mulu's bats roost in Mulu's caves but feed in forests outside the park and in Brunei. The majority are Wrinkled-lipped Bats *Tadarida plicata*. In the USA, *T. braziliensis* forages up to 65km away to feed on insects. In Europe, *T. teniotis* forages up to 100km from the roost (Arlettaz 1990). Four Bornean nectar bats, 2 *Rousettus* spp. and 2 *Eonycteris* spp. forage up to 50km away. Fukuda (2009), (p. 96).

2 Cave-dwelling, local foragers include the Dusky Fruit Bat (p. 88), which feeds on a wide range of local fruits. Cave entrances at Mulu are surrounded by *Caryota* palms and fig trees, from seeds defecated by bats. Cave-dwelling *Rhinolophus* and *Hipposideros* insect bats also forage locally (pp. 103–9).

3 Sedentary residents with flexible roosting habits are also found at Mulu. These bats occupy a local feeding territory utilizing a variety of roosting sites including old birds' nests, banana leaves and hollow trees. Sedentary fruit bats include the 2 short-nosed fruit bats (p. 86). Most vesper bats (p. 118) are sedentary residents.

4 Frugivorous nomads fly long distances to find fruiting patches of forest. They use a variety of temporary roosts near the food source. Fruit-eating nomads include flying foxes (p. 85), Horsfield's Fruit Bat (p. 86), Dyak Fruit Bat (p. 88) and the 2 megaerop tail-less fruit bats (p. 94). These bats are rare at Mulu.

Bats of Deer Cave (Hall 1996). All bats listed usually only roost in caves. Only *E. spelaea* eats fruit.

Eonycteris spelea (nectar) (p. 96)	*Hipposideros cervinus* (p. 108)	*Coelops robinsoni* (p. 108)
Emballonura alecto (p. 112)	*H. dyacorum* (p. 108)	*Miniopterus australis* (p. 116)
Rhinolophus borneensis (p. 104)	*H. galeritus* (p. 106)	*Cheriomeles torquatus* (p. 136)
R. philippensis (p. 104)	*H. diadema* (p. 106)	*Chaerephon plicata* (abundant) (p. 134)

View from the Bat Observatory at Deer Cave Mulu, where tourists gather to watch the emergence of up to 3 million Wrinkle-lipped Bats from Deer Cave at dusk. When rain is imminent no bats may emerge.

DO BRUNEI'S FORESTS FEED SARAWAK'S BATS? The map shows the likely foraging range of Mulu's cave-dwelling, long-distance foraging bats, chiefly *Tadarida plicata*. Cave-dwelling *Rousettus* and *Eonycteris* bats trapped at Tasek Merimbun most likely originated from Mulu's caves about 50km distant at the closest point. The majority of Sarawak's forests within a 65km radius from Mulu have been logged, whilst Brunei's forests are mostly intact. Logging causes changes to bat species, but the bat population survives (p. 126). However, the conversion of logged forest to oil palm around Mulu will result in a bat population collapse, with the remnant bats largely dependent on Brunei's adjacent virgin forests for food.

Collapse in bat populations at Niah: The evidence for this projected scenario at Mulu is the collapse in bat populations at the Niah Caves in NW Sarawak (p. 366). Niah's bats do not have the advantage of living next to Brunei's extensive unlogged virgin forests.

Wrinkle-lipped Bat *Tadarida plicata*, the most common Mulu cave bat. The long, narrow wings enable this bat to fly at 65km an hour. Illustration from Thomas Hardwicke (1830).

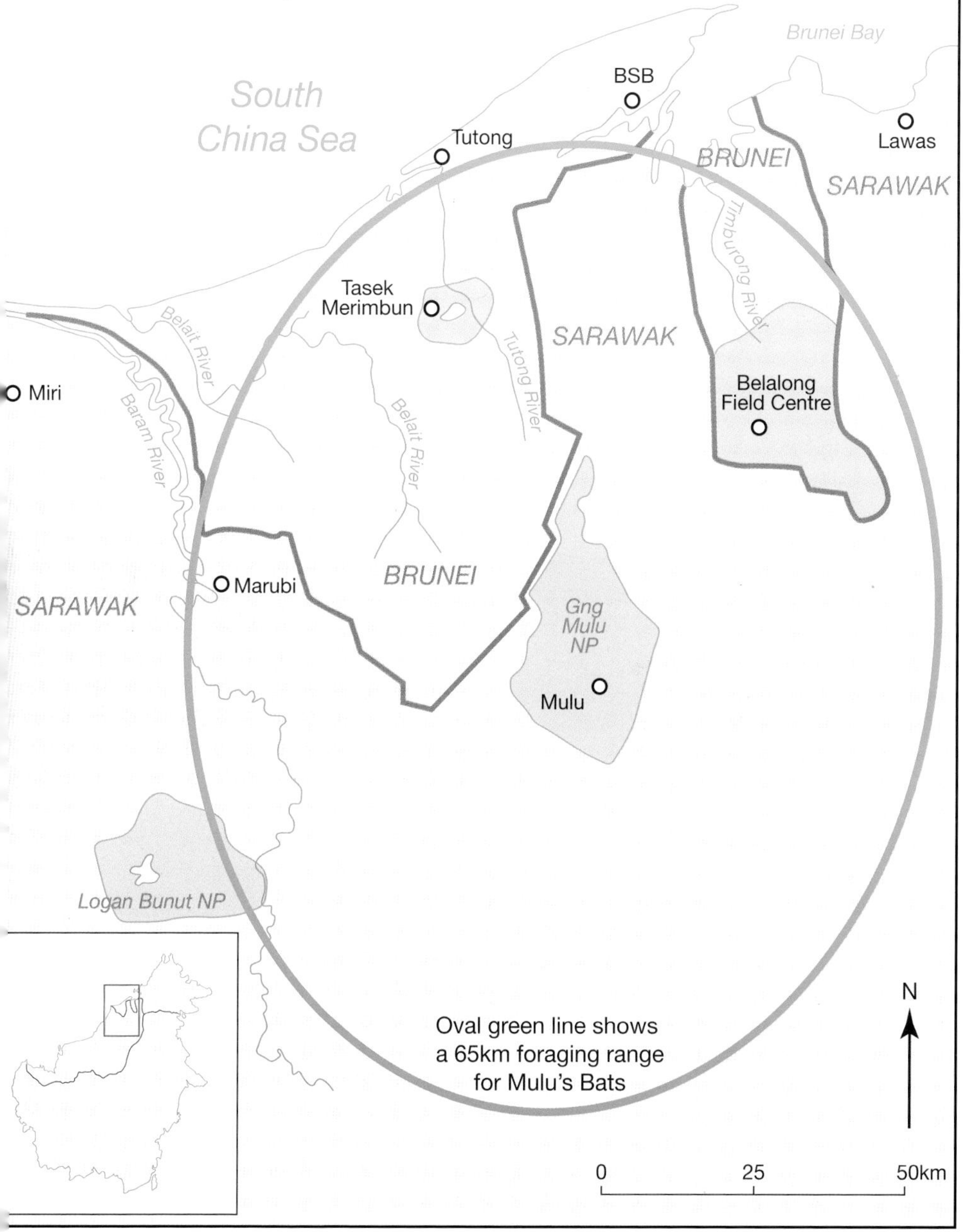

KALIMANTAN 1: OVERVIEW

KALIMANTAN The rapidly developing Indonesian province of Kalimantan occupies 72.5% of southern Borneo and hosts c. 80% of Borneo's Orangutans and other large mammals. Large areas of remote virgin forest remain, but about half is scheduled for conversion to oil palm. If this planned conversion proceeds, a minimum of 15,000 Orangutans will die, almost a quarter of the world population (pp. 32 and 188). Listed below are some national parks and sites of interest for wildlife. Currently it is possible to drive from Tawau in E Sabah anti-clockwise around Borneo to Tg Selor in E Kalimtantan. The road-less gap of 200km between Tg Selor and Tawau is best accessed by speedboat from Pulau Tarakan up the Sebuku, Sembakung and Sesayap Rivers. The forested headwaters of these rivers host a small nomadic population of Pigmy Elephants from Sabah (p. 288).

1 Betung Kerihun A large, mountainous park on the Indonesian/Sarawak border with many primates (p. 364).

2 Danau Sentarum and Kapuas Lakes 800km² of seasonal wetlands surrounded by swamp forest. Ramsar Site.

3 Gunung Niut 1,400km² of hill and montane forest. Highest point 1,709m. Remnant extinct volcano can be viewed from Gng Penrissen in Sarawak.

4 Bukit Baka and Bukit Raya Access from the Kapuas River. 1810km² of lowland dipterocarp up to montane forest. This area includes part of the Schwaner mountain range, and the highest peak is Bukit Raya at 2,278m.

5 Gunung Palung National Park surrounding an extinct volcano with a wide range of habitats (p. 377).

6 Karimata Islands Host to an endemic race of the Red Langur.

7 Natuna Islands p. 387.

8 Lamandau 64,000ha protected forest site for Orangutan release by the Orangutan Foundation UK (p. 378).

9 Belantikan Hulu Remote hill forest surveyed for wildlife and Orangutan release.

10 Murung Raya Bukit Batikap Remote hill forest used for Orangutan release. See www.heartofborneo.org

11 Tanjung Puting 4,160km² of peat-swamp forest (p. 378).

12 Sabangau 20km south-west of Palangkaraya. 6,300km² of peat-swamp forest (p. 380).

13 Barito Ulu Research Area 1,950km² of hill forest in the headwaters of the Barito River.

14 Meratus Mountains 2,460km² of geographically isolated hill and montane forest north-east of Bandjarmasin. Highest point is Gng Besar 1,907m. Largely unprotected.

15 Gunung Lumut Isolated community hill forest between Balikpapan and the Meratus Mountains.

16 Sungai Wain Protection Forest 100km² water-catchment forest north of Balikpapan (p. 382).

17 Bukit Soeharto 620km² of lowland dipterocarp forest between Balikpapan and Samarinda, the site of E Kalimantan's forest research centre and Yasuma's (1994) mammal records. Badly affected by fire and squatters

18 Mahakam Lakes and Mahakam River 4,000km² (p. 322).

19 Kutai 2-hour drive north of Samarinda. 2,000km² of beach, swamp and lowland primary forest damaged by coal mining, land squatting and forest fires. Highest point is Gng Tandung Mayang (397m). See below.

20 Wehea Protected Forest Community forest with the last known population of Kutai Grey Langurs (p. 164).

21 Sangkulirang (Mangkalinat) Peninsula Large area of karst limestone with many bat caves.

22 Derawan Islands Includes Maratua, Kakaban and Sangkalaki. Best Borneo site for dolphin watching (p. 314).

23 Kayan Mentarang 13,650km². Large area of hill forest (p. 384).

24 Pulau Tarakan From here a speedboat gives access to remote NE Kalimantan.

WILD SUMATRAN RHINOS AT KUTAI In 2013, WWF Indonesia produced video-camera footage of one (possibly two) adult Sumatran Rhinos in W Kutai in E Kalimantan. These photos show the last known Sumatran Rhinos anywhere in the wild in Borneo. Camera-trapping surveys are now so widespread that if there were any other wild rhinos left their presence would almost certainly be detected. Given the scarcity of rhinos there is no chance that there is a viable breeding population at Kutai, and these wild rhinos urgently need to be captured so that they can participate in the established rhino breeding programmes currently underway either in Sabah at Tabin, or Sumatra at Way Kambas without any further delay (p. 298). www.wwf.or.id.

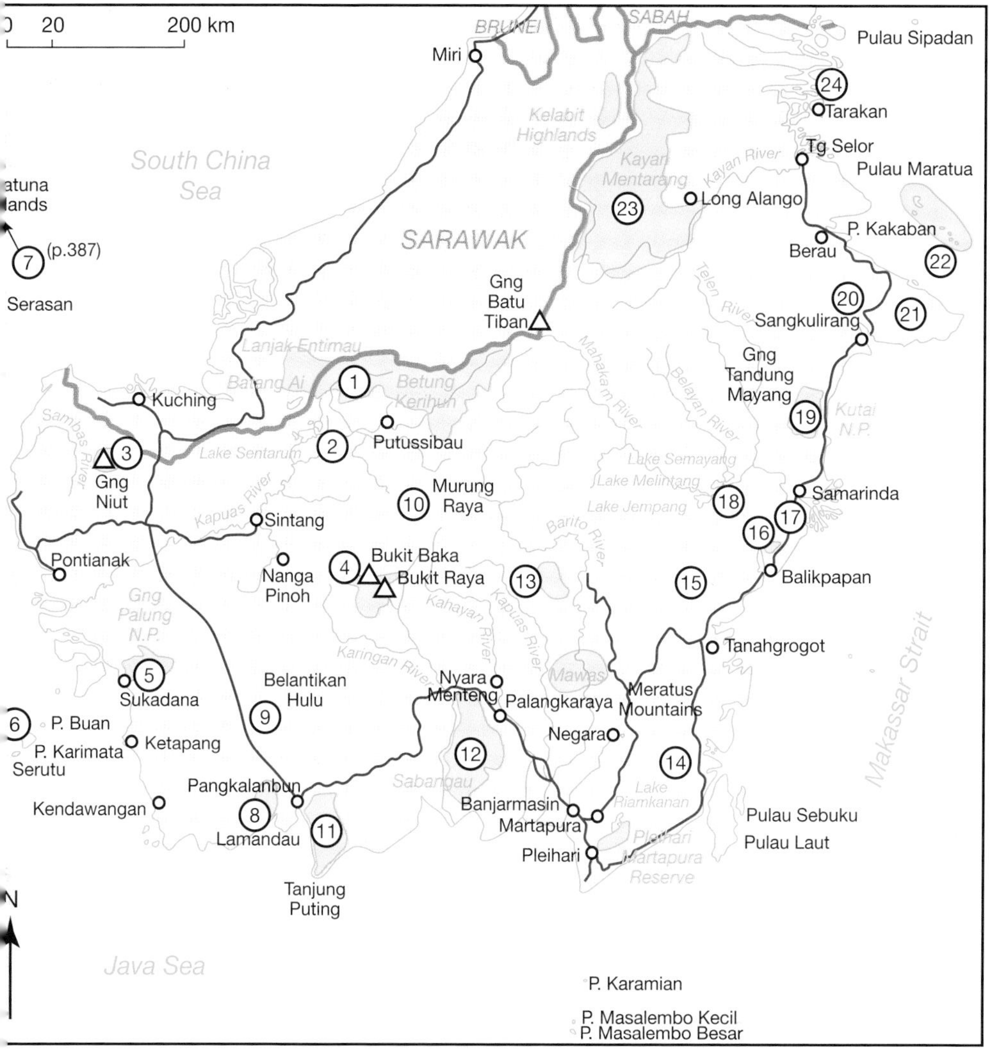

Wild Sumatran Rhinoceros rolling in a mud wallow at Kutai in E Kalimantan in October 2013. (Photo: WWF-Indonesia/PHKA)

KALIMANTAN 2: GUNUNG PALUNG

GUNUNG PALUNG NATIONAL PARK (1°13´S, 110°14´E) 900km² One of Borneo's finest wildlife reserves, and the site of Cabang Panti, one of Borneo's most important field research centres. The park is dominated by the U-shaped granitic remnant of an extinct volcano, with a long summit ridge topped by two peaks, Gunung Panti (1,050 m) and Gunung Palung (1,116 m). Gng Palung is interesting ecologically for two reasons (1) Seven distinct forest types occur within a small area enabling diversity comparisons across habitats and altitudinal gradients. (2) Gng Palung is close to the coast and both fauna and flora are subject to the Massenerhebung effect in which temperature drops faster on small coastal mountains compared with larger inland mountains. Two relict montane birds are found near the summit Grey-throated babbler and endemic Chestnut-crested Yuhina.(See Phillips 2014).

Access By plane or boat from Pontianak to Ketapang, then drive 2 hours to Sukadana and from there journey to several access points. Tourists can stay overnight at Lubuk Baji, a forest rest hut 2.5 hours walk into the forest. Obtain your permit from the Park headquarters in Ketapang. Bona fide researchers who want to work at Cabang Panti should apply to the Indonesian government agency, RISTEK, that handles research permits as well as contact Dr Cheryl Knott of the Gunung Palung Orangutan Project (GPOP). www.savegporangutan.org. or Dr. Andrew Marshall.

Vegetation The Park contains areas of mangrove and beach forest along the coast. Inland, there are large areas of peat-swamp, freshwater swamp forest, kerangas and riverine alluvial terraces. Most of the lowlands are dipterocarp forest growing on sandstone which changes to hill dipterocarp forest on the ridges. The vegetation becomes moss covered and stunted in the summit area due to the low cloud base. The dipterocarp forest is subject to extreme mast fruiting (masting) events, the result of ENSO droughts (p.14) and these dominate the breeding cycles of the forest mammals.

Mammals The Orangutan population is estimated at 2,500 and there are large numbers of Red Langurs and gibbons. Tarsiers, slow loris, Proboscis Monkeys, Silvered Langurs and macaques also occur.

CABANG PANTI RESEARCH STATION was founded by Dr Mark Leighton in 1983.
Orangutan research initiated by Cheryl Knott in 1992 has continued ever since and includes the collection of long-term reproductive and behavioural data on numerous named Orangutans. Urine and faecal samples are obtained from wild Orangutans (usually when they wake in the early morning) to determine hormonal condition and parasite load in relation to changes in forest fruiting and diet.
Studies on Red Langurs and gibbons were initiated and continue to be supervised by Dr Andrew Marshall (see Marshall 2004, Marshall & Leighton 2006, and Marshall (2008).
Dipterocarp masting was studied by Lisa Curran and Leighton in 1985–1999 during four masting episodes with an average interval of 3.7 years. With the exception of a minor mast in 1994, all masts occurred during ENSO years. Curran found that all dipterocarp seed were predated, unless masting occurred over a very wide area (a regional scale) due to the intense predation by locally resident mammals, as well as by nomadic pigs that arrived from outside the park (see Curran & Leighton 2000).
Figs Laman & Weiblen (1998) recorded 56 species of figs at Gng Palung, noting that the large stranglers fruit out of synchrony with dipterocarps, thus providing an important fallback food for many mammals.
Local education and conservation Researchers and staff of organize and participate in many local conservation and educational projects as part of GPOP's conservation program – the Gunung Palung Orangutan Conservation Program, also known locally as Yayasan Palung. See www.savegporangutans.org

GIBBONS AND SQUIRRELS: FOOD COMPETITORS AT GNG PALUNG Marshall at al (2009) studied the comparative diets of gibbons and other frugivores at Gng Palung based on 4090 feeding observations between 1985–1992. During fruit masting Gibbons preferred sugar rich primate fruit particularly Artabotrys a lianas in the *Annonaceae* (p. 187), *Aglaia* fruit (Meliacea) (p. 64), *Garcinia* fruit (mangosteen) and *Disopyros* fruit (persimmon). p. 172). Less favoured fruit included *Nepthelium* (Rambutan) (pp. 217 and 218), *Palaquium* p. 95 and *Xanthophyllum* p. 182). During lean periods when primate fruit was unavailable gibbons ate figs (p. 76), and when there were no figs they ate leaves. Gibbons food competitor was **Prevost Squirrel** with a 50% dietary overlap. Orangutan diet overlapped by 48% but Orangutans forage in larger trees. Long-tailed Macaques also had a dietary overlap of 48% but they tend to forage lower down in smaller trees so are not important competitors.

Garcinia mangostana

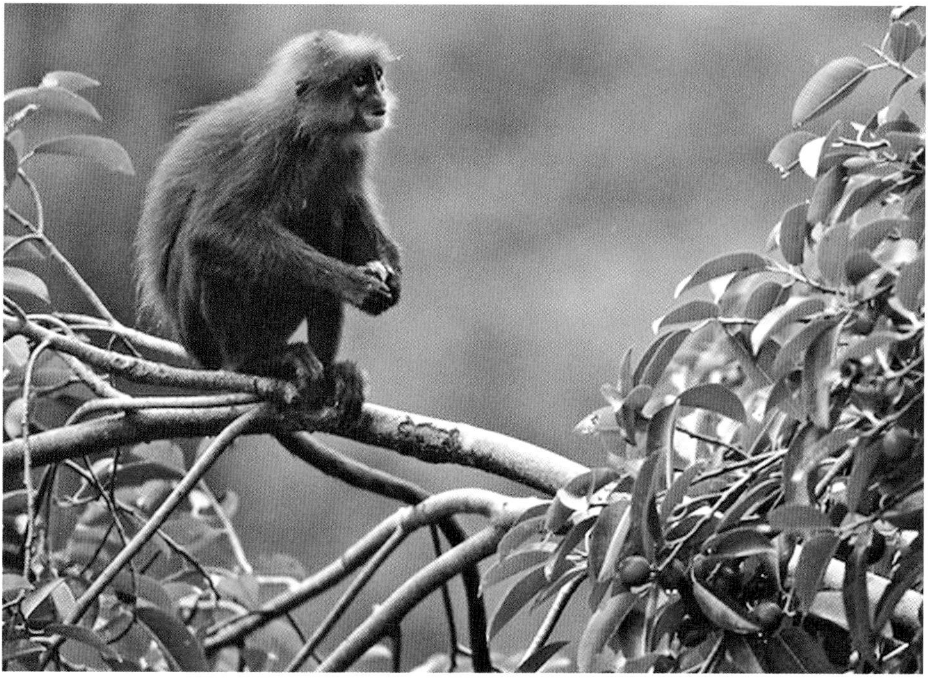

Red Langur feeding on *Ficus dubia*, a large strangling fig at Gunung Palung. Strangling figs fruit out of synchrony with most forest trees, and are an important source of fallback food for primates during inter-mast lean periods. (Photo: Tim Laman, www.timlaman.com)

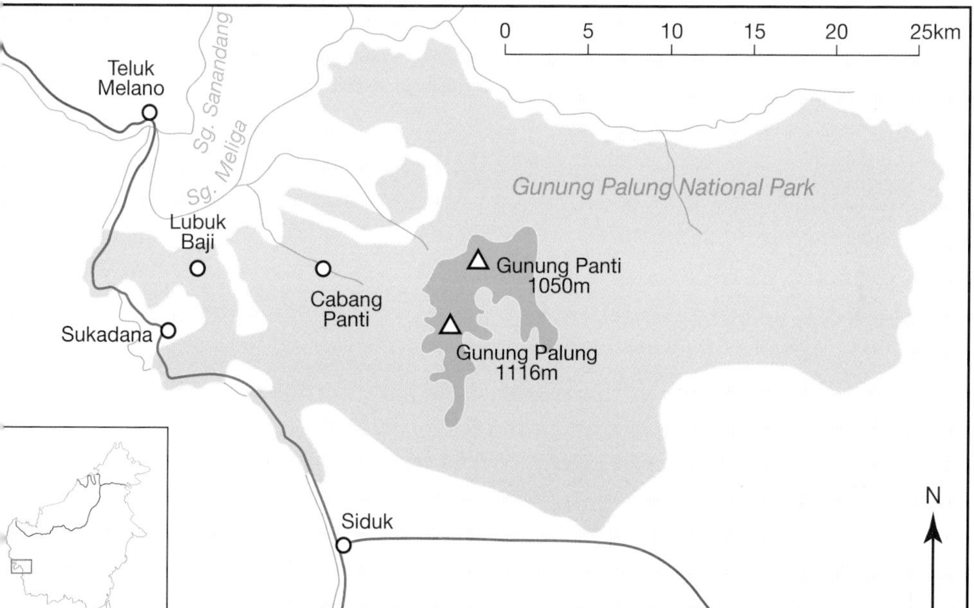

KALIMANTAN 3: TANJUNG PUTING

TANJUNG PUTING (C Kalimantan: 3°4´S, 111°059´E) 4,160km^2 Most famous for the 4,000 Orangutans, but retains a nearly complete range of Borneo's larger mammal wildlife as well. About 50% of the park is seasonally flooded peat-swamp forest. Trees typically have stilt roots or air-breathing roots. Another 40% is mainly dry-land stunted kerangas forest on poor soil, with *Nepenthes* and ant plants common. About 10% is degraded grassland (*lallang*) following cultivation. Along the coast there are extensive nipah palm forests that grow in brackish water. There is a small area of mangroves around the Kumai River mouth.

Access By plane from Jakarta to Pangkalanbun, then by road to Kumai, then by speedboat (1½ hours) along the Kumai and Sekonyer Rivers to Camp Leakey.

Accommodation Widely available outside the park at Rimba Lodge or in the park itself at Tg Harapan. Many tourists rent 'sleep on board' *klotoks* (motor boats), which are moored in the river at night.

Climate Heaviest rains are in Nov–May. June–October months are less wet.

Mammals 4,000 wild Orangutans and large populations of Red Langur, Proboscis Monkey and White-bearded Gibbon. Rescued Orangutans are no longer released at Tg Puting. Silvered Langur, and Long-tailed and Pig-tailed Macaques, are common. The monkeys often sleep in riverside trees at night to avoid attacks from Clouded Leopards. Peat-swamp forests can support large populations of primates because the majority of trees fruit year round, not in annual or in multi-year masting episodes typical of lowland dipterocarp forest.

Reptiles Both the man-eating Saltwater Crocodile and the rare fish-eating False Gharial *Tomistoma schelegii*, which only occurs in black-water peat-swamp rivers, are common (p. 177). Monitor lizards are abundant.

Birds Of Bornean hornbills, 5 out of 8 occur here; 218 bird species have been recorded, including birds rare elsewhere in Borneo: Storm's Stork, Lesser Adjutant, Dusky Heron, Bornean Bristlehead, Black Partridge, Crestless Fireback and Crested Fireback. Large heron colony breeds along Sg Buluh Besar River (May–Aug).

PEAT-SWAMP FORESTS OF BORNEO After Sabangau, Tg Puting is one of the largest area of contiguous peat-swamp forest in Borneo, and although logged in the past most of the forest remains largely intact.

Global warming Peat-swamp forest grows on a layer of peat up to 15m deep, the result of waterlogged soils in which organic matter fails to decay. If peat-swamp forest is drained for agriculture, the land sinks and the peat starts to decay, releasing large amounts of carbon dioxide, a major cause of global warming.

Fire-prone forest Logged and drained peat-swamp forest easily catches fire and can burn underground, causing large-scale pollution (haze). In coastal areas drainage of peat causes the peat to fall below sea level, resulting in salty peat in which little will grow.

Vegetation Peat-swamp forest is especially rich in 3 favoured timber trees, *Tetramerista glabra* (Miyapok, primate dispersed), *Gonystylus bancanus* (Ramin, hornbill and fish dispersed) and *Shorea albida* (Alan bunga, wind dispersed and mast fruiting), and is therefore a target for both legal and illegal logging. Experience shows that unlike lowland dipterocarp, forest peat-swamp forest is very difficult to re-afforest. Overall less than 20% of peat-swamp forest in Borneo remains intact, and large areas such as at Binsulok FR (Klias) in Sabah and the 1 million ha of the failed Mega Rice Project at Sabangau remain a barren wilderness. See map, p. 381.

Peat-swamp Forest	Original Area km^2	Intact in 2010 est.
Sabah	1,200	20%
Brunei	900	80%
Sarawak	17,000	20%
Kalimantan	60,000	30%

Data from Wetland International (2010)

ORANGUTAN FOUNDATION
A FUTURE FOR ORANGUTANS, FORESTS & PEOPLE

ORANGUTAN CONSERVATION AT TG PUTING started at Camp Leakey in a project initiated by Birute Galdikas, described in Galdikas (1995), *Reflections of Eden*. Tg Puting is the most important wildlife tourist site in Kalimantan where visitors can watch several generations of wild Orangutans being fed twice daily. Locally rescued Orangutans are now released at the nearby Lamandau protected forest in a project run by Ashley Leiman of the Orangutan Foundation UK, which also sponsors guard posts at Tg Puting, research projects at Pondok Ambung in Tg Puting and wildlife research at Belantikan Hulu (unprotected forest) in CW Kalimantan, which has a population of some 6,000 Orangutans. The Orangutan Foundation UK also organizes tours to visit Tg Puting and volunteer groups to work on Orangutan conservation projects in Kalimantan. See www.orangutan.org.uk.

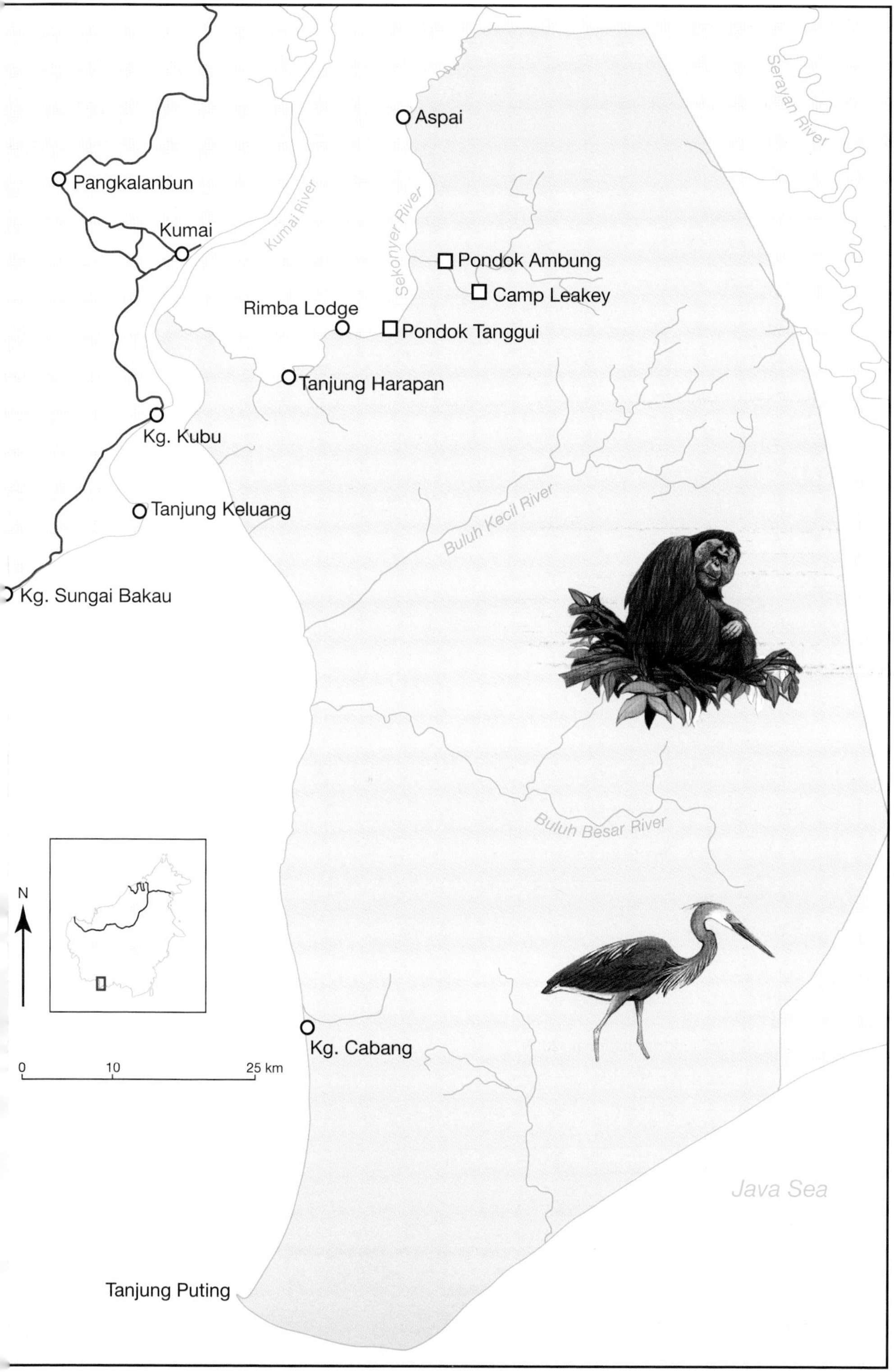
Aspai
Pangkalanbun
Kumai
Kumai River
Sekonyer River
Serayan River
Pondok Ambung
Camp Leakey
Rimba Lodge
Pondok Tanggui
Tanjung Harapan
Kg. Kubu
Tanjung Keluang
Buluh Kecil River
Kg. Sungai Bakau
Buluh Besar River
N
Kg. Cabang
0
10
25 km
Java Sea
Tanjung Puting

KALIMANTAN 4: SABANGAU

SABANGAU NATIONAL PARK (2°34´S, 113°38´E) 6,300km² Located 20km south-west of Palangka Raya. The core 50km² of the Sabangau peat-swamp forest in C Kalimantan is managed by the Centre for International Cooperation in Sustainable Management of Tropical Peatlands (CIMTROP), based at the local University of Palangka Raya. CIMTROP sponsors research by Ou Trop, the Orangutan Tropical Peatland Project, at the Setia Alam Research Station, one of Borneo's most active field centres and natural laboratories, with both local and international students studying peat-swamp wildlife, vegetation and ecology

Access By plane from Jakarta to Palangka Raya, a city in C Kalimantan. Palangka Raya is also the location of the Kalaweit (gibbon) centre (p. 184) and BOS Nyaru Menteng, the largest Orangutan rehabilitation centre in Borneo and a focus for efforts to preserve Kalimantan's remaining lowland forests. Setia Alam is about an hour from Palangka Raya by bus, boat and foot.

Climate There is rain almost every day throughout the year apart from in a drier period in June–Sept.

Research Setia Alam is surrounded by a grid of boardwalk transects through the often flooded peat-swamp forest. Long-term research projects organized by Ou Trop include the ecology of Orangutans, Red Langurs, White-bearded Gibbons and butterflies, and peat-swamp forest phenology and restoration. Camera traps are used to record and monitor local populations of wildlife, including Clouded Leopards, Marbled Cats and Sun Bears. Applications for bona fide research are welcome, but there are no facilities for casual tourists without research permits. Contacts: info@outrop.com, www.outrop.com.

PRIMATES OF SABANGAU The peat-swamp forest at Sabangau hosts the largest populations with some of the highest densities of scarce primates in Borneo.

Red Langurs Estimated population 75,000. See Ehlers Smith et al. (2013). Populations varied between different habitats, but in mixed swamp forest reached 2.52 groups per km², with an average group size of 6.95 individuals giving a density of 17.51 per km², almost as high as lowland dipterocarp forest at Sepilok (p. 162).

Gibbons Estimated 30,000 individuals (OUTROP 2013). Gibbon populations are estimated by triangulating (3 observers) or quadrangulating (4 observers) the early-morning calls. See Cheyne et al. 2008, 2010, 2012, 2013.

Orangutans Estimated 6,900 individuals (OUTROP 2013). Research by Harrison et al. 2009, 2010, 2011 and Morrogh Bernard et al. 2003, 2008, 2011, 2014 has established that Sabangau can support high densities of Orangutans because the peat-swamp forest is non-masting and produces fruit year round (pp. 16 and 44).

Diversity of mammals in peat-swamp forest Both the abundance and diversity of birds, mammals and insects in peat-swamp forest is known to be significantly lower than that in lowland dipterocarp forest, so why are primates so abundant at Sabangau? There are two possible explanations. The swampy forest is not easily accessible to humans and limits hunting and farming. Mammal populations in dipterocarp forests are limited by the carrying capacity of the habitat in the lean season between mast fruiting whilst at Sabangau trees fruit continuously throughout the year, with no lean season to limit mammal populations.

WILD CATS AND CLOUDED LEOPARD AT SABANGAU The only wild cat not recorded from Sabangau is the Bay Cat, whilst the Clouded Leopard is locally common (p. 274). A camera-trap survey by Cheyne et al. (2013), which placed 54 camera traps in the 50km² research plot for 45 months in 2008–2012 found that 5 males and 1 female Clouded Leopard were present. The camera traps were placed along obvious trails, which may have biased the results (p. 276). Using capture-recapture software, Clouded Leopard density was estimated at 0.72–4.41 individuals per 100km².

BATS, HOLLOW TREES AND POOR SOILS
Nutrient-poor soils such as kerangas, coastal sand and peat-swamp forests in Borneo are particularly rich in hollow trees. Abundant hollow trees in peat-swamp forest include *Shorea albida* (Alan bunga), *Dactylocladus stenostachys* (Jongkong) and *Combretocarpus rotundus* (Keruntum). See Brown (1955) re Sarawak. It is possible that these trees have evolved hollow interiors to encourage roosting colonies of bats and flying squirrels so that their faeces will contribute valuable nutrients to the trees. See Kunz (1982) and Voigt (2015), and pp. 70 and 131.

Sabangau is named after a common bird-dispersed shrub of poor soils, *Glochidion littorale* (Phyllantaceae), ubiquitous throughout coastal Borneo.

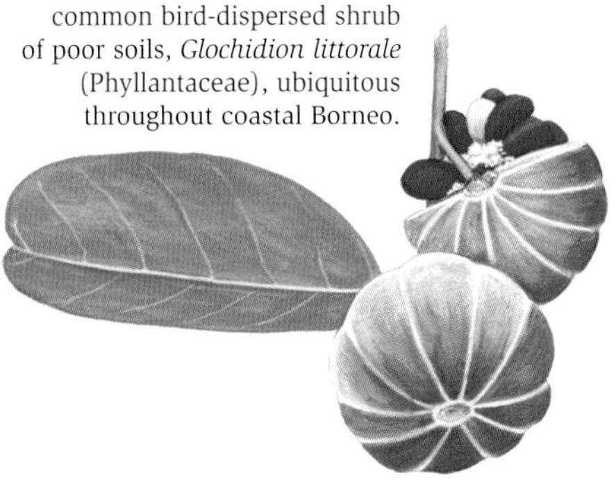

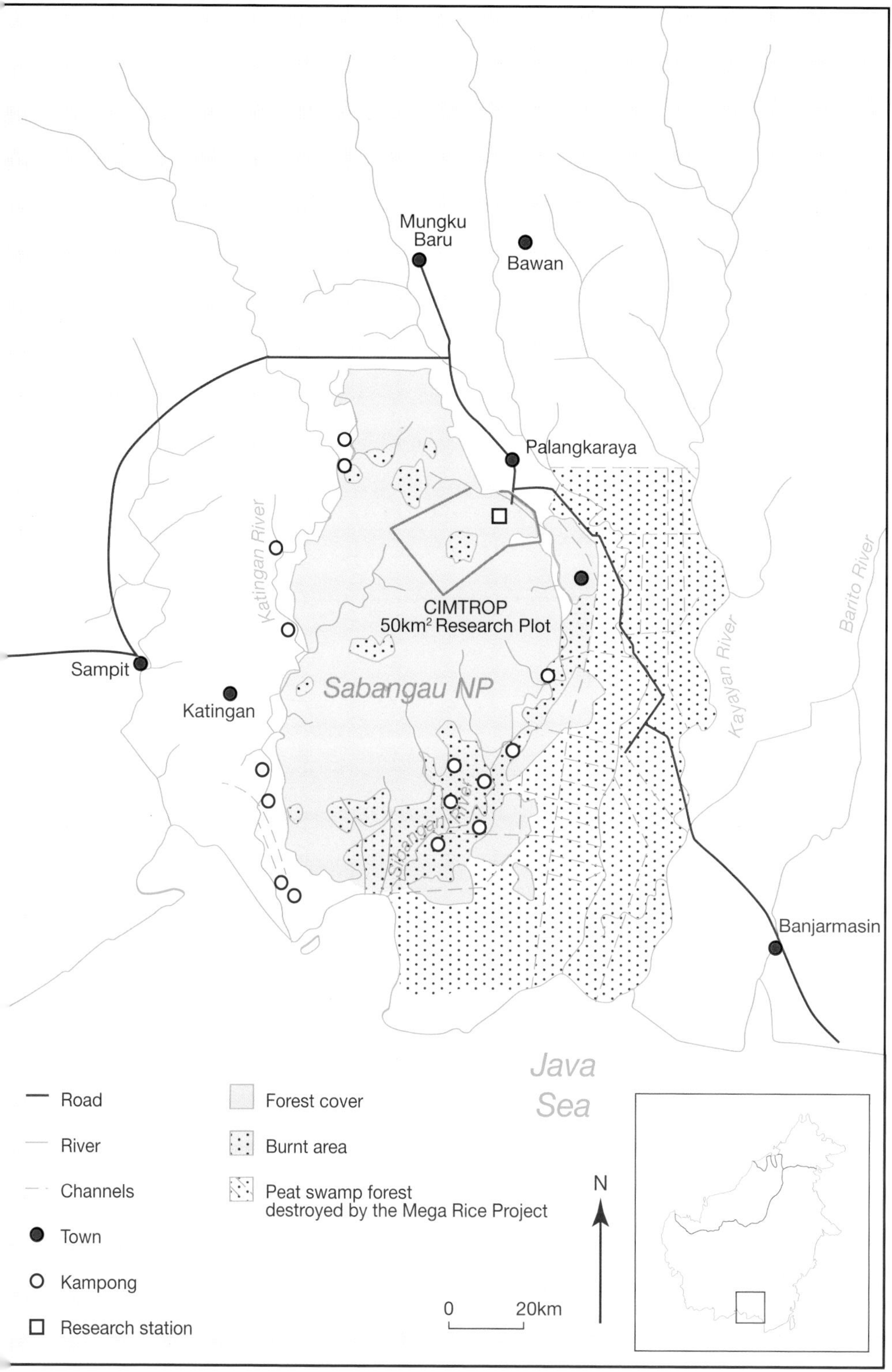
Mungku
Baru
Bawan
Palangkaraya
Katingan River
CIMTROP
50km² Research Plot
Sampit
Katingan
Sabangau NP
Sabangau River
Kayayan River
Barito River
Banjarmasin
Java
Sea
Road
River
Channels
Town
Kampong
Research station
Forest cover
Burnt area
Peat swamp forest
destroyed by the Mega Rice Project
N
0
20km

KALIMANTAN 5: SUNGAI WAIN AND BALIKPAPAN

SUNGAI WAIN 100km² of watershed protection forest with a large reservoir near the park headquarters providing water to the Pertamina refinery and Balikpapan city. Sungai Wain is the single most important area of lowland dipterocarp forest accessible in E Kalimantan. Despite damage by fire in the past, it remains ecologically rich with an incredibly high diversity of birds, mammals and plants.

Access About a 1-hour drive from Balikpapan city or Sepinggan Airport.

Accommodation Home stays can be arranged with the Sg Wain park authorities. Email: Pak Agusdin at agusdin_wain@yahoo.co.id. Day tours can be arranged by any hotel in Balikpapan.

Climate The climate is slightly seasonal, but in ENSO years droughts of several months may occur with arson and fires affecting vast areas of Kalimantan. The driest months are usually Aug–Nov.

Mammals Sungai Wain was a release and research site for rehabilitated Orangutans and a small number of Sun Bears for many years (see Fredriksson 2012). Red Langurs are more common than Kalimantan Grey Langurs (p. 162). Three-striped Ground Squirrels (p. 212) and Splendid Treeshrews (p. 148) are common. Pen-tailed Treeshrews occur in the swamp forest at the start of the main trail (Pak Agusdin).

Birds This rare fragment of lowland dipterocarp forest is the only accessible locality in Borneo where the endemic Bornean Peacock Pheasant can be seen.

Plants The *Shorea laevis* dipterocarp forest at Sg Wain is more open and dryer than elsewhere in Borneo, with abundant palms, including the endemic *Borassodendron borneensis* (Bandang), which produces a large anachronistic fruit originally dispersed by elephants (p. 290). The fruits are chewed but not dispersed by Sun Bears. The pith of the leaves provide a fallback food for Orangutans during lean seasons. The forest is also rich in wildlife-friendly trees of the Sapotaceae family (Nyatoh), including *Madhuca* (p. 196) and *Palaquium* (p. 95).

BALIKPAPAN (1°16´S,116°51´E) This is a rapidly expanding city at the centre of both a coal and oil boom, with E Kalimantan's only international airport (Sepinggan).

Samarinda and the Mahakam Lakes – Birding and Dolphin Watching Samarinda, 2 hours north of Balikpapan, is the gateway to the Mahakam River and Lakes. The best time to visit the Mahakam Lakes is Jul–Aug, at the beginning of the dry season, when waterbirds congregate around the reduced lakes and Irrawaddy Dolphins are most easy to see.

Samboja Lestari 20km² Large Orangutan and Sun Bear rescue and rehabilitation centre a 45-minute drive from Balikpapan Airport. An ambitious project founded by the botanist/ecologist Willie Smits to restore agricultural land to forest, combined with the enrichment planting of wildlife-friendly fruit trees. Good-quality lodge accommodation needs advance booking. Day visits are possible on Saturdays only. www. sambojalodge.com

Balikpapan Sun Bear Education Centre Kawasan Wisata Pendidikan Lingkungan Hidup (KWPLH) is a 10ha environmental education facility located 23km north of Balikpapan. A popular, successful educational site with rescued Sun Bears on the outskirts of Balikpapan. Website: http://en.kwplh.beruangmadu.org. Email: info.kwplh@beruangmadu.org.

Balikpapan Bay and mangroves A survey by Stanislav Lhota estimated the Proboscis Monkey population in the mangroves around the Bay at 1,400, one of the largest breeding groups in Borneo, whilst a marine mammal survey by Budiyono and Kreb found that Balikpapan Bay contained significant populations of Irrawaddy Dolphins and Short-finned Porpoise. The mangroves are unprotected and large areas near the oil terminal on the bay are scheduled for development. See www.mongabay.com

CATASTROPHIC FIRES IN EAST KALIMANTAN During the ENSO-related droughts of 1983 and 1997–1998, several millions of hectares of logged forest in E Kalimantan, including nearly half of Sg Wain, caught fire, leaving only a core area of 5,000ha unburnt. This forest is slowly regenerating, but it will take many decades for it to re-establish. Repeat fires occurred during the extreme ENSO event in 2015.

In Borneo virgin forest is unlikely to burn during droughts because the microclimate of virgin forest retains the humidity inside the forest. During extreme ENSO-related droughts even primary forests burn readily, with extreme [up to 90%] subsequent mortality of ancient trees. Where forest has been damaged by logging, previous fires and small-scale cultivation, the extra sunlight dries out the forest, the humidity is lost and forests may easily burn during droughts.

The Utang Resident
Coelites euptychioides
This striking nymphalid butterfly of undisturbed forest is locally common at Sg Wain. The large false eyes on the underwing are probably deimatic markings to startle a pursuing predator when the butterfly settles, whilst the additional smaller eyes are probably deception markings to convince predators that the head is on the rear wing. In the Bornean rainforest that has been ecologically stable for millions of years, it is extremely unlikely that any species that is not fully adapted to that environment will survive. See p. 233 and Honor Phillipps (2016), *A Naturalist's Guide to the Butterflies of Borneo*. Also see Wickler (1968) and Howse (2010, 2014) for more information on deceptive markings in butterflies and other animals.

Photo: Honor Phillipps

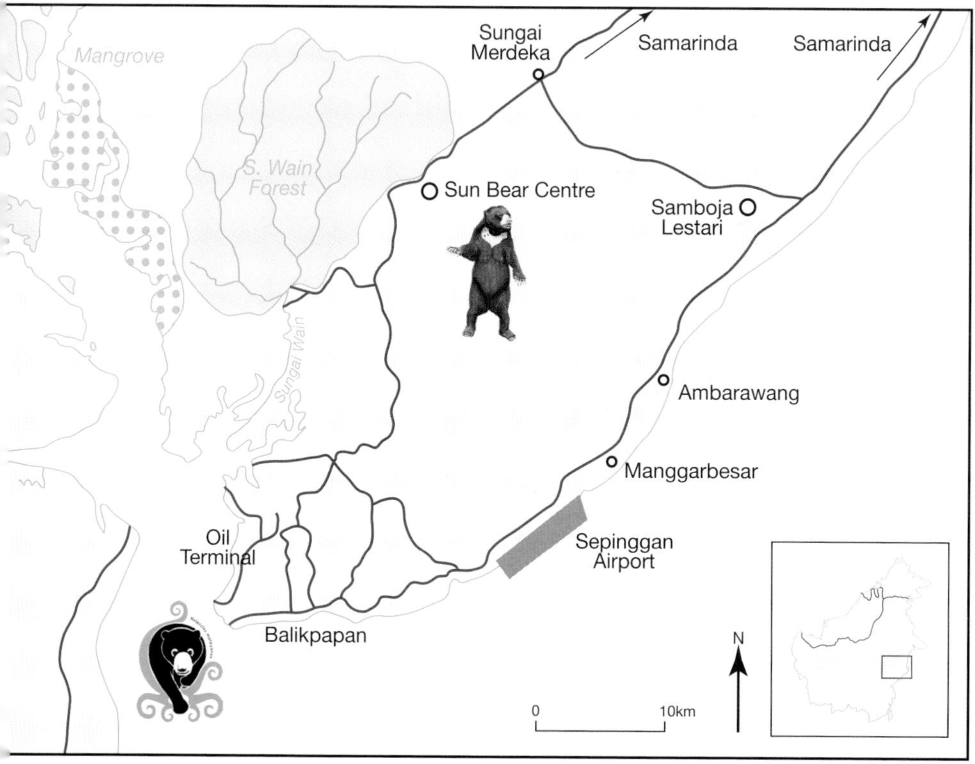

KALIMANTAN 6: KAYAN MENTARANG

KAYAN MENTARANG NATIONAL PARK (8°22´N, 123°57´E) 13,650km² In the far north-west corner of Kalimantan on the mountainous borders of Sabah and Sarawak, in the very heart of Borneo, lies Borneo's largest national park, encompassing the remote headwaters of two rivers, the Kerayan/Mentarang/Malinau/Sesayap River, which reaches the sea near Pulau Nunukan, and the Iwan/Lurah/Bahau/Kayan River, which reaches the sea near Tg Selor. The park is mainly rugged hill forest intercepted by numerous river valleys rising from 200m to Gng Harun (2,160m). A population of about 15,000 Lun Bawang and Kenyah (Dayak swidden farmers), along with small numbers of hunter-gatherer Penans, live in small villages along the rivers that border or enter the park. The Christian Dayak rice farmers arrived from NE Sarawak about 100 years ago, originally for head hunting, and later settled.

Acommodation WWF Indonesia helped draft the park management plan, and maintains 5 field posts along the park borders and a field research centre at Lalut Birai. Park headquarters is based in Samarinda and visits are best arranged by tour companies in Samarinda, which can make travel arrangements and book home stays.

Access By speedboat from Tarakan up the Sesayap River, or from Tg Selor up the Kayan River. To access remote villages use flights operated by Christian missionaries. These flights are often irregular with limited baggage capacity.

Access by walking from Sarawak The park is criss-crossed by rugged jungle tracks connecting villages in different river valleys. A popular trek is a walk from Bakelalan or Bario in Sarawak to Long Bawan in Kalimantan. You must bring your passport, and if you fly out from Long Bawan to Tarakan, Berau (Tg Selor) or Samarinda, your passport must be stamped with a full Indonesian visa, which is only obtainable in Kuching.

Climate Rain falls most afternoons.

What to see Kayan Mentarang is one of the most scenic areas of Borneo, with most of Borneo's rare montane birds found on the higher peaks. However, large mammals are scarce as subsistence hunting is permitted. Merchants from Berau and Samarinda visit villages regularly to collect Helmeted Hornbill beaks, pangolin scales, bezoar stones, singing birds and other illegally poached forest products.

The Penan Benlalui hunters of the Lurah River Valley were the subject of a 21-month field study in 1990–1992 by Rajindra Puri, and many of Puri's observations are quoted in this book. Although the Penan population has largely settled in Kenyah villages and does some swidden farming, the Penans continued to subsist mostly on wild pig meat and sago from wild sago palms (see pp. 52 and 302, and Puri 2000).

BEZOAR STONES, RHINOCEROS HORNS AND ANCIENT JARS For at least the last 1,000 years, a trade in forest products that continues today has connected the interior tribes of Borneo's hill forests with markets in S China. Traditional trade items include edible swiftlet nests, rattan vines for making mats and furniture, hornbill ivory, kingfisher feathers, bezoar stones from langurs and porcupines, Sun Bear body parts, bees' wax, resin (dammar) from dipterocarp trees for varnish, camphor wood for incense (gaharu), pangolin scales and cinnamon bark [cassia].

A typical trade route before 1819 1. Nomadic Penan hunter trades rhino horn with settled Dayak swidden farmer for salt, knives and pots. 2. Dyak farmer trades rhino horn with visiting Malay trader from the coast. 3. Back at the river mouth port the rhino horn is exchanged for cloth, ceramics, iron tools and brass coins from Guandong (Canton) brought by a Chinese merchant (supercargo). 4. Chinese trading junks arrived with the north-east monsoon in November and returned with the aid of the south-west monsoon in June (p. 10). Kalimantan trading sultanates in the early 1800s included Pontianak, Ketapang, Banjarmasin, Kutai and Bulungan. The E Sabah trade was controlled by the Sultan of Sulu based on Jolo island (the Philippines), whilst the NW Borneo trade was centered on Brunei.

After Singapore was founded in 1819, direct trade with China collapsed and Singapore-based European and Arab merchant-captains in large, well-armed sailing boats dominated. European manufactures including guns and gunpowder, arak (palm spirit) and opium, were exchanged for Bornean forest products, which were traded to China via Singapore. Due to the lack of roads all interior trade was by river boat. The most important coastal river mouths (Malay: *kuala*) were controlled by wealthy Muslim Malay sultans often descended from Yemeni Arab traders. Conrad's novels *Lord Jim* and *Aylmer's Folly* are about the struggle between two Singapore-based merchant captains to dominate the Berau River trade in E Kalimantan. Smaller rivers around Borneo were serviced by Bugis traders (originally from S Sulawesi) in locally built sailing craft (*pinisi*). Until about 100 years ago this forest products trade was sustainable, but the advent of professional poachers with shotguns has led to a collapse in the Borneo populations of hornbills, langurs, rhinoceroses and pangolins, the direct result of unsustainable demand from China.

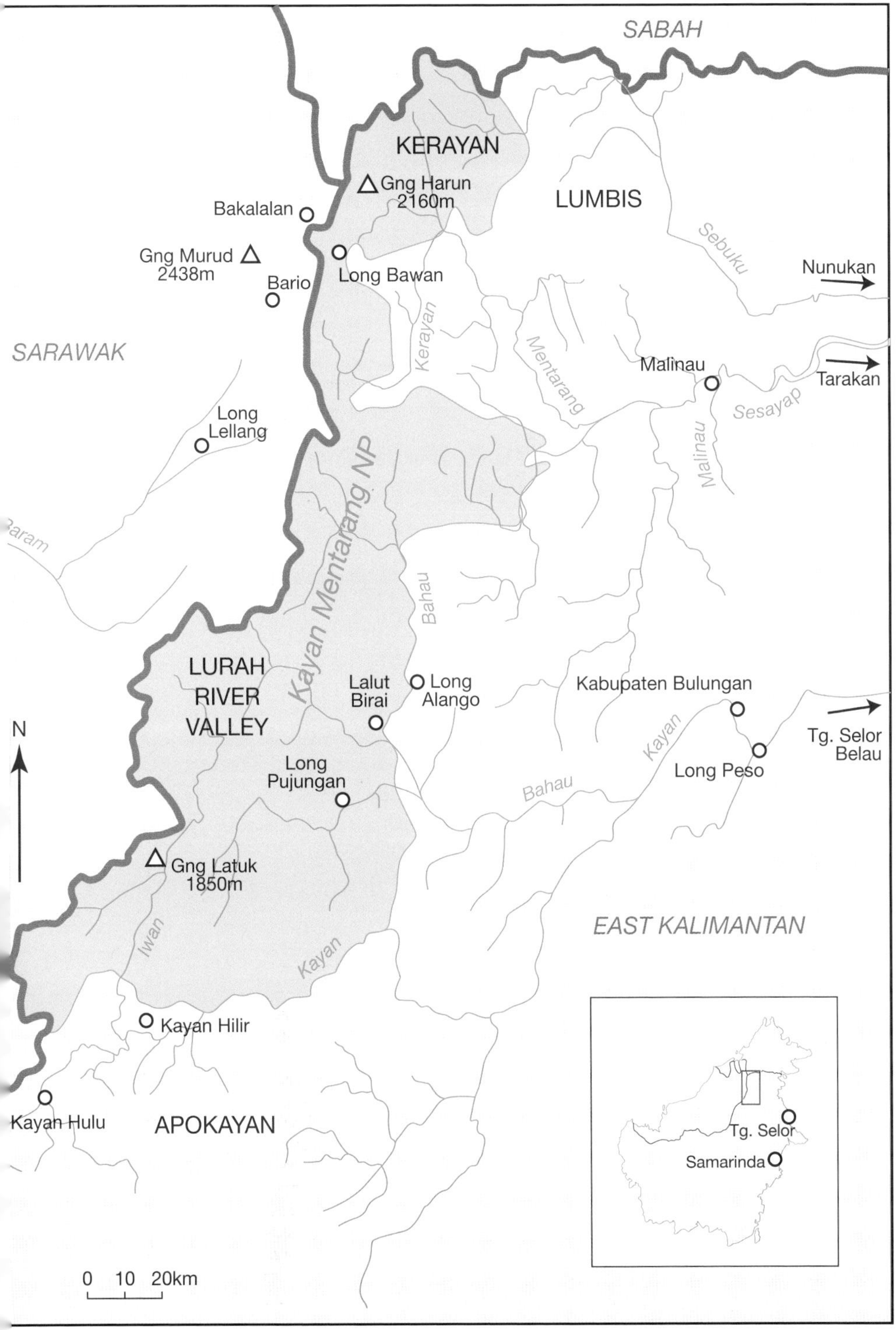

SABAH
KERAYAN
Gng Harun
2160m
LUMBIS
Bakalalan
Gng Murud
2438m
Long Bawan
Bario
Sebuku
Nunukan
Kerayan
Mentarang
SARAWAK
Malinau
Tarakan
Sesayap
Long
Lellang
Malinau
Kayan Mentarang NP
Baram
Bahau
LURAH
RIVER
VALLEY
Lalut
Birai
Long
Alango
Kabupaten Bulungan
Kayan
Tg. Selor
Belau
N
Long
Pujungan
Long Peso
Bahau
Gng Latuk
1850m
EAST KALIMANTAN
Iwan
Kayan
Kayan Hilir
Kayan Hulu
APOKAYAN
Tg. Selor
Samarinda
0 10 20km

KALIMANTAN 7: NATUNA ISLANDS

NATUNA ISLANDS Starting some 18,000 years ago, the forested Sunda Basin was slowly covered by rising sea levels, creating the South China Sea. Today this shallow sea is dotted with hundreds of small islands, previously the hills and mountains of the Sunda Basin. The largest island is Bunguran Besar (Natuna Besar), 1,605km^2, dominated by Gng Ranai at 1,035m. Sparsely populated with Indonesian fisher folk and an Indonesian naval base, Bunguran Besar is located in the centre of the drowned Mollengraf and North Natuna River deltas, with a water catchment that covered most of Thailand, the Malay Peninsula, Sumatra, Java and Borneo. The organic matter deposited by these two large rivers now forms one of the world's largest natural gas fields (p. 168).

Access There is an airport on Bunguran next to the small town of Ranai. You can fly to Ranai from Pontianak in Kalimantan or from Batam Island, a 40-minute ferry ride from Singapore. There are small hotels near the airport.

Relict fauna of Sundaland It is taken for granted in this book that the fauna of Sundaland, including Borneo, Sumatra, Java and the Malay Peninsula, has been similar for the last 2.6 million years. Differences would naturally arise due to varied habitats, local climates and dispersal barriers such as large rivers. When sea levels rose a relict fauna of living fossils was left behind on the Natuna Islands, now a living museum of Sundaland's bio-diversity.

Natuna zoology The Natuna islands are on the shipping lanes between Borneo and Singapore and were fully investigated by early zoologists, including Everett (1893), Hose (1894), Abbott (1900), Knight (1907), Chasen (1928) and de Fontaine (1931). **References:** Banks (1949), Chasen (1935, 1940), Lammertink et al. (2003), Miller (1901), Meijaard (2003), Nijman & Meijaard (2008), Oberholser (1932), Paeadiso (1971), Rothschild (1884).

Do the mammals of the Natuna Islands belong to Borneo or the Malay Peninsula? Early zoologists argued pointlessly whether the Natuna Islands fauna belonged to Malaya or Borneo. The answer is that the fauna is a relic of the Sunda Basin fauna that was originally common to both. This relict fauna may answer questions such as 1. Were the extinctions on these islands random, or 2. Did small generalist mammals survive better than larger mammals with specialized habitat niches? For zoologists a re-examination of Natuna mammal DNA is likely to be rewarding.

ODDITIES OF THE NATUNA ISLANDS FAUNA There has been no comprehensive review of the fauna of the Natuna Islands since Chasen's classic *Handlist of Malaysian Mammals* (1940) and the islands are not covered in Medway (1969, 1977) and Payne et al. (1985). Some zoological oddities are listed below for future researchers (p. 168).

1 **Primates** Bunguran only has a *Presbytis* Langur, whilst Serasan only has a *Trachypithecus* Langur.

2 On **Bunguran** occur pangolin, slow loris, Sunda Skunk and a colugo but no tarsier, whilst on Serasan there is a tarsier, a colugo and a Pen-tailed Treeshrew but no slow loris, pangolin or Sunda Skunk.

3 **Pigs** The wild pig on Bunguran is the Malayan *Sus scrofa* NOT the Bornean *S. barbatus* (p. 300).

4 **Malayan Shrew** *Crocidura malayana* has been collected both on P. Serasan and P. Panjang in the S Natuna Islands but not so far on the Bornean mainland. (Listed as *C. aagaardi* in Chasen 1935).

5 **Sunda Tree Mouse** *Chiropodomys gliroides* occurs on Bunguran Besar but not mainland Borneo (p. 240).

6 **Squirrels** Chasen (1940) lists *Ratufa affinis* (Borneo) for P. Bunguran Besar and *R. bicolor* (Malaya) for P. Lagong 25km^2 just off the south coast of Bunguran (p. 210).

7 **Bats** Paeadiso (1971) makes a good argument that mystery bat *Cynopterus sphinx* is common on Serasan where Everett found *Cynopterus* in large parties feeding on coconut nectar (Thomas & Hartert, 1894), (p.86).

SPLENDID TREESHREW *Tupaia splendidula* is an uncommon endemic of S Kalimantan with 2 races in the Natuna Islands. The type illustration by Joseph Wolf (1865) is of *T. s. lucida* from Pulau Laut (p. 148).

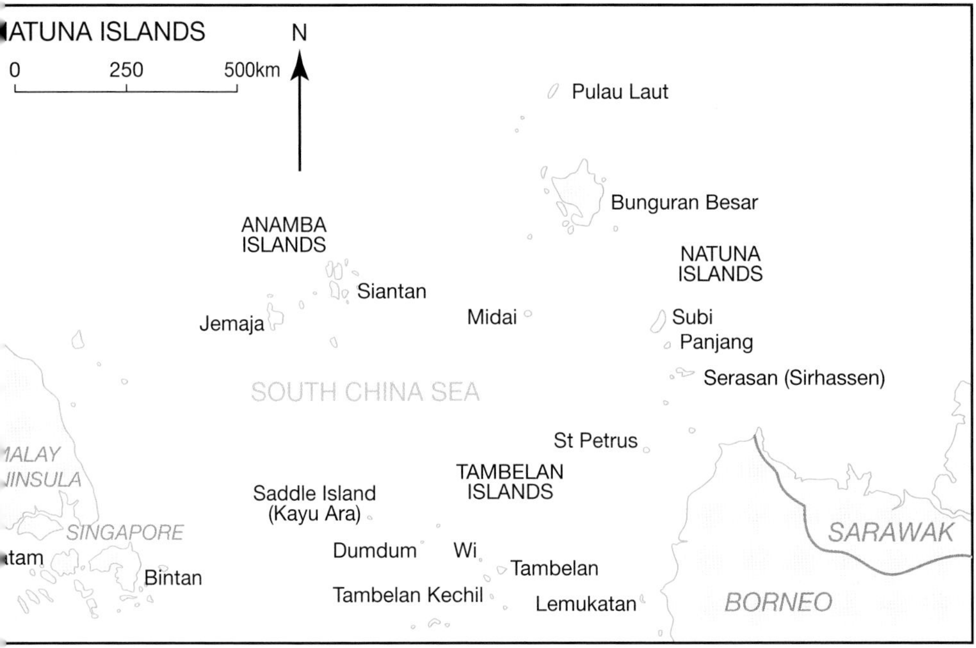

ATUNA ISLANDS
N
0
250
500km
Pulau Laut
Bunguran Besar
ANAMBA ISLANDS
NATUNA ISLANDS
Siantan
Jemaja
Midai
Subi
Panjang
Serasan (Sirhassen)
SOUTH CHINA SEA
St Petrus
TAMBELAN ISLANDS
Saddle Island (Kayu Ara)
SINGAPORE
SARAWAK
Dumdum
Wi
Tambelan
tam
Bintan
Tambelan Kechil
Lemukatan
BORNEO

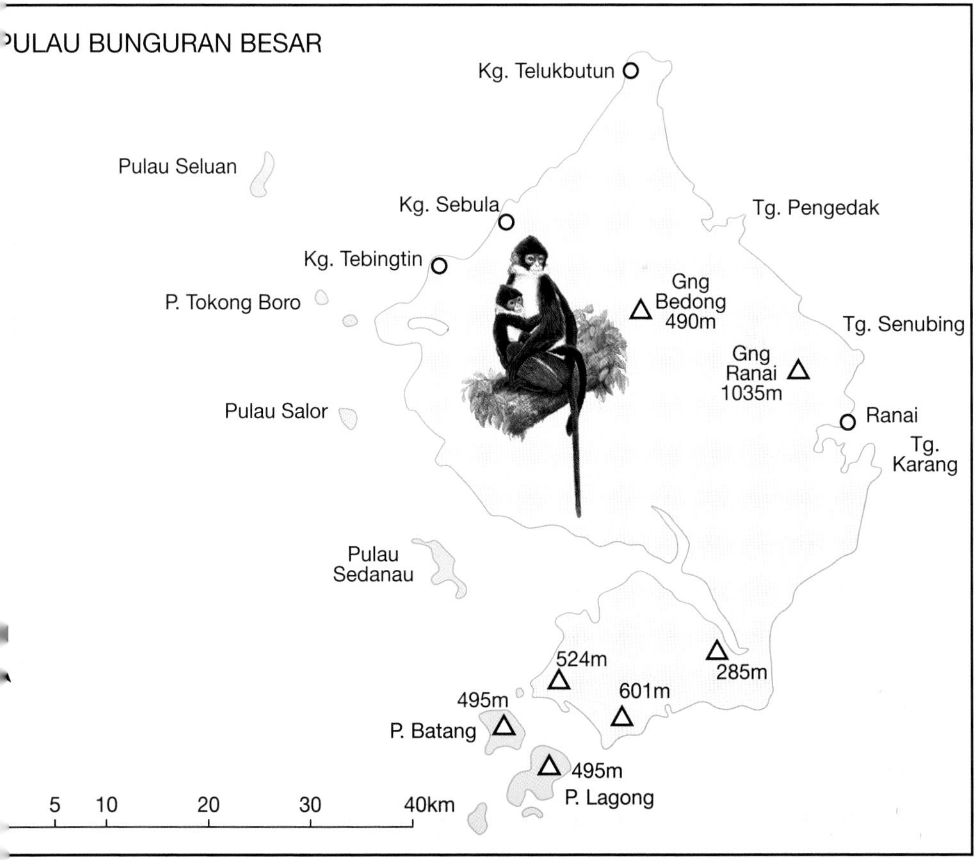

ULAU BUNGURAN BESAR
Kg. Telukbutun
Pulau Seluan
Kg. Sebula
Tg. Pengedak
Kg. Tebingtin
P. Tokong Boro
Gng Bedong 490m
Tg. Senubing
Gng Ranai 1035m
Pulau Salor
Ranai
Tg. Karang
Pulau Sedanau
524m
285m
495m
601m
P. Batang
495m
P. Lagong
5
10
20
30
40km

SELECTED BIBLIOGRAPHY

A full list of references can be downloaded from **www.Borneomammals.com**

Abdullah, M. T. & Hall, L. S. (1997) Abundance and distribution of fruit bats and other mammals in the tropical forest canopy in Borneo. *Sarawak Museum Journal* 51(72): 63–74.

Agoramoorthy, G. (2013) Proboscis Monkeys of Borneo: In-situ and Ex-situ conservation. LAP, p. 108.

Ahmad, A. H. (1994) The ecology of mousedeer in a Bornean rainforest, Sabah, Malaysia. MSc thesis, Aberdeen.

Alfred, R. et al. (2012) Home Range and Ranging Behaviour of Bornean Elephant (*E. maximus borneensis*) Females. PLOS

Allen, G. M. & Coolidge, H. (1940) Mammal and bird collections of the Asiatic Primate Expedition: Mammals. *Bulletin of the Museum of Comparative Zoology*, Harvard, 87:131–166.

Ancrenaz, M. et al. (2004) Determination of ape distribution and population size using ground and aerial surveys: a case study with orang-utans in lower Kinabatangan, Sabah, Malaysia. *Animal Conservation* (Nov. 2004)

Ashton, P. (2015) *On the Forests of Tropical Asia: Lest the Memory Fade*. Kew. 748pp.

Banks, E. (1931) A popular account of the mammals of Borneo. J. Malayan Br. Roy. *Royal Asiatic Soc.*, 139pp.

Barker, G. et al. (2013) (ed.) Rainforest foraging and farming in Island Southeast Asia. *The Archaeology of the Niah Caves, Sarawak*, vol. 1, McDonald Institute Cambridge. 410pp.

Barlow, C. (2000) *The Ghosts of Evolution*, Basic Books, 290pp. Anachronistic fruit – mainly Americas.

Bates, P. J. J. & Harrison, D. L. (1997) *Bats of the Indian Subcontinent*. Harrison Zoological Museum, Sevenoaks.

Bennett, E., Caldecott, J. O. & Davison, G. E. H. (1987). A wildlife survey of Ulu Temburong, Brunei. *British Medical Journal*.

Bennett, E. L & Gombek, F. (1993) *Proboscis Monkeys of Borneo*. Natural History Publications (Borneo).

Bennett, E. L. (1998) *The Natural History of the Orangutan*. Natural History Publications (Borneo).

Bintaja, R., et al. (2005) Modelled atmospheric temperatures and global sea levels over the past million years. *Nature* 437: 125–128.

Blate, G. M., Peart, D. R. & Leighton, M. (1998) Post-dispersal predation on isolated seeds: a comparative study of 40 tree species in a Southeast Asian rainforest. *Oikos* 82: 522–538. Gunung Palung.

Blundell, A. G. & Peart, D. R. (2004) Density-dependent population dynamics of a dominant rainforest canopy tree. *Ecology* 85:704:715

Bock, Carl (1881) *The Head-Hunters of Borneo: Travel Up the Mahakkam and Down the Barito*. Sampson, Low. 344pp.

Bolick, L. (2013) Orangutan density variation and nest tree selection in logged Bornean peat swamp and Sundaland heath forest, PhD thesis, University of California, Davis, 277pp.

Boonratana, R. (1997) A statewide survey to estimate the distribution and density of the Sumatran Rhinoceros, Asian Elephant and Banteng in Sabah, Malaysia. WWF Sabah.

Brodie, J.E. et al. (2009) Functional differences within a guild of tropical mammalian frugivores. *Ecology* 90:688-698

Budiyono & Kreb (2015) Berau Cetacean Conservation Project, Final Technical Report YK-RASI.

Caldecott, J. O. (1986) An ecological and behavioural study of the Pig-tailed Macaque. S. Karger.

Campos-Arceiz, A. (2012) Asian tapirs are no elephants when it comes to seed dispersal. *Biotropica*, vol. 44, no. 2.

Cannon, C. H., Curran, L. M., Marshall, A. J. & Leighton, M. (2007) Longterm reproductive behaviour of woody plants across seven Bornean forest types in the Gng Palung National Park (Indonesia). *Ecology Letters* 10: 956–969.

Cannon, C. H., Morley, R. J. & Bush, A. B. G. (2009) The current refugial rainforests of Sundaland are unrepresentative of their bio-geographic past and highly vulnerable to disturbance. *PNAS*, vol. 106, no. 27.

Chasen, F. N. (1940) A handlist of Malaysian mammals. *Bulletin of the Raffles Museum* 15: 209pp.

Chasen, F. N. & Kloss, C. B. (1931) On a collection of mammals from the lowlands and islands of North Borneo. *Bulletin of the Raffles Museum* 6.

Cheyne S. M. (2008) Gibbon feeding ecology and diet characteristics. *Folia Primatologica* 79: 320.

Cheyne S. M, Thompson, C. J. H., Phillips, A. C., Hill, R. M. C. & Limin, S.H. (2007) Density and population estimate of gibbons (*Hylobates albibarbis*) in Sabangau catchment, Central Kalimantan, Indonesia. *Primates* 49: 50–56.

Cheyne, S. M. & Macdonald, D. W. (2011) Wild felid diversity and activity patterns in Sabangau peat-swamp forest, Indonesian Borneo. *Oryx*, vol. 45, no. 1.

Chivers, D. J. (ed.) (1980) Malayan Forest Primates: Ten Years' Study in Tropical Rainforest. Springer. 364pp.

Colon, C. P. (2002) Ranging behaviour and activity of the Malay Civet (*Viverra tangalunga*) in a logged and an unlogged forest in Danum Valley, East Malaysia. *Journal of Zoology* (London) 257: 473–485.

Corlett, R. T. & Primack R. B. (2011) *Tropical Rain Forests* (2nd edn). Wiley-Blackwell, New Jersey.

Corlett, R. (2009) *Ecology of Tropical East Asia*. Oxford University Press.

Corner E. J. H. (1952) Wayside trees of Malaya. *Kew Bulletin*, vol. 44, no. 2.

Cranbrook, Earl of & Piper, P. J. (2007) The Javan Rhinoceros in Borneo. *Bulletin of the Raffles Museum* 55 (1).

Cranbrook, Earl of (V) & Piper, P. J. (2009) Borneo records of Malay tapir, *Tapirus indicus* Desmarest: a zooarchaeological and historical review. *International Journal of Osteoarchaeology* 19(4), 491–507.

Crompton, R. H. & Andau, P. M. (1987) Ranging, activity rhythms, and sociality in free-ranging *Tarsius bancanus*. *International Journal of Primatology* 8 (1): 43–71.

Curran, L. M. & Leighton, M. (2000) Vertebrate responses to spatiotemporal variation in seed production of mast-fruiting Dipterocarpaceae. *Ecological Monographs* 70(1): 101–128.

Curran, L. M. (1994) The ecology and evolution of mast-fruiting in Bornean Dipterocarpaceae: a general ectomycorrhizal theory. PhD thesis, Princeton.

Cusack, J. (2011) Characterizing small mammal responses to tropical forest loss and degradation in northern Borneo using capture-mark-recapture methods. MSc thesis, Imperial College.

Davies, A. G. & Payne, J. (1982) A faunal survey of Sabah. Kuala Lumpur: WWF Malaysia.

Davies, A. (1991) Seed-eating by Red Leaf Monkeys (*Presbytis rubicunda*) in dipterocarp forest of northern Borneo. *International Journal of Primatology* 12, 119–144.

Davis, D. D. (1958) Mammals of the Kelabit Plateau, northern Sarawak. *Fieldiana Zoology* 39: 119–147.

Davis, D. D. (1962) Mammals of the lowland rain-forest of North Borneo. *Bulletin of the Chicago Natural History Museum* 31: 1–129.

den Tex, R-J. et al. (2010) Speciation dynamics in the SE Asian tropics: putting a time perspective on the phylogeny and biogeography of Sundaland tree squirrels, Sundasciurus. Smithsonian Libraries

Denzinger, A. & Schnitzler, H. U. (2013) Bat guilds, a concept to classify the highly diverse foraging and echolocation behaviors of microchiropteran bats. *Frontiers in Physiology* 4: 164.

DeWalt et al. (2006) Liana habitat associations and community structure in a Bornean tropical forest (Sepilok). *Plant Ecology* 186:203–216

Dietz, C. et al. (2009) *Bats of Britain, Europe and Northwest Africa*. A & C Black, London, 400pp.

Dinerstein, E. (2003) *The Return of the Unicorns*. Columbia University Press, NYC. 316pp.

Dove, M. R. (1983) Swidden Agriculture in Indonesia: the subsistence strategies of the Kalimantan Kantu. De Gruyter Mouton.

Ehlers Smith, D. A. (2015) The ecology and conservation of *Presbytis rubicund*, PhD thesis.

Emmons, L. H., Nais, J. & Biun, A. (1991) Fruit and consumers of *Rafflesia keithii*. *Biotropica*. 23 (2)

Emmons, H. L. (2000) *Tupai, A Field Study of Bornean Treeshrews*. University of California, Davis. 269pp.

Epstein, J. H. et al. (2009). *Pteropus vampyrus*, a hunted migratory species with a multinational home-range and a need for regional management. *Journal of Applied Ecology* vol. 46, issue 5, pp. 991–1002.

Fooden, J. (1995) *Systematic Review of Southeast Asian Longtail Macaques* Macaca fascicularis. *Zoology*, no. 81.

Francis, C. M. (2008) *A Field Guide to the Mammals of South-East Asia*. New Holland Publishers. 392pp.

Francis, C. M. et al. (2010) The role of DNA barcodes in understanding and conservation of mammal diversity in Southeast Asia. PLOS one.

Fredriksson, G. M., Wich, S. A. & Trisno (2006) Frugivory in Sun Bears (*Helarctos malayanus*) is linked to El Nino-related fluctuations in fruiting phenology, E Kalimantan. *Biological Journal of the Linnean Society*

Galdikas, B. M. (1995) *Reflections of Eden. My life with the Orangutans of Borneo*. Gollancz, London. 408pp.

Gardner, P. (2014) The natural history, non-invasive sampling, activity patterns and population genetic structure of the Bornean Banteng *Bos javanicus lowi* in Sabah, Malaysian Borneo. PhD thesis, Cardiff.

Goossens, B. et al. (2005) Patterns of genetic diversity and migration in increasingly fragmented and declining Orang-utan *Pongo pygmaeus* populations from Sabah, Malaysia. National Centre for Biotechnology Information.

Grafe, T. U. et al. (2011) A novel resource-service mutualism between bats and pitcher plants. Biology Letters 7.

Hall, G. S. et al. (2004) Biogeography of fruit bats in Southeast Asia, *Sarawak Museum Journal* 81.

Hanbury-Tenison, R. (1980) *Mulu the Rainforest*. Weidenfeld & Nicolson, London. 176pp.

Handbook of the Mammals of the World, vols 1–3, Carnivores, Hoofed Mammals, Primates. Lynx Edicions, Barcelona.

Harrison, J. (1961) The natural food of some Malayan mammals. *Bulletin of the National Museum, Singapore* 30.

Harrison, M. E., Morrogh-Bernard, H. C. & Chivers, D. J. (2010) Orangutan energetics and the influence of fruit availability in the nonmasting peat-swamp forest of Sabangau, Indonesian Borneo. *International Journal of Primatology* 31: 585–607.

Harrison, T. (1966) Bats netted in and around Niah Great Cave, 1965–1966. *The Sarawak Museum Journal* 14: 229–233.

Hazebroek, H. P. & Morshidi, A. (2000) *National Parks of Sarawak*. Natural History Publications (Borneo).

Hill, J. E. (1959) A North Bornean pygmy squirrel, *Glyphotes simus* Thomas and its relationships. *Bulletin of the British Museum*, vol.5, no. 9.

Hobbs, J. J. (2004) Problems in the harvest of edible birds' nests in Sarawak and Sabah. *Biodiversity and Conservation*. 13.

Hodgkison, R., S. T. Balding et al. (2004) Habitat structure, wing morphology, and the vertical stratification of Malaysian fruit bats, *Journal of Tropical Ecology* 20: 667–673.

Hopkins, H. C. F., Huxley, C. R., Pannell, C..M., Prance, G.T. & White, F. (1998) *The biological monograph: the importance of field studies and functional syndromes for taxonomy and evolution of tropical plants*. Kew.

Hornaday, W. T. (1885) Two years in the jungle. The experiences of a hunter and naturalist in India, Ceylon, the Malay Peninsula and Borneo. Charles Scribner's Sons.

Hose, Charles (1893) *A Descriptive Account of the Mammals of Borneo*. Edward Abbott.

Hua, P. et al. (2013) Dispersal, mating events and fine scale genetic structure in the Lesser Flat-headed bats. PLOS one.

Hubbell, S. P. (2001) *The Unified Neutral Theory of Biodiversity and Biogeography*. Princeton, New Jersey.

Husson, S. et al. (2009) Orangutan distribution, density, abundance and impacts of disturbance. Orangutans: Geographic variation in behavioral ecology and conservation. Oxford Scholarship Online.

Jaaman, S. A. (2010) *Marine Mammals in E Malaysia Distribution and Interactions with Fisheries*. VDM 265pp.

Janecka, J. E. et al. (2008) Evidence for multiple species of Sunda Colugo. *Current Biology* 18: 21.

Janzen, D. H. (1974) Tropical Blackwater Rivers, Animals, and Mast *Fruiting* by the Dipterocarpaceae. *Biotropica*, vol. 6, no. 2.

Johns, A.D. (1983) Ecological effects of selective logging in a West Malaysian rainforest. PhD thesis, Cambridge.

Kanamori, T. et al. (2010) Feeding Ecology of Bornean Orangutans (*Pongo pygmaeus morio*) in Danum Valley, Sabah, Malaysia. A 3-year record including two mast fruiting. *American Journal of Primatology*, vol. 72, no. 9.

Kavanagh, M. (1982) Lanjak Entimau, a Management Plan. WWF Malaysia.

Khan, F. A. A. et al. (2008) Using genetics and morphology to examine species diversity of Old World bats: report of a recent collection from Malaysia. *Museum of Texas Tech University* 281: 1–28.

Kingston, T., Lim, B. L. & Zubaid, A. (2006) *Bats of Krau Wildlife Reserve*. UKM, Bangi. 148pp.

Kitayama, K. (1992) An altitudinal transect study of the vegetation on Mount Kinabalu. *Vegetatio* 102.

Kiyono Y. & Hastaniah (2000) Flowering and fruiting phenologies of dipterocarp at Bukit Soeharto, East Kalimantan. In: Guhardja et al. (eds), *Rainforest Ecosystems of East Kalimantan*. Springer Publishing, NYC, pp. 121–128.

Knott, C. D., Thompson, M. E. et al. (2010) Female reproductive strategies in orangutans, evidence for female choice and counterstrategies to infanticide in a species with frequent sexual coercion. *Proceedings of the Royal Society*, London.

Kofron, C. P. (2002) The bats of Brunei Darussalam, Borneo. *Mammalia* 66: 259–274.

Kumaran, J. V. et al. (2011) Comparative distribution and diversity of bats from selected localities in Sarawak. *Borneo Journal of Resource Science and Technology* 1: 1–13.

LaFrankie, J. V. (2010) *Trees of Tropical Asia, an Illustrated Guide to Diversity*. Manila.

Lambert F. (1990) Some notes on fig-eating by arboreal mammals in Malaysia. *Primates* 31: 453–458.

Lammertink et al. (2003) Population size, and conservation of the Natuna Leaf Monkey *Presbytis natunae* endemic to the island of Bunguran, Indonesia. *Oryx*.

Leighton, M. & Leighton, D. R. (1983) Vertebrates' responses to fruiting seasonality within a Bornean rain forest, In: S. L. Sutton et al. *Whitmore and Management* (2nd edn). Blackwell. Oxford, pp. 181–196.

Lekagul, B. & McNeely, J. A. (1988) *Mammals of Thailand* (2nd edn). Association for the Conservation of Wildlife.

Lhota, S., Loken, B. et al. (2012) Discovery of Miller's Grizzled Langur (*Presbytis hosei canicrus*) in Wehea forest confirms the continued existence and extends known geographical range of an endangered primate. *American Journal of Primatology*, vol. 74, no. 3.

Lim, B. L. & Muul, I. (1978) Small mammals. In Kinabalu Summit of Borneo. Kota Kinabalu, Sabah: The Sabah Society Monograph, pp. 403–458.

Lim, C. K. & Cranbrook, Earl of (2014) *Swiftlets of Borneo: Builders of Edible Nests*, Natural History Publications (Borneo).

Lim, N. (2007) *Colugo: The Flying Lemur of South-east Asia*. Draco Publishing, Singapore.

Lim, N. T. L. & Ng, P. K. L. (2008) Home range, activity cycle and natal den usage of a female Sunda Pangolin *Manis javanica* (Mammalia: Pholidota) in Singapore. *Endangered Species Research*, vol. 3.

Lim, N. T. & Ng, P. K. L. (2010) The abundance of Flying Lemurs (*Cynocephalus variegatus*) in Singapore. Nanyang Technological University.

Lyon, M W. (1913) Monograph of the Treeshrews. US Nat. Mus., vol. 45.

MacArthur, R. H. & Wilson, E. O. (1963, 1967) Equilibrium Theory of Island Biogeography. Princeton University Press.

MacKinnon, J. R. (1974) *In Search of the Red Ape*. Collins, London and New York. 222pp.

MacKinnon, J. R. (1975) *Borneo*. The World's Wild Places, Time-Life Books, London. 184pp.

MacKinnon, K. (1978) Stratification and feeding differences among Malayan Squirrels. *Malayan Nature Journal* 30, 593–608.

MacKinnon, K. et al. (1996) *The Ecology of Kalimantan*. Periplus Editions, Singapore. 802pp.

Marshall, A. (2010) Effects of habitat quality on primate populations in Kalimantan: gibbons and leaf monkeys as case studies. In: Supriatna J. & Gursky-Doyen S. (eds). *Indonesian Primates*. Springer Science. pp. 157–177.

Marshall, A. G. (1985) Old World phytophagous bats (Megachiroptera) and their food plants: a survey. *Zoological Journal of the Linnean Society* 83: 351–369.

Marshall, A. J. & Wrangham, R. W. (2007) Evolutionary consequences of fallback foods. *International Journal of Primatology* 28.

Mather, R. J. (1992) A field study of hybrid gibbons in Central Kalimantan, Indonesia. PhD thesis, Cambridge.

Matsubayashi, H. & Lagan, P. (2014) Natural salt-licks and mammals in Deramakot. Sabah Forestry Department.

Matsuda I. et al. (2009) The feeding ecology and activity budget of proboscis monkeys. *American Journal of Primatology* 71: 115.

McConkey, K. & Galetti, M. (1999) Seed dispersal by Sun Bears in C Borneo. *Journal of Tropical Ecology* vol. 15 (2).

McConkey, K. R. & Chivers, D. J. (2007) Influence of gibbon ranging patterns on seed dispersal distance and deposition site in a Bornean forest, *Journal of Tropical Ecology*.

Medway, L. (1959) 300,000 bats. *Sarawak Museum Journal* 8: 667–679.

Medway, L. (1978) *Mammals of Borneo: Field Keys and an Annotated Checklist.* Royal Asiatic Society.

Medway, Lord (1983) *The Wild Mammal of Malaya (Peninsula Malaysia) and Singapore.* Oxford University Press.

Meijaard, E. (2003) Mammals of south-east Asian islands and their Late Pleistocene environments. Journal of Biogeography, vol. 30, no. 8.

Meijaard, E. et al. (2010) Declining orangutan encounter rates from Wallace to the present suggest the species was once more abundant. PLOS one.

Meijaard, E. & Groves, C. (2004) The biogeographical evolution and phylogeny of the genus *Presbytis*, *Primate Report* vol. 68, pp. 71–90.

Meijaard, E. & Nijman, V. (2000) Distribution and conservation of the Proboscis Monkey (*Nasalis larvatus*) in Kalimantan, Indonesia. *Biological Conservation* 92.

Mitchell, A. H. (1994) Ecology of Hose's Langur (*Presbytis hosei*) in logged and unlogged dipterocarp forest of NE Borneo. (Tabin Willife Reserve), PhD thesis, Yale.

Mjoberg, E. G. (1930) *Forest Life and Adventures in the Malay Archipelago.* William Morrow.

Mohd Azlan, J. et al. (2003) Diversity, relative abundance and conservation of chiropterans in Kayan Mentarang NP. *Sarawak Museum Journal* 79: 251–265.

Mohd Ridwan, A. R. & Abdullah, M. T. (2012) Population genetics of the Cave-dwelling Dusky Fruit Bat, *Penthetor lucasi*, based on four populations in Malaysia. *Pertanika Journal of Tropical Agricultural Science* 35 (3).

Morley, R. J. (2000) *Origin and Evolution of Tropical Rain Forests.* Wiley-Blackwell, New Jersey. 378pp.

Morrogh-Bernard, H., Husson, S., Page, S. E. & Rieley, J. O. (2003) Population status of the Bornean Orang-utan in the Sebangau peat swamp forest. *Biological Conservation* 110: 141–152.

Motley, J. & Dillwyn, L. L. (1855) *Contributions to the Natural History of Labuan and the Adjacent Coasts of Borneo.* John van Voorst, London. 62pp.

Mumford, A. (2009) A preliminary assessment of seed dispersal by two ape species in the Sabangau. Honour's thesis, Oxford, 42pp.

Munds, R. A., Nekaris, K. A. I. & Ford, S. M. (2013) Taxonomy of the Bornean slow loris, with new species *Nycticebus kayan* (Primates, Lorisidae), *American Journal of Primatology* 75 (1).

Munshi-South, J., Emmons, L. H. & Bernard, H. (2007) Behavioral monogamy and fruit availability in the Large Treeshrew (*Tupaia tana*) in Sabah, Malaysia. *Journal of Mammalogy* 2007.

Musser, G. G. & Newcom C. (1983) Malaysian murids and the giant rat of Sumatra. Bull. *American Museum of Natural History* 174:

Nakabayashi, M. (2015) Feeding ecology of three frugivorous civets in Borneo, PhD thesis, Kyoto.

Nakagawa, M. et al. (2007) A preliminary study of two sympatric *Maxomys* rats in Sarawak, spacing patterns and population dynamics. (Lambir during dipterocarp masting). *Raffles Bulletin*, 55 (2).

Nakashima, Y. et al. (2010) Functional uniqueness of a small carnivore as seed dispersal agents: a case study of the common palm civets in the Tabin Wildlife Reserve, Sabah. *Oecologia* 164: 721–730.

Nasir, D. (2012) *Behavioural Ecology of the Sunda Colugo.* Lambert Academic Publishing, Saarbrücken. 140pp.

Nekaris, A. et al. (2013) Mad, bad and dangerous to know: the biochemistry, ecology and evolution of slow loris venom. *Journal of Venomous Animals and Toxins including Tropical Diseases.* 19:21.

Ng, F. S. P. (2014) *Tropical Forest Fruits, Seeds, Seedlings and Trees.* Forest Research Institute Malaysia, Kuala Lumpur. 430 pp.

Niemitz, C. (1984) Activity rhythms and use of space in semi-wild Bornean tarsiers, with remarks on wild spectral tarsiers. In: C. Niemitz (ed.), *Biology of Tarsiers.* Gustav Fischer Verlag, Stuttgart.

Nijman, V. & Meijaard, E. (2008) Zoogeography of primates in insular SE Asia: species area relationships and the effects of taxonomy. *Contributions to Zoology*, 77 (2).

Nijman, V. (2010) Ecology and Conservation of the Hose's Langur Group (Colobinae: *Presbytis hosei, P. canicrus, P. sabana*): A Review in Indonesian Primates (eds) Sharon Gursky, Jatna Supriatna.

Nor, S. M. (1996) The mammalian fauna on the islands at the northern tip of Sabah (Banggi and Balembangan). *Fieldiana: Zoology* 83: 1–51.

Nor, S. M. (1997) An elevation transect study of small mammals on Mt Kinabalu. PhD thesis, Illinois.

Norhayati, A. (2001). Frugivores and fruit production in primary and logged tropical rainforests. PhD thesis, Malaysia.

Nowak, R. M. (1999) *Walker's Mammals of the World.* Johns Hopkins University Press, Maryland.

Oppenheimer, S. (1998) *Eden in the East: The Drowned Continent of Southeast Asia.* Oxford. 488pp.

Pannell, C. M. (1997) Solving problems in the taxonomy of Aglaia (Meliaceae): functional syndromes and the biological monograph. Proceedings of the Third International Flora Malesiana Symposium, pp. 163–170.

Patou, M. L., Wilting, A. et al. (2010) Evolutionary history of the *Paradoxurus* palm civets – a new model for Asian biogeography. *Journal of Biogeography* 37: 2077–2097.

Payne, J. & Francis C. M. (1998) *A Field Guide to the Mammals of Borneo*. Sabah Society and WWF.

Payne, J. & Prudente, C. (2008) *Orangutans: Behaviour, Ecology and Conservation*. New Holland, London.

Phillipps, Q. & Philllipps, K. (2014) *Phillipp's Field Guide to the Birds of Borneo*. Beaufoy Publishing, London.

Piper, P., Rabett, R. & Barker, G. (2013) A zoologist with a taste for the past: the Earl of Cranbrook's contribution to zooarchaeological research in Southeast Asia. *Raffles Bulletin* supplement no. 29.

Piper, P. J., Cranbrook, Earl of & Rabett, R. J. (2007) Confirmation of the presence of the Tiger in Late Pleistocene and Early Holocene Borneo. *Malayan Nature Journal* 59(3): 259–267

Puri, K. K. (2005) Deadly dances in the Bornean rainforest. Hunting knowledge of the Penan Benalui. KITLV.

Rajamani, L. et al. (2006) Indigenous use and trade of Dugong in Sabah, Malaysia. *Ambio*, vol. 25, no. 5.

Rajaratnam, R. (1992) Differential habitat use by primates in Samunsam Wildlife Sanctuary, Sarawak. WWF Malaysia.

Rajaratnam, R. et al. (2007) Diet and habitat selection of the Leopard Cat in an agricultural landscape in Sabah (Tabin). *Journal of Tropical Ecology* 23: 2: 209–217.

Richards, P. W. (1952) *The Tropical Rain Forest. An Ecological Study*. Cambridge University Press, 450pp.

Ridley, H. (1930) The dispersal of plants throughout the world. L. Reeve & Co. 744pp.

Roberta, C. T. T. et al. (2010). In: Mohamed et al. (eds), *Lanjak Entimau Wildlife Sanctuary: Hidden Jewel of Sarawak*. Academy of Sciences Malaysia.

Ross, J. et al. (2013) Recent camera trap records of Malay Weasel in Sabah, Borneo. *SCC*, vol. 49.

Ross, J. et al. (2013) The occurrence of reddish-orange mongooses *Herpestes* in the Greater Sundas and the potential for their field confusion with Malay Weasel *Mustela nudipes SSC 46*

Ross, J., Hearn, A. et al. (2013) Activity patterns and temporal avoidance by prey in response to Sunda Clouded Leopard predation risk. ZSL.

Roubik, D. W., Sakai, S. & Kaim, H. (eds) (2005). Pollination ecology and the rainforest, Sarawak studies. Ecological studies 174. Springer Science.

Ruedi, M. (1996) Phylogenetic evolution and biogeography of Southeast Asian shrews (genus *Crocidura*: Soricidae). *Biological Journal of the Linnean Society* 58: 197–219.

Russon, A. E. (1999) *Orangutans, Wizards of the Rain Forest*. Firefly. 222pp.

Sakai, S., Harrison, R. D., Momose, K. et al. (2006) Irregular droughts trigger mass flowering in a seasonal tropical forests in Asia (Lambir). *American Journal of Botany*. vol. 93, no. 8.

Samejima, H. et al. (2012) Camera-trapping rates of mammals and birds in a Bornean tropical rainforest under sustainable forest management. *Forest Ecology and Management* 270: 248–256. Deramakot.

Sazali, S. N. et al (2011) Phylogenetic Analysis of the Malaysian *Rhinolopus* and *Hipposideros* inferred from partial mitochondrial DNA cytochrome *b* gene sequences. *Pertanika Journal of Tropical Agricultural Science* 34 (2).

Schilthuizen, M. (2008) *The Loom of Life. Unravelling Ecosystems*. Springer Science. 167pp.

Schuster, G., Smits, W. & Ullal, J. (2012) Thinkers of the jungle. The Orangutan Report.

Sebastian, A. (2003) ITTO Project Joint Biodiversity Expedition in Kayan Mentarang National Park.

Sha, J. C. M., Bernard, H. & Nathan, S. (2008) Status and conservation of Proboscis Monkeys (*Nasalis larvatus*) in Sabah, East Malaysia. *Primate Conservation*. 23, 107–120.

Shanahan, M. & Debski, I. (2002) Vertebrates of Lambir Hills National Park, Sarawak. *Malayan Nature Journal* 56 (1).

Sheldon, F. H., Lim, H. C. & Moyle, R. G. (2015) Return to the Malay Archipelago: the biogeography of Sundaic rainforest birds, *Journal of Ornithology*.

Simmons, N. B. (2005) Order Chiroptera, pp. 312–529. In: Wilson, D. E. & Reeder, D. A. (eds), *Mammal Species of the World. A Taxonomic and Geographic Reference* (3rd edn, vol. 1). Baltimore, 743pp.

Smits, W. T. M. (1994) Dipterocarpaceae: mycorrhizae and regeneration. Thesis. Tropenbos Series No. 9.

Soedjito, H. (ed) (1998) Report ITTO Borneo Biodiversity Expedition 1997 to Bentuang Karimun NP. WWF.

Soepadmo, E. et al. (1999–2011) *Tree Flora of Sabah and Sarawak*, vols 1–8. Sabah Forestry Department.

Start, A. & Marshall, A. G. (1975) Nectarivorous bats as pollinators of trees in West Malaysia. In: *Tropical Trees: Variation, Breeding and Conservation*, J. Burley & B. T. Styles (eds), pp. 141–150. Academic Press.

Struebig, M. J. et al. (2012) Bat diversity in the lowland forests of the Heart of Borneo. *Biodiversity Conservation*.

Stuebing, R. et al. (2014) *A Field Guide to the Snakes of Borneo*. Natural History Publications (Borneo). Kota Kinabalu, 319pp.

Sun, I-F. (2007) Seed predation during general flowering events of varying magnitude in a Malaysian rain forest. *Journal of Ecology* 95, 818–827.

Suyanto, A. & Struebig, M. J. (2007) Bats of the Sangkulirang limestone karst formations, East Kalimantan – a priority region for Bornean bat conservation. *Acta Chiropterologica* 9: 67–95.

Suyitno, A. & Wulffraat, S. (2012) The Elephant Groups of East Kalimantan, WWF Indonesia.

Thompson, C. J. H. (2004) Agile gibbons: vocalizations as indicators of geographic isolation. BSc, Anglia.

Thorington Jr, R. W. et al. (2012) *Squirrels of the World*. Johns Hopkins University Press, Maryland. 458pp.

Thornton, I. (1996) *Krakatau. The Destruction and Reassembly of an Island Ecosystem*. Harvard Univ. Press. 335pp.

Tingga, R. C. T. (2010) Morphology and genetic variation of aethalops (Chiroptera: Pteropodidae) using mitochondrial and nuclear genes. MSc thesis, UMS. Kota Samarahan.

Tuen, A. A., Abdullah, M. T. et al. (2002) Mammals of Balambangan Island, Sabah *Journal of Wildlife and Parks*. 20: 75–82.

Turner, A. (2011) Impact of logging on Paleotropical bat assemblages: what value do secondary forests hold for biodiversity conservation? Sabah, Borneo. MSc thesis, East Anglia.

Van der Meer, L. et al. (2008) Evidence for scatter-hoarding in a tropical peat swamp forest in Malaysia. JSTOR.

Vander Wall, S. B. (2001) The Evolutionary Ecology of Nut Dispersal. JSTOR.

Van Schaik, C. (2004) *Among Orangutans. Red apes and the rise of human culture*. Bellknap.

Veron G., Patou, M. L. et al. (2014) How many species of *Paradoxurus* civets are there? New insights from India and Sri Lanka. *Journal of Zoological Systematics and Evolutionary Research*.

Vogel, E., Knott, C., Crowley, B. C., Blakely, M. D., Larsen, M. & Dominy, N. (2012) Bornean Orangutans at the brink of protein bankruptcy. *Biology Letters*, v.8, 2012, p. 333.

Voris, H. K. (2000) Maps of Pleistocene sea levels in Southeast Asia: shorelines, river systems and time durations. *Journal of Biogeography*.

Wallace, A. R. (1865) *The Malay Archipelago*. John Beaufoy Publishing.

Wearn, O. R. et al. (2013) Assessing the status of wild felids in a highly disturbed commercial forest reserve in Borneo and the implications for camera trap survey design. PLOS one.

Webb, C. O. & Peart, D. R. (1999) Seedling density dependence promotes coexistence of Bornean rainforest trees, *Ecology* 80 (6), 1999, pp. 2006–2017.

Wells, K. & Bagchi, R. (2005) Eat in or take away – seed predation and removal by rats (Muridae) during a fruiting event in a dipterocarp rainforest. *Raffles Bulletin of Zoology* 53: 281–286.

Wells, K. (2002) Diversity, dynamics and spacing patterns of a small mammal community in a primary rainforest in Sabah, Malaysia. Comparing an arboreal and terrestrial habitat. MSc thesis, Wurzburg.

Wells, K. et al. (2011) Pitchers of *Nepenthes rajah* collect faecal droppings from both diurnal and nocturnal small mammals and emit fruity odour. *Journal of Tropical Ecology* 27: 347–353.

Wells, K., Pfeiffer, M., Lakim, M. B. & Linsenmair, K. B. (2004) Use of arboreal and terrestrial space by a small mammal community in a tropical rain forest in Borneo. *Journal of Biogeography* 31: 641–652.

Whitehead, John (1893) *The Exploration of Kina Balu*. Gurney and Jackson.

Whitmore, T. C. (1984) *Tropical Rain Forests of the Far East*. Clarendon, Oxford.

Whittaker, R. (2007) *Island biogeography: ecology, evolution, and conservation*. OUP.

Whittaker, R. J. & Jones, S. H. (1994)The role of frugivorous bats and birds in the rebuilding of a tropical forest ecosystem. *Journal of Biogeography* 21: 689–702.

Wich, S. A. et al. (2012) Understanding the impacts of land-use policies on a threatened species: is there a future for the Bornean Orang-utan? PLOS one.

Wickler, W. (1968) *Mimicry in Plants and Animals*. McGraw-Hill. 256pp.

Wiens, F. et al. (2008) Chronic intake of fermented floral nectar by wild treeshrews. PNAS.

Wilson, D. E. & Reeder, D. M. (2005) *Mammal Species of the World: a Taxonomic And Geographic Reference* (3rd edn). Johns Hopkins University Press, Maryland.

Wilting A., Samejima, H. & Mohamed, A. (2010) Diversity of Bornean viverrids and other small carnivores in Deramakot Forest Reserve, Sabah, Malaysia. *Small Carnivore Conservation* 42: 10–13.

Wong, S. T., Servheen, C., Ambu, L. & Norhayati, A. (2005). Impacts of fruit production cycles on Malayan Sun Bears and Bearded Pigs in lowland tropical forest of Sabah, *Journal of Tropical Ecology* 21: 627–639.

Yasuda, M., Miura, S. & Hussein, N. A. (2000) Evidence for food hoarding behaviour in terrestrial rodents in a Malaysian lowland rainforest. *Journal of Tropical Forest Science* 12: 164–173.

Yasuma, S. (1994) *An Invitation to the Mammals of Kalimantan*. JICA and DG of Higher Education Indonesia.

Yasuma, S. & Abdullah M. A. (1996 and 1997) *An Invitation to the Mammals of Brunei Darussalam* (2 vols). JICA and Forestry Department of Brunei Darussalam, Bandar Seri Begawan.

Yasuma, S. & Andau, M. (2000) *Mammals of Sabah, Part 2, Habitat and Ecology*. JICA and SWD. 331 pp.

Yasuma, S. et al. (2003) *Mammals of the Crocker Range: A Field Guide*, Sabah Parks.

Yeager, C. P., Silver, S. C. & Dierenfeld, E. S. (1997) Mineral and phytochemical influences on foliage selection by the Proboscis Monkey (*Nasalis larvatus*). *American Journal of Primatology* 41, 117–128.

INDEX OF COMMON NAMES

INDEX OF SCIENTIFIC NAMES

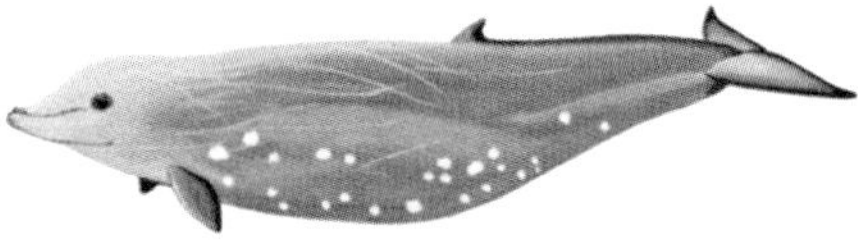

GLOSSARY

Allee Effect Alternative name for Positive Density Dependence (p. 298). See also **NDD**.

Aposematic markings Usually black-and-white/yellow stripes or bright red/orange colours on animal bodies, which warn potential predators that the target is either toxic or dangerous, e.g. p. 26 mimicry, p. 162 Red Langur, p. 252 Malay Weasel, p. 260 Linsang, p. 273 mongoose and cockroach. See also Mimicry below.

Aposematic smells Bad smells that warn of nasty animals, e.g. p. 141 Moonrat, p. 252 Malay Weasel.

Bezoar stones See p. 165 grey langurs, p. 152 pangolin, p. 244 porcupines.

Big Bang Plants that flower and fruit in one big bang, e.g. Monocarpic palms, dipterocarps, feeding nomadic animals, as compared with Steady State plants that flower and fruit continuously, feeding resident animals.

BSC (Biological Species Concept) and **PSC (Phylogenetic Species Concept)** See p. 168 on what makes a species.

Camouflage Colouration that makes animals hard to see (crypsis), or disguises them as something else (mimesis), e.g. Bay Cat, which exhibits both crypsis and mimesis of mousedeer, p. 282.

Comber, Jim Orchid fanatic who described the wildlife in the Crocker Range, p. 208.

Commensalism When one species benefits without any benefit to another, e.g. rats and humans p. 226.

Conspecific The same species.

Convergent evolution When different species resemble each other, e.g. p. 110 bats, p. 216 gliding mammals.

Cryptic species Many bats are so similar that they can only be told apart by DNA (p. 108, DNA barcoding).

Deimatic markings Markings that startle or deceive predators, e.g. p. 102 moth, pp. 224, 232 squirrel tails.

Density compensation When the populations of 2 species are inversely related, e.g. p. 162 Red and grey langurs.

Ecosystem engineers Mammals that alter their habitats to their own benefit, e.g. p. 288 rhinos and elephants.

Hose, Charles Wrote the first comprehensive book on Borneo's mammals (pp. 217, 242).

Larder-hoarding Storage of **Orthodox seeds** near the home/nest for later consumption by rodents during a **Lean period**, e.g. pp. 42–43, p. 245 porcupines. See also **Scatter hoarding.**

Lean period In dipterocarp forest the period between forest **Mastings** when only **Steady State** plants are fruiting. Many mammal populations are limited by starvation in the lean period, which occupies most of the time. In peat-swamp forest there is little masting and no lean period leading to high primate populations.

LGM, or Last Glacial Maximum The last cold period in Bornean history 23,000–18,000 years ago, with temperatures *c.* 5°C lower than today. Montane forest covered large areas of the lowlands, and Borneo was joined by land to Sumatra, Java and the Malay Peninsula, due to sea water being frozen in glaciers.

Low, Sir Hugh English botanist who produced the first list of Borneo's mammals (pp. 143, 70, 200).

Masting Simultaneous flowering/fruiting of the majority of forest trees in any one area. In cold seasonal climates most trees mast annually in autumn. In dry climates most trees mast annually in the dry season. In Sundaland's dipterocarp forests most trees mast at irregular long intervals triggered by ENSO droughts (pp. 12–13 phenology, p. 42 seed predation, p. 49 bamboos, p. 54 dipterocarps, p. 60 oaks).

Mimicry When harmless species copy the coat patterns of dangerous animals for defence or warning (Batesian mimicry), or when dangerous mammals copy the coat patterns of dangerous animals to reduce predation (Müllerian mimicry). See p. 26 mimicry examples, p. 157 primates.

Monocarpic Plants that flower once, set seeds and die, e.g. pp. 50–51 many palms. When only one stem in the whole clump flowers once and dies, it is known as **Hapaxanthic**, e.g. p. 53 *Eugeissona* palms.

Morph Variation in coat colour that occurs regularly in the same species, e.g. Sarawak Langurs vary between red and black, Red Langurs have a white morph and Silvered Langurs have a reddish morph. Some black mammals, e.g. Sun Bear and Black Flying Squirrel, are sometimes found in an erythristic (reddish) morph.

Motley, James Engineer who co-authored an early illustrated book on the wildlife of Labuan (pp. 139, 196).

Mutualistic Associations When different species benefit from an association, e.g. pollination. See p. 32 seed dispersal, p. 144 treeshrew + bird, p. 180 macaque + bird, p. 186 gibbon + hornbill, p. 304 egret + cattle, p. 303 ground cuckoo + pigs, p. 247 pheasant + Sun Bears.

NDD or Negative Density Dependency Also known as the Janzen Connell effect. Due to species specific predation (e.g. rats, fungi), most rainforest seeds have a higher chance of survival the further away they are dispersed from the parent tree (p. 30 oil palm, p. 43 seed predation, p. 44 why so many trees?).

Noyau When a male's territory overlaps the smaller territories of several females, e.g. Sun Bear, Slow Loris.

Obligate A one-to-one **Mutualistic** relationship between different species essential for survival. Obligate relationships are rare because of the risk of extinction, so most relationships between plants and mammals are generalist and involve more than one partner for both pollination and seed dispersal (p. 44).

[Orth]odox seeds Seeds with a hard coat and low water content most common in cold and dry climates, which [are] slow to germinate and evolved for scatter and larder hoarding by rodents. **See Recalcitrant Seeds**.

[Per]ianal glands Glands around the anus that can scent mark faeces to indicate sexual status for breeding or **Resource marking**, e.g. p. 262 civets.

[Po]lygyny When a male animal has more than one female mate, e.g. p. 156 langurs, p. 304 Banteng.

[Po]pulation Cycle Some Bornean mammals with large fluctuations in food supply vary more than ten times [in] numbers. This applies particularly to mammals that feed on dipterocarp seeds, e.g rodents and pigs and their [p]redators. See p. 13 pigs, p. 228 rodents, p. 278 wild cats.

Recalcitrant Seeds Seeds with a soft seed coat and high water content (e.g dipterocarps), which germinate rapidly. In Borneo recalcitrant seeds predominate in lowland forest, whilst **Orthodox seeds** (e.g acorns) predominate in the (cooler) mountains. The probable reason for this is that fungal growth is slower in cool conditions.

Resource marking Otters and some civets mark food resources they use regularly (p. 258 otters and streams),

Resource partitioning When similar mammals split available food resources both within and between species by size or sometimes by diet speciality, e.g. p. 187 primates, p. 309 deer, p. 258 otters, p. 279 male and female Clouded Leopards, p. 294 rhinos.

SARs or Species Area Relationships The larger the area the more species it will have. This applies to both national parks and islands. For conservation planning parks should always be as large as possible. Many parks in Borneo, e.g. Matang, Bako and Sepilok, are too small to host the full diversity of Borneo's plants and animals (p. 168 primates and islands).

Scatter-hoarding The random hiding of **Orthodox seeds** by rats and squirrels near a fruiting tree so that they can be recovered for later consumption. Scatter hoarding is a form of seed dispersal because some scatter-hoarded seeds are never recovered (p. 42, p. 212 squirrels, p. 232 acorns). See also **Larder-hoarding**.

Secondary seed dispersal Most tree seeds have evolved more than one form of dispersal, e.g. a fallen belian fruit may be swallowed whole by a rhino (primary disperser). The defecated seed is then larder hoarded by a porcupine (secondary dispersal) (p. 37 belian seed, p. 244 porcupines).

Sequestered poisons Many Bornean butterflies are known to sequester (store) the poisons from their toxic larval food plants, which in turn makes their own body toxic. This is then advertised to potential predators with **Aposematic markings**. It is probable that many Bornean animals also sequester poisons in their diet and advertise this fact with aposematic markings and/or smell. See p. 34 Argus Pheasant, p. 124 beetles and bats, p. 129 *Phoniscus* bats, p. 138 shrews, p. 150 large treeshrews, p. 141 Moonrat, p. 160 slow loris, p. 252 Malay Weasel, p. 255 Teledu, p. 352 bats).

Shelford, Robert W. Entomologist and curator of the Sarawak Museum in Kuching, 1897–1905 (p. 272).

Steady State Some Bornean plants, e.g. bananas, gingers, *Sonneratia*, *Terminalia* and understorey bat figs, flower and fruit steadily throughout the year, providing food locally for resident mammals (mainly bats). These plants also provide fallback food for nomadic mammals (mainly bats) when **Big Bang** trees are not flowering or fruiting (p. 94 bananas, pp. 72–72 bananas and gingers).

TCM or Traditional Chinese Medicine Many Bornean animals are threatened by poaching to supply demand for TCM, including pangolin scales (p. 152), bezoars (p. 164) and rhino horn (pp. 298–99). There is no scientific evidence that these supposed 'medicines' have any beneficial effects on humans.

Whitehead, John English ornithologist. The first person recorded to climb Low's Peak on Kinabalu (pp. 207, 230, 332, 334).

THE AUTHORS

Quentin Phillipps has a broad interest in the history, wildlife and natural history of Borneo. He was born in Sandakan Sabah in 1951 and grew up on Tuaran Rubber Estate. He was educated at Sabah College, Kota Kinabalu; Bedales School, Hampshire, UK; and King's College Cambridge, where he studied Japanese and economics. Currently he divides his time between London, where he owns a property business, and Tg Aru, Kota Kinabalu. Quentin is the joint author (with his sister Karen) of the bestselling *Phillipps' Field Guide to the Birds of Borneo*, now in the third edition. He is currently working on a monograph of the 150 species of Bornean fig.

Karen Phillipps was born in Sandakan and educated at Bedales School, Hampshire, UK, and Camberwell College of Arts and Technology, London, where she studied graphic design. She has illustrated numerous books on Asian wildlife, including *A Field Guide to the Birds of Borneo, Sumatra, Java and Bali* (1993), *Mammals of Borneo* (1985), *A Colour Guide to Hong Kong Animals* (1981), *A Field Guide to the Birds of China* (2000), *The Birds of Hong Kong and South China* (now in the tenth edition), *The Birds of Sulawesi* and *A Field Guide to the Birds of Borneo* (2009, 2011, 2014). Karen spent many years living in Hong Kong and travelling in Borneo and the Far East, and is currently resident in the Algarve, Portugal.

BORNEO'S HIGHEST MOUNTAINS

SABAH	metres
Kinabalu	4095
Trus Madi	2643
Tambuyukon	2579
Minduk Sirung	2050
Alab	1964

BRUNEI	
Pagon	1850
Retak	1618
Tudal	1181

SARAWAK	
Murud	2423
Mulu	2376
Lawi	2046
Lawit	1767
Dulit	1369

KALIMANTAN	
Siho	2574
Makita	2500
Mantam	2467
Bukit Raya	2278
Lian Pran	2240
Kong Kemul	2053
Batu	2029
Menjoh	2002
Menyapa	2000
Harden (Harun)	1992
Kerihun	1980
Gunung Besar	1892
Lesung	1730
Pancung Apang	1728
Niut	1709

SITE INDEX IN THIS BOOK (left column
INDEX TO MAP OPPOSITE (right column

The Heart of Borneo Initiative is a multinational project co-ordinated by the WWF to conserve 220,000km^2 of forested highlands in central Borneo. 'Borneo's forests, water and biological diversity are critical for prosperity of the entire island. The continued maintenance of their natural and cultural wealth is of local, national and global importance. At the very heart of Borneo there lies a uniquely rich, largely forested landscape. It straddles the transboundary highlands of Brunei, Indonesia and Malaysia, and reaches out through the foothills into the adjacent lowlands. Our vision for the Heart of Borneo is that partnerships at all levels ensure effective management of a network of protected areas, productive forests and other sustainable land-uses. Borneo's magnificent heritage is thereby sustained forever.' Vision Statement approved by representatives of Brunei, Malaysia and Indonesia at the Heart of Borneo conference in Bali, 12 February 2007. www.panda.org, www.wwf.de (Germany), www.wwf.or.id (Indonesia), www.wwf.org.uk (UK), www.wwf.org.my (Malaysia), www.wwf.nl (Netherlands), www.worldwildlife.org (USA).